Flash® 8 ActionScript Bible

Joey Lott and Robert Reinhardt

WILEY

Wiley Publishing, Inc.

May there be peace within and among all beings.
This book is dedicated to the light that shines within you and without you.

—Joey

Flash® 8 ActionScript Bible

Published by
Wiley Publishing, Inc.
10475 Crosspoint Boulevard
Indianapolis, IN 46256
www.wiley.com

Copyright © 2006 by Wiley Publishing, Inc., Indianapolis, Indiana

Published simultaneously in Canada

ISBN-13: 978-0-471-77197-5
ISBN-10: 0-471-77197-X

Manufactured in the United States of America

10 9 8 7 6 5 4 3 2 1

1O/SY/RS/QV/IN

For general information on our other products and services or to obtain technical support, please contact our Customer Care Department within the U.S. at (800) 762-2974, outside the U.S. at (317) 572-3993 or fax (317) 572-4002.

Library of Congress Cataloging-in-Publication Data

Reinhardt, Robert, 1973–
  Flash 8 ActionScript bible / Joey Lott and Robert Reinhardt.
      p. cm.
  Includes index.
  ISBN-13: 978-0-471-77197-5 (paper/website)
  ISBN-10: 0-471-77197-X (paper/website)
  1. Computer animation. 2. Web sites—Design. 3. Flash (Computer file) 4. ActionScript (Computer program language)
I. Lott, Joey. II. Title.

TR897.7.R464 2005
006.6'96—dc22

2005029253

About the Authors

Joey Lott has written several books on Flash and ActionScript. He lives in Los Angeles.

Robert Reinhardt, Director of Multimedia Applications for Schematic (`www.schematic.com`), is internationally regarded as an expert on multimedia application development, particularly in Macromedia Flash. Robert is the lead author of the *Flash Bible* series and *Flash ActionScript Bible* (Wiley). He has developed multimedia courses for educational facilities in Canada and the United States and has been a featured speaker at several Web conferences. Robert also provides multimedia consulting through his company, [theMAKERS], and is a writing partner for CommunityMX.com.

Credits

Executive Editor
Chris Webb

Development Editor
Sara Shlaer

Technical Editor
J. Matthew Sutton

Production Editor
Felicia Robinson

Copy Editor
Foxxe Editorial Services

Editorial Manager
Mary Beth Wakefield

Production Manager
Tim Tate

**Vice President and
Executive Group Publisher**
Richard Swadley

**Vice President and
Executive Publisher**
Joseph B. Wikert

Project Coordinator
Ryan Steffen

Graphics and Production Specialists
Beth Brooks
Denny Hager
Barbara Moore
Lynsey Osborn
Alicia B. South

Quality Control Technicians
Laura Albert
Leeann Harney

Proofreading and Indexing
TECHBOOKS Production Services

Contents at a Glance

Contents

Part III: Working with Display Objects 241

Chapter 13: Using Display Objects 243

Chapter 14: Working with Movie Clips 269

Part VI: Using Components   579

Acknowledgments

A book such as this one gets published only with the help of many people. The journey from start to completion involves the generous assistance of many people.

Thanks to everyone at John Wiley & Sons for their diligent work to make this book possible. We'd like to specifically thank Chris Webb for his dedication to the project through many editions. And many thanks to Sara Shlaer for her enthusiasm and her work editing this manuscript.

We'd like to thank Matt Sutton for his thorough technical edits, for checking each line of code, and for the many helpful comments. Matt's contributions are apparent each time the examples work.

Thanks to Margot Maley Hutchinson of Waterside for picking up this project.

The Flash team at Macromedia continues to be a great resource, and we'd like to thank every person on the team for the help they provided. In particular, we'd like to thank Gary Grossman, Erica Norton, Matt Wobensmith, Werner Sharp, Nivesh Rajbhandari, Mike Downey, Jen deHaan, and Peter deHaan.

The Flash community is a great resource. Many thanks to those that are willing to ask questions, speak about differing points of view, challenge popular wisdom, and publish their investigations and discoveries. That makes learning ActionScript so much more accessible.

And thank *you*. It is you, the readers that make this book possible. And your comments help improve each edition.

Joey's acknowledgments: Robert, my friend, thank you for everything. Thank you for seeing the potential, and for opening the opportunity to work on this book. Thank you to my parents, my sister, and everyone that has given so generously of their friendship, love, and support. Thanks from beyond the beyond for all that is.

Introduction

Flash has begun to mature as a product, and ActionScript has begun to mature as a language. That represents both opportunity and challenge to you. As a mature language, ActionScript provides a broad spectrum of features and functionality. The possibilities are limitless: There is great opportunity to build new, innovative, useful, and interesting applications using Flash and ActionScript. However, with that opportunity comes the challenge of learning how to use ActionScript effectively. If you want to express your thoughts and feelings well, you need the right language for communicating them. Likewise, with ActionScript the challenge is to learn the language so that there is a natural flow of expression that is seamless from its conception to its manifestation in code.

Our goal with this book is to provide you with the resources to learn the language so that you can express yourself elegantly and eloquently. We make every attempt to meet you right where you are in your journey, and to provide you with the support to get where you want to go. As you can see by the page count of this book, ActionScript is not a short topic. In fact, if you're new to ActionScript it may seem overwhelming. However, it's our intention to make learning ActionScript accessible. In this book, you'll find that we've organized the topics in a way that we feel is most accessible to readers.

How to Get the Most Out of This Book

You can read and utilize this book in many ways. If you are a beginning programmer, or even if you might benefit from a review of basic programming, we encourage you to read Part I first. Parts II and III are essential for nearly anyone who wants to use ActionScript. Whether you're new to programming or simply new to ActionScript, you'll want to read those chapters. Following that, you can browse the chapters and sections that most interest you. ActionScript is a large subject, and you will likely find that you will master one part at a time.

Intermediate and advanced ActionScript developers can also benefit from the book. You can turn to any chapter as a reference. Even an advanced ActionScript developer might not know all the details about a particular topic, or what's changed in the newest version of Flash. If you want to update your knowledge, learn more about a topic, or just brush up on it, read the chapter for reference.

Keep the book on your desk. Read sections over and over. Try the exercises. You'll learn more each time. At first, just getting a `MovieClip` object to move across the screen may be difficult. But upon returning to the same exercise months later, you will undoubtedly discover something you didn't notice before.

Conventions Used in the Book

Throughout the book, when we refer to application menus, the menu names and nested menu items are separated by arrow icons. For example, to open a new Flash document within Flash 8, you can select the New option from the File menu. We indicate that in the text by suggesting you choose File ⇨ New.

Although the icons are pretty standard and self-explanatory (they have self-explanatory labels), here's a brief explanation of what they are and what they mean.

Tip   Tips offer you extra information that further explains a given topic or technique, often suggesting alternatives or workarounds to a listed procedure.

Note   Notes provide supplementary information to the text, shedding light on background processes or miscellaneous options that aren't crucial to the basic understanding of the material.

Cross-Reference   If you want to find related information to a given topic in another chapter or section, look for the cross-reference icon.

Web Resource   When you see this icon, you will find Web URLs that point to further information about the topic at hand.

On The Web Site   This icon points out files or other material available on the book's web site.

New Feature   This icon indicates a new important feature to the specific application.

Also, many code samples that are printed in this book have lines of code that are too long to fit on one line. These lines of code are broken into two or more lines and end with the line continuation symbol, ⊃. This symbol should not be typed into the actual code of your Flash document. Simply continue to type the following line(s) of code on the same line in the Actions panel. For example, you would type the following line all on the same line in the Actions panel:

```
mPhoto._accProps.description = "Picture of attendees at the round table    ⊃
    discussion";
```

Because Flash is available for both the Windows and Mac OS X operating systems, when applicable we provide keyboard shortcuts for both. In many cases the Ctrl key in a Windows environment is analogous to the Command key on the Macintosh, which we represent using the ⌘ symbol. You'll also notice that many keyboard shortcuts are denoted using a + symbol when Flash requires that you press several keys at the same time. For example, the notation Shift+N indicates that you should press and hold the Shift key while then pressing the N key.

How This Book Is Organized

We've reorganized this edition of the book in ways that we think will make it most approachable and helpful. The eight parts of the book are outlined in the following sections.

Part I: Getting Started with Flash 8 ActionScript

When you build a building, the first thing you do is lay the foundation. Doing so helps to ensure a sturdy base from which something can be created. Part I aims to provide you with basic information and practical exercises that can assist you in getting a fundamental understanding of ActionScript and programming in general. You'll learn all about how ActionScript works, where to place it, how to write it, syntax, structure, and much more.

Part II: Using Core Classes

In Part II you'll learn about some of the core classes in ActionScript. Flash 8 ActionScript is based on the ECMA specification. Although ActionScript introduces features beyond the scope of the ECMA specification, it also incorporates the core functionality. Therefore, the core classes are those classes that are part of the ECMA specification—classes such as Array, Date, Number, and Math. You'll use the core classes in nearly every ActionScript project.

Part III: Working with Display Objects

Flash has a library of classes for representing data visually. Those classes define objects that wecall *display objects*—objects such as movie clips, buttons, text fields, and so forth. In Part III you'll learn about working with display objects. You learn basics such as using buttons, movie clips, and text fields. You'll also learn more advanced topics such as programmatic drawing, filter effects, and working with bitmap data.

Part IV: Scripting Player Control

In Part IV you can learn about working with player-level classes. You'll learn to script mouse and key detection, work with context menus, and determine how content will scale within the player. You'll also learn how to print Flash content, and how to detect the user's Flash Player capabilities.

Part V: Working with Media

Some of the most popular features of Flash involve working with media such as sound and audio. In Part V you can read about using the Sound class to programmatically work with sound. You'll also learn how to use the NetStream and Video classes to work with video.

Part VI: Using Components

By encapsulating functionality, components can provide a simple drag-and-drop solution to what might otherwise require hundreds or even thousands of lines of code. In Part VI you'll learn about the user interface components that are included with Flash, as well as how to create your own components.

Part VII: Managing Data

Part VII discusses how to manage data using ActionScript. Flash Player has many data capabilities, and in Part VII you can read about each. You'll learn how to send data across Flash Player instances using `LocalConnection`, and how to store locally persistent data using `SharedObject`. You'll also learn how to use URL-encoded data and XML data, how to work with socket connections, web services, Flash Remoting, and file uploads and downloads.

Part VIII: Working with Flash in Context

Flash content can be used in many contexts. While the possibilities are limitless, you can read about some common ways in which you're likely to use Flash content. In Part VIII you learn how to use Flash content in a browser, how to make content accessible, and how to build stand-alone Flash content.

Getting in Touch with Us

The official web site for this book is:

    www.rightactionscript.com/asb

At the site you'll find code examples, updates, notes, and more.

You can also find the code examples at:

    www.wiley.com/go/actionscriptbible

We appreciate your feedback. If you have found this book to be helpful, please let us know. And if you have suggestions for ways we might improve subsequent editions, please let us know that as well. You can contact Joey by email at joey@person13.com.

Getting in Touch with Macromedia

Macromedia wants to constantly improve Flash in ways that help you. The only way they get to know how you are using Flash (or how you'd like to use Flash) is if you send them feedback. The more feedback you can provide, the better equipped they are to adapt Flash to your requests. In order to hear from you, Macromedia has set up a system by which you can sub-mit your feedback at:

    www.macromedia.com/support/email/wishform/?6213=9

If there are features that work particularly well for you, let Macromedia know. If there are features that are not working for you, let them know. And if there are things that Flash does not do that you'd like it to do, let Macromedia know that as well.

Regardless of your geographic location, you always have access to the global Flash community for support and the latest information through the Macromedia Online Forums:

    http://webforums.macromedia.com/flash

You can also visit Macromedia's new Designer & Developer Center, where you can find the latest news and tutorials for Macromedia software:

    www.macromedia.com/devnet

For inspiration and motivation, check out the site of the day, weekly features, and case studies at:

    www.macromedia.com/showcase

Getting Started with Flash 8 ActionScript

✦ ✦ ✦ ✦

✦ ✦ ✦ ✦

Introducing Flash 8

With Flash 8, you can build a tremendous variety of projects — from games to commerce applications to prototypes and beyond. Regardless of the type of project, there are some common threads when building Flash applications. One of those common threads is the subject of this book — ActionScript. In this chapter, we'll look at the sorts of things you can do with ActionScript in Flash 8. We'll also discuss the new features so that you can get a sense of what topics you'll be able to learn in this book.

Understanding the Capabilities of Flash 8

The Macromedia Flash authoring tool was originally an animation tool, but it is so much more than that today. From the early days when it was known as FutureSplash to the Flash 8 version today, Flash has always excelled as a vector-drawing and animation tool. Even though animation is still a large part of what Flash does, now it is only a fraction of the Flash toolset. Here are the broad categories available in Flash 8 authoring:

✦ **Vector graphics** — Vector drawings are made up of many lines and curves and fills, each defined by a set of coordinates and the paths along them. These paths — vectors — are described via mathematical functions. Because mathematical formulas are used to store and create the image, they are resolution-independent and can be resized arbitrarily smaller or larger with no loss of quality. Also, images based on calculations are generally smaller in file size than bitmap images, which is an advantage for bandwidth-limited Web delivery.

✦ **Bitmap graphics** — Bitmap (a.k.a. *raster*) images are made up of a grid of pixels. Every pixel's color and location in the grid must be stored individually, which usually (but not always) means larger file sizes than images made of vector calculations. Although Flash handles bitmap graphics, the program is not built for direct image manipulation on a pixel level; rather, Flash is primarily an image handler. Flash can retain JPEG compression of imported JPEG files, as well as apply lossless or custom lossy compression to imported bitmap images.

✦ **Animation** — Flash is an excellent tool for vector animation, given that the native file format is vector-based. Color and alpha effects can be applied over time by using Flash's built-in tweening, by using a series of manually modified keyframes, or by controlling symbols with ActionScript. Time-based animations can also be streamed so that playback can begin before the entire Flash movie has downloaded into the Flash Player.

✦ **Multimedia authoring** — Flash can import a wide range of media formats in addition to standard vector and bitmap image formats. For example, Flash is capable of importing video directly into the authoring environment. Flash can also import audio files in most common formats at author-time or dynamically stream MP3 audio at runtime. Both of these can be used to enhance your productions and animations. You can manipulate these assets with ActionScript and add interactive functionality to them.

✦ **Dynamic content** — Flash can incorporate dynamically loaded information into your productions. Text, images, and MP3s can be loaded into the movie at runtime, and information can also be sent from the movie to a server or database.

✦ **Rich Internet Applications** — Since the release of Flash MX, Macromedia has coined the term Rich Internet Applications, or RIAs, to refer to a new breed of Web applications that use Flash Player technology to access sophisticated enterprise-level server applications. Several technologies have been developed by Macromedia, including Flash Remoting and Flash Communication Server (also known as FlashCom, or FCS), to add enterprise-level features to Flash content. Flash Remoting is the fastest means of sending and receiving data from a Flash movie to server-side applications, whereas Flash Communication Server can enable simultaneous interaction among several users in real time. FlashCom can also deliver live or prerecorded audio/video to Flash movies as well.

The preceding list is only a general overview of some of the capabilities of Flash. Don't think that you have to be limited by that list. Flash can be a great tool for rapid prototyping of applications, it's often an easy way to build simple utility applications (data viewers/parsers, slideshow presentations, etc.), and you'll likely find more unusual ways to use Flash as well.

Looking at What's New in Flash 8

Flash is a product that practically defies definition. Flash 8, the latest version of Flash, doesn't do anything to help anyone impose limits on the application. It adds new functionality, improved compile time, improved player performance. This section offers a look at some of the new features of Flash 8.

✦ **Improved text rendering** — One of the features of Flash Player 8 that Macromedia likes to brag about is the new Saffron text engine. Saffron is a technology that significantly improves font rendering at small point sizes. Flash Player 8 integrates the new text engine seamlessly, and you will likely notice font-rendering improvements without any extra coding. It also adds a few new properties to text fields that enable you to manage the font rendering programmatically. In Flash Player 8, you can programmatically control the font thickness and sharpness. You can also control how the text aligns to the pixel grid, which enables text to appear more legibly at smaller font sizes.

✦ **Programming bitmaps** — One of the neatest new features of Flash 8 is the `BitmapData` class. The `BitmapData` class lets you work with bitmaps programmatically. You can copy nearly any graphical data to a `BitmapData` object — whether from a movie clip or even from a video frame — and apply lots of effects or modify the pixels.

✦ **Bitmap caching** — Although one of the benefits of Flash Player is that it can render vector data (which is much more bandwidth-friendly than raster graphics), it can also have difficulty rendering complex vector data. When a vector movie clip moves, Flash Player redraws the artwork from the vector data. Even if the movie clip simply moves one pixel to the left, Flash Player has to redraw the entire movie clip. For simple vectors, that's okay. But when the vectors are complex, it can be difficult for Flash Player. The effect is that animations can playback slowly or unevenly.

Flash Player 8 introduces bitmap caching. Using bitmap caching, you can tell Flash Player to treat a movie clip like a bitmap surface rather than a vector. That means that when the movie clip moves, the bitmap surface is simply translated, and Flash Player doesn't have to redraw anything. Used judiciously, the bitmap caching feature can drastically improve playback of some animations.

✦ **Blend Modes** — Blend modes let you specify how an object will appear in relation to everything underneath it.

✦ **Filters** — Filters offer a vast new array of runtime-applied effects, from blurs and drop shadows to complex color transforms. Filters enable effects that Flash alone simply could not accomplish previously. The filters are scriptable, and you can programmatically adjust the settings at runtime in order to achieve animated effects.

✦ **Improved JavaScript and browser interaction** — Integrating Flash into a container was frequently dubious at best. The new `ExternalInterface` class simplifies and improves Flash Player connectivity to the container application. In many cases, that means Web browsers and JavaScript. Using `ExternalInterface`, not only can you call JavaScript functions from Flash, but you can reliably call ActionScript functions from JavaScript as well.

✦ **File uploading and downloading functionality** — Until Flash 8, HyperText Markup Language (HTML) forms had one major advantage over Flash in that they allowed the user to browse to and upload a file, while Flash did not. However, Flash 8 resolves that issue with the new `FileReference` class. Using `FileReference`, it is possible to allow a user to open a file browse dialog box and upload that file to a server from Flash. You no longer have to use pop-up HTML forms or any of the workarounds devised previously.

✦ **Loading PNG, GIF, and Progressive JPEG files** — Flash Player 6 and Flash Player 7 were capable of loading nonprogressive JPEG content at runtime. However, they did not load progressive JPEG, GIF, or PNG content — all of which are supported in Flash Player 8. Using the same APIs used to load standard JPEG files, you can now load any of those formats at runtime.

✦ **IME** — For those building applications for use with non-ASCII character sets, the IME class provides improved support for input method editors (IMEs).

✦ **New drawing features** — Flash Player 8 has new drawing features that translate to the ActionScript drawing API. Specifically, Flash Player 8 lets you manage options like whether or not to scale the thickness of lines as the container movie clips are scaled, what type of line end caps to use (round, square, or none), and how to join lines (round, bevel, or using miter joints).

New to Flash Player 8, you can also apply gradients to lines, and there are advanced controls over gradients in general. Plus, you can apply bitmap fills programmatically.

✦ **New video codec** — Flash Player 8 supports a new video codec — On2 VP6. The new codec not only means better-quality video, but it also supports alpha channel encoding. That means that you can playback Flash video with an encoded alpha channel, and content on layers underneath the video will be displayed through transparent sections of the video.

Getting Started with Flash 8 ActionScript

Flash is far too complex and intricate a topic to discuss in complete detail within one book. For that reason, the *Flash 8 ActionScript Bible* focuses on ActionScript, rather than the Flash IDE and related topics such as timelines, motion and shape tweens, making symbols, and the like. I assume that if you are reading this book you are already familiar and comfortable with the basics of the Flash IDE and the associated concepts. You don't have to be a Flash expert to learn from this book. However, you do need to know what keyframes and movie clip symbols are.

 Note   For a great general reference on Flash, see the latest edition of the *Flash Bible* series from Wiley Publishing.

Assuming that you're comfortable with the basics of Flash, the next chapter introduces you to the basics of ActionScript.

 Web Resource   We'd like to know what you thought about this chapter. Visit www.rightactionscript. com/asb/comments to fill out an online form with your comments.

Summary

✦ Flash 8 is a powerful tool for working on a vast array of projects — from animation to rich Internet applications.

✦ Flash 8 has many capabilities, and understanding those can help you plan the scope of each project.

✦ Flash 8 has many new ActionScript features that you can learn and utilize to build new types of applications.

✦   ✦   ✦

Learning ActionScript Basics

✦ ✦ ✦ ✦

In This Chapter

Understanding ActionScript as a language, and learning what you can do with it

Examining the event-event handler model in Flash and ActionScript

Using the Actions panel to author your code

✦ ✦ ✦ ✦

Before you can effectively start working with anything new, you first have to do a few things:

✦ Gather a general overview of the topic, understanding the scope of what you can hope to accomplish.

✦ Learn the basic mechanics of the medium. In other words, you want to have a broad understanding of how the pieces fit together to make a whole.

✦ Familiarize yourself with the tools of the trade, so to speak. You want to be comfortable with the environment within which you are working.

This chapter covers each of these fundamentals so you can begin working with ActionScript. First, you learn about what ActionScript is and what it can do. Then, you read about how ActionScript functions at a very high level. And last, you become familiar with the Actions panel, which is the initial "command center" for ActionScript within Flash.

Introducing ActionScript

ActionScript is the programming language used to send instructions to your Flash movie. It is how you "talk" to your Flash movie, telling it exactly what you want it to do. The more effectively and fluently you are able to communicate in ActionScript, the more effective you will be in creating Flash movies that do what you want.

Note   This book uses the terms *coding, scripting,* and *programming* interchangeably. Although each is sometimes used in a more specific context, nothing is implied by using one term over the other in each instance.

To help you understand what ActionScript is, it is helpful to understand the similarities between ActionScript and something you already know — human languages. Any human language is merely a collection of symbols and sounds used to represent ideas. The same is true of any programming or scripting language. ActionScript, for example, is merely a collection of words and symbols with the purpose of communicating instructions to the Flash movie. Additionally, human languages have syntax and vocabulary that are specific to that language, but not wholly dissimilar to those of other languages.

The same is true of scripting languages. Not only is ActionScript similar to other scripting languages in many ways, but you may also find that with the right perspective it is quite similar to the English language.

Programming languages are in many ways remarkably similar to the languages humans use to communicate. Therefore, although hearing a foreign language might seem like gibberish at first, with a little training, you can begin to share your ideas with people in a language they understand. It is much the same with ActionScript. Think of this book as your language teacher. You'll start in this chapter by developing an understanding of the ActionScript culture, the environment, and the tools you can use to begin your ActionScript journey. Then, in Chapter 3 you look at and investigate the parts of speech and the syntax and structure. With these fundamentals under your belt, you'll be well on your way to communicating with Flash.

ActionScript is based on the ECMA-262 specification, although it does not adhere to it fully. If you want to learn more, you can read about it at the ECMA web site at www.ecma-international .org.

Learning What You Can Do with ActionScript

Before you dive into the details of ActionScript, let's first briefly discuss what you can do with it. Presumably, you already have at least some minimal experience with Flash, and you are familiar with the playback of the timeline. The default behavior in Flash is such that when an SWF (the compiled Flash movie format) is opened in a player, the timeline begins to play automatically. In many cases, this is not, in and of itself, problematic. However, when the play-head reaches the end of the timeline, it then loops back to the beginning of the timeline and starts playing it again. Often you want an animation to play only one time and then stop at the end. To prevent the Flash movie from looping the playback, you actually have to give it the instruction to stop. You can do this by placing one line of code on the last frame. That one line of code looks like this:

```
stop();
```

With this first command, you can see that ActionScript really can read very much like English. The command (or statement) stop() instructs the Flash movie to stop playback. Of course, you can do many more complex things with ActionScript besides a simple stopping of the playback. Using ActionScript, you can load external data into your movie for the purposes of creating dynamic, user-specific customizations or even e-commerce applications. Using ActionScript, you can create nonlinear, interactive presentations and animations. The possibilities with ActionScript are practically limitless, and they allow you to create Flash applications with tremendous potential. In fact, there is very little that you can think up that cannot be accomplished with ActionScript.

Creating Your First ActionScript

All right, so far this all sounds great, right? We've suggested that ActionScript is perhaps not going to be as difficult and baffling as it might seem at first. We've even shown you a sample ActionScript statement that reads pretty much just like plain English. But there's still nothing like a working example to demonstrate a point.

So, let's create your first ActionScript. In this example, we introduce a statement that can prove invaluable during Flash development. The trace() statement causes Flash to display a message in the Output panel when you are playing the movie in the test player. Although the `trace()` statement is not used during production, it is a great way to perform simple debugging (more complex debugging is covered in Chapter 6), and it is an excellent first statement for learning ActionScript.

When you use the `trace()` statement, you need to tell Flash what message you want to display in the Output panel. To do this, you simply place the quoted message within the opening and closing parentheses. For example:

```
trace("All the world's a stage");
```

Note   Technically, the value between the parentheses of a statement such as `trace()` does not need to be a quoted value, as in the previous example. However, it does need to evaluate to a string. You can find more discussion of this topic in Chapter 3 in the discussion of variables and datatypes.

Now that you've looked at the `trace()` statement, you may be wondering where this statement goes so that Flash will do something with it. At this point, you have the statement ready to go, but you need to actually "speak" it to Flash to get Flash to do what you want — which is to display the message in the Output panel.

The most fundamental technique for adding ActionScript code to a Flash movie is to use the Actions panel. We'll examine this panel in much more detail later in this chapter (see "Understanding the Actions Panel"). For the purposes of getting up and running with ActionScript in this example, simply complete the following steps. You'll read about the theory in more depth in just a moment.

1. Open a new Flash document.

2. Select the first keyframe of the default layer of the main timeline.

3. Open the Actions panel by choosing Window ⇨ Actions or by pressing F9.

4. The right portion of the Actions panel is the Script pane. Type the following code into the Script pane:

```
trace("All the world's a stage");
```

5. Test the movie by choosing Control ⇨ Test Movie or by pressing Ctrl+Enter (Windows) or ⌘+Enter (Macintosh).

When you've tested the movie in this way, you should see the Output panel open and display the following:

```
All the world's a stage
```

Tip   If the Output panel does not open and display the message, make sure that `trace()` actions have not been omitted. You can do this by selecting File ⇨ Publish Settings. In the Publish Settings dialog box, select the Flash tab, and make sure that Omit trace actions is *not* checked.

Understanding the Event Model: How ActionScript Works

In the simplest form, ActionScript can be viewed as simple commands, called *statements*, given to the Flash player. This is not unlike giving commands to a trained dog. The difference is that (one hopes) Flash responds the same way to the same commands with consistency, whereas Rover might not be so easily persuaded to sit or roll over when he has the idea of chasing the mail carrier.

It is also important to understand the bigger picture within which ActionScript works. One of the most important things to understand in Flash with respect to ActionScript is the concept of events and event handlers.

Events are those things that occur and can trigger another action or actions to happen. An *event handler*, on the other hand, can catch and process the event. Therefore, an event can occur independently, whether or not an event handler exists. And an event handler can exist independently of the occurrence of an event. However, without an event to trigger the event handler to respond, the event handler merely sits dormant, so to speak. It is much like pushing a button on the outside of a house to ring a bell on the inside. Pushing the button (the event) does nothing as long as there is not a bell (event handler) waiting to ring (action) inside. And the bell inside does not ring until the button is pushed. Here is another analogy to help you better understand this concept. An answering machine sits and waits until someone calls the phone line. The answering machine does nothing but sit there listening until the phone line is called. The answering machine represents the event handler. The call represents the event. And the answering machine recording a message represents the action that occurs when the event handler handles the event.

In Flash, the events can be grouped into several categories. The two most common types of events are what we'll call *time-based* and *user-based*. The most common time-based example is that of the playhead entering a new frame. Each time this happens, it is an event. User-based events include mouse and keyboard activity.

The event handlers in Flash are those things that are equipped to handle specific events. Just like a lock and key, the event handlers accept only the events they are explicitly designed to handle. When you place your desired actions within the context of that event handler, they can execute when that event occurs. For example, if you create code within an event handler that handles mouse clicks, a keystroke entered by the user will never trigger that code. But if the mouse is clicked, the event is handled, and the code is executed.

Assigning Actions

As just discussed, Flash needs all actions to be placed within event handlers. There are two basic types of event handlers — keyframes and event handler methods. When you place ActionScript code on a keyframe, it is executed when the playhead enters the frame. When you place code within an event handler method, the code is executed when the corresponding event occurs. There are many types of event handler methods, as you'll see in the section "Event Handler Methods."

Note   In addition to keyframes and event handler methods, it is also possible to add code to Flash 5-style event handlers directly on `MovieClip` and `Button` instances. However, we do not recommend this practice, as event handler methods allow much more programmatic and runtime control.

Keyframes

If you've worked with Flash at all, you're likely already familiar with keyframes. Keyframes are integral to any type of Flash development, be it simple motion tweens or complex ActionScript-driven applications. Each new layer in a timeline always has a single keyframe on the first frame. You can also insert new keyframes by selecting a frame and choosing Insert ➪ Timeline ➪ Keyframe or by pressing F6. You can recognize a keyframe in a timeline because it is represented by a circle within the frame (see Figure 2-1). When no code has been assigned to the keyframe, and when no content has been placed on the stage for the keyframe, it is represented by an unfilled circle. If you add ActionScript code to the keyframe, an "a" appears above the circle. And if you add content to the stage for a keyframe, the circle is filled.

Figure 2-1: A keyframe is indicated by a circle within the frame on the timeline; in this figure there are four keyframes — each showing the different ways a keyframe can be represented depending on the status (code/no code, content/no content).

To place code on a keyframe, do the following:

1. Select the keyframe.

2. Open the Actions panel either by choosing Window ➪ Actions or by pressing F9.

3. In the Actions pane (lower-right portion of the Actions panel) type the code (as shown in Figure 2-2).

Tip

As a best practice, consider always creating a layer specifically for ActionScript code. Use a consistent name such as Actions for the layer, and keep the layer at the top of the timeline so it is easy to locate.

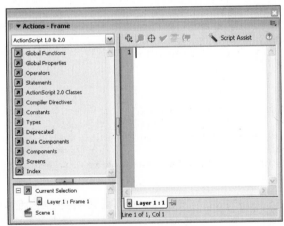

Figure 2-2: Adding code to a keyframe using the Actions panel.

Code placed on keyframes will run as soon as the playhead enters the frame during runtime (as the movie is playing). On one hand, this means that if you place code on a keyframe on the first frame of the main timeline, it will execute as soon as the movie starts playing. On the other hand, if you place code on a keyframe on a later frame, such as the hundredth frame of the main timeline, the code on the later keyframe will not execute until the playhead has entered that frame.

Note All we're trying to do at this point is introduce the basics of where and how to add ActionScript to a Flash movie. If you want more detailed information and examples, you'll find it as you continue reading this chapter and the next.

Event Handler Methods

You can also place your code within an event handler method. Event handler methods are actually quite simple, but a thorough explanation requires slightly more background information than you've yet learned. So, for the time being, we'll cover how to implement basic event handler methods without going into the theory. Don't worry. We will discuss the theory at a later point. When you first start taking a foreign language course, you are generally taught some basic expressions for saying "hello" and "how are you?" without necessarily understanding the theory. You just need to know these basic phrases to get by at first, and you later back them up with a deeper knowledge. Likewise, you should understand how to use event handler methods now, and later you can back them up with a greater understanding.

Event handler methods are always applied to objects such as `Button` and `MovieClip` instances. To accomplish this, complete the following steps:

1. Create an object instance. For example, drag a Movie Clip symbol onto the stage.

2. Make sure that the instance has a name. In the case of a `MovieClip` or `Button` instance that you have created on the stage during authoring time, you should select the instance on the stage and enter an instance name via the Property inspector (see Figure 2-3).

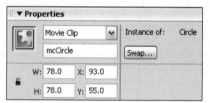

Figure 2-3: Naming a MovieClip instance in the Property inspector.

3. If you have not done so already, create a new layer specifically for ActionScript. (We'll refer to this as the Actions layer.)

4. If the object (such as the `MovieClip` object) has been created on a frame other than the first frame, create a keyframe on the Actions layer at the same frame.

5. Select the appropriate keyframe on the Actions layer, and open the Actions panel either by choosing Window ⇨ Actions or by pressing F9.

6. Add the event handler method code to the keyframe. For example:

```
mCircle.onRelease = function ():Void {
  trace("All the world's a stage");
};
```

The structure for an event handler method is always the same, although the specific details may change depending on what object, what event, and what actions you are using. The general structure is as follows:

```
objectName.eventHandlerMethodName = function ():Void {
    Actions to occur on event handling go here.
};
```

In the example in Step 6, the object name was `mCircle`, the event handler method name was `onRelease`, and when the event was handled the code instructed Flash to display a message in the Output panel. The name of the object variable is always the instance name you have assigned to the item on the stage. For example, if you create a button named `btAnimate`, and you want to assign the same event handler method to it as in the previous example, your code would look like this:

```
btAnimate.onRelease = function ():Void {
    trace("All the world's a stage");
};
```

You should choose the event handler method name from the list of predefined method names that are available for the specific type of object. In each of the relevant chapters in this book, you can read about the available event handler methods for a type of object. In the preceding examples, we used the name `onRelease` because that is an event handler method that is available for both `Button` and `MovieClip` instances. That event handler method is invoked when the instance is clicked on and then released.

Another key point to understand with event handler methods is that they should be defined within a keyframe. This part might seem a little confusing because earlier we stated that actions should be defined *either* on a keyframe *or* within an event handler method. And now, we're telling you to define the event handler method on a keyframe. This might appear to be a contradiction. In fact, the definition of the event handler method should be defined on a keyframe, but the execution of the code within the event handler method is deferred until the corresponding event takes place. For example, in Step 6 in the preceding example, the `trace()` action does not occur when the playhead enters the keyframe. Instead, the event handler method is defined. Then, at any point after that, if the event (in the example, the event is the click and release of a `MovieClip` object named `mCircle`) occurs, the `trace()` action is executed.

Understanding the Actions Panel

If you owned the world's most sophisticated and powerful computer, but all you knew how to do was check your email with it, you might feel that the computer was a very limited thing. Similarly, if you are using Flash, but you do not familiarize yourself with all that is available within it, you are limiting your experience and the power that you can wield with it. For this reason, having a thorough understanding of the environment in which you write ActionScript can be extremely important.

Opening the Actions Panel

The Actions panel can be toggled open and closed either through the Flash menus or by keyboard shortcuts. To open and close the Actions panel using the Flash menus, choose Window ⇨ Actions. If the menu item is checked, it means that the panel is already opened, and selecting it will close the panel. Otherwise, if unchecked, selecting the menu option will open the Actions panel. However, it is generally far easier and faster to use the F9 keyboard shortcut to toggle the Actions panel open and closed.

Once the Actions panel has been opened, there are a few things to consider.

✦ The Actions panel defaults to being docked at the bottom of the Flash window, just above the Property inspector. You can undock the Actions panel if you prefer by clicking on the panel by the gripper in the upper-left corner (as shown in Figure 2-4) and dragging it so that it is displayed as being undocked (no dark outline) and releasing it. When clicking on the gripper, make sure that the cursor changes to the cross-arrows as shown in Figure 2-4. Likewise, if you have undocked the panel, and you want to redock it, you can click on the panel on the gripper in the upper-left corner and drag it over an area of the window until the outline is displayed as docked. Then, release it. Or, you can also choose a layout from the Window ⇨ Workspace Layout menu option. When you do this, however, be aware that the entire panel layout will adjust to the selected panel set.

Figure 2-4: Click the gripper on the Actions panel to dock and undock it.

✦ The title of the Actions panel should always read Actions – Frame (see Figure 2-5) before you add any code to it. If it says Actions – Movie Clip or Actions – Button, you should make sure that you have selected the correct frame, and not an object instance on the stage. This is a common mistake that people make — beginners and experts alike. If you accidentally place code on a `MovieClip` or `Button` instance instead of a frame, you will get an error when you try to export the movie. The error will read something like this:

```
**Error** Scene=Scene 1, layer=Layer 1, frame=1:Line 1:

Statement must appear within on handler
```

or

```
**Error** Scene=Scene 1, layer=Layer 1, frame=1:Line 1:

Statement must appear within onClipEvent handler
```

We don't promote the use of ActionScript on instances in these ways. So, if you get these kinds of messages, it means you have probably accidentally placed the code on an instance rather than on a frame. Simply locate the `MovieClip` or `Button` instance on which the code has been accidentally placed, open the Actions panel, and then move the code to the correct frame.

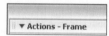

Figure 2-5: The Actions panel displays Actions – Frame when a frame has been selected.

✦ You can use the shader feature of the Actions panel to show and hide the panel while the title bar remains visible. To accomplish this, click anywhere on the Actions – Frame title to toggle the visibility of the panel.

The Actions panel consists of two main parts, as you can see in Figure 2-6. On the left is the Actions toolbox, and on the right is the Script pane. The lower portion of the Actions toolbox contains the Script Navigator. It is intended to allow you to navigate through all the scripts you have added to your movie.

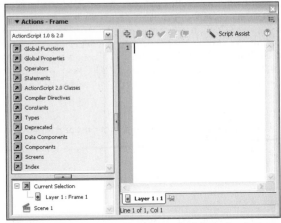

Figure 2-6: The Actions panel: On the left is the Actions toolbox with the Script Navigator, and on the right is the Script pane.

Working with the Actions Toolbox

On the left side of the Actions panel is the Actions toolbox. Within the Actions toolbox, you find all the available ActionScript actions, operators, classes, and so on categorized according to definition and use. You will find that everything is organized into *folders* with names such as Global Functions, Statements, Operators, and so on. Each folder can, in turn, contain subfolders. Clicking a folder expands it to reveal any items and/or subfolders contained within it. For example, if you expand the Global Functions folder, you will see several subfolders revealed within it, and if you expand one of those subfolders, you will see that the subfolder contains items indicated by circular icons, as shown in Figure 2-7.

Figure 2-7: Expanding a folder in the Actions toolbox reveals its contents.

You can add actions to the Script pane by either double-clicking the item in the Actions toolbox or by dragging it from the Actions toolbox to the Script pane. It is important to understand that the Actions toolbox is a potentially useful feature, but it is not the only way to add actions.

If you find that it works well for you, use it. If not, rest assured that it is not a better way than the other methods discussed later in this chapter.

The Actions panel pop-up menu offers an option to View Esc Shortcut Keys (see Figure 2-8). When this option is toggled to on, the Esc shortcut key combinations appear next to each item in the Actions toolbox where applicable. This useful feature provides a quick reference.

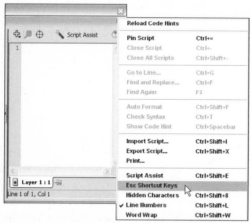

Figure 2-8: Select the View Esc Shortcut Keys option from the Actions panel menu to display the Esc sequences next to items in the Actions toolbox.

Working with the Script Navigator

The Script Navigator can be found in the lower portion of the Actions toolbox. The Script Navigator (see Figure 2-9) has several top-level items within it. Current Selection is always an option, and when you expand that item, you can choose the current selection, be it a frame or an object. Then, there are top-level items for each of the scenes in your movie. If you expand one of the scene items, you can select from all the frames and/or object instances within the scene that currently contain code. Lastly, if any library symbols contain code internally, and if any instances of those symbols have been placed within your movie, those symbols show up under the top-level item named Symbol Definition(s). When you expand one of those items, you can select from a list of scripts within the symbol.

By selecting a script in the Script Navigator, that script becomes the current script and is displayed in the Script pane.

If you want to adjust the size of the Script Navigator, you can use the mouse, click on the resize bar between the Script Navigator and the rest of the Actions toolbox, and drag the resize bar to where you want it.

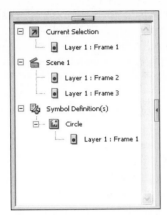

Figure 2-9: The Script Navigator allows you to select from available scripts in your movie.

Working with the Script Pane

The Script pane is, for most ActionScript developers, the focal point of the Actions panel. It is via the Script pane that you can add ActionScript code to your movies, and hence, it is an indispensable element.

Figure 2-10 shows the Script pane. At the top of the Script pane is the toolbar that allows you to quickly and easily access some of the functionality built into the Actions panel such as syntax checking and auto-formatting. The main portion of the Script pane consists of a text area in which you can type code. And at the bottom of the Script pane there are a few more options for tabbing and pinning scripts that you'll learn about in just a moment.

Figure 2-10: You can add code to your movies in the Script pane.

In the figure, a `trace()` action has already been added. On your own computer, you will notice that before you add any code to the Script pane, the majority of the options on the toolbar are disabled. After you add some code to the Script pane, the options become available, as shown in the preceding figure. Starting from the left, the toolbar options are as follows:

✦ **Actions Add Menu** — You can add code to the Script pane not only by typing or by selecting an item from the Actions toolbox, but you can also choose an item from the Actions Add Menu, and it will appear in the Script pane.

✦ **Find and Replace** — You can use the Find option to search for text within the current script. Use the Replace option to find instances of particular text, and replace them with some other text.

✦ **Insert Target Path** — This option offers you a graphical interface alternative for choosing a target path to a `MovieClip` instance.

✦ **Check Syntax** — You can use this option to check the syntax of a script before trying to export the movie. If any errors occur, they will be displayed in the Output panel.

✦ **Auto Format** — You can use this option to have Flash format your code for you for optimal readability. See "Working with Formatting" later in this chapter for more details.

✦ **Show Code Hint** — This option reveals code hinting for the currently selected code, if available. You can read more about code hinting in the section "Using Code Hinting."

✦ **Debug Options** — Choose from this option's menu items to assist with setting debugging options in your script. See Chapter 6 for more information on debugging.

✦ **Script Assist** — Script Assist is the updated version of a feature that was previously called Normal Mode. When using Script Assist the Actions Panel behaves differently, and we don't recommend it if you plan to write more than a few lines of code. Script Assist is useful for people who feel uncomfortable writing code, and only want to add minimal ActionScript. We don't discuss Script Assist in this book.

✦ **Help** — Open the Help panel.

Managing Scripts

When you are creating simple Flash applications, you may have only a single script within the entire document. In such cases, you don't have to concern yourself with how you are going to keep multiple scripts at hand. However, when you start adding scripts to multiple frames, within symbols, and so forth, it can quickly become a hassle to switch back and forth between more than one script. Fortunately, the current version of Flash improves upon the pinning functionality and includes tabbing on the Script pane so that you can have more than one script open at the same time. This functionality allows you to open a script, pin it so that it remains open, and then open an additional script. You can then tab between the two scripts without having to continuously open and reopen the same scripts, as in previous versions of Flash.

To open and pin several scripts, do the following:

1. Open a script in the Script pane. For example, open the script on the first frame of the main timeline by selecting that frame. Figure 2-11 shows how the tab at the bottom of the Script pane will indicate that the script has been opened.

Figure 2-11: The Script pane tab indicating that the open script is from layer 1, frame 1.

2. Next, click the pin button next to the tab. This toggles the state of the button and pins the current script. It then opens a second tab to the left of the first. Figure 2-12 shows this. The new tab will open to the pinned script.

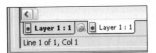

Figure 2-12: After you have pinned a script, the second tab appears.

3. Now, you can select a second script. The second script appears in the original tab, while the pinned script remains opened in the new tab. Figure 2-13 shows an example in which a script from frame 2 has been opened in addition to the pinned script.

Figure 2-13: The pinned script from frame 1 is opened at the same time as the unpinned script from frame 2.

4. You can pin more than a single script if you want. If we continued this example, we could also pin the script from frame 2 and then open a script from frame 3, as shown in Figure 2-14.

Figure 2-14: You can pin more than one script at a time.

You can also use the keyboard shortcuts to quickly pin and unpin scripts. To pin the current script, press Ctrl+= or ⌘+=. To unpin the current script, press Ctrl+- or ⌘+-. You can also unpin all pinned scripts either by selecting the Close All Scripts option from the Actions panel menu or by pressing Ctrl+Shift+- or ⌘+Shift+-.

Setting Actions Panel Preferences

The Actions panel has its own set of preferences that you can adjust to your liking. You can access the preferences either from the Actions panel pop-up menu (the Preferences menu item) or by opening the Preferences dialog box (Edit ⇨ Preferences) and selecting the ActionScript preferences tab. Figure 2-15 shows the ActionScript preferences.

As you can see from the picture, the ActionScript preferences are categorized into four groups: Editing Options, Text, Syntax Coloring, and Language. Let's take a closer look at each of these sections.

Figure 2-15: The ActionScript Preferences tab.

Editing Options

Flash is capable of automatically detecting and placing indentation in your code as you write it. For instance, after you type the following and press Enter, Flash can automatically indent the next line:

```
if(true){
```

Then, when you type the next closing brace (}), Flash automatically unindents that line. In the ActionScript Editor preferences, you can turn off Automatic Indentation by unchecking the box, or you can adjust the amount that it indents (Tab size). By default, the Tab size is set to 4, meaning the tab value is equal to the width of four spaces.

Code hinting is on by default. You can turn it off by unchecking the box, and you can adjust the rate at which the code hints appear. By default, code hints appear immediately. You can use the slider to change the number of seconds before code hints appear. For more information regarding code hinting in general, see the section "Using Code Hinting."

Additionally, you can select the format that Flash uses to open/import or save/export a file.

Font

You can adjust the font and font size that are used in the Script pane by changing the preferences in the Text section of the ActionScript Editor preferences.

Open/Import/Save/Export

You can specify the file-encoding format to use for opening/importing/saving/exporting ActionScript files. The default setting in Flash 8 is UTF-8. You can optionally select the value of Default Encoding, which uses the default encoding for the operating system of the computer on which Flash is running.

Reload Modified Files

When an open file is modified outside of Flash, Flash can reload it. It can do so automatically (always) or it can detect the change, and notify you (prompt). Optionally, you can specify that you don't want Flash to reload such files.

Syntax Coloring

The Actions panel has a syntax-highlighting feature that you can modify in the ActionScript Editor preferences. After unchecking the Syntax coloring box, all text appears in black on white within the Script pane. Leaving the box checked, however, color-codes your script. Six types of syntax are distinguished for the purposes of color coding:

✦ Foreground is anything that doesn't fall into any other category.

✦ Background.

✦ Keywords include all the items grouped within the Statements folder in the Actions toolbox as well as items grouped in Compiler Directives.

✦ Comments.

✦ Identifiers include predefined class names, constants, predefined functions, properties, and methods.

✦ Strings include all quoted strings.

You can modify the colors used to suit your own preferences.

Language

The Language portion of the ActionScript preferences allows you to adjust the ActionScript 2.0 settings. We discuss this in greater detail in upcoming chapters.

Working with Formatting

ActionScript gives you flexibility in how you format your code. With a few exceptions, you can use spaces, carriage returns, and indentation as you please without affecting the way in which the code works. There are many styles for writing code that programmers choose to adopt. But whatever style they choose, chances are good that each programmer will remain fairly consistent with his or her own style. Doing so ensures that the code remains more readable.

For several reasons, you may find that your code is not consistently formatted. For example, you might be drawing together snippets of code from various sources, or you simply might not have applied consistent formatting along the way. Flash offers you an auto-formatting feature that you can access either from the Actions panel toolbar or from the Actions panel pop-up menu. Auto Format follows a set of rules that you can adjust, and formats the selected code uniformly.

The rules that the Auto Format feature follows are set in the Auto Format preferences, which can be opened from the standard Flash Preferences window. From the Preferences window, select the Auto Format option. In the preferences (shown in Figure 2-16), you have five check boxes from which you can alter the formatting style. Below those options is a preview. If you check and uncheck the boxes, you can see how the formatting style changes.

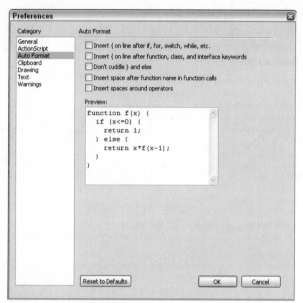

Figure 2-16: The Auto Format preferences.

Using Code Hinting

Using code hints, Flash can give you a hint for syntax of certain code structures as well as methods and properties for objects. When you type certain code elements in the Script pane, Flash automatically recognizes them and pops up a hint. The addition of strong typing to ActionScript (see Chapter 3 for more details) has enabled even greater flexibility in code hinting.

There are two types of code hints. Tooltip code hints (see Figure 2-17) appear as pale yellow pop-ups, showing the correct syntax for a recognized statement or code snippet. Menu code hints (see Figure 2-18) appear as drop-down menus from which you can choose the appropriate selection.

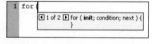

Figure 2-17: A tooltip code hint.

Figure 2-18: A menu code hint.

There are two ways to get code hints to display. By default, code hints are invoked automatically as soon as any recognized snippet, object, or variable is entered into the Script pane. However, you can also invoke a code hint manually by one of three methods:

✦ Pressing the code hint button on the Actions panel toolbar

✦ Choosing Show Code Hint from the Actions panel pop-up menu

✦ Pressing Ctrl+Spacebar (Windows) or ⌘+Spacebar (Mac)

When invoking code hints manually, the cursor must be located after the opening parenthesis and before the closing parenthesis. Or, if it is an object/variable, the cursor must be after the dot operator (.) and before the semicolon (;).

You can adjust the speed at which code hints are invoked (from 0 to 4 seconds) or even turn off automatic code hinting altogether in the ActionScript preferences. (See the section "Setting Actions Panel Preferences" for more information.)

Obviously, in order for Flash to be able to open the correct code hints, it needs to recognize the type of code that is being entered. When you enter code snippets such as the following:

```
for (
```

Flash is able to recognize that code snippet because a `for` statement always starts the same way. So, as soon as you type in that code, Flash is able to recognize it for code hinting. Additionally, there are some other keywords that happen to be the names of what we called top-level objects or classes such as `Math` or `Stage` that are capable of invoking code hints because `Math` and `Stage` both happen to be classes that don't need to be instantiated (more on this in Chapter 3). However, when you want Flash to provide code hinting for variables and instantiated objects, you need to provide Flash some assistance in determining what code hints to offer.

Cross-Reference See Chapter 3 for more information on variables and Chapter 5 for more information on objects.

To see the problem, let's first examine the following code. Even though you have not yet read about variables (variables are discussed in depth in Chapter 3), the following line of code should not be too perplexing. It's simply assigning a value to a variable named `firstName`.

```
var sFirstName = "Joey";
```

Then, once the variable has been defined, if you try, on another line, to invoke code hinting for the code, you will not get any hints.

You do not get any code hints because Flash does not recognize the data type of the variable `firstName`. There are several options for how you can provide this information to Flash:

✦ **Use strong typing** — Strong typing is a new feature introduced in Flash MX 2004, and it is the preferred way to tell Flash what type of code hinting to provide. When you use strong typing, you can declare a variable (more on variables in Chapter 3) to be of a particular type such as String, Date, MovieClip, and so on. Then, if and when you type the variable name later in the code, Flash already knows the type of the variable, and it is able to provide the proper code hinting. Not only does strong typing provide the means by which Flash can offer code hinting, but it also provides additional benefits such as compile-time error checking. We'll take a closer look at strong typing in Chapter 3, but for now, here is an example of how to declare a strongly typed variable:

```
var sFirstName:String = "Joey";
```

The `var` keyword tells Flash that you are declaring a variable. The name of the variable is followed by a colon and then the type of data the variable will represent — in this case it will be string data. The rest of the statement looks the same as before.

✦ **Use a code hint suffix in the variable name** — For example, `sFirstName_str` uses the `_str` suffix, which Flash will recognize as indicating a string variable. This is a technique that was introduced in Flash MX prior to strong typing.

✦ **Declare the data type in a specially formatted comment** — For example:

```
// String sFirstName;
```

You need to use only one of the preceding techniques if you want to tell Flash which type of code hinting to provide you for each variable. As already mentioned, the strong typing technique is the preferred approach as it also offers additional benefits that you'll read about in Chapter 3.

Using the Help Panel

The Help panel is the primary point of access to Flash and ActionScript reference material and documentation within Flash 8. You can locate Help documents that concern ActionScript in various ways:

✦ Open the Help panel, choose the Table of Contents option from the Help panel toolbar, and navigate to the document(s) via the contents of the folders that appear in the left pane.

✦ Open the Help panel, select the Search option from the Help panel toolbar, search for a keyword, and select from the search results.

✦ Open the Help document for a particular item in the Actions toolbox. You can right-click or ⌘-click an item in the Actions toolbox and choose the View Help option from the context menu. The Help panel will open and display the relevant Help document.

✦ Open the Help document for a snippet of code in the Script pane. You can right-click or ⌘-click a snippet of code in the Script pane and choose the View Help option from the context menu. Flash will open the Help panel, and if it is able to locate documentation on the snippet, it displays that information.

You can also update the Help panel's contents. If you have an Internet connection, you can click the Download Help Contents button in the Help panel toolbar (it is labeled Update).

Summary

✦ ActionScript enables you to programmatically control your Flash movies.

✦ Events are those things in Flash that can trigger an action to occur. Event handlers are those things that can detect events.

✦ All ActionScript code must occur within an event handler.

✦ ActionScript is added to keyframes, `MovieClip` objects, and `Button` objects by way of the Actions panel.

✦ The Actions panel has many configurable features (preferences), allowing you to customize your ActionScript authoring environment.

✦   ✦   ✦

Constructing ActionScript

In This Chapter

Using variables and understanding the data they can represent

Working with data using expressions

Instructing the Flash movie with statements

Controlling the flow of code using control structures

If you decide to work as a car mechanic, you learn the names and functionality of all the common parts of cars. Learning ActionScript is very similar in that respect because it is a good idea to learn what all the basic terms mean and how they function within the whole. This will aid you, not only in thinking through your own code, but also in communicating it to others.

For the purposes of learning about how ActionScript works, we're going to examine it syntactically in smaller pieces. Of course, as with any language, these pieces are not useful in isolation. For example, to create a complete sentence in English, you normally need to use both a noun and a verb at the minimum. But if you examine each of the pieces, learn how they are structured, and learn how they fit together to create correct syntax, you'll be much better prepared to communicate with Flash. Flash is not nearly as tolerant about syntactical errors in ActionScript — even minor ones — as a human might be when listening to you speak in English, or any other human language. If you accidentally drop a preposition or conjugate a verb incorrectly, the listener will generally be able to understand the meaning from the context of the conversation. But Flash does not know about the context. Flash does not know what you are trying to accomplish. It only knows how to do each instruction, exactly as you provide it. Therefore, the simple omission of a parenthesis can cause Flash to misunderstand you. For this reason, it is especially important to have a good understanding of the syntax of ActionScript.

Fortunately, ActionScript is composed of only a handful of elements that repeat many of the same structural patterns. So even though Flash demands perfect syntax, the structure of the language is simple enough that you'll be up and running in no time.

In this chapter, we take a look at variables and datatypes, operators and expressions, and statements and control structures.

Understanding Datatypes

When we talk about data, we're talking about information or values. These values can be of many types. For example, even in a very simple movie you might still have a number, some text, and a `MovieClip` instance. All three of these examples are data of different types — what ActionScript calls *datatypes*.

Flash is actually capable of performing datatype conversions when necessary. However, this can lead to some poor coding practices on the part of ActionScript developers. For this reason, the ActionScript 2.0 standards require that you pay closer attention to the datatypes you are using.

In ActionScript, you'll work with many different datatypes. However, for the sake of understanding how these datatypes work, you can consider them in two basic categories: primitive types and reference types. The primitive types are called *primitive* because they are the basic foundational datatypes, not because they lack importance. The reference datatypes are called reference types because they *reference* the primitive types.

Primitive datatypes include strings, numbers, Booleans, undefined, and null. We'll examine each of these primitive datatypes a little more closely in this chapter. Reference datatypes are all objects, which is the subject of much of the rest of this book, so we'll defer the majority of the discussion of reference datatypes to those later chapters.

Working with Strings

Strings are characters or words. String values must always be enclosed in either single quotes or double quotes. Here are a few examples of strings:

```
"a"
'b'
"1"
"Joey"
'123'
'abc'
"****"
```

Strings are used whenever you want to work with characters or words. For example, you can use strings to populate text fields in your movie, or you can use strings to programmatically create names for new MovieClip instances. You've also already seen how strings can be used with actions such as trace(). The trace() action requires that you provide it with a message to display in the Output panel. That message must evaluate to a string value.

```
trace("I know him; Marley's Ghost!");
```

As already mentioned, you can use either double quotes or single quotes when defining a string value. Which you choose is often purely a matter of personal preference. There are two rules that you must follow, however, if you want your code to work without error. First, you must have a matching closing quote for every opening quote. And whichever type of quote you use to open the string literal must be used to close it. In other words, mismatched quotes are not allowed. Here are two examples of correctly matched quotes on string literals:

```
"here is a string"
'here is a string'
```

And here are three examples of incorrect quotes on string literals:

```
"here is a string'
'here is a string"
"here is a string
```

There are times when more than personal preference might dictate which type of quotes you choose to use. Notice what would happen if you tried the following:

```
trace('I know him; Marley's Ghost!');
```

Note The semicolon at the end of a line denotes the end of an expression or a statement. It is similar to a period in an English sentence.

This line of code would actually cause an error because it would interpret the apostrophe as the closing quote and then fail to know what to do with the remainder of the string. This is easily remedied by using double quotes around the string:

```
trace("I know him; Marley's Ghost!");
```

The inverse is true as well, of course — if you want to use a double quotation mark as a character in a string literal, you can use single quotes around the entire value. The problem arises when you want to use both single and double quotation marks as characters within a string literal. There is an easy way to accommodate this: by using special characters. To learn more about special characters, see Chapter 11.

Working with Numbers

In Flash, all numbers are treated as the *number* datatype. Positive, negative, floating point, integer, and so forth, are all simply considered numbers, with no further differentiation generally required on your part.

To define a number, you need only type the number without any quotes. The following are examples of numbers.

```
6
12
-1
3.3
1.8
```

Number datatypes allow you to perform all kinds of mathematical operations, as shown in the following examples:

```
trace(5 + 5);  // Displays: 10
trace(5 - 4);  // Displays: 1
trace(5 / 2);  // Displays: 2.5
```

It is important to understand when to use numbers and when to use strings. If you try to use a string when you really want to use a number, you can end up with unexpected results. For example:

```
trace("5" + "5");  // Displays: 55
```

In the example, the resulting value of addedAges is "55", not 10 (as you may expect). This is because ActionScript treats the two values as strings and concatenates them, rather than adding the numeric values.

Note *Concatenation* refers to when two string values are appended. You can read more about concatenation operations in Chapter 11.

However, it should also be understood that there are legitimate reasons for numbers to be treated as strings. For example, even though a phone number is composed of numbers, it is usually treated as a string. And if you want to format the phone number with spaces, parentheses, dashes, and so on, it is necessary that the phone number be treated as a string by enclosing the value in quotation marks.

Using Booleans

Boolean data is data that can hold only two values: `true` and `false`. Boolean variables are used to test conditions within your Flash movie. Boolean values are used commonly in *conditional expressions* within statements such as the `if` statement and control structures such as the `for` and `while` statements. For more information about conditional statements and control structures, read the section "Using Statements That Control Flow: Control Structures" later in this chapter.

Understanding the undefined and null Datatypes

ActionScript has two additional primitive datatypes — `undefined` and `null` — with which you'll want to familiarize yourself. In order to have a better understanding of these datatypes, it is useful to first be familiar with variables. Therefore, we'll interweave the discussion of these two datatypes with the discussion of variables later in this chapter.

Casting Data

ActionScript allows you to tell Flash to convert a value to a specific datatype by what is known as *casting*. When you cast a value, you use the following syntax:

```
Datatype(value)
```

For example, you can cast a string to a number as follows:

```
Number("123")
```

When you are casting data you have to be careful. Some casting will have unexpected results. For example, the numeric value of 0 can be converted to a Boolean `false`, and any nonzero value will be converted to `true`. For example:

```
trace(Boolean(0));  // Displays: false
trace(Boolean(1));  // Displays: true
```

Therefore, if you convert the string values of `true` and `false`, they will both convert to the Boolean `true` value because both string values are nonzero values.

```
trace(Boolean("true"));   // Displays: true
trace(Boolean("false"));  // Displays: true
```

Using Variables

In Flash movies you're going to be using a lot of data. Now, with all that data floating around, you're going to want some way to keep track of it. This is where variables become very useful.

A *variable* is a named container that you can use to hold or reference some particular data. Once you have created a variable, you can store and retrieve data in the variable. Although a variable can contain only one value at a time, you can use the same variable to contain or reference different data at different times. For example, if you create a variable named nYear, it may contain the value of 2005 at one point, but at another point it may contain the value 2006.

Consider a rental storage space as a metaphor for a variable. You can rent a space (declaring the variable), and when you do so, you can begin to place things in that space (assigning data to the variable). At a later time, you may want to view the things from the storage space (retrieving the value from the variable), or you may decide to place other contents in the storage space (assigning a new value to the same variable). And when you are done with the storage space, you can stop renting it (deleting the variable).

Declaring Variables

Before you can meaningfully use a variable, you must first bring it into being by *declaring* it. Flash 8 and ActionScript 2.0 let you declare variables using *strong typing*. Strong typing means that when you create the variable, you also specify the type of data that it can hold. When you export your movie, Flash then makes sure that you consistently tried to store the correct type of data in that variable. If Flash detects that you mismatched the datatype with the variable at any point, an error message is generated, alerting you to the fact. This is helpful for ensuring that your Flash applications are well planned and designed using good coding practices.

To declare a variable using strong typing, use the following pattern:

```
var variableName:Datatype;
```

The var keyword lets Flash know that you are declaring a variable. The variable name is up to your choosing, but it should follow the rules for variable naming (see the next section, "Naming Variables"). A colon separates the name of the variable and the name of the datatype, and there should be no space between the name, colon, or datatype. If you have code hinting turned on, you should get a drop-down list of built-in datatypes from which you can select. Alternatively, if you have defined your own custom datatype (see Chapter 5), you can declare a variable of that type as well. You'll also see that the line ends with a semicolon.

Here is an example in which you declare a variable named nQuantity as a number:

```
var nQuantity:Number;
```

Now, you've declared a variable with the name nQuantity, and you've told Flash that all values you assign to the variable must be numbers. The variable has been created, but you have not defined any value for it yet. If you use trace() to display the value of the variable, you can see that this is so:

```
trace(nQuantity);
```

When you test this, you should see the value undefined appear in the Output panel. The value undefined is a special value that Flash uses for any variable that has not yet been assigned any value.

Once a variable has been declared, you can assign a value to it using a simple assignment statement with an equals sign:

```
var nQuantity:Number;
nQuantity = 6;
```

You can also declare the variable and assign a value, or initialize the variable, all on one line:

```
var nQuantity:Number = 6;
```

In addition to the undefined value, there is another special value, *null*, that you can assign to a variable that indicates that the variable does not contain any other, specific value. While undefined is used to indicate no value has been assigned to a variable, you can use null to indicate that a variable has *intentionally* been left without any other value. It is often a good practice to initialize your variables to some value other than undefined. And because null allows you to quickly distinguish between values intentionally or unintentionally left without another value, it is a good practice to initialize your variables to null when you don't have any other specific value to assign to them:

```
var nQuantity:Number = null;
```

You can use a variable in any situation in which you could use the value the variable contains. You've already seen an example of this with the trace() actions. You can use a variable to tell Flash what message to output:

```
var sMessage:String = "Welcome!";
trace(sMessage);
```

You can also perform other kinds of operations using variables, just as you would on the actual values themselves. For example:

```
var nQuantity:Number = 6;
var nPrice:Number = 9.99;
trace(nQuantity * nPrice);   // Displays: 59.94
```

Naming Variables

Now that you've looked at declaring and defining variables, the next thing to examine is how to name the variables. There are two main parts to this discussion. First, there is the matter of using valid variable names that Flash will understand, so we'll look at the rules for naming variables. Second, we'll examine some additional guidelines for naming variables that, while not strictly enforced by Flash, will aid you in creating more readable code.

The following are the rules that you must follow for Flash to be able to understand your variable names:

✦ The first character must be an underscore (_), a dollar sign ($), or a letter. The first character *cannot* be a number. Although underscores and dollar signs are allowable as the first character, in practical application, you will almost always start the variable name with a letter.

✦ The subsequent characters must be underscores (_), dollar signs ($), letters, *or* numbers.

✦ Variable names can have no spaces.

✦ The name cannot be a keyword or other special value recognized by Flash. For example, the names MovieClip, true, String, and undefined are not allowable variable names because they already have other meanings in ActionScript.

✦ The name must be unique (within its scope). If you create two variables with the same name in the same scope (more on scope in Chapters 4 and 5), the latter will overwrite the former.

Next, let's talk about some good naming conventions that you can use. First, because you'll want to be using strong typing with all your variables, it is a good idea to have a convenient way to be reminded of what type of value a variable can hold. A system named *Hungarian notation* has been devised that can assist in this. For our purposes, we'll use a modification of Hungarian notation specifically designed for ActionScript. With this system, you can prefix each variable name with a character (or, in some cases, several characters) that can help you to remember what type of datatype the variable can hold. You may have already seen this in the previous examples in this chapter. When we define a variable named nQuantity, the variable name is prefixed with the character n. This tells us that the variable holds a number value. Table 3-1 shows a list of other recommended prefixes.

 Note   Hungarian notation is a convention originally credited to Charles Simonyi, a Hungarian who was Chief Software Architect at Microsoft. He suggested naming conventions that later were adopted by many developers for many different languages.

Table 3-1: Modified Hungarian Notation ActionScript Prefixes for Common Classes

Prefix	Datatype
a	Array
bmp	BitmapData
b	Boolean
bt	Button
c	Color
cam	Camera
cm	ContextMenu
cmi	ContextMenuItem
d	Date
lc	LocalConnection
lv	LoadVars
m	MovieClip
mcl	MovieClipLoader
mic	Microphone
n	Number
nc	NetConnection
ns	NetStream
o	Object
pj	PrintJob

Continued

Table 3-1 *(continued)*

Prefix	Datatype
rs	RecordSet
s	String
snd	Sound
so	SharedObject
t	TextField
tf	TextFormat
vid	Video
xml	XML
xmls	XMLSocket

Note   The preceding table lists suggested prefixes for common classes. It is not comprehensive of every possible class in ActionScript.

This modified Hungarian notation convention is completely optional, but it can be very useful. It helps not only you, but also others who may read your code. By adding the appropriate prefix to the variable name, it makes it immediately clear what type of datatype the variable can hold.

It's also important when naming your variables to make the names as descriptive as possible. For example, the variable name nQuantity is much more descriptive than nQ. Of course, the level of descriptiveness required depends on the context. For example, if your Flash application deals with quantities of widgets as well as cogs, nQuantity might not be sufficiently clear. It would be better, in such a case, to have variables named nQuantityCog and nQuantityWidget, for example. The more descriptive the variable name, the better, in most situations. Just remember, though, that most likely you'll be typing the same variable name multiple times, so it is important to achieve the correct balance between descriptiveness and name length. You can always use abbreviations in the variable names if appropriate. For example, rather than defining a variable named nQuantityWidget you might find it easier to define a variable named nQntyWidget.

Remember that you cannot use spaces in your variable names. However, when you want to make your variable names descriptive, the names will often consist of more than one word. There are two conventions that are commonly used when naming variables with multiple words. The first of the two conventions is to use the underscore (_) to separate your words in the variable name. An example of this method follows:

```
var sFirst_name:String = "Joey";
```

The second of these conventions is what is known as the *interCap* method (also known as studlyCaps or camelCaps). The word "interCap" refers to the capitalization of the first letter of each word subsequent to the first, using no spaces or underscores — internal capitalization. An example of this method is the following:

```
var sFirstName:String = "Joey";
```

It would behoove you to use one of these conventions. Pick one that you like, and if you decide you prefer the other one later on, switch to it. In this book we tend to prefer the interCap method, so you see a preference for it in the examples. But neither convention is more correct or offers any advantages over the other one.

It is also important to remember that ActionScript is case-sensitive. This means that sFirstName, sFirstname, SfirstName, and so on are all different variables. If you accidentally type the name of a variable with incorrect capitalization, the result will be that Flash will not recognize that the variable is defined. Here is an example:

```
var sFirstName:String = "Joey";
trace(sFirstName);  // Displays: Joey
trace(sfirstName);  // Displays: undefined
```

Using Expressions

Anyone who has taken even very basic arithmetic (using addition and subtraction and the like) has worked with expressions. Expressions are simply those parts of statements that evaluate to be equal to something. Here are some very simple examples:

```
1
"abcd"
nQuantity
```

Even though these examples are all either simple values or variables, they all evaluate to a single value, and therefore, are considered expressions. Slightly more complex (although still simple) expressions might look something like this:

```
1 + 1
"a" + "b"
nQuantity * nPrice
```

Expressions are an important part of ActionScript. You use expressions in all kinds of situations. For example, you can use an expression within a trace() statement:

```
trace("Welcome!");
```

You can also use expressions in variable assignment statements:

```
var nQuantity:Number = 6;
var nPrice:Number = 9.99;
var nTotal:Number = nQuantity * nPrice;
```

We'll also look at other kinds of expressions that perform comparisons and tests. For example:

```
6 < 10
55 == 56
```

In the preceding examples, we use comparison operators to determine how two values compare. The first expression is determining whether 6 is less than 10. That expression evaluates to true. The second expression determines whether 55 is equal to 56. That expression evaluates to false.

There are many other examples of expressions, and we'll examine some of them throughout the rest of this chapter.

Working with Operators

As you have seen, expressions can be composed of a single value. But expressions can also be more complex by combining several different values to make one expression. In expressions involving multiple values, there are two types of ActionScript elements involved: *operands* and *operators*. The *operands* are the values on which the operation acts. The *operators* determine the action taken. In the expression 4 + 5, for instance, there are two values, or operands — 4 and 5 — and there is one operator: the plus operator (+).

In the Actions toolbox you can see that the operators are grouped into six categories: arithmetic, assignment, bitwise, comparison, logical, and miscellaneous. The following sections take a closer look at each of these groups, and the operators of which they are composed. We'll look at each of these groups in the order they are listed in the Actions toolbox, with the exception of the bitwise operators. We'll look at the bitwise operators after the rest because, except in specialized situations, you are more likely to use the other operators than you are to use bitwise operators.

Working with Arithmetic Operators

The arithmetic operators should be familiar to you because they are, for the most part, the operators you used in math class. They are the operators used on number operands for mathematical computations. The result of an operation using an arithmetic operator is a number value. Table 3-2 lists all the arithmetic operators.

Table 3-2: Arithmetic Operators

Operator	Name	Example	Result
+	Plus	x + y	x + y
- -x	Minus/Negation	x - y x - yx *	 (-1)
*	Multiply	x * y	x * y
/	Divide	x / y	x / y
%	Modulo	x % y	Remainder of x / y

The addition, subtraction, multiplication, and division operators don't really require any discussion. They work just as you would expect them to.

The modulo operator (%) may be new to you. Even if it is not new, you might need a little refresher on what it does. Quite simply, it returns the value of the remainder after the first operand is divided by the second. In the following example, we use the modulo operator with a variable nYear and the second operand of 4. The result is 0. This means that 2004 is divisible by 4. In practical terms, the implication of this is that the year 2004 is a leap year.

```
var nYear:Number = 2004;
trace(nYear % 4); // Displays: 0
```

Also worth pointing out is that the minus and negation operators use the same character, but operate differently. The negation operator has the same effect as multiplying a number by –1. For example, this operation:

```
y = -x;
```

is the same as this operation:

```
y = x * (-1);
```

Working with Assignment Operators

Table 3-3 presents a rather daunting list of operators that all fall under the category of *assignment operators*. But don't be scared off just yet. In fact, there is only one fundamental operator in the bunch — the equals sign (=). This one should not be a new operator to you. It does just as you would expect it to do: It assigns the value of the operand on the right to the operand on the left. The remainder of the operators are compound assignment operators that function as shortcuts, as you'll see in a moment.

In the following example, the operand on the left (nQuantity) is assigned the value of the operand on the right (6):

```
nQuantity = 6;
```

Of course, you might want to use expressions that are slightly more complex than simply nQuantity = 6. You might, for instance, want to add several operands together on the right side of the equals sign operator, as in the following:

```
nQuantity = 6 + 36 + 24;
```

In this case, you notice that the addition takes place before the assignment. In other words, nQuantity is assigned the value of the sum of 6, 36, and 24, not just the value of 6. This is due to the operator precedence of the plus operator (+) being greater than that of the assignment operator (=). See the section later in this chapter titled "Considering Operator Precedence." Additionally, you can find a complete list of operators and their precedence in the Flash Help system.

Table 3-3: Assignment Operators

Operator	Name	Example	What It Means
=	Equals (assignment)	x = y	x = y
+=	Add by value	x += y	x = x + y
-=	Subtract by value	x -= y	x = x - y
*=	Multiply by value	x *= y	x = x * y
/=	Divide by value	x /= y	x = x / y
%=	Modulo by value	x %= y	x = x % y
<<=	Left shift by value	x <<= y	x = x << y

Continued

Table 3-3 *(continued)*

Operator	Name	Example	What It Means
>>=	Right shift by value	x >>= y	x = x >> y
>>>=	Right shift zero fill by value	x >>>= y	x = x >>> y
&=	Bitwise AND by value	x &= y	x = x & y
|=	Bitwise OR by value	x |= y	x = x | y
^=	Bitwise XOR by value	x ^= y	x = x ^ y

As mentioned, there is really only one fundamental operator in the assignment operator category — the equals sign. Each of the additional operators merely saves you some time typing. For example, the following expression:

```
nQuantity += 6;
```

is the shorthand version of the following:

```
nQuantity = nQuantity + 6;
```

Either of the two preceding expressions means that you want Flash to add 6 to the current value of nQuantity. It just so happens that the former variation is shorter and quicker to type.

The operators that are compounded with the equals (=) operator are either mathematical operators or bitwise operators (covered in the following sections of this chapter). In each case, the compound operator follows the same pattern. For example:

```
nQuantity *= 6;
```

is the same as:

```
nQuantity = nQuantity * 6;
```

Working with Comparison Operators

Comparison operators allow you to compare operands. The result of a comparison is a Boolean value: true or false. These operators are most often used in expressions called *conditionals* within if...else blocks, and *control of flow* expressions within for and while blocks. (You learn about these types of statements later in this chapter.) But the basic premise is that if the conditional expression evaluates to true, a block of code is executed, and if it evaluates to false, the block of code is skipped over.

Using comparison operators (see Table 3-4), you can compare strings, numbers, and Boolean values. These primitive datatypes are equal only if they contain the same value. You can also compare reference data types such as objects, functions, and arrays. But reference data types are equal only if they reference the same object, whether or not they contain the same value.

Table 3-4: Comparison Operators

Operator	Name
==	Equals
!=	Not equals
>	Greater than
<	Less than
>=	Greater than or equal
<=	Less than or equal
===	Strict equality
!==	Strict inequality

Perhaps the most common mistake made in programming is confusing the *equality* equals operator (==) with the *assignment* equals operator (=). In fact, even among seasoned professionals, it is not uncommon to make this error on occasion. The difference is so tiny in print, but the result is so drastic. Take, for instance, the following example:

```
var nQuantity:Number = 999;
if (nQuantity = 4){
trace("if condition true");
}
trace(nQuantity);
```

What would you expect this code to do? Even if you don't know what some of the code structures mean, you can probably figure out that after nQuantity is assigned a value of 999, you want the code to check to see *if* nQuantity is equal to 4. If that condition is true, it should write a message to the Output panel. Finally, it writes the value of nQuantity to the Output panel.

You might expect that the final value of nQuantity is still 999. But because the wrong operator was mistakenly used in the if condition (nQuantity = 4), nQuantity has been assigned the value of 4! Can you see the problems that have been caused by one missing character? So, the corrected code looks more like this:

```
var nQuantity:Number = 999;
if (nQuantity == 4){
trace("if condition true");
}
trace(nQuantity);
```

Any datatype can be compared using the equality operators. String characters are first converted to the ASCII values and then compared, character by character. Therefore, "a" is less than "z" and lowercase letters have higher values than their uppercase counterparts. Tables 5-5 and 5-6 show examples of numbers and strings being compared, using the equality operators along with the resulting value of the expression.

Table 3-5: Number Comparison

Expression	Result
6 == 6	true
6 != 6	false
6 > 6	false
6 < 6	false
6 >= 6	true
6 <= 6	true

Table 3-6: String Comparison

Expression	Result
"Joey" == "Joey"	true
"joey" != "Joey"	true
"joey" > "Joey"	true
"Joey" < "Joseph"	true

The only two operators in this category that you have not yet looked at are the strict equality (===) and strict inequality (!==) operators. These operators work much like the nonstrict counterparts (== and !=) with one difference: They don't perform datatype conversions automatically. What this means is that when using the regular equality equals operator (==), Flash automatically converts the operands to the same datatype before testing for equality. Therefore, the values 5 and "5" are equal when testing using the regular equality operator (==) but not when using the strict equality operator (===). Table 3-7 gives some examples of the difference between using regular and strict equality operators.

Table 3-7: Strict Equality and Inequality Operators

Regular	Regular Result	Strict	Strict Result
6==6	true	6===6	true
6!=6	false	6!==6	false
6=="6"	true	6==="6"	false
6!="6"	false	6!=="6"	true

Working with Logical Operators

As you learned with comparison operators, sometimes you want to check for equality in an expression before performing a certain statement or group of statements. But there are times when you want to check multiple conditions before some statement or statements execute. This is when you should use the logical operators to link your conditions. There are also times when you simply want to see whether some expression is not true. Again, you should use a logical operator. Table 3-8 shows the logical operators.

Table 3-8: Logical Operators

Operator	Name
&&	And
||	Or
!	Not

The following is an example of creating a script that checks for a user's login and password before admitting them. Without using the logical AND operator (&&), you can write your code as follows:

```
if (sUsername == "Joey"){
  if (sPassword == "isAwesome"){
    trace("That is the correct username and password.");
  }
}
```

This works, but it is inefficient. Just imagine if you want to check for 5 or 10 conditions! You can easily simplify the code like this:

```
if (sUsername == "Joey" && sPassword == "isAwesome"){
  trace("That is the correct username and password.");
}
```

This new condition is checking to make sure that *both* expressions are true in one single line.

Now, imagine a situation in which you have a block of code that you want to execute if either one of two conditions is true. This is a perfect example of when to use the logical OR operator (\|\|). The next example shows how you might use this operator:

```
if (sLocation == " California" || sLocation == "Florida"){
  trace("Yay for oranges!");
}
```

In this case, you want to output a message if the location is equal to California *or* Florida.

The third and final logical operator is the NOT operator (!). You use this operator when you want to test for an expression *not* being true. The simplest example of an expression using the logical NOT operator is the following:

```
!true
```

A more real-world example is something like this one:

```
if (!(sLocation == "California") && !(sLocation == "Florida")){
   trace("Your location is not California and not Florida");
}
```

In this example, you combine the logical NOT operator with the logical AND operator to create a more complex expression. And, of course, you can combine all three of the logical operators to create complex expressions of multiple joined simpler expressions.

Working with String Operators

There is no string operator category in the Actions panel. And you should already recognize the string operators (see Table 3-9) from the mathematical and assignment operator discussions. We're discussing them here because they function slightly differently when used with strings instead of numbers. The join operator (+) is reused in a slightly different way to join, or concatenate, the strings. The result of any use of the plus operator to join two strings is a new string. The join by value operator (+=) is also used to work with string values, not just number values.

Table 3-9: String Operators

Operator	Name	Example	Result
+	Join	"x" + "y"	"xy"
+=	Join by value	x += "y"	x = x + "y"

Working with Miscellaneous Operators

In addition to the other categories for operators you can find in the Actions toolbox, there are six operators that are categorized as miscellaneous. Table 3-10 lists these operators, which are explained in the following sections.

Table 3-10: Miscellaneous Operators

Operator	Name	Example	Result
++	Increment	x++	x = x + 1;
--	Decrement	x--	x = x - 1;
?:	Conditional	(x == y) ? a : b	If x equals y then a. Otherwise, b
instanceof	instanceof	nQuantity instanceof Number	True if nQuantity is a number, false if not
typeof	typeof	typeof nQuantity	"number" (assuming nQuantity is a number)
Void	Void	n/a	n/a

Using the Increment and Decrement Operators

The increment and decrement operators are shorthand operators. The following examples are equivalent:

```
x++;
++x;
x = x + 1;
```

As are the next three:

```
y--;
--y;
y = y - 1;
```

Notice that it does not matter whether the increment or decrement operator appears before or after the operand. But there are some cases in which this distinction is important. You should note that when using the increment and decrement operators in conjunction with an assignment operator (=), the order matters. For instance, this operator:

```
y = x++;
```

and the following operator are not equivalent:

```
y = ++x;
```

In the first example, the x is incremented *after* y is set equal to its value. The result is that x has a value of one greater than y. However, in the second example, x is incremented *before* y is set equal to its value. So in the second example, x and y are equal. This is due to (you guessed it) operator precedence.

Using the Conditional Operator

All the operators you have learned about so far are what are known as *unary* and *binary operators*, meaning that they operate on one and two operands, respectively. ActionScript has one operator that can operate on three operands (a *ternary* operator). ActionScript's one ternary operator is the conditional operator (?:).

The three operands that the conditional operator works on are as follows: the conditional expression, the expression to use if the condition is true, and the expression to use if the condition is false.

```
(conditional expression) ? expression a : expression b
```

Most often, the conditional operator is used in assignment statements when you want a shorthand way of assigning one of two values to a variable, depending on the result of a condition. For example, consider the scenario in which you want to display the number of seconds remaining in a countdown. For every value except 1, you'll want to use a label of "seconds" after the number. But when only one second is remaining, you want to use a label of "second" instead. To make this decision, you can use the conditional operator. For this example, assume that the number of seconds has already been calculated and assigned to a variable named nSeconds, and we'll assume that the variable, sLabel has already been declared.

```
sLabel = (nSeconds == 1) ? "second" : "seconds";
```

The same result can be achieved using an if/else statement (see the section "Using Statements That Control Flow: Control Structures"), but it takes more lines of code.

```
if(nSeconds == 1) {
  sLabel = "second";
}
else {
  sLabel = "seconds";
}
```

Using the typeof Operator

The typeof operator works on a single operand, and it returns the name of datatype of the operand. For example:

```
var nQuantity:Number = 6;
trace(typeof nQuantity); // Displays: number
```

Table 3-11 lists the types of operands and the value that a typeof operation will return.

Table 3-11: Return Values for typeof Operations

Operand Type	Return Value
String	string
Number	number
Boolean	boolean
Function	function
MovieClip	movie clip
All other types	object

Using the instanceof Operator

The instanceof operator returns true or false depending on whether or not the first operand is an instance of the class specified (or an instance of a subclass of that class) as the second operand. (See more about classes in Chapter 5.)

```
trace(mCircle instanceof MovieClip);
```

Assuming that mCircle is the name of a MovieClip instance, the preceding statement would output true.

Understanding Bitwise Operators

The bitwise operators are a group of operators available within ActionScript that are seldom used and usually only in specific cases. The purpose of this class of operators is to allow you lower-level manipulation of numbers within Flash for faster operations. If you don't want to, or if you don't feel comfortable learning bitwise operations, don't feel obligated to do so.

More often than not you can use other operations in place of bitwise operations (although the bitwise operations will likely be more efficient). However, if you are interested, read on. There are some scenarios in which working with bitwise operations can be convenient. Extracting and synthesizing color values is one such example of the usefulness of bitwise operations.

All the bitwise operators convert any operands to the 32-bit equivalent before performing any operations. Table 3-12 lists all the bitwise operators.

Table 3-12: Bitwise Operators

Operator	Name
&	Bitwise AND
|	Bitwise OR
^	Bitwise XOR (exclusive or)
<<	Bitwise Left Shift
>>	Bitwise Right Shift
>>>	Bitwise Unsigned Right Shift
~	Bitwise Not

Using Bitwise AND

The bitwise AND operator (&) converts both of the operands to 32-bit format and then compares each of the bits of each operand. If the corresponding bits in the two values are 1, that bit in the resulting value is 1. Otherwise, the bit in the resulting value is 0. So, the bit in the resulting value is 1 only if the corresponding bits in the first operand *and* the second operand are 1. The following example results in z being equal to 210:

```
var x:Number = 1234;
var y:Number = 4567;
var z:Number = x & y;
```

Why? Here's a closer look:

x	0000 0000 0000 0000 0000 0100 1101 0010
y	0000 0000 0000 0000 0001 0001 1101 0111
z	0000 0000 0000 0000 0000 0000 1101 0010

Using Bitwise OR

The bitwise OR operator (|) operates in much the same way as the bitwise AND operator, except that the OR operator checks to see whether the corresponding bit in either the first operand *or* the second operand is 1. If either bit is 1, the bit in the resulting value is set to 1, as shown in the following example:

```
var x:Number = 1234;
var y:Number = 4567;
var z:Number = x | y;
```

This time, the result is 5591. Don't worry if you can't figure this out in your head! You can use Flash to check the results. Here is a closer look:

x	0000 0000 0000 0000 0000 0100 1101 0010
y	0000 0000 0000 0000 0001 0001 1101 0111
z	0000 0000 0000 0000 0001 0001 1101 0111

Understanding 32-Bit Integers

Computers speak in binary. Everything that computers do is a matter of 1s and 0s. But because humans are better able to communicate in decimal (base-10) numbers, applications such as Flash convert all the "human" numbers into binary. This conversion can slow down things a bit, so sometimes developers may want to work with the binary values themselves.

Integers are classified in most languages as ranging from approximately negative to positive two billion. This is because this is the range that can be represented by 32 *bits*. Bits are the smallest components of data. They are the fundamental binary unit. They can be on or off, which means they can have a value of 1 or 0. Incidentally, 8 bits are called a byte, and 1,024 bytes are a kilobyte. The accompanying table shows some examples of decimal numbers represented as 32-bit integers.

Number	32-Bit Representation
1	0000 0000 0000 0000 0000 0000 0000 0001
2	0000 0000 0000 0000 0000 0000 0000 0010
3	0000 0000 0000 0000 0000 0000 0000 0011
4	0000 0000 0000 0000 0000 0000 0000 0100
5	0000 0000 0000 0000 0000 0000 0000 0101
1978	0000 0000 0000 0000 0000 0111 1011 1010
2147483648	0111 1111 1111 1111 1111 1111 1111 1111
−1	1111 1111 1111 1111 1111 1111 1111 1111
−2	1111 1111 1111 1111 1111 1111 1111 1110
−3	1111 1111 1111 1111 1111 1111 1111 1101
−2147483648	1000 0000 0000 0000 0000 0000 0000 0000

The bits are numbered from right to left, from 0 to 31. If you look at this table, you notice that all positive values have a 0 value in the bit 31 position. Likewise, all negative values have a 1 value in the 31-bit position. This is because the 31st bit holds the value of the sign in signed 32-bit integers.

Using Bitwise XOR

The bitwise XOR (^, exclusive or) operator is the same as the bitwise OR operator, except that it sets the bits in the resulting value equal to 1 *exclusively* when the corresponding bit in one of, but not both, the operands is 1. Using the example again, z results in 5381 this time:

```
var x:Number = 1234;
var y:Number = 4567;
var z:Number = x ^ y;
```

Here is a closer look:

x   0000 0000 0000 0000 0000 0100 1101 0010

y   0000 0000 0000 0000 0001 0001 1101 0111

z   0000 0000 0000 0000 0001 0001 0000 0101

Using Bitwise Left Shift

The bitwise left shift (<<) operator simply shifts bits 0 to 30 (preserving the sign) of the first operand over to the left by the value of the second operand. The following example results in y having a value of 12:

```
var x:Number = 3;
var y:Number = x << 2;
```

Following is a simple chart that shows this bit shift:

x   0000 0000 0000 0000 0000 0000 0000 0011

y   0000 0000 0000 0000 0000 0000 0000 1100

The result of a bitwise left shift is the equivalent of multiplying the first operand by 2 to the power of the second operand. In other words, the following:

```
a << n
```

is a shortcut way to write the following in ActionScript:

$a * 2^n$

Using Bitwise Right Shift

The bitwise right shift (>>) operator shifts bits 0 to 30 (preserving the sign) of the first operand to the right by the value of the second operand. In this example, you can see how the right shift and left shift operators are the inverse of one another because y ends up with a value of 3:

```
var x:Number = 12;
var y:Number = x >> 2;
```

Following is a simple chart that shows this bit shift:

x   0000 0000 0000 0000 0000 0000 0000 1100

y   0000 0000 0000 0000 0000 0000 0000 0011

You can see then that in most cases then, the bitwise right shift operator is the same as dividing the first operand by 2 to the power of the second operand.

The bitwise unsigned right shift operator (>>>) works the same as the signed counterpart (>>), except that it shifts all the bits to the right and therefore does not preserve the sign:

```
var x:Number = -12;
var y:Number = x >>> 2; // y = 1073741821
```

Here is what the shift of the bits looks like:

```
x    1111 1111 1111 1111 1111 1111 1111 1011

y    0011 1111 1111 1111 1111 1111 1111 1101
```

Using Bitwise NOT

The bitwise NOT operator (~), also called the *one's complement operator,* works by inverting all the bits in the operand. The following are equivalent:

```
var x:Number = ~6;
var x:Number = -(6+1);
```

Working with Bitwise Operations

You may be wondering why you would want to use bitwise operations. The truth is that in the majority of smaller Flash applications, bitwise operations are not going to have a big impact one way or the other. But in larger applications, it is possible to see performance gains by using bitwise operations in place of Boolean operations whenever possible because bitwise operations save the steps of converting between binary and Boolean data. With enough operations, this can add up.

Even if you are not concerned with faster computing in your application, convenience can still be a factor when determining whether to use bitwise operations. Once you become comfortable with the bitwise operators, you may well find that there are plenty of scenarios in which it is simply more convenient to use the bitwise operators. In contrast to bitwise operations, the Boolean equivalents often take a little more code.

Bitwise operations are often more convenient when working with RGB color values and when working with a series of related Boolean flags. In the case of the RGB color values, bitwise operations can be used to quickly extract the color parts (red, green, and blue) from the single RGB value, or to synthesize a single RGB value based on the red, greed, and blue parts. In the case of related Boolean flags, often it is more convenient to group these values together into a single number — each bit of which can represent one of the Boolean flags. Let's take a closer look at each of these scenarios.

Using Bitwise Operations with Color

As you may or may not know, RGB color values are composed of three values: red, green, and blue — each ranging from 0 to 255. Often, this is represented by a six-digit hexadecimal (base-16) number such as 00FF00 (green). In the hexadecimal representation, the red, green, and blue values are in pairs (for instance, 00, FF, and 00). What you might not realize is that this is easily represented in binary. The red, green, and blue values are represented by 1 byte (8 bits) each. You may notice that the maximum value for a pair in the hexadecimal representation is 255, and the maximum value for a byte is 255. The following chart shows the binary representation of an RGB color value (the same as 00FF00 in hexadecimal):

Red	Green	Blue
0000	1111	0000
0000	1111	0000

It's important to note that the bytes can be shifted by doing a left bitshift of 8, and the bitshifted bytes can be added using the bitshift or (|) operator. The following example shows how you can assemble a color value from the red, green, and blue parts:

```
var nRed:Number = 123;   // 0111 1011
var nGreen:Number = 45;  // 0010 1101
var nBlue:Number = 78;   // 0100 1110

// 0111 1011 0010 1101 0100 1110
var nRGB:Number = nRed<<16 | nGreen<<8 | nBlue;
```

You can also use bitwise operations to extract the red, green, and blue parts from an RGB value. Simply use the bitshift right operator (>>) in conjunction with the bitwise AND (&) operator. Shift the bits of the RGB value to the right by 16 and combine that value with 0xFF using an AND operation to extract the red part. Then, perform the same operation, but shift the bits to the right by only 8 to extract the green part. And simply combine the RGB value with 0xFF using bitwise AND to extract the blue part.

```
var nRedPart:Number = nRGB >> 16 & 0xFF;
var nGreenPart:Number = nRGB >> 8 & 0xFF;
var nBluePart:Number = nRGB & 0xFF;
```

Note   ActionScript uses 0x*NNNNNN* to indicate hexadecimal representation of a number. Therefore, 0xFF is the equivalent of the decimal representation 255. You can read more about numbers in Chapter 8.

Using Flag Variables

The other useful implementation of bitwise operations is in working with flag variables. A flag variable is a sort of glorified setting-tracking variable conglomerate. It is a way of using a single variable to keep track of multiple settings. For example, the 3-byte RGB value is a sort of complex flag variable. It allows for a single variable to keep track of three settings in one value.

The more common type of flag variable, however, uses each bit much like a Boolean variable — but more efficiently. In this way, a single variable can be used instead of multiple Boolean variables. The following chart shows how the bits of a flag variable can be thought of as Boolean variables describing the state of an animation within an object:

Bit Position	3	2	1	0
Bit position meaning	Is it visible?	Is it playing?	Is it draggable?	Is it right-side up?
Bit value	1	0	0	1
Bit value meaning	It is visible.	It is not playing.	It is not draggable.	It is right-side-up.

Each bit has a decimal value that works out to be 2 raised to the power of its bit position. In other words, if bit 0 is on (has a value of 1), the decimal value is 1 (or 2^0). If bit 1 is on, then the decimal value is 2 (or 2^1). For this reason, it is good to create some variables where the name describes the function of the bit and the value is the decimal value of that bit when on. For example:

```
var RIGHT_SIDE_UP:Number = 1;
var DRAGGABLE:Number = 2;
var PLAYING:Number = 4;
var VISIBLE:Number = 8;
```

You can then use these variables to turn the bits in your flag variable on and off through bitwise operations. You can turn a bit on using the bitwise OR operator:

```
var nFlag:Number |= VISIBLE; // Make it visible
```

You can turn a bit off (called *clearing a bit*) by using both the bitwise AND the bitwise NOT operators:

```
nFlag &= ~PLAYING; // Make it stop playing
```

And you can toggle a bit by using the bitwise XOR operator:

```
nFlag ^= DRAGGABLE; // Toggle draggability on and off
```

Considering Operator Precedence

It is important to remember your basic rules of operator precedence, or order of operations, from high school algebra. (We bet you never thought you would use *that* again!) What this means is that the operators in your expression perform in order, according to a hierarchy or precedence, and may yield different results from what you want if you are not careful. For example, the following results in the value of 177 instead of 65, as you might expect:

```
var nAverageScore:Number = 90 + 78 + 27 / 3;
```

This is because the division operator (/) has higher precedence than the addition operator (+), so the division is performed before the addition. In order to accommodate for this, you can use parentheses to enclose the part of the expression you want to have perform its operations first, as in the following example:

```
var nAverageScore:Number = (90 + 78 + 27) / 3;
```

In the previous example, operators enclosed in parentheses take precedence over other operators. For this reason, the "better safe than sorry" approach to operator precedence is recommended. Use parentheses to encapsulate the operations you want to take precedence over others, which saves a great deal of debugging later on and makes your expressions more reader-friendly when you need to go back to them. It also saves you time by not having to look up precedence each time.

Using Comments Effectively

There are times in every programmer's experience when she or he has to revisit some old code. What you may find is convoluted logic that you swear you could never have written. But the truth is that you did—you just cannot remember what you were thinking when you wrote it. No matter how much you think you will remember what you were thinking, chances are you will not, which is why comments are so helpful.

Comments are exactly what they sound like. They are a way for you to write, in your own words, what the purpose of the code is at any point. Your comments are never interpreted by Flash; they are for your own benefit later on. So, feel free to be as verbose as you need to be.

Of course, you need to signify to Flash that what you are typing is a comment, not a part of the code. You do this by using characters to indicate a comment. There are two styles for doing this that are recognized in ActionScript. The first is a multiline comment indicated by /* at the beginning, and */ at the end. For example:

```
/* This is the first line of my first comment.
   And this is the second line.*/
```

This style is most appropriate when you want to give an in-depth comment about the logic or function of a particular piece of code.

The second style of comment is the single-line comment, which is indicated by //, as follows:

```
// This is a single-line comment.
```

These comments are often useful for indicating the meaning of a particular line of code, as shown in the following instance:

```
// Keeps track of how many widgets the user has selected.
var nQuantity:Number = null;
```

In this case, the comment gives an idea of the function of the variable that is being declared.

Another very important function of comments is what is known as "commenting out" code. As you already know, comments are not interpreted in your Flash movie at runtime. In other words, they are not seen by your program; they serve only as reminders for you. Sometimes, when you are debugging your code, it can be useful to omit certain statements or blocks of statements for the time being. A clever way to do this is to simply make the code into a comment, thus preventing it from being executed. This saves you from having to delete and retype code. Here is an example of code that has been commented out:

```
//for (var i = 0; i < 5; i++){
//var nQuantity:Number *= 2;
//}
```

When you want to comment out more than one line of code, as in the preceding example, it can sometimes be more convenient to use multiline comments as shown here:

```
/*
for (var i = 0; i < 5; i++){
  var nQuantity:Number *= 2;
}
*/
```

Working with Statements

One of the basic building blocks of ActionScript are *statements*. Statements are the equivalent of sentences in the English language. They are stand-alone commands or instructions given to a Flash movie.

You've already seen a lot of statements up to this point. For example, the following is a statement:

```
trace('"Mr. Sherlock Holmes, I believe?" said she.');
```

The following is also a statement, the likes of which you've also already seen:

```
var sName:String = "Sherlock Holmes";
```

There are additional types of statements that have not yet been formally introduced. The following types of statements in ActionScript are discussed in this chapter:

✦ **Action/function calls** — These include built-in actions and functions such as `trace()` and `play()`. They also include custom functions and methods, topics that are covered in Chapters 4 and 5.

✦ **Variable declaration/assignment**

✦ **Built-in keyword statements** — These include statements such as `continue` and `return`.

✦ **Control structures** — These include structures that group together other statements, and either loops the execution of those statements or makes the execution conditional.

Understanding Statement Syntax

Conceptually, you can say that there are two types of statement syntax. These two types can be differentiated by their complexity. The first kind of statement syntax is for simple statements that generally occupy a single line of code. An example of this kind of statement is as follows:

```
var sBookTitle:String = "ActionScript Bible";
```

You may have noticed that most of the statements in this book thus far have ended in a semicolon. The semicolon is what tells Flash that what precedes it is a complete statement, just like a period in an English sentence. The second type of statement syntax applies to complex, or compound statements. These types of statements can actually contain statements (substatements). Examples of these types of statements are the `if` and `for` statements that are discussed in the next section. The `if` statement, for example, allows you to set a condition that must be met in order for the substatements to be executed. An example of a simple `if` statement is:

```
if(nQuantity > 0) {
  trace("Thank you for your order.");
}
```

Even though you have not yet read about the `if` statement, you can probably understand what the preceding example says. It simply checks to see whether the condition (`nQuantity > 0`) is true. If so, it executes the `trace()` substatement. The substatement is enclosed in the opening and closing curly braces. It is possible to have more than one substatement within the curly braces. For example:

```
if(nQuantity > 0) {
  trace("Thank you for your order.");
  trace("An email has been sent to you.");
}
```

The syntax for the `if` statement is the same for all of the statements in the control structures category, covered in the next section. The basic syntax is as follows:

```
parentStatement {
  substatement(s)
}
```

The substatements enclosed in the curly braces make up what is known as a *statement block*. Notice that the statement block is *not* followed by a semicolon.

Using Statements That Control Flow: Control Structures

Control structures group multiple substatements together and control the flow of code execution. We examine six control structures in this chapter:

✦ if — This statement makes the execution of the substatements conditional.

✦ for — This statement loops the substatements a specific number of times.

✦ for...in — This statement loops through the properties of an object (see Chapter 5 for more information on objects).

✦ while — This statement loops the substatements until a condition is no longer met.

✦ do while — This statement loops the substatements until a condition is no longer met just as a while statement. But a do while statement always executes the substatements at least once.

✦ switch — This statement selects and executes specific substatements determined by the value of the expression you specify.

Working with the if Statement

There are times in your code when you want certain statements to execute only *if* a condition is met. For instance, you might want a message to be displayed only if a certain user has logged in. To accomplish this, you use the if statement. For example:

```
if (sUsername == "Arun"){
  sMessage = "hello, Sir!";
}
```

All if statements begin with the keyword if. Immediately following the if keyword is the condition in parentheses, and after the condition is the statement block (the code encapsulated in curly braces). If the condition is true, the statement block is executed. Otherwise, the statement block is skipped, and the code is resumed immediately following the closing curly brace.

There are a couple of variations on the if statement: the if...else statement and the if...else if statement. If you want to display a custom greeting for a particular user, as in the previous example, but display a different greeting for everyone else, you can use the if...else statement. It functions the same way as the if statement, but if the condition is false, the block of code in the else portion of the statement is executed as follows:

```
if (sUsername == "Arun"){
  sMessage = "hello, Sir!";
}
else{
  sMessage = "hi";
}
```

If you have a different personalized greeting for several users, you can use the if...else if variation, as follows:

```
if (sUsername == "Arun"){
  sMessage = "hello, Sir!";
}
else if (sUsername == "Carolyn"){
  sMessage = "hi, mom! :)";
}
```

Of course, you can combine if...else and if...else if, as follows:

```
if (sUsername == "Arun"){
  sMessage = "hello, Sir!";
}
else if (sUsername == "Carolyn"){
  sMessage = "hi, mom! :)";
}
else{
  sMessage = "hi";
}
```

Working with the for Statement

A for statement uses an index or a counter to loop through the block of code a set number of times. The following is an example of a for statement that loops 25 times:

```
for (var i:Number = 0; i < 25; i++){
  trace(i);
}
```

Notice that inside the parentheses are three expressions separated by semicolons (;). The first of these expressions (var i:Number = 0) is the *initialization expression* that sets the initial value of the index (i). This expression is evaluated only the first time the for statement header is encountered. The second expression (i < 25) is the *conditional expression* that is tested on each iteration through the for statement. As long as the condition is met, the block of code executes. The final expression (i++) is the *updating expression*, and it is processed after each iteration. This expression can manipulate the value of the index in any way, although the use of the increment (++) and decrement (--) operators is most common.

Note

Note that the index variable need not be declared in the initialization expression. It can be declared prior to that, and then the initialization expression can merely assign the initial value to the variable. The following illustrates how the previous example can be rewritten such that the index variable is declared just prior to the for statement.

```
var i:Number;
for(i = 0; i < 25; i++) {
  trace(i);
}
```

You may notice that the index variable, i, does not use the modified Hungarian notation. Using single-letter variable names in for statements is a convention used in programming. Typically, the variable name i is used first.

You use for loops when you want to loop through a block of code a known number of times. Even though it is a known number of times, that does not mean that the number cannot be dynamic. The number of times can be determined by a hard-coded integer value, as in the previous example, or by a variable or expression that evaluates to an integer value. Often, `for` loops are used with arrays to loop through each element of the array, as in the following example:

```
for (var i:Number = 0; i < aTitles.length; i++){
  trace(aTitles[i]);
}
```

Note that `for` loops do not have to initialize with 0, nor do they have to use the increment operator as the previous two examples have shown. Additionally, the expressions can be compound by using the logical AND (&&), OR (||), and NOT (!) operators as well as the conditional operator (?:). Here are some examples of valid `for` loops:

```
for (var i:Number = 25; i > 0; i--){
  trace(i);
}

for (var i:Number = (aTitles.length * 10); i > -50; i -= 5){
  trace(i);
}

for (var i:Number = 50; i > -50; i -= (i > 0 || i < -30) ? 5 : 10){
  trace(i);
}
```

It is even possible to perform more complex initializations and increments by adding additional expressions separated by commas. For example:

```
for(var i:Number = 0, a:Number = 25; i < 25; i++, a -= 2) {
  trace(i + " " + a);
}
```

In the preceding example, the variable i is initialized to 0, and the variable a is initialized to 25. Then, at the end of each iteration, i is incremented by 1 and a is decremented by 2. One important thing to notice with this form is that the `var` keyword is used only once in the compound initialization expression regardless of how many variables you initialize. This is a form that you are not likely to see all too often, but it can be convenient in some scenarios.

You can also work with nested `for` loops — `for` loops inside of `for` loops. This is an extremely useful practice in many cases. Often, when working with multiple arrays, nested `for` loops are invaluable. When you do use nested `for` loops, you need to be very aware of which `for` loop's index you are using within the block of code. It is probably the most common mistake to use the wrong index and end up with unexpected results. Also, be aware that nested `for` loops need to use different names for their index variables. The outermost `for` loop conventionally still uses i, whereas the nested `for` loops would use j, k, l, and so on, respectively. The following is an example of nested `for` loops:

```
var j:Number;
for (var i:Number = 0; i < 3; i++){
  trace(i);
  for (j = 100; j > 97; j--){
    trace("\t" + j);
  }
}
```

This example outputs the following:

```
0
   100
   99
   98
1
   100
   99
   98
2
   100
   99
   98
*/
```

Working with the while Statement

A `while` statement helps you to execute a block of statements repeatedly *while* a condition is true. The structure of the `while` statement is the following:

```
while (condition){
  statements
}
```

Many programmers are confused about when to use the `while` statement versus when to use the closely related `for` statement. Essentially, the `for` statement is a more compact form of the `while` statement, and for that reason, you can often use them interchangeably. For example, consider the following `while` statement:

```
var i:Number = 0;
while(i < 25) {
  trace(i);
  x++;
}
```

This `while` loop could be written as a `for` loop as follows:

```
for(var i:Number = 0; i < 25; i++) {
  trace(i);
}
```

However, a `for` statement is a specialized looping statement that is generally designed to loop a specific, known number of times, even if that number is dynamic. A `while` statement, on the other hand, can be used even when the number of times is unknown. For example, you can use a `while` statement to loop through the elements of an array until it encounters an element that is null.

```
var nIndex:Number = 0;
while(aValues[nIndex] != null && nIndex < aValues.length) {
  trace(aValues[nIndex]);
  nIndex++;
}
```

The preceding `while` statement could be written as a `for` statement using a nested `if` statement and a `break` statement. However, you'll notice that the `while` statement is slightly more straightforward and reads more clearly.

```
for(var i:Number = 0; i < aValues.length; i++) {
  if(aValues[i] == null) {
    break;
  }
  trace(aValues[i]);
}
```

Working with the do while Statement

There is a variation on the `while` statement called the `do while` statement. Notice that in a `while` statement, the condition is tested at the beginning of the statement, so that if it is `false` the first time through, the block of code is never executed. But with the `do while` statement, the condition is placed at the end of the block of code, so the statements in the block are executed *at least* once. Here is an example:

```
do{
  counter++;
} while (!keyPressBoolean)
```

Using break and continue in Statement Blocks

In any looping statement, there are times when you want to break out of the loop in order to prevent an infinite loop, or simply because a condition has been satisfied and there is no longer any point in wasting resources looping through something. To do this, you should use the `break` statement, which is used within the code block of a `while` or `for` statement. When encountered, it stops the loop, and resumes the code immediately following the close of the `while` or `for` statement.

An example of when you might use a `break` statement is as follows: Consider that you have an array (more on arrays in Chapter 7) named `aTitles` that contains the names of the titles of many books. You can use a `for` statement to loop through all the elements of the array to try to find the element that matches a particular title. Now, what if the title happens to be the first element of the array? In that case, you will have found the match right away, and there would not be any point in continuing to search through the rest of the elements. You can use the `break` statement to tell Flash to stop looping through the elements once a match has been found.

```
for (var i:Number = 0; i < aTitles.length; i++){
  if(aTitles[i] == "ActionScript Bible") {
    trace("Title found.");
    break;
  }
}
```

The `break` statement is also used within the `switch` statement, as you will see in the next section, "Working with the switch Statement."

Sometimes, you want to skip over a certain iteration in a loop, which is when the `continue` statement is handy. The `continue` statement is very similar to the `break` statement because it stops the current iteration of a loop wherever it is encountered. But rather than breaking out of the loop, it simply returns to the condition and continues the loop.

The use of `continue` can be useful to avoid errors. For instance, dividing by 0 causes an error. Actually, Flash is smart enough to not generate an error, but it returns infinity as a result, which can be undesired. The following example shows how to use `continue` to avoid dividing by 0:

```
for (var i:Number = -10; i < 10; i++){
  if (i == 0){
    continue;
  }
  trace(100/i);
}
```

In this example, the loop iterates from –10 to –1, essentially skips 0, and resumes with 1 to 9. Notice that it is important where you place the `continue` statement in the code block. If it comes at the end of the code block, it is of little value to you because the rest of the block has already executed.

Working with the switch Statement

Using the `switch` statement is very similar to writing a series of `if` statements. It is slightly different, however, and you may find that it suits your needs better on occasion. The basic structure of a `switch` statement is:

```
switch(expression){
  case testExpression:
    statement;
  [case testExpression2:
    statement;
  default:
    statement;]
}
```

The way it works is that it tests to see if the expression evaluates to be strictly equal to the test expressions. If it is strictly equal, it executes all the remaining statements in the `switch` block. An example might help to make this clearer:

```
var nQuantity:Number = 6;
switch(nQuantity){
  case 10:
    trace("10");
  case 6:
    trace("6");
  case 1:
    trace("1");
}
```

In this example, the following would be displayed in the Output panel:

```
6
1
```

because `nQuantity` evaluates strictly to be equal to 6. Therefore, it executes the statements from that `case` to the end of the `switch` code block. This might not have been exactly what you expected. You might have expected it to execute only the `trace("6")` statement. You can easily accomplish this by adding a `break` statement:

```
var nQuantity:Number = 6;
switch(nQuantity){
  case 10:
    trace("10");
    break;
  case 6:
    trace("6");
    break;
  case 1:
    trace("1");
}
```

You might also want to have a sort of catchall, an equivalent to the `else` statement, in the event none of the cases are met. You can accomplish this by adding a `default` statement:

```
var nQuantity:Number = 6;
switch(nQuantity){
  case 10:
    trace("10");
    break;
  case 6:
    trace("6");
    break;
  case 1:
    trace("1");
    break;
  default:
    trace("none of the cases were met");
}
```

Web Resource We'd like to know what you thought about this chapter. Visit `www.rightactionscript .com/asb/comments` to fill out an online form with your comments.

Summary

✦ Variables are one of the fundamental pieces of ActionScript. They provide a way to give a name to the value they store.

✦ There are three primitive datatypes in ActionScript: string, number, and Boolean. In addition, there are two special values that have no datatype: `null` and `undefined`.

✦ Operators allow you to manipulate operands and form expressions. Using operators, you can perform a wide range of tasks — from adding and subtracting to joining strings together.

✦ It is important to use comments in your code. Comments are not executed in the program, but they serve as reminders to you about the logic and function of your code.

✦ Control structures are statements that enable you to control the flow of your code. You can use `if` statements to execute a block of code *only* if a condition is true. You can use `for` and `while` loops to repeatedly execute a block of code.

✦   ✦   ✦

Working with Functions

Y ou've learned a lot so far. You've learned all of the basic building
blocks of ActionScript. If you thought all of that was exciting,
then hold on to your hat because in this chapter you're going to take
it to the next level. Using functions you can create reusable code,
readable code, portable code. With functions, you can write efficient,
neatly organized, well-maintained code in place of long, unwieldy rou-
tines. Sounds exciting, doesn't it? So let's get to it.

Understanding Programming with Functions

Functions are a revolution. Writing code without functions is like publishing books without a printing press. In the days before the printing
press, books were copied by hand. The publishing business was
much less productive, to say the least. Then, along came the printing
press. Suddenly, a plate could be made one time, and many copies
could be made from that one plate. The printing press was a revolution. It enabled more copies of more books to be made more quickly.
There was much less redundant effort being put into the process.
Likewise, programming without functions means you have to write
each line of code over and over if you want to accomplish the same
(or similar) tasks within the application. But when you write a function, you can encapsulate the statements, and you can invoke that
function (the group of statements) repeatedly, without having to
rewrite the same code. That's working smarter.

Functions are a way of grouping together a block of code in which
execution is deferred until invoked (directly or indirectly) from
within the main routine of the code. In other words, a function is
a way of packaging up a block of code that performs a particular
task when (but not before) it is called.

Functions offer many advantages over unstructured programming.
These advantages include:

✦ Code becomes more readable by eliminating clutter and redundant bits of code.

✦ The program becomes more efficient by reusing functions
rather than retyping the entire block of code each time.

✦ A function becomes a centralized point for making changes. By making a change to the function, that change is applied in each instance the function is invoked.

✦ Well-written functions can be reused through many programs. In this way, you can develop a library of functions that can be used to build many kinds of programs without starting from scratch every time.

✦ Encapsulating code in a function provides the basis for user interaction. Without functions, the application runs as a single routine. With functions, a user-initiated action can invoke a function.

Defining Custom Functions

You have read some of the advantages of using functions in your ActionScript code. Now, you need to learn how to write them. Writing a function is also called *defining* a function or *declaring* a function.

A function is actually a statement, and it uses syntax similar to some of the other statements you saw in Chapter 3, such as `if` and `for`. Therefore, the following syntax should be somewhat familiar already:

```
function functionName():datatype {
  statements
}
```

Here are some of the key points to notice in the function syntax:

✦ The `function` keyword tells Flash that you are defining a function. When you define a function you must always include the `function` keyword as shown.

✦ The function name is a name that you choose. It should follow the same naming rules as a variable. Also like naming variables, it is a good idea to give your function a name that indicates what it does. A name such as `someFunction` is probably not as good a name as `drawNewCircle`.

✦ All function definitions must include a pair of parentheses following the function name. Although it is not shown in the preceding code block, it is possible to add what are known as *parameters* within the parentheses. You'll read about parameters in more detail later in the chapter. But regardless of whether a function defines any parameters, the parentheses must be in the definition.

✦ The parentheses should be followed by a colon and a valid datatype name. The datatype is for the type of data that the function will return. You'll look at returning data later in this chapter. For the time being, use the `Void` name. This means that the function does not return a value.

✦ The body of the function is defined by an opening and closing curly brace (`{ }`).

Now that you've examined the basic syntax, take a look at a very simple example function:

```
function displayGreeting():Void {
  trace("Hello.");
}
```

Calling Functions

We defined the term *function* as a block of code in which execution is deferred. This means that a function can be defined, but nothing will happen until you invoke it, or call it. You can test this for yourself by creating a new Flash movie with the following code on the first frame of the main timeline:

```
function displayGreeting():Void {
  trace("Hello.");
}
```

When you test your movie, you will see that nothing happens, even though there is a `trace` action in the code. So, now that you know how to *define* functions, you need to learn how to use them in your programs by *calling* them.

To call a function, you need to use the name of the function followed by the parentheses, which is called the *function call operator*. When you invoke a function, the call to the function is, itself, a statement. Therefore, you should use a semicolon after the statement. Here is an example that defines a function and then invokes it. If you want to follow along and test this yourself then simply place the code on the first frame of the main timeline.

```
function displayGreeting():Void {
  trace("Hello.");
}
displayGreeting();
```

The result of the preceding code is that when you test the movie, the following should appear in the Output window:

```
Hello.
```

Passing Parameters

Some functions you write do not need any information to be passed to them. For example, the `displayGreeting()` function shown in the preceding section did not require any parameters.

Note   ActionScript does not enforce symmetry between the parameter list defined for a function and the number of parameters passed to the function when called. So, technically, `displayGreeting()` does not *require* any parameter. That is, Flash will compile the code without errors even if you pass no parameters to a function that defines a parameter list. However, that does not mean that the function will work as expected. If you do not pass it the parameters it expects, it is not likely to work correctly.

On the other hand, many functions that you write require parameters to be passed to them. For example, you could make the `displayGreeting()` function much more interesting if it were possible to display a personalized greeting using different names. With a parameter, this is quite simple to accomplish. Here is how the modified function might look:

```
function displayGreeting(sFirstName:String):Void {
  trace("Hello, " + sFirstName);
}
```

Once the function has been defined in this way, you can invoke it and pass it different values for the parameters. Here are some examples:

```
displayGreeting("Joey");   // Displays: Hello, Joey
displayGreeting("Robert");  // Displays: Hello, Robert
```

A parameter is a variable within a function in which the value is assigned when the function is invoked. As you can see by the example with displayGreeting(), the parameter is named sFirstName, and the value of that variable is set each time the function is invoked. When the function is invoked with the value Joey, the variable is assigned that value. Or, if the same function is invoked with the value Robert, the variable is then assigned that value.

The parameter (variable) is declared within the parentheses of the function definition. You may notice that the declaration of a parameter is similar, yet slightly different from the declaration of a regular variable. First of all, the declaration is similar in that you are asked to create a name for the parameter and define the datatype. However, when you declare a parameter you should not use the var keyword. Nor should you use a semicolon. And you cannot initialize a parameter within the parentheses. The following are *incorrect* examples, and will result in errors.

```
// Do not use the var keyword.
function displayGreeting(var sFirstName:String):Void {
  trace("Hello, " + sFirstName);
}

// Do not use a semicolon.
function displayGreeting(sFirstName:String;):Void {
  trace("Hello, " + sFirstName);
}

// Do not try to initialize the variable in the parentheses.
function displayGreeting(sFirstName:String = "Arun"):Void {
  trace("Hello, " + sFirstName);
}
```

What if you want to use multiple parameters in your function? That's quite simple. When you define your function, you can declare multiple parameters by separating them by commas. Likewise, when you invoke the function, you can pass it multiple values by simply delimiting them using commas. Here is an example of the displayGreeting() function definition with multiple arguments:

```
function displayGreeting(sFirstName:String, sGreeting:String):Void {
  trace("Hello, " + sFirstName + ". " + sGreeting);
}

// Displays: Hello, Joey. Good morning.
displayGreeting("Joey", "Good morning.");
```

You may notice that when you start adding more and more parameters to the parameters list in a function definition, the code starts to run off the side of the editor. You can opt for turning on word wrap in the Actions panel. Or, you can also place each parameter (or groups of parameters) on new lines in the definition. This is a common convention because it makes it easier to read the function's parameter list when it consists of many parameters. The syntax remains the same. The only difference is that you are adding new lines between each parameter in the list to make it easier to read. For example:

```
function displayGreeting(sFirstName:String,
                         sGreeting:String):Void
{
   trace("Hello, " + sFirstName + ". " + sGreeting);
}
```

Passing Parameters by Value or by Reference

When you pass parameters to functions, those parameters are passed in one of two ways: by value and by reference. The difference has to do with datatype. Primitive datatypes such as string, number, and Boolean are passed by value. That means that the literal value is passed to the function, and any connection with the variable from which the value came is severed. In other words, after a value is passed to a function, any variable that was used to pass that value along is left alone. Here is an example:

```
function incrementByOne(nValue:Number):Number{
   nValue++;
   return nValue;
}
var nQuantity:Number = 5;
var nQuantityPlusOne:Number = incrementByOne(nQuantity);
trace(nQuantity);
trace(nQuantityPlusOne);
```

The Output window displays the following:

```
5
6
```

In this example, even though the value of nQuantity is passed to the function, and that value is increased by one within the function, nQuantity retains its value of 5. Why? Because the *value* of nQuantity was passed to the function, and not the variable itself. That value was then assigned to a parameter named a within the function, incremented, and returned. The returned value was then assigned to a new variable named nQuantityPlusOne.

On the other hand, when reference datatypes (see Chapter 5 for more information on objects and reference datatypes) are passed as an argument, they are passed by reference. This means that an object that is passed to a function is a reference to the actual object. The result is that anything you do to the object reference within the function affects the object itself. No copy of the object is made. Here is an example using a MovieClip instance named mBox:

```
function move(mA:MovieClip, x:Number, y:Number):Void{
   mA._x = x;
   mA._y = y;
}
move(mBox, 100, 100);
```

The preceding example moves a MovieClip object named mBox to 100,100 on the stage. You can read more about MovieClip objects in Chapters 13 and 14.

Working with the arguments Property

All the functions you've looked at thus far either do not use any parameters, or the parameters are declared as a parameters list within the parentheses. However, regardless of whether or not a function declares any parameters, all parameters passed to the function are stored in a special array named `arguments`. Each function has an `arguments` variable (object) that is created within it when the function is called.

Using the arguments Object to Reference Other Functions

Every `arguments` object has two special properties that reference functions. These properties, `caller` and `callee`, although not often used, can be useful in some circumstances — especially when developing highly abstract functions.

The `caller` property of the `arguments` object returns a reference to another function, if any, that called the current function. If the current function was not called from another function, the `caller` property has a `null` value.

```
function function1():Void{
  function2();
}

function function2():Void{
  if(arguments.caller == function1)
    trace("function2 called from function1");
  else
    trace("function2 not called from function1");
}

function1();
function2();
```

In this example, the Output window displays the following:

```
function2 called from function1
function2 not called from function1
```

The `callee` property of a function's `arguments` object is a reference to the function itself. It may not be apparent immediately why this is useful. But consider the scenario of an anonymous (see the section "Creating Anonymous Functions") recursive function (see the section "Creating Recursion") for a moment. You can write a function literal that is capable of calling itself recursively as follows:

```
var fFactorial:Function  = function(nOperand:Number):Number{
  if(nOperand > 0){
    return nOperand * arguments.callee(nOperand-1);
  }
  else{
    return 1;
  }
}
```

ActionScript does not enforce symmetry between the number of arguments in the function definition and the number of arguments passed to the function when it is called. What that means is that any values that are not passed in the call, but are defined in the argument string for the function, have an `undefined` value. And any values that are passed in the function call that are in addition to the arguments defined for the function are discarded.

Therefore, it is entirely possible to define no parameters in the function declaration but rather rely on using the `arguments` object. Here is an example of how you can use the `arguments` object as an array:

```
function traceParams():Void{
  for(i = 0; i < arguments.length; i++){
    trace(arguments[i]);
  }
}
traceParams("one", "two", "three");
```

In this example, the following is displayed in the Output window:

```
one
two
three
```

In the majority of functions it is far better to declare the parameters. The `arguments` object is mostly useful when you are overloading a function (see the next section "Overloading a Function") or other similar situation. The `arguments` object is mentioned here for completeness and also as a reference for when it is mentioned later in this chapter and in other parts of the book.

Returning a Value from a Function

Up to this point, you've mainly looked at functions that serve as subroutines. That is, the functions can serve to break up the main routine into smaller, more manageable pieces. On the one hand, in the cases where a function operates as a subroutine in that fashion, the function does not need to return a value. On the other hand, sometimes you want to create a function that performs some calculations or operations and then returns a value. You can use the `return` statement within a function to return a specified value. The syntax for a `return` statement is as follows:

```
return value;
```

When you use the `return` statement to return a value from a function, you should specify the datatype that is being returned. You do this in the function definition just after the parenthesis. In the examples up to this point the return type has been `Void`. But when you return a string you should set the return type to `String`, when you return a number you should set the return type to `Number`, and so on.

Here is an example of a function that calculates the area of a rectangle and returns the value as a number.

```
function calculateArea(nA:Number, nB:Number):Number {
  var nArea:Number = nA * nB;
  return nArea;
}
```

As soon as a `return` statement is encountered, Flash exits the function. So, if any other code remains after the `return` statement, it is not encountered. For example:

```
function calculateArea(nA:Number, nB:Number):Number {
  var nArea:Number = nA * nB;
  return nArea;
  trace("The area is: " + nArea);
}

calculateArea(6, 6);
```

In the preceding example, the `trace()` statement is never executed. This is because the code in the function stops executing after the `return` statement.

Following is an example that uses several `return` statements. Obviously, only one of the `return` statements can be encountered in any given call to the function. But in this case, one `return` statement occurs if a condition is met, and the other occurs if the condition is not met. The function accepts two parameters — an array (of strings) and a string value. This function searches through the array using a `for` statement until it finds an element that matches the string. Once it finds the match, it returns the index. If no match is found the function returns `null`.

```
function findMatchingIndex(aTitles:Array,
                           sTitle:String):Number
{
  // Loop through all the elements in the array.
  for(var i:Number = 0; i < aTitles.length; i++) {

    // If one of the elements matches the value of sTitle
    // the return the index. This will cause the function to
    // stop executing.
    if(aTitles[i] == sTitle) {
      return i;
    }
  }

  // If no match was found then (and only then) this
  // statement is encountered.
  return null;
}
```

Cross-Reference For more information on arrays, see Chapter 7.

Regardless of what a function does, if it returns a value, chances are good that you should invoke the function as part of an expression. For example, the `calculateArea()` function could be used in the following way:

```
var nArea:Number = calculateArea(6, 6);
```

Essentially, the function becomes a value just like a string, number, variable, and so on. Therefore, just as the following is a valid, yet not-too-useful ActionScript statement:

```
6;
```

so too is this:

```
calculateArea(6, 6);
```

You want to actually use the returned value in some meaningful way. You can use a function that returns a value in any of the same situations in which you would use a variable. You already saw the `calculateArea()` function used in an assignment statement. Here is another example in which the function is used as part of a conditional expression.

```
if(calculateArea(6, 6) > 18) {
   trace("The area is more than 18.");
}
```

Referencing Functions

You can reference a function by its name. When you use the function name in conjunction with the function call operator (parentheses) the function is invoked. But the name by itself serves as a reference to the function. This means that you can actually use the function name to assign a reference to a variable, for example. Once you have assigned a reference to the function to a variable, you can invoke the function using that variable name in conjunction with the function call operator. Here is an example:

```
function calculateArea(a:Number, b:Number):Number {
   var nArea:Number = a * b;
   return nArea;
}
var fArea:Function = calculateArea;
trace(fArea(6, 6));
```

In the next section, you'll see how you can use this fact to assign anonymous functions to variables. And later in the book, you'll see examples in which a reference to a function can be passed into an object to be used as a callback at a later point.

Creating Anonymous Functions

Thus far you have examined how to define functions using the standard, named function syntax. In addition, there is another way of defining a function using an *anonymous function,* which allows you to create a function that does not have a name. The function can then be assigned to a variable.

Here is the syntax for an anonymous function:

```
function():datatype {
   statements
};
```

You might notice that the syntax between a standard function declaration and an anonymous function is quite similar. There are really only two differences: First, the anonymous function does not include a function name. And second, the anonymous function should be followed by a semicolon, whereas a standard function declaration should not.

As mentioned, you typically want to assign the anonymous function to a variable. Otherwise, the function falls *out of scope* (meaning that it becomes undefined) as soon as it is defined. Here is an example of an anonymous function assigned to a variable:

```
var fSayHi:Function = function(sName:String):Void {
  trace("Hi, " + sName);
};
fSayHi("Joey"); // Displays: Hi, Joey
```

As you can see, you can invoke an anonymous function using the variable to which it has been assigned.

Understanding Scope

Scope is the area within which something is defined within ActionScript. Some things are defined only within a timeline. Others are defined within the scope of an entire movie. And yet, others can be defined only within a function. Two types of scope need to be examined in terms of functions: variable scope and function scope. *Variable scope* is the scope of variables within a function; *function scope* is the scope of a function within a movie.

Variable Scope

When you declare a variable inside of a function properly, the variable is what's known as a *local variable*. A local variable means that when you declare a variable within a function, its definition does not persist after the function call. This is a good way to avoid naming conflicts with other variables.

The following is an example of a function that declares and initializes a local variable named sMessage. The local variable is defined within the function. But if you try to use trace() to display the value of the variable outside of the function, the result will be undefined.

```
function testScope():Void {
  var sMessage:String = "hello, world!";
}
testScope();
trace(sMessage); // Displays: undefined
```

In a large program with many functions, using local variables helps to ensure that you will have fewer conflicts between variables with the same name. Although you should always attempt to use unique names for your variables, it is possible that you will reuse the same name for a variable in different functions. If each has the same scope, one might interfere with the other, leading to undesired values and results. Another possible reason to use local variables is for memory management. Even though it might not be a really significant amount, every variable that is defined in your program takes up memory. If you are not using a variable for anything, but it is still defined, it is a waste of memory. By using local variables, the memory is freed up after the function is finished.

Parameters are treated as local variables — having scope within the function, but not outside it. You can see this with the following example:

```
function testParameterScope(sMessage:String):Void {
  trace(sMessage);
}
testParameterScope("Hello");  // Displays: Hello
trace(sMessage); // Displays: undefined
```

In contrast with this, variables declared outside of the function, but on the same timeline in which the function is defined, can be used within the function. For example:

```
function testScopeTimeline():Void {
  trace(sMessage);
}
var sMessage:String = "Hello";
testScopeTimeline(); // Displays: Hello
```

In this example, the variable sMessage is defined outside of the function, but it is available within the function.

Function Scope

As you've seen thus far, when you declare a function, it is scoped to the timeline on which it has been defined. That means that it can be called from within the same timeline by its name or outside that timeline if a target path is used. If you want to use the function within the same timeline, this is not difficult. If you want to use the function from within another timeline, it is slightly less convenient. And if you want to use the function from within an object that has no timeline, it becomes particularly challenging.

Creating Recursion

Recursion is when a function calls itself from within the function body. This is a necessary process in some cases. The classic example of recursion is that of calculating the factorial of a number. As a refresher, remember that a factorial of a number n is given by the formula:

```
n * (n-1) * (n-2) ... * 1
```

For example, the factorial of 5 is 120 (5 * 4 * 3 * 2 * 1). To create a function that calculates the factorial of a number, you have to use recursion. The following code shows a function that does just that.

```
function factorial(nOperand:Number):Number{
  if(nOperand > 0){
    return nOperand * factorial(nOperand - 1);
  }
  else{
    return 1;
  }
}
```

Recursion is a pretty simple concept, but it is often a new concept to people who have not written a lot of code. For this reason, it can sometimes be a bit confusing. To see how the recursion in this example works, look at what happens when the function is invoked. In this case, we use a small number to keep it short:

```
trace(factorial(3));
```

When the factorial() function is first called, it is called with a value of 3. It executes the statement within the if statement because n is greater than 0. The statement instructs the function to return the value of the expression n * factorial(n-1). In order to evaluate the expression, the function must call itself (factorial(n-1)). This time, when factorial() is called, it is called with a value of 2. Again, the value of n is greater than 0, so the first return statement is executed. And once again, the function calls itself. This time, it is with a value of 1. The same process is run again with factorial() being called one more time with a value of 0. On this function call, however, n is no longer greater than 0, so 1 is returned and the function is not called again.

You should be very careful to make sure that your recursive functions have a limit to the number of recursions that can take place. Consider what would happen if the function from this example were written like this:

```
function factorial(nOperand:Number):Number{
  return nOperand * factorial(nOperand - 1);
}
```

The function would keep calling itself forever. This infinite loop would most likely lead to a crash. Fortunately, Flash has a safeguard against this, and after a set number of recursions, the ActionScript is disabled in the movie. If you use this sort of function of infinite recursion (meaning that there is no condition that will cause the recursion to stop) in your movie, you get a message like this in the Output window when you test it:

```
256 levels of recursion were exceeded in one action list.
This is probably an infinite loop.
Further execution of actions has been disabled in this movie.
```

Overloading a Function

Overloading a function normally involves having multiple functions with the same name, but with different numbers and/or types of parameters. This can be useful in a lot of situations. For example, you could have a function named calculateArea() that calculates the area of a rectangle based on two parameters (the lengths of the sides). But you might also want to have a calculateArea() function that calculates the area of a circle based on a single parameter (the radius). The trouble is that, as already mentioned, ActionScript does not require symmetry between the number of parameters defined for a function and the number of parameters passed to it. That means that you cannot have two functions with the same name — even if they expect different numbers of parameters. And, therefore, you cannot truly overload a function using ActionScript.

Instead, you can simulate function overloading by using if statements or a switch statement in the function to check for the number of parameters. The following shows how you can write a function that calculates the area of either a rectangle or a circle depending on the number of parameters it is passed (determined by arguments.length). While not an overloaded function in the strictest sense, it is the ActionScript equivalent.

```
function calculateArea():Number {
  switch(arguments.length) {
    case 1:
      var nRadius:Number = arguments[0];
      return (Math.PI * (nRadius * nRadius));
    case 2:
      var nA:Number = arguments[0];
      var nB:Number = arguments[1];
      return (nA * nB);
    default:
      return null;
  }
}
```

Writing for Reusability

When writing functions, keep in mind the importance of portable or reusable code. Ideally, you should strive to make your functions as generalized and as encapsulated as possible. A function should typically operate like a black box: This means that the activity of a function should be essentially independent of the rest of the program. A well-written function should be able to be plugged into many different programs, like a master key fits many different locks.

You should write your functions with the idea of reusability. Here are some points to remember when writing generalized functions:

✦ **In general, do not use variables that have been defined outside the functions**—The variables (and objects) that are used within your functions should be declared within the function or passed to the function as parameters. If you need to assign a value to a variable that will be used outside the scope of the function, consider using a `return` statement instead. Because a function can return only one value at a time, you may find that using a `return` statement seems limiting. If this is the case in your function, then probably one of two things is happening: Either the values you want to return are related values, and you can put them into an array or object and return that, or they are unrelated, and your function should be broken up into multiple functions.

There are exceptions to this rule of functions that are completely portable. Sometimes you simply want to use a function to group together some functionality in a movie for the purposes of organizing your code into subroutines. In such cases, it is acceptable to directly access variables and objects declared outside of the function.

✦ **Give your functions names that describe the task they perform**—This helps you to easily identify what a function does when you are looking for it again. If you find this difficult because your function does many things, consider breaking up that function into multiple functions. Even though you want to write generalized functions, they should perform specific tasks.

While these guidelines are generally useful, sometimes it simply is not appropriate to write a really generalized function. If the task for which you are writing a function is very specific to a program you are working on, trying to make it too generalized may not be useful or efficient.

Using Built-In Functions

Thus far, you've learned how you can create custom functions in ActionScript. Typically, it is these custom functions to which people are referring when they talk about functions. However, there are many other *built-in functions* in ActionScript that you can use in much the same way as you would use a custom function. The Actions toolbox contains a folder named Global Functions; inside this folder are additional subfolders containing all the built-in functions. Many of these functions have been replaced by classes and methods (see Chapter 4), and therefore it is best to use the newer replacements. For example, all of the timeline control, movie clip control, and printing functions have been replaced by methods. But there are some global, built-in functions that are still useful. Some of these functions include:

✦ `fscommand ()`—This function is used only in very specific circumstances. The `fscommand()` function enables your Flash movie to communicate with the player. You can read more about this function in Chapters 38 and 40.

✦ `setInterval()`/`clearInterval()` — These functions enable you to instruct Flash to invoke other functions at specific, timed intervals. See the following section, "Creating Interval Functions," for more information.

✦ `escape()`/`unescape()` — These functions are used to convert text to and from URL-safe format. See Chapter 11 for more information.

✦ `getTimer()` — The `getTimer()` function returns the number of milliseconds since the Flash movie began playing. This can be potentially useful for some timed processes in which great accuracy and precision are not required. For instance, you may want to have certain loops in your movie "time out," and `getTimer()` is an appropriate function to use in these cases. For instance, you may have a movie that waits for a response from a server. But if no response is obtained after 30 seconds or so, you might want to stop waiting and alert the user that the server is not responding.

✦ `trace()` — The `trace()` function is one you've already seen throughout this book. It is useful for displaying messages while testing your Flash applications.

✦ `isFinite()`/`isNaN()` — These functions test whether or not a value is finite or even a valid number.

✦ `parseFloat()`/`parseInt()` — These functions parse a number from a string.

Cross-Reference   For more information on the `isFinite()`/`isNaN()` and `parseFloat()`/`parseInt()` functions, see Chapter 8.

Creating Interval Functions

One very useful thing that you can do with functions is to create interval functions utilizing the `setInterval()` command. Using `setInterval()`, you can specify a function and an interval (in milliseconds) on which the function should be continually called. The command returns an ID that can be used to stop the interval at a later point. Here is the standard syntax for `setInterval()` when used with a function:

```
setInterval(function, interval [, param1 ... , paramN])
```

The first parameter for `setInterval()` should be a reference to the function. That means that you should *not* include the function call operator. In other words, if you are using `setInterval()` with a custom function, `writeMessage()`, the first parameter for `setInterval()` is simply `writeMessage`.

The `interval` parameter is given in milliseconds. If you pass a value of 1000 for the `interval` parameter, the function is called once approximately every second. Be aware, however, that the interval on which the function is called is not exact. Flash calls the function as close to the interval as possible. But the processor on the computer on which the player is running has an impact on how accurately the interval is maintained.

You can optionally pass parameters to the function by way of the `setInterval()` action. Any parameters passed to `setInterval()` subsequent to the first two (required) parameters, are passed along to the function. For example, the following shows a function, `writeMessage()`, that takes two parameters. Using `setInterval()` you can tell Flash to call this function every 1000 milliseconds and to also pass two values to the function.

```
function writeMessage(sName:String, sMessage:String):Void {
   trace("Hello, " + sName + ". " + sMessage);
}
var nWriteInterval:Number = setInterval(writeMessage, 1000, "Joey",
"Good morning.");
```

One common mistake that Flash developers make with setInterval() is thinking that variables passed to the function through setInterval() will be evaluated each time the function is invoked. For example, the preceding code could be rewritten as:

```
function writeMessage(sName:String, sMessage:String):Void {
   trace("Hello, " + sName + ". " + sMessage);
}
var sNameParam:String = "Joey";
var sMessageParam:String = "Good morning.";
var nWriteInterval:Number = setInterval(writeMessage, 1000, sNameParam,
sMessageParam);
```

It is tempting to believe that subsequently changing the values of sNameParam and/or sMessageParam would result in a different value being displayed in the Output window. However, the variables sNameParam and sMessageParam are not evaluated each time the function writeMessage() is invoked. Instead, they are evaluated one time — when setInterval() is called. Those values are then used for each call to the function. Therefore, even if you change the values of the variables, the same values will be passed to the function.

Next let's look at an example of a test you can use to check the precision with which Flash is able to invoke the interval function. You can place the code on the first frame of the main timeline of a new Flash document.

```
function traceTimer():Void {
   trace(getTimer());
}
var nTimerInterval:Number = setInterval(traceTimer, 200);
```

When you test this, you see that the function is called at intervals that are regularly close to 200 milliseconds apart, but the interval is not precise.

Frame rate can also have an influence on how you use setInterval() if you use setInterval() to affect animation on the stage. The movie updates the stage only visually at a rate equal to the frame rate of the movie. That means that if some process occurs within the movie at a rate higher than that of the frame rate, it is not reflected in the appearance on the stage at a rate higher than the frame rate. So, if you were to use setInterval() to move a MovieClip instance across the stage and the frame rate is set at 1fps (frames per second), whereas the interval at which the function is being called is 10 milliseconds, it is likely that the movement seen on the stage would be choppy. You can remedy this easily by using the updateAfterEvent() action in the function being called by setInterval(), as shown in the following code. The updateAfterEvent() action instructs Flash to update the display regardless of the frame rate.

```
function moveRight(mA:MovieClip):Void {
   mA._x++;
   updateAfterEvent();
}
var nMoveRInterval = setInterval(moveRight, 10, mCircle);
```

You can also define an anonymous function within setInterval() instead of passing the name or a reference to a function.

```
var nTimerInterval:Number = setInterval(function()
{trace(getTimer());}, 200);
```

Now that you know how to set an interval for a function to be called, you probably want to know how to stop the function from being called. In other words, you want to know how to clear the interval. This is done very simply by calling the clearInterval() function, which takes a single parameter — the ID for the interval that should be cleared. Remember that setInterval() returns an ID that can be used to point to the interval. This ID can then be used as a parameter for clearInterval() to clear the desired interval. The following code stops an interval for which the ID has been assigned to nTimerInterval.

```
clearInterval(nTimerInterval);
```

Web Resource   We'd like to know what you thought about this chapter. Visit www.rightactionscript .com/asb/comments to fill out an online form with your comments.

Summary

✦ Functions are a way of grouping together blocks of code that you can use again and again by calling them by name or reference.

✦ Functions can act as subroutines, or they can perform some algorithm and return a value.

✦ Functions can be named or anonymous. Each of these two types has different advantages and disadvantages.

✦ Using the arguments object created for a function, you can invoke a calling function, invoke an anonymous function recursively, and work with the arguments that have been passed to the function as an array rather than as separate variables.

✦ It is desirable to define generalized functions that can be used in many different contexts.

✦   ✦   ✦

Getting to Know Objects

Objects are quite possibly the most powerful structures with which you can work in ActionScript. An object is simply a programming structure that has certain intrinsic qualities and characteristics. In that way, an object in ActionScript is not unlike an object you can hold in your hand. This chapter takes a look at objects, their blueprints (classes), as well as other important object-oriented programming (OOP) concepts. And, along the way, we hope the chapter demystifies OOP in general.

Introducing Objects

Let's take a moment and really examine what an object is, what it does, and how you can use objects to assist in programming. As mentioned in the introduction to this chapter, an object is a programming construct that has intrinsic qualities and characteristics. This is really the same idea as a tangible object you can see. For example, a book is an object. Books have intrinsic qualities — each book has a title, an author, a publisher, a page count, and so on. In programming terms, these qualities or characteristics are called *properties*.

In addition to having properties that are descriptive, objects can also perform actions. Your computer is an object. It is capable of performing actions such as turning on and off, opening and closing applications, and so on. Cars can accelerate, birds can fly, and so on. These are all examples of actions that objects can perform. When programmers talk about the actions that ActionScript objects can perform, they call them *methods*.

Understanding Object Blueprints

Objects can be categorized according to the blueprint from which they were created. This is true of nonprogramming objects as well. You can categorize all cars as car objects. Clearly not all cars are exactly the same. Even two cars that rolled off the same line one after the other are going to have some differences, and cars of different make, model, and year are going to be quite different. Nonetheless, all cars can be said to have similar characteristics such as having tires, engines, steering wheels, and so on. Likewise, all cars (okay, well, all *running* cars) are capable of the action of accelerating, braking, and the like. It is possible to say, therefore, that cars all derive from the same fundamental blueprint.

In this same way, objects in ActionScript can be categorized based on the type of blueprint from which they have been derived. In programming terms, the blueprint is called a *class*. The class defines all the basic properties and methods for any objects that are derived from it. For example, a class with which you may already be familiar, the MovieClip class, defines properties such as _x and _y as well as methods such as play(). These properties and methods are defined in the class and then each MovieClip object inherits them.

If you look in the Actions toolbox you should find a folder named ActionScript 2.0 Classes. In that folder are several subfolders organizing all the built-in classes in ActionScript. Using ActionScript you can create objects from the built-in classes as well as from custom classes that you (or someone else) have created. First, let's take a look at the built-in classes. Then, later on in the chapter you learn how you can create your own custom classes.

Creating an Object

Before you tell Flash to create an object, all you have is the blueprint — the class. You need to specifically tell Flash that you want it to create an instance of that class. An *instance* of a class is synonymous with an object that is derived from the class. In most cases, you create an instance of a class by invoking the class's constructor. The *constructor* is a special function that shares the name of the class and creates a new instance. The constructor should be invoked as part of a new statement, and the returned value (the new instance) can be assigned to a variable.

```
var variableName:datatype = new ClassName();
```

The datatype you should use to declare the variable should match the name of the class from which you are instantiating the object.

The constructor function, just like any other function, may or may not accept parameters. This depends entirely on how the constructor has been defined. In subsequent chapters, you'll get a chance to review the constructors for all the built-in classes, and so you'll know what, if any, parameters their constructors expect. Also, when you use code hinting in the Actions panel, you can quickly see what parameters a given constructor may expect.

To begin with, let's take a look at the most basic kind of object there is — an Object object. The Object class is the most fundamental class in all of ActionScript, so it is a good place to start. Here is how you can create a new Object instance using the constructor.

```
var oFirstObject:Object = new Object();
```

You can now use the instanceof operator to verify that oFirstObject is, in fact, an instance of the Object class.

```
trace(oFirstObject instanceof Object);  // Displays: true
```

Now that you've seen how to create a basic Object object, how about creating a String object? When you create a String object using the constructor, you typically will want to pass the constructor a string literal (a quoted string) as a parameter.

```
var sTitle:String = new String("ActionScript Bible");
```

Again, you can test to verify that the new object is actually an instance of the String class.

```
trace(sTitle instanceof String);  // Displays: true
```

Accessing Object Properties

Many classes have properties defined such that instances of the class inherit those properties. For example, the String class defines a length property. You can see this if you look in the Actions toolbox. The length property holds the value of the number of characters in the string. For example, if you define a String object as follows:

```
var sTitle:String = new String("ActionScript Bible");
```

then the length property of that object (sTitle) will have a value of 18 because the value ActionScript Bible has 18 characters. If you create another String object:

```
var sName:String = new String("Joey Lott");
```

the object (sName) would have a length property with a value of 9.

The preceding examples created two String objects, named sTitle and sName. Each of these objects was derived from the same blueprint — the String class. Therefore, both of these objects inherited the same set of properties and methods, including the length property. However, the objects don't have the same *value* for the property. Even though the objects share the same blueprint, they are still able to operate independently of one another.

To access a property of an object you need only use the name of the object, a dot, and the name of the property — in that order and without spaces. This syntax is called *dot syntax* because, rather obviously, it uses a dot. For example, you can access the length property of a String object named sTitle in the following manner:

```
sTitle.length;
```

Now, although the preceding statement is perfectly valid ActionScript, it clearly would not be very useful. The length property yields a value, and you likely want to do something with that value. Therefore, you can use a property in exactly the same ways that you can use a variable. In fact, a property is essentially a variable that is associated with an object. Here are a few examples of how you can use the length property:

```
trace(sTitle.length);
if(sTitle.length > 12) {
  trace("The title has more than twelve characters.");
}
var nLengthDelta:Number = sTitle.length - sName.length;
```

Properties can differ from normal variables in one way, however. Typically, you can both read and write to a variable. For example:

```
var nQuantity:Number = 15; // Write
trace(nQuantity);  // Read
nQuantity = 16;  // Write again
trace(nQuantity);  // Read again
```

Many properties work in the same way. For example, you can read and write the _x and _y properties of a MovieClip object. On the other hand, some properties are *read-only properties*. That means that you can read the property value, but you cannot assign a new value to the property directly. The _currentframe property of a MovieClip object is an example of this. Even if you try to assign a new value to the property, it will not take. Here is an example with a MovieClip instance named mCircle. Assume that its timeline is stopped on frame 1.

```
trace(mCircle._currentframe);  // Displays: 1
mCircle._currentframe = 6;  // Will not take
trace(mCircle._currentframe);  // Displays: 1
```

Accessing Object Methods

A method is, as we have already discussed, an action that an object can take. That is a very high-level explanation of a method. In more technical terms, a method is a function that has been associated with an object. Therefore, when accessing the method of an object, you use the same terminology as when accessing a function — you say that the method is called or invoked. Furthermore, you use the same function call operator [()] to invoke a method, and you can pass parameters to a method in the same way as you pass parameters to a function.

The differences between a method and a function are:

✦ When invoking a method you use dot syntax as with a property. That means that you use a dot between the name of the object and the method call.

✦ When you invoke a method, Flash automatically knows to perform the action specifically for that one object. This is unlike a function. A function does not inherently perform any action on any particular object.

The following is an example in which a method is invoked on an object. First, a String object is created. Next the substr() method is invoked. This method returns a portion of the original string starting at the specified index (0), and containing the specified number of characters (12).

```
var sTitle:String = new String("ActionScript Bible");
var sSubject:String = sTitle.substr(0, 12);
trace(sSubject);  // Displays: ActionScript
```

Methods can perform all sorts of actions. In the preceding example, you saw how a method can extract a portion of a string and return it. ActionScript classes have methods that do everything from playing a sound to loading an Extensible Markup Language (XML) document to creating new text fields. Throughout the upcoming chapters, you will get an opportunity to see almost all of the methods built into ActionScript.

Working with Static Properties and Methods

Thus far you've read about properties and methods that are invoked from instantiated objects. For example, you can create a new String object and then read the value of the length property or invoke the substr() method. When you do so, the property or method that is accessed is specific to that particular object. In other words, the substr() method acts upon the specific String object from which it is invoked — not from any other object.

However, there are some properties and methods that are invoked from the class itself, and not from an instantiated object. These kinds of properties are called *static properties* and the methods invoked from a class are called *static methods*. The reason for static properties and methods may not seem clear at first, but when you take a look at the specific static properties methods available within ActionScript, the purpose should become obvious.

Here are a few examples of the static properties available within ActionScript: From the Math class you can read static properties such as PI and SQRT2 and from the Key class you can read static properties such as ENTER, SPACE, and CAPSLOCK. If you look at the names of these static properties, even if you didn't know anything about ActionScript, you can probably guess what values they represent. The static property Math.PI, for example, holds the value of the mathematical pi (~3.142). The Key.SPACE static property holds the key code value for the space key on the keyboard. Because these values don't change with each instance of the class, there is no need to have to access the values from instances. In fact, you cannot even create an instance of some of these classes such as Math and Key because there is no need to create instances that would all be exactly the same. There would not be any possible benefit derived from creating an instance of the Math class, for example. Why? Because the Math class serves simply as a container for mathematical static properties and static methods.

> **Note** There are a handful of built-in classes that have static methods. Some examples of static methods include Mouse.hide(), Math.sqrt(), and Selection.getFocus(). As with the static properties, when you look at the static methods, it becomes apparent why they are invoked from the class. Consider the Mouse.hide() method. There is only one mouse, and so there is no need to create multiple instances of the Mouse class. Likewise, only one selection can be made at a time. Therefore, there is no need to instantiate the Selection class.

As you continue through the rest of the book, we'll point out static properties and static methods as they are relevant.

> **Note** You may have noticed that some of the static properties mentioned in the preceding paragraphs (for example, Key.SPACE) use uppercase characters. Read-only static properties are also called constants, and by convention they are in uppercase characters.

Adding New Object Properties

Some of the built-in ActionScript classes are what we refer to as *dynamic* classes. This means that you can add new properties (and methods as discussed in the next section) to instances even if those properties are not defined for the class. To define a new property for an object instantiated from a dynamic class (such as Object) all you need to do is assign a new value to it as though it already existed for the object. Here's an example:

```
var oDynamicObject:Object = new Object();
oDynamicObject.dynamicProperty = "New property value";

// Displays: New property value
trace(oDynamicObject.dynamicProperty);
```

If you look in the Actions toolbox you will see that the Object class does not define any property named dynamicProperty. But once the object was instantiated, you can create the new property for that object (and only that object).

Adding New Object Methods

Dynamic classes enable you to define not only custom properties for the instances but also custom methods. Typically, adding custom methods to an object is not a particularly good practice. But for some scenarios you could encounter, it is potentially useful. Therefore, for the sake of completeness, we include a brief discussion of this feature here.

You can add a new method to an object in much the same way that you can add a new property — simply by defining the method and assigning it to a custom property of the object. We have already covered all the information you need to accomplish this. Let's revisit it here: First, in Chapter 4, we covered how to assign a function literal to a variable and how to then invoke the function by way of the variable. Then, earlier in this chapter we mentioned that methods are, in fact, functions associated with an object. Therefore, combining these two pieces of information, you can assign a custom method to an object as in the following example:

```
var oDynamicObject:Object = new Object();
oDynamicObject.dynamicMethod = function():Void {
  trace("Method invoked");
};

// Now, call the method.
ODynamicObject.dynamicMethod();
```

Note   Although several classes are dynamic, there are only a few for which it is considered a good practice to define custom properties and/or methods for instances. The `Object` class is one such example. As you'll read in subsequent chapters, the `Object` class is frequently used to make associative arrays, and thus it is valid to add custom properties to instances. The `LoadVars` and `LocalConnection` classes are two examples of other dynamic classes for which it is necessary to define custom properties and/or methods for instances. In those cases, it is an inherent part of how the classes work. However, while some other classes are dynamic, it is not generally considered a good practice to define custom properties and/or methods for instances. A common example is the `MovieClip` class. The `MovieClip` class is dynamic, and many programmers do add custom properties and methods to `MovieClip` instances. However, the code is generally much more scalable and much more readable when custom properties and methods are not added. If it seems necessary, there are likely better ways to accomplish the same thing. For example, if an object needs additional properties and/or methods, it is generally better to define a subclass of the class as described in this chapter.

Defining Event-Handler Methods

We first mentioned event-handler methods back in Chapter 2. They are specially named methods that exist for certain types of objects that Flash automatically invokes when a corresponding event occurs. For example, the `onPress()` event-handler method is automatically invoked for a `MovieClip` object when the user clicks the instance with the mouse. However, by default these event-handler methods are not defined. That makes sense because what you want to occur when the event happens is up to you. So, you have to define the method.

Once an object that accepts event-handler methods has been created, you can define the event-handler method(s) using essentially the same technique as outlined in the earlier section "Adding New Object Methods." The only difference is that in this case, you want to assign the function literal to the specific event-handler method name. The following is an example in which the `onPress()` event-handler method is defined for a `MovieClip` object named `mCircle`:

```
mCircle.onPress = function ():Void {
  trace("You clicked the circle.");
};
```

Cross-Reference   We discuss event-handler methods in more detail in Chapter 13.

Telling Objects to Talk to Themselves

Admit it. You talk to yourself. And that's exactly what you want to help objects to accomplish as well. You see, when you create a custom method for an object, or when you define an event-handler method, you need to be able to tell an object to address itself. For example, if you define an `onPress()` method for a `MovieClip` object, you might want to be able to reference the object's properties from within that method. As you've already learned, you use dot syntax when accessing properties, and that will hold true in this scenario as well. The only thing you need to know is what name an object uses to refer to itself. In ActionScript, you can use the keyword `this` to reference an object from within its own methods. Here's an example in which a `MovieClip` instance named `mCircle` references its own `_xscale` and `_yscale` properties within an `onPress()` event-handler method. The result is that when the user clicks the instance, the `MovieClip` object scales up by 50 percent.

```
mCircle.onPress = function():Void {
  this._xscale = 150;
  this._yscale = 150;
};
```

And, of course, you can reference an object's methods in the same way, using the `this` keyword within a custom method or event-handler method definition. In this example, when the user clicks the `MovieClip` instance named `mCircle`, the object's timeline begins to play back.

```
mCircle.onPress = function():Void {
  this.play();
};
```

The `this` keyword is always a reference to the current object. In the preceding examples, `this` referred to the `MovieClip` instance `mCircle`. Internally, most objects don't not know their own name. They know only how to refer to themselves as `this`.

Displaying the Time with an Object

Now that you have learned about variables, functions, and objects, it's about time you created a Flash application that utilizes some of the things you have learned. In this exercise, you'll create a new Flash application that uses a function and a simple `Date` object to write the current time to the Output panel.

1. Open a new Flash document. Save the document as `displayTime.fla`.

2. Select the first frame of the default layer on the main timeline, and open the Actions panel. You can open the Actions panel either by pressing F9 or by choosing Window ➪ Development Panels ➪ Actions.

3. In the Script pane type the following code:

```
displayTime();
function displayTime():Void {
  var dNow:Date = new Date();
  var nHours:Number = dNow.getHours();
  var nMinutes:Number = dNow.getMinutes();
  var nSeconds:Number = dNow.getSeconds();
  trace("Hours: " + nHours);
```

```
      trace("Minutes: " + nMinutes);
      trace("Seconds: " + nSeconds);
   }
```

4. Test the movie.

If all went according to plan, you should see something that looks similar to Figure 5-1. Of course, your number values will be different. They should match up with the current time on your computer. If you test the movie again, you should see a different time displayed.

Figure 5-1: Sample output from the Flash application.

Now, take a closer look at the code in this application. First, you want to create a function named `displayTime()` that returns no value. Therefore, the function should be declared as `Void`.

```
function displayTime():Void {
  // function statements to go here
}
```

Next, within the function you want to create a new `Date` object. We discuss the `Date` class in further detail in Chapter 10. For now, simply know that when you call the `Date` constructor with no parameters, Flash automatically creates a new object representing the computer's current time.

```
var dNow:Date = new Date();
```

Next, you want to extract the hours, minutes, and seconds parts from the object. If you look in the ActionScript 2.0 Classes ➪ Core ➪ Date ➪ Methods folder in the Actions toolbox, you will see that, among many others, there are three methods that suggest they might do exactly what you want. The `getHours()`, `getMinutes()`, and `getSeconds()` methods return the hours, minutes, and seconds parts of the `Date` object as numbers. You can assign those values to variables for convenience.

```
var nHours:Number = dNow.getHours();
var nMinutes:Number = dNow.getMinutes();
var nSeconds:Number = dNow.getSeconds();
```

You can then use `trace()` to display the results:

```
trace("Hours: " + nHours);
trace("Minutes: " + nMinutes);
trace("Seconds: " + nSeconds);
```

The function has been successfully defined. The only remaining step is to invoke the function:

```
displayTime();
```

Working with MovieClip Objects

The `MovieClip` class belongs to a small conceptual group of built-in ActionScript classes that are not instantiated in the standard way using a constructor. Instances of the `MovieClip`, `Button`, and `TextField` classes are objects that can be created at authoring time by dragging or drawing an instance on the stage. (You'll also see how to create instances of these programmatically in subsequent chapters.) Even if you weren't aware of it, every time you created a movie clip or button on the stage and every time you drew a dynamic or input text field, you were creating an object.

When it comes to working with movie clips in ActionScript, you cannot use a constructor to instantiate them. For example, this code will not create a new `MovieClip` instance on the stage:

```
mCircle:MovieClip = new MovieClip();
```

Instead, when you create the instance at authoring time, you should make sure to give it an instance name via the Property inspector. Figure 5-2 shows an instance of a circle movie clip placed on the stage and the name `mCircle` entered into the Property inspector. If you don't see the Property inspector in your version of Flash, choose Window ➪ Properties to show it.

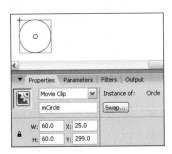

Figure 5-2: Creating an instance of a movie clip on the stage and naming it with the Property inspector.

You should also name button and text field instances in the same way when you create them at authoring time. The Property inspector for a button looks almost identical to the Property inspector for a movie clip. The Property inspector for a text field looks slightly different, as shown in Figure 5-3. When you want to create a text field at authoring time, you can use the text tool to draw the text shape on the stage. Then, from the Property inspector, make sure to choose either Dynamic or Input text. Static text is not an object.

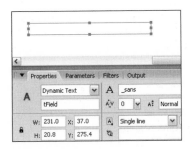

Figure 5-3: Creating a TextField object and naming it with the Property inspector.

Once you have created a new `MovieClip`, `Button`, or `TextField` object, you can invoke the properties and methods in the same way as with any other object. For example, if you have created a `MovieClip` instance named `mCircle`, then you can access the `_x` property using standard dot syntax:

```
trace(mCircle._x);
```

The only caveat at this point is that the ActionScript that references the object must be on the same timeline on which the object has been created. In other words, the object must exist within the same scope in which you are attempting to reference it. If you create a new `MovieClip` object on the main timeline, then you can reference it from ActionScript on the main timeline.

Displaying the Time Using a Movie Clip

In the section "Displaying the Time with an Object," you created a Flash application with a function that displays the time in the Output panel when invoked. In this exercise, you will modify that idea just slightly such that the time gets displayed when the user clicks a `MovieClip` instance on the stage.

1. Open a new Flash document, and save it as `displayTimeWithMovieClip.fla`.

2. Create a new Movie Clip symbol. You can accomplish this by pressing Ctrl+F8 on Windows or ⌘+F8 on the Mac. Or, you can choose Insert ⇨ New Symbol.

3. The Create New Symbol dialog box appears. In the Name field, type **Circle**. Make sure the Movie Clip option is selected, and click OK.

4. The new symbol should open in editing mode. Use the Oval tool to draw a filled circle. The exact size and color of the circle is not particularly important. Just make sure that it is visible and large enough that a user can click on it.

5. Return to the main timeline.

6. Rename the default layer Circle.

7. Open the library and drag an instance of the Circle symbol onto the stage.

8. With the instance selected on the stage, give it a name via the Property inspector. Name the instance `mCircle`.

9. Create a new layer. Name the layer Actions.

10. Select the first (and only) frame of the Actions layer and open the Actions panel.

11. Add the following code to the Script pane:

```
mCircle.onPress = function():Void {
  var dNow:Date = new Date();
  var nHours:Number = dNow.getHours();
  var nMinutes:Number = dNow.getMinutes();
  var nSeconds:Number = dNow.getSeconds();
  trace("Hours: " + nHours);
  trace("Minutes: " + nMinutes);
  trace("Seconds: " + nSeconds);
};
```

12. Save the document and test the movie. When you click on the circle you should see the current time values displayed in the Output panel. Each time you click on the circle a new, updated set of values should be appended to the list in the Output panel.

Now that you've had an opportunity to complete the steps in this exercise, you're ready to take a closer look at what's going on.

First, you simply created a new Movie Clip symbol containing circle artwork. This is probably already a familiar process to you. Once you created the symbol, the next step was to create a new instance of it on the stage. So, you returned to the main timeline, dragged an instance from the library onto the stage, and named the new instance.

It is a good practice to create your ActionScript code on its own layer. This is helpful when you need to locate your code. Therefore, the next thing you did was create a new layer named *Actions* specifically for this purpose. With that layer created, you then added the code to the keyframe on the layer. You may have noticed that the code looked remarkably similar to the code from the previous exercise. In fact, the majority of the code is identical. The only difference is that now the code is encapsulated in an event-handler method instead of a regular function, and the code is invoked when the event occurs instead of manually invoking the function as before. The onPress() event-handler method is used here because it handles the event of the user clicking on the object with the mouse.

Creating Interval Methods

In Chapter 4, you learned how to create interval functions using the setInterval() statement. Because methods are special kinds of functions, it is possible to create interval methods in much the same way that you created interval functions. In fact, you still use the same setInterval() command. The difference is that you need to provide setInterval() with some slightly different parameters because Flash now needs to know not just the function to invoke, but also the object from which to invoke the function (method).

When you want to use the setInterval() command to create an interval method, use the following syntax:

```
setInterval(object, functionName, interval[,
param1 ..., paramN]);
```

Other than a slight difference in the syntax, the setInterval() command works the same when invoking a method of an object as when invoking a function. The method is invoked at the specified interval; if any parameters are specified, they are passed on to the method with each call, and the setInterval() command returns an ID that can be used to stop the interval later using clearInterval().

It is important that the parameters you pass to setInterval() are of the correct type. The first parameter should be a reference to the object whose method you want to invoke. In contrast, the second parameter is not a reference to the method, but rather the name of the method as a string. The third parameter should be a number value specifying the interval in milliseconds. Here is an example that tells Flash to invoke the nextFrame() method of a MovieClip object named mCircle at an interval of approximately once per second.

```
var nFrameInterval:Number = setInterval(mCircle, "nextFrame", 1000);
```

Cross-Reference   If you need any more information on the `setInterval()` statement and how it operates in general, refer back to Chapter 4.

Understanding the Object Class

The `Object` class is the most basic and fundamental class in ActionScript. In fact, all the other classes in ActionScript are based on this basic class. Because the `Object` class is so basic, it does not serve a specific purpose like many other classes. For example, the `String` class deals specifically with strings, and it enables you to perform all kinds of tasks specific to strings. Likewise, the `ColorTransform` class enables you to work with colors programmatically. The `Object` class does not pertain to any specific tasks. Instead, the most common use of the `Object` class is to create simple objects that act as containers for related properties. Programmers often refer to this kind of construct as an *associative array* or a *hashtable*. An associative array is simply a basic object with properties that have something in common. For example, you could create an associative array that contains information about a car. The object could have properties such as `make`, `model`, and `exteriorColor`. In ActionScript the code to create such an object would look like this:

```
// First, create the new Object object.
var oCar:Object = new Object();

// Next, define new properties and values.
oCar.make = "Oldsmobile";
oCar.model = "Alero";
oCar.exteriorColor = "blue";
```

Remember that most of the built-in ActionScript classes are dynamic, meaning that you can add new properties to an instance, even if they are not defined within the class. In the case of an `Object` object used as an associative array, you can also refer to the custom properties as *keys*. In the preceding example, the associative array named `oCar` has three keys — `make`, `model`, and `exteriorColor`.

Associative arrays can be useful for grouping together related data. For example, in the preceding example it makes sense to group together the three pieces of data (the make, model, and exterior color) because they all pertain to the same car. You could, alternatively, create three variables such as the following:

```
var sCarMake:String = "Oldsmobile";
var sCarModel:String = "Alero";
var sCarExteriorColor:String = "blue";
```

However, grouping these values together as keys of a single associative array has several advantages. First, it makes it easier to see the relatedness between the data if they are all grouped together in a single object. And second, it is much easier to pass that data to a function or method — or to return that data from a function or method — if it is grouped together in a single object.

Creating Object Literals

You can create `Object` objects not only with the constructor as shown previously but also using object literal syntax. Object literal syntax is:

```
{property1:value1[, ... propertyN:valueN]}
```

For example, you can create the same oCar object from the previous section, using the following object literal syntax:

```
var oCar:Object = {make:"Oldsmobile", model:"Alero", exteriorColor:"blue"};
```

As you can see, this syntax can sometimes be more concise. This is one of the advantages of object literal syntax. Another advantage is that you can create the object inline within a function call or the like; if a function or method expects an Object object as a parameter, you can define the object right within the function or method invocation. For example, the following shows a function named displayCarInformation() that expects a single object parameter. Then, you can invoke the function and define the parameter value inline.

```
function displayCarInformation(oCarInfo:Object):Void {
  trace("Make: " + oCarInfo.make);
  trace("Model: " + oCarInfo.model);
  trace("Exterior Color: " + oCarInfo.exteriorColor);
}

displayCarInformation({make:"Oldsmobile", model:"Alero", exteriorColor:"blue"});
```

The result of the preceding code is that the following is displayed in the Output panel:

```
Make: Oldsmobile
Model: Alero
Exterior Color: blue
```

It is important to keep in mind that there is a time and place for object literals and a time and place for objects created using the constructor. If you want to simply define an object inline within a function call, use the object literal syntax. On the other hand, if the object is going to have many properties/keys, defining the object with object literal notation might be less readable than defining the object using standard constructor syntax.

Accessing Associative Array Keys and Values

In the preceding sections, you've already seen how to create an associative array. You have also seen one of the two ways of accessing keys and values in an associative array. The first way uses dot syntax — which should already be familiar to you. However, there are certain limitations to dot syntax. The two primary issues that arise with dot syntax and associative arrays are:

✦ The key names must follow the variable naming rules. For example, the key name exteriorColor is valid, but the name Exterior Color is not because it contains a space.

✦ There is no way to use variables to dynamically access the keys and values of an associative array when using dot syntax.

The solution to all of this is to use what programmers call *array-access notation*. When you use array-access notation, the basic syntax looks like the following:

```
object[key]
```

For example, the following statement uses dot syntax.

```
oCar.make = "Oldsmobile";
```

That same statement can be rewritten in array-access notation as follows:

```
oCar["make"] = "Oldsmobile";
```

Notice that the name of the key is in quotes. In other words, when using array-access notation the key is specified as a string.

You can use array-access notation in the same situations in which you can use dot syntax. For example, you can both assign a value to a key and read the value from the key as shown here.

```
oCar["make"] = "Oldsmobile";
trace(oCar["make"]);
```

Because the key is specified as a string when using array-access notation, you can use key names that you cannot use in dot syntax. For example, you cannot do the following:

```
oCar.Exterior Color = "blue";   // Will cause an error
```

However, you can do this:

```
oCar["Exterior Color"] = "blue";   // Correct
```

Creating keys such as `Exterior Color` can be useful in several scenarios. For example, the key names can be user-generated or can come from another source such as a database. In such a case, you cannot necessarily guarantee that the key names will follow variable naming rules. Another example is that you may want to display the names of the keys and their values to the user. In that case it is probably preferable to display a value such as `Exterior Color` instead of `extColor`.

When you use array-access notation you can also use variables for the keys. For example:

```
var sKeyName:String = "make";
trace(oCar[sKeyName]);   // Displays: Oldsmobile
```

Using variables as the key names can be quite useful in many situations. For example, if the names of the keys are unknown (they are retrieved from an outside source or specified by the user), the use of variables is what enables you to create such an application.

Looping through Object Properties

If you have created an associative array, it is often useful to be able to loop through all the keys and values even if you don't necessarily know the key names. For this purpose, you can use the `for...in` statement. The `for...in` statement syntax is:

```
for(var property:String in object) {
  statements
}
```

When Flash encounters a `for...in` statement, it automatically loops through all the enumerable (more on enumerable and non-enumerable properties later in this chapter) properties of the specified object. Through each iteration, the next property name is assigned to the variable `property`. The name of the variable is up to you. Within the body of the `for...in` statement (inside the curly braces), you can use the variable to access the corresponding value in the associative array. Here is an example that creates an associative array and then uses a `for...in` statement to iterate through all the keys and values, and finally writes those to the Output panel.

```
var oCar:Object = new Object();
oCar["Make"] = "Oldsmobile";
oCar["Model"] = "Alero";
oCar["Exterior Color"] = "blue";

for(var sKey:String in oCar) {
  trace(sKey + ": " + oCar[sKey]);
}
```

The result in the Output panel is:

```
Exterior Color: blue
Model: Alero
Make: Oldsmobile
```

Notice that the order in which Flash iterates through the keys in the associative array does not match the order in which the keys were assigned to the object. They are returned in the reverse order from which they were added. If you need to control the order, you should use an integer-indexed array — an instance of the `Array` class.

 For more information on `Array` objects see Chapter 7.

Creating Custom Classes

Now that you've had a chance to learn about objects in general, and you've created a few instances of objects based on built-in classes, the natural progression is to next delve into creating custom classes. Note that in many cases creating custom classes is considered to be an advanced topic. Furthermore, the majority of the remaining chapters in this book do not specifically rely on your having an understanding of how to create your own classes. Therefore, if you prefer, you are welcome to momentarily skip this portion and move on to the next. Also, as you read this section, if there are any parts that are not completely clear to you, don't worry. ActionScript is not the sort of thing that you are likely to master in a day . . . or a week . . . or a year. Even experts that have been working with ActionScript for years continue to learn things daily. So keep an open mind, and you'll have some fun with custom classes.

Understanding the Purpose of Custom Classes

You've looked through the Actions toolbox. Perhaps you've flipped through the table of contents of this book. You've seen that ActionScript has a whole slew of built-in classes. They seem to do just about everything. So, why would you want to create your own custom class?

Good question. The answer is: To make your programming a little easier, a little more easily understood, and a little easier to share and reuse. Every application involves different types of concepts that can be grouped together. A storefront application would involve concepts such as products, users, shopping basket, and so forth. Each of these concepts can be modeled as a class by grouping together the common characteristics and actions. For example, each user can have a name, a password, and a shipping address. These are the characteristics of a user. Likewise, a user can perform actions such as logging in, checking out, and so on. A storefront application is likely to have many users. So, it is convenient to create a single class that helps to describe all users in generic terms. Then, each specific user can be an instance of that class.

Custom classes are not limited to creating something that describes a user in a storefront application. You can create custom classes that describe just about anything. If you are creating a message board application, you might create classes to describe threads, posts, and categories. In a whiteboard application you might create classes to describe lines, shapes, and so on. Classes can also describe less tangible types of objects. Some classes can be used to create objects for sending and receiving and otherwise working with data. The possibilities for classes are limitless.

Working with the Classpath

All ActionScript classes should be defined in AS files located in a directory within Flash's classpath. AS files refer to text files saved with the file extension .as. The Flash classpath is a list of directories to which Flash will automatically look for these AS files. By default the classpath consists of the following two directories:

✦ The same directory to which the FLA file has been saved. This is convenient for classes that pertain only to one project. But for classes that you are likely to reuse in multiple projects, this is not the recommended location.

✦ The Classes directory in what Macromedia refers to as the user configuration directory. This directory is found in the following locations depending on your operating system.

```
Windows 98 and ME: C:\[Windows Directory]\
Application Data\Macromedia\
Flash 2004\[language]\Configuration\Classes

Windows NT: C:\[Windows directory]\profiles\
[user name]\Application Data\Macromedia\
Flash 2004\[language]\Configuration\Classes

Windows 2000 and XP: C:\Documents and Settings\
[user name]\Application Data\Macromedia\Flash
2004\[language]\Configuration\Classes

Mac OS Classic (Mac OS 8.x and above) Single-User:
Hard Disk:System Folder:Application
Support:Macromedia:Flash 2004:[language]:Configuration:Classes

Mac OS Classic (Mac OS 8.x and above) Multi-User:
Hard Disk:Users:[user name]:
Documents:Macromedia:Flash 2004:[language]:Configuration:Classes

Mac OS X: Hard Disk/Users/[user name]/Library/
Application Support/Macromedia/
Flash 2004\[language]\Configuration\Classes
```

You can also add your own directories to the classpath. Flash actually enables you to set two classpaths. First l, you can add a directory to the global Flash classpath that is active for all Flash documents. You can also specify a classpath for each FLA file. You just need to add a directory to one or the other. If the directory is intended to hold classes that may well be used in other FLA files, it is wise to include that directory in the global classpath. If you simply want to add another directory to the classpath for a single FLA (meaning that in all likelihood the class files are going to be used by only that one FLA), you should add that directory to the classpath for the FLA.

To edit the global classpath, do the following:

1. Choose Edit ➪ Preferences or press Ctrl+U on Windows or ⌘+U on the Mac.

2. Choose the ActionScript tab in the Preferences dialog box.

3. In the Language section near the bottom of the ActionScript preferences screen, click the ActionScript 2.0 Settings button.

To edit the document-level (FLA-specific) classpath, do the following:

1. Choose File ➪ Publish Settings or press Ctrl+Shift+F12 on Windows or ⌘+Shift+F12 on the Mac.

2. Click the Flash tab in the Publish Settings dialog box. If the Flash tab is not shown, first select the Format tab and make sure that Flash (.SWF) is checked.

3. Make sure that ActionScript 2.0 is selected for the ActionScript Version option, and then click the Settings button to the right of the drop-down menu.

Whether working with the document-level or the global classpath, you can add, remove, or reorder directories in the same ways.

You can add a new directory to the classpath by clicking the Add New Path button (the button with the plus sign) and typing the path to the directory in the new entry that is made following the other, existing paths. The path can be either a relative or absolute. The global classpath (assuming you have not already changed it) has two default entries in the classpath. These entries are $(UserConfig)/Classes (which points to the Classes directory in the user configuration directory) and . (which refers to the same directory to which the FLA is saved).

You can remove a path from the classpath by selecting the entry from the list and clicking the Remove Selected Path button (the button with the minus sign).

You can also reorder the directories in the classpath. Flash searches for classes in the directories in the order they are listed. This means that if you have two classes with the same name in two different directories in the classpath, Flash uses the one that it encounters first.

Also, be aware that Flash always searches in the document-level classpath first. That means that if you have two classes with the same name, the one found in the document-level classpath will be used instead of the one in the global classpath.

If you plan to create many classes that you want to make accessible globally to your FLA files, you might consider creating a directory for those files and adding it to the global classpath. You can save your custom classes to the user configuration directory's Classes directory. However, you may find that navigating to that directory may prove tiresome because it is nested within many parent directories. A directory such as C:\ActionScriptClasses may be much easier for the purposes of saving and editing the AS files.

Making AS Files

To create your AS files, you need nothing other than a text editor. Although you can use any text editor you want for this purpose, if you are working with Flash Professional, you can use the integrated Script window. The Script window provides you with color coding, code hinting, and syntax checking — things that a regular text editor is not likely to do.

To create a new AS file using the Script window in Flash Professional, do the following:

1. Choose File ➪ New or press Ctrl+N on Windows or ⌘+N on the Mac.

2. In the General tab, select ActionScript File from the list.

3. Click OK. A new document will open up in the Script window.

If you have Flash Basic, you do not have the ActionScript Editor built into the IDE as with Flash Professional. In that case, you'll need to use a different editor. Even if you have Flash Professional you may find that the ActionScript Editor simply doesn't have the features you'd like in an editor. In either case, there are a variety of third-party editors available:

✦ **PrimalScript** — A commercial product with excellent features and ActionScript 2.0 support. PrimalScript has better code-hinting than the ActionScript Editor. It also has better project management and version control integration. Learn more at `www.sapien.com`.

✦ **FDT** — A plug-in for the popular editor, Eclipse. You can download Eclipse for free from `www.eclipse.org`. FDT leverages the features of Eclipse, but provides added ActionScript support. Learn more at `www.powerflasher.net`.

✦ **Seppy** — A free ActionScript editor. Learn more at `www.sephiroth.it/python/sepy.php`.

✦ **Scite** — A free ActionScript editor. Learn more at `www.bomberstudios.com/sciteflash`.

Creating a Simple Class

Each class must be defined in its own file. The name of the file must correspond to the name of the class. For example, if you want to create a `Car` class, the name of the file should be `Car.as`.

Within the file, all the code should be enclosed in the following code structure:

```
class ClassName {
   // The rest of the code goes here.
}
```

Every class definition must begin with the keyword `class`. This helps Flash to know that what is being defined is a class. The body of the class is enclosed in curly braces as shown.

The `ClassName` in the preceding syntax example should be the name of the class such as `Car`. The names of classes follow the same rules as variables. Your class names cannot contain any spaces or other special characters. Typically, class names contain only letters, and perhaps, in rare occasions, numbers (but the name can never start with a number). By convention, class names begin with capital letters. Capital letters help to distinguish classes from instances. Therefore, following this convention, `Car` is a better choice for a class name than `car`.

Defining Properties for a Class

Once you have told Flash that you are creating a class by using the syntactical structure described in the last section, the next step is to determine what properties you want to define for the class. For example, in a `Car` class you might want to define properties such as `make`, `model`, and `exteriorColor`.

When defining a class's properties, you need to decide whether they should be public or private. A public property is one that can be accessed directly from instances, whereas a private property cannot be accessed from the instances. The difference between declaring a public or private member is simply the difference between using the `public` or `private` keyword in the declaration. The syntax for a public member declaration is as follows:

```
public var memberName:datatype;
```

The syntax for a private member declaration is:

```
private var memberName:datatype;
```

You probably have noticed that declaring a public or private class member is almost identical to declaring a standard variable. You need to add only the additional `public` or `private` keyword at the beginning of the declaration.

> **Note** You might sometimes see classes in which public members are declared without the use of the `public` keyword. If you do not specify public or private, Flash defaults to public. However, it is a good practice to always explicitly declare the member to be public when it is public.

You might wonder why you would ever want to define private members — properties that cannot be directly accessed from the instances of the class. After all, isn't the entire purpose of a property that it can be accessed from the instances? It may surprise you to find out that we actually recommend that you make *all* properties private. Instead of allowing the property to be directly accessed from the instances of the class, you create special methods called *getter* and *setter* methods that handle the getting and setting of the property values. This practice is called *data hiding*, and it is encouraged in all object-oriented programming. The reasons may not be immediately apparent. But with a little investigation they become obvious:

✦ If you allow the values of members to be directly retrieved and set from the instances, you open up the possibility for data corruption. For example, if you create a `Car` class, you may want to ensure that the value for the `exteriorColor` property is one of the valid options. For example, `red`, `silver`, `green`, and so on would be valid colors. But you don't want the color to be accidentally set to `rabbit`, `dog`, or `cow`. Using a setter method enables you to ensure the quality of the data. Another example: The same `Car` class might have a `mileage` member. Obviously, the mileage on a car cannot be negative. Using a setter method enables you to ensure that the value is always positive.

✦ Another reason for getter and setter methods is that they enable you to perform other tasks when the value is retrieved or set. It might be that two or more members are interrelated, and the value of one affects the values of the others. Using a setter method enables you to perform the appropriate checking and assignments.

✦ Using getter and setter methods allows you to create read-only (or, theoretically write-only) properties in addition to standard read-write properties. By defining only a getter method, and no setter method, for example, the property is a read-only property. This is useful for properties that are dependent on the values of other properties. For example, an `area` property of a `Circle` class could be a read-only property whose value is dependent on the value of a read-write property named `radius`.

Therefore, we suggest that you create only private members in your classes, and that you expose them by way of getter and setter methods only. We also recommend that you begin the names of all private members with an underscore (_). For example, the private member declarations for an example Car class might look like this:

```
private var _sMake:String;
private var _sModel:String;
private var _sExteriorColor:String;
```

Using the underscore to differentiate private members is a standard programming convention. When you use underscores you can readily distinguish between local variables and private class properties used within methods.

Once you have declared the private members for your class, the next step is to define the corresponding getter and setter methods. The syntax for a getter method is as follows:

```
public function get propertyName():datatype {
  // Method code goes here. At some point there should be
  // the following:
  // return correspondingPrivateMember;
}
```

The syntax for a setter method is:

```
public function set propertyName(valueParam:datatype):Void {
  // Method code goes here. At some point there should be
  // the following:
  // correspondingPrivateMember = valueParam;
}
```

As you can see, the syntax for getter and setter methods is quite similar to the syntax for regular functions. The differences are simply that the getter and setter method declarations should include the public keyword and that the keyword get or set should come just before the method name. The method name is the name of the property as it should be accessible from the instances. Commonly the getter and setter method names will be quite similar to the corresponding private properties, differing only by an underscore and a prefix. For example, if the private property is called _sMake, then the corresponding getter and setter methods will be called make.

Here is an example of simple getter and setter methods that correspond to the _make member.

```
public function get make():String {
  return _make;
}

public function set make(sMake:String):Void {
  _sMake = sMake;
}
```

When you have defined getter and setter methods, you can then access those methods from an instance using the getter and setter method name as though it were a property of the instance. Here is an example. First, create a simple Car class. If you want to follow along you'll need to create this class in an AS file named Car.as. This file should be saved in your Flash classpath.

```
class Car {
  private var _sMake:String;

  public function get make():String {
    return _sMake;
  }

  public function set make(sMake:String):Void {
    _sMake = sMake;
  }
}
```

Then, in a new Flash document, on the first frame of the default layer of the main timeline, you can create an instance of the Car class and then get and set the values as shown here:

```
var crTest:Car = new Car();
trace(crTest.make);  // Displays: undefined
crTest.make = "Oldsmobile";
trace(crTest.make);  // Displays: Oldsmobile
```

Notice that you didn't define a public property named make for the Car class. Instead, you created a private member named _sMake and defined getter and setter methods named make. Flash then knows that any time you access the make property from an instance of the class, it should invoke the getter or setter method. You can test to see that you cannot directly access the private member _sMake with the following addition to the FLA code:

```
trace(crTest._sMake);
```

When you add that code and then try to test the movie, you should get the following error message:

```
The member is private and cannot be accessed.
```

If you are following along, you should delete or comment out the line that is causing the error. This line just verifies that the private member was, indeed, private.

You can also test to make sure that Flash is actually invoking the getter and setter methods. By adding some simple trace() actions, you can clearly see that the methods are, in fact, being invoked:

```
class Car {
  private var _sMake:String;

  public function get make():String {
    trace("Getting the value...");
    return _sMake;
  }

  public function set make(sMake:String):Void {
    trace("Setting the value...");
    _sMake = sMake;
  }
}
```

Defining Methods for a Class

Like properties, methods can be either public or private. Public methods are accessible from the instances of the class. Private methods are accessible only from other methods within the class. Private methods are useful for encapsulating certain logic or processes that you want to use internally within the class.

The syntax for a public method is:

```
public function methodName([parameterList]):datatype {
  // Method code goes here.
}
```

The syntax for a private method is almost identical:

```
private function methodName([parameterList]):datatype {
  // Method code goes here.
}
```

Here's an example of a public method for a Car class:

```
public function drive(bStart:Boolean):Void {
  if(bStart) {
    trace("Car is driving.");
  }
  else {
    trace("Car is stopped.");
  }
}
```

And here is an example of how to invoke the preceding method from an instance of the Car class named crTest.

```
crTest.drive(true);   // Displays: Car is driving.
crTest.drive(false);  // Displays: Car is stopped.
```

Creating a Constructor

If you don't explicitly define a constructor method for your class, Flash automatically creates an empty constructor for you (in the compiled code, not in the AS file). On one hand, this means that, as you saw in the preceding example with the Car class, you can create an instance of the class using a constructor that does not require any parameters. For example:

```
var crTest:Car = new Car();
```

On the other hand, there are at least two good reasons to explicitly define a constructor for your class:

✦ If you define a constructor, even if it doesn't require any parameters, you can perform initialization when the instance is created.

✦ You can define a constructor that accepts parameters. For example, a Car constructor might accept parameters that set the values for some of the properties.

The correct syntax for a constructor method is:

```
function ClassName([parameterList]) {
  // Constructor code goes here.
}
```

A constructor method should never return a value; therefore, it is unnecessary (and incorrect) to declare a return type. There are specific cases in which you might want to define a private constructor. However, in most cases the constructor is public.

Here is an example of a constructor for the Car class:

```
public function Car(sMake:String) {
  _sMake = sMake;
}
```

In ActionScript, you cannot currently have more than one constructor per class. If you want to mimic overloaded constructors, you can create a single constructor that determines the number or parameters and then invokes the correct private method. The following is an example of a Car class that mimics overloaded constructors:

```
class Car {
  private var _sMake:String = null;
  private var _sModel:String = null;
  private var _sExteriorColor:String = null;

  public function Car() {
    switch(arguments.length) {
      case 3:
        _sExteriorColor = arguments[2];
      case 2:
        _sModel = arguments[1];
      case 1:
        _sMake = arguments[0];
    }
  }

}
```

In the preceding example, when the constructor is called with no parameters no additional actions take place. If the constructor is called with one parameter, then the _sMake property is set. If the constructor is called with two parameters, then the _sModel *and* _sMake properties are set (notice there are no break statements). If the constructor is called with three parameters, then the _sExteriorColor, _sModel, and _sMake properties are set.

Adding Static Properties to a Class

You learned earlier about static properties in some of the built-in ActionScript classes. You can also define static properties in your own, custom classes. To create a static property, all you need to do is use the static keyword in the declaration. Here is the basic syntax for a static property declaration:

```
static publicPrivateModifier var propertyName:Datatype;
```

Static properties can be useful when you want to associate a value or some values with a class, but you don't need to create copies of the value in each instance. Often static properties are constants, and you'll assign a value to the property in the declaration statement. Here is an example in which an array (see Chapter 7 for more on arrays) is created as a constant in the Car class. This constant holds the possible values for the exterior color.

```
static public var EXTERIOR_COLORS:Array = ["red", "silver", "gold", "white",
"blue"];
```

Remember, static properties are always accessed from the class, not from an instance. Therefore, you would always access the EXTERIOR_COLORS constant as Car.EXTERIOR_COLORS. This is true even within a regular public or private method of a class. For example, within a method of the Car class you would still access the constant as Car.EXTERIOR_COLORS.

As noted previously, constant names are always in uppercase by convention.

Note   Even though the EXTERIOR_COLORS static property is intended to behave like a constant, it does not strictly enforce read-only behavior. Technically, a constant ought to be read-only. If you want to ensure that the values of a constant aren't overwritten you can define the constant using a getter method as follows.

```
static public function get EXTERIOR_COLOR():Array {
   return ["red", "silver", "gold", "white", "blue"];
}
```

Adding Static Methods to a Class

You can also add static methods to custom classes. Static methods are methods that are accessed directly from the class itself. The syntax for a static method is:

```
static publicPrivateModifier function methodName([paramList]):datatype {
   // Method code goes here.
}
```

Within a static method you cannot access the public or private members of a class, and the keyword this is not accessible.

Making Your First Class

In this exercise, you create a Car class. You'll build the class in stages so that you can see how each step works.

1. Create a new Flash document. Save this file as car.fla.

2. Create a new AS file. Save this file as Car.as. Make sure to save the file to the same directory as the FLA file. This will ensure that the AS file is in the classpath for the FLA.

3. In the AS file, define a simple Car class with three private members, _sMake, _sModel, and _sExteriorColor. Define the getter and setter methods for them as well.

```
class Car {

   private var _sMake:String = null;
```

```
  private var _sModel:String = null;
  private var _sExteriorColor:String = null;

  public function get make():String {
    return _sMake;
  }

  public function set make(sMake:String):Void {
    _sMake = sMake;
  }

  public function get model():String {
    return _sModel;
  }

  public function set model(sModel:String):Void {
    _sModel = sModel;
  }

  public function get exteriorColor():String {
    return _sExteriorColor;
  }

  public function set exteriorColor(sExteriorColor:String):Void {
    _sExteriorColor = sExteriorColor;
  }
}
```

4. In the FLA file, create an instance of the `Car` class, set the properties, and then use the `trace()` action to display the values.

```
var crTest:Car = new Car();
crTest.make = "Oldsmobile";
crTest.model = "Alero";
crTest.exteriorColor = "blue";
trace(crTest.make);
trace(crTest.model);
trace(crTest.exteriorColor);
```

5. Test the movie. You should see the following in the Output panel.

```
Oldsmobile
Alero
blue
```

Once you have tested the movie, close the SWF file and return to the FLA file.

6. In the AS file, add a constructor that allows you to specify the make, model, and exterior color as you create the object. The class definition should look like the following (changes are shown in bold).

```
class Car {

  private var _sMake:String = null;
  private var _sModel:String = null;
```

```
      private var _sExteriorColor:String = null;

      public function get make():String {
        return _sMake;
      }

      public function set make(sMake:String):Void {
        _sMake = sMake;
      }

      public function get model():String {
        return _sModel;
      }

      public function set model(sModel:String):Void {
        _sModel = sModel;
      }

      public function get exteriorColor():String {
        return _sExteriorColor;
      }

      public function set exteriorColor(sExteriorColor:String):Void {
        _sExteriorColor = sExteriorColor;
      }

      public function Car(sMake:String,
                          sModel:String,
                          sExteriorColor:String)
      {
        _sMake = sMake;
        _sModel = sModel;
        _sExteriorColor = sExteriorColor;
      }

  }
```

7. In the FLA file, change the code to the following:

```
var crTest:Car = new Car("Oldsmobile", "Alero", "blue");
trace(crTest.make);
trace(crTest.model);
trace(crTest.extColor);
```

8. Test the movie. You should get the same results as before. When you have tested the movie, close the SWF file and return to the FLA file.

9. In the AS file, add a getter method named description. Notice that you have not defined a private member named _sDescription. In this case, description is based on the values of the other properties.

```
class Car {

  private var _sMake:String = null;
```

```
private var _sModel:String = null;
private var _sExteriorColor:String = null;

public function get description():String {
  var sDescription:String = "";
  sDescription += "Model: " + _sModel + "\n";
  sDescription += "Make: " + _sMake + "\n";
  sDescription += "Exterior Color: " + _sExteriorColor + "\n";
  return sDescription;
}

public function get make():String {
  return _sMake;
}

public function set make(sMake:String):Void {
  _sMake = sMake;
}

public function get model():String {
  return _sModel;
}

public function set model(sModel:String):Void {
  _sModel = sModel;
}

public function get extColor():String {
  return _sExteriorColor;
}

public function set extColor(sExteriorColor:String):Void {
  _sExteriorColor = sExteriorColor;
}

public function Car(sMake:String,
                    sModel:String,
                    sExteriorColor:String)
{
  _sMake = sMake;
  _sModel = sModel;
  _sExteriorColor = sExteriorColor;
}

}
```

10. In the FLA file, change the code to the following:

```
var crTest:Car = new Car("Oldsmobile", "Alero", "blue");
trace(crTest.description);
```

11. In the AS file, add a read-only property named `mileage`:

```
class Car {

    private var _sMake:String = null;
    private var _sModel:String = null;
    private var _sExteriorColor:String = null;
    private var _nMileage:Number;

    // Define only a getter method for mileage to make it
    // a read-only property.
    public function get mileage():Number {
        return _nMileage;
    }

    public function get description():String {
        var sDescription:String = "";
        sDescription += "Model: " + _sModel + "\n";
        sDescription += "Make: " + _sMake + "\n";
        sDescription += "Exterior Color: " + _sExteriorColor + "\n";

        // Add the mileage to the description.
        sDescription += "Mileage: " + _nMileage + "\n";
        return sDescription;
    }

    public function get make():String {
        return _sMake;
    }

    public function set make(sMake:String):Void {
        _sMake = sMake;
    }

    public function get model():String {
        return _sModel;
    }

    public function set model(sModel:String):Void {
        _sModel = sModel;
    }

    public function get extColor():String {
        return _sExteriorColor;
    }

    public function set extColor(sExteriorColor:String):Void {
        _sExteriorColor = sExteriorColor;
    }

    public function Car(sMake:String,
```

```
                              sModel:String,
                              sExteriorColor:String)
  {
     _sMake = sMake;
     _sModel = sModel;
     _sExteriorColor = sExteriorColor;

     // Initialize the mileage to 0.
     _nMileage = 0;
  }

}
```

12. In the AS file, add a private member named _nDriveInterval. Next, add a public method named drive() that accepts a Boolean parameter. If the parameter value is true then the method sets an interval method. If the parameter value is false, the method clears the interval. You'll also need to define a private method named incrementMileage(). This is the method that gets called at an interval when the drive() method is invoked with a value of true.

```
class Car {

   private var _sMake:String = null;
   private var _sModel:String = null;
   private var _sExteriorColor:String = null;
   private var _nMileage:Number;
   private var _nDriveInterval:Number;


   public function get mileage():Number {
      return _nMileage;
   }

   public function get description():String {
      var sDescription:String = "";
      sDescription += "Model: " + _sModel + "\n";
      sDescription += "Make: " + _sMake + "\n";
      sDescription += "Exterior Color: " + _sExteriorColor + "\n";
      sDescription += "Mileage: " + _nMileage + "\n";
      return sDescription;
   }

   public function get make():String {
      return _sMake;
   }

   public function set make(sMake:String):Void {
      _sMake = sMake;
   }

   public function get model():String {
      return _sModel;
```

```
    }

    public function set model(sModel:String):Void {
      _sModel = sModel;
    }

    public function get extColor():String {
      return _sExteriorColor;
    }

    public function set extColor(sExteriorColor:String):Void {
      _sExteriorColor = sExteriorColor;
    }

    public function Car(sMake:String,
                        sModel:String,
                        sExteriorColor:String)
    {
      _sMake = sMake;
      _sModel = sModel;
      _sExteriorColor = sExteriorColor;
      _nMileage = 0;
    }

    // The drive() method should accept a Boolean parameter.
    public function drive(bStartDrive:Boolean):Void {

      // If the parameter value is...
      if(bStartDrive) {

        // ... true, tell Flash to start invoking the
        // incrementMileage() method of this class at a
        // rate of approximately once every second. Assign
        // the interval ID to _driveIntervalID.
        _nDriveInterval = setInterval(this,
                                       "incrementMileage",
                                       1000);
      }
      else {

        // ... otherwise, clear the interval.
        clearInterval(_nDriveInterval);
      }
    }

    // The incrementMileage() method is a private method
    // that simply increments the value of _mileage by 1.
    private function incrementMileage():Void {
      _nMileage++;
    }
  }
```

13. In the FLA file, create a new Movie Clip symbol named `DriveCar`. In the symbol, draw a filled circle.

14. On the main timeline, rename the default layer to Actions, and create a new layer named Artwork.

15. On the Artwork layer, drag an instance of the `DriveCar` Movie Clip symbol. Name the object `mDriveCar`.

16. Select the Actions layer, and open the Actions panel. Modify the code so that it reads as follows:

```
var crTest:Car = new Car("Oldsmobile", "Alero", "blue");

// Define an onPress() event-handler method. When the
// user clicks on the MovieClip, Flash tells the Car
// object to invoke the drive() method, and it passes
// it a value of true.
mDriveCar.onPress = function():Void {
  crTest.drive(true);
};

// Define an onRelease() event-handler method. When
// the user releases the click on the MovieClip, Flash
// tells the Car object to stop driving by invoking
// the drive() method with a value of false. Also, use
// the trace() action to output the description
// property value.
mDriveCar.onRelease = function():Void {
  crTest.drive(false);
  trace(crTest.description);
};
```

17. Test the movie. Click and hold the circle for a few seconds. Then, when you release the click, the current description should display in the Output panel. Do this a few times. Notice that the mileage keeps increasing cumulatively.

In this exercise, when the user clicks the circle, the `Car` object's `drive()` method is invoked, telling the object to start driving. Internally, that method sets an interval by which the private method `incrementMileage()` is invoked once per second. This interval continues as long as the user holds down the mouse button clicked. As soon as the button is released, the `drive()` method is again invoked — this time telling the `Car` object to stop driving. This causes the interval to be cleared, so the mileage is no longer incremented. However, the value for the mileage is not reset. Thus, the next time the user clicks the circle, the mileage increases even more.

Working with Advanced Class Topics

Now you have learned all the basics needed to create simple classes. The next step is to examine some of the more advanced topics. These topics include working with packages (organizing your classes), extending classes (creating parent/child relationships between classes), creating and implementing interfaces (rules for how to create a class), and making dynamic classes.

Organizing Your Classes with Packages

It is a good idea to organize your classes. This is true for several reasons. First of all, and likely rather apparently, organizing your classes helps you to locate classes and to remember what their purposes are. In addition, it is likely that you will download and install custom classes that were designed by others. It is possible, therefore, for you to end up with classes with the same name. If all your classes simply go in one directory, you have difficulty trying to have classes with the same name.

You organize your classes the same way that you would organize other files on your computer — using directories. In object-oriented terminology, these organizational directories are called *packages*. These directories (and their subdirectories, if applicable) should be placed somewhere within the classpath.

Consider the following scenario: You have created three classes — Rabbit, Hummingbird, and Ladybug. Now, these classes all happen to be related because they are animals. It makes sense to then package them together into an animal package. You can accomplish this by doing two things:

✦ First, you need to make a slight modification to the code in the AS file. The name of the class should reflect the package. Packages are indicated using dot syntax. For example, the Rabbit class should be declared as follows:

```
class animal.Rabbit {
  // Class code goes here.
}
```

✦ The AS file should be moved within the appropriately named directory. In the case of the Rabbit class, the AS file should be placed within a directory named animal.

You can create subpackages as well. For example, if you wanted to, you could create subpackages such as mammal, bird, and insect within the animal package. The same rules apply. For example, if you want to place the Rabbit class in the mammal subpackage, you need to first modify the class definition as follows:

```
class animal.mammal.Rabbit {
  // Class code goes here.
}
```

Then, you need to create a subdirectory named mammal within the animal directory, and move the AS file into that subdirectory.

Now that you have created the Rabbit class within the animal.mammal package, you can also have other types of Rabbit classes — for example, a Rabbit class in the car.vw package.

Once you have created a class within a package, you have to be careful how to reference that class. Classes, even within the same package, cannot reference one another using the simple class name as you've done up to now. If you have a Rabbit class and a RabbitFood class within the animal.mammal package, you *cannot* create a new RabbitFood instance within the Rabbit class as follows:

```
var rfVeggies:RabbitFood = new RabbitFood();
```

Instead, you have to tell Flash where it can find the RabbitFood class. You can do this in one of two ways:

✦ Use the fully qualified name (including package) when declaring the variable. For example:

```
var rfVeggies:animal.mammal.RabbitFood =
new animal.mammal.RabbitFood();
```

✦ Use an `import` statement to tell Flash where to look for the classes.

The same holds true for classes in different packages. If you have a `PetAdoptions` class within a package named `pets.group`, you *cannot* simply create a new instance of the `Rabbit` class within the `PetAdoptions` class using the following code:

```
var rBunny:Rabbit = new Rabbit();
```

In most cases, an `import` statement is the preferred choice. It makes it easier to see what classes are being used, and it makes for less code for you to type (at least, assuming that you are defining more than one instance of a given class). The syntax for the `import` statement to import a single class is:

```
import package[.subpackages].ClassName;
```

For example, you can import the `Rabbit` class as follows:

```
import animal.mammal.Rabbit;
```

Alternatively, you can also import an entire package or subpackage. The * is a wildcard that tells Flash to import all the classes in a class or subclass. The basic syntax is:

```
import package[.subpackages].*;
```

For example, you can import all the classes in the `animal.mammal` package as follows:

```
import animal.mammal.*;
```

Note   Using the asterisk will only import the classes in the `animal.mammal` package. If there are classes in a package called `animal.mammal.primate`, the `import` statement will not recurse into that package. You would need to add another `import` statement to import the classes in the `primate` subpackage. Furthermore, importing a class does not necessarily cause Flash to compile the class into the SWF. Only classes that are referenced are compiled into the SWF.

The `import` statement or statements should always appear at the top of an AS file if used. An `import` statement should never appear within a class definition. For example, if you want to import the `Rabbit` class in the `PetAdoptions` class, your code will look something like:

```
import animal.mammal.Rabbit;

class pets.group.PetAdoptions {
   // Class code goes here.
}
```

The same issue occurs not only in other AS files but also within an FLA file. If you want to use a packaged class within your FLA, you need to tell Flash how to find the class. Again, you can declare the instance using the fully qualified name of the class. Or, you can use an `import` statement. When you use an import statement in your FLA files, you should place the statement(s) at the top of the rest of the code.

Extending Classes

One of the most powerful things you can do with classes is to establish parent-child relationships between them. When you create a class that is a child of another class, that class is said to *extend* the parent class. Programmers often refer to the parent class as the superclass and the child class as a subclass.

The reasons for extending classes might not be readily apparent. The purpose is twofold: First, it is good for organizational purposes. Second, you can define shared characteristics and functionality in the superclass and then create multiple subclasses that inherit the common, core elements, while also adding their own specific characteristics and functionality. For example, the Rabbit class might extend a more generic superclass such as Mammal. The Mammal class can define the types of things that all subclasses share in common. Then, not only the Rabbit class, but also any other subclasses such as Elephant, Rhinoceros, or Squirrel will also be able to inherit the common elements without having to redefine them each time.

To create a class that extends another, you can use the keyword extends in the class declaration. The basic syntax is as follows:

```
class ClassName extends SuperClassName {
  // Class definition goes here.
}
```

Here is an example of a Mammal class. This class defines a single property with getter and setter methods:

```
class animal.mammal.Mammal {

  private var _sName:String;

  public function get name():String {
    return _sName;
  }

  public function set name(sName:String):Void {
    _sName = sName;
  }

}
```

The Mammal class is the superclass. One of the subclasses of the Mammal class might be Rabbit. Here is an example of the Rabbit class that extends Mammal.

```
import animal.mammal.Mammal;

class animal.mammal.Rabbit extends Mammal {

  public var _sColoration:String;

  public function Rabbit(sName:String, sColoration:String) {
    _sName = sName;
    _sColoration = sColoration;
```

```
   }

   public function get coloration():String {
     return _sColoration;
   }

}
```

Notice that `Rabbit` does not have a `_sName` property defined within it. However, within the constructor method you see that the value of the `_sName` member is assigned. This is possible because the `Rabbit` class inherits that member, as well as the getters and setters, from the superclass. Therefore, if you use the following code in an FLA file, it will work without difficulty:

```
import animal.mammal.Rabbit;

var rBunny:Rabbit = new Rabbit("William", "White and Brown");

trace(rBunny.name);  // Displays: William
trace(rBunny.coloration);  // Dislays: White and Brown
```

A superclass of one class can be the subclass of another. For example, the `Mammal` class is the superclass of `Rabbit`. But `Mammal` could also be the subclass of another superclass — maybe a class named `Animal`. A class inherits everything from the entire chain of superclasses. So in the example in which `Animal` is the superclass of `Mammal`, and `Mammal` is the superclass of `Rabbit`, the `Rabbit` class inherits from both `Animal` and `Mammal`. It inherits from `Mammal` directly and indirectly from `Animal` (because `Mammal` inherits directly from `Animal`). In fact, the `Object` class is the superclass for any class in which no superclass has been explicitly defined. Therefore, all classes inherit from `Object` either directly or indirectly.

When you extend a class, you sometimes want to implement particular methods in the subclass slightly differently than in the superclass. For example, all classes inherit the `toString()` method from the `Object` class. But you might want to *override* the `toString()` method for a particular class. In other words, you might want to define a method named `toString()` in the `Rabbit` class that is specific to that class. To do so is not complicated; you simply declare a method in the `Rabbit` class with the same name. If Flash encounters a `toString()` method in the `Rabbit` class, for example, it will not look any farther up the superclass chain.

There is another scenario that can occur, however. Sometimes you want to use the functionality of the superclass method, but you want to add some additional code to the subclass's implementation of it. For example, the `Mammal` class might have a method named `eat()`. You might want to allow Flash to use the functionality of that method, but in addition, you want the `Rabbit` class implementation to reduce the amount of rabbit food that the rabbit has left. In such a case, you can use the `super` keyword to refer to the superclass. Here is an example of the `Rabbit` implementation of the `eat()` method:

```
public function eat():Void {
  // First, call the eat() method of the superclass.
  super.eat();

  // Code goes here to decrement the amount of rabbit food.
}
```

Before moving on to another topic, we should also mention, for the sake of clarity, that you can extend built-in classes just as you can extend custom classes. This means that you can create classes that extend `String`, `Array`, or `XML` to name a few. You can even extend the `MovieClip` class, although it requires a few additional steps, which are discussed in Chapter 30.

Creating Interfaces

Interfaces declare what methods a class must define. Any class that *implements* the interface must include the methods that are declared in the interface. This set of rules in the interface helps to ensure that any class that implements the interface does what it is supposed to do (at least in structure). Interfaces do not describe what methods do. They simply state the names of methods alone with any parameters and return types.

An *interface* determines what methods an implementing class must define. While the utility of interfaces may not be immediately apparent, they are nonetheless quite helpful in advanced programming. Interfaces are key to modular designs that enable different datatypes implementing the same interface to be used interchangeably. For example, an application may allow a user to send messages via email, SMS, instant messenger, or various other protocols. Each protocol may be represented in ActionScript by a class (`protocol.Email`, `protocol.SMS`, `protocol.IM`, etc.). If each protocol class has the same basic programming interface (e.g., `setMessage()` and `send()`), then the instances of the classes can be used interchangeably within the application.

The formal interface construct is not specifically required in order to ensure interchangeability of classes. For example, you can simply define `setMessage()` and `send()` methods in each of the protocol classes discussed in the previous paragraph. However, a formal interface provides several benefits:

✦ You can document interfaces using API documentation software. That means that formal interfaces will show up in the API documentation so that you and your team can reference them.

✦ A formal interface will cause the compiler to check that an implementing class does define the required methods. For example, you may inadvertently not define `send()` within the `Email` protocol class as discussed in the previous paragraphs. Without a formal interface the compiler will succeed without any notification, even though the application won't work as you planned. You might determine the cause quickly, but it also might take some time. With a formal interface the compiler will throw an error telling you exactly what you've done incorrectly. That means you can quickly implement the method, and the application will work.

✦ It is possible to declare variables, properties, and parameters as interface types. That means, for example, you can declare a parameter as an interface type, and then you can pass the function or method any object of a type that implements that interface. That makes code potentially more flexible and scalable.

Writing an Interface

Many of the same concepts that you learned about creating classes apply to creating interfaces, so you don't have too much new material to learn.

Each interface should be in its own AS file. The name of the file should correspond to the name of the interface. For example, if the name of the interface is `IMessageSender`, the name of the AS file should be `IMessageSender.as`.

Within the AS file, you should declare the interface. The syntax is very similar to the syntax for a class declaration. The difference is that the interface declaration uses the `interface` keyword instead of the `class` keyword. The interface should be declared using the following syntax:

```
interface InterfaceName {
  // Interface code goes here.
}
```

The interface name should follow the same naming rules as variables and classes. As a best practice, name your interfaces starting with a capital *I* to indicate interface. For example, use interface names such as `IMessageSender` or `IPolygon`.

The interface definition should consist of public, non-implemented methods only. You cannot declare any members within the interface. For example, the following would cause an error:

```
interface IMessageSender {
  private var _msToSend:Message;  // Incorrect.
}
```

A non-implemented method definition consists of everything within a regular method definition except the curly braces and everything contained within them. Here is an example of a non-implemented method:

```
public function send():Void;
```

You cannot declare private methods in an interface. Trying to do so will cause an error. Furthermore, it wouldn't be of any benefit since the point of an interface is to declare the *publicly accessible* interface.

You cannot declare getter or setter methods in an interface either.

As with classes, you can place interfaces in packages. Furthermore, the way in which you place a class in a package is identical to the way in which you place an interface in a package — place the AS file in the directory, and add the package to the interface declaration.

```
// Assume that data.Message is another custom class.
import data.Message;

interface protocol.IMessageSender {
  public function send():Void;
  public function setMessage(msObject:Message):Void;
}
```

You can also define interfaces that extend other interfaces. When you do so, simply use the `extends` keyword much like you would in a class declaration. For example, you may want to define an interface `protocol.ISender` that declares `send()`. That interface may be implemented by some classes that send data that isn't necessarily a message.

```
interface protocol.ISender {
  public function send():Void;
}
```

Then, you can define `protocol.IMessageSender` so that it extends `protocol.ISender`:

```
import data.Message;
import protocol.ISender;

interface protocol.IMessageSender extends ISender {
  public function setMessage(msObject:Message):Void;
}
```

Implementing an Interface

A class can implement one or more interfaces. To implement an interface, you use the `implements` keyword in the class declaration. Here is the basic syntax for a class that implements a single interface:

```
class ClassName implements InterfaceName {
  // Class code goes here.
}
```

To implement multiple interfaces you need only to list the interfaces using comma delimiters:

```
class ClassName implements Interface1Name, Interface2Name, Interface3Name {
  // Class code goes here.
}
```

And if you want to declare a class that both extends a superclass and implements one or more interfaces, you should use the following syntax:

```
class ClassName extends SuperClassName implements InterfaceName {
  // Class code goes here.
}
```

Using an Interface

To illustrate how interfaces can work, let's build a simple example. In the following example we'll define one interface (`IShape`) and two classes (`Circle` and `Square`) that implement the interface. Then, we'll define a class (`ShapeRowContainer`) that has a method that expects a parameter of a type that implements the IShape interface. That means any class that implements that interface can be used interchangeably with the method. In the example, the classes that implement `IShape` must define a method called `getDimensions()`. The `getDimensions()` method returns an object with width and height properties. The `ShapeRowContainer.addShape()` method relies on the interface to determine whether or not it can add the shape to the container.

The `IShape` interface is simple. It looks like the following:

```
interface IShape {

  public function getDimensions():Object;

}
```

The classes that implement `IShape` are also rather simple. `Circle` is:

```
class Circle implements IShape{

  private var _nX:Number;
```

```
    private var _nY:Number;
    private var _nRadius:Number;

    public function Circle(nX:Number, nY:Number, nRadius:Number) {
      nX = nX;
      nY = nY;
      nRadius = nRadius;
    }

    public function getDimensions():Object {
      return {width: 2 * _nRadius, height: 2 * _nRadius};
    }

}
```

And Square **is as follows:**

```
class Square implements IShape {

    private var _nX:Number;
    private var _nY:Number;
    private var _nSide:Number;

    public function Square(nX:Number, nY:Number, nSide:Number) {
      _nX = nX;
      nY = nY;
      nSide = nSide;
    }

    public function getDimensions():Object {
      return {width: _nSide, height: _nSide};
    }

}
```

Then, ShapeRowContainer **is defined as follows:**

```
class ShapeRowContainer {

  private var _aShapes:Array;
  private var _nWidth:Number;
  private var _nHeight:Number;

  public function ShapeRowContainer(nWidth:Number, nHeight:Number) {
    _nWidth = nWidth;
    _nHeight = nHeight;
    _aShapes = new Array();
  }

  public function addShape(shObject:IShape):Boolean {

    // If the height of the shape is greater than the
    // height of the container, return false.
```

```
      if(shObject.getDimensions().height > _nHeight) {
        return false;
      }

      // Add up the sum of the widths of the shapes in the
      // container.
      var nSum:Number = 0;
      for(var i:Number = 0; i < _aShapes.length; i++) {
        nSum += _aShapes[i].getDimensions().width;
      }

      // If the sum of the widths of the current shapes
      // and the new shape is greater than the width of
      // the container, then return false. Otherwise, add
      // the shape.
      if(nSum + shObject.getDimensions().width > _nWidth) {
        return false;
      }
      else {
        _aShapes.push(shObject);
        return true;
      }
    }
  }
```

You can then make a new Flash document, save it to the same directory as the class files, and use the following code on the main timeline:

```
// Make a new ShapeRowContainer that is 200
// by 200.
var srcInstance:ShapeRowContainer = new ShapeRowContainer(200, 200);

// Make two circles and two squares.
var cirA:Circle = new Circle(0, 0, 50);
var cirB:Circle = new Circle(0, 0, 400);
var sqA:Square = new Square(0, 0, 100);
var sqB:Square = new Square(0, 0, 200);

var bAdded:Boolean;

// Add the circles and squares to the container,
// and trace whether or not they were added.
// It will add cirA, but not cirB because the
// dimensions of cirB are greater than the container.
// It will add sqA, but not sqB because the cumulative
// width of cirA, sqA, and sqB is greater than the width
// of the container.
bAdded = srcInstance.addShape(cirA);
trace(bAdded);
bAdded = srcInstance.addShape(cirB);
trace(bAdded);
bAdded = srcInstance.addShape(sqA);
trace(bAdded);
bAdded = srcInstance.addShape(sqB);
trace(bAdded);
```

Making Dynamic Classes

If you recall from an earlier discussion in this chapter, some of the built-in ActionScript classes are dynamic. That means that you can create new, custom properties for objects derived from those classes, even if those properties are not defined in the class. This is not so, by default, for custom classes. For example, consider the following simple class:

```
class Book {
  private var _sTitle:String;

  public function Book(sTitle:String) {
    _sTitle = sTitle;
  }
}
```

If you then make an instance of the class, and you attempt to add a custom property (pageCount) to the instance, it will cause the compiler to throw an error:

```
var bkExample:Book = new Book("ActionScript Bible");
bkExample.pageCount = 1000; // This will not work.
```

When you try to add custom properties to nondynamic classes, you will get a compile error telling you as much.

Now, before we reveal how to make a class dynamic, consider whether or not you really need to make the class dynamic. Generally, it is not a good practice. You typically want to define your classes so that they work in a very specific way. If you find you are defining all kinds of dynamic properties for instances, you should consider whether or not you are really using the instances of the class properly, whether or not the class needs to be redefined, or whether you should, perhaps, create a new class to handle the specific needs.

If you have decided that you have good reason to make your class dynamic, all you need to do is add the dynamic keyword to the beginning of the class declaration.

```
dynamic class ClassName {
  // Class code goes here.
}
```

If you extend any dynamic class, the subclass is not automatically dynamic. For example, if you create a subclass of one of the built-in ActionScript classes, the subclass is not dynamic unless you use the dynamic keyword in the class declaration.

Web Resource We'd like to know what you thought about this chapter. Visit www.rightactionscript .com/asb/comments to fill out an online form with your comments.

Summary

✦ A *class* is a blueprint that ActionScript uses to know how to define instances. Those instances are called *objects*, and each object defined from the same blueprint shares common traits.

✦ An object can have properties and methods. The *properties* are essentially variables that are associated with the object. The *methods* are essentially functions associated with the object.

✦ Objects can be used as associative arrays. An *associative array* is a collection of data that is indexed by name.

✦ You can create your own custom classes. An ActionScript 2.0 class must be defined in an external AS file stored within the classpath.

✦ Packages are a good way to organize your classes and avoid naming conflicts.

✦ Interfaces provide a set of guidelines to which all implementing classes must agree. That can be helpful to ensure that a group of classes use a uniform set of methods.

✦   ✦   ✦

Debugging and Error Handling

You've read through the first chapters of this book and worked on some of the exercises provided. You next try to apply the concepts you have learned to create your own project with ActionScript. Everything seems to be going perfectly . . . until you test your movie and discover that nothing is working as planned! First of all, take a deep breath and know that even the very best have this happen quite frequently. Next, read this chapter and learn what techniques are available to help you solve the problems.

Anyone who has development experience in any language and for any platform knows that good debugging skills are absolutely essential to a successful project. Debugging simply means troubleshooting and finding the causes of errors in the program. And debugging skills are as important to ActionScript as they are for any other language.

If you find yourself trying to determine what is not working with your Flash movies in almost every project, don't think you are alone. Having errors and oversights in your code is not necessarily a mark of poor programming skills. Rest assured that you are in good company. The real issue is not in having errors, but in how well you are able to troubleshoot them. Consider it a puzzle. It can even be a lot of fun to track down the culprit. But as with any game, it can be frustrating if you are not equipped with the proper tools and know-how. The purpose of this chapter is to acquaint you with successful debugging techniques in ActionScript so that you are ready to sort out what is going on.

This chapter explores several interrelated topics. First, the chapter looks at where mistakes are commonly made and then it describes the steps you can take during production to help avoid them in the future. Next, it looks at how to add special code to your movies that handles errors when they occur. And last, the chapter covers the ways to debug your Flash applications when errors still occur.

Troubleshooting Your Flash Application

Troubleshooting an application is something all Flash developers have to do frequently while creating their productions. Countless problems can occur during development, but most of them fall into the following categories:

✦ A problem with your computer system

✦ A bug in the Flash authoring application

✦ A application works incorrectly—or simply doesn't work at all

Probably the most common problem you will encounter is a problem right in your application. The least common problem is finding a bug in Flash software. When you first find an error, you should determine which one of these types of issues is occurring.

Discovering Computer System Issues

Every once in a while your computer just needs to be rebooted. This just seems to be the way of things. If you are working on your Flash document and encountering unexplainable errors, try restarting the computer. Developers have spent countless hours trying to discern a problem in their code when the problem was merely that the computer needed to be restarted. It sounds simple. But sometimes simple is what works. So, keep this in mind — especially when your application works one moment and then stops working the next with no significant changes to the code.

Note   If Flash crashes while you are authoring a Flash document, it's a good idea to reboot before you resume working on your file.

It is also possible, although less likely, that an error could occur on your computer system that would both affect your Flash document and not be fixed by restarting. One way to determine whether this is the case is to move your Flash document to another computer and test it there. If your Flash document works on another computer, that should indicate that the problem is with your computer. In the unlikely event that you should have this happen, you should try reinstalling the Flash authoring application. If that does not help, try consulting with a professional.

Encountering Bugs in Flash

Encountering a software error in Flash does not happen very often. Every version of Flash has gone through extensive testing to find any problems and correct them before public release. However, it is possible you may encounter an oddity (an undocumented "feature") or find a bug with the software during development.

When you think you have found a bug with the program, there are several steps you should take before assuming that this is the source of your problem and reporting it to Macromedia:

1. Make sure this problem is with Flash itself and does not have to do with your operating system, movie, browser, or external languages or servers.

2. Check all documentation and errata, and search the tech notes on Macromedia's web site to see whether the problem has been reported and whether there are established workarounds for it. A good place to start is at www.macromedia.com/support/flash.

3. Ask other people in the Flash community if they can reproduce this problem on different computers. If you don't have a Flash friend handy on your instant messenger client, post your problem to one of Macromedia's Flash newsgroups (listed at www.macromedia.com/support/forums) or a Flash user forum such as were-here.com.

You can find these and other resources described in the "Finding Help in the Flash Community" section later in this chapter.

If you determine that there is an error with the software, you can report bugs or feature requests at www.macromedia.com/support/email/wishform.

Detecting Errors in the Flash Document

If the problem with your movie is not with the operating system, there could be a mistake in the Flash document (.fla file). You have published your movie, but it is not functioning the way you intended. Perhaps it is running inconsistently on your system, or across several platforms or browsers. Maybe certain elements simply do not work at all. These types of problems are a large part of what will be covered in this chapter. But before you look to your code, there are several troubleshooting steps you can take.

1. Consider the history of building your production and the last point at which it worked correctly. You might want to save a new copy of the movie, and work backward by deleting elements and seeing whether certain older parts of your movie work on their own.

2. Verify that the problem happens in a new Flash document (.fla file). Test individual sections to see if they work by copying and pasting your problematic instances and code into a new Flash document. Your problem may lie in individual sections or perhaps with interactions between these and other parts of the movie. You can narrow down your problems by isolating your error.

3. Consider *where* you are testing your movie. As strange as it sounds, Flash movies can behave differently in the stand-alone player (or Test Movie mode) than they do in a web browser. You may need to run your tests in the browser, or perhaps even live on a server. If you are working with several scenes, you can cut down on your troubleshooting requirements by testing individual scenes. You may also consider the earlier step at this point of copying a portion of your application into a new file and testing it.

4. Check the player versions (including revisions) you are using with the Flash movie. It is also possible to have a different version running in the Test Movie environment within Flash than the Flash Player plug-in you have installed with your browser. Stand-alone players are frequently released at a different time than browser players, so you may find that you have to work with different versions. Regularly check Macromedia's web site for the latest versions of the Flash Player plug-in and stand-alone players.

Of course, many of the errors you will encounter and have to troubleshoot will concern ActionScript. Typos and instance or variable naming are two of the most common errors you will encounter. You will learn about how to find these errors and many more in your code in the next section.

Finding Errors in Your Application

After you have taken some time to review the steps mentioned in the preceding section, your application *still* may not function properly. This section reviews common problems that occur as you author Flash documents.

It's common that many of your Flash applications will not be perfect in the first version or draft of the Flash document. As you develop an application, several problems can happen along the way. This section covers typical problems that occur during development. Walking through these steps may save you a lot of time during the troubleshooting process.

Troubleshooting a movie can often take as long as (or longer than) the development and production process, particularly if you are working on several integrated Flash movies in a large project, or if you are learning the tools or ActionScript features in Flash. However, even seasoned developers run up against common and/or simple errors along the way.

Errors that you will encounter in your Flash application can be categorized into two types:

✦ **Compile-time errors** — These types of errors occur when Flash attempts to compile (export) your movie. Compile-time errors are often the simplest to discover because Flash will actually give you a message with details telling you that an error has occurred.

✦ **Runtime errors** — Detecting these types of errors can sometimes be a subtler art. When a runtime error occurs it means that your ActionScript code is syntactically correct, but somewhere in your code is faulty logic.

Fixing compile-time errors is generally a straightforward process. For example, if you try to assign a number value to a string variable, you will get a compile-time error message in the Output panel. You can read the error message and locate the problematic code relatively quickly. The main difficulty that developers have with compile-time errors is simply not reading the error messages. As funny as it might seem, it is fairly common for developers to close the Output panel without regarding the message. Then, they wonder why their application doesn't work. So, the primary tip for working with compile-time errors is simply to read the error messages.

Because detecting and fixing runtime errors can be seemingly more complicated, let's take a closer look at some of the common issues that might occur.

Detecting Naming Conflicts and Problems

Unintentionally giving two objects or instances the same name is an easy mistake to make and is quite common during development. Making sure each of your objects has a unique name should be one of the early steps taken when you troubleshoot your movie.

Another common mistake is misspelling the names of objects, function, instances, and frame labels in your movie. It is easy to get confused — particularly if your names are different on labels, layers, symbols, instances, objects, variable names, or linkage identifiers. If a particular object or event is not happening when it should, check — and double-check — the names (and references) to the affected object(s). Verify an object's name in the Property inspector (if applicable) and in any actions referring to the object. It is surprisingly easy to accidentally omit or add an extra letter to a name (such as changing dog to dogs) when you type the text into the Property inspector or the Actions panel.

Problems also occur if you duplicate a `MovieClip` instance and then forget to change the instance name. This can create errors when you are trying to manipulate one of the instances using ActionScript. If two `MovieClip` objects have the same name, and that name or object reference is targeted with an action, only one object will respond.

Caution   Watch out that you don't accidentally "overwrite" an object. For example, if you create a `Sound` object named `sndOne` in one area of your code and later create another object on the same timeline with the same name of `sndOne`, the former object will be replaced with the new one. You can certainly plan to do this with your code, but many beginners unintentionally replace objects with new ones.

Troubleshooting may become unnecessarily frustrating when a duplicated or forgotten instance is hidden underneath a graphic, is an object on a lower layer, or is an empty text field. Use the Movie Explorer (Window ➪ Movie Explorer or Alt+F3 or Option+F3) to help you track down multiple instances with the same name. This method applies only to physical instances that you may have created on the stage — you can't use the Movie Explorer to find dynamically created instances in ActionScript.

Naming Variables

It is also important to make sure your variable names include *only* letters, numbers, and underscores. Also, the first character of your variable names cannot be a number. For a review of variable naming rules, see Chapter 3.

Additionally, we strongly recommend that you adopt a standard naming convention. This is also discussed in Chapter 3.

Using Reserved Words

Another mistake is to use reserved words as instance names in a Flash movie. There are many words that should never be used as variable or instance names because they result in a conflict. You should always avoid using predefined constructs of the ActionScript language when naming anything in your movie. This will help you avoid conflicts and make your code more readable. For example, object names such as `System`, `Key`, and `Stage` should not be used as variable or instance names. Using the suggested modified Hungarian notation convention (see Chapter 2) should help alleviate this issue.

Watching for Case-Sensitivity

Because ActionScript 2.0 is a case-sensitive language, if you are inconsistent with your use of case in your code, you will find that things don't work as you expect. Let's take a look at a few examples.

Variable and class names as well as stored values are case-sensitive. If you declare a variable named `sTitle` and you then later have a typo in which you use a variable named `stitle`, the latter will be undefined. And unfortunately, because of legacy support, the ActionScript compiler will not necessarily catch that error. So, be sure to review your code to make sure you have been consistent with you capitalization for variable names. Also, a consistent naming convention can help you to keep consistent use of case in variable and class names.

Cross-Reference   See Chapter 3, "Constructing ActionScript," for more information on variable naming conventions. See Chapter 5, "Getting to Know Objects," for more information on class-naming conventions.

ActionScript is also case-sensitive when comparing string values. For example, the string literal values of `ActionScript Bible` and `actionscript bible` are not the same. You can see this for yourself with the following `trace()` actions.

```
trace("ActionScript Bible" == "actionscript bible");
```

Also, keywords and identifiers are case-sensitive in Flash. For example, the following ActionScript will return an error to the Output panel:

```
btMessage.onRollOver = Function () {
  trace("message");
};
```

The keyword `function` should not be capitalized. Likewise, `var`, `this`, `while`, `else`, and `typeof` are a few other examples of code in ActionScript that are case-sensitive. An easy way to tell if you have correct case is if your ActionScript is color-coded in the Actions panel. If a piece of code appears blue (or whatever color you have assigned to identifiers and keywords), you know you have the correct case.

Using Expressions and Strings

A common cause of error is the misuse or confusion between expressions and strings when writing ActionScript. When you are referring to a variable, object, or function, you should not have quotation marks around the name. However, when you are writing a string, you should use quotation marks. If you do not use quotations, the code will be sent as a value (or object reference) as opposed to a string.

Finding Conflicts in Frame Actions

Sometimes, you run into problems with conflicting actions on frames. This can occur when conflicting code is placed at the same frame number, but in different layers. On frame 1, for example, you may have a `stop()` action in layer 2 and a `play()` action in layer 3. But what exactly happens in such conflicting circumstances?

The answer is that Flash has a specific order in which it executes the actions on a frame. It starts at the first line of code on the topmost layer, and it continues sequentially through all the code on that layer for that frame. Then, it moves next to the next layer from the top. It continues this until all the actions on the frame have been executed. Therefore, if the topmost layer contains a `stop()` action, but the next layer contains a `play()` action, the movie will play and not stop on that frame.

Importing Images, MP3s, and Video

Flash Player 8 allows developers to dynamically load JPEG (progressive and nonprogressive), GIF, and PNG and MP3 files into Flash movies at runtime. If you are having trouble dynamically loading images, check that they are a valid format. Flash Players 6 and 7 can load only standard JPEG images.

Another problem may arise when you try to import certain MP3 files at author time. You may get the following error message during an import session:

```
One or more files were not imported because there
were problems reading them.
```

This error message can result because Flash 8 isn't able to import MP3 files with a bit rate higher than 160Kbps. MP3 files with this bit rate or higher need to be imported via QuickTime. If this does not work, and you have QuickTime installed, ensure that you have the latest version of the software installed. Note, however, that the user does not need to have QuickTime installed to load high-bit-rate MP3 files into Flash Player 7 at runtime. This issue only affects MP3 files that you want to work with in the authoring environment.

Caution You also see the previous error if you are trying to import certain kinds of images. A *complete* install of QuickTime is necessary to import TGA, TIF, PNG, PCT, PIC, SGI, QTIP, or PSD files. If you have a *minimal* install of QuickTime, you see the same error as previously.

When you are working with video files, you may also run into some problems with QuickTime Flash movies and correct version support. In QuickTime 6, Flash 5 and earlier is supported. Therefore, if you are attempting to publish a SWF track inside a QuickTime movie with a version not supporting the Flash version, you get the following error:

```
The installed version of QuickTime does not have a
handler for this type of Macromedia Flash movie.
```

You, therefore, need to publish your movie in version 5 or earlier. The version of QuickTime on your computer affects your ability to publish, so make sure you have the latest available version installed.

Publishing Your Movies

When you publish your movie, your content may not appear or sound as you expect it to. It is easy to make mistakes with imported content or forget to adjust your settings within the Flash authoring environment to control your content when it is published.

If you have imported uncompressed bitmap or audio files, you can adjust the compression settings for each media file in the Library panel. It is not advisable to recompress already compressed files because it may have a negative effect on the quality of your Flash movies (SWF files). If your file size is too large after you have published your movie, go back to the Library panel, and adjust export settings for the media files. Remember that the settings in the Library override what is set in the Publish Settings dialog box. However, if the Override sound settings check box is selected in Publish Settings in the sound area of the Flash tab, any compression settings for sound assets in the Library will be ignored.

Tip On the Flash tab of the Publish Settings dialog box, select the Generate Size Report check box in the Options area. When you publish or test your Flash movie, this option creates a text file that outlines the number of bytes used by each element in the Flash movie. You can view this text file directly in the Output panel when you use the Control ➪ Test Movie command to view your Flash movie in the authoring environment of Flash 8.

Another publishing-related problem is the accidental overwriting of HTML files. In any Flash project, you likely create (or modify) a custom HTML document to display your Flash movie. If you are working with a custom HTML page in the same directory (or folder) as your Flash movie and document, it is a good idea to make sure your Publish Settings' Format tab does not have the HTML check box selected. Thus, you will not accidentally overwrite your custom HTML document when the Flash movie is published.

Including Hidden Layers

A common mistake during Flash is to forget about locked or hidden layers. Collapsed layer folders can hide several layers from your view. It is easy to forget about `MovieClip` objects on hidden layers. Additionally, ActionScript on layers within collapsed layer folder can be easily overlooked as you troubleshoot your code. You should also remember that any content on Guide layers is not published in your Flash movie (SWF file).

Caution Although ActionScript attached to content in a Guide layer is not exported with your final Flash movie (SWF file), actions on keyframes in a Guide layer will be exported. The only way to temporarily omit code from executing is to comment the code in the Actions panel.

Fixing Blurry Text

Blurry text has been a long-standing issue in the Flash community. Text blurring in published movies is caused when your fonts are anti-aliasing when published. The X and Y position of text on the stage and the font size of text are two important things to consider if you want to avoid blurriness.

The top-left X- and Y-coordinates of any text field should be whole numbers (integers), such as 10, 15, 23, and so on. These values can be adjusted in the Info panel or the Property inspector. If text is placed on integers that have not been rounded, anti-aliasing will be applied. Also, if you are working with text inside a Movie Clip, try to position the Movie Clip at an integer as well.

Note Make sure that the registration point in the Info panel is set to use the top-left corner of selected items.

When you specify a font face and a font size, it is important to know what the intended sizes of the font should be—fonts are designed to work optimally at specific point sizes. Make sure that you use only multiples of this intended size (an 8-pt font should be set at 8 pts, 16 pts, 32 pts, and so on). At other points, blurriness occurs because anti-aliasing is applied.

It is advisable to work with fonts made specifically for Flash and that have also been proven to work well in the Flash environment. Fonts that have been well designed and tested look and work a lot better in your movies, even when placed deeply within many nested layers of Movie Clips. This is when blurring most likely occurs.

Web Resource A respected source of reliable pixel fonts for use with Flash is `www.miniml.com`. The intended size is 8 pts. Some fonts are free, and others are available for a modest cost.

Tip Even if you have made sure your font is not blurry, ensure that it is actually legible for your audience. Some fonts commonly used in Flash movies are barely legible, even to those with perfect eyesight. Despite the popularity of small fonts, make sure that what you say on your site at the very least can be read by those viewing your movie.

Another solution to the blurry text problem is to use Dynamic (or Input) text fields that don't embed the fonts assigned to them. Any nonembedded (or device) font is aliased in any field type (Static, Dynamic, or Input).

From an ActionScript point of view, any scaling of the Flash movie may cause text to blur as well. If text legibility is a concern, make sure that you use the following `scaleMode` of the `Stage` object on frame 1 of your Flash movie:

```
Stage.scaleMode = "noScale";
```

See Chapter 22 for more information on the `scaleMode` property of the `Stage` object.

Considering External Issues

Many problems you encounter are associated with the web browser or the Flash Player environment. The operating system and version (for example, Windows XP or Mac OS X) can also introduce problems for Flash movies.

Watching for Browser Caching

Most browsers will cache Web content that is displayed on a web page. When you click the refresh button in the browser's toolbar, usually the content — even if it's in the cache — will be reloaded from the web server. However, some browsers, such as Internet Explorer, are known to be stubborn with the refresh of Flash movie (SWF file) content. Even when you upload a new version of the movie to your server, you still see the cached version online. One of the quickest ways to view a new version of a SWF file is to append a variable onto the end of your movie's URL, such as `www.rightactionscript.com/file.swf?index=2324`. Another way to escape this is by working with meta-refresh tags in your HTML file or by changing your file's name.

Netscape does not seem to suffer from these caching issues. Remember to hold down the Shift key when you click the refresh button. In Netscape, this forces the movie to reload from the URL instead of the cache.

Considering Platform Issues

There are differences in the way a movie is handled on a Mac as opposed to a Windows machine. Published movies play differently in the browsers across these two platforms. Macs have been known to handle frame rates differently, and monitors display colors in a different way, too. We recommend that you test your movies on different platforms and in different browsers when testing and troubleshooting your productions.

Server Issues

Sometimes, errors in your movie don't occur until it has been uploaded to a server. If this is the case, try it on a different server(s) to see if the problem continues to occur. If not, it may be an issue with the MIME settings on the server. MIME types may need to be set up to include those for Flash movies (SWF files).

You can find more information about server issues and MIME types on Macromedia's web site at `www.macromedia.com/support/flash/ts/documents/tn4151.html`.

As you saw in the beginning of this chapter, your errors can occur in many different areas: the server, external scripts or elements, the browser or platform, and, of course, the movie itself. You need to determine where the source of the problem is during the troubleshooting process.

Finding Help in the Flash Community

You may get to the point when you simply cannot find an error in your code, or your movie still doesn't work despite everything you've tried. There are no errors reported in the Output panel when you check your code in the Actions panel or when you test your movie. You have checked your code syntax with references in this book or the Help panel in the Flash 8 authoring environment, yet your movie still seems to behave unpredictably. What is the next step?

 You could be dealing with a bug or errata in documentation and may need to find a workaround. Macromedia's Flash support area of its web site (www.macromedia.com/support/flash) has an extensive collection of searchable tech notes. These can be very helpful when you are dealing with unexplainable errors and problems. Tech notes include information on the player and authoring, errata, and tutorials.

Another recommendation is to check the archives of the many extensive Flash communities online, and approach other coders about your problem.

After you feel you have exhausted all of the possible solutions, it is a good idea to turn to those around you for assistance. The Flash community is a wonderful resource for inspiration, ideas, code, and even support and troubleshooting. It is very common to find someone who has already experienced your problem and can help you resolve the issue. Flash communities are most easily found online, but if you are lucky, your own city may have an active Flash Users Group where you can discuss Flash in person with fellow developers.

 A starting place for finding a local Flash Users Group is on the Macromedia web site at www .macromedia.com/v1/usergroups.

The following resources are just a few of the online communities of Flash users. Most of these sites also contain tutorials and resources, as well as the forums. You may even come across undocumented features useful to your application. Most of these forums have searchable archives, which may be a quick way to resolve your problem instead of waiting for an answer on a message board.

✦ www.were-here.com—A large part of this site is focused on an extensive and busy community forum.

✦ www.ultrashock.com—Some of the community's giants hang out in the Ultrashock forums. A respected resource by many, Ultrashock is a great place to hang out and ask and learn from the masters.

✦ www.flashkit.com—Flash Kit is well known for being a great place to find content for your Flash movies and tutorials to help you learn. Flash Kit also has a busy Web forum, in which you can share tricks, ideas, and seek help for your problems.

✦ chattyfig.figleaf.com—You can join email-based forums from this location. Be sure to read the etiquette FAQ at this web site before emailing the list. These groups are very high volume email lists, so you had better prepare your inbox before signing up!

✦ `webforums.macromedia.com/flash`—Macromedia forums are a great place to find help from others in the community, and also Team Macromedia volunteers and employees. You can also access these forums as newsgroups using the `forums.macromedia.com` server.

Preventing Errors

Now that you have considered many of the possible errors you can run into when working on a production, you should look at how to prevent these common mistakes before they happen. Adopting these practices inevitably helps you avoid the previously discussed errors, which means that you will save time and frustration during production.

Planning before Development

Planning your productions is perhaps the most important step in the development process. It is also the primary method you can use to prevent errors in production. If you develop your concept and goals before you begin production in Flash, you will probably encounter fewer problems and errors along the way. Keep the following points in mind:

✦ **Use good communication practices**—Effective communication between the members on your team also helps you avoid problems in your production. Flowcharts, notes, diagrams, and mockups all reduce redundant work and errors because of misunderstandings. Determine the best ways to streamline the communication process and spread information among all members in your development team.

You should also remember to establish healthy communication with clients. If you have a firm grasp on what your clients want to see in their product, you will probably save a lot of time and money in the long run. A happy client is a paying client, so it is well worth the effort to keep in close contact with your client and know what he or she wants to receive.

✦ **Simplify the production**—Before you start your movie, you should try to find a way to reach your goals in the simplest way possible. The act of planning in itself should help you achieve this. However, it is a good idea to consider your ActionScript during the planning stage as well. Either create pseudo-code or sketch out rough ideas as to which objects, functions, or properties you are going to use and where. Create data flowcharts, and note what you will use for facilitating this transfer (for example: `LoadVars`, XML, and Flash Remoting).

During the planning phase, you should also determine the easiest way to structure your movie. You want to take the fewest steps possible, with the simplest data and movie structure to achieve your predetermined goals. Your navigation and its usability should also be considered. The most simple and streamlined projects encounter fewer problems and errors along the way.

Using Versioning

Saving files incrementally is called *versioning*, and it can greatly help you when you encounter problems with your movie. If you have older versions of the document you can revert back to, you can determine which area of the movie has errors. You also have a version of the file with which to "start over."

One way to use versioning is simply to use the Save As option to save new copies of files. However, what is frequently a better option is to use versioning software such as CVS. CVS, which stands for Concurrent Versions System, is a standard in versioning software. It is open source, and binary versions are available for download for most common operating systems. While it is beyond the scope of this book to discuss any single versioning application, you can read more about CVS and download the latest version at `www.nongnu.org/cvs`. Versioning software such as CVS is quite helpful because it manages the archives, lets you work on teams by merging changes to files, and lets you quickly rollback to a previous version of a file.

Tip   Saving often during development is a good idea in case your computer crashes or freezes up. Backing up documents in different locations can also help if your file is corrupted or lost. This is particularly important if you are working with the same file on different platforms.

Note   Flash Professional has a Projects panel that enables you to configure projects to integrate directly with Visual Source Safe, a commercial versioning application from Microsoft.

Testing Your Movie

Frequent testing of your movie is very important for pinpointing errors. It is much easier to troubleshoot and fix your errors if you combine frequent testing with versioning. Usually, you have to fix only one thing (your latest modifications) instead of having to locate all your errors at once. This is much easier than attempting to debug all of your errors all at once.

When testing your movie, it is also important to consider the different kinds of computers that will play your movie to your audience. You may decide to author toward a target audience who will most likely have one certain kind of computer. Or, perhaps you may require your movie to work well across a wide spectrum of capabilities. Whatever the case may be, testing on different kinds of platforms, browsers, processors, and connections helps determine what fixes and optimizations should take place.

There are many useful tools in the test environment (Control ➪ Test movie, or Ctrl+Enter or ⌘+Enter). The Bandwidth Profiler and the ability to list all the objects and variables within a movie help developers optimize and debug their movies. The following sections offer some useful practices and tools for testing your movies.

Testing Your Movie with Server-Side Scripts

When you are working on a large integrated production, it can often be very difficult to determine the source of the error you are encountering. If you are using server-side scripts, it is a good idea to develop your script with an HTML interface, instead of with Flash. That way, you can determine whether your problem is in the server-side script, or in your ActionScript or Flash movie. After your server-side script is in working order, move on to integrating the scripts with Flash, so you will know that any problems you encounter in your production will be with your Flash movie, and not your server-side scripts.

Working with the Bandwidth Profiler

The Bandwidth Profiler can help you determine whether you need a preloader for your movie. This feature shows a graphical depiction of how your movie will download on various connections. The profiler lets you see when playback will be halted because not all frames are loaded. From this information, you can either modify your movie to include a preloader or distribute your content differently on the timeline.

Tip A known problem with the Bandwidth Profiler is how the streaming graph uses the uncompressed SWF file size to generate the report. Flash 8 reduces the size of your movies using compression when you publish them. Therefore, when you use the feature to Show Streaming, the download speed and depiction in the Profiler are not entirely accurate.

Correcting Choppy Movie Playback

When a movie is played online, sometimes you may notice that it does not run smoothly. You can generate a size report, which can help you optimize your movie. This option is found in the Publish Settings dialog box. The report generates a numerical report and helps you determine which frames are slowing during playback. You may choose to either restructure or eliminate some content from these frames so your movie plays smoothly.

Tip A preloader can help when playback is choppy. Flash content plays back as a progressive download. That means that as soon as enough has buffered, it starts to playback. However, it is possible that the playback can get ahead of the download, causing pauses and stuttering. A preloader tells the movie to begin playback only after a specified amount has downloaded.

Testing Platforms and Browsers

It is likely that many, if not most, of your end users will be on a Windows computer using Internet Explorer. However, we don't recommend that you create your movies with only this setup in mind. You should be aware of what the other browsers are capable of and the differences that exist between them. Many other browsers such as Firefox, Netscape, Safari, and Opera have picked up market share in the past few years. If you are aware of these differences and test your movies in different situations, you will be able to author your movies with fewer errors along the way.

Web Resource You can find more information on Internet Explorer for Macintosh and Flash authoring at Macromedia's web site at `www.macromedia.com/support/flash/ts/documents/mac_ie_issues.htm`.

ActionScript Placement

Generally, as you start to write more sophisticated code, we recommend you place most code in class files. However, when you are starting out writing code it's more likely that you'll place the code within the Flash document rather than class files. We strongly recommend that you keep the code within your Flash documents as centralized as possible (meaning that you should try to put all your code in just a few easy-to-find places). When you are debugging your movie, it can be difficult to find all your code if it is scattered on many timelines, frames, and instances. Therefore, you should keep your code in a few centralized areas, so you do not have to search (and perhaps miss) a few places where code has been applied.

If you have been working with ActionScript for some time now, it is possible you may have gotten in the habit of adding ActionScript directly to object instances on the stage. If so, you may find it beneficial to consult Chapters 2 and 13 to see how you can place all your ActionScript code on keyframes. This makes is much simpler to locate your code.

Working with Compatible Actions

When looking at the Flash Player statistics, it is important to consider which version of the Flash player has been installed in your target population. A statistic showing that 98.3 percent of computers have the Flash player installed does not mean that 98 percent of all browsers have the latest version of the plug-in installed. This number includes *all* versions of the player.

When you develop a movie, you should determine your prospective audience. Will most of your users have Flash Player 8, or will a number of them still only be using Flash Player 7 or even Flash Player 6? Different versions of the Flash Player will display varying content on the audience's computer. You need to author your movie in a specific way to be compatible with different Flash Player versions.

Web Resource   You can find up-to-date information about Flash Player statistics at Macromedia's web site at `www.macromedia.com/software/player_census`.

A movie authored entirely with code compatible with earlier players must be published in an earlier version number under the Flash tab in Publish Settings. Refer to Figure 6-1 to see this drop-down menu. For example, if all code within your movie uses Flash 5 actions, and you publish your movie as version 8, it will not necessarily be fully compatible with Flash Player 5. You should publish your movie as version 5 for full compatibility.

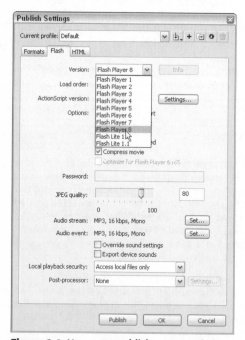

Figure 6-1: You must publish your movie in an earlier version for your actions to be compatible with a particular version of the Flash Player.

The best way to test the compatibility of your movie is by downloading old versions of the plug-in and running your movie through the different players.

Web Resource You can download old versions of the Flash Player from Macromedia for testing purposes. You can find them at www.macromedia.com/support/flash/ts/documents/oldplayers.htm.

Catching Errors Programmatically

ActionScript has structures that you can use to programmatically manage some errors using the try, catch, and finally statements. You can use these to build programmatic error checking right into your application.

Working with Basic try/catch Statements

The try and catch statements are typically used together. The basic syntax is:

```
try {
  // Code to try.
}
catch (erObject:Error) {
  // Code to run if the try code throws an error.
}
```

When Flash encounters a try block, it first attempts to run the try block's substatements. Within the try block, it is possible that something can throw an error (more on this in a moment). As soon as an error is thrown, the remainder of the try block is skipped, and the catch block code is run.

The difficulty is that you have to tell Flash to throw an error if some condition is or is not met. For example, you may want to tell Flash to process some data, but in order to do so, the condition must be met that the user has successfully entered a username. If the username is not entered then the rest of the code might fail. So, you want to check, within the try block, to see if the username has been entered. If not, then you want to tell Flash to throw an error. You do this by using a throw statement. The throw statement takes a single parameter — the object you want to throw. Typically, the object should be an instance of the Error class (or a subclass of Error). Here is a simple example that illustrates how this works:

```
// Assume that you have an input TextField object named
// tUsername that is on the stage. Here, assign the input
// value to a string variable.
var sUsername:String = tUsername.text;

// Flash will first attempt to run the code in the try
// block.
try {

  // If the user has not entered a username...
  if(sUsername == "") {

    // ...use a throw statement to throw a new Error
```

```
            // object. This tells Flash to stop running the rest
            // of the code in the try block, and jump immediately
            // to the catch block.
            throw new Error();
          }

          // Rest of try block code goes here. For the purposes
          // of this example, we'll use a trace() statement to
          // see when this code is run.
          trace("The try block ran successfully.");

        }
        catch (erObject:Error) {

          // If an error is thrown, the catch statement block is
          // invoked. The Error object that was thrown is
          // passed to the catch block (more on this in a
          // moment.) For the purposes of this example, we'll use
          // a trace() statement to see when this code is run.
          trace("An error was thrown.");
        }
```

If you want to place the preceding code on a frame of the same timeline in which an input TextField object named tUsername is defined, you can test for yourself to see the results. If tUsername has no value, an error is thrown and the catch block is invoked. Otherwise, if tUsername has a value, the try block runs successfully, and the catch block is never invoked.

At this point, you may be wondering how a try/catch combination is any more than a glorified if statement. First, one of the benefits of a try/catch combination is that as soon as an error is thrown in the try block, the remainder of the try block code is skipped, and the catch block is invoked. Accomplishing this task with simple if statements would require a lot of nested statements. The try/catch combination is much simpler to implement.

Another benefit of try/catch that might not be immediately apparent is that errors can be thrown from within functions and methods that are invoked within the try block. For example:

```
    function checkUsername(sUsernameParam:String) {
      if(sUsernameParam == "") {
        throw new Error();
      }
    }

    var sUsername:String = tUsername.text;

    try {
      checkUsername(sUsername);
    }
    catch (erObject:Error) {
      trace("An error was thrown.");
    }
```

The preceding code does essentially the same thing as the previous example, but uses a function to check whether the username has been entered. Although this is a fairly simple example, it illustrates that an error can be thrown from within a function that is invoked within a try block.

The `finally` statement can also be used in conjunction with `try` and `catch`. The code within the `finally` block always runs, regardless of whether there was an error thrown. The finally block can be useful for "cleaning up." You can use `try` and `finally` together:

```
try {
  // Code to try.
}
finally {
  // Code to run regardless.
}
```

Or, you can use `try`, `catch`, and `finally`:

```
try {
  // Code to try.
}
catch (erObject:Error) {
  // Code to run if the try code throws an error.
}
finally {
  // Code to run regardless.
}
```

Understanding Error Objects

In the previous examples with `try` and `catch`, you saw that in order for Flash to know to break out of a `try` statement you must throw an error. The `catch` statement then catches that error. You use the built-in `Error` class to create your errors. For example:

```
throw new Error();
```

The `Error` class has two constructor options — the first requires no parameters. The second takes a string parameter specifying a message to assign to the object. The message can then be retrieved within the `catch` statement using the `message` property of the caught object.

```
var sUsername:String = tUsername.text;
try {
  if(sUsername == "") {
    throw new Error("Missing Username.");
  }
}
catch (erObject:Error) {
  trace(erObject.message);  // Displays: Missing Username.
}
```

Note   `Error` objects also have another property — `name`. The `name` property allows you to specify an arbitrary name for the error type. Flash doesn't inherently do anything with that value. However, it is accessible from the object within the `catch` statement.

Typically, you will want to create subclasses of `Error`. These subclasses can assist you in throwing and catching different types of errors. You can have multiple `catch` clauses associated with a single `try` statement. Each catch clause must handle a different datatype. For example:

```
var sUsername:String = tUsername.text;
var erToThrow:Error;
try {
  if(sUsername == "") {
    throw new EmptyStringException();

  }
  if(sUsername == undefined) {
    throw new UndefinedException();
  }
}
catch (erObject:EmptyStringException) {
    // Code to handle error.
}
catch (erObject:UndefinedException) {
  // Code to handle error.
}
```

The preceding code assumes that you have defined classes named `EmptyStringException` and `UndefinedException` that subclass `Error`.

Throwing Exceptions

If you are familiar with exception handling in other languages, you might initially find ActionScript exception handling to be somewhat limited because unlike other languages, ActionScript's built-in class methods do not throw errors automatically. This is something that may or may not change in the future. But one thing that you can do is to make sure that all your own custom functions and methods do throw errors when appropriate.

Debugging Your Flash Application

Perhaps you've already reviewed your application using the troubleshooting steps outlined earlier in this chapter, but you are finding that your application still does not work as you want. Flash provides several tools you can use to go through your code to discover where the errors are occurring. Primarily, you'll look at the following:

✦ **The Output panel** — The Output panel is really quite simplistic. But don't discount it on account of that simplicity. Often you may find that the Output panel is simple to use and can assist you in locating errors relatively effectively.

✦ **The Debugger panel** — The Debugger panel is more sophisticated than the Output panel. You can do more complicated and intricate tasks, such as stepping through your code piece by piece.

Using the Output Panel

The Output panel can be an invaluable resource for simple debugging of ActionScript in your Flash movies. The Output panel is available when you test your movie in the Flash application, and it allows you to view the following:

✦ `trace()` output

✦ A list of all variables (and their values) in the movie

✦ A list of all objects in the movie

trace

Hey, if it works, it works. And nothing can be more truly said of trace(). Despite its simplicity, don't be misled into thinking that trace() is not useful. Throughout this book, you have seen trace() used time and time again, so you should be familiar with its function by now. It simply takes a single value as a parameter and displays it in the Output panel when testing the Flash movie.

The trace() action is a great place to start when debugging ActionScript because of its simplicity and ease of use. The learning curve with trace() is very small. All you need is to know when to apply it.

Tip   When you use trace() actions in your Flash document, they are only for the purpose of testing. There is no need to include them in the final published movie. It would be painful, however, to have to go through and manually remove the trace() actions that you had put into the document in the first place. Fortunately, you can easily omit these actions in the published file by checking the Omit Trace Actions check box in the Flash movie's Publish Settings dialog box. This will simply omit all the trace() actions in the published movie without your having to actually remove them from the code.

The first rule of debugging when using trace() actions is to drill down to the problem. Sometimes, you will have a pretty good idea of where the problem is. For example, you may have an error that you know is related to a specific for loop. But other times, you may not know where the problem is at all. In such cases, it is best to start with the largest scope and then narrow it down to where the specific error is occurring. The following code shows an example of when you might want to use such a technique:

```
var nValue:Number;
var bIsOne:Boolean;
for(var i:Number = 0; i < 4; i++){
  for(var j:Number = 0; j < 3; j++){
    for(var k:Number = 0; k < 5; k++){
      nValue = i + j + k;
      if(nValue = 1){
        bIsOne = true;
      }
    }
  }
}
```

In this example, the if statement in the innermost for loop evaluates as true every time because the assignment operator (=) is used instead of the comparison operator (==). But depending on how the bIsOne variable is used in the rest of the code, it could be tricky to spot the problem right away. So, it can be really helpful to use trace() here to narrow down the problem. Start with the largest scope — the outermost for loop — and add a trace() action that will output useful debugging information such as the value of i:

```
var nValue:Number;
var bIsOne:Boolean;
for(var i:Number = 0; i < 4; i++){
  trace("i:" + i);
  for(var j:Number = 0; j < 3; j++){
    for(var k:Number = 0; k < 5; k++){
      nValue = i + j + k;
      if(nValue = 1){
        bIsOne = true;
```

```
        }
      }
    }
  }
```

This outputs the following:

```
i: 0
i: 1
i: 2
i: 3
```

This looks correct, so the problem is probably not in the outermost `for` loop. Next, try placing a `trace()` action in the next `for` loop:

```
var nValue:Number;
var bIsOne:Boolean;
for(var i:Number = 0; i < 4; i++){
  for(var j:Number = 0; j < 3; j++){
    trace("j:" + j);
    for(var k:Number = 0; k < 5; k++){
      nValue = i + j + k;
      if(nValue = 1){
        bIsOne = true;
      }
    }
  }
}
```

This outputs the following:

```
j: 0
j: 1
j: 2
j: 0
j: 1
j: 2
j: 0
j: 1
j: 2
j: 0
j: 1
j: 2
```

Again, this looks about right. So, move on to the next smaller scope until something looks amiss. In this example, you would keep placing `trace()` actions and testing the movie until you reached the `if` statement. At that point, you would see that it evaluates to `true` every time, and this should indicate to you that there is a problem. Closer examination will show you that you simply used the wrong operator.

Listing the Variables

Another useful selection that the Output panel makes available is the List Variables option. You can choose this option from the Debug menu when testing your movie. This option simply displays all the current variables and their values and can be very useful for determining whether or not a variable is even being created, as well as what value is being assigned a variable. To see how the feature works, place the following code on the first frame of the main timeline of a new Flash document.

```
var sTitle:String = "ActionScript Bible";
var nReaders:Number = 1000000;
var oCar:Object = {make:"Oldsmobile", model:"Alero"};
```

Then test the movie, and select List Variables from the Debug menu. The following will be displayed in the Output panel:

```
Level #0:
Variable _level0.$version = "WIN 8,0,0,0"
Variable _level0.sTitle = "ActionScript Bible"
Variable _level0.nReaders = 1000000
Variable _level0.oCar = [object #1, class 'Object'] {
    model:"Alero",
    make:"Oldsmobile"
}
```

Note   The output for List Variables is not updated automatically when values change. You must choose the List Variables option every time you want updated information. For movies in which you want to see updated data frequently, it might be a good idea to use the Debugger window.

Listing the Objects

You can use the List Objects option (available from the Debug menu when testing your movie) to view the Button, MovieClip, and TextField objects in your movie. This can be a really useful tool — for example, when you are using duplicateMovieClip() or attachMovie() to dynamically add MovieClip objects to a movie. If some of the MovieClip objects do not seem to be appearing, you might want to consult the List Objects output to see whether they are being created, or whether they are there, but just not visible. The following shows an example of the List Objects data that might be displayed in the Output panel.

```
Level #0: Frame=1
  Shape:
  Movie Clip: Frame=1 Target="_level0.mCircle"
    Shape:
  Movie Clip: Frame=1 Target="_level0.mSquare"
    Shape:
  Edit Text: Target="_level0.tUserInput" Variable= Visible=true Text = "
```

Notice that again the output is grouped by level. In this example, only level 0 exists, but if other levels existed, then the objects on those levels would appear grouped by level. Notice, too, that each object lists the object type (Movie Clip indicating a MovieClip object, Button indicating a Button object, and Edit Text indicating a TextField object) and absolute target path to the object. Nested objects are indicated by indention.

Debugging Using the Debugger

The Debugger is a more sophisticated and complex means of debugging, appropriate when any of the following conditions are true:

✦ Using the Output panel techniques has not helped to solve the problem.

✦ You want to see real-time updates of variable and property values.

✦ You want to be able to set values of variables while testing the movie.

✦ You are using breakpoints in your ActionScript code, and want to be able to step through it while the movie is running.

✦ The movie you want to debug is running from a remote location.

There are two ways to run the Debugger, depending on where the movie being debugged is running:

✦ Debugging the movie from the Flash authoring application (local debugging)

✦ Debugging the movie running in a web browser or in the stand-alone debug player (remote debugging)

Once the Debugger is running, however, the process is the same for both local and remote debugging.

Local Debugging

Local debugging is done when the movie is running in the test player within the Flash authoring application. You can run the Debugger by choosing Control ⇨ Debug Movie instead of the normal Test Movie option. This opens the movie in the debug test player and automatically opens the Debugger window as well.

Remote Debugging

You can also debug movies remotely. This means that you can debug a movie playing in the stand-alone debug player. Macromedia has debug players available for download at the following site:

```
http://www.macromedia.com/support/flash/downloads.html
```

Exporting the Movie for Debugging

The first step in debugging a movie remotely is to export the movie with debugging enabled. To do this, open Publish Settings (File ⇨ Publish Settings), choose the Flash tab, and check the box next to Debugging Permitted.

When you enable debugging for a movie, you have the option of adding a password. This ensures that only people with the password can open the movie with the Debugger. You can set the password in the same Publish Settings dialog box.

When a movie is published with debugging enabled, it generates both a SWF and an SWD file. Both files should be kept together when moved. The SWD file contains additional information specifically for the purposes of debugging.

Opening the Debugger Window

When performing remote debugging, you must ensure that Flash is currently running on the machine from which you wish to use the Debugger. You can manually open the Debugger window if you want (Window ⇨ Debugger); otherwise, it will be automatically opened when the debug player attempts to make a connection (see the next section). Either way, for the Debugger to be able to receive connections from the debug player, you must enable remote debugging. To do this, open the Debugger window and choose Enable Remote Debugging from the pop-up menu accessible from the icon at the top right.

Opening the Movie for Debugging

Once you have a movie with debugging enabled, you can open that movie in the debug player:

1. Open the debug player.

2. Choose File ➪ Open.

3. Enter the location of the movie (SWF) you want to debug. It may be on the local hard disk (`movie.swf`), or on a web server (`www.server.com/movie.swf`).

4. Click OK.

Once the movie is opened in the debug player, you should be prompted to select the machine on which you want to run the Debugger. You can choose either the localhost, or you can specify an address for another computer. Either one will work as long as Flash is currently running on the specified machine and the remote debugging is enabled for the Debugger.

When you have clicked OK for the selection, the player attempts to connect to the Debugger on the specified computer. If it can make the connection, the Debugger is opened for the movie. When the movie is connected to the Debugger, the movie is initially paused to allow for the setting or removal of *breakpoints* (discussed later in this chapter).

Note   If the debug player cannot find the SWD file, you will not be automatically prompted to select a location for the Debugger. If this happens you can still run remote debugging (although perhaps with less functionality) by right-clicking (or Command-clicking on a Mac) in the movie (that has been opened in the player) and choosing the Debugger menu option.

Understanding the Debugger Window

Regardless of whether you are using local or remote debugging, the functionality within the Debugger window is the same. The Debugger is composed of several sections (see Figure 6-2):

✦ The status bar indicates whether the Debugger is active. If it is active, the status bar will display the location of the movie being debugged.

✦ The Display list (top left) allows you to choose from the display objects in the movie.

✦ The Properties, Variables, Locals, and Watch lists allow you to see values, and (in some cases) edit values for properties and variables.

✦ The Call Stack viewer displays the stack trace, if any.

✦ The Code View pane (with accompanying jump menu and toolbar) allows you to view the code in the movie (if there is an SWD file). The Code View pane is on the right side of the panel.

Viewing and Setting Variables and Properties

One of the benefits of the Debugger is that it allows you to see real-time values for properties and variables in your movies. For example, if a `MovieClip` object is moving, you can see the `_x` and `_y` properties being updated in real time in the Properties list. You can even set many properties and variables in your movie.

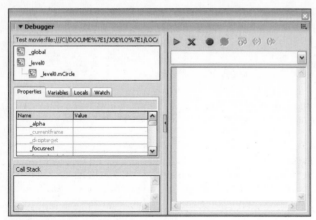

Figure 6-2: The Debugger and its parts.

The Properties List

The Properties list allows you to view and set properties of the object selected in the display list. The properties in the Properties list include only the predefined properties that are shared by all graphical objects. Table 6-1 lists the properties.

Table 6-1: Properties List Elements

Property Name	Is It Editable?
_alpha	Yes
_currentframe	No
_droptarget	No
_focusrect	No
_framesloaded	Yes
_height	No
_highquality	Yes
_name	Yes
_quality	Yes
_rotation	Yes
_soundbuftim	Yes
_target	No
_totalframes	No
_url	No
_visible	Yes

Property Name	Is It Editable?
_width	Yes
_x	Yes
_xmouse	No
_xscale	Yes
_y	Yes
_ymouse	No
_yscale	Yes

If the property is editable, you can change the value, and it will be reflected in the movie that is being debugged.

The Variables List

The Variables list is very much like the Properties list. It displays any variables in an object except for those listed in the Properties list. For example, the _level0 object always has at least one variable in it ($version), which has a value of the player version. TextField objects will always have a whole list of variables that are the properties not included in the Properties list, such as autoSize and text. Any user-defined properties and variables show up in the Variables list as well.

The Locals List

The Locals list includes only local variables. You can really do only so much with the Locals list when you have set breakpoints (discussed later in this chapter) within a function or have stepped into (also discussed later in this chapter) a function. Otherwise, the Locals list operates just like the Variables list or the Properties list.

The Watch List

The Watch list is a list of variables that you can put together. It is useful for being able to monitor variables from different objects at the same time. You can add only variables from the Variables and Locals lists to the Watch list, not from the Properties list. To add a variable to the Watch list, you can do one of the following:

✦ In the Variables or Locals list, right-click or Command-click the variable you want to add to the Watch list, and select Watch from the menu.

✦ In the Watch list, right-click or Command-click, and choose Add from the menu. In the Name column, type in the full path to the variable you want to add.

To remove a variable from the Watch list, right-click or Command-click the variable and choose Remove from the menu.

Working with Breakpoints

One of the great features of debugging in Flash is the ability to use breakpoints and to step through the code. Breakpoints are points within the code that you can set on which the movie playback will pause during debugging. They are useful for determining where problems are occurring within the code.

Setting and Removing Breakpoints

You can set and remove breakpoints either in the Actions panel, when authoring the movie, or in the Debugger, when debugging the movie. Setting the breakpoints in the Actions panel is advantageous if you want to have the breakpoints remembered from one debugging session to the next. Breakpoints set in the Actions panel are saved as part of the Flash document. On the other hand, setting breakpoints in the Debugger is advantageous for one-time tests that you don't need to have recalled the next time you debug the movie. You can also remove breakpoints in the Debugger that were set in the Actions panel without affecting the breakpoints that are saved to the document.

To set breakpoints in the Actions panel:

1. Place the cursor in the line of code to which you want to add a breakpoint.

2. Do one of the following:

   • Right-click or Command-click, and select Set Breakpoint from the menu.

   • Choose Set Breakpoint from the Debug Options menu in the toolbar.

To remove a single breakpoint in the Actions panel:

1. Place the cursor in the line of code from which you want to remove a breakpoint.

2. Do one of the following:

   • Right-click or Command-click, and select Remove Breakpoint from the menu.

   • Choose Remove Breakpoint from the Debug Options menu in the toolbar.

And you can remove all breakpoints from a document by doing one of the following:

   ✦ Right-click or Command-click anywhere in the Actions panel, and choose Remove All Breakpoints from the menu.

   ✦ Choose Remove All Breakpoints from the Debug Options menu in the toolbar.

Setting and removing breakpoints in the Debugger are very similar. When a movie is first opened for debugging, it is paused specifically so that you can add or remove breakpoints within the code. You can use the Jump menu to select the group of code to which you want to add or remove breakpoints.

To set a breakpoint in the Debugger:

1. In the Code View pane, place the cursor in the line of code to which you want to add a breakpoint.

2. Do one of the following:

   • Right-click or Command-click, and select Set Breakpoint from the menu.

   • Click the Toggle Breakpoint button in the toolbar.

To remove a single breakpoint in the Debugger:

1. In the Code View pane, place the cursor in the line of code from which you want to remove a breakpoint.

2. Do one of the following:

   • Right-click or Command-click, and select Remove Breakpoint from the menu.

   • Click the Toggle Breakpoint button in the toolbar.

And you can remove all breakpoints from the movie by doing one of the following:

✦ Right-click or Command-click anywhere in the Actions panel, and choose Remove All Breakpoints from the menu.

✦ Click the Remove All Breakpoints button in the toolbar.

Stepping through the Code

Once you have set breakpoints, you can begin stepping through the code. When the movie has begun playing (you must first choose Continue), it pauses when a breakpoint is encountered. The current line of code is indicated by a yellow arrow in the margin.

In the Debugger toolbar (see Figure 6-3), you will find the following options for stepping through code:

✦ **Continue (F10)** — A movie is paused when first being debugged, so you must choose to continue when you want the movie to begin playing. Continue can be chosen any time the movie is stopped to resume playback until the next breakpoint is reached.

✦ **Stop Debugging (F11)** — At any point, you may stop debugging the movie. When you choose this option, the movie continues to play normally without any breakpoints, and the Debugger is inactivated.

✦ **Toggle Breakpoint** — To temporarily enable or disable a breakpoint in the code, select the line and click the Toggle Breakpoint button.

✦ **Remove All Breakpoints** — Assuming that there are breakpoints set in the application, you can remove all of them (for the duration of the debugging session) by clicking the Remove All Breakpoints button.

✦ **Step Over (F7)** — Choosing to step over will move the playback to the next line of code and pause again.

✦ **Step In (F6)** — Choosing to step in will step into a function or method. If the current line does not contain a function or method call, then stepping in is the same as stepping over.

✦ **Step Out (F8)** — Stepping out is the reverse of stepping in. If the current line is within a function or method, then choosing Step Out will move the playback to the line after which the function or method was called. It finishes executing the function first.

 **Figure 6-3:** The Debugger toolbar.

An Exercise in Debugging

In this brief exercise, you will familiarize yourself with debugging using the Debugger. You will edit values for properties and variables, create a Watch list, set and remove breakpoints, continue, step over, step in, step out, and stop debugging.

1. Open a new Flash document, and save it to your local hard disk.

2. Rename the default layer to Objects, and add a new layer named Actions.

3. On the Objects layer, draw a square with the rectangle drawing tool.

4. Select the square, and convert it to a Movie Clip symbol by choosing Modify ⇨ Convert to Symbol or by pressing F8. Name the symbol Square, and click OK.

5. Name the instance of the square `mSquare` using the Property inspector.

6. On the Objects layer, use the Text tool to create a Dynamic Text box (a `TextField` object) on the stage. Make sure the color of the text will be visible on the movie's background.

7. Name the `TextField` object `tDebugText` using the Property inspector.

8. On the Actions layer, add the following code:

```
// Define a function to call later on
function showMessage() {
  tDebugText.text = sMessage + " " + nCounter;
  nCounter++;
}

function rotateMovieClip() {
  showMessage();
  mSquare._rotation += 15;
}

var sMessage:String = "default message";
var nCounter = 0;

// Create an interval for the text to change
var movieClipRotaterInterval:Number = setInterval(rotateMovieClip,
1000);
```

9. Set a breakpoint on the following line:

```
mSquare._rotation += 15
```

(You are setting this breakpoint solely for the purpose of removing it in the Debugger. It is just for exercise.)

10. Now debug the movie (choose Control ⇨ Debug Movie).

11. In the Debugger, choose Actions for Scene 1: Frame 1 of Layer name Actions from the jump menu.

12. Choose the line of code with the breakpoint, and remove the breakpoint.

13. Choose the previous line of code:

```
showMessage();
```

and add a breakpoint.

14. Now choose Continue; the movie will play until it reaches the breakpoint and pauses.

15. Choose Step Over to step over `showMessage()`. Notice that the function is still executed. You are not stepping over the execution of the function. All you are doing is telling Flash you don't want to debug within the function.

16. The application should now be paused on the next line. Even though you have not set a breakpoint there, Flash automatically goes to and pauses on the next line of code after you do a Step Over. Click Step Out to cause Flash to finish with the function. The function will automatically be called again (because of the interval you set) and Flash will pause at the breakpoint again.

17. Choose Step Out. Notice that this time Flash does not pause on the next line of code. Instead, the function call is finished and because of the interval, the function is called again.

18. Choose Step In to step into the function `showMessage()`.

19. Choose Step Out.

20. In the Display list, select `_level0`.

21. Click the Variables list tab, and notice the values of `nCounter` and `sMessage`. What happens if you change these values and then click Step Out?

22. Choose Stop Debugging.

We'd like to know what you thought about this chapter. Visit `www.rightactionscript` `.com/asb/comments` to fill out an online form with your comments.

Summary

✦ Common errors can occur in several areas of your movie. You may have to troubleshoot your computer system, the movie within a player, the movie within browsers, server-side scripts, or the code or instances within the movie itself.

✦ Certain types of errors are very easy to make when authoring a movie. Perhaps the most common error is with naming instances and spelling errors.

✦ Improper variable scoping and incorrectly defined paths are common mistakes in Flash authoring.

✦ Resources for help are easy to find online from the established and helpful Flash community and the Macromedia web site.

✦ You can adopt certain practices to help prevent common mistakes from occurring in the first place, including naming conventions and regular testing and saving.

✦ Tracking down errors in your code is called debugging.

✦ Flash 8 allows you to use the Output panel and the Debugger for debugging your movies.

✦ When using the Output panel for debugging, you can use `trace()` actions as well as the List Variables and List Objects features.

✦ The Debugger is a sophisticated tool that allows you to view real-time changes in variables as well as step through each line of code.

✦ The Debugger can be run with local or remote movies.

✦ Breakpoints allow you to pause on lines of code while the movie is playing.

✦ ✦ ✦

Using Core Classes

◆   ◆   ◆   ◆

◆   ◆   ◆   ◆

Working with Arrays

Arrays (ordered data structures) are among the simplest yet most useful objects in ActionScript. Your programs will benefit many times over from the proper use of arrays. Many tasks that you might try to do using multiple variables, `String` object methods, and `for` and `while` loops can be handled much more efficiently with an array. For example, an array can be much more efficient than storing related values in separate variables with incremental names (for example, `sTitle0`, `sTitle1`, `sTitle2`, and so on) or than storing the values in a list (for example, `"value1, value2, value3, value4"`). By the time you have finished this chapter, you should be armed with some powerful tools for making your ideas come to life with ActionScript.

Creating Ordered Structures

In most programs, there comes a time when you work with groups of related data. Sometimes this data comes in the form of lists, such as the following:

```
var sEmployees:String = "Arun, Peter, Chris,
Heather";
```

If you want to handle the data as a single string, the previous example works just fine. But what happens when you want to work with each piece of data individually? A comma-delimited list is too awkward and difficult to work with. It might require complicated loops and many variables to accomplish even a simple task, such as sorting the list alphabetically. Here is a perfect case for an array.

Arrays are simply ordered data structures. These structures are composed of *elements* — values with indices that correspond to those values. In other words, each value has a unique identifier by which it can be referenced. In the case of arrays created using the `Array` class, these indices are numbers. For instance, in the previous example, you could restructure the `sEmployees` string into an array in which Arun would have an index of 0, Peter an index of 1, Chris an index of 2, and Heather an index of 3.

Tip   Notice that the first index mentioned was a 0. Much like other languages, ActionScript uses zero-indexed arrays, meaning the first element of an array in ActionScript has an index of 0, not 1.

You can think of a basic array like a table from a spreadsheet program. In its basic form, an array is a single column with as many rows as it has elements. The employee example can be graphically represented like this:

Index	Value
0	Arun
1	Peter
2	Chris
3	Heather

There are many examples of arrays in real life. Libraries keep all the books in order according to the unique numbers assigned to the books. If you know the index, you can find it in order. The same is true of driver's license numbers, license plate numbers, Social Security numbers, and so on. Examples of *arrays*, collections of organized data with unique indices, are all around us.

Creating Arrays

Now that you have a general sense of what an array is, you need to know how to create one. All arrays are instances of the `Array` class, and as such, you can create instances using the `Array` constructor. There are three variations with the constructor:

✦ **No parameters** — This option creates a new array with zero elements. You'll read the different alternatives for adding new elements to such an array in the next section.

```
// Create a new array with zero elements.
var aEmployees:Array = new Array();
```

✦ **A single parameter specifying the number of elements** — This option creates a new array with the specified number of elements. However, each element is left undefined. You then need to assign values to each of the elements. This is discussed in the next section.

```
// Create a new array with four elements.
var aEmployees:Array = new Array(4);
```

✦ **A list of parameters, each of which is a new value to insert into a new element in the array** — For example, a constructor called with three parameters will create a new array with three elements. The parameter values are assigned to the new elements.

```
// Create a new array with zero elements.
var aEmployees:Array = new Array("Arun", "Peter", "Chris",
                                 "Heather");
```

In addition to creating arrays with the constructor, you can also create array literals. An *array literal* is still an instance of the `Array` class, just as an array created with the constructor. The only difference is that the array literal notation is slightly more condensed. With array literal notation you tell Flash to create a new array using square brackets. Within the square brackets you can provide a list of elements to add to the array. Here is an example:

```
var aEmployees:Array = ["Arun", "Peter", "Chris", "Heather"];
```

You may notice that the array literal notation essentially is no different from the third variation of the Array constructor. Why would you then choose one over the other? Generally, one is not any better than the other. It is largely a matter of preference. In fact, you can also use array literal notation as an alternative to the first variation of the constructor.

```
var aEmployees:Array = [];
```

The preceding creates a new array with zero elements. It is only the second variation on the constructor that is somewhat awkward to mimic using array literal notation.

Adding Values to an Array

In the preceding section, you learned how to create a new array. Often, after you have created an array, the next thing you want to do is add new elements and/or assign values to existing elements. Let's take a look at some of the ways you can do this.

Assigning Values Using Array-Access Notation

Array-access notation allows you to assign values to specific elements in an array if you know the index of the element. The basic syntax for assigning a value to an element using array-access notation is:

```
arrayName[index] = value;
```

Here is a specific example that creates a new array with four undefined elements. Then, using array-access notation, you can assign new values to the array.

```
var aEmployees:Array = new Array(4);
aEmployees[0] = "Arun";
aEmployees[1] = "Peter";
aEmployees[2] = "Chris";
aEmployees[3] = "Heather";
```

A simple way to see the contents of an array is to use a trace() action to write the contents to the Output panel. You can allow Flash to implicitly convert the array to a string, or you can explicitly invoke the toString() method. In either case, when the array is converted to a string, it is represented as a comma-delimited list.

```
trace(aEmployees.toString());
```

The result of the preceding trace() action is:

```
Arun,Peter,Chris,Heather
```

As you can see, the array contains four elements with the values that you assigned them. Also, in this example, notice that the first element of the array has an index of 0. As mentioned earlier, all ActionScript arrays are zero-indexed.

Another quality of ActionScript arrays is that they size dynamically. This means that if you assign a value to an element that has not yet been created, Flash automatically creates that element, and any other elements with indices between. For example, you can assign a value to an element with index 9 of the aEmployees array:

```
aEmployees[9] = "Ruth";
```

If you then use a trace() action to see the contents of the array, you'll see the following in the Output panel:

```
Arun,Peter,Chris,Heather,undefined,undefined,undefined,undefined,undefined,Ruth
```

Notice that the first four elements remain the same. A value of Ruth has been assigned to the tenth element. Because the tenth element did not previously exist, it was automatically created. However, because the fifth through ninth elements didn't exist either, they were also created with undefined values. You cannot create an array with gaps in the indices. The indices must always be contiguous.

Appending Values to the End of an Array

When you are dynamically adding elements to an array it is sometimes difficult to keep track of the number of elements. Fortunately, ActionScript offers a convenient and simple way to append elements to an array using the push() method.

The push() method accepts one or more parameters and automatically appends those values to the end of the array. Here is an example:

```
var aEmployees:Array = ["Arun", "Peter", "Chris", "Heather"];
aEmployees.push("Ruth");
trace(aEmployees.toString());
```

The result is:

```
Arun,Peter,Chris,Heather,Ruth
```

You are not limited to adding a single element at a time. Here is another example:

```
var aEmployees:Array = ["Arun", "Peter", "Chris", "Heather"];
aEmployees.push("Ruth", "Hao", "Laura");
trace(aEmployees.toString());
```

The result is:

```
Arun,Peter,Chris,Heather,Ruth,Hao,Laura
```

The push() method always appends new elements, even if all the existing elements have undefined values. Therefore, be careful when you want to insert values in an array with undefined elements. For example:

```
var aEmployees:Array = new Array(2);
aEmployees.push("Ruth", "Hao", "Laura");
trace(aEmployees.toString());
```

In this example, the Output panel will display the following:

```
undefined,undefined,Ruth,Hao,Laura
```

The first two elements remain undefined.

Prepending Elements to the Beginning of an Array

Appending elements to an array is enough of a challenge without using the push() method. Prepending elements to the beginning of an array without the use of a built-in method would be a struggle. Fortunately, you can rely on the built-in unshift() method.

The unshift() method works in much the same way as the push() method, but it adds the new elements to the beginning of the array instead of the end. Any existing elements are shifted (or *un*shifted, if you will) to higher indices. For example, if you use unshift() to add one new element to an array, the new element is inserted at index 0 and all the existing elements' indices are incremented by one.

The following is an example of the unshift() method:

```
var aEmployees:Array = ["Arun", "Peter", "Chris", "Heather"];
aEmployees.unshift("Ruth", "Hao", "Laura");
trace(aEmployees.toString());
```

And this is the resulting output:

```
Ruth,Hao,Laura,Arun,Peter,Chris,Heather
```

Inserting Elements into an Array

You have already seen how to append and prepend elements to an array. How about inserting elements into an array, not necessarily at the beginning or end? Once again, ActionScript provides a method for that very purpose. You can use the splice() method to insert new elements into an array starting at a given index. All subsequent elements are shifted to accommodate the new elements.

The basic syntax to use the splice() method to insert new elements is:

```
arrayName.splice(startingIndex, numberOfElementsToDelete,
    element1[,...elementN]);
```

As you can see from the syntax, not only does the splice() method have the capability of inserting new elements into an array, but it can also remove existing elements at the same time. The first parameter of the method is the starting index. For example, if you want to begin inserting and/or removing elements at the second element, you specify a value of 1. The second parameter is the number of elements to delete. If you don't want to remove any elements but only to insert new elements, you should specify a value of 0. Otherwise, indicate the number of elements to remove, and Flash removes that many elements from the array starting with the specified index. Then, for the remaining parameters in the splice() method, you should indicate the values for the element or elements you wish to insert into the array. The following is an example of the splice() method being used to insert three new elements into an array:

```
var aEmployees:Array = ["Arun", "Peter", "Chris", "Heather"];
aEmployees.splice(3, 0, "Ruth", "Hao", "Laura");
trace(aEmployees.toString());
```

The preceding code will display the following in the Output panel:

```
Arun,Peter,Chris,Ruth,Hao,Laura,Heather
```

Removing Elements from an Array

Of course, if you have the ability to add elements to an array, you also should have the ability to remove elements from an array. Let's take a look at some of the ways you can achieve this.

Removing the Last Element of an Array

You can use the `pop()` method to remove the last element from an array. Because the `pop()` method always removes the last element, it does not require any parameters. The method returns the removed value in the event that you want to do something with it other than simply remove it from the array. The following is an example of how to use the `pop()` method:

```
var aEmployees:Array = ["Arun", "Peter", "Chris", "Heather"];
var sAnEmployee:String = String(aEmployees.pop());
trace(aEmployees.toString());
trace(sAnEmployee);
```

The Output panel will display the following:

```
Arun,Peter,Chris
Heather
```

Removing the First Element of an Array

Like the `pop()` method, the `shift()` method removes and returns an element from the array, but instead of removing the element from the end of the array, the `shift()` method removes the element from the beginning of the array. All subsequent elements are shifted such that their indices are decremented by one. The following is an example of the `shift()` method:

```
var aEmployees:Array = ["Arun", "Peter", "Chris", "Heather"];
var sAnEmployee:String = String(aEmployees.shift());
trace(aEmployees.toString());
trace(sAnEmployee);
```

The Output panel will display the following:

```
Peter,Chris,Heather
Arun
```

Removing Elements from Within an Array

You've seen how to remove elements from the beginning and end of an array, but how about elements that are not at the beginning or end? You can use the `splice()` method to accomplish this. We've already seen how to use this method to insert new elements into an array. You can use the same method with only the first two parameters in order to simply remove elements. The method not only removes the specified elements but also returns a new array containing the removed elements. The following is an example:

```
var aEmployees:Array = ["Arun", "Peter", "Chris", "Heather"];
var aRemovedEmployees:Array = aEmployees.splice(2, 2);
trace(aEmployees.toString());
trace(aRemovedEmployees.toString());
```

The preceding code will result in the following display in the Output panel:

```
Arun,Peter
Chris,Heather
```

Reading Data from Arrays

You can read the data from an array using array-access notation to access one element at a time. For example:

```
var aEmployees:Array = ["Arun", "Peter", "Chris", "Heather"];
trace(aEmployees[0]);  // Displays: Arun
trace(aEmployees[1]);  // Displays: Peter
trace(aEmployees[2]);  // Displays: Chris
trace(aEmployees[3]);  // Displays: Heather
```

You can use array-access notation to access any element, and you can use this syntax in any situation in which you can use a variable.

Often you will find that you want to read all the elements of an array. For example, if you have an array of the names of the months of the year, you might want to be able to read all those elements in order to display them to the user. Using a `for` statement and a special property, `length`, of the array, you can loop through all the elements of an array with just a few lines of code.

The `length` property of an array returns the number of elements in the array. Knowing the number of elements in the array and knowing that all arrays are zero-indexed, you can quickly construct a `for` statement to loop through the elements of an array from first to last. Here is an example:

```
var aEmployees:Array = ["Arun", "Peter", "Chris", "Heather"];
for(var i:Number = 0; i < aEmployees.length; i++) {
  trace(aEmployees[i]);
}
```

The preceding example will display the values in the array one at a time in the Output panel as follows:

```
Arun
Peter
Chris
Heather
```

Notice that the `for` statement condition checks to see if i is less than the number of elements in the array — not less than or equal to. Because arrays are zero-indexed, the greatest index value will always be exactly one less than the number of elements in the array. For example, an array with six elements will have index values of 0, 1, 2, 3, 4, and 5. The greatest index value of 5 is one less than the number of elements in the array.

Now, how about if you want to loop through the elements of the array starting with the last element and working backward? No problem. Just change the `for` statement expressions slightly. Instead of initializing the loop at 0 and running until less than the number of elements, you should initialize the loop at one less than the number of elements and run until equal to zero, decrementing by one each time:

```
var aEmployees:Array = ["Arun", "Peter", "Chris", "Heather"];
for(var i:Number = aEmployees.length - 1; i >= 0; i--) {
  trace(aEmployees[i]);
}
```

The preceding example will display the values in the array one at a time in the Output panel as follows:

```
Heather
Chris
Peter
Arun
```

In fact, you can come up with just about any set of conditions on which to loop through an array. Depending on what you are trying to accomplish, you might want to skip every other element, begin looping in the middle of the array, and so on.

Using Different Types of Arrays

There are many ways to approach arrays. What determines how you will treat an array in your programming is the functionality you require from it. In different scenarios, different approaches to using arrays will be more appropriate than others. This section outlines different ways to use arrays in your programs.

Working with Single-Dimension Arrays

The arrays you have seen in this chapter so far are called *single-dimension arrays*. That is, they are single columns of indexed data. You create these arrays in many ways — through the use of array literals and different Array constructors. Some examples of a single-dimension array are the following:

```
var aLetters:Array = ["a", "b", "c"];
var aNoLetters:Array = new Array();
var aMoreLetters:Array = new Array("d", "e", "f");
```

Working with Parallel Arrays

There are occasions in your programming when you will have two groups of data that are related. For example, you might be working with data such as employee names and their corresponding phone numbers. Each employee has a phone number, and you want a way to connect the two pieces of data together. You could create a single array in which each element is a string containing both pieces of data, separated by a delimiter such as a colon (:):

```
var aEmployees:Array = new Array();
aEmployees.push("Arun:555-1234");
aEmployees.push("Peter:555-4321");
aEmployees.push("Chris:555-5678");
aEmployees.push("Heather:555-8765");
```

Then you could use String object methods to extract the names and the birthdays when you want to use them:

```
// The split() method separates string by specified
// delimiter into a new array.
var aEmployees:Array = new Array();
aEmployees.push("Arun:555-1234");
```

```
aEmployees.push("Peter:555-4321");
aEmployees.push("Chris:555-5678");
aEmployees.push("Heather:555-8765");
var aTempEmployeeInfo:Array = null;
for(var i:Number = 0; i < aEmployees.length; i++) {
  aTempEmployeeInfo = aEmployees[i].split(":");
  trace("Employee:" + aTempEmployeeInfo[0]);
  trace("Phone Number:" + aTempEmployeeInfo[1]);
}
```

The preceding will result in the following display in the Output panel:

```
Employee:Arun
Phone Number:555-1234
Employee:Peter
Phone Number:555-4321
Employee:Chris
Phone Number:555-5678
Employee:Heather
Phone Number:555-8765
```

Although that works, it is somewhat overly complex when all you want to do is something as simple as store and retrieve a name and corresponding phone number. A much easier way to solve this problem is to use what are known as *parallel arrays*.

The idea behind parallel arrays is simply to create two (or more) arrays in which the elements with the same indices are related. So using the employee scenario, you could create two parallel arrays as follows:

```
var aEmployeeNames:Array = ["Arun", "Peter", "Chris", "Heather"];
var aEmployeePhone:Array = ["555-1234", "555-4321", "555-5678", "555-8765"];
```

Then it is much easier to retrieve the corresponding elements from each array than to try and parse through a string as you did earlier. All you need to do is to access the elements with the same index from each array:

```
var aEmployeeNames:Array = ["Arun", "Peter", "Chris", "Heather"];
var aEmployeePhone:Array = ["555-1234", "555-4321", "555-5678", "555-8765"];
for(var i:Number = 0; i < aEmployeeNames.length; i++) {
  trace("Employee:" + aEmployeeNames[i]);
  trace("Phone Number:" + aEmployeePhone[i]);
}
```

This displays the following in the Output panel:

```
Employee:Arun
Phone Number:555-1234
Employee:Peter
Phone Number:555-4321
Employee:Chris
Phone Number:555-5678
Employee:Heather
Phone Number:555-8765
```

Notice that this is the same output as before, but the code is simplified.

You are not limited to using just two arrays with corresponding data. You can use as many as you need and can manage. Let's continue on with the same employee example and imagine that you want to add one additional piece of information about each employee. Perhaps you want to add the number of years employed. You could then easily add a third parallel array:

```
var aEmployeeYears:Array = [5, 7, 3, 1];
```

Working with Multidimensional Arrays

You can think of the standard, single-dimension array as being a single column of data. Many other languages support what are known as multidimensional arrays. You can think of a two-dimensional array, for example, as a grid where each element is determined by two indices — a row and a column index. A three-dimensional array can be thought of as representing three-dimensional space, and each element is determined by three indices — the row, column, and depth. In ActionScript, you can represent this construct using an array of arrays. Here is an example:

```
var aEmployees:Array = new Array();
aEmployees.push(["Arun", "555-1234"]);
aEmployees.push(["Peter", "555-4321"]);
aEmployees.push(["Chris", "555-5678"]);
aEmployees.push(["Heather", "555-8765"]);
for(var i:Number = 0; i < aEmployees.length; i++) {
  trace("Employee:" + aEmployees[i][0]);
  trace("Phone Number:" + aEmployees[i][1]);
}
```

The preceding code creates a new array, aEmployees, and appends to it four elements that are, themselves, arrays. Then, notice that each value is accessed using two indices. The first index specifies the row (the element of the outermost array), whereas the second index specifies the column (the element of the innermost arrays). The result is very similar to what you achieved using parallel arrays in the earlier section. In fact, parallel arrays and two-dimensional arrays can be used almost interchangeably.

Of course, you can create arrays as elements of arrays that are, themselves, elements of an array. Such a scenario would mimic a three-dimensional array. You can even create arrays of greater dimensions, although once you get beyond three or four dimensions, it can become confusing.

Working with Arrays of Objects

Another type of array that can be useful is an array of associative arrays. We discussed associative arrays in Chapter 5. As a quick refresher, however, an associative array is an object with named indices called *keys*. Arrays of associative arrays can be useful when you have a list of data in which each element is composed of various, named subelements. For example, this same employee/phone number example is a good candidate for this type of construct. Here is an example:

```
var aEmployees:Array = new Array();
aEmployees.push({employee:"Arun", phone:"555-1234"});
aEmployees.push({employee:"Peter", phone:"555-4321"});
aEmployees.push({employee:"Chris", phone:"555-5678"});
```

```
aEmployees.push({employee:"Heather", phone:"555-8765"});
for(var i:Number = 0; i < aEmployees.length; i++) {
  trace("Employee:" + aEmployees[i].employee);
  trace("Phone Number:" + aEmployees[i].phone);
}
```

Converting Arrays to Lists

A single string that represents a group of related data is often called a *list*. Here's a simple example of a list:

```
var sEmployees:String = "Arun,Peter,Chris,Heather";
```

The character used between each element in the list is generally called a *delimiter*. Although any character can be used as a delimiter, one of the most common is the comma.

When you have an array of elements, there are various reasons why you might want to convert it to a list. One of the most common uses of lists is in sending values to a server-side script, but that is certainly not the only possible use. In any case, when you want to convert an array to a list you can use the join() method. The join() method returns a new list (a string) containing all the elements of the array delimited by the character you specify. You specify the delimiter as a parameter of the join() method. Here is an example:

```
var aEmployees:Array = ["Arun", "Peter", "Chris", "Heather"];
var sEmployees:String = aEmployees.join(",");
trace(sEmployees);
```

The Output panel will display the following:

```
Arun,Peter,Chris,Heather
```

You may notice that in this case the join() method results in the same value as the toString() method. However, the toString() method does not allow you to specify a delimiter other than the comma. With join() you can use any delimiter you want. For example:

```
var aEmployees:Array = ["Arun", "Peter", "Chris", "Heather"];
var sEmployees:String = aEmployees.join(";");
trace(sEmployees);
```

The Output panel will display the following:

```
Arun;Peter;Chris;Heather
```

On the other hand, sometimes you have a list that you want to convert to an array. You can convert any list into an array using the String class split() method. The split() method asks that you specify the delimiter it should use to determine the elements of the list. Here is an example:

```
var sEmployees:String = "Arun,Peter,Chris,Heather";
var aEmployees:Array = sEmployees.split(",");
```

The result of the preceding code is a new array with four elements.

Creating New Arrays from Existing Arrays

The Array class provides you with several ways to create new arrays based on an existing array. There are two basic scenarios in which you will create a new array from existing elements:

✦ You want to add together the elements of several arrays to create a new array.

✦ You want to create a new array that contains a subset of the elements of the original.

Concatenating Arrays

You can create a new array that contains the elements of several other arrays using the concat() method. You invoke the method from an array and pass it parameters specifying the other arrays whose elements you want to add to the new array. Flash then creates a new array and adds all the elements of the original arrays to the new one. Here is an example:

```
var aEmployeesExec:Array = ["Arun", "Peter", "Chris", "Heather"];
var aEmployeesNew:Array = ["Gilberto", "Mary"];
var aEmployeesStaff:Array = ["Ayla", "Riad"];
var aEmployeesAll:Array = aEmployeesExec.concat(aEmployeesNew, aEmployeesStaff);
trace(aEmployeesAll.toString());
```

In the example, the Output panel will display the following:

```
Arun,Peter,Chris,Heather,Gilberto,Mary,Ayla,Riad
```

The newly created array, aEmployeesAll, contains copies of all the elements of the other arrays.

You can also use the concat() method without any parameters as a shortcut to creating a copy of an array. Here is an example:

```
var aEmployees:Array = ["Arun", "Peter", "Chris", "Heather"];
var aEmployeesCopy:Array = aEmployees.concat();
```

Extracting Subsets of Array Elements

The slice() method (not to be confused with splice()) returns a new array containing a subset of elements from the original. When you invoke the slice() method, you specify the starting and ending indices of the array. Flash then returns a new array containing all the elements between those indices, including the first, but not the last. Here is an example:

```
var aEmployeesAll:Array = ["Arun", "Peter", "Chris", "Heather",
                           "Gilberto", "Mary", "Ayla", "Riad"];
var aEmployeesExec:Array = aEmployeesAll.slice(0, 4);
var aEmployeesNew:Array = aEmployeesAll.slice(4, 6);
var aEmployeesStaff:Array = aEmployeesAll.slice(6);
trace(aEmployeesExe.toString());
trace(aEmployeesNew.toString());
trace(aEmployeesStaff.toString());
```

In this example the Output panel will display the following:

```
Arun,Peter,Chris,Heather
Gilberto,Mary
Ayla,Riad
```

Sorting Arrays

An important feature of arrays is that you can sort them. There are different sorting algorithms that developers use, but fortunately you don't have to concern yourself with them because ActionScript provides methods that take care of all of that for you. We examine three sorting methods more closely in the following sections:

  ✦ sort() — This method sorts regular, single dimension arrays.

  ✦ sortOn() — This method sorts arrays of associative arrays based on one of the keys of the associative arrays.

  ✦ reverse() — This method reverses the order of the elements.

Sorting Simply

The most basic type of sort you can perform on an ActionScript array is an alphabetical sort. To achieve an alphabetical sort, simply create your array and invoke the sort() method with no parameters. This is a very useful type of sort to perform. For example, in the sample array used throughout this chapter, you can quickly sort the elements in alphabetical order as follows:

```
var aEmployees:Array = ["Arun", "Peter", "Chris", "Heather"];
aEmployees.sort();
trace(aEmployees.toString());
```

The Output panel displays the elements in alphabetical order:

```
Arun,Chris,Heather,Peter
```

It is important to keep in mind that any sort is going to likely reorder the elements — meaning new indices for some elements. Be sure that before you perform a sort on an array you are not relying on any particular indices for any particular elements. For example, if you are using parallel arrays, and you sort one of them, the array elements will no longer correspond.

A simple sort works wonderfully when you want to sort an array of strings in ascending alphabetical order. However, ActionScript also provides you with some ways of performing more complex sorting.

Sorting More Complexly

There are six types of complex sorts from which you can choose when you use the sort() method. Five of these complex sorts rely on the Array sorting flag constants. The following sections take a look at each of them.

Sorting Numerically

When the sort() method sorts the elements, it generally compares all the elements as though they were string values. This is true, even if the values are numeric. And this can lead to some unexpected sort orders when you want to sort an array of numbers. You can test this for yourself with the following code:

```
var aNumbers:Array = [10, 1, 2, 15, 21, 13, 33, 3];
aNumbers.sort();
trace(aNumbers.toString());
```

What you'll see in the Output panel, should you try this, is the following:

```
1,10,13,15,2,21,3,33
```

Clearly these values are not sorted in numerical order. But they are sorted in the correct order if they are treated as strings. The only problem is that you don't want to compare them as strings. You want to compare them as numbers. Fortunately, the Array class has a constant, Array.NUMERIC, that allows you to sort the values numerically. All you need to do is pass this constant to the sort() method.

```
var aNumbers:Array = [10, 1, 2, 15, 21, 13, 33, 3];
aNumbers.sort(Array.NUMERIC);
trace(aNumbers.toString());
```

Now, in the Output panel the correctly ordered numbers will appear:

```
1,2,3,10,13,15,21,33
```

Sorting in Descending Order

Thus far you've seen how to sort arrays in ascending order. That is the default setting. But with the Array.DESCENDING constant you can tell Flash to sort your array in descending order instead. Here is an example:

```
var aEmployees:Array = ["Arun", "Peter", "Chris", "Heather"];
aEmployees.sort(Array.DESCENDING);
trace(aEmployees.toString());
```

This causes the array to sort in reverse alphabetical order. The following will be displayed in the Output panel:

```
Peter,Heather,Chris,Arun
```

Sorting Regardless of Case

When Flash compares two strings, the cases of the values are a factor. Uppercase characters are sorted before lowercase characters. Therefore, if you perform a simple sort on an array in which the initial case of the words is not consistent, you should be aware that the sorted array may be other than you expect. Here is an example:

```
var aWords:Array = ["orange", "Sedona", "apple", "Caracas"];
aWords.sort();
trace(aWords.toString());
```

In this case, the array will be sorted as follows:

```
Caracas,Sedona,apple,orange
```

Although that is the default behavior, you can explicitly tell Flash to perform a case-insensitive sort using the `Array.CASEINSENSITIVE` constant. Here is an example:

```
var aWords:Array = ["orange", "Sedona", "apple", "Caracas"];
aWords.sort(Array.CASEINSENSITIVE);
trace(aWords.toString());
```

With the simple addition of the constant as a parameter to the `sort()` method, the array will now be sorted as follows:

```
apple,Caracas,orange,Sedona
```

Sorting and Testing for Unique Values

You can also use the `sort()` method to test and ensure that the values of the array are unique. If you pass the `sort()` method the `Array.UNIQUESORT` constant, then it has the following behavior:

✦ If the elements of the array are all unique, the array is sorted alphabetically in ascending order.

✦ If there are one or more duplicate elements, the `sort()` method returns 0 and the array is not sorted.

Here is an example of the `sort()` method with the `Array.UNIQUESORT` constant:

```
var aEmployees:Array = ["Arun", "Peter", "Chris", "Heather"];
if(aEmployees.sort(Array.UNIQUESORT) != 0) {
  trace(aEmployees.toString());
}
else {
  trace("Array has duplicate elements, and has not been sorted. ");
  trace(aEmployees.toString());
}
```

The preceding code will display the sorted array because `aEmployees` has no duplicate entries:

```
Arun,Chris,Heather,Peter
```

If you modify the first line of code as follows:

```
var aEmployees:Array = ["Arun", "Peter", "Chris", "Heather", "Arun"];
```

you can see that the `sort()` method catches the duplicate element, and the array is not sorted:

```
Array has duplicate elements, and has not been sorted.
Arun,Peter,Chris,Heather,Arun
```

Getting Sorted Indices

Another option available to you is to use the `sort()` method to return an array of indices that represent the sorted elements. This option does not sort the original array but gives you a way to access the element in a sorted order. When you invoke the `sort()` method and pass it the `Array.RETURNINDEXEDARRAY` constant, Flash does not modify the original array, but rather returns a new array containing elements representing the indices from the original.

The order of the elements in the new array can be used to access the elements from the original array in sorted order. Here is an example:

```
var aEmployees:Array = ["Arun", "Peter", "Chris", "Heather"];
var aSortedIndices:Array = aEmployees.sort(Array.RETURNINDEXEDARRAY);
trace(aEmployees.toString());
trace(aSortedIndices.toString());
for(var i:Number = 0; i < aSortedIndices.length; i++) {
  trace(aEmployees[aSortedIndices[i]]);
}
```

This example will display the following in the Output panel:

```
Arun,Peter,Chris,Heather
0,2,3,1
Arun
Chris
Heather
Peter
```

You can see that the original array is not modified. The new array contains number elements that represent the indices of the original array. If you loop through the elements of the new array and use those values as the indices to access the values from the original array, you can access the values from the original array in ascending alphabetical order.

Sorting with Multiple Flags

So great, you say, you can perform a case-insensitive search. You can even perform a descending order search. But what if you want Flash to sort using both criteria at the same time? No problem, says Flash. Simply use the bitwise OR operator (|) to join together all of the constants you want Flash to use for the sort. Here is an example:

```
var aWords:Array = ["orange", "Sedona", "apple", "Caracas"];
aWords.sort(Array.DESCENDING | Array.CASEINSENSITIVE);
trace(aWords.toString());
```

The Output panel will display the following:

```
Sedona,orange,Caracas,apple
```

Sorting with Custom Algorithms

If none of the built-in sorting options is what you are looking for, you can use a custom sorting algorithm instead. For the most part, the sorting options discussed previously should work for just about any scenario you might have with a single-dimensional array containing strings or numbers. In the next section, we also discuss how to use the sortOn() method to sort arrays of associative arrays. Therefore, custom algorithms are less and less likely to be essential.

Should you need to use a custom sorting algorithm, here's how it works:

1. First, you create a function that Flash will use to sort the elements. The function should accept two parameters. Flash will automatically pass it two elements at a time (called a and b). Within the function you need to put in place the logic to determine which element should be sorted before the other. Once you have determined the order you can return one of three values:

      a. 1 — a should be sorted after b.

      b. –1 — b should be sorted after a.

      c. 0 — leave the original order of a and b.

  2. When you call the `sort()` method, pass it a reference to the custom sorting function. Flash handles the rest.

Here's a basic example that uses a custom sorting algorithm to perform a case-insensitive sort that sorts in descending alphabetical order. You can also achieve the same results by first performing a sort with the `Array.CASEINSENSITIVE` and `Array.DESCENDING` flags.

```
function sorter(a:String, b:String):Number {
  if(a.toUpperCase() > b.toUpperCase()) {
    return -1;
  }
  else if(a.toUpperCase() < b.toUpperCase()) {
    return 1;
  }
  else {
    return 0;
  }
}var aWords:Array = ["orange", "Sedona", "apple", "Caracas"];
aWords.sort(sorter);
trace(aWords.toString());
```

The output is:

```
Sedona,orange,Caracas,apple
```

The following is another example that is more complex. In this example, the function sorts the array's values first according to the type of value (name of city or name of country) and then alphabetically:

```
function isInArray(sElement:String, aArray:Array) {
  for(var i:Number = 0; i < aArray.length; i++) {
    if(sElement == aArray[i]) {
      return true;
    }
  }
  return false;
}
function sorter(a:String, b:String):Number {
  var aCountries:Array = ["Mexico", "Vietnam", "Japan"];
  var aCities:Array = ["Caracas", "Paris", "Berlin"];
  if((isInArray(a, aCountries) && isInArray(b, aCities)) ||
(isInArray(b, aCountries) && isInArray(a, aCities))) {
    return 1;
  }
  if(a.toUpperCase() > b.toUpperCase()) {
    return 1;
  }
  else if(a.toUpperCase() < b.toUpperCase()) {
```

```
      return -1;
    }
    else {
      return 0;
    }
}
var aPlaces:Array = ["Berlin", "Vietnam", "Japan", "Caracas",
                     "Mexico", "Paris"];
aPlaces.sort(sorter);
trace(aPlaces.toString());
```

The output is:

```
Japan,Mexico,Vietnam,Berlin,Caracas,Paris
```

Sorting Arrays of Associative Arrays

You can use the sortOn() method to sort an array's elements by key name if the elements of the array are all associative arrays. For example, consider the following array:

```
var aCars:Array = new Array();
aCars.push({make: "Oldsmobile", model: "Alero", extColor: "blue"});
aCars.push({make: "Honda", model: "Accord", extColor: "red"});
aCars.push({make: "Volvo", model: "242", extColor: "red"});
```

With this array, you may want to sort its elements by make, model, or exterior color. With the sortOn() method, this is as simple as a single method call. But sortOn() can do more. Let's take a look at a few of the options available with the sortOn() method.

Sorting by a Single Key

The simplest type of sort with sortOn() is to sort an array based on a single key. In these cases, you need only to pass the name of the key to the sortOn() method as a single, string parameter. Here is an example:

```
function displayArray(aArray:Array) {
  var sElement:String = null;
  for(var i:Number = 0; i < aArray.length; i++) {
    sElement = "";
    for(var key in aArray[i]) {
      sElement += aArray[i][key] + " ";
    }
    trace(sElement);
  }
}

var aCars:Array = new Array();
aCars.push({make: "Oldsmobile", model: "Alero", extColor: "blue"});
aCars.push({make: "Honda", model: "Accord", extColor: "red"});
aCars.push({make: "Volvo", model: "242", extColor: "red"});
aCars.sortOn("make");
displayArray(aCars);
```

In this example, you first define a function that displays the contents of the array. Because the array's elements are not simple string or number values, a `toString()` call will not yield a value for displaying the contents of the array. So the `displayArray()` function simply loops through the contents of the array and displays each element's values. Next, you define the array. The array consists of three associative arrays, all with the same keys, but different values. Then, you invoke the `sortOn()` method, telling it which key to sort on. The display in the Output panel looks like this:

```
Honda Accord red
Oldsmobile Alero blue
Volvo 242 red
```

Notice that the elements have been sorted alphabetically by the value of the make. If you want to sort on the model instead, you can simply invoke `sortOn()` with the value of `model` instead of `make`. In that case the output will be as follows:

```
Volvo 242 red
Honda Accord red
Oldsmobile Alero blue
```

And, of course, you can also sort on the exterior color if you want. In order to do that, you simply invoke the `sortOn()` method with the value of `extColor`.

Sorting on Multiple Keys

When you are sorting arrays of associative arrays, it can be useful not only to be able to sort on a single key, but also on multiple keys. For example, if you have an array of associative arrays that describe cars, as in this example, you might want to tell Flash to sort it by make, and then by model, and finally by exterior color. The `sortOn()` method has a built-in option for this kind of sorting. All you need to do is pass the `sortOn()` method an array of the key names on which you want to sort, in the order you want Flash to sort them. Here is an example:

```
function displayArray(aArray:Array) {
  var sElement:String = null;
  for(var i:Number = 0; i < aArray.length; i++) {
    sElement = "";
    for(var key in aArray[i]) {
      sElement += aArray[i][key] + " ";
    }
    trace(sElement);
  }
}

var aCars:Array = new Array();
aCars.push({make: "Oldsmobile", model: "Alero", extColor: "blue"});
aCars.push({make: "Honda", model: "Accord", extColor: "red"});
aCars.push({make: "Volvo", model: "242 DL", extColor: "red"});
aCars.push({make: "Oldsmobile", model: "Alero", extColor: "red"});
aCars.push({make: "Honda", model: "Accord", extColor: "gold"});
aCars.push({make: "Volvo", model: "242", extColor: "white"});
aCars.push({make: "Oldsmobile", model: "Aurora", extColor: "silver"});
aCars.push({make: "Honda", model: "Prelude", extColor: "silver"});
aCars.push({make: "Volvo", model: "242", extColor: "red"});

aCars.sortOn(["make","mode","extColor"]);
displayArray(aCars);
```

In this example the Output panel will display the following:

```
Honda Accord gold
Honda Accord red
Honda Prelude silver
Oldsmobile Alero blue
Oldsmobile Alero red
Oldsmobile Aurora silver
Volvo 242 DL red
Volvo 242 red
Volvo 242 white
```

Notice that the array has been sorted first by make, so all the elements with the same make are grouped together. Then, within each make group the elements are sorted by model. Therefore, the Accords are sorted before the Prelude, for example. And then, within each model group the elements are sorted by exterior color. For example, the gold Accord is sorted before the red Accord.

It is very important that when you want to sort on multiple keys you pass the sortOn() method a *single* parameter. The single parameter is an array. If you try and pass the sortOn() method multiple key name parameters, the sort will not be correct.

Sorting with Sort Flags

You can also use all the same sorting flags with sortOn() that you can use with sort(). If you are sorting on a single key, the first parameter for the sortOn() method is still the key name. Then, you can pass the method a sorting flag constant as the second parameter. Here is an example:

```
function displayArray(aArray:Array) {
  var sElement:String = null;
  for(var i:Number = 0; i < aArray.length; i++) {
    sElement = "";
    for(var key in aArray[i]) {
      sElement += aArray[i][key] + " ";
    }
    trace(sElement);
  }
}

var aCars:Array = new Array();
aCars.push({make: "Oldsmobile", model: "Alero", extColor: "blue"});
aCars.push({make: "Honda", model: "Accord", extColor: "red"});
aCars.push({make: "Volvo", model: "242", extColor: "red"});
aCars.sortOn("make", Array.DESCENDING);
displayArray(aCars);
```

The result of this sort is:

```
Volvo 242 red
Oldsmobile Alero blue
Honda Accord red
```

You can also use sorting flags when sorting with multiple keys. The first parameter should still be an array of the keys on which you want to sort. The second parameter should be the sorting flag constant. Here is an example:

```
function displayArray(aArray:Array) {
  var sElement:String = null;
  for(var i:Number = 0; i < aArray.length; i++) {
    sElement = "";
    for(var key in aArray[i]) {
      sElement += aArray[i][key] + " ";
    }
    trace(sElement);
  }
}
var aCars:Array = new Array();
aCars.push({make: "Oldsmobile", model: "Alero", extColor: "blue"});
aCars.push({make: "Honda", model: "Accord", extColor: "red"});
aCars.push({make: "Volvo", model: "242 DL", extColor: "red"});
aCars.push({make: "Oldsmobile", model: "Alero", extColor: "red"});
aCars.push({make: "Honda", model: "Accord", extColor: "gold"});
aCars.push({make: "Volvo", model: "242", extColor: "white"});
aCars.push({make: "Oldsmobile", model: "Aurora", extColor: "silver"});
aCars.push({make: "Honda", model: "Prelude", extColor: "silver"});
aCars.push({make: "Volvo", model: "242", extColor: "red"});
aCars.sortOn(["make","mode","extColor"], Array.DESCENDING);
displayArray(aCars);
```

The Output panel for this example will display the following:

```
Volvo 242 white
Volvo 242 red
Volvo 242 DL red
Oldsmobile Aurora silver
Oldsmobile Alero red
Oldsmobile Alero blue
Honda Prelude silver
Honda Accord red
Honda Accord gold
```

And, of course, whether you are sorting on single or multiple keys, you can combine multiple sorting flags using the bitwise OR operator.

Reversing an Array

With the sorting flags that are now available, there is little need for the reverse() method anymore. But should you want to quickly and simply reverse the order of an array's elements, you can use this method:

```
aEmployees.reverse();
```

We'd like to know what you thought about this chapter. Visit www.rightactionscript .com/asb/comments to fill out an online form with your comments.

Summary

✦ Arrays are indexed data structures in which each piece of data, called an *element*, has a unique index by which it can be referenced.

✦ Arrays can be created as array literals using the constructor methods or as a returned value from a method such as `slice()` or `concat()`.

✦ You can use the array access operator (`[ ]`) to read and write to the elements of an array. You place the index of the element you want to read or write to between the square brackets of the operator. Numbered indices start with 0.

✦ There are many ways to work with arrays. The basic array is the single-dimensional, numbered indices array. You can work with multiple arrays with corresponding elements in what are known as parallel arrays. And you can even create arrays of arrays to provide support for more complex collections of data.

✦ You can sort your arrays using many of ActionScript's built-in sorting options.

✦   ✦   ✦

Using Numbers

Chances are good that in the majority of Flash applications, you'll be using numbers. Numbers show up when you're using ActionScript to animate objects, calculate prices, and determine quantities, and in many scenarios in which you might not even have thought of numbers. In this chapter, you get a chance to learn more about different types of numbers and how to work with them.

Understanding Number Types

Although all numbers in ActionScript are classified as the Number datatype, there are different types of numbers with which you can work. The following sections examine some of these types.

Note   All numbers are of the Number datatype. That means that Flash Player works with all numbers to the same degree of precision. Unlike many programming languages, ActionScript does not formally differentiate between, for example, integers and floating-point numbers.

Integers and Floating-Point Numbers

The first category of numbers is base-10. These numbers should be familiar to you. They are the numbers that you use to count in everyday life. But within this category, you can have two classifications of precision: integers and floating-point numbers.

Integers are whole numbers, including 0 and negative values. The following are examples of integers:

```
1, 25, 0, -36, -3, 2932
```

Integers are the numbers you use to count whole things. For instance, you count frames in integer values — you cannot have anything between two frames. You use integers as indices for arrays, and you use integers to count most items (for example, people, paper clips, and pens).

There are, however, times when you require more precision in your numbers (for instance, when you are working with monetary values). Imagine the chaos that would ensue if banks worked only in integer values! In other words, $3.50 is not the same as $3. In these cases, you need more precision in your numbers. That is what floating-point numbers are for.

Floating-point numbers are also called *fractional numbers* because they can include fractions of integer values. Examples of floating-point numbers are:

```
2.1, -32.012, 3.14, 3833.222223
```

Because integers and floating-point numbers fall under the same datatype (and same class as well) in ActionScript, you don't need to do anything fancy to perform operations with both types of values together. For instance, you can use any of the mathematical operators using both types of numbers as operands:

```
5.1 + 3;        // results in 8.1
22 - 98.2223;   // results in -76.2223
5 % 2.1;        // results in 0.8
```

However, you should be aware that ActionScript automatically adjusts the precision of the number value to whatever is necessary. In other words, you might have noticed that adding a floating-point number to an integer results in a floating-point value. But when you add two (or more) floating-point values together that add up to a whole number, the precision of the resulting value is less than the precision of the operands. For example:

```
3.2 + 4.1 + 0.7;  // results in 8, not 8.0
```

In the previous example, even though all the operands have a precision to one decimal place, the result lost that precision. In most cases, this is not a problem.

Decimal Numbers

The type of numbers you work with most often are numbers in base-10, also known as decimal numbers. The term "decimal" simply means that multiplying a number by 10 to the power of n moves the decimal point n places without affecting the value of the digits of the number. In fact, decimal numbers can be represented in this fashion:

```
1.23 * 10² = 123
```

In ActionScript, the letter e with a plus sign (+) or minus sign (-) is used to create this kind of notation:

```
var nDecimalOne:Number = 1.23e+2;   // results in 123
var nDecimalTwo:Number = 1.23e-2;   // results in 0.0123
```

Notice that for numbers in which the exponent is positive and is less than 15, ActionScript writes the values (to the Output panel, for instance) in full form. But any number that has an integer part greater than or equal to 1000000000000000 is automatically converted to this exponential format. Likewise, with negative exponents, the cutoff is –5.

Other Bases for Numbers

As we alluded to earlier, base-10 (also known as decimal — *deci* means 10) is not the only base for numbers. Among the more commonly used are binary (base-2), octal (base-8), and hexadecimal (base-16). ActionScript supports numeric bases from 2 to 36.

If you have no clue about what any of this means, don't worry. You are not alone. But the idea is really quite simple. To start with, take a closer look at the world of base-10 numbers. When you count, you start with 0 and go up to 9, increment the value of the next column (tens, hundreds, thousands, and so on), and start over with 0 again. In other words, you have only 10 digits to cycle through in each column: 0 through 9.

You could just as easily work with fewer or more digits, however. Take, for instance, binary numbers — the kind of numbers that your computer can understand. Binary has the root *bini*, which means two. Therefore, the base for binary numbers is 2. Table 8-1 shows some binary numbers with their decimal equivalents.

Table 8-1: Binary Numbers

Binary	Decimal
0	0
1	1
10	2
11	3
100	4
101	5
110	6

Likewise, you can work with bases that are greater than 10 (in which case, letters are used to represent values greater than 9). For example, the hexadecimal value a is the equivalent of the decimal value of 10. (Hexadecimal refers to numbers in base-16.) Therefore, the letters *a* through *f* are used in addition to 0 through 9. Table 8-2 shows some hexadecimal values with their corresponding decimal values.

Table 8-2: Hexadecimal Numbers

Hexadecimal	Decimal
a	10
b	11
c	12
2c	44
2d	45
5b	91
7b	123

Converting Strings to Numbers

If you work with any external data, be it from XML, CGI script, PHP, ColdFusion, or any other source, chances are good that you will need to convert a primitive string datatype to a number datatype. Although ActionScript tries to handle the conversion for you in many cases, it is still good form to make sure these conversions are done properly. Otherwise, you might end up with unexpected results.

Let's take a look at several of the ways you can convert strings to numbers.

Casting to a Number

You can convert any string to a number by *casting* it. To cast from a string to a number, you use the following syntax:

```
Number(stringValue)
```

Here are a few examples:

```
var nOne:Number = Number("468");      // 468
var nTwo:Number = Number("23.45");    // 23.45
var nThree:Number = Number("abc");    // NaN (Not a Number)
var nFour:Number = Number("0101");    // 65 (Octal)
```

Casting a string to a number will work just fine in many situations. However, when you cast from a string to a number, you don't get to control the precision of the number value it parses. That is to say, if you are interested only in the integer part of a string value, you have to go through several steps to strip the fractional part:

```
var nOne:Number = = Number("13.3");   // 13.3
nOne = Math.floor(nOne); // 13
```

Cross-Reference

The `floor()` method is a method of the `Math` class. It returns the integer part of the value passed to it. For rounding values you would use the `Math` class's `round()` method. All the methods of the `Math` class are discussed in Chapter 9.

Alternatively, you can use the `parseInt()` and `parseFloat()` methods to afford more control over precision when converting from a string to a number.

Converting to a Number with Precision

ActionScript offers two additional functions for parsing number values from strings: `parseInt()` and `parseFloat()`.

The `parseInt()` function always tries to convert the string value to an integer, even if the string represents a floating-point number. The `parseFloat()` function, on the other hand, always attempts to convert the string to a number with the greatest precision possible. If the string represents a floating-point number, `parseFloat()`converts it to a floating-point value. If the string represents an integer, `parseFloat()` converts it to an integer.

Here are some examples:

```
var nOne:Number = parseInt("13.3");    // 13
var nTwo:Number = parseFloat("13.3");  // 13.3
var nThree:Number = parseInt("54");    // 54
var nFour:Number = parseFloat("54");   // 54
```

You can also parse number values from strings with bases other than 10 using the parseInt() function. The function takes a second optional parameter, allowing you to specify the numeric base:

```
var nOne:Number = parseInt("11", 10);    // 11
var nTwo:Number = parseInt("11", 2);     // 3
var nThree:Number = parseInt("gg", 17);    // 288
```

Furthermore, if you omit the second parameter, ActionScript attempts to parse the number value using the most appropriate base. As you have seen, often this is base-10, but that is not always the case. For instance, octal (base-8) numbers are represented in ActionScript by a leading 0. So, any string (representing an integer) that begins with 0 is converted as an octal number:

```
var nOne:Number = parseInt("0101");  // returns 65
```

For this reason, it is usually a good idea to always specify the base of the number you are parsing from a string. Typically, you parse number values from strings returned from a server, so the values and formats are unknown. It is much simpler to just specify the base (probably base-10, in most cases) than to worry about invalid return values.

Tip   You can also convert hexadecimal string representations to numbers using parseInt() and Number(). For example:

```
var nColorValue:Number = parseInt("0xFF0000");
```

This technique can be particularly useful for converting user-entered hexadecimal strings to their correct numeric equivalents.

Detecting When a Number Is Not a Number

There are times when numbers are not numbers at all. You saw in the previous section that sometimes when a string cannot be parsed to return a number value, the functions simply return the special NaN value. Also, in cases of division by 0, the returned value is NaN. It is a good idea to check for this unexpected result whenever you are parsing numbers from strings. If it goes unnoticed, it can result in a whole set of errors.

The way to check for NaN values is to use the isNaN() function. The function takes a single parameter (the value in question) and returns a Boolean value — true if the value is not a number, or false if the value is a number. Here is an example of how to use the isNaN() function to verify the values parsed from a string:

```
var sValue:String = "abc";
if (isNaN(sValue)){
    trace("not a number");
}
else{
    trace("number");
}
```

Dealing with Infinite Values

There are times when values are recognized by ActionScript as numbers, but the values are out of the range that ActionScript can understand. This can result in undesirable results if not caught.

Flash uses the constants `Number.POSITIVE_INFINITY` and `Number.NEGATIVE_INFINITY` to represent the positive and negative numbers that are out of the range of acceptable values. You can use these constants in your code if you want to represent infinite numbers. But more often than not, you want to detect and catch infinite values rather than intentionally work with them. ActionScript provides a built-in function that enables you to determine whether a value is within the valid range of numbers. The `isFinite()` function takes a parameter (the value to be tested) and returns a Boolean value. It returns `false` if the number is out of range (not finite, or infinite), or `true` if the value is within the valid range.

```
trace(isFinite(10));  // Displays: true
trace(isFinite(Number.POSITIVE_INFINITY));   // Displays: false
```

Handling Minimum and Maximum Values

There are limits to how large and how small the number values that ActionScript works with can be. The largest number value is 1.79769313486231e+308, and the smallest value is 4.94065645841247e-324. If you are like most people, you probably are not going to remember those values off the top of your head. Therefore, ActionScript has two built-in constants with those values. They are `Number.MAX_VALUE` for the largest number value and `Number.MIN_VALUE` for the smallest value.

It is a good idea to use these properties to make sure that the numbers you are working with in your scripts are all within the acceptable range.

Note   The `MAX_VALUE` and `MIN_VALUE` properties hold the largest and smallest possible *positive* values for numbers in ActionScript. The largest and smallest *negative* values for numbers are the negative counterparts:

```
-Number.MAX_VALUE;
-Number.MIN_VALUE;
```

Working with Number Instances

For the most part, when you work with numbers in ActionScript, you work with primitive numbers instead of instances of the `Number` class. However, you *can* create instances of the `Number` class using the constructor as follows:

```
var nInstance:Number = new Number(primitiveVal);
```

In most situations, there are no advantages to creating an instance of the `Number` class as opposed to simply working with a number primitive. The primary situation in which it is advantageous to create a `Number` instance is when you want to create a string that represents the number in a nondecimal base — for example, if you want to display a numeric value in hexadecimal format.

The toString() method of the Number class is overloaded so that you can specify a radix. The default value, if none is specified, is 10. But if you specify 16, for example, Flash generates a hexadecimal string representation of the number. Here is an example:

```
var nVal:Number = new Number(123);
trace(nVal.toString(16));  // Displays: 7b
```

We'd like to know what you thought about this chapter. Visit www.rightactionscript .com/asb/comments to fill out an online form with your comments.

Summary

✦ Numbers can be integers (whole numbers) or floating-point values (fractional numbers).

✦ ActionScript can understand number values in bases other than 10 — from base-2 to base-36.

✦ You can convert a string value to a number value by casting or with the parseInt() and parseFloat() functions. Only parseInt() allows you to specify a base (for non-base-10 values) for the conversion.

✦ When ActionScript attempts to work with a value that it cannot recognize as a number, it assigns it a NaN value (not a number). You can test for NaN using the isNaN() function.

✦ ✦ ✦

Using Math

I f you tend to shy away from anything with the word "math" in it, you're not alone. It brings up difficult memories of high school algebra classes, perhaps. But by not delving deeper into the Math class and the use of math in your animations, you are cheating yourself out of some powerful techniques. This chapter gently guides you through using math in your Flash applications.

As you have already seen, ActionScript operators take care of all the fundamental mathematical operations such as addition, subtraction, multiplication, and division. The Math class, therefore, does not concern itself with such things. As you will learn in this chapter, you can use the Math class to generate random numbers, perform trigonometric or exponential functions, and much more.

◆   ◆   ◆   ◆

In This Chapter

Discovering when to use math in your Flash applications

Generating random numbers

Working with trigonometric functions

Working with additional constants and methods of the Math class

◆   ◆   ◆   ◆

Performing ActionScript Math

You might be asking yourself, "What in the world could I ever use math for in Flash?" Well, as you will see in this chapter, you can do some pretty amazing stuff using math to power your Flash movies. Of course, it is not appropriate in every scenario. But if you want to create a project that can calculate areas of objects or even a simple interest-bearing account, you need the Math class. But what is even more important is how you can use Flash in your movies to create visual effects. Animations can occur on mathematically determined paths. And the Math class is frequently necessary when you want to create artwork with the Drawing API (see Chapter 10).

Physics studies how things move, among other things. And at the heart of physics (at least Newtonian physics) is mathematics. There is no way around it. So, if you want to move things in your Flash movie — controlling them with ActionScript and you want to bring more life into them — you need to master how to use mathematics in your code.

In this chapter, you will see how to use the properties and methods of the Math class in your Flash movies. It is not enough just to know which method to use to take one number to the power of another. You need to know how to apply it in the context of your Flash movie.

Learning about ActionScript Math

As with several other classes in ActionScript, Math is a static class. This means that you never instantiate Math objects. You never create a Math object using new and a Math constructor method. Instead, you access the properties and methods directly from the class:

```
Math.propertyOrMethod;
```

This makes sense when you look at the functionality that the Math class makes available. The Math class essentially does little more than group together a bunch of related mathematical functions and constants. There would not be a need to create multiple instances of Math objects simply to find the cosine of an angle, for instance.

Working with the Math Constants

There are a handful of mathematical constants you can access directly from the Math class. Table 9-1 shows a list of the properties and their values.

Table 9-1: Math Constants

Property	Value	Description
E	~2.718	Base of natural logarithm
LN10	~2.302	Natural logarithm of 10
LN2	~0.693	Natural logarithm of 2
LOG10E	~0.434	Base-10 logarithm of E
LOG2E	~1.442	Base-2 logarithm of E
PI	~3.142	π
SQRT1_2	~0.707	Square root of ½
SQRT2	~1.414	Square root of 2

The Math class constants are the values of frequently used numbers in mathematics. However, with the exception of PI, it would be entirely possible to obtain the rest of the values by means of the methods of the Math class. That fact, along with the fact that the value Π happens to be central to a great many operations, makes PI perhaps the most important of the properties of the Math class.

Finding Absolute Values

The absolute value method abs() takes a single parameter — a number. It returns the distance of that number from 0. In other words, any positive value returns itself. Any negative value returns itself negated (made positive).

It can be useful to use abs() for determining whether a value is between a positive and negative counterpart. For example, the following if statement

```
if(nValue < 10 && nValue > -10) {
  // Code goes here.
}
```

can be rewritten in the following way using the `abs()` method:

```
if(Math.abs(nValue) < 10) {
  // Code goes here.
}
```

Rounding and Truncating Numbers

The three methods, `round()`, `ceiling()`, and `floor()`, are quick and easy ways to ensure that you are always working with an integer value. There are plenty of times when this is important. For instance, when instructing a timeline to go to a frame number, you must specify an integer value. After all, there is not a 23.232 frame.

Each of these three methods takes one parameter — a number value to be converted to an integer. The `round()` method is the function that should seem most familiar to you. If you think back to grade school math, you can probably recall having to round numbers. The idea is that the initial value (the parameter) is converted into the integer value that is nearest to it. In other words, if the starting value is n.5 or greater, where n is the integer part of the value, the `round()` method returns n+1. If the starting value is less than n.5, the method returns n. For example:

```
trace(Math.round(5.75));  // Displays: 6
trace(Math.round(93.3));  // Displays: 93
```

On the other hand, there are times when you will want to find the next-nearest higher or next-nearest lower integer value for a number. In these cases, you will want to use the `ceil()` or `floor()` methods of the `Math` class.

The `ceil()` method returns the next-highest integer value of the number passed it as an argument. If the initial value is an integer already, the method returns the same number. Otherwise, it returns the integer part of the number plus one:

```
trace(Math.ceil(5.75));  // Displays: 6
trace(Math.ceil(93.3));  // Displays: 94
trace(Math.ceil(93));  // Displays: 93
```

The `floor()` method is the counterpart to `ceil()`. But rather than return the next highest integer, it returns the next-lowest integer. Just like `ceil()`, if the value passed to the method is already an integer, it returns the same number. Otherwise, it returns the integer part of the value:

```
trace(Math.floor(5.75));  // Displays: 5
trace(Math.floor(93.3));  // Displays: 93
trace(Math.floor(93));  // Displays: 93
```

The methods `round()`, `ceil()`, and `floor()` all have a great many applications within your ActionScript code. You should use these methods anytime you want to ensure that you are working with a whole number value. For example, if you are performing math operations on values representing people, you likely want to make sure that you end up with a whole number value. If you created a contest that allowed 8.3 people to win, it could prove problematic.

You can also use these methods to round or truncate to decimal place values. The basic idea is to first multiply the value you want to round, or truncate by 10 to the power of the number of desired decimal places. For example, if you want to end up with two decimal places you should multiply the number by 100. Then, use the `round()`, `ceil()`, or `floor()` method (depending on what kind of operation you want to perform). Last, divide the value by the same number you initially used to multiply. Here is an example:

```
var nValue:Number = 6.39639;
nValue *= 100;
nValue = Math.floor(nValue);
nValue /= 100;
trace(nValue);  // Displays: 6.39
```

Generating Random Numbers

Creating random numbers in an application is an important feature. It allows for games to vary with each playing. It is an essential part of any card game or casino-style game. You might even come up with applications for randomness in controlling animations. Whatever your application of randomness, you need to learn how to work with the `random()` method of the `Math` class.

The `random()` method is the only method of the `Math` class that does not take any parameters. The method always returns a floating-point value between 0 and 0.999999, inclusive. Although this may not immediately seem useful, consider that you can simply multiply the returned value by any other number you want to yield a value between 0 and that number. A general formula for this is:

```
var randomFloat:Number = Math.random() * n;
```

where n is the highest possible value you want to work with. So, if you want to work with a random number between 0 and 45, you can use the following statement:

```
var nRandomFloat:Number = Math.random() * 45;
```

But what if you want to generate a random number within a range that does not start with 0? The answer: Just add the starting value to the end of the equation. So, if you want to work with a range of numbers between 20 and 30, first figure what the size of the range is (10) and then the starting point (20), and put it together:

```
var nRandomFloat:Number = (Math.random() * 10) + 20;
```

But in many cases, you will want to work with integer values. As you can see, none of the examples so far can guarantee an integer value. For instance, the previous line of code can generate a value of 20, 25, or 30, but it can also generate a value of 23.345, 26.102, or 29.0004. This is no good if you want to use the random number to control something that requires an integer value. But if you combine this `random()` method with the `floor()` method, you can achieve exactly that goal.

The technique is very similar to creating a random floating-point number. Now, you'll use the `floor()` method to truncate the random number, thus ensuring an integer. Here is an example:

```
var nRandomInteger:Number = Math.floor(Math.random()*10);
```

In this example, the right side of the expression returns a random integer value between 0 and 9. Remember that a range from 0 to 9 is a range of 10 possible values. If you want to generate a range of 10 values starting with 1, you can use the following code:

```
var nRandomInteger:Number = Math.floor(Math.random()*10) + 1;
```

At this point, you might be asking, "Why use `floor()`? Why not use `round()`?" Those are good questions. By using the `floor()` method you can ensure that the randomness is equally distributed. If you use `round()`, the likelihood of the minimum or maximum values in the range being generated is only half the chance of any other number in the range.

To give you an idea of how you might use `random` numbers in your movies, consider the scenario of a game program that uses dice. If you are working with one six-sided die, you want to generate a random number between 1 and 6 each time a button is pressed:

```
mRollDie.onRelease = function():Void {
  var nValue:Number = Math.floor(Math.random() * 6) + 1;
  trace(nValue);
}
```

Finding the Greater or Lesser of Two Numbers

In some cases, you want to compare two values, and work with either the greater or the lesser of the two. An example is a comparison between two test scores, in which you want a simple and fast way to choose the higher of the two. For these cases, there are the `max()` and `min()` methods, respectively. Each method simply takes the two values to be compared and then returns one of those values. In the case of `max()`, the maximum of the two values is returned. In the case of `min()`, the minimum value is returned.

```
trace(Math.min(25, 2));   // Displays: 2
trace(Math.max(25, 2));   // Displays: 25
```

Working with Exponents and Square Roots

Arguably one of the most important theorems in mathematics is the Pythagorean theorem, named for the Greek mathematician who discovered it. Basically, it states that for any right triangle (a triangle with a 90-degree angle, as you can see in Figure 9-1), the sum of the square of the two adjacent sides between which the right angle is formed is equal to the square of the hypotenuse (the side opposite the right angle). In other words:

$a^2 + b^2 = c^2$

Figure 9-1: The sides of a right triangle.

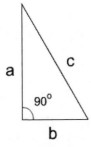

This is enormously powerful for you when working in a coordinate system such as Flash. It means that given any two of the sides of a right triangle, you can find the value of the other (and the angles between, as you will learn later). "But why would this possibly be of any importance," you ask?

Simple. Imagine that you want to move something a fixed distance in a diagonal direction. You are not given any methods for the `MovieClip` object that allow you to move objects in diagonals. In fact, you can move objects only in the X and Y directions. But do not lose hope. Given that you know the hypotenuse and one other side of the right triangle formed by the diagonal along which you want to move your object, you can solve for the missing side.

One way to work with exponents (such as squaring a number) and square roots in ActionScript is with the `pow()` and `sqrt()` methods of the `Math` class. The `pow()` method takes two parameters — the value to be raised to a power and the power to which to raise the first number (the exponent):

```
Math.pow(val, exponent);
```

The `sqrt()` method takes one parameter — the value whose square root you want:

```
Math.sqrt(val);
```

You can use both of these methods together to work with the Pythagorean Theorem, as in the following example:

```
/*
We know the hypotenuse and the one side of the triangle,
and want to find the value of the third side.
*/
var nHypotenuse:Number = 5;
var nA:Number = 3;
var nB:Number;  // unknown

// Given that a^2 + b^2 = hypotenuse^2
nB = Math.sqrt(Math.pow(nHypotenuse, 2) - Math.pow(nA, 2));
```

Of course, solving for an unknown side of a triangle is not the only application of the `pow()` and `sqrt()` methods. But when working with a Cartesian coordinate system (a simple x and y grid as in Flash), this can turn out to be a really useful tool for plotting coordinates of `MovieClip` objects.

You might also want to use the `pow()` method when working with any kind of interest-bearing account or value. It is entirely possible that you might want to do such calculations for real-life scenarios, or maybe even as part of a role-playing or strategy game you design. The calculation for finding compound interest is the following:

```
newValue = originalValue * (1 + rate/cp)^(cp*t)
```

In this equation, `cp` is the number of compounding periods per year (12 if it is compounded every month), and `t` is the number of years. This sort of equation can be represented in ActionScript in the following way:

```
var nNew = nOrig * Math.pow((1 + nRate/nCp), (nCp*nT));
```

Using Trigonometric Functions in ActionScript

Chances are that you never thought you would actually want to apply anything you learned in trigonometry. We hope this section will make you rethink that. You can do some powerful things with basic trigonometric functions.

Let's start out with a simple example. You know how to move `MovieClip` objects along a motion guide using Flash's authoring tools. But what about using ActionScript to do it? Of course, moving a `MovieClip` object along a straight line is no big challenge. But how do you attempt to move it along a path in the shape of a circle, for example?

This is exactly where the `Math` class's trigonometric methods become really useful. But first, you have to know some of the basics of trigonometry and circles. There are a few fundamental properties of any circle. First, you must have an *origin* for the circle: a point directly in the center. And second, you must have a *radius:* the length from the center to the edge of the circle. If you take two axes, one for Y and one for X, that run perpendicular to one another and intersect at the center of your circle, you see that the axes always form a right triangle, as shown in Figure 9-2. The lengths of the sides (a and b) are the same as the length of the radius of the circle.

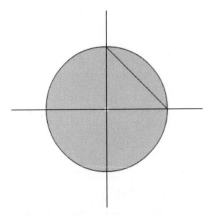

Figure 9-2: The axes intersect at a circle's center to form a right triangle.

When you have a triangle, especially a right triangle, some really interesting formulas surface that enable you to derive almost any unknown value when given at least two of the others. When you are working with a circle, one value remains constant: the radius, or the hypotenuse of the triangle. The thing that varies is the angle (Θ) between the radius and the X-axis that runs through the center of the circle. But if you know these two values for a right triangle, you can derive the X- and Y-coordinates using the following formulas:

```
sin(Θ) = y/hypotenuse
cos(Θ) = x/hypotenuse
```

Or in more usable format:

```
y = sin(Θ) * hypotenuse
x = cos(Θ) * hypotenuse
```

Therefore, if you know the radius of a circular path, and you continually increment the angle value, you can form right triangles over and over, and derive the corresponding X- and Y-coordinates, thus moving an object around in a circular path.

There is only one little catch when doing this in ActionScript — the Math class trig methods work with *radians*, not degrees. A radian is the measure of an angle in terms of Π. But don't worry; there is an easy conversion between degrees and radians:

```
radians = (π * degrees)/180
```

After you have a radian measurement for the angle, you can then use the trigonometric methods of the Math class. Here is the basic syntax for sin(), cos(), and tan():

```
Math.sin(radians)
Math.cos(radians)
Math.tan(radians)
```

This next example shows how to revolve a MovieClip object (on the main timeline) around a circular path.

First, to make it easier, you want to adjust the _x and _y properties of the main movie clip, as well as set up a few properties of the revolving object mcBall.

```
// Place 0,0 of the main object at the center of the stage
this._x = 275;
this._y = 200;

// Use the attachMovie() method to add a MovieClip to the
// stage from a library symbol with a linkage id of
// "Circle". For more information on attachMovie()
// see Chapter 14.
this.attachMovie("Circle", "mBall", 0);

// Declare and initialize two variables. The nPathRadius
// variable determines the radius of the circle path
// along which the MovieClip should move. The nDegrees
// variable should be initialized to 0.
var nPathRadius:Number = 100;
var nDegrees:Number = 0;

// Define a custom function that we'll call repeatedly using
// setInterval().
function moveInCircle():Void {

  var nRadians:Number = nDegrees * (Math.PI / 180);

  // Derive x and y coordinates.
  var nX:Number = nPathRadius * Math.sin(nRadians);
  var nY:Number = nPathRadius * Math.cos(nRadians);

  // Move the object.
  mBall._x = nX;
  mBall._y = nY;

  // Increment degrees.
  nDegrees++;

  // Update the view on stage.
  updateAfterEvent();
```

```
};

// Use setInterval() to call the moveInCircle() function
// repeatedly.
setInterval(moveInCircle, 10);
```

This is just one example of how to use trigonometric functions in your animations.

For the sake of thoroughness, you should also be familiar with the inverse trigonometric functions available as methods of the Math class. ActionScript provides four methods for inverse trig functions: asin(), acos(), atan(), and atan2(). The first three take a parameter (a sine value, a cosine value, and a tangent value, respectively), and return a value of the corresponding angle as measured radians:

```
Math.asin(sineValue)
Math.acos(cosineValue)
Math.atan(tangentValue)
```

Calculating Natural Logarithms and Exponentials

The exp() and log() methods of the Math class are probably most suited for things other than animation. Natural logarithms (logarithms with base e) and their counterpart exponential functions are often used for plotting graphs. Don't let that discourage you from using them in creative ways to control your animations, but also be aware that they can serve other purposes.

First, you need to know what the two methods are. The exp() method requires one parameter: a number. It then raises e (Math.E) to the power of that number. In other words:

```
Math.exp(5) == Math.pow(Math.E, 5)
```

The log() method takes one parameter as well: a number. It then returns the natural logarithm of that number:

```
Math.log(number);
```

These two methods are related in the following way:

```
Math.log(x) = y
```

and:

```
Math.exp(y) = x
```

You can use these types of methods to plot graphs of stock market trends. It is common practice to plot the natural log of the indices versus time. Therefore, if you receive stock market data from, let's say, an XML document, you can use the log() method of the Math class to plot the values on a graph.

There are some more powerful techniques for which both the exp() and the log() methods are useful. Although probably not something you will need in all your Flash movies, you can use the log() method to approximate integrals and derivatives. And you can use the exp() method to approximate hyperbolic trig functions. These sorts of approximations can be useful for finding areas under curves or for finding values in physics equations (such as the velocity at a point in time given a constant acceleration).

And the fourth inverse trig function, `atan2()`, takes two parameters (an X- and a Y-coordinate), and returns the angle formed by the right triangle measured in radians:

```
Math.atan2(x, y)
```

Using inverse trig functions is really useful if, for example, you know an angle's sine, cosine, or tangent; or you know the X and Y values of the sides of a triangle and want to know the angle measurement. You can use this in real situations if you know, for example, a `MovieClip` object's position and you want to rotate another `MovieClip` relative to the first.

 We'd like to know what you thought about this chapter. Visit `www.rightactionscript` `.com/asb/comments` to fill out an online form with your comments.

Summary

✦ Math is an essential tool for creating advanced animations and Flash applications. The ActionScript `Math` class provides the advanced mathematical functionality to accommodate these mathematical needs.

✦ `Math` is a static class. Therefore, you never create an instance of the class, but always access the properties (constants) and methods directly from the `Math` class itself.

✦ You can use `Math.random()` to make random numbers for many purposes in Flash applications.

✦ You can use basic trigonometry to calculate nonlinear paths along which to move objects.

✦   ✦   ✦

Working with Dates and Times

✦   ✦   ✦   ✦

In This Chapter

Learning about time zones and how your computer keeps track of time

Creating a Date object to work with current, past, and future dates and time

Complete coverage of all the Date methods and constructors

✦   ✦   ✦   ✦

ActionScript's Date class allows you a great deal of control over creating objects that store date and time information. Date objects store date information including year, month, date, day, hour, minute, second, and millisecond. You can create a Date object for just about any date. Although you could create variables and arrays to accomplish much the same thing, a Date object has built-in functionality to make working with dates a bit easier.

Working with Computer Dates

In order to understand Date objects, you must first understand three points:

✦ What time zones are and how they work

✦ Where Flash retrieves the time and date information

✦ How Flash calculates time and date information

In the days before computers, telephones, and even trains, time was kept locally, and there was no standardization on a global scale. Each town would keep its own time by setting the clockmaker's clock to 12:00 noon when the sun was at the center of the sky. This meant that times would vary from town to town. But with the advent of global travel and communications, it became necessary to have some kind of standardization of time internationally. So, in the late nineteenth century, the idea of time zones was proposed and quickly adopted. Although not every country and region adheres perfectly to the time zones, the world is divided up into roughly 24 parts — one for each hour in a day. Each zone is one hour ahead of the zone directly to the west. The contiguous states of the United States are divided into four zones. Thus, when it is 12:00 noon in Los Angeles, it is 2:00 in the afternoon in St. Louis or Chicago, and it is 3:00 in the afternoon in New York. Understanding time zones is necessary in understanding Date objects.

Note   The description of how time zones work is very simplified. Some areas of the world don't use time as most of the world knows it at all, and thus have no need for time zones. Additionally, some areas use time zones that are half an hour apart from other time zones instead of an hour. And last, to confuse matters even more, the practice of Daylight Savings Time has been adopted in many places in the world. In those areas, clocks are offset by an hour for approximately half the year. This practice is used in some places and not in others, which means that the difference between some time zones is not always uniform. If a deeper understanding of time zones is important to your application, you might want to deepen your understanding beyond the extremely simplified explanation given in this chapter.

What Is UTC?

In order to make time zones work, there has to be a standard and center from which all time is based. The center for the Earth's time zones is in Greenwich (pronounced GREN-ich), England. It is known as Greenwich Mean Time, or GMT. However, as time went on, global efforts produced more accurate ways of measuring time — to one-billionth of a second. This new time, though essentially the same as GMT, is called Coordinated Universal Time, and is abbreviated UTC.

Note   Coordinated Universal Time is abbreviated UTC, and not CUT, because of the way the name originated. At first, the name was Universal Time, abbreviated UT. Variations on Universal Time were abbreviated with numbers to indicate version such as UT0, UT1, UT2, and so on. When the name Coordinated Universal Time was chosen, the abbreviation UTC was agreed upon to adhere to the format of the earlier abbreviations.

UTC is always the reference point for all other time zones. Computers measure time in UTC and then offset the value to account for time zones. For instance, Los Angeles is eight hours behind UTC, so it has an offset of –8.

Computer Time

If you ask yourself where time and date information comes from in your programs, including Flash, it might appear to be a mystery. The answer is that it comes from the computer itself, which keeps track of time in very small fractions of a second in the computer's hardware clock. The computer then has a software clock as part of the operating system (Windows XP, Mac OS X, and so on) that offsets the value from the hardware clock to produce a UTC time and date. The software clock also allows you to modify settings such as time zone and daylight savings time. In this way, your computer can display local times and dates, which are more meaningful than UTC times and dates.

This means that Flash has access to both the UTC and the local time of the computer on which the Flash movie is playing. This is a very important point that can cause confusion for beginning programmers. Even though many Flash movies are served from a remote location, the movie itself is played within the Flash Player on a user's local machine. What this means is that the current dates and times reported by your Date objects are based entirely on the user's local settings, hardware, and software. If the user's clock is off, your calculations may not work.

Caution   If you intend to use the Date object as a timer in your Flash movie, it is best to perform a simple check to make sure that the user's clock is even running! You can do this by querying for the time and then querying again and seeing if there is a difference between the times.

If having accurate current dates is important to the functionality of the Flash movie you are authoring, you can use a slightly more advanced technique to compare the value of the user's time to the time on a remote server. If you want to do this, you need to use some kind of server-side scripting together with an XML object, a LoadVars object (both discussed in Chapter 33), or Flash Remoting, discussed in Chapter 36.

ActionScript Time

ActionScript works with all dates in milliseconds. Just as time zones have a point of reference from which they are all derived, so do dates in ActionScript. The point of reference for all dates in ActionScript is January 1, 1970, also called the Epoch, and all dates are measured in milliseconds from that starting date. If you create a Date object that uses the current date of the local computer, it queries the local computer for the date and then converts it to milliseconds from January 1, 1970. The next section discusses in more detail the formatting issues with ActionScript Date objects.

Creating a Date Object

The first thing you need to know when creating a Date object is how to instantiate an object using the Date constructor method. There are several variations on the Date constructor, and your usage depends on what you want to accomplish. Let's look at the options.

Getting the Current Date and Time

If you want to create a Date object that contains the current local date and time, simply use the Date constructor method with no parameters. Here is an example:

```
var dNow:Date = new Date();
```

This constructor captures the time of the local computer to the precision of a millisecond.

Note   Even though the precision of the time returned by a Date object is milliseconds, it does not mean that it is necessarily accurate to the same degree. Precision merely refers to how small of a unit is used in the measurement. Hence, milliseconds are more precise than seconds. However, the clock interrupt of a computer often varies the value returned by up to 55 milliseconds or so. For this reason, it is best to not depend on a reading from the Date object for accuracy beyond seconds.

You can verify that the preceding code did, in fact, create an object that represents the current date and time by using trace():

```
var dNow:Date = new Date();
trace(dNow.toString());
```

You should see a string representation of the current date and time in the Output panel if you test the preceding code. The string will look something like the following, but of course, your exact values will be different:

```
Thursday Jun 15 20:07:48 GMT-0700 2006
```

This is the default manner in which Flash converts a Date object to a string. Later in this chapter you'll see how you can format your Date object output differently.

In many situations, it can be useful to create an object that contains the current local date and time. The following are a few such circumstances:

✦ Creating a value to insert into a database when the user registers, makes a purchase, posts a message, and so on.

✦ Creating a value to display to the user, showing the current date and/or time.

✦ Getting the current date and time to compare with another value. For example, you may want to make sure that a user's account has not yet expired.

Making a Date Based on Epoch Milliseconds

You can also create `Date` objects that represent specific times other than the current time. There are two basic ways to accomplish this with the `Date` constructor. Let's first look at how you can create a new `Date` object based on Epoch milliseconds. Recall from the earlier discussion that the Epoch milliseconds are the number of milliseconds from midnight of January 1, 1970 to the time and date you are referencing. Now, of course, it is not common for humans to think in terms of Epoch milliseconds, and if we asked you the Epoch millisecond value for your birthday it is doubtful that you would know. But computers do tend to think in terms of Epoch time — be it milliseconds or, in some cases, seconds. For this reason, it is a convenient way for your Flash application to communicate with other applications. This is especially true if you are using server-side scripts and databases with your Flash application, and you are using either a `LoadVars` or an `XML` object to load and send your data.

To create a `Date` object based on Epoch milliseconds, use the following syntax:

```
var dDateObject:Date = new Date(epochMilliseconds);
```

Typically, when you instantiate a `Date` object using Epoch milliseconds, you'll be retrieving the milliseconds value from another source. For the purposes of this example, you can just hard-code a value:

```
var dSometime:Date = new Date(1150354800000);
trace(dSometime.toString());
```

Depending on your local time zone offset value, the Output panel will display something very close to the following:

```
Thu Jun 15 00:00:00 GMT-0700 2006
```

Making a Date Based on Year or Month

Another option for the constructor is to pass it numeric values indicating the year, month, and so on, for the date and time you want to represent. The basic syntax for this option is:

```
var dDateObject:Date = new Date(year, month, date, hour,
  minute, second, millisecond);
```

Each of the parameters expects a number — an integer, to be exact — value, as shown in Table 10-1.

✦ The `year` parameter can be any full four-digit year, such as 1875 or 2675. You can also pass the `Date` constructor any integer value from 0 to 99, and ActionScript will interpret it to mean a date from 1900 to 1999. This means that a value of 100 will produce a `Date` object for the year 100, not 2000; but a value of 99 will result in a `Date` object for the year 1999, not 99. If you want to work with dates before the year 99, you need to actually pass the constructor function a negative value for the `year` parameter. The value you pass will be subtracted from 1900, the reference point for ActionScript dates with two-digit year values. Passing a value of –1850 creates a Date object for the year 50.

✦ Perhaps the most likely place for an error when creating a `Date` object is in passing the correct `month` value. Most cultures represent the months numerically, starting with 1 and ending with 12. Thus, it is natural enough to think of January as the month with the index of 1. But remember from the discussion of arrays that ActionScript is a 0-indexing language. Therefore, when creating a `Date` object, January is represented by the number value 0, and the last month, December, is represented by the number value 11.

✦ The `date` parameter is the parameter that refers to the day of the month. If for no other reason but to make it confusing, `date` is the only property of the `Date` object that has a 1-index. Therefore, the first day of the month is represented by the number value of 1. The last possible day in any month is 31, although some months obviously do not have 31 days. For example, the last day in February will have a value of 28 on non-leap-years and 29 on leap years.

✦ The `hour`, `minute`, `second`, and `millisecond` values are integer values used for the time of day component of the `Date` object. Each of these value ranges starts with 0, not 1. Therefore, with 24 hours in a day, the first hour, midnight, is represented by the number value 0, and the last hour, 11 p.m., is represented by the number value 23. The values for `minute` and `second` range from 0 to 59, and `millisecond` values range from 0 to 999.

Table 10-1: Date Constructor Parameters

Parameter	Meaning	Value Range
year	Calendar year	0-99, 99 and up, –1801 and down
month	Integer index of month	0 to 11
date	Integer index of day of month	1 to 31
hour	Integer index of hour in day	0 to 23
minute	Integer index of minute in hour	0 to 59
second	Integer index of second in minute	0 to 59
millisecond	Integer index of millisecond in second	0 to 999

You must always specify at least the year and month when creating a `Date` object in this way. Any of the subsequent values that you leave undefined will default to 0 (or 1 in the case of the date parameter). Here are a few examples:

```
var dSometime1:Date = new Date(2006, 5);
trace(dSometime1.toString());
var dSometime2:Date = new Date(2006, 5, 15);
trace(dSometime2.toString());
var dSometime3:Date = new Date(2006, 5, 15, 6);
trace(dSometime3.toString());
var dSometime4:Date = new Date(2006, 5, 15, 6, 55);
trace(dSometime4.toString());
var dSometime5:Date = new Date(2006, 5, 15, 6, 55, 33);
```

```
trace(dSometime5.toString());
var dSometime6:Date = new Date(2006, 5, 15, 6, 55, 33, 24);
trace(dSometime6.toString());
```

The Output panel will display the following:

```
Thu Jun 1 00:00:00 GMT-0700 2006
Thu Jun 15 00:00:00 GMT-0700 2006
Thu Jun 15 06:00:00 GMT-0700 2006
Thu Jun 15 06:55:00 GMT-0700 2006
Thu Jun 15 06:55:33 GMT-0700 2006
Thu Jun 15 06:55:33 GMT-0700 2006
```

Note   As with all examples in this chapter, if you test this code you might get slightly different values due to time zone offsets.

Tip   You might notice that the last two strings are the same, even though one specified the milliseconds and the other did not. The actual values are different by 24 milliseconds. The string that Flash generates with the `toString()` method does not display to the precision of milliseconds.

When you create a new `Date` object in this way, make sure that you always include at least both the year and month parameters. If you specify only one parameter, Flash interprets that to mean the Epoch milliseconds. For example:

```
var dSometime:Date = new Date(2006);
trace(dSometime.toString());
```

You might expect this to create a date and time representing the year 2006. But, instead, because Flash interprets the parameter to mean Epoch milliseconds, the Output panel displays something like the following (depending on your time zone offset):

```
Wed Dec 31 16:00:02 GMT-0800 1969
```

Working with Date Objects

The ActionScript `Date` class has a rather daunting number of methods available to it, as shown in Table 10-2. Although at first glance, the methods can appear a bit overwhelming, don't worry. At a closer look, you notice that these methods can be easily grouped into only four categories. The first group of methods is called `get` because the method names all start with the word "get," and these methods are responsible for *getting* the values of the properties of the `Date` object from which they are invoked. The second group of methods is called `set` because the method names all start with the word "set," and these methods are responsible for *setting* the values of the properties of the `Date` object from which they are invoked. The third group of methods is called inherited because they are the methods inherited from the `Object` object. And finally, there is the one static method that is invoked directly from the `Date` class.

Table 10-2: Date Object Methods

Category	Method	Description
get	getFullYear()	Returns four-digit value of year
	getYear()	Returns integer value of year relative to 1900
	getMonth()	Returns integer value of month of year
	getDate()	Returns integer value of day of month
	getDay()	Returns integer value of day of week
	getHours()	Returns integer value of hour of day
	getMinutes()	Returns integer value of minutes of hour
	getSeconds()	Returns integer value of seconds of minute
	getMilliseconds()	Returns integer value of milliseconds of second
	getTime()	Returns integer value of milliseconds from 1/1/70
	getTimezoneOffset()	Returns integer value of minutes offset from UTC
	getUTCFullYear()	Returns four-digit value of year
	getUTCMonth()	Returns integer value of month of year
	getUTCDate()	Returns integer value of day of month
	getUTCDay()	Returns integer value of day of week
	getUTCHours()	Returns integer value of hour of day
	getUTCMinutes()	Returns integer value of minutes of hour
	getUTCSeconds()	Returns integer value of seconds of minute
	getUTCMilliseconds()	Returns integer value of milliseconds of second
set	setFullYear()	Sets four-digit value of year
	setYear()	Sets integer value of year relative to 1900
	setMonth()	Sets integer value of month of year
	setDate()	Sets integer value of day of month
	setHours()	Sets integer value of hour of day
	setMinutes()	Sets integer value of minutes of hour
	setSeconds()	Sets integer value of seconds of minute
	setMilliseconds()	Sets integer value of milliseconds of second
	setTime()	Sets integer value of milliseconds from 1/1/70
	setUTCFullYear()	Sets four-digit value of year
	setUTCMonth()	Sets integer value of month of year
	setUTCDate()	Sets integer value of day of month
	setUTCHours()	Sets integer value of hour of day
	setUTCMinutes()	Sets integer value of minutes of hour
	setUTCSeconds()	Sets integer value of seconds of minute
	setUTCMilliseconds()	Sets integer value of milliseconds of second
inherited	toString()	Returns the string value of the Date object
static	UTC()	Returns the milliseconds since 1/1/1970 for a specified date

Note For the purposes of most calculations, whether you use UTC or local time is of little importance, as long as you stick with one or the other. But when you need to take time zone differences into consideration, pay attention to which you are using.

Get Methods

The get methods allow you to retrieve the properties of your Date objects. You may notice that the get methods include several methods for getting the day of the week. However, notice that there are not any analogous methods in the set methods. This is because the day of the week is not an independent variable, so to speak. Its value is determined by the value of the year, month, and date.

Getting the Year

There are several methods available to return the value of your Date object's year. If you are working with local time, you can use either getYear() or getFullYear(). If you need to work with UTC, you can opt for the getUTCFullYear() method.

The difference between getYear() and getFullYear() is that getYear() returns an integer representing the difference between the Date object's year and the year 1900, whereas getFullYear() returns the value of the actual year. For example:

```
var dWhen:Date = new Date(1978, 9, 13);
trace(dWhen.getYear());    // Displays: 78
trace(dWhen.getFullYear());  // Displays: 1978
```

The difference becomes much more apparent when working with dates before 1900. For example:

```
var dThen:Date = new Date(1779, 6, 4);
trace(dThen.getYear());    // Displays: -121
trace(dThen.getFullYear());  // Displays: 1779
```

You can also use getUTCFullYear() to determine the UTC year that corresponds to a given local date. If you want to know what the year in England was when your local time was December 31, 1964 at 8 p.m., you could do the following:

```
var dThen:Date = new Date(1964, 11, 31, 20, 0, 0, 0);
trace(dThen.getUTCFullYear());
```

Getting the Month

You can return the month value of your Date object with the getMonth() and getUTCMonth() methods. Both methods return an integer from 0 to 11, representing January through December. The getMonth() methods returns the integer value of the local month, whereas the getUTCMonth() method returns the integer value of the corresponding month in UTC.

Getting the Date

You can use the getDate() and getUTCDate() methods to return the values of the local day of the month and the corresponding day of the month UTC, respectively. These values can be integers from 1 to 31. For example:

```
var dThen:Date = new Date(1523, 3, 13);
trace(dThen.getDate());    // Displays: 13
```

Getting the Day

As we mentioned earlier, ActionScript Date objects actually calculate the value of the day of the week based on the year, month, and date values. You cannot set the day value for a Date object, but you can retrieve it using getDay() or getUTCDay(). Both methods return the day of the week as an integer from 0 to 6. A value of 0 corresponds to Sunday, and a value of 6 corresponds to Saturday. Here is an example:

```
var dWhen:Date = new Date(1978, 9, 13, 20);
trace(dWhen.getDay());
trace(dWhen.getUTCDay());
```

The first value that this example will display is a 5 because the day of the week was a Friday. The second value depends on the time zone offset. If my local time zone is on Pacific Standard Time, it will return 4, or Thursday, because the time in Greenwich, England is eight hours ahead.

Getting the Hours, Minutes, Seconds, and Milliseconds

You can retrieve the `hour` value of your `Date` objects using the `getHours()` and `getUTCHours()` methods. These methods return integers from 0 to 23 for the local date and the UTC corresponding date, respectively. For example:

```
var dThen:Date = new Date (2727, 9, 27, 5);
trace(dThen.getHours());   // Displays: 5;
trace(dThen.getUTCHours()); // Displays: 5 + offset
```

In much the same way, you can use `getMinutes()`, `getUTCMinutes()`, `getSeconds()`, `getUTCSeconds()`, `getMilliseconds()`, and `getUTCMilliseconds()`. The `minutes` and `seconds` are given in integer values from 0 to 59. The `milliseconds` are given in integer values from 0 to 999.

Getting the Time

There are occasions when you want to work with dates in terms of `millisecond` values. The `getTime()` method returns an integer value of milliseconds elapsed since midnight of January 1, 1970 UTC. The usefulness of this method might not be apparent at first. But imagine if you wanted to create a new `Date` object and give it the value of another `Date` object, essentially creating a copy. You *could* do the following:

```
var dOriginal:Date = new Date();
var nYear:Number = dOriginal.getFullYear();
var nMonth:Number = dOriginal.getMonth();
var nDate:Number = dOriginal.getDate();
var nHour:Number = dOriginal.getHours();
var nMinute:Number = dOriginal.getMinutes();
var nSecond:Number = dOriginal.getSeconds();
var nMillisecond:Number = dOriginal.getMilliseconds();
var dCopy:Date = new Date(nYear, nMonth, nDate, nHour, nMinute,
nSecond, nMillisecond);
```

But the preceding is quite laborious, especially when compared with the following code that accomplishes the same thing.

```
var dOriginal:Date = new Date();
var dCopy:Date = new Date(dOriginal.getTime());
```

Getting the Time Zone Offset

So far, you have seen that you can work with either local dates *or* UTC dates. However, as long as you know the offset between the two, you can work with both together. The `getTimezoneOffset()` method returns an integer value of the difference between the local time and the UTC in minutes. Here is an example of the `getTimezoneOffset()` method in use:

```
var dNow:Date = new Date();
trace("Your time zone offset: " + dNow.getTimezoneOffset() + " minutes");
```

Set Methods

The `set` methods of `Date` objects allow you to set the individual attributes of the object you are working with. Once you have created a `Date` object, you can modify the year, month, date, hours, minutes, seconds, milliseconds, and time since midnight of January 1, 1970.

Setting the Year

You can set the year value of a `Date` object by using the `setYear()`, `setFullYear()`, and `setUTCFullYear()` methods. These methods are very similar to their `get` method counterparts. Each takes a parameter. The `setYear()` method can take any integer value between 0 and 99 to set the object's year to 1900 through 1999. If you pass it a value outside the 0 to 99 range, it interprets the value literally. For instance:

```
var dSometime:Date = new Date();
dSometime.setYear(5);  // Set the year to 1905
```

But:

```
dSometime.setYear(105);  // sets the year to 105
```

The `setFullYear()` method takes an integer parameter that is interpreted literally in all ranges, even 0 to 99. Thus:

```
dSometime.setFullYear(5);  // Set the year to 5
```

And as you might expect, `setUTCFullYear()` takes an integer value that is interpreted literally in all ranges. It then sets the UTC year value to that year. When the local date value is displayed, it will reflect the UTC change plus the time zone offset.

Setting the Month

You can set the local and UTC month values using the `setMonth()` and `setUTCMonth()` methods, respectively. Both methods require an integer value from 0 to 11. For example:

```
dSometime.setMonth(0);  // Set the month to 0, January
```

If you set the value of the month greater than 11, the year value of the object will increment. In other words, a value of 12 results in the year value increasing by 1, and the month value set to 0. For example:

```
var dSometime:Date = new Date(2003, 5, 23);  // June 23, 2003
dSometime.setMonth(12);  // January 23, 2004
```

You can also pass negative values to these methods. When you do this, it starts with 0, January, and subtracts. Thus, a value of –1 is the same as saying December of the previous year. For example:

```
var dSometime:Date = new Date(2003, 5, 23); // June 23, 2003
 dSometime.setMonth(-1);  // December 23, 2002
```

Setting the Date

You can use the `setDate()` and `setUTCDate()` methods to set the day of the month for a `Date` object. Both methods require a single parameter of an integer value from 1 to 31. For example:

```
dSometime.setDate(23);  // Set the day of the month to 23
```

Just like the methods for setting the month value, if you pass these methods values greater than the number of days in the month, the month will increment. For example:

```
var dSometime:Date = new Date(3433, 1, 8);  // February 8, 3433
dSometime.setDate(29);  // March 1, 3433
```

And just as with the methods for setting the month value, you can also pass negative values to the methods. For example:

```
var dSometime:Date = new Date(3433, 1, 8);   // February 8, 3433
dSometime.setDate(-1);  // January 30, 3433
dSometime.setMonth(-1);  // December 30, 3432
```

Note that because the date portion of a `Date` object is 1-indexed, setting the date to –1 sets the date value to two days prior to the beginning of the month value. A value of 0 passed to the `setDate()` method would set the date value to one day prior to the beginning of the month.

Setting the Hours, Minutes, Seconds, and Milliseconds

As you might expect, you can also set the hour, minutes, seconds, and milliseconds of your `Date` objects for both local time and UTC. The methods for doing this are `setHours()`, `setUTCHours()`, `setMinutes()`, `setUTCMinutes()`, `setSeconds()`, `setUTCSeconds()`, `setMilliseconds()`, and `setUTCMilliseconds()`.

Each method takes integer values as parameters. Hours range from 0 to 23. Minutes and seconds range from 0 to 59. And milliseconds range from 0 to 999. Here is an example:

```
var dSometime:Date = new Date(2020, 0, 1);
dSometime.setHours(5);
dSometime.setMinutes(30);
dSometime.setSeconds(5);
dSometime.setMilliseconds(900);
trace(dSometime.toString());
```

The Output panel will display something like the following (depending on time zone offset):

```
Wed Jan 1 05:30:05 GMT-0800 2020
```

And like the other `set` methods, you can also increment the other values by setting an attribute higher than its uppermost value. For instance, if you added the following line to the previous example, the resulting date would have a `seconds` value of 6 and a `milliseconds` value of 0.

```
dSometime.setMilliseconds(1000);
```

Likewise, you can also pass any of these methods negative values. Let's use the same example again to illustrate this:

```
dSometime.setSeconds(5);  // Set the seconds value back to 5
dSometime.setMilliseconds(-1);  // 05:30:04:999
```

Setting the Time

You learned about the getTime() method earlier. The setTime() method is the counterpart in the set methods category. It allows you to set the value of your Date object with an integer of the number of milliseconds since midnight on January 1, 1970. (For an example, refer to the explanation of getTime()).

```
var dOriginal:Date = new Date();
var dCopy:Date = new Date(dOriginal.getTime());
```

You can just as easily write this in the following way using the setTime() method of the dCopy object:

```
var dOriginal:Date = new Date();
var dCopy:Date = new Date();
dCopy.setTime();
```

Inherited Methods

The toString() method is inherited from the Object class, and, as you've already seen, it returns a string representing the value in the following format:

```
Day Mon dd hh:mm:ss GMT+/-Time Zone Offset yyyy
```

Note   The toString() method is implicitly invoked in any situation in which you try to use a Date object as a string. The examples in this book generally call the method explicitly to be clear.

Static Methods

All the methods you have looked at so far are invoked from Date objects that have been instantiated using the Date constructor. However, there is one method that is invoked directly from the Date class.

UTC() is a method that returns the time value in milliseconds UTC from midnight on January 1, 1970 UTC of the date specified in the arguments. The UTC() method takes the same arguments as the Date constructor: year, month, date, hour, minutes, seconds, milliseconds. The following is an example of the UTC() method:

```
var nUTCDate:Number = Date.UTC(1970, 0, 1, 0, 0, 0);
```

In this example, nUTCDate would have a value of 0 because the UTC date create is the same as the starting date, January 1, 1970, and thus 0 milliseconds have elapsed for this date. Parameters that are omitted are set to 0, so the preceding example could be written as:

```
var nUTCDate:Number = Date.UTC(1970, 0, 1);
```

The UTC() static method could be useful as a shortcut to creating a local date if you know the UTC date. For instance, the following code is the longhand way of doing just this:

```
var dLocal:Date = new Date();
dLocal.setUTCFullYear(1970);
```

```
dLocal.setUTCMonth(0);
dLocal.setUTCDate(1);
dLocal.setUTCHours(0);
dLocal.setUTCMinutes(0);
dLocal.setUTCSeconds(0);
dLocal.setUTCMilliseconds(0);
```

Or, using the `UTC()` method, you could write the same thing in this way:

```
var nUTCDate:Number = Date.UTC(1970, 0, 1);
var dLocal:Date = new Date(nUTCDate);
```

Working with Advanced Date and Time Issues

If you plan to work with dates and times extensively, especially for the purposes of displaying values to the user, you may find it useful to create a new custom `DateTime` class that extends the `Date` class. To do this, complete the following steps:

1. Open a new AS file.

2. In the AS file add the following code:

```
class DateTime extends Date {
  static var SEC:Number = 1000;
  static var MIN:Number = DateTime.SEC * 60;
  static var HOUR:Number = DateTime.MIN * 60;
  static var DAY:Number = DateTime.HOUR * 24;
  static var YEAR:Number = DateTime.DAY * 365;
  static var LEAPYEAR:Number = DateTime.DAY * 366;

  static var DAYS:Array = new Array("Sunday",
                                    "Monday",
                                    "Tuesday",
                                    "Wednesday",
                                    "Thursday",
                                    "Friday",
                                    "Saturday");
  static var MONTHS:Array = new Array("January",
                                      "February",
                                      "March",
                                      "April",
                                      "May",
                                      "June",
                                      "July",
                                      "August",
                                      "September",
                                      "October",
                                      "November",
                                      "December");

  function DateTime() {
    var nArgs:Number = arguments.length;
```

```
      switch (nArgs) {
        case 0:
          super();
          break;
        case 1:
          super(arguments[0]);
          break;
        case 2:
          super(arguments[0], arguments[1]);
          break;
        case 3:
          super(arguments[0], arguments[1], arguments[2]);
          break;
        case 4:
          super(arguments[0], arguments[1], arguments[2],
                arguments[3]);
          break;
        case 5:
          super(arguments[0], arguments[1], arguments[2],
                arguments[3], arguments[4]);
          break;
        case 6:
          super(arguments[0], arguments[1], arguments[2],
                arguments[3], arguments[4], arguments[5]);
          break;
        case 7:
          super(arguments[0], arguments[1], arguments[2],
                arguments[3], arguments[4], arguments[5],
                arguments[6]);
          break;
      }
    }

    public function toFullDisplay():String {
      var sDay:String = DateTime.DAYS[this.getDay()];
      var sMonth:String = DateTime.MONTHS[this.getMonth()];
      var sDisplay:String = sDay + " ";
      sDisplay += sMonth + " ";
      sDisplay += String(this.getDate()) + ", ";
      sDisplay += String(this.getFullYear());
      return sDisplay;
    }

    public function toUSDisplay(sSpacer:String):String {
      if(sSpacer == undefined) {
        sSpacer = "/";
      }
      var sDisplay:String = "";
      sDisplay += zeroFill(this.getMonth() + 1) + sSpacer;
      sDisplay += zeroFill(this.getDate()) + sSpacer;
      sDisplay += String(this.getFullYear());
```

```
    return sDisplay;
}

public function toEuroDisplay(sSpacer:String):String {
  if(sSpacer == undefined) {
    sSpacer = "/";
  }
  var sDisplay:String = "";
  sDisplay += zeroFill(this.getDate()) + sSpacer;
  sDisplay += zeroFill(this.getMonth() + 1) + sSpacer;
  sDisplay += String(this.getFullYear());
  return sDisplay;
}

private function zeroFill(nVal:Number):String {
  if(nVal < 10) {
    return ("0" + String(nVal));
  }
  else {
    return String(nVal);
  }
}

static function toDateTime(dDateObj:Date):DateTime {
  return new DateTime(dDateObj.getTime());
}

public function parseDateTime(sDateTimeStr:String):Void {
  var bTimeZonePlus = false;
  var aDateTime:Array = sDateTimeStr.split("T");
  var aDateParts:Array = aDateTime[0].split("-");
  var aTimeOffset:Array = aDateTime[1].split("-");
  if(aTimeOffset.length == 1) {
    bTimeZonePlus = true;
    aTimeOffset = aDateTime[1].split("+");
  }
  var aTimeParts:Array = aTimeOffset[0].split(":");
  var aOffset:Array = aTimeOffset[1].split(":");
  var nYear:Number = parseInt(aDateParts[0], 10);
  var nMonth:Number = parseInt(aDateParts[1], 10) - 1;
  var nDay:Number = parseInt(aDateParts[2], 10);
  var nHour:Number = parseInt(aTimeParts[0], 10);
  var nMinutes:Number = parseInt(aTimeParts[1], 10);
  var nSeconds:Number = parseInt(aTimeParts[2], 10);
  var nOffset:Number = parseInt(aTimeOffset[1], 10);
  if(bTimeZonePlus) {
    nHour -= nOffset;
  }
  else {
    nHour += nOffset;
  }
```

```
      var nEpochMillis:Number = Date.UTC(nYear, nMonth, nDay,
                                    nHour, nMinutes, nSeconds,
                                    0);
      this.setTime(nEpochMillis);
    }

    public function isLeapYear():Boolean {
      var nYear:Number = this.getFullYear();
      if (nYear % 4 != 0) {
        return false;
      }
      else if (nYear % 400 == 0) {
        return true;
      }
      else if (nYear % 100 == 0) {
        return false;
      }
      else {
        return true;
      }
    }

  }
```

3. Save the file as `DateTime.as`. Save the file to a directory in your global Flash classpath.

The preceding code is just an example to get you started. You may want to modify the code to suit your own application development needs. However, the example code is a good starting point. Now let's take a closer look at the example code.

First, you declare the class to extend `Date`. No matter what modifications you might make to the class, you should make sure that `DateTime` always extends `Date`. By extending the `Date` class, you ensure that you can use all the same functionality of the built-in `Date` class by way of a `DateTime` object.

```
class DateTime extends Date {
```

Next, you define some constants that may be useful. The first set of constants is helpful for performing date math (see the section "Performing Date Math"). The second set of constants contains arrays of string values that correspond to the numeric day of week and month values:

```
static var SEC:Number = 1000;
static var MIN:Number = DateTime.SEC * 60;
static var HOUR:Number = DateTime.MIN * 60;
static var DAY:Number = DateTime.HOUR * 24;
static var YEAR:Number = DateTime.DAY * 365;
static var LEAPYEAR:Number = DateTime.DAY * 366;

static var DAYS:Array = new Array("Sunday",
                                   "Monday",
                                   "Tuesday",
                                   "Wednesday",
                                   "Thursday",
                                   "Friday",
                                   "Saturday");
```

```
static var MONTHS:Array = new Array("January",
                                    "February",
                                    "March",
                                    "April",
                                    "May",
                                    "June",
                                    "July",
                                    "August",
                                    "September",
                                    "October",
                                    "November",
                                    "December");
```

Next, you define the constructor for the `DateTime` class. You need to define only the constructor because the `Date` class has overloaded constructors, and so you need to tell `DateTime` how to call the correct superclass constructor depending on the number of parameters:

```
function DateTime() {
  var nArgs:Number = arguments.length;
  switch (nArgs) {
    case 0:
      super();
      break;
    case 1:
      super(arguments[0]);
      break;
    case 2:
      super(arguments[0], arguments[1]);
      break;
    case 3:
      super(arguments[0], arguments[1], arguments[2]);
      break;
    case 4:
      super(arguments[0], arguments[1], arguments[2],
            arguments[3]);
      break;
    case 5:
      super(arguments[0], arguments[1], arguments[2],
            arguments[3], arguments[4]);
      break;
    case 6:
      super(arguments[0], arguments[1], arguments[2],
            arguments[3], arguments[4], arguments[5]);
      break;
    case 7:
      super(arguments[0], arguments[1], arguments[2],
            arguments[3], arguments[4], arguments[5],
            arguments[6]);
      break;
  }
}
```

The first method displays the full date, including the name of the day and the name of the month:

```
public function toFullDisplay():String {
  var sDay:String = DateTime.DAYS[this.getDay()];
  var sMonth:String = DateTime.MONTHS[this.getMonth()];
  var sDisplay:String = sDay + " "
  sDisplay += sMonth + " "
  sDisplay += String(this.getDate()) + ", "
  sDisplay += String(this.getFullYear());
  return sDisplay;
}
```

The toUSDisplay() and toEuroDisplay() methods return the date in U.S. or European format. In both cases, you can specify the character you want to use between the month, day, and year. The default is a forward slash.

```
public function toUSDisplay(sSpacer:String):String {
  if(sSpacer == undefined) {
    sSpacer = "/";
  }
  var sDisplay:String = "";
  sDisplay += zeroFill(this.getMonth() + 1) + sSpacer;
  sDisplay += zeroFill(this.getDate()) + sSpacer;
  sDisplay += String(this.getFullYear());
  return sDisplay;
}

public function toEuroDisplay(sSpacer:String):String {
  if(sSpacer == undefined) {
    sSpacer = "/";
  }
  var sDisplay:String = "";
  sDisplay += zeroFill(this.getDate()) + sSpacer;
  sDisplay += zeroFill(this.getMonth() + 1) + sSpacer;
  sDisplay += String(this.getFullYear());
  return sDisplay;
}
```

The zeroFill() method is a private method that is used by the preceding methods in order to make sure the month and date are always two digits. For example, if the month is 9, you display 09.

```
private function zeroFill(nVal:Number):String {
  if(nVal < 10) {
    return ("0" + String(nVal));
  }
  else {
    return String(nVal);
  }
}
```

The static `toDateTime()` method can be invoked from the `DateTime` class. You can pass it a `Date` object, and it returns a new `DateTime` object representing the same value:

```
static function toDateTime(dDateObj:Date):DateTime {
  return new DateTime(dDateObj.getTime());
}
```

The `parseDateTime()` method accepts a string and parses the string into a `DateTime` object. The example method accepts and parses a string in the following format: yyyy-mm-ddThh:nn:ss+/-hh:mm. For example, 2003-07-17T00:19:05-05:00 indicates July 17, 2003 at 12:19:05 a.m. with a time zone offset of –5 hours.

```
public function parseDateTime(sDateTimeStr:String):Void {
  var bTimeZonePlus = false;
  var aDateTime:Array = sDateTimeStr.split("T");
  var aDateParts:Array = aDateTime[0].split("-");
  var aTimeOffset:Array = aDateTime[1].split("-");
  if(aTimeOffset.length == 1) {
    bTimeZonePlus = true;
    aTimeOffset = aDateTime[1].split("+");
  }
  var aTimeParts:Array = aTimeOffset[0].split(":");
  var aOffset:Array = aTimeOffset[1].split(":");
  var nYear:Number = parseInt(aDateParts[0], 10);
  var nMonth:Number = parseInt(aDateParts[1], 10) - 1;
  var nDay:Number = parseInt(aDateParts[2], 10);
  var nHour:Number = parseInt(aTimeParts[0], 10);
  var nMinutes:Number = parseInt(aTimeParts[1], 10);
  var nSeconds:Number = parseInt(aTimeParts[2], 10);
  var nOffset:Number = parseInt(aTimeOffset[1], 10);
  if(bTimeZonePlus) {
    nHour -= nOffset;
  }
  else {
    nHour += nOffset;
  }
  var nEpochMillis:Number = Date.UTC(nYear, nMonth, nDay,
                                     nHour, nMinutes,
                                     nSeconds, 0);
  this.setTime(nEpochMillis);
}
```

The `isLeapYear()` method returns `true` if the year is a leap year and `false` otherwise:

```
public function isLeapYear():Boolean {
  var nYear:Number = this.getFullYear();
  if (nYear % 4 != 0) {
    return false;
  }
```

```
      else if (nYear % 400 == 0) {
        return true;
      }
      else if (nYear % 100 == 0) {
        return false;
      }
      else {
        return true;
      }
    }
```

The `toDateTime()` method allows you to set a `DateTime` object based on a `Date` object:

```
    static function toDateTime(dDateObj:Date):DateTime {
      return new DateTime(dDateObj.getTime());
    }
```

Creating a DateTime Object

Once you have defined the `DateTime` class, you can create a `DateTime` object in essentially the same ways that you can create a `Date` object. Here are a few examples:

```
    var dtNow:DateTime = new DateTime();
    var dtWhen:DateTime = new DateTime(2003, 6, 21);
    var dtThen:DateTime = new DateTime(123456789);
```

Working with Date Methods

You can work with all the same `Date` methods for a `DateTime` object. This includes all the `get` and `set` methods as well as the `toString()` method and the static `UTC()` method.

Performing Date Math

When working with dates, you will undoubtedly find that you want to do calculations from time to time — calculations about differences between two dates, or forming a new date by adding to or subtracting from an existing one. When this happens, you should convert all your values to milliseconds. Remember, this is the format ActionScript is storing all your date information in.

If you work with the `DateTime` class, you already have constants for seconds, minutes, hours, days, weeks, and even years in terms of milliseconds. This should make it simpler to perform date and time math. For instance, you can now calculate the date three days and one minute from now with the following code:

```
var dtNow:DateTime = new DateTime();
var nSoon:Number = dtNow.getTime() + (3 * DateTime.DAY) + DateTime.MIN;
var dtSoon = new DateTime(nSoon);
```

Displaying the Date

When you work with the example `DateTime` class, you have three options for displaying the date: full date display, U.S. format, and European format. Here are a few examples:

```
var dtWhen:DateTime = new DateTime(2005, 5, 15);
trace(dtWhen.toFullDisplay());
trace(dtWhen.toUSDisplay());
trace(dtWhen.toEuroDisplay());
trace(dtWhen.toUSDisplay("-"));
trace(dtWhen.toEuroDisplay("-"));
```

The Output panel will display the following:

```
Thursday June 15, 2005
06/15/2005
15/06/2005
07-15-2005
15-06-2005
```

Creating a DateTime Object from a Date Object

There are plenty of scenarios in which you might have a `Date` object that you want to convert to a `DateTime` object. For example, if you retrieve a date from the server using Flash Remoting, you might retrieve a `Date` object. If you then want to display that value to the user or utilize any of the other `DateTime` methods, you should first convert the `Date` object to a `DateTime` object. You can accomplish this with the static `toDateTime()` method:

```
var dtServerDate:DateTime = DateTime.toDateTime(dFromServer);
```

Parsing a Date String into a DateTime Object

In many scenarios, you can retrieve a string that represents a date. You can use the `parseDateTime()` method to parse the string into a `DateTime` object. The example method parses strings such as 2003-07-17T00:19:05-05:00. Here is an example:

```
var dtBlogDateTime:DateTime = new DateTime();
dtBlogDateTime.parseDateTime("2003-07-17T00:19:05-05:00");
```

Detecting Leap Years

The `isLeapYear()` method simply returns `true` or `false`. You can see if a given `DateTime` object represents a leap year or not with this method:

```
var dtNow:DateTime = new DateTime();
trace(dtNow.isLeapYear());
```

Web Resource

We'd like to know what you thought about this chapter. Visit www.rightactionscript .com/asb.comments to fill out an online form with your comments.

Summary

✦ ActionScript Date objects enable you to work with past, present, and future dates and time. You can construct Date objects with specific times or allow the constructor function to query the local computer for the current time and date information.

✦ The Date object works with all date information in terms of milliseconds from midnight on January 1, 1970. You can use the methods of the Date object to work with user-friendly values such as year, month, date, day, hour, minutes, seconds, and milliseconds. You can also use some methods to work directly with the milliseconds value.

✦   ✦   ✦

Working with Strings

Thus far in the book you've had the opportunity to see a lot of string values. What you've primarily seen have been string literals, which are *primitive string data*. The String class is a wrapper class in that it provides some additional functionality around a primitive datatype — in this case the primitive string type. As a primitive type, a string cannot do much. For example, a string cannot report the number of characters it contains. Instead, you need to first create a String object. This chapter looks at the String class and discusses how it applies to your applications.

Understanding Primitives and Objects

The primitive string type is a value. Although useful, it cannot do more than be a value. The String class allows you to instantiate a String object that can do much more. For example, a String object can report the number of characters in the value, and it can convert the value to all uppercase or all lowercase. If all you want is to have a simple value, you should work with a primitive type. Most of the time this will suffice, and there is no need to use the extra resources to create a String object. However, if you want to work with the additional functionality of the String class, you should create a String object. There are two ways you can accomplish this. The preferred way is to use a constructor. The String constructor requires that you pass it the primitive string value you want it to wrap. Here is an example:

```
var sTitle:String = new String("ActionScript
Bible");
```

The new String object, sTitle, wraps the primitive value of ActionScript Bible. Once you have created the object, you can utilize the properties and methods. For example:

```
trace(sTitle.length); // Displays: 18
```

Note   Technically, you can also pass a `String` object to a `String` constructor. Flash automatically calls the `toString()` method of the `String` object to convert it to a string primitive value. However, the same does not work for other datatypes. For example, you cannot simply pass a `Date` object to a `String` constructor. You would need to explicitly call the `toString()` method:

```
// This code causes an error because Flash will not
// automatically convert the Date object to a string.
var dToday:Date = new Date();
var sDate:String = new String(dToday);

// This code will work because it calls the toString()
// method explicitly.
var dToday:Date = new Date();
var sDate:String = new String(dToday.toString());
```

The second way you can create a `String` object is to allow Flash to implicitly create a `String` object by simply invoking a property or method of the `String` class from a primitive string value. For example:

```
trace("ActionScript Bible".length);  // Displays 18
```

With this second technique, Flash actually creates a new `String` object on the fly. However, this is poor coding, and it is not recommended. Although it will work, there are at least two downsides:

✦ There is no way to manage the object because it is created and then essentially lost in memory. It is better to create the object explicitly so that you can manage it.

✦ If you are going to invoke properties and/or methods from the same string value several times, Flash will create several `String` objects. This is wasteful. If you explicitly create a `String` object, only one object needs to be created.

Getting and Setting Primitive Values

The `String` class is treated as a wrapper class because it wraps a primitive value and provides additional functionality. In the previous section, you saw how to set the primitive value for a `String` object. You set the value when you instantiate it with the constructor. For example:

```
var sTitle:String = new String("ActionScript Bible");
```

To get the primitive value from the object, you can use one of three techniques:

✦ **Call the valueOf() method.** The `valueOf()` method of any class returns the primitive value if one exists:

```
trace(sTitle.valueOf()); // Displays: ActionScript Bible
```

✦ **Call the toString() method.** This method returns the string representation of any type of object if available. In the case of a `String` object, the string representation is a string primitive:

```
trace(sTitle.toString()); // Displays: ActionScript Bible
```

✦ **Simply use the object as is.** By default, the `toString()` method of an object is called if you attempt to use it where Flash is expecting a string. This is not necessarily the recommended technique, but it works:

```
trace(sTitle); // Displays: ActionScript Bible
```

Joining Strings

The `concat()` method of a `String` object allows you to concatenate one or more primitive string values with the primitive string value of the object. The concatenated value (which is a primitive string) is returned and the `String` object's value is unaffected. Here is an example:

```
var sTitle:String = new String("ActionScript Bible");
trace(sTitle.concat(" rocks!")); // Displays: ActionScript Bible rocks!
trace(sTitle.valueOf()); // Displays: ActionScript Bible
```

Notice that the value of `sTitle` remained unchanged in the preceding example. If you want to concatenate values and then reassign the new value to the `String` object, you need to do the following:

1. Call the `concat()` method to return the new primitive string.

2. Pass the primitive string to a new `String` constructor.

3. Assign that new `String` object to the same variable as the original `String` object.

Here's an example:

```
var sTitle:String = new String("ActionScript Bible");
sTitle = new String(sTitle.concat(" rocks!"));
trace(sTitle.valueOf()); // Displays: ActionScript Bible rocks!
```

Of course, the `concat()` method is not the only option for concatenating strings. In Chapter 5 you learned how to work with the string concatenation operator (+) for this purpose. There is no reason why you should abandon this practice now. In fact, most of the time you'll still see the string concatenation operator used instead of the `concat()` method. For one thing, it is more convenient. And for another, it is more flexible because it allows you to both prepend and append values. Here's an example:

```
var sTitle:String = new String("ActionScript Bible");
trace("the" + sTitle.valueOf() + " rocks!");
// Displays: the ActionScript Bible rocks!
```

Regardless of which technique you use, however, there are some special considerations when working with strings in general. Some of these things were mentioned briefly in Chapter 3, but the following sections elaborate a bit more.

Escaping Characters

When you are forming string values you should be careful to escape characters when necessary. If you recall from the discussion in Chapter 3, there are several situations in which you need to escape characters. One of the most common is when you are working with quotation marks within a string. It is important that you make sure that the starting and ending quotation marks for the string literal match up and that there are no rogue matches inline. Here's an example of a string literal that would yield an error:

```
var sPhrase:String = 'Ain't ain't a word.'; // error
```

The problem is that the apostrophes inline will be interpreted by Flash as single quotation marks, and the first of the two will match up with the starting single quote. The simplest solution in this case is to use double quotation marks around the string literal instead of single ones. The following change makes the code valid:

```
var sPhrase:String = "Ain't ain't a word."; // correct
```

The same goes for inline double quotes. Typically, if you are going to use inline double quotation marks, then you should use single quotation marks around the string literal. Here's an example:

```
var sQuote:String = '"hello"';
```

But the problem occurs when you want to use both double and single (apostrophes) quotation marks inline. For example:

```
var sPhrase:String = '"Ain't" ain't a word.';
```

In the preceding example, even if you use double quotation marks instead of single quotation marks around the string literal, there will be an error. In such cases you can use the backslash to escape the problematic characters. The backslash tells Flash to interpret the following character in a special way. In the case of a quotation mark, it tells Flash to interpret the quotation mark literally rather than thinking that it should try to match it to a starting or ending quotation mark around the string. Here is the corrected example:

```
var sPhrase:String = '"Ain\'t" ain\'t a word.';
```

The backslash can be used to escape any other special characters, as you'll see in the next section.

Nonvisible Characters

There are some special characters with which you should familiarize yourself. To begin with, let's take a look at the backslash. Obviously, the backslash character has a special function when used in a string literal, so it is not displayed. So, in the event that you wish to display a backslash in a string, you must place another backslash in front of it:

```
trace("\"); // Displays:
trace("\\"); // displays: \
```

There are some additional special character combinations to note. Table 11-1 shows a list of some of the special characters.

Table 11-1: Nonvisible Characters

Character Sequence	Meaning
\b	Backspace
\t	Tab
\n	Newline
\r	Carriage return
\f	Form feed

Here's an example of the newline character used in a string:

```
trace("line one\nline two");
```

The preceding code will display the following in the Output panel:

```
line one
line two
```

If you want to display one of the values literally rather than as the interpreted value, you need to escape it with a backslash. For example, if you want to display \n literally, instead of a newline, you can add an additional backslash just before it. For example:

```
trace("\\n");  // Displays: \\n
```

Avoiding Common Mistakes

There are a handful of mistakes that developers seem to make. Even highly experienced developers make mistakes. However, the difference is that with some education you can more easily troubleshoot when you do make a mistake. The first point for consideration is that it is always a good idea to consult the Output panel when there is an error. All too often, when a developer tests the movie and the Output panel pops up, he or she immediately dismisses and closes it rather than learning what is wrong. This might seem obvious, but it is the first common mistake. After you have successfully located the line or lines causing the problem, it is likely that it is one of the following common mistakes:

✦ There is a mismatched quotation mark somewhere in the string.

✦ Because the backslash character is not frequently used in displays, it is fairly common to forget how to use it. This mistake is essentially the same mistake as in the previous bullet point. The difference is, however, that the first mistake will cause errors, whereas this mistake will not. The rather frustrating result of this mistake is simply a failure to display the string as desired.

✦ Another really common mistake is to omit the concatenation operator (+) when joining multiple strings. For instance, it is easy enough to forget an operator in a line such as the following:

```
var sGreeting:String = "hello, " + sUsername +     ⤶
". today is " dToday;
```

Unfortunately, this results in an error because of the missing operator just before dToday. So, the correct line reads as follows:

```
var sGreeting:String = "hello, " + sUsername +     ⤶
". today is " + dToday;
```

✦ It is also common to accidentally omit quotation marks when joining multiple string literals, or even sometimes at the beginning or end of a single string literal. For instance:

```
var sValue:String = "this is string one." + " " + this is string two";
```

This code clearly does not work. But sometimes, it can be hard to see the missing quotation marks. The correct line reads as follows:

```
var sValue:String = "this is string one." + " " +     ⤶
"this is string two";
```

✦ It is a common mistake to use the = operator instead of the += operator when appending strings such as the following:

```
var sVal:String = "string one.";
sVal += "string two.";
sVal = "string three.";
```

This results in a string with the value of string three. The problem is that the last line uses just the assignment operator instead of the += operator. The correct code reads as follows:

```
var sVal:String = "string one.";
sVal += "string two.";
sVal += "string three.";
```

✦ When you are retrieving string values from a database or other server-side datasource, you sometimes find that extra whitespace characters have been added to the beginning and/or end of the string value. Depending on your usage of the string, that extra whitespace might not have much effect. If you are having some kind of issue with your code that could potentially be caused by such extra whitespace, you can add a simple debugging test by outputting the string value with a character such as a ' or a | at the beginning and end so that you can see if there are any extra nonvisible characters. For example, if you have a variable named sValue, you would use the following:

```
trace("|" + sValue + "|");
```

Then, when you test the application you will be able to quickly see if there is extra whitespace. If the value of sValue is some text, and there is no extra whitespace, it will appear as:

```
|some text|
```

On the other hand, if there is an extra space at the end of the text, you can see it:

```
|some text |
```

Working with Character Codes

When you are working with strings, there are many characters that you can display beyond the standard characters on the keyboard. Doing so requires the use of the character codes. Each character has a numeric value associated with it. For instance, the letter "a" has the character code of 97. There is a separate character code for upper- and lowercase letters. In the discussion of the charCodeAt() and fromCharCode() methods later in this chapter, you learn how to generate a list of the character codes.

Determining the Number of Characters

Every String object has a length property that reports the number of characters in a String object. You've already seen this used in several of the previous examples.

```
var sTitle:String = new String("ActionScript Bible");
trace(sTitle.length);  // Displays: 18
```

All characters in a String object's value are counted. This includes spaces, punctuation, and special character sequences. Even the backspace sequence counts as a character. This might seem counterintuitive, but it is true nonetheless.

Working with Substring Values

A substring is a string that is made up of a portion of another string. For example "accord" is a substring of "accordion". A substring can be a single character or the entire original string. The slice(), substring(), and substr() methods of the String class are all used for selecting a substring value. Each works in a slightly different way, but all return a new string value without changing the String object. In addition, the charAt() method returns a single-character substring.

substr

The substr() method allows you to select a substring by specifying a starting point and a length. Each character in a String object's value is assigned an index. The first character has an index of 0, the second has an index of 1, and so on. Figure 11-1 helps to illustrate this.

0	1	2	3	4	5	6	7	8	9	10	11	12	13	14	15	16	17
A	c	t	i	o	n	S	c	r	i	p	t		B	i	b	l	e

Figure 11-1: The characters in a String object each have an index starting with 0.

The following is an example of how to use the substr() method:

```
var sTitle:String = new String("ActionScript Bible");
trace(sTitle.substr(6, 6));  // Displays: Script
trace(sTitle.substr(0, 6));  // Displays: Action
trace(sTitle.substr(0, 12)); // Displays: ActionScript
```

In this example, the value assigned to the String object is ActionScript Bible. Then, you can display various substrings such as Script, Action, and ActionScript.

You may optionally omit the second parameter. When you do this, it returns a substring starting at the specified index and going to the end of the original string. For example:

```
var sTitle:String = new String("ActionScript Bible");
trace(sTitle.substr(6));  // Displays: Script Bible
```

It is also worth noting that you can specify negative values for a starting index. Specifying a negative value simply counts backward from the end of the string where -1 is the last character. So, the previous example can also be written as follows:

```
var sTitle:String = new String("ActionScript Bible");
trace(sTitle.substr(-12, 6));  // Displays: Script
```

However, it does not work to specify negative values for the length parameter.

substring

There are other times when it is more convenient to specify a starting and ending index for the substring value you are selecting. You can do this by using the substring() method of the String class. This method returns a substring starting with the starting index specified and containing all the characters up to, but not including, the ending index. Here's an example:

```
var sTitle:String = new String("ActionScript Bible");
trace(sTitle.substring(6, 12));  // Displays: Script
```

Notice that the value passed for the ending index, 12, is one greater than the index of the last character returned. Also, with the substring() method, you cannot use negative numbers for the indices.

slice

You can use the slice method to extract a substring as well. This method works similarly to both substr() and substring(). The method takes two parameters, a starting and ending index, just as substring() does. And just as with substring(), the returned value contains the characters from the starting index up to, but not including, the ending index. However, unlike substring(), the second parameter is optional. If omitted, the last index of the string is used. Additionally, using slice(), you can specify the indices with negative numbers where -1 is the last character in the string. Here's an example:

```
var sTitle:String = new String("ActionScript Bible");
trace(sTitle.slice(6, 12));  // Displays: Script
trace(sTitle.slice(6));  // Displays: Script Bible
trace(sTitle.slice(-12));  // Displays: Script Bible
```

charAt

When you want to parse through a string, one character at a time, you can take advantage of the charAt() method. The method takes one parameter, a value for an index within the string. This method returns a new one-character string that contains the value of the character at the specified index.

```
var sTitle:String = new String("ActionScript Bible");
var sChar:String = sTitle.charAt(0);
```

The preceding will return a value of A. You can employ the use of a for loop to loop through the characters of a string, one at a time:

```
var sTitle:String = new String("ActionScript Bible");
for (var i:Number = 0; i < sTitle.length; i++){
    trace(sTitle.charAt(i));
}
```

Notice that the charAt() method is really a simplified version of the substr(), substring(), or splice() methods.

Finding Substrings

There is often a need to search a string for the occurrence of a substring. You can use the indexOf() and lastIndexOf() methods to do this. These methods take the same parameters and operate in much the same way. They both require one parameter — the substring for which to perform the search. And for each, there is a second optional parameter, the starting point for the search within the string. In each case, if the substring is not found, a value of -1 is returned. Otherwise, the value of the index of the first character of the found substring is returned. For example:

```
var sTitle:String = new String("ActionScript Bible");
trace(sTitle.indexOf("ActionScript")); // Displays: 0
trace(sTitle.indexOf("i"));  // Displays: 3
trace(sTitle.lastIndexOf("i"));  // Displays: 14
trace(sTitle.indexOf("i", 4));  // Displays: 9
trace(sTitle.lastIndexOf("i", 12));  // Displays: 9
trace(sTitle.indexOf("q"));  // Displays: -1
trace(sTitle.lastIndexOf("g"));  // Displays: -1
```

You can use either of these methods in a while statement to find all the occurrences of a substring. Here's an example:

```
var sTitle:String = new String("ActionScript Bible");
var nMatch:Number = sTitle.indexOf("i");
while(nMatch != -1) {
  trace(nMatch);
  nMatch = sTitle.indexOf("i", nMatch + 1);
}
```

The preceding code will result in the following output:

```
3
9
14
```

Notice that within the while statement each call to indexOf() is passed not only the substring to match but also the starting index from which to search. The starting index for each search should be one more than the previous match to ensure that you don't keep getting the same match (and, therefore, an infinite loop!).

The indexOf() and lastIndexOf() methods can be particularly useful for form validation — for example, when you want to make sure that a particular type of value has been entered into a field. For instance, you might want to ensure that a valid email address has been entered into a field. A really simple check for a valid email address is to make sure that it contains both a @ and a . within it:

```
var nCheckOne:Number = sEmail.indexOf("@");
var nCheckTwo:Number = sEmail.lastIndexOf(".");
if (nCheckOne!= -1 && nCheckTwo!= -1 && nCheckOne < nCheckTwo){
    trace("good email address");
}
```

Tip   Although the basic `indexOf()` and `lastIndexOf()` methods can be useful for simple pattern matching, as shown in the example, regular expressions are much better suited to
matching complex patterns.

Getting a Character Code

Sometimes you may want to work with numeric values instead of characters in your strings.
There are several reasons why you might want to do this. For example, in order to compare
some special characters you might find you need to compare the character codes rather than
the characters themselves. You can easily do this by using the `charCodeAt()` method of the
`String` object. The method takes a single parameter — an index within the string. It then
returns the character code for the character at that index. For example:

```
var sTitle:String = new String("ActionScript Bible");
trace(sTitle.charCodeAt(12));   // Displays: 32
```

Using Character Codes to Get Characters

The `fromCharCode()` method is a static method of the `String` class. This method returns a
new string primitive value with the character that corresponds to the character code you
specify. This can be useful when you want to work with characters that are not part of the
standard keyboard. For example, you might want to display the copyright symbol in your
Flash movie. You can do this quite simply if you know that the character code for the copyright symbol is 169. You can try it out by using the following code:

```
trace(String.fromCharCode(169));
```

You can easily generate a list of characters and their codes by using the `trace()` function in
a `for` loop to write them to the Output panel. The following code outputs the first 150 characters and codes:

```
for(var i:Number = 0; i < 150; i++){
   trace(i + ": " + String.fromCharCode(i));
}
```

Note   See `www.w3.org/MarkUp/html-spec/html-spec_13.html` for a list of character
codes. The list uses HTML markup codes, but if you omit the &# preceding each code and
the ; following each code, the same numbers work in ActionScript.

Converting a String into an Array

There are occasions when you have strings of delimited values that you want to split apart
into an array of values. The `split()` method does just that. This is particularly useful when
you have passed values to your Flash movie from another application, and some values were
from an array. As you'll read in later chapters, when you utilize the `LoadVars` class to load
data, you can pass name-value pairs only, not complex data structures such as arrays.
However, you can convert the array to a delimited string on the server before passing it to
Flash. And when it is in Flash, you can parse it into an array again. The `split()` method

requires one parameter — the delimiter (this was optional in previous versions of Flash). The method then returns a new array populated by the values from the string. The following is an example:

```
var sValue:String = "a,b,c,d,e,f";
var aValues = sValue.split(",");
for (i = 0; i < aValues.length; i++){
    trace(aValues[i]);
}
```

This example outputs the following:

```
a
b
c
d
e
f
```

If you use another delimiter in the string, you need to specify it as the argument for the split() method appropriately. For example:

```
var sValue:String = "a b c d e f";
var aValues = sValue.split(" ");
for (i = 0; i < aValues.length; i++){
    trace(aValues[i]);
}
```

This example outputs the same output as the previous example.

Caution   Make sure that you specify the correct delimiter when you call the split() method. Otherwise, Flash will not know how to correctly split the string.

Tip   Using an empty string ("") as the delimiter for the split() method will create an array containing each of the characters of the string.

Changing the Case of a String

The toLowerCase() and toUpperCase() methods are both fairly intuitive. The toLowerCase() method returns a new string with all the uppercase letters converted to lowercase. And the toUpperCase() method returns a new string with all the lowercase letters converted to uppercase. In other words, calling either method returns a string with all letters either uppercase or lowercase. Here are some examples:

```
var sTitle:String = new String("ActionScript Bible");
trace(sTitle.toLowerCase());  // Displays: actionscript bible
trace(sTitle.toUpperCase());  // Displays: ACTIONSCRIPT BIBLE
trace(sTitle.valueOf());  // Displays: ActionScript Bible
```

Notice that the value of the original String object is unaffected.

The toLowerCase() and toUpperCase() methods are particularly useful for comparing strings in a case-insensitive manner. For example:

```
var sTitleOne:String = new String("ActionScript Bible");
var sTitleTwo:String = new String("ActionScript bible");
trace(sTitleOne.valueOf() == sTitleTwo.valueOf());
trace(sTitleOne.toUpperCase() == sTitleTwo.toUpperCase());
```

In the preceding example, the first trace() outputs false, whereas the second outputs true because upper- and lowercase letters are not equal. Therefore a B and a b are not going to match. However, if you convert the string values to all uppercase (as in this example) or all lowercase prior to comparing them, you can get a case-insensitive comparison.

Passing String Values to and from Applications

Earlier in this chapter, we used the word "escape" to mean placing a backslash character before a character within a string literal so that Flash interprets it literally instead of with any special meaning. The term "escape" is also used to signify something else in ActionScript and in general Web development. When passing values to and from applications, particularly in URLEncoded format, it is important that special characters be converted to another standard format when being passed back and forth. Consider, for instance, that the & and = characters have special meanings in name-value pairs being passed to and from applications. Therefore, it is important that these characters be converted to another form while being exchanged between applications. This encoding process is called *escaping* the string.

Because of the importance of encoding these special characters, there is a function within ActionScript that specifically takes care of this process. The escape() function can be called at any time to convert a string to the encoded equivalent. This saves you a great deal of time and energy when the need arises. Note that the escape() function does not make changes to the existing string, but returns a new string. Here is an example:

```
var sTitle:String = new String("ActionScript Bible");
trace(escape(sTitle));  // Displays: ActionScript%20Bible
```

The %20 is a hexadecimal escape sequence that represents a space. Because spaces are not permitted in values passed via the HTTP protocol, it must be encoded. These hexadecimal escape sequences are standard, and just about every programming language has a library or built-in function to encode and decode them.

Likewise, there is a function, unescape(), that decodes any string that is URL-encoded. So, for instance, if you were loading a variable from another application, you might need to call the unescape() function to display it properly. Like the escape() function, the unescape() function does not modify the existing string, but returns a new string. The following is an example of the unescape() function:

```
var sTitle:String = new String("ActionScript%20Bible");
trace(unescape(sTitle));  // Displays: ActionScript Bible
```

Most of the time, Flash automatically unescapes all string values without requiring that you explicitly call the unescape() function.

Web Resource   We'd like to know what you thought about this chapter. Visit www.rightactionscript .com/asb/comments to fill out an online form with your comments.

Summary

✦ Strings are primitive datatypes for which the String class is a wrapper class. This simply means that a String object contains the string value and provides additional functionality.

✦ There are character sequences or combinations used in place of special characters with other meanings within a string.

✦ The String class includes methods for finding substrings and matching substrings.

✦ When passing values to and from other applications, it can be important to make sure that the name-value pairs are properly URL-encoded, with all characters escaped. This means that characters such as spaces are substituted with other characters or sequences of characters. You can do this easily with the escape() function (the opposite of which is the unescape() function).

✦ ✦ ✦

Applying Regular Expressions

◆   ◆   ◆   ◆

In This Chapter

Familiarizing yourself
with regular expressions

Learning the
metacharacters for
creating regular
expressions

Installing the RegExp
class

Using the RegExp
methods

Using the regular
expression String
methods

◆   ◆   ◆   ◆

gramming
stead of
r expres-
as well as
he custom

U   ons

n matching
ern within a
llows a partic-
placements of

a String
e:

ript Bible");
ipt");

il address format is
nly do you want to
u also want to make
er. You *can* accom-
nown in the following

omeserver.com");

```
            .adex = sEmail.lastIndexOf(".");
if(nAmpIndex == -1 || nDotIndex == -1) {
  bValidEmail = false;
}
if(!(nAmpIndex > 0)) {
  bValidEmail = false;
}
if(!(nDotIndex > nAmpIndex)) {
  bValidEmail = false;
}
```

```
if(!(nDotIndex < sEmail.length - 1) || !(nDotIndex > nAmpIndex + 1)) {
  bValidEmail = false;
}
trace(bValidEmail);
```

As you can see in the preceding example, this simple check can involve a lot of code. Furthermore, the preceding code doesn't even verify the email address syntax with a high degree of precision. A more precise test can be accomplished using a regular expression and just a few lines of code, as shown in this example:

```
var sEmail:String = new String("someone@someserver.com");
var reEmail:RegExp = new RegExp("^([\\w\\-\\.]+)@(([\\w
\\-]{2,}\\.)+[\\w\\-]{2,3})$");
trace(reEmail.test(sEmail));
```

Note   The previous example does not work unless you've installed the `RegExp` class. Instructions on how to do this are provided later in this chapter.

This is just one simple example of the power of regular expressions. Throughout this chapter, you will learn many more, but the following section looks at regular expressions in general before examining ActionScript's implementation of them.

Looking at How Regular Expressions Work

ActionScript does not have a built-in implementation of regular expressions. Therefore, standard notation for a regular expression is not recognized within ActionScript. In this overview, regular expressions are presented within the `//` operator, which is not recognized by ActionScript. This convention is convenient for this generalized discussion; later in the chapter you will see how to use regular expressions in ActionScript, which uses the same concepts but is implemented slightly differently.

In its simplest form, a regular expression can be the characters that form the substring for which you want to search, as shown in the following example:

```
/abc/
```

This regular expression matches the strings `"abc"`, `"abcd"`, and `"0123abcd"`. It does not match `"ab"`, `"cba"`, or `"fred"`, however.

Case-Sensitivity, Global Pattern Matching, and Multiline Matches

The regular expression `/abc/` also does not match `"Abc"`, `"aBc"`, or `"ABC"`, because regular expression matching is case-sensitive. However, you can specify that a case-insensitive match should be done using the `i` flag. For example, the following code matches the strings `"abc"`, `"ABC"`, `"aBc"`, `"abCde"`, and so on because the regular expression has been flagged as case-insensitive:

```
/abc/i
```

Although the regular expression `/abc/` finds a match in the string `"abcabc"`, it finds only one match instead of two. This is because the regular expression matches only the first match it finds, by default. However, with the `g` flag (for global), you can specify that the expression should match *all* instances of the pattern that it finds within a string. For example, the following matches `"abc"` twice in `"abcabc"`:

```
/abc/g
```

One additional flag can be set for a regular expression. By default, all matches are performed on strings as a single line of characters — including newlines as another character. With an `m` flag, however, you can specify that a match is to be performed on a multiline string. This only affects the results of the match if the `^` or `$` metacharacters are used (see Table 12-1). For example, the following code matches only the first occurrence of `"abc"` in the string `"abcdefghi\nabcdefghi"`:

```
/^abc/
```

By setting the `m` flag (along with the `g` flag) as follows, the expression matches both occurrences of `"abc"`:

```
/^abc/mg
```

This is explained in more detail under the discussion of assertions later in this chapter.

Creating More Complex Patterns

Regular expressions would not do much good if all you could do was search for simple patterns such as `/abc/`. The real power of regular expressions is realized when you use *metacharacters,* characters that have special meaning to the regular expression, to create complex patterns. So far, you have seen how to match an exact substring using a regular expression such as `/abc/`. This is fine if you want to match a string such as `"abc"`. However, what if you want to match `"aabbcc"`, `"abcccc"`, or `"aaabc"` as well? Using the + character within the regular expression, you can create a pattern that matches all these strings:

```
/a+b+c+/
```

This is just one example of a more complex pattern. Table 12-1 describes all the metacharacters that can be used in a regular expression.

Table 12-1: Special Characters for Regular Expressions

Metacharacter	Category	What It Does
\	Escape	Matches the literal character that it precedes if that character is otherwise normally treated as a metacharacter: `/\^/ matches "^" or "abc^"`.
^	Assertion	Matches a pattern to the beginning of a string only: `/^abc/ matches "abc"`, but not `"123abc"`. When used with the multiline flag set to `true`, the `^` assertion matches a pattern to the beginning of each line.
$	Assertion	Matches a pattern to the end of a string only: `/abc$/ matches "123abc"`, but not `"abc"`. When used with the multiline flag set to `true`, the `$` assertion matches a pattern to the end of each line.

Continued

Table 12-1 *(continued)*

Metacharacter	Category	What It Does
\b	Assertion	Matches a pattern to a word boundary: `/abc\b/` matches `"abc"` or `"abc 123"`, but not `"abc123"`. `/\babc/` matches `"abc"`, `"abc 123"`, or `"abc123"` but not `"123abc"`.
\B	Assertion	Matches a pattern to a nonword boundary: `/abc\B/` matches `"abc123"` but not `"abc"` or `"abc 123"`. `/\Babc/` matches `"123abc"` but not `"abc"`.
*	Quantifier	Matches 0 or more of the characters preceding it: `/a*bc/` matches `"abc"`, `"bc"`, or `"aaabc"`.
+	Quantifier	Matches one or more of the characters preceding it: `/a+bc/` matches `"abc"` or `"aaabc"`, but not `"bc"`.
?	Quantifier	Matches none or one of the characters preceding it: `/a?bc/` matches `"abc"` or `"bc"` but not `"aaabc"`.
{n}	Quantifier	Matches the character it precedes *n* times: `/a{3}bc/` matches the three `"a"`s in `"aaabc"`, the first three `"a"`s in `"aaaaabc"` but not `"abc"`.
{n,}	Quantifier	Matches the character it precedes at least *n* times: `/a{3,}bc/` matches the three `"a"`'s in `"aaabc"` and the five `"a"`'s in `"aaaaabc"` but not `"abc"`.
{n,m}	Quantifier	Matches the character it precedes at least *n* times and no more than *m* times: `/a{3,4}bc/` matches the three `"a"`s in `"aaabc"` and the four `"a"`'s in `"aaaaabc"` but does not match either `"abc"` or `"aaaaabc"`.
x|y	Or	Matches either x or y: `/a|b/` matches `"abc"`, `"ac"`, and `"bc"`, but not `"cdefg"`. `/abc|def/` matches `"abcdef"`, `"abc"`, and `"def"`.
()	Group	Groups characters and patterns together, as in the following: `/(abc)*def/`, which matches `"abcdef"` and `"abcabcdef"` but not `"abc123def"` or `/a(b|c)d/`, which matches `"abd"` or `"acd"`, but not `"abcd"`.
[]	Character Ranges	Matches any of the characters in the brackets: `/[abc]/` matches `"a"`, `"bcdef"`, `"cdef"`, `"abc"`, and so on. Does not match `"def"`. Ranges can be specified using a dash: `/[a-z]/` matches `"a"`, `"b"`, `"c"`, `"r"`, `"z21"`, and so on. Does not match `"R"`, `"2"`, or `"35"`.
[^]	Character Ranges	Matches any characters except those within the brackets: `/[^abc]/` matches `"def"`, `"xyz"`, and `"123"`, but not `"abc"` or `"a123"`.
.	Special Character	Matches any character.

Metacharacter	Category	What It Does
[\b]	Special Character	Matches a backspace.
\d	Special Character	Matches any digit. Same as [0-9].
\D	Special Character	Matches any nondigit. Same as [^0-9].
\f	Special Character	Matches formfeed.
\n	Special Character	Matches newline.
\r	Special Character	Matches carriage return.
\t	Special Character	Matches tab.
\v	Special Character	Matches vertical tab.
\w	Character Ranges	Matches any alphanumeric character, including underscore Same as [a-zA-Z0-9_].
\W	Character Ranges	Matches any non-alphanumeric character, including underscore Same as [^a-zA-Z0-9_].
\s	Character Ranges	Matches any whitespace character. Same as [\f\n\r\t\v].
\S	Character Ranges	Matches any non-whitespace character. Same as [^\f\n\r\t\v].
\n	Grouped Match	Matches the *n* grouped component, where *n* is an integer from 1 to 9: /(s)tar\1/ will match "stars" but not "star" or "start". /s(t)ar\t/ will match "start" but not "stars". In a more generic form: /([A-Z])[A-Z]+\1/i will match "stars", "treat", and "abracadabra".

Note

The regular expression-specific special characters, \n (where *n* is an integer from 1 to 9), \b, \B, \d, \D, \s, \S, \w, and \W, should all appear in your ActionScript code with double slashes in front of them (for example, "\\b\\w"). However, because many of the special characters (\f, \r, \n, \t, \v) are already recognized by Flash, these characters should not appear with double slashes. Instead, they should appear with single slashes (for example, "\f\n"). You will see examples of this in the code examples throughout this chapter.

Assertions

The ^, $, \b, and \B metacharacters are all *assertions*. These metacharacters assert where the match must occur within a string. The ^ metacharacter requires that the match occur at the beginning of the string (or the beginning of a line if the m flag is on for the regular expression). The $ metacharacter requires that the match occur at the end of the string (or the end of a line if the m flag is on for the regular expression).

/^Action/ matches the first "Action" in "ActionScript Bible is about ActionScript", but it will not match anything in "the ActionScript Bible is about ActionScript" because "Action" must appear at the beginning of the string.

/Script$/ matches the last "Script" in the same string.

The \b metacharacter requires that the match occur at a word boundary, and the \B metacharacter requires that a match occur anywhere *except* a word boundary.

/\bd/i matches the "D" in "Durga" but not the "d" in "Radha".

/a\b/i matches the last "a" in "Radha" but not the "a" in "Ram".

/\Bd/i matches the "d" in "Radha" but not the "D" in "Durga".

/a\B/i matches the "a" in "Ram" but not the "a" in "Durga".

Quantifiers

The quantifier metacharacters enable you to specify a quantity of times that a match should be made, as follows:

✦ The * metacharacter requires that the preceding character or grouped pattern be matched 0 or more times.

✦ The + metacharacter requires that the preceding character or grouped pattern be matched one or more times.

✦ The ? metacharacter requires that the preceding character or grouped pattern be matched 0 or one time.

✦ The {n} metacharacter matches the preceding character or grouped pattern *n* times.

✦ The {n,} metacharacter matches the preceding character or grouped pattern at least *n* times.

✦ The {n,m} metacharacter matches the preceding character or pattern at least *n* times but only up to *m* times.

/ActionScript*/ matches "ActionScrip", "ActionScript", and "ActionScriptt", but not "AactionScript".

/ActionScript+/ matches "ActionScript" or "ActionScriptt", but not "ActionScrip".

/ActionScript?/ matches "ActionScript" or "ActionScrip", but not "ActionScriptt".

/A{3}ctionScript/ matches "AAActionScript", but not "ActionScript" or "AActionScript".

/A{3,}ctionScript/ matches "AAActionScript" or "AAAActionScript", but not "ActionScript".

/A{1,2}ctionScript/ matches "ActionScript" or "AActionScript", but not "AAActionScript".

Grouping Together Patterns

The ( ) metacharacter enables you to group together patterns in a regular expression. To understand this, consider the following example:

```
/Action*Script/
```

This expression matches "ActionScript" or "ActionnScript", and so on. But if the grouping metacharacter is used, as in:

```
/(Action)*Script/
```

the regular expression still matches "ActionScript", but no longer matches "ActionnScript". Instead, it will now match "Script", "ActionScript", and "ActionActionScript". Why? Because the * metacharacter attempts to match 0 or more instances of the preceding grouped pattern, instead of just the preceding character.

Using parentheses also accomplishes another task. Characters and patterns grouped in parentheses within a regular expression are remembered when a match is made, as shown in the following example:

/(abc*)defg/ will match "abcccdefg" and remember the substring "abccc".

/(abc*)def(g)/ will match "abcccdefg" and remember the substrings "abccc" and "g".

> **Note**   When we say that the regular expression instance will remember a substring, we mean that each of the substrings matching the grouped pattern is stored in an array that can be accessed later.

Matching One Pattern or Another

You can use the | metacharacter to match the pattern on either side of it:

/Action|Script/ matches "Action" or "Script" in "Action adventure", "Script adventure".

Be careful when you use the | metacharacter because it matches the entire pattern on either side of the metacharacter:

/recogniz|se/ matches "recognize" (American English spelling) and "recognise" (British English spelling), but it also matches "recognizant" and "rise".

If you want to match *only* "recognize" or "recognize", you should group part of the expression with parentheses:

/recogni(z|s)e/ matches *only* "recognize" or "recognise".

Creating Subsets and Ranges

You can create subsets and ranges of characters you want to try to match using the square brackets ([ ]) around the characters. For example, you can write a regular expression to accomplish the same task as /recogni(z|s)e/ as follows:

```
/recogni[sz]e/
```

Another example is:

```
/ca[rtb]/
```

which matches `"car"`, `"cat"`, and `"cab"`.

You can also specify ranges of characters using a dash (-) between the starting and ending characters in the range:

/[a-r]/ matches any character from `"a"` to `"r"`.

/[a-z]_[0-9]/ matches any lowercase character and any digit separated by an underscore (that is, – `"t_4"`).

You can also specify subsets and ranges that must *not* appear in the string to a match to be made. To do so, you simply enclose the subset and/or ranges in the square brackets with a caret ([^]), as shown in the following example:

/[^crb]at/ matches `"mat"`, `"fat"`, `"pat"`, `"sat"`, and so on, but does not match `"cat"`, `"rat"`, or `"bat"`.

Additionally, the \w, \W, \s, and \S metacharacters are shorthand versions of [a-zA-Z0-9_], [^a-zA-Z0-9_], [\f\n\r\t\v], and [^\f\n\r\t\v], respectively.

Working with the RegExp Class

Now that you have learned the fundamentals of regular expressions, the next step is to learn how to use them in ActionScript. Although future versions of ActionScript might include a RegExp class, when working with Flash 8, you need to either write your own class or use one that has already been written.

Fortunately, an excellent RegExp class exists already. Pavils Jurjans wrote a RegExp class for Flash 5 and Flash MX. We have converted this class to an ActionScript 2.0 version. You can find the Flash 5/MX version (in case you are working with an older version of Flash) as well as the new ActionScript 2.0 version at his web site at http://www.jurjans.lv/flash/RegExp.html. Although the class is written in ActionScript, it is surprisingly fast. Throughout this chapter, you learn how to use the ActionScript 2.0 version of the RegExp class for your own projects.

Note   Before you can do anything else with the RegExp class, you must have a copy of the code. The file is called RegExp.as, and you can find it at http://www.jurjans.lv/flash/RegExp.html. Copy this file to a location in your global Flash classpath. The class is available for free, but do feel free to make a donation via his web site if you benefit from the class.

If You Know JavaScript

If you are familiar with JavaScript regular expressions, you should read this section to ensure that you understand some of the key differences between using regular expressions in JavaScript versus ActionScript. If you are not familiar with regular expressions in JavaScript, you can skip to the next section.

The ActionScript implementation of regular expressions adheres as closely to the JavaScript implementation as possible, but there are a few differences. The major difference is simply that ActionScript does not currently allow for regular expression literals. In JavaScript, the following is allowed:

```
re = /abc/;  // This only works in JavaScript.
```

However, in ActionScript, there is no such thing as a regular expression literal. You must always use the constructor to create a regular expression object in ActionScript:

```
// This works in JavaScript and ActionScript.
var reCase:RegExp = new RegExp("abc");
```

Creating a Regular Expression Object

After you have the class included in your project, you must create a regular expression object before you can do anything with regular expressions. To create a regular expression object, just call the RegExp constructor. The constructor requires one parameter and allows for a second optional parameter. The required parameter is a string representing the regular expression. For example, the regular expression /abc/ would be represented as the following in ActionScript:

```
var reCase:RegExp = new RegExp("abc");
```

Then, if you want to add any flags to the regular expression, you can specify them as a string in the second parameter. To make the preceding example case-insensitive, you can add the i flag:

```
var reCase:RegExp = new RegExp("abc", "i");
```

To flag it to match globally and multiline, the following will work:

```
var reCase:RegExp = new RegExp("abc", "gm");
```

The second parameter can appear in any permutation of the three flags. For example, "gim" and "igm" are the same thing.

If you want to change the regular expression after an object has been created, you can do so by calling the compile() method, which takes the same parameters as the constructor. For example, you can modify the previously created object in the following way:

```
reCase.compile("def", "i");
```

Because backslashes already escape characters in strings, it is important to remember that you need to use double-backslashes within the regular expression string to create some of the metacharacters. For example, the regular expression /\w/ is created in ActionScript as follows:

```
var reCase:RegExp = new RegExp("\\w");
```

Note Notice that in the previous example, the \w character is preceded by an additional slash (\\w instead of \w). This is an example of how the regular expression-specific characters (\n [where *n* is an integer from 1 to 9], \b, \B, \d, \D, \s, \S, \w, and \W) are always written with two slashes in quoted strings. Remember that some of the other special characters (\f, \n, \r, \t, \v) are written with only the one preceding slash.

Regular expression objects (instances of the `RegExp` class) include several properties. The `ignoreCase`, `global`, and `multiline` properties are each Boolean properties that indicate whether the `i`, `g`, and `m` flags are set for the regular expression. These properties are read-only. You can modify them only by recompiling the regular expression.

Regular expression objects also have a source property that returns the string value of the regular expression used, as shown in the following example:

```
var reCase:RegExp = new RegExp("abc", "ig");
trace(reCase.source);
reCase.compile("(a)[^b]c*");
trace(reCase.source);
```

This displays the following:

```
abc
(a)[^b]c*
```

Matching Using a Regular Expression Object

The `RegExp` class includes two methods for regular expression objects that match regular expressions in strings. Each method is invoked from a regular expression object and is passed a parameter (the string that is to be used for the match).

The `test()` method is the simpler of the two methods. `test()` returns `true` if the regular expression is matched at least once to the string parameter and returns `false` if it is not:

```
var reCase:RegExp = new RegExp("abc");
trace(reCase.test("aBc"));   // Displays: false;
reCase.compile("abc", "i");
trace(reCase.test("aBc"));   // Displays: true;
```

This is useful if you simply want to know whether at least one match exists. For example, you might want to determine whether an email address is valid. If that is all you want to know, you can use the `test()` method:

```
var sEmail:String = new String("someone@someserver.com");
var reEmail:RegExp = new RegExp("^([\\w\\-\\.]+)
@(([\\w\\-]{2,}\\.)+[\\w\\-]{2,3})$");
trace(reEmail.test(sEmail));
```

The `exec()` method, however, provides a little more detail in its feedback. Whereas `test()` returns only `true` or `false`, `exec()` returns `null` if no matches are found, or an array of the current match if a match is made. The array contains indexed elements. The 0 element is the matched substring. The remaining elements (1 through *n*) are remembered substrings (those matched to characters and patterns enclosed in parentheses in the regular expression). The returned array also includes two properties in addition to those of a normal array: the `index` property and the `input` property. The `index` property is the integer value of the string index for the first character of the matched substring in the string. The `input` property is the string that is passed to the `exec()` method. The following code demonstrates how to use the `exec()` method.

```
var reCase:RegExp = new RegExp("abc");
var sVal:String = new String("aBcdefabCdefABC");
var aMatch:Array = reCase.exec(sVal);
```

```
trace(aMatch + " - " + aMatch.index);
// Try it again with the case insensitive and global
// flags set.
reCase.compile("abc", "ig");
aMatch = reCase.exec(sVal);
trace(aMatch + " - " + aMatch.index);
aMatch = reCase.exec(sVal);
trace(aMatch + " - " + aMatch.index);
aMatch = reCase.exec(sVal);
trace(aMatch.toString() + " - " + aMatch.index);
aMatch = reCase.exec(sVal);
trace(aMatch + " - " + aMatch.index);
```

The preceding code displays the following in the Output panel:

```
null - undefined
aBc - 0
abC - 6
ABC - 12
null - undefined
```

In the first exec() call, the result is null because no match was found in the string. When the regular expression is recompiled with the i and g flags, the same exec() call returns an array with the first match found in the string: "aBc" with a starting index of 0. The next call to exec() returns an array with the second match: "abC" with a starting index of 6. The third call to exec() returns an array with the third match: "ABC" with a starting index of 12. The fourth call to exec() returns null again because no more matches exist within the string. Incidentally, if the exec() method were called again and the same trace() function were called, the following would be appended to the Output panel display:

```
aBc - 0
```

This is because the lastIndex property of the regular expression object (re) would be reset to 0. The lastIndex property is discussed just a bit later in this chapter.

The following code shows an example of remembered substrings as elements of the returned array.

```
function display(aMatchParam):Void {
  trace("Input: " + aMatchParam.input);
  trace("  Found: " + aMatchParam[0]);
  trace("     At: " + aMatchParam.index);
  for(var i = 1; i < aMatchParam.length; i++){
    trace("        Remembered Match " + i + ": " +
aMatchParam[i]);
  }
}

var reCase:RegExp = new RegExp("(The|hooray for)* *(Action)
*(Script)* *(Bible)* *(rocks|rules|is awesome)*", "i");
var aMatch:Array = reCase.exec("action");
display(aMatch);
aMatch = reCase.exec("The script rules");
display(aMatch);
```

```
aMatch = reCase.exec("ActionScript rocks");
display(aMatch);
aMatch = reCase.exec("hooray for ActionScript");
display(aMatch);
aMatch = reCase.exec("The ActionScript Bible is awesome");
display(aMatch);
```

This example displays the following in the Output panel:

```
Input: action
  Found: action
    At: 0
      Remembered Match 1:
      Remembered Match 2: action
      Remembered Match 3:
      Remembered Match 4:
      Remembered Match 5:
Input: The script rules
  Found: The script rules
    At: 0
      Remembered Match 1: The
      Remembered Match 2:
      Remembered Match 3: script
      Remembered Match 4:
      Remembered Match 5: rules
Input: ActionScript rocks
  Found: ActionScript rocks
    At: 0
      Remembered Match 1:
      Remembered Match 2: Action
      Remembered Match 3: Script
      Remembered Match 4:
      Remembered Match 5: rocks
Input: hooray for ActionScript
  Found: hooray for ActionScript
    At: 0
      Remembered Match 1: hooray for
      Remembered Match 2: Action
      Remembered Match 3: Script
      Remembered Match 4:
      Remembered Match 5:
Input: The ActionScript Bible is awesome
  Found: The ActionScript Bible is awesome
    At: 0
      Remembered Match 1: The
      Remembered Match 2: Action
      Remembered Match 3: Script
      Remembered Match 4: Bible
      Remembered Match 5: is awesome
```

In addition to returning an array, the exec() method also modifies the regular expression object if matches are found. The lastIndex, ignoreCase, global, multiline, and source properties are all modified in the regular expression object (the RegExp class instance).

The lastIndex property is the index in the string that should be used as the starting point for the next match. This is how the object remembers not to search from the beginning of the string again each time (if the global flag is set). You can read and write to this property to move the starting point of the next match:

```
var reCase:RegExp = new RegExp("abc", "ig");
var sVal:String = "aBcdefabCdefABC";
var aMatch:Array = reCase.exec(sVal);
trace(aMatch + " - " + reCase.lastIndex);
aMatch = reCase.exec(sVal);
trace(aMatch + " - " + reCase.lastIndex);
aMatch = reCase.exec(sVal);
trace(aMatch + " - " + reCase.lastIndex);
aMatch = reCase.exec(sVal);
trace(aMatch + " - " + reCase.lastIndex);
aMatch = reCase.exec(sVal);
trace(aMatch + " - " + reCase.lastIndex);
```

As it is, this code will display the following in the Output panel:

```
aBc - 3
abC - 9
ABC - 15
null - 0
aBc - 3
```

However, notice what happens if the lastIndex property is set to a different value (changes to the previous code are shown in bold):

```
var reCase:RegExp = new RegExp("abc", "ig");
var sVal:String = "aBcdefabCdefABC";
var aMatch:Array = reCase.exec(sVal);
trace(aMatch + " - " + reCase.lastIndex);
reCase.lastIndex = 0;
aMatch = reCase.exec(sVal);
trace(aMatch + " - " + reCase.lastIndex);
reCase.lastIndex = 0;
aMatch = reCase.exec(sVal);
trace(aMatch + " - " + reCase.lastIndex);
reCase.lastIndex = 0;
aMatch = reCase.exec(sVal);
trace(aMatch + " - " + reCase.lastIndex);
reCase.lastIndex = 0;
aMatch = reCase.exec(sVal);
trace(aMatch + " - " + reCase.lastIndex);
```

Now the Output panel displays the following:

```
aBc - 3
aBc - 3
aBc - 3
aBc - 3
aBc - 3
```

String Methods and Regular Expressions

The `RegExp` class adds several methods to the `String` class. These methods provide additional functionality to `String` objects by utilizing the `RegExp` class. The following four methods are discussed here: `match()`, `search()`, `replace()`, and `split()`.

Matching

The `match()` method of the `String` object takes a regular expression object as a parameter and returns an array of all the matches. Unlike the array returned by the `RegExp` class `exec()` method, the `match()` method returns an array of all the matches in the `String` object (each as an element) and does not have any additional properties beyond those of any other array. If no matches are found, the method returns `null`:

```
var reCase:RegExp = new RegExp("(\\w)+", "g");
var sVal = new String("abc def ghi");
var aMatches:Array = sVal.match(reCase);
trace(aMatches.toString()); // ["abc", "def", "ghi"]
reCase.compile("(\\w){3}\\B", "g");
aMatches = sVal.match(reCase);
trace(aMatches.toString());  // null
```

Searching

The `search()` method of the `String` object is very similar to the `test()` method of the `RegExp` class. The differences are that the `search()` method is invoked from a `String` object and passed a `RegExp` object as a parameter (instead of the other way around for the `test()` method) and that the method returns the index of the match if one is made or returns `-1` if no match is made:

```
var reCase:RegExp = new RegExp("\\s(\\w)+\\s", "g");
var sValue:String = new String("abc def ghi");
trace(sValue.search(reCase));              // 3
reCase.compile("(\\w){3}\\B", "g");
trace(sValue.search(reCase));              // -1
```

Replacing

You can use the `replace()` method of the `String` object to easily replace patterns within a `string` value. The method takes two parameters: the regular expression object and the string that should replace any matched patterns:

```
var reCase:RegExp = new RegExp("shoot|crud|darn", "gi");
var sVal = new String("Shoot! More darn regular expression crud!");
var sRepl = sVal.replace(reCase, "%#@$");
trace(sRepl);
```

This example replaces `"Shoot"`, `"darn"`, and `"crud"` in the string value and displays the following to the Output panel:

```
%#@$! More %#@$ regular expression %#@$!
```

Within the replacement string (the second parameter), you can use special values $1 to $9 to indicate the first nine remembered substrings:

```
var reCase:RegExp = new RegExp("(\\w+) (\\w+)", "gi");
var sVal = new String("ActionScript Bible");
var sRepl = sVal.replace(reCase, "$2, $1");
trace(sRepl);
```

The preceding example writes the following to the Output panel:

```
Bible, ActionScript
```

Tip   If you want to replace the text with the string "$2" instead of with the second matched substring, you can escape the $2 character with two slashes ("\\$2"). For instance, in the previous example, you can substitute this line:

```
rStr = str.replace(re, "\\$2, $1");
```

and the output would become:

```
$2, ActionScript
```

Splitting

The String class already has a split() method, but that method is enhanced by the regular expression version that replaces it when you install the RegExp class. The new split() method works just as the regular split() method does, by splitting a string into an array of strings based on the delimiter passed to it as a parameter. If that parameter is a string, the split() method works the same as before. However, if the parameter passed to it is a RegExp object, the split() method uses the regular expression as the delimiter. The following example shows how a string value can still be used as the delimiter:

```
var sVal:String = new String("ActionScript Bible");
var aVals:Array = sVal.split(" ");
```

In the preceding example, the string is split into an array with elements "ActionScript", and "Bible". The same split() method can be called using a RegExp object instead of a string as the delimiter:

```
var reCase:RegExp = new RegExp("[ ,]", "ig");
var sVal = new String("ActionScript Bible, Flash Bible");
var aVals:Array = sVal.split(reCase);
```

In this case, the array that is returned has the following elements: "ActionScript", "Bible", "Flash", and "Bible".

The Top-Level RegExp Object

The RegExp class has 13 static read-only properties that are automatically set, depending on the results of the regular expression object operation.

The lastMatch property is the string containing the last match made by the regular expression. For example:

```
var reCase:RegExp = new RegExp("def", "gi");
var sVal = new String("abcdefghi");
var sMatches:Array = sVal.match(reCase);
trace(RegExp.lastMatch); // Displays: def
```

Along with the `lastMatch` property are the `leftContext` and `rightContext` properties. These properties contain the strings to the left and to the right of the last matched string:

```
var reCase:RegExp = new RegExp("c(a|o)w", "gi");
var sVal = new String("the cow does not caw.");
var aMatches:Array = sVal.match(reCase);
trace(RegExp.lastMatch);  // Displays: caw
trace(RegExp.leftContext);  // Displays: the cow does not
trace(RegExp.rightContext); // Displays: .
```

The RegExp class also keeps track of the first nine remembered matched components and the last matched component. The first nine are stored in the $1 through $9 properties, and the last is stored in the `lastParen` property, as shown in the following example:

```
var reCase:RegExp = new RegExp(".*(\\b\\w+ain).*(\\b\\w+ain)    ⊃
.*(\\b\\w+ain).*(\\b\\w+ain)\\.", "gi");
var sVal = new String("the rain in Spain falls mainly          ⊃
on the plain.");
var aMatches = sVal.match(reCase);
trace(RegExp.lastParen);  // Displays: plain
trace(RegExp.$1);  // Displays: rain
trace(RegExp.$2);  // Displays: Spain
trace(RegExp.$3);  // Displays: main
trace(RegExp.$4);  // Displays: plain
```

We'd like to know what you thought about this chapter. Visit `www.rightactionscript` `.com/asb/comments` to fill out an online form with your comments.

Summary

✦ Regular expressions provide a way to match patterns within strings.

✦ Using the metacharacters of regular expressions, you can create increasingly complex patterns that go beyond searching for a specific substring.

✦ ActionScript does not include a native RegExp class. This chapter covers the class originally written by Pavils Jurjans.

✦ RegExp objects enable you to match patterns within strings passed to their methods as parameters.

✦ The RegExp class adds several methods to the String class, enabling String objects to take advantage of regular expression-matching.

✦   ✦   ✦

Working with Display Objects

P A R T

◆   ◆   ◆   ◆

In This Part

Chapter 13
Using Display Objects

Chapter 14
Working with
Movie Clips

Chapter 15
Drawing
Programmatically

Chapter 16
Transforming Colors

Chapter 17
Applying Filters

Chapter 18
Using the Bitmap API

Chapter 19
Working with Text Fields
and Selection

Chapter 20
Formatting Text

◆   ◆   ◆   ◆

Using Display Objects

Chances are good that if you've worked with Flash for any time at all, you've worked with MovieClip, Button, and TextField objects. And you may not even have known you were working with objects. But every time you create an instance of a MovieClip or Button symbol, and anytime you draw a dynamic or input text field, you are creating an ActionScript object. If you are new to ActionScript, you might not have actually controlled these objects with code yet. Perhaps you have animated these objects using tweens, and maybe you have added masks at authoring time. But these same things and more can be achieved using ActionScript with MovieClip, Button, and TextField objects.

The fact that ActionScript has objects that are represented visually makes it unique as a programming language. In fact, this is largely to your advantage. In the face-to-face world we think of objects as *things* — things we can see. But in most programming languages an object is difficult to grasp as a concept because you cannot typically see the object. In ActionScript, however, you can actually see MovieClip, Button, and TextField objects. This makes ActionScript an ideal language for learning object-oriented concepts.

If you recall for a moment what you've learned about objects so far in this book, you can see that those concepts apply to MovieClip, Button, and TextField instances, even if you don't yet know any of the ActionScript behind these types of objects. For example, you just read that objects must be derived from a class that determines shared qualities and actions. You can see that this is true of all MovieClip instances, for example. All MovieClip instances have qualities such as their X- and Y-coordinates on stage and their dimensions. Likewise, they have shared actions such as playing and stopping the timeline. These are some of the readily visible qualities and actions of all MovieClip objects.

In this chapter we'll look at the MovieClip, Button, and TextField classes, and to a certain extent the Video class. The four aforementioned classes are what we call the *display object classes* because they are the four datatypes in ActionScript that have visible representation on the stage. While each of the classes is unique in many respects, they also have some common functionality. That common functionality is the main focus of this chapter. Additionally, in this chapter we'll look at the MovieClip and Button classes in more detail. The TextField and Video classes each have their own chapters, and therefore we'll defer detailed discussion of those topics until then.

Creating Display Objects at Authoring Time

In this chapter, you'll learn about two ways of creating display objects — at authoring time and at runtime. Some display objects can be created only at authoring time, while others can be created both at authoring time and at runtime. You're probably already familiar with the process for creating an authoring time instance of most of the display object types, whether you know it or not. For example, if you want to create a MovieClip or Button instance, all you need to do is to create a MovieClip or Button symbol and then drag an instance from the library to the stage. If you want to create a TextField object, you can select the Text tool, set the text type (using the Property inspector) to either Dynamic Text or Input Text (Static Text is not accessible to ActionScript), and draw the object on the stage.

When you create an instance of a display object at authoring time, you have the opportunity to give a name to that instance — that object. You can do so by selecting the object on stage and typing a value into the <Instance Name> field within the Property inspector (see Figure 13-1).

Figure 13-1: The <Instance Name> field in the Property inspector.

When you give an instance a name in this way, you are giving a name to the object, enabling you to reference it from within ActionScript. This is important so that you can access the properties and methods of that object to be able to affect it with ActionScript. The variable-naming rules (see Chapter 3) apply to naming display objects as well. And you should be sure that you give each instance a name that is unique within its scope. For example, if you create two MovieClip instances on the same timeline with the same name of mCircle and then try to target one of them, Flash will not know which one you are referencing.

Because every object has to have a name, even if you don't provide a name for an object, it is assigned one by Flash. Every unnamed instance has a name of instanceN where N is an integer value from 1 upward. The first unnamed object is instance1, the second is instance2, and so on. If you ever see these instance names showing up (in the Output panel or in the Debugger panel, for example), you will know that you have neglected to name an instance somewhere.

Addressing Display Objects

To begin with, let's look at the simplest example of how to *address*, or *target*, a display object. If you have created an instance during authoring time, you can address that instance using ActionScript on the same timeline by simply using the instance name. You can then use dot syntax with the instance just as you would with any other type of object. For example, if you have created a MovieClip instance named mCircle on the first frame of the main timeline, you can add the following code to tell the instance to play back its own timeline:

```
mCircle.play();
```

So, if you need to reference a display object from the same timeline on which it has been created this is all you need to know. However, there are other situations that often arise in which you will want to be able to target a display object from another timeline. Let's take a look at some of those situations and what ActionScript to employ.

Targeting Nested Instances

Display objects can be nested within other `MovieClip` objects. An example of this kind of nesting of objects would be a `MovieClip` symbol of a car within which are four instances of a wheel `MovieClip` symbol. Let's say that the wheels are given instance names of `mWheel1`, `mWheel2`, `mWheel3`, and `mWheel4` within the car symbol. You then might create an instance of the car symbol on the main timeline and name the instance `mCar`. At this point, you would have a single `MovieClip` object on the main timeline, but within that single instance would be four nested objects — the wheels. In order to create the animation effect of the car starting and stopping, you would surely want to also instruct the nested wheel instances to start and stop at the appropriate times. So, you then need a way to target the wheel instances from the main timeline. Nested instances are treated by Flash as properties of the parent instance. Therefore, to access the nested instances, you need merely use the following syntax:

```
parentMovieClip.nestedInstance.methodOrProperty
```

The following code shows how you could target the wheel instances within the car object and instruct them to play their respective timelines. The `play()` method is a `MovieClip` method that tells the targeted object to play its own timeline.

```
mCar.mWheel1.play();
mCar.mWheel2.play();
mCar.mWheel3.play();
mCar.mWheel4.play();
```

You can extend this knowledge to objects nested within nested objects. Take a look at another example to illustrate this. In this example, assume that you've created a `MovieClip` on the main timeline, and you've named the instance `mStore`, and within `mStore` there are nested objects, among which is an instance named `mShelf1`. Also within `mShelf1` are nested objects, among which is `mProduct1`. If you want to then target `mProduct1` from the main timeline, and instruct Flash to move it so that its x coordinate is 100, you could use the following code:

```
mStore.mShelf1.mProduct1._x = 100;
```

For reasons you will read about in a moment, you should not try to nest display objects within other `Button` or `TextField` instances if you want to target them with ActionScript. However, you *can* nest `Button` and `TextField` instances within `MovieClip` objects just as you would nest `MovieClip` objects within `MovieClip` objects. And you can target a nested `Button` or `TextField` instance in the same way. For example, the following code positions a `Button` instance named `btHorn` within its parent `MovieClip`, `mCar`.

```
mCar.btHorn._x = 25;
```

Working with Absolute Addressing

Every Flash movie has a main `MovieClip` object whose existence is inherent in the Flash movie; it cannot be added or removed. This is simply because it is the necessary *root* of all the content of a movie. As a result, all other `MovieClip` objects within a Flash movie are properties of the main `MovieClip` object. The main `MovieClip` object is sometimes called the main timeline, and it has a specific identifier by which it can be referenced in ActionScript: _root.

The _root reference is a global property that addresses the main `MovieClip` object from any timeline, thereby enabling you to reference an absolute target. For this reason, targeting a `MovieClip` using _root is called *absolute addressing*.

Using absolute addressing, you always target a `MovieClip` using a top-down approach. For example, if the main timeline contains a `MovieClip` object named mA, which in turn contains a `MovieClip` object named mB, this means mB can be addressed from any other timeline in the same movie as:

```
_root.mA.mB;
```

Although it may be tempting to do otherwise, it's best to use the _root reference sparingly, if at all. When one movie is loaded into another (you'll see how to do this in Chapter 14), the _root reference can change. It always has to reference the main timeline — and there can be only one actual main timeline. If a movie is loaded into another, the loaded movie's main timeline can become a nested instance of the loader movie. For this reason, it's best to give preference to relative addressing, the next subject you are going to examine.

Working with Relative Addressing

Although we didn't call it such, the addressing we examined using the car and wheel example was *relative addressing*. No absolute reference was used, but instead the addressing was always relative to the timeline from which the code was being issued. For example, if the main timeline contains a `MovieClip` object named mCar, you can issue the following command successfully from the main timeline:

```
mCar.play();
```

But if you issue that same command from within another timeline, it will not work. Why? Because Flash is looking for a `MovieClip` instance with that name relative to the timeline in which the code is placed.

Using relative addressing is often a good idea when you want to target a `MovieClip` object whose location is known relative to the timeline on which the code is given. This is useful for creating modular pieces within your Flash movie. Relative addressing enables you, for instance, to create a `MovieClip` symbol containing nested `MovieClip` objects and code to instruct those nested objects. They can then be placed anywhere in the path hierarchy of your Flash movie and still operate as expected. Relative addressing is useful, therefore, for creating a sort of timeline independent of code.

You have seen how to target nested `MovieClip` objects from within a parent `MovieClip` object. The example with the car and nested wheels demonstrates how objects nested within another `MovieClip` can be addressed relatively. But it is also useful for an object to be able to address both itself and its own parent (if any) `MovieClip` in a relative fashion.

First, let's look at how a `MovieClip` can address itself. You've actually already seen how to do this back in Chapter 5 when you were learning about objects. Remember that a `MovieClip` is an object, so all the things that applied to objects in general are going to apply to `MovieClip` instances as well. Therefore, using the this keyword, you can tell a `MovieClip` instance to address itself. Why would you want to have a MovieClip address itself, you ask? The most common case for this is within a method definition such as an event-handler method. For example, you might want a `MovieClip` instance to begin playing back its own timeline when the user clicks it. The following is the code that tells an instance `mCar` to play its own timeline when the user clicks it:

```
mCar.onPress = function():Void {
  this.play();
};
```

In the same situation you can use the `this` keyword to tell a `MovieClip` where to start looking for nested instances. For example, if you want to not only tell the `mCar` instance to play its own timeline when clicked, but also the timelines of the nested wheel `MovieClip` objects, you need to use the `this` keyword to tell Flash that the nested instances are located within the `mCar` object.

```
mCar.onPress = function():Void {
  this.play();
  this.mWheel1.play();
  this.mWheel2.play();
  this.mWheel3.play();
  this.mWheel4.play();
};
```

If you neglect to include the `this` keyword in the preceding examples it will not work as expected. Flash does not assume `this` if you don't include it.

Next, look at how a `MovieClip` can address its container. Each `MovieClip` has a built-in property named `_parent` that is a reference to its container `MovieClip`. Because `_parent` is a property of the object, remember to use the `this` keyword first to tell Flash which object's `_parent` property you are referencing. Here is an example in which when a `MovieClip` instance is clicked, it tells its parent `MovieClip` object's timeline to play.

```
mCircle.onPress = function():Void {
  this._parent.play();
};
```

MovieClip objects can act as containers, which is not the case for other sorts of display objects. Therefore, while you can reference nested objects within MovieClip instances, you cannot do that using other display objects such as Button instances. However, every display object type can be placed within a container, and therefore every display object has a `_parent` property that references the container. For example, assuming that `btPlay` is a Button instance, the following tells the container object to play.

```
btPlay.onPress = function():Void {
  this._parent.play();
};
```

Accessing Nested Instances with Array-Access Notation

As you may recall from the discussion in Chapter 5, objects can be treated like associative arrays in ActionScript. This fact creates some important possibilities when targeting nested display objects.

Because nested display objects are treated by Flash as properties of the container object, that means that in addition to using standard dot syntax, you can also use array-access notation. For example, the following two lines are equivalent:

```
mCar.mWheel1.play();
mCar["mWheel1"].play();
```

You may be wondering why you would ever want to use array-access notation to address nested instances. Array-access notation is preferable in some scenarios because it enables you to dynamically evaluate the nested instance name. For example, for various reasons you may not want to hardcode the actual nested instance name into the code. Instead, you might want to use a variable whose value is determined by user input. The problem is that using dot syntax Flash doesn't have any way of knowing you want it to try and evaluate a variable. Instead, it will think you are trying to target an instance with that variable name.

```
var sInstance:String = "mWheel1";
mCar.sInstance.play();    // Incorrect
```

The preceding example tells Flash to try to find a nested instance named sInstance, not mWheel1. But if you use array-access notation, Flash first evaluates the expression in the array-access operator (the square brackets).

```
var sInstance:String = "mWheel1";
mCar[sInstance].play();
```

Another very good use of array-access notation is when you have a group of sequentially named nested instances that you want to target. In the previous example, mCar had four sequentially named nested instances: mWheel1 through mWheel4. You can use a for statement to target all the nested instances:

```
for(var i:Number = 1; i <= 4; i++) {
  mCar["mWheel" + i].play();
}
```

Of course, in the preceding example there are only four nested instances, so the benefit might appear minimal. However, there is a substantial benefit when there are many nested instances or when the number of nested instances is dynamic and, therefore, unknown to you.

Handling Events

Chapter 2 discussed the basic event model that ActionScript uses. Recall that events can occur within Flash movies. These events can be things such as the playhead entering a frame, a user clicking the mouse, or an object getting keyboard focus, to list just a few. When these events occur, Flash automatically looks for and invokes special event-handler methods. These event-handler methods are left undefined by default. Therefore, you can define these event-handler methods for MovieClip, Button, and TextField instances (Video objects don't handle any events) to tell Flash which actions to call when an event occurs. Each event-handler method corresponds to a particular event. For example, the onPress() event-handler method for MovieClip and Button objects is called only when the press event occurs (when the user clicks the mouse on the instance) for a particular object. Let's take a closer look at the event-handler methods for display objects.

Handling Button Events

Both `Button` and `MovieClip` instances are capable of handling button events. Therefore, all the event-handler methods described in the following sections apply both to `MovieClip` and `Button` instances.

✦ **onPress, onRelease, and onReleaseOutside** — Probably the most commonly used event-handler methods are the `onPress()`, `onRelease()`, and possibly `onReleaseOutside()` methods. These methods enable basic button functionality for a `Button` or `MovieClip` instance. The `onPress()` method is invoked when the user clicks the instance. The `onRelease()` method is invoked when the user releases the mouse click while the cursor is still over the instance. And the `onReleaseOutside()` method is invoked when the user has clicked the instance, but then releases the mouse click after having dragged the mouse cursor off the instance.

Often, the `onPress()` or `onRelease()` methods are used on their own. In such cases, which you use depends entirely on whether you want the action to occur as the user first clicks the instance or after he or she releases the click. On the other hand, sometimes both methods are used in conjunction with one another. For example, when creating draggable `MovieClip` instances (discussed in Chapter 14), you want the instance to start dragging when the user first clicks it, but you want the instance to stop dragging once the user releases the click.

✦ **onRollOver and onRollOut** — The `onRollOver()` and `onRollOut()` methods are invoked when the user mouses over and mouses out of an instance, respectively. These methods are, quite obviously, helpful for creating rollover effects.

✦ **onDragOver and onDragOut** — The `onDragOver()` method is invoked when the user clicks a `Button` or `MovieClip` instance, drags the mouse off the instance while still holding the click, and then drags the mouse back over the instance. The `onDragOut()` method is invoked when the user clicks an instance and then drags the mouse cursor out of the instance. Be careful with these methods because they will not work if another instance has focus. For example, you cannot detect a drag over if you are simultaneously dragging another `MovieClip`. In such cases, you may find it better to use the `hitTest()` method, described in the section "Checking for Overlapping" in Chapter 14.

Handling MovieClip Events

The former group of event-handler methods is applicable to both `MovieClip` and `Button` instances. This second group of methods, however, can be applied only to `MovieClip` instances. Take a look at what these methods are, and what events they handle.

✦ **onUnload** — The `onUnload()` method is automatically invoked when a `MovieClip` instance is removed from the stage with a `removeMovieClip()` method (discussed in Chapter 14). This method can be useful for handling any kind of actions you want to occur when a `MovieClip` has been removed. For example, you may want to automatically load another instance, move to another screen, alert the user, and so on.

✦ **onEnterFrame** — The `onEnterFrame()` method is invoked at the same frequency of the movie's frame rate, regardless of whether the playhead is moving. The `onEnterFrame()` method can be a way to create animation effects and continual monitoring within a movie. However, this technique is somewhat limited by the fact that it works at the frame rate. Therefore, you may find that the onEnterFrame() method gets called too frequently or too infrequently for your particular application. Instead, this example gives preference to interval functions and methods as discussed in Chapters 4 and 5. Using interval functions and methods enables you to set the frequency at which they are called — be it once an hour or once every 10 milliseconds.

✦ **onMouseDown and onMouseUp** — The onMouseDown() and onMouseUp() events occur when the mouse button is pressed and released, respectively. Unlike onPress() and onRelease(), the onMouseDown() and onMouseUp() event handlers are called when the mouse button is pressed and release regardless of where the mouse is in relation to the movie clip. Frequently, the events are better handled by a Mouse class listener as discussed in Chapter 21. However, it's perfectly acceptable to handle the events with the onMouseDown() and onMouseUp() methods assigned to a movie clip.

✦ **onMouseMove** — The onMouseMove() method is called every time the mouse moves. Like onMouseDown() and onMouseUp(), the onMouseMove() method responds to the mouse regardless of where it is in relation to the movie clip. Also like those methods, mouse movements are often better handled by a Mouse class listener, but that doesn't mean it's incorrect or inappropriate to use the event-handler method for a movie clip.

✦ **onKeyDown and onKeyUp** — The onKeyDown() and onKeyUp() methods are called when a key is pressed and released. Key presses are better handled by Key class listeners discussed in Chapter 21.

Focus Events

MovieClip, Button, and TextField instances are each capable of handling focus events. Focus events occur when keyboard focus moves to or from an object. When an instance receives focus within the movie, the onSetFocus() method is invoked for that object. Likewise, when the instance loses focus, the onKillFocus() method is invoked. Focus events are discussed in more detail in Chapter 19.

Using MovieClip Objects as Buttons

As you've already seen, MovieClip objects are capable of handling all the same events as Button objects. And, because MovieClip objects provide much more robust functionality coupled with the fact that MovieClip objects can contain addressable, nested instances, in many cases MovieClip objects are preferable to Button objects when working with ActionScript.

Although MovieClip objects are often preferable to Button objects, this is not to say that you can never use Button objects. The key is to understand what the limitations of Button objects are, and to learn to discern when to use a MovieClip instead. By and large, if you are creating simple applications and if you want to utilize the button states that are inherent to Button instances (up, over, down), Button objects may be a good option. The problem occurs when you want to start creating more dynamic, complex applications. When you want to add instances to the stage at runtime, remove instances programmatically, or programmatically change the artwork or label of a button, a `MovieClip` instance will work when a `Button` instance cannot.

The single drawback to using `MovieClip` objects instead of `Button` objects is that unlike `Button` instances they don't have built-in button states. For example, if you define the up, over, and down states for a `Button` symbol, the instances of that symbol will automatically respond to those states during runtime, whereas MovieClip instances don't have that default behavior. However, with just a little extra effort it is possible to create up, over, and down states for a `MovieClip` object as well. You can achieve this by creating keyframes within the `MovieClip` symbol's timeline with frame labels of _up, _over, and _down, respectively. Once the `MovieClip` object is set to handle a button event, Flash automatically looks for these frame labels when the states are triggered. If the labels are found, Flash automatically goes to and stops on those frames. In addition, however, you should also place a `stop()` action on the first frame of the `MovieClip` symbol's timeline. Otherwise, the timeline will continue to play until a button event occurs.

You can also specify a hit area for a `MovieClip` object that is acting like a `Button`. All `MovieClip` objects have a `hitArea` property. If the `hitArea` property is undefined, the hit area of the `MovieClip` object is the object itself. But by assigning a reference to another `MovieClip` object to the property, the referenced object becomes the hit area instead. For example, you could make a `MovieClip` object called `mHitArea` the hit area of a `MovieClip` called `mCircle` with the following assignment statement:

```
mCircle.hitArea = mHitArea;
```

The referenced object can overlap the `Button`-like `MovieClip`, but it does not have to. Having the referenced object (the hit area object) in another part of the stage can be really useful for creating complex rollover effects, for instance. And the referenced object does not even need to be visible for the hit area to be active.

Practicing Targeting

In this exercise, you are going to get to practice what you've learned so far in this chapter. You'll create a new Flash application that contains artwork of a cartoon person as well as his coat, hat, glasses, beard, shoes, and cane. You will add ActionScript code that enables the user to click the various accessories, and toggle them as either visible or not.

1. For this exercise, there's a starter FLA file on the Web site. This file contains the artwork for the application. Open `person_starter.fla` from the web site. Save it to your local disk as `person001.fla`.

2. On the stage, you should see an instance of the Man `MovieClip` symbol. Select this object, and give it an instance name of `mMan`.

3. Edit the Man `MovieClip` symbol. Within this symbol you will find that there are multiple layers, each containing its own `MovieClip` instance. None of the instances have yet been named. You should give each a name. The objects should be named `mHat`, `mGlasses`, `mBeard`, `mCoat`, `mShoes`, `mCane`, and `mBody`.

4. Return to the main timeline, and add the following code to the first frame of the Actions layer:

```
setHandlers();

function setHandlers():Void {

  // Loop through all the nested MovieClip objects in
  // mMan.
  for(var sInstance:String in mMan) {

    // If the MovieClip is mBody, skip it.
    if(sInstance == "mBody") {
      continue;
    }


    // When the user clicks on the accessory, toggle
    // the transparency between 100 and 0.
    mMan[sInstance].onRelease = function():Void {
      this._alpha = (this._alpha == 100) ? 0 : 100;
    };
  }
}
```

5. Save and test the movie.

When you test the movie, you should be able to click each of the accessories and have them disappear and reappear. Let's take a closer look at the code to make sure everything is clear.

First, you define a function so that you can encapsulate some of the code. Within the function you use a for...in statement to loop through all the nested MovieClip objects within the mMan instance. Remember, you named all those nested instances — mHat, mGlasses, and so on. Although you could specify the same code for each nested instance one at a time, a for...in statement is more efficient in this case.

```
for(var sInstance:String in mMan) {
```

Within the for...in statement, the first thing you want to do is check to see whether the name of the current nested MovieClip is mBody. If so, you use a continue statement to skip to the next instance because you don't want to make mBody clickable.

```
if(sInstance == "mBody") {
  continue;
}
```

Within the onRelease() event-handler method, you want to toggle the value of _alpha between 100 and 0 with each click. If _alpha is 100 then set it to 0, and if it's 0 then set it to 100.

```
this._alpha = (this._alpha == 100) ? 0 : 100;
```

Working with Appearance Properties

Display objects share a common set of properties that afford you the ability to read and programmatically alter the appearance of the instances. Table 13-1 lists these appearance properties.

Table 13-1: Appearance Properties

Property	Description
_x	X-coordinate within parent `MovieClip`
_y	Y-coordinate within parent `MovieClip`
_width	Width of object in pixels
_height	Height of object in pixels
_xscale	Scale of the object in the X direction, in percentage
_yscale	Scale of the object in the Y direction, in percentage
_alpha	Transparency of the object
_visible	Can be set to make the object either visible or invisible
_rotation	Rotation of the object in degrees
_xmouse	X-coordinate of the mouse within the object's coordinate space
_ymouse	Y-coordinate of the mouse within the object's coordinate space

The next section takes a closer look at each of the appearance properties and explains how you can work with these properties in your own applications.

Working with Coordinates

The stage of a Flash movie is measured in pixels from the upper-left corner, and each `MovieClip` or `Button` symbol's internal coordinates are measured from the center point of the symbol's own canvas. Of course, the artwork within a `MovieClip` or `Button` instance may not be placed such that the center aligns with the center of the canvas. `TextField` and `Video` objects also have internal coordinates, but the contents of a `TextField` or `Video` object are always placed such that the internal 0,0 point is at the upper left of the object. Every display object within any container has X- and Y-coordinate values relative to their own. If an object is on the main timeline with coordinates of 0,0, it will appear so that its internal 0,0 point is at the upper-left corner of the stage.

Display objects have two properties that tell about their own location within its container's coordinate space. The properties are _x and _y — the X- and Y-coordinates, respectively. You can read or write these properties using dot syntax. Here is an example in which the coordinates of a `MovieClip` instance, `mCircle`, are displayed in the Output panel.

```
trace(mCircle._x);
trace(mCircle._y);
```

Not only can you read the values from these properties, but you can also set the values. This enables you to programmatically place the instances on the stage. Also, when combined with an interval function, for example, it allows you to create animation effects. Here is an example in which an instance named mCircle is placed at 0,0 within its parent's coordinate space.

```
mCircle._x = 0;
mCircle._y = 0;
```

This technique works well for moving graphical objects to absolute locations, and it can be very handy for initializing a movie with objects in set places. But sometimes, you want to move an object relative to its current location. You can also combine the reading and writing of these properties to move graphical objects in this relative fashion:

```
mCircle._x = mCircle._x + 1;
mCircle._y = mCircle._y + 1;
```

Or, of course, you can use a compound operator to write the same thing in shorthand:

```
mCircle._x += 1;
mCircle._y += 1;
```

Or even the following:

```
mCircle._x++;
mCircle._y++;
```

You can also use an interval function or method to continually update the X- and Y-coordinates of an object. Here is an example:

```
function animate():Void {
  mCircle._x++;
  mCircle._y++;
  updateAfterEvent();
}

// Next, set an interval at which Flash should call the
// function.
var nAnimateInterval:Number = setInterval(animate, 50);
```

You can even read and write the _x and _y properties of the _root object. Although you cannot use this to move the Flash Player around, you can change the _root MovieClip object's position within the player. By default, _root is located with 0,0 at the upper-left corner of the stage. However, you can move _root's position within the player in order to move the entire contents of your movie.

Working with Dimensions

Every display object has a height and a width, measured in pixels. And every display object has properties, _height and _width, which allow you to read and write these values. Just like _x and _y, you can set the height and width of an object to absolute values:

```
mCircle._height = 10;
mCircle._width = 20;
```

And you can also assign these values relative to the current height and width:

```
mCircle._height *= 2;
mCircle._width *= 2;
```

Display objects can be be scaled in both the X and Y directions using the _xscale and _yscale properties. These values are given in percentages. Setting a graphical object's _xscale property to 50, for example, would result in the object appearing to be squished to half its original width:

```
mCircle._xscale = 50;
```

If you want to scale an object while maintaining the original aspect ratio, you should be sure to set the _xscale and _yscale properties to the same value. Otherwise, the object will appear to be squished. Also, to reset an object to the original size after having scaled it, simply set the _xscale and _yscale properties back to 100.

The _root object, like all MovieClip objects, also enables you to work the _height, _width, _xscale, and _yscale properties. You can get and set these properties for _root just as with any other object. But remember, you will be able to set the properties only of the _root object, not the player itself. Setting the properties of _root will change the dimensions of the main MovieClip object within the player, just as with any other MovieClip object. Because _root happens to contain all other objects within a movie, however, setting these properties can be an effective way to scale or alter the dimensions of the entire movie.

When you set any of the dimensions properties of a display object, that object is scaled uniformly. For example, Figure 13-2 shows a rectangle with rounded corners and stars in each corner.

Figure 13-2: A rectangle with rounded corners and stars in the corners.

Figure 13-3 shows the rectangle (a movie clip) scaled uniformly. Notice that the corners appear squished.

Figure 13-3: A uniformly scaled rectangle.

New to Flash 8 it is possible to use the scale9Grid property to specify that a movie clip object ought to scale nonuniformly. Figure 13-4 shows the same rectangle scaled with scale9Grid settings applied.

Figure 13-4: A scale9Grid scaled rectangle.

The scale9Grid property expects a value of type flash.geom.Rectangle. The Rectangle class lets you define a rectangular region that scales uniformly. Figure 13-5 shows how scale9Grid works. Notice that rectangular region defined in the inner part of the rectangle can scale uniformly without causing the movie clip to appear squished or stretched. That also indirectly defines eight additional regions — four corners and regions to the right, top, left, and bottom. The corners do not scale, the right and left regions scale only in the Y direction, and the regions on the top and bottom only scale in the X direction.

Figure 13-5: An illustration of the scale9Grid regions.

The `Rectangle` constructor expects four parameters — the X-coordinate of the upper-left corner, the Y-coordinate of the upper-left corner, the width of the rectangle, and the height of the rectangle. The following code defines a `Rectangle` that has the upper-left corner at 100,100, and it is 50 x 200.

```
import flash.geom.Rectangle;

var rctRegion:Rectangle = new Rectangle(100, 100, 50, 200);
```

To better understand `scale9Grid`, complete the following short exercise.

1. Open `scale9Grid_starter.fla` from the Web site, and save it as `scale9Grid.fla` to your local disk.

2. Note that a movie clip instance is already placed on the stage. It has an instance name of `mShape`. Within the movie clip is a rectangle with rounded corners. The rounded corners have radii of 20 pixels. Each corner also has a star drawn within it.

3. Select the first keyframe of the Actions layer, and add the following code:

```
function onMouseMove():Void {
  mShape._xscale = _xmouse / 550 * 500;
  mShape._yscale = _ymouse / 400 * 500;
}
```

4. Test the movie. Notice that when you move the mouse, the rectangle scales uniformly.

5. Edit the code on the Actions layer as follows. Changes are bolded.

```
import flash.geom.Rectangle;

// Define the scale9Grid with a rectangle that has the upper
// right corner at 20,20 and has a width and height that are 40
// pixels less than the width and height of the movie clip.
mShape.scale9Grid = new Rectangle(20, 20, mShape._width - 40,
mShape._height - 40);

function onMouseMove():Void {
  mShape._xscale = _xmouse / 550 * 500;
  mShape._yscale = _ymouse / 400 * 500;
}
```

6. Test the movie. This time note how the movie clip scales.

Working with Transparency and Visibility

Display objects in ActionScript can have different levels of transparency—from 0 (completely transparent) to 100 (completely opaque). Each object has a property called _alpha, which contains a value from 0 to 100 to describe the transparency of the object. You can set the property of the object in an absolute fashion:

```
mCircle._alpha = 50;
```

And you can set the value in a relative fashion:

```
mCircle._alpha--;
```

Setting the _alpha property in this relative manner allows you to create programmatic fade-ins and fade-outs for your animations:

```
function fadeOut(mClip:MovieClip):Void {
  if(mClip._alpha > 0){
    mClip._alpha--;
    updateAfterEvent();
  }
  else {
    clearInterval(nFadeInterval);
  }
};
var nFadeInterval:Number = setInterval(fadeOut, 100, mCircle);
```

Note   Be careful when working with the _alpha property because its values can range below 0 and beyond 100. But obviously, the display of the property cannot exceed 0 percent (completely transparent) or 100 percent (completely opaque). That means that if you increment or decrement beyond these values, you might not see any visible differences, but the value of the property can still be getting larger or smaller. It is good to impose limits through conditional statements:

```
if (mCircle._alpha > 0 && mCircle._alpha < 100)
```

Related to the _alpha property, yet with important differences, is the _visible property of graphical objects. The _visible property has two possible values: false (for not visible) and true (visible).

At first glance, the differences between setting _alpha to 0 and _visible to false might not be clear (no pun intended.) But the subtle difference is an important one. If a graphical object has event handlers for Button events, the Button events will remain active, even when the _alpha property is set to 0. However, when _visible is set to false, the Button events are no longer active. As you can see, both properties can be very advantageous over the other in different situations.

You can set the _alpha and _visible property values for _root, as well as any other MovieClip object. Doing so to _root has the effect of changing the transparency or visibility of the entire movie.

Note   Text fields must have the font embedded for the _alpha property to work properly. With device fonts setting the _alpha property to anything less than 100 will cause the text to disappear.

Note Flash Player works with alpha values using a range of 0 to 255, but the _alpha property ranges from 0 to 100. If you notice that incrementing or decrementing _alpha is causing some unexpected values, try incrementing or decrementing a variable, and assigning the vale of that variable to _alpha instead.

```
var nAlpha:Number = 0;
var nInterval:Number = setInterval(updateAlpha, 100);

function updateAlpha():Void {
nAlpha++;
mClip._alpha = nAlpha;
if(nAlpha == 100) {
  clearInterval(nInterval);
}
}
```

Working with Rotation

By default, a graphical object is rotated 0 degrees, unless otherwise specified by the author. But by setting the value of the _rotation property of your graphical object, you can spin the object by degrees. Positive values are in the clockwise direction, whereas negative values are in the counterclockwise direction. The range of values for _rotation is from -180 to 180. However, you can assign values outside of that range, and Flash will automatically convert them to something within the range. You could, for example, set the _rotation property to a value of 720, and the graphical object would appear just as if the _rotation was set to 0 (because 720 is twice 360, meaning two full rotations). This is useful for continual incrementing or decrementing of the _rotation property of an object because you do not have to concern yourself with remaining within a specific range of values, as you might with the _alpha property.

You can set the _rotation property of a graphical object, just as you did with many other properties — both in an absolute:

```
mCircle._rotation = 45;
```

or a relative manner:

```
mCircle._rotation++;
```

You can also set the _rotation property for _root. Remember, doing so simply alters the _root MovieClip object's orientation within the player.

Note Text fields must have fonts embedded for the _rotation property to work. Otherwise, setting the _rotation property of a text field with device fonts causes the text to disappear.

Working with Mouse Coordinates

The _xmouse and _ymouse properties (both read-only) of display objects return the X- and Y-coordinates of the mouse cursor within that object's internal coordinate space. Remember that because every object has its own coordinate space, the _xmouse and _ymouse properties of any two objects may not necessarily be equal. In fact, they will be equal only if the two objects happen to have their registration points aligned. As you'll see later on, the _xmouse and _ymouse properties can be very helpful when creating advanced rollover effects.

Working with Self-Describing Properties

Display objects are able to describe certain things about themselves such as their name, location, and origin with the _name, _target, and _url properties. Each of the four display object types have _name properties. However, the Video class does not define _target and _url properties.

The _name property returns the instance name for a display object. Using the _name property, as you'll see in examples throughout the book, is quite useful when using associative arrays with display object instance names as the keys.

The _target property is little used in recent versions of Flash. It returns the target path to the object, but in Flash 4 syntax. If you ever have a practical need to get an object's target path, a better option is to use the targetPath() function. You can pass this function a display object reference, and it returns a string indicating the target path in dot syntax.

The _url property returns a string indicating the location from which the object's contents were loaded. If the contents were loaded from a Web server then the value is in the form of an absolute URL such as http://www.flashsupport.com/test.swf. If the contents were loaded locally then the value is an absolute path to the location on the local computer. The _url property can be useful in special situations in which you want to, for example, make sure that your application can be run exclusively from a particular URL. You can achieve this by inserting a single blank keyframe before all the rest of the content in the movie and adding the following code:

```
if(this._url != "http://yourdomain/path/file.swf") {
  this.stop();
}
```

Tweening Programmatically

You can programmatically tween display objects by updating the display properties at an interval. For example, the following code moves a movie clip called mClip from left to right across the stage.

```
mClip._x = 0;
var nInterval:Number = setInterval(tweenObject, 100, mClip, "_x", 10, 550);

function tweenObject(oObject:Object, sProperty:String, nIncrement:Number,
nEndPoint:Number):Void {
  oObject[sProperty] += nIncrement;
if(oObject[sProperty] == nEndPoint) {
  clearInterval(nInterval);
}
}
```

However, using the mx.transitions.Tween class, you can simplify programmatic tweens.

Starting a New Tween

As soon as you construct a new Tween object it starts. The Tween class is in the mx.transitions package, so normally you'll want to import the class before constructing it.

```
import mx.transitions.Tween;
```

The Tween constructor accepts the following parameters. All but the last parameter are required.

✦ **Display object**—A reference to the display object to tween.

✦ **Property**—The name of the property (as a string) to tween.

✦ **Easing function**—A reference to an easing function. Read the section "Adding Easing to Programmatic Tweens" for more details. You can also use null to apply no easing.

✦ **Start value**—The start value for the tweened property.

✦ **End value**—The end value for the tweened property.

✦ **Duration**—The number of frames over which the tween is to occur. Optionally, you can specify a value in seconds. If the value is in seconds you must specify true for the next parameter.

✦ **Use seconds**—By default the tween duration is in frames. However, you can optionally specify a value of true that tells Flash to interpret the duration as seconds rather than frames. A null, undefined, or false value causes the tween to interpret the duration as frames.

The following constructs a new Tween object that causes a movie clip called mClip to move from 0 to 550 across the stage from left to right in 10 seconds.

```
var twMoveClip:Tween = new Tween(mClip, "_x", null, 0, 550, 10, true);
```

Adding Easing to Programmatic Tweens

You can specify a reference to an easing function as the second parameter to the Tween constructor to apply easing to the tween. Although you can write a custom easing function, it's much simpler to use one of the many easing functions in the classes within the mx.transitions.easing package. Within the package are the following classes—Back, Bounce, Elastic, Regular, and Strong. Each of those classes has the following static methods—easeIn(), easeOut(), easeInOut(). Additionally, the package contains the None class with the static method easeNone(), which is the equivalent to specifying null when constructing the Tween object. You can use references to any of those methods as the second parameter to the Tween constructor. The simplest way to understand the easing methods is to test them with the following exercise.

1. Open a new Flash document, and save it as tweensEasing.fla.

2. Make a new Movie Clip symbol called Circle.

3. Within Circle draw a 25 x 25 circle aligned to 0,0 (so the upper-left corner of the bounding box is aligned with 0,0).

4. Set `Circle` to Export for ActionScript in the Linkage properties. Use `Circle` as the linkage identifier.

5. On the first keyframe of the main timeline add the following code.

```
import mx.transitions.Tween;
import mx.transitions.easing.*;

// Populate aEasingMethods with each of the easing methods -
// Back.easeIn, Back.easeOut, Back.easeInOut, Bounce.easeIn,
// Bounce.easeOut, etc.
var aClasses:Array = [Back, Bounce, Elastic, Regular, Strong];
var aEasingMethods:Array = new Array();
for(var i:Number = 0; i < aClasses.length; i++) {
  aEasingMethods.push(aClasses[i].easeIn);
  aEasingMethods.push(aClasses[i].easeOut);
  aEasingMethods.push(aClasses[i].easeInOut);
}

var mClip:MovieClip;
var nDepth:Number;
var nX:Number = 20;
var oClips:Object = new Object();

// For each of the easeing methods make a new instance of Circle.
for(var i:Number = 0; i < aEasingMethods.length; i++) {
  nDepth = this.getNextHighestDepth();
  mClip = this.attachMovie("Circle", "mClip" + nDepth,
nDepth,{_x: nX, _y: 50});

  // Set nX so the next circle is to the right of the current
  // circle.
  nX += mClip._width + 5;

  // Add a new element to oClips using the circle movie clip
  // instance name as the key and the easing method as the value.
  oClips[mClip._name] = aEasingMethods[i];

  // When the user clicks on the circle start a new tween of _y.
  // Use the easing method reference stored in oClips for the
  // movie clip that is clicked.
  mClip.onPress = function():Void {
    var twMove:Tween =  new Tween(this, "_y",
oClips[this._name], 50, 350, 2, true);
  };
}
```

6. Test the movie. Click on each circle one at a time, and you'll see the effects of each easing type.

Pausing and Resuming Tweens

You can pause and resume tweens with the stop() and resume() methods, respectively. The following exercise illustrates the stop() and resume() methods.

1. Open tweensEasing.fla, and save it as tweensPause.fla.

2. Edit the code on the first frame as follows. Changes are bolded.

```
import mx.transitions.Tween;
import mx.transitions.easing.*;

var aClasses:Array = [Back, Bounce, Elastic, Regular, Strong];
var aEasingMethods:Array = new Array();
for(var i:Number = 0; i < aClasses.length; i++) {
  aEasingMethods.push(aClasses[i].easeIn);
  aEasingMethods.push(aClasses[i].easeOut);
  aEasingMethods.push(aClasses[i].easeInOut);
}

var mClip:MovieClip;
var nDepth:Number;
var nX:Number = 20;
var oClips:Object = new Object();

// Use a variable to keep track of the current Tween.
var twCurrent:Tween;

for(var i:Number = 0; i < aEasingMethods.length; i++) {
  nDepth = this.getNextHighestDepth();
  mClip = this.attachMovie("Circle", "mClip" + nDepth,
nDepth, {_x: nX, _y: 50});
  nX += mClip._width + 5;
  oClips[mClip._name] = aEasingMethods[i];
  mClip.onPress = function():Void {
    var twMove:Tween =  new Tween(this, "_y",
oClips[this._name], 50, 350, 2, true);

    // Set the current tween to twMove. Also set bPaused to false
    // since the tween is obviously running.
    twCurrent = twMove;
    bPaused = false;
  };
}

// Keep track of whether the tween is paused or not.
var bPaused:Boolean;

// When the user clicks the mouse toggle the playback of the
// current tween.
function onMouseDown():Void {
  if(bPaused) {
```

```
    twCurrent.resume();
  }
  else {
    twCurrent.stop();
  }
  bPaused = !bPaused;
}
```

Additional Methods for Tween Objects

In addition to the stop() and resume() methods, Tween objects define the following methods.

✦ **continueTo(end point, duration)** — Tells the tween to use a new end point and duration.

✦ **fforward( )** — Tells the tween to jump to the end point.

✦ **rewind( )** — Tells the tween to jump to the starting point.

✦ **nextFrame( )** — Tells the tween to go to the next point.

✦ **prevFrame( )** — Tells the tween to go to the previous point.

✦ **start( )** — Tells the tween to start again from the beginning.

✦ **yoyo( )** — Tells the tween to reverse the direction and run again.

Adding Listeners to Tween Objects

Tween objects dispatch events, and you can register listener objects to handle those events. A listener object can have any of the following methods defined.

✦ **onMotionChanged( )** — Each time the tween updates the property value, the onMotionChanged() method of a listener object is called. The method is useful if you want to update additional properties, for example.

✦ **onMotionFinished( )** — When the tween reaches the end point, it calls the onMotionFinished() method on the listener objects.

✦ **onMotionStopped( )** — When the tween is stopped, listeners are notified by way of the onMotionStopped() method.

✦ **onMotionResumed( ):** When the tween is resumed, listeners are notified by way of the onMotionResumed() method.

✦ **onMotionStarted( )** — When the tween is started, listeners are notified by way of the onMotionStarted() method. The method is not called when the Tween object is constructed. It is called when the start() or yoyo() methods are called.

Listener object methods are passed the Tween object as a parameter

You can add a listener object using the addListener() method. The method expects one parameter — the reference to the listener object.

The following exercise uses a listener object to cause the tweens to yo-yo continuously.

1. Open tweensEasing.fla, and save it as tweensListeners.fla. (Note that tweensEasing.fla is the document from two exercises ago.)

2. Edit the code on frame 1 as follows. Changes are bolded.

```
import mx.transitions.Tween;
import mx.transitions.easing.*;

var aClasses:Array = [Back, Bounce, Elastic, Regular, Strong];
var aEasingMethods:Array = new Array();
for(var i:Number = 0; i < aClasses.length; i++) {
  aEasingMethods.push(aClasses[i].easeIn);
  aEasingMethods.push(aClasses[i].easeOut);
  aEasingMethods.push(aClasses[i].easeInOut);
}


var mClip:MovieClip;
var nDepth:Number;
var nX:Number = 20;
var oClips:Object = new Object();

// Each time the onMotionFinished() method is called, restart the
// tween in the reverse direction.
var oListener:Object = new Object();
oListener.onMotionFinished = function(twObject:Tween):Void {
  twObject.yoyo();
};

for(var i:Number = 0; i < aEasingMethods.length; i++) {
  nDepth = this.getNextHighestDepth();
  mClip = this.attachMovie("Circle", "mClip" + nDepth,
nDepth, {_x: nX, _y: 50});
  nX += mClip._width + 5;
  oClips[mClip._name] = aEasingMethods[i];
  mClip.onPress = function():Void {
    var twMove:Tween =  new Tween(this, "_y",
oClips[this._name], 50, 350, 2, true);

    // Add the listener object.
    twMove.addListener(oListener);
  };
}
```

Enabling Button-Like Behavior

The default setting for all MovieClip and Button objects is that they are enabled to handle button events. Therefore, if you define an event-handler method for the object, when the corresponding event occurs, the method will be invoked. However, there are times when you might want to temporarily disable the object from handling button events. For example, you may want to disable a submit button for a form until all the required fields have been filled.

You can set the `enabled` property of any `MovieClip` or `Button` object to either `true` or `false`. The default setting is `true`. If you set the property to `false`, the object is temporarily disabled from handling button events.

```
mCircle.enabled = false;  // Temporarily disable.
```

You can set the `enabled` property of a MovieClip or Button object at anytime, and you can switch back and forth between `true` and `false`. You might opt to do this at specific points in a movie to disable a `Button` or a `MovieClip` when you don't want the user to be able to interact. For example, you may have a `Button` that, when clicked, attempts to load another movie into the player by way of a `MovieClipLoader` object (see Chapter 14 for more details). However, once the user has clicked the `Button`, you may want to disable the `Button` until the movie has been successfully loaded.

Another button-like behavior for `MovieClip` and `Button` objects is the automatic changing of the cursor icon when the user mouses over the object. When the user mouses over any enabled object with button event-handler methods applied to it, the cursor icon becomes a hand icon. This default behavior is expected in most situations. However, you may want to modify this behavior in some circumstances. You can disable the hand cursor by setting the `useHandCuror` property to `false`. If you later want to re-enable the hand cursor, all you need to do is set the `useHandCursor` property to `true` again.

```
mCircle.useHandCursor = false;  // Turn off hand cursor.
```

Tab-Switching, Focus, and Menus

The Tab key allows a user to switch focus between display objects of a movie. `Button`, `MovieClip`, and `TextField` objects are all tab-switchable. By default, all `Button` objects, input `TextField` objects, and `MovieClip` objects handling `Button` events are enabled for tab-switching; and the ordering is dependent solely upon the Flash Player's own default algorithms. However, by taking advantage of the `tabEnabled` and `tabIndex` properties of the tab-switchable display objects, you can determine which objects are tab-switchable, and in what order they should be switched.

The `tabEnabled` property of graphical objects can be set to either `true` or `false`. By default, it is undefined. When the value is either `true` or undefined, the object is included in the tab-switching for the movie. However, you can set the property to `false` to remove the object from those between which the user can tab. This is useful when you have objects within the movie that you do not want to be enabled for tab-switching. For example, if you create a form in Flash, you may well want the elements of the form to be enabled for tab-switching. These might include `TextField` objects, menu `MovieClip` objects, and `Button` objects. However, you may also have other `MovieClip` objects with `Button` event handlers within the movie that are not part of the form. By default, these objects would be included in the tab-switching. But you can disable them by setting their `tabEnabled` properties to `false`.

Note   When an SWF is embedded in an HTML page, focus can shift away from Flash Player entirely. That can occur when the user presses tab after having shifted focus through each of the objects in the focus list. At that point focus moves away from Flash Player and to the web browser. You can instruct Flash to maintain focus with the `seamlessTabbing` attribute/parameter of the embed and `object` tags in HTML. Simply set the attribute/parameter to `false`.

Also, it can often be advantageous to set the order in which objects are switched. By default, the order is determined by the objects' coordinates within the movie. But this may not always be the order in which you want them to be switched. You can, therefore, set the `tabIndex` property of each object to determine the order in which it will be switched. The `tabIndex` property can be assigned any positive integer value, but it should be unique from that of any other object in the movie at that point in the timeline. If any object has a `tabIndex` property defined, all other objects are removed from the tab-switching order.

Additionally, when `Button` and `MovieClip` objects are enabled for focus and have been selected using the keyboard, by default a yellow rectangle outlines the object of focus. This is intended so that a user can see where the focus is in a movie. However, you can turn off this focus rectangle with the `_focusrect` property. There is a global `_focusrect` property that allows you to turn off focus rectangles for the entire movie, but not for individual objects.

```
_focusrect = false;
```

Additionally, you can also set this property for each graphical object individually so that some objects have focus rectangles when selected, and others do not:

```
mCircle._focusrect = false;
```

The global `_focusrect` property is set to `true` by default. Each object's `_focusrect` property has a `null` value by default. Either a `null` or a `true` value turns on the focus rectangle. Setting the property to `false` turns off the focus rectangle.

MovieClip-Specific Tab-Switching and Focus-Related Properties

`MovieClip` objects have two additional properties that deal with focus and tab-switching, which are not needed for `Button` objects. Because `Button` objects can receive focus by default, there is no need to ever specifically instruct them to be able to receive focus. `MovieClip` objects, on the other hand, are not able to receive focus in their default state. As stated in the previous section, `MovieClip` objects can receive focus when they have an attached event handler or event-handler method for `Button` events. In other words, when `MovieClip` objects act like `Button` objects, they can receive focus. Additionally, by setting the `tabIndex` property of a `MovieClip` object, it will be included in the tab-switching order, regardless of whether or not it handles `Button` events. But you can also force a `MovieClip` object to be able to receive focus by setting the `focusEnabled` property to `true`. However, just by setting the `focusEnabled` property to `true`, the `MovieClip` object will not be included in the tab-switching order. In this manner, the only way to get the object to receive focus is through the `Selection.setFocus()` method (discussed in more detail in Chapter 19):

```
mCircle.focusEnabled = true;
Selection.setFocus(mCircle);
```

When a `MovieClip` object has nested, or child, graphical objects that are tab-switching-enabled, they are automatically included in the automatic tab ordering (if no `tabIndex` properties have been set for any of the graphical objects). It may be the case, however, that you would prefer that they *not* be included in the tab order. For example, it might be that the children of a `MovieClip` are menu items for a menu `MovieClip`, and you want for the Tab key to switch between menus, but not the items of the menus. In that case, you would want to set the `tabChildren` property of the parent `MovieClip` object to `false`. The property is `undefined`, by default. If it is either `undefined` or set to `true`, the child objects of the `MovieClip` object are included in the automatic tab ordering.

Tracking Objects As Menus

In their default state, `Button` objects and `MovieClip` objects behave in the following manner: When moused over, the object registers an over state. When clicked, the object registers a down state. As long as the mouse click is maintained, the object registers a down state, even if the mouse cursor is moved off of the object and over another. And because only one object at a time can handle the mouse events, no other objects will register over states, even if the mouse cursor is moved over them, as long as another object is in a down state. Although this is a wanted behavior in many cases, it is not what you want when you work with menus. This sort of behavior is contrary to how people expect menus to behave.

Conventionally, when a menu is clicked and the mouse click is maintained, the user expects that the menu will drop down to reveal the items that can then be navigated by dragging the still-clicked mouse over the items, each item highlighting as it is moused over. When the mouse click is released, the user expects that the item the mouse was over to then be selected, the resulting operation to be performed, and the menu to close. To accommodate this kind of behavior, ActionScript includes the `trackAsMenu` property for `Button` and `MovieClip` objects. By default, the property is `false`. However, setting it to `true` for a `Button` or `MovieClip` will change that object's behavior, so that even if the mouse button is still held down and the mouse is moved over another object, the new object will receive the mouse event and register the down state instead of the first object.

Web Resource We'd like to know what you thought about this chapter. Visit `www.rightactionscript` `.com/asb/comments` to fill out an online form with your comments.

Summary

✦ Each time you drag an instance of a `MovieClip` or `Button` symbol onto your movie, you are creating a `MovieClip` or `Button` object. You should always name your instances so that you can address them with ActionScript.

✦ You can address named `MovieClip` and `Button` objects to tell them what you want them to do via ActionScript. Addresses are either absolute or relative, with preference being given to relative addresses.

✦ Handling events with `MovieClip` and `Button` objects is accomplished by defining event-handler methods.

✦ The appearance properties for `MovieClip` and `Button` objects enable you to programmatically set an object's location, dimensions, rotation, and so on.

✦   ✦   ✦

Working with Movie Clips

The MovieClip class is one of the most prominent classes in Flash 8 because it is the fundamental container display object. Even the main timeline is a movie clip. In this chapter you'll learn about using ActionScript specifically to work with MovieClip objects — from managing timeline playback to loading image and SWF content, and much more.

Affecting Timeline Playback

All `MovieClip` objects have timelines. In some cases, the timelines consist of only a single frame. But when a `MovieClip` object's timeline has multiple frames, it can be useful to affect the playback programmatically.

There are a handful of methods that enable you to affect the playback of a timeline. They are as follows:

✦ **play( )** — This method instructs the `MovieClip` object's timeline to start playback from the current frame until it is told to stop.

✦ **stop( )** — This methods instructs the `MovieClip` object's timeline to stop playback on the current frame.

✦ **gotoAndPlay( )** — This method instructs a `MovieClip` object's timeline to go to a specific frame and begin playback from that frame. The method requires a parameter that can either be the frame number or a string specifying a frame label within the timeline.

✦ **gotoAndStop( )** — This method instructs a `MovieClip` object's timeline to go to a specific frame and stop on that frame. As with `gotoAndPlay()`, this method can accept either a frame number or a frame label as the parameter.

✦ **nextFrame( )** — This method instructs a `MovieClip` object's timeline to go to and stop on the frame just following the current frame.

✦ **prevFrame( )** — This method instructs a `MovieClip` object's timeline to go to and stop on the frame just previous to the current frame.

In addition to the methods just described, there are two properties that report information about a `MovieClip` object's timeline. The `_currentframe` property returns the frame number of the current frame and the `_totalframes` property returns the total number of frames in a `MovieClip`. Although both of these properties are read-only, they can still be useful. By dividing the `_totalframes` value by the `_currentframe` value, you can obtain a ratio that you can use to create, for example, a slider to control the playback of a `MovieClip` object's timeline.

Creating MovieClip Objects Programmatically

Not only can you create `MovieClip` objects at authoring time by dragging instances onto the stage from the library, but you can also create them programmatically using ActionScript. The following sections explore some of the options for accomplishing this and discuss the benefits of each.

Understanding Stacking Order within Flash Movies

Before discussing the `MovieClip` methods for programmatically creating other `MovieClip` objects, you need to first consider an issue that is key to understanding how to work with all of them. Flash uses an internal concept of *depths* to determine stacking order of objects on the stage. Let's take a closer look at this idea.

You are probably already familiar with how layers work within your Flash movies. In the Flash authoring application, you can create, reorder, and delete layers from timelines within the movie. Contents of a layer placed above others will appear above the contents of the layers below. Layers are a means of creating a Z-axis within two-dimensional spaces. This is a convention seen in many other applications, and should not be unfamiliar to you. What you might not know is that there are several additional possible levels of stacking order that can take place within a Flash movie.

But layers are an authoring time convention only. Once Flash has exported the movie, the SWF doesn't know anything about layers. Instead, everything in the movie is converted into a depth. A depth is a numeric value that Flash uses to determine the Z-axis placement of an object. Objects with higher depth values appear in front of objects with lower depths. Each `MovieClip` object has its own internal depths. Therefore, depth 1 within `_root` does not interfere with depth 1 of a nested `MovieClip` object. However, within each `MovieClip` each depth can contain only one object. Therefore, if you attempt to create a new instance at the same depth as another object, the original object will be overwritten.

Flash automatically assigns unique depths to instances created during authoring time. The first instance within each `MovieClip` is given a depth of -16384. Subsequent objects are given incrementally higher depths (-16383, -16382, and so on). Flash uses these very low numbers so that they are not likely to interfere with instances you create programmatically. It is suggested that you begin creating new programmatically generated instances with a depth of 0.

When you create a lot of `MovieClip` objects (and `TextField` objects as well), it can become somewhat of a chore to keep track of what depths have been used. Remember, if you accidentally add a new instance at a depth that is already used, the new object will overwrite the existing instance. Due to this, Flash MX 2004 introduced the new `getNextHighestDepth()` method. This method always returns the next highest depth (starting from 0) within the `MovieClip` from which it is called. For example, to get the next highest depth within an instance named `mCircle` you can use the following code:

```
var nDepth:Number = mCircle.getNextHighestDepth();
```

However, getNextHighestDepth() does not verify that the MovieClip doesn't already have another instance at that depth. In other words, you can rely on getNextHighestDepth() exclusively as long as you use the method to generate the depths for all instances you create programmatically. However, if you also create instances with hardcoded depths, you'll need to verify that the depth returned by getNextHighestDepth() has not already been taken. For this purpose another new method was introduced in Flash MX 2004 that enables you to check to see if any instances currently occupy a given depth. The method getInstanceAtDepth() checks to see if a MovieClip contains any nested instances at a specified depth. If so, it returns the instance name as a string. Otherwise, it returns undefined:

```
var sInstance:String = mCircle.getInstanceAtDepth(1);
if(sInstance == undefined) {
  trace("mCircle does not have any instances at depth 1.");
}
else {
  trace("instance, " + sInstance + " found.");
}
```

Here's an example of how to use both getNextHighestDepth() and getInstanceAtDepth() to ensure that the new depth value is unique:

```
var nDepth:Number = this.getNextHighestDepth();
while(this.getInstanceAtDepth(nDepth) != undefined) {
  nDepth = this.getNextHighestDepth();
}
```

Remember, however, that if you use getNextHighestDepth() exclusively to generate the depths you use, you can dispense with the complexities of having to use getInstanceAtDepth() to check.

Additionally, you can change the depth of any existing MovieClip object using the swapDepths() method. The swapDepths() method accepts one of two types of parameters: either the name of the object (as a string) with which you want to exchange depths or the new depth value you want to assign to the instance. If you pass the method the name of an object then that object must reside within the same timeline as the object from which you are invoking the method. For example, if mCircle and mSquare are on the same timeline then you can use the following code:

```
mCircle.swapDepths("mSquare");
```

However, if mCircle and mSquare are on different timelines, the preceding code will not work.

If you pass swapDepths() a number value, Flash will change the depth of the MovieClip to that value. If any object already resides on that depth, the object on that depth is assigned the depth that had previously been assigned to the object that just took its depth.

The result of swapDepths() is that the two objects (assuming that there are actually two objects involved) change their order along the Z-axis. Therefore, the object that previously appeared behind will then appear in front.

You can get a MovieClip object to report its own depth using the getDepth() method. This can be very important in situations when you want to decide if two objects should change their depths or not. For example, if two objects begin to overlap you may want to make sure a specific one appears in front. You already know how to use swapDepths() to change the order of the two objects. But if the object you want in front is *already* in front, calling that method can have the exact opposite effect from what you want. So, it is a good idea to compare the depths of the two objects first. You can use the `getDepth()` method to get the depths of the two objects and compare them. The following example first checks to see whether `mCircle` is in front of `mSquare`. If so, it changes the order.

```
if(mCircle.getDepth() > mSquare.getDepth()) {
  mCircle.swapDepths(mSquare);
}
```

Creating Duplicate MovieClip Objects

You can actually tell Flash to create a duplicate of any `MovieClip` object in your movie (excepting `_root`) using the `duplicateMovieClip()` method. If you have created a `MovieClip` instance during authoring time you can create a duplicate of it. You can even create a duplicate of an instance that was created during runtime (such as an instance created using `duplicateMovieClip()`—duplicates of duplicates).

Note   While you can duplicate MovieClip objects into which images and SWF content have been loaded, the loaded content will not get duplicated. For SWF content you will have to load it a second time. For images you can either load the image a second time, or you can use the `BitmapData` class as discussed in Chapter 18.

In its basic format, the `duplicateMovieClip()` method takes two parameters—the name and the depth for the new, duplicate instance. For example:

```
mCircle.duplicateMovieClip("mNewCircle", this.getNextHighestDepth());
```

The new, duplicate instance is created in the same timeline as the original instance. It is assigned the new instance name and depth. The new instance is a duplicate of the original, and Flash duplicates the values of the majority of its properties. For example, the duplicate instance has the same values for `_x`, `_y`, `_width`, `_height`, `_xscale`, `_yscale`, and `_alpha` as the original at the time of duplication. But some properties' values are not copied. For example, regardless of whether or not the original's `_visible` property was set to `false`, the duplicate's `_visible` property defaults to `true`. In addition, regardless of the `_currentframe` value for the original, the duplicate always begins with the playhead at frame 1. Event handler methods are not duplicated. Nested instances that were created programmatically are not duplicated either.

You can use the `duplicateMovieClip()` method to create multiple duplicates at once with the aid of a `for` statement. Here is an example that creates `MovieClip` instances named `mCircle0` through `mCircle6`.

```
for(var i:Number = 0; i < 7; i++) {
  mCircle.duplicateMovieClip("mCircle" + i, this.getNextHighestDepth());
}
```

In some cases, you may be creating a duplicate instance that uses a variable to name the object. The preceding code is an example of this. In such a case, it can sometimes be cumbersome to have to write out the target path to the instance after it has been duplicated. For example, if, within the preceding for statement you wanted to instruct each duplicate instance to play its timeline and to set the `_x` and `_y` properties to random values, you could write the code as follows:

```
for(var i:Number = 0; i < 7; i++) {
  mCircle.duplicateMovieClip("mCircle" + i, this.getNextHighestDepth());
  this["mCircle" + i].play();
  this["mCircle" + i]._x = Math.random() * 300;
  this["mCircle" + i]._y = Math.random() * 300;
}
```

However, the `duplicateMovieClip()` method also returns a reference to the newly created instance. You can utilize the reference to make your job a little easier. Here is an example of how you could rewrite the preceding code:

```
var mDuplicate:MovieClip;
for(var i:Number = 0; i < 7; i++) {
  mDuplicate = mCircle.duplicateMovieClip("mCircle" + i,
  this.getNextHighestDepth());
  mDuplicate.play();
  mDuplicate._x = Math.random() * 300;
  mDuplicate._y = Math.random() * 300;
}
```

When you create duplicate `MovieClip` instances, remember that the duplicates will have the same X-and Y-coordinates as the original by default. Therefore, unless you set the _x and _y properties it may not seem that any duplicates were created. You can set the _x and _y properties after creating the duplicate as shown in the preceding code. Or, alternatively, you can use an `init` object when calling the `duplicateMovieClip()` method. For more information on the `init` object, see the section "Working with Initialization Objects."

Adding MovieClip Objects from the Library Programmatically

Duplicating `MovieClip` instances is great assuming you already have an instance on the stage to duplicate. But if you don't already have any authoring-time instances on the stage you're not going to be able to accomplish much with `duplicateMovieClip()`. Instead, you'll want to use the `attachMovie()` method. This method enables you to add new `MovieClip` instances to your movie from `MovieClip` symbols in the library.

When you want to use the `attachMovie()` method to programmatically add instances from the library you'll need to do a little preplanning. Here's why: Flash exports into the SWF only the symbols that are actually used in the movie. This is a feature that makes sure that your SWF files are not filled with unused symbols. But if you want to use some of those symbols programmatically, you need to make sure that Flash exports them in the SWF. To accomplish this you should do the following:

1. Open the library (choose Window ➪ Library or F11).

2. Select the Movie Clip symbol in the library that you want to add programmatically.

3. Either from the library menu or from the right-click/⌘-click menu, choose the Linkage option (see Figure 14-1).

Figure 14-1: Select the Linkage option for a symbol.

4. In the Linkage Properties dialog box, select the Export for ActionScript box. When you select that box, the Export in first frame box is also selected by default. Leave that box selected as well.

5. Give the symbol a linkage identifier name. In the Linkage Properties dialog box, enter the value. By default Flash will fill in the same name as that of the symbol.

6. Click OK to close the dialog box.

Congratulations. You've just told Flash to export the symbol so that you can access it programmatically. And you've assigned it a linkage identifier by which you will be able to specify to Flash which symbol you want to reference. The preceding steps are for assigning linkage settings to a symbol that you already created. You can also assign linkage settings to a symbol as you are creating it. From either the Create New Symbol or Convert to Symbol dialog box, you can choose to show the advanced settings by clicking the Advanced button, as shown in Figure 14-2. (If your dialog box already shows the advanced settings your button will read *Basic*, and you don't need to click it.) From the advanced settings, you can set the linkage settings at the time you create the symbol. You can always change them later if you want by accessing the linkage settings for the symbol.

Figure 14-2: Click Advanced to adjust the advanced settings.

Now that you've accomplished all the preliminary work, the next step is to write the ActionScript code to add an instance of the symbol programmatically. The attachMovie() method creates the new instance nested within the MovieClip from which it is called. For example, if you call the method from an instance named mContainer, the new instance will be nested within mContainer.

The method itself requires at least three parameters — the linkage identifier of the symbol, the name for the new instance, and the depth for the new instance. Here's an example that creates a new instance of a symbol with the linkage identifier Circle. The new instance is named mCircle, and it is nested within a MovieClip instance named mHolder:

```
mHolder.attachMovie("Circle",
                    "mCircle",
                    mHolder.getNextHighestDepth());
```

Notice that in this example, the getNextHighestDepth() method obtains a new depth *within* mHolder. This is because the new instance is being created within mHolder. So, you want to make sure that you are providing a valid depth for use within that timeline, not the parent.

When you create a new instance using attachMovie(), the new instance is always placed at 0,0 of the parent object's coordinate space. For example, if you create a new instance within _root, the new object will appear in the upper-left corner of the stage. You can, of course, assign new values to the _x and _y properties immediately after you create the instance. Additionally, you can use an init object to accomplish this. See "Working with Initialization Objects" for more information. As with the duplicateMovieClip() method, the attachMovie() method returns a reference to the newly created instance. And, as with duplicateMovieClip() this can be helpful when you would otherwise have to type long or awkward target paths.

Working with Initialization Objects

When you are creating new instances using duplicateMovieClip() and/or attachMovie(), often you want to initialize the new object with certain values. For example, you might want to assign each instance X- and Y-coordinate values so that the instances don't overlap (with duplicateMovieClip()) or so that the instance does not appear at 0,0 (with attachMovieClip()). As you've already seen, it is possible to set these values immediately after creating the new instance. But ActionScript also includes an option by which you can assign these property values when creating the new object. In order to accomplish this, both the duplicateMovieClip() and the attachMovieClip() methods accept an additional, optional parameter called an *initialization object*. An initialization object is an Object instance to which you have assigned properties and values that correspond to the properties for the new MovieClip instance you want to create. For example, you can create a new initialization object with _x and _y properties. Flash will then automatically assign the values from the initialization object to the corresponding properties in the new MovieClip instance. You can create the initialization object using an Object constructor. However, in many cases you may find it more convenient to use object literal notation to define the initialization object inline within the attachMovie() or duplicateMovieClip() method. In the following example, a new MovieClip instance is attached using attachMovie(). The first three parameters remain as before — the linkage identifier, the new instance name, and the depth. Additionally, an initialization object is defined with _x and _y properties.

```
mHolder.attachMovie("CircleSymbol",
                    "mCircle",
                    mHolder.getNextHighestDepth(),
                    {_x: 50, _y: 60});
```

In the preceding example the new instance is initialized with an X-coordinate of 50 and a Y-coordinate of 60.

Likewise, you can utilize an initialization object with `duplicateMovieClip()`. Here's an example:

```
mCircle.duplicateMovieClip("mNewCircle",
                           this.getNextHighestDepth(),
                           {_x: 50, _y: 60});
```

If you recall, we said earlier that when you create a duplicate `MovieClip` using `duplicateMovieClip()` none of the event handlers of the original are copied to the duplicate. However, with the initialization object you can conveniently copy all those event handler method definitions to the duplicate. As mentioned previously, all classes extend, either directly or indirectly, the `Object` class. Therefore, any type of object, including a `MovieClip` object, can serve as an initialization object. With this in mind, if you want a duplicated `MovieClip` to contain all the same event handler methods as the original, you can use the original object as the initialization object. Here is an example. Assuming that `mCircle` is a `MovieClip` instance with an X-coordinate of 0, the following code will duplicate it and move the duplicate so that the duplicate is to the right of `mCircle`. Notice that `mCircle` has an `onPress()` event handler method. However, `mNewCircle` will not respond to mouse events because the event handler method is not copied to the duplicate.

```
mCircle.onPress = function():Void {
  trace(this._name);
};

mCircle.duplicateMovieClip("mNewCircle", this.getNextHighestDepth());
mNewCircle._x = 100;
```

If you specify `mCircle` as the initialization object when calling `duplicateMovieClip()`, then the `onPress()` event handler method is copied:

```
mCircle.onPress = function():Void {
  trace(this._name);
};

mCircle.duplicateMovieClip("mNewCircle", this.getNextHighestDepth(),
mCircle);
mNewCircle._x = 100;
```

Creating Empty MovieClip Objects

Why in the world would you want to create an *empty* `MovieClip` instance? Although an empty `MovieClip` object may not immediately appear useful, it is exactly its emptiness that makes it such a powerful object. Here are two of the most common uses of empty `MovieClip` objects:

✦ **Attaching several MovieClip instances within the empty MovieClip object** — Nesting the objects within the single parent makes it simple to move, resize, or otherwise alter the entire group.

✦ **Loading content** — As you'll see shortly, you can load other SWF files or image files from external sources into a `MovieClip` instance. It is very useful to be able to programmatically create an empty `MovieClip` for this purpose.

You can create a new empty `MovieClip` instance with the `createEmptyMovieClip()` method. This method creates a new instance nested within the `MovieClip` from which it is called. The method requires two parameters — the name and depth for the new instance. Here is an example:

```
this.createEmptyMovieClip("mExternalSWFHolder", this.getNextHighestDepth());
```

The `createEmptyMovieClip()` method creates the new instance at 0,0 within the coordinate space of the parent object. Unlike `duplicateMovieClip()` and `attachMovie()`, the `createEmptyMovieClip()` method does not accept an initialization object. If you want to change the placement of the new object, you have to set the _x and _y properties of the new instance after it has been created. Also, like `duplicateMovieClip()` and `attachMovie()`, the `createEmptyMovieClip()` method returns a reference to the new instance.

Removing MovieClip Objects

The `removeMovieClip()` method, when invoked from a `MovieClip` object will remove the object from the stage. From time to time when you call `removeMovieClip()` on some MovieClip objects there may appear to be no effect. That is likely because the depth of the instance is out of range for the `removeMovieClip()` method. The method can only remove objects with depths within a certain range; otherwise, it does nothing. Authoring time instances default to depths outside of the range. Additionally, the `getNextHighestDepth()` method often returns numbers outside of the range. However, just because an instance is outside of the range doesn't mean you cannot use `removeMovieClip()`. It just means you have to move it within the range before calling `removeMovieClip()`. As you already learned, the `swapDepths()` method can move a MovieClip to a specified depth if you pass it a number. A depth of 0 is within the valid range for which `removeMovieClip()` will work. Therefore, simply call `swapDepths()` with a parameter of 0 before calling `removeMovieClip()`.

```
mCircle.swapDepths(0);
mCircle.removeMovieClip();
```

Loading External Content

Not only can you programmatically create `MovieClip` instances, but you can also load external content programmatically. You can load SWF files as well as many types of image files (progressive and nonprogressive JPEG, GIF, and PNG.) If you are authoring to Flash Player 6 or 7, you can load SWF files as well as nonprogressive JPEG files. If you are authoring to earlier versions of the player you can load only SWF files.

Loading external content can be of great benefit when creating Flash applications. Here are just a few scenarios in which loading external content can be beneficial:

✦ Your application consists of several parts, and you have different teams working on each part. You can have each team create its own SWF, and you can load the multiple SWF files into a single framework.

✦ Your application consists of some parts that you know will be updated frequently. You can make those parts into their own SWF files and load them into the main SWF. This makes updating the application more manageable.

✦ Your application consists of dynamically generated catalog or inventory contents. If the images in your application need to be generated dynamically based on database lookups and user input, you can make this possible by loading the image files programmatically.

✦ Your application is a news application that provides up-to-date articles with images. The article contents are loaded from a database (see Chapter 33 for more information on loading data) and the images that accompany the article reside on the server.

Let's take a closer look at how to achieve these results.

Note   This book discusses using `MovieClipLoader`, which was introduced in Flash Player 7. If you want to author to an earlier version of the player, use the `loadMovie()` method. You can read more about `loadMovie()` in the Flash Help panel.

Loading SWF Content

Let's look at how you can load SWF content into your movie at runtime. To load content, you'll need a MovieClip object that can hold it. When you load SWF content into a MovieClip, the new content replaces anything within the existing object, so it's frequently a good idea to make new MovieClip objects for each SWF you want to load into the application. As you learned in the previous section, one convenient way to make a new MovieClip object is to use the `createEmptyMovieClip()` method.

You can use a `MovieClipLoader` object to load content into `MovieClip` instances. You can make a new `MovieClipLoader` object using the constructor as part of a new statement. The constructor doesn't require any parameters:

```
var mlSWFLoader:MovieClipLoader = new MovieClipLoader();
```

Once you have a `MovieClip` object into which you can load the SWF content, and once you've instantiated a `MovieClipLoader` object, you can next use the `loadClip()` method of the `MovieClipLoader` object to load the content. The `loadClip()` method requires two parameters — the URL of the content and the container `MovieClip` object. The URL can be relative or absolute. Here is an example that uses a relative URL:

```
mlSWFLoader.loadClip("circles.swf", mCircleSWFHolder);
```

The preceding line of code searches for an SWF file named `circles.swf` that is in the same directory as the loading SWF. Assuming that `circles.swf` can be found at `http://www .person13.com/asb/circles.swf`, you can use an absolute URL as follows:

```
mlSWFLoader.loadClip("http://www.person13.com/asb/circles.swf",
mCircleSWFHolder);
```

When you load an SWF, everything within the container object is replaced. That is, the entire timeline of the instance is replaced. The majority of the appearance properties will retain their values, however. For example, `_x`, `_y`, `_alpha`, and so on, will remain the same as prior to the loading of the content. The exception to this is that you should not set the `_height` and `_width` properties of an empty `MovieClip` object until after the content has loaded. If you set the `_height` and `_width` properties of an empty `MovieClip` before the content has loaded, the content will not show.

When you load an external SWF into a `MovieClip` object, the loaded contents will be aligned within the `MovieClip` object just as they were in the external SWF. But remember, the upper-left corner of the stage for the main timeline is 0,0. Therefore, when you load an external SWF into a `MovieClip` object, it is not centered within the object. All the content appears to the right and below the center point (which is 0,0).

The following code is an example that, when placed on a frame of the main timeline, loads an SWF into the movie.

```
this.createEmptyMovieClip("mCirclesSWFHolder",
this.getNextHighestDepth());
var mlSWFLoader:MovieClipLoader = new MovieClipLoader();
mlSWFLoader.loadClip("http://www.person13.com/asb/circles.swf",
mCirclesSWFHolder);
```

For more complex scenarios, you can also send variables along with the request for the external SWF. You can do so by using a query string as part of the URL. The following code illustrates using a query string.

```
this.createEmptyMovieClip("mCirclesSWFHolder",
this.getNextHighestDepth());
var mlSWFLoader:MovieClipLoader = new MovieClipLoader();
mlSWFLoader.loadClip("http://www.person13.com/asb/circles.swf?nCircles=
20", mCirclesSWFHolder);
```

Loading Image Content

In addition to loading SWF content, you can also load image content into your Flash movies. As of Flash Player 8, you can load both progressive and nonprogressive JPEG, GIF, and PNG images.

To load JPEG content you use a `MovieClipLoader` object, just as when you load an SWF. The only difference is that you provide a URL to an image resource instead of an SWF resource. The `loadClip()` method works the same way with image files as with SWF files. The loaded content replaces the timeline of the `MovieClip` object into which it loads. Here is an example:

```
this.createEmptyMovieClip("mImageHolder", this.getNextHighestDepth());
var mlImageLoader:MovieClipLoader = new MovieClipLoader();
mlImageLoader.loadClip("http://www.person13.com/asb/image2.jpg", mImageHolder);
```

However, you should be aware of the implications of the `MovieClip` object's timeline being replaced by image data. Once the image data loads, the object can no longer be fully treated as a `MovieClip` object. If you want to continue to be able to work with the loaded content as though it were a `MovieClip` object, there is a simple solution: You can create a nested `MovieClip` object into which you load the image content. Then, the parent `MovieClip` object will contain the nested image and you can still work with the parent as a `MovieClip` object. Here is an example:

```
this.createEmptyMovieClip("mImageHolder", this.getNextHighestDepth());
mImageHolder.createEmptyMovieClip("mImage", mImageHolder.getNextHighestDepth());
var mlImageLoader:MovieClipLoader = new MovieClipLoader();
mlImageLoader.loadClip("http://www.person13.com/asb/image2.jpg",
mImageHolder.mImage);
```

Monitoring Loading

`MovieClipLoader` objects rely on listener objects to monitor the progress of loading content. The listener object for a `MovieClipLoader` instance is simply an object with any of the following methods defined:

✦ **onLoadStart( )** — This method is invoked when content begins to load. The method is passed a reference to the `MovieClip` object into which the content is being loaded.

✦ **onLoadProgress( )** — This method is invoked continually each time data is loaded. At each interval the method is passed three parameters — a reference to the `MovieClip` object into which the content is being loaded, the number of loaded bytes, and the number of total bytes.

✦ **onLoadInit( )** — The `onLoadInit( )` method is called once the data has loaded and is initialized. In many cases, you ought to use the `onLoadInit( )` method rather than `onLoadComplete( )`.

✦ **onLoadComplete( )** — This method is invoked when the content has completed loading. It is passed a reference to the `MovieClip` object into which the content is being loaded.

Here is an example of a simple `MovieClipLoader` listener object:

```
var oListener:Object = new Object();
oListener.onLoadStart = function (mHolderClip:MovieClip):Void {
    trace(mHolderClip + " started loading.");
};
oListener.onLoadProgress = function(mHolderClip:MovieClip,
                                    nLoaded:Number,
                                    nTotal:Number):Void
{
    trace(mHolderClip + " loaded " + nLoaded + " of " + nTotal + "bytes");
};
oListener.onLoadInit = function(mHolderClip:MovieClip):Void {
  trace(mHolderClip + " initialized");
};
oListener.onLoadComplete = function(mHolderClip:MovieClip):Void {
    trace(mHolderClip + " completed loading");
};
```

To use the `MovieClipLoader` listener, complete the following steps:

1. Create the `MovieClip` object into which you are going to load the content. For example:

```
this.createEmptyMovieClip("mHolder",
                          this.getNextHighestDepth());
```

2. Instantiate a `MovieClipLoader` object with the constructor. For example:

```
var mlLoader:MovieClipLoader = new MovieClipLoader();
```

3. Create a listener object.

4. Use the `addListener( )` method to add the listener object to the `MovieClipLoader` instance.

```
mlLoader.addListener(oListener);
```

5. Invoke the `loadClip()` method from the `MovieClipLoader` object.

Monitoring the load progress for SWF and image content is important for several reasons:

✦ When you monitor load progress, you can report to the user how much of the content has downloaded. This is important when the download might potentially take some time. You want to assure the user that something is happening and that he or she is not just waiting for nothing.

✦ You cannot do too much with a `MovieClip` until the content has loaded. Although you can adjust some of the appearance properties, the object will not report accurate dimensions until it has loaded completely. Also, you cannot assign any custom properties to the instance until after the content has loaded because if you assign the properties first they will be overwritten. SWFs and images load asynchronously. That means that after you instruct Flash to try and load the content, the content begins to load in the background while the rest of the actions are run in the movie. Therefore, you need a way to be able to detect when the content has loaded before you try to do anything with it. The `MovieClipLoader` class offers you this kind of functionality—the listener's `onLoadComplete()` method is invoked once the entire content has been loaded, and the `onLoadInit()` method is called once the data is initialized.

Unloading Content

You can unload SWF content from a `MovieClip` object in one of two ways:

✦ You can load new content into the `MovieClip` object. This will replace the previously loaded content.

✦ You can call the `unloadClip()` method from the `MovieClipLoader` object.

The `unloadClip()` method will unload the content that had previously been loaded into the object. The method requires one parameter—a reference to the `MovieClip` object from which you want to unload the content. This method cannot remove content from objects if the content was not loaded with a `MovieClipLoader` in the first place. Also, because a `MovieClip` into which image data has been loaded cannot be treated as a `MovieClip` any longer, you cannot unload image data. Instead, if you want to remove an image you should make sure that you have loaded the content into a nested `MovieClip` as previously recommended. Then you can use the `removeMovieClip()` method to remove the parent object.

When you use `unloadClip()`, the original timeline is not retrieved. Once you have loaded content into a `MovieClip` object, the original timeline cannot be retrieved. That means that you should be careful not to indiscriminately load content into `MovieClip` objects if you want to retain the original contents in them.

Opening Web Pages

The `getURL()` method allows you to communicate with Internet browser programs. It will communicate with the browser program from which the movie is being played, or from the default browser if the movie is being played from a projector or other application. Typically, this method is used to change the URL of the current browser window. However, you can also use it to launch new windows and send JavaScript commands.

You must always specify a URL as a string as a parameter when calling the getURL() method. For example:

```
this.getURL("http://www.person13.com.com");
```

If the Flash movie containing the preceding code is being viewed in a browser window, the window's location will change to the specified URL. Otherwise, if the movie is being viewed as a projector or in the stand-alone Flash Player, it will launch a new browser window of the computer's default browser with the specified URL.

You can also pass a second optional parameter: a window/frame name as a string. This allows you to open URLs in other browser windows or frames without redirecting the current window and losing the Flash movie in the process:

```
this.getURL("http://www.person13.com", "_blank");
```

Note   The JavaScript property _blank indicates that a new, blank browser window should be opened. _blank is not a keyword and has no significance, within ActionScript. To learn more about JavaScript, Danny Goodman's *JavaScript Bible, 5th Edition* (Wiley Publishing, 2004) is an excellent resource.

You can pass a third optional parameter: the HTTP method for sending variables. However, note that since sending variables via getURL() utilizes custom properties assigned to the MovieClip object, it is not recommended. If you do have a legitimate reason to do so, you can specify a string value of either GET or POST. When you pass this third parameter to the getURL() method, you send any custom properties of the MovieClip object from which the method is invoked as string values in URLEncoded format. There is one exception: Nested MovieClip objects are not sent. Custom properties refer to those properties that you, the author, have created. Predefined properties such as _alpha and _totalframes are not included. It is also important to understand what values are being sent. Primitive data types such as numbers and Booleans are easily converted to string values. But other data types may yield unexpected results. For instance, custom objects will have the value of "[object Object]" when converted to strings. Also note that because all the properties of the MovieClip object are converted to strings before they are sent, none of the properties of nested objects are sent. This means that you have to be very careful that any values that you need to send using the getURL() method are properties of the MovieClip object from which you invoke the method. Here is an example of the getURL() method invoked from a MovieClip object named mCircle:

```
mCircle.getURL("http://www.person13.com/", "_blank", "GET");
```

If the mCircle MovieClip object had two custom properties, radius and velocity, the location in the browser might look something like this:

```
http://www.person13.com/?radius=100&velocity=12
```

You can also use the getURL() method to make calls to JavaScript functions in the HTML page within which the Flash movie is embedded. To do this, simply use the following technique:

```
mObject.getURL("javascript:functionName([parameters])");
```

Creating Draggable MovieClip Objects

Draggable MovieClip objects can be utilized in many ways. Here are just a few examples:

✦ Windows containing various content that the user can move around the stage.

✦ Drag-and-drop functionality. For example, you can enable a user to drag an item from a catalog of your online store, and drop it into her basket.

✦ Games. All kinds of games utilize draggable objects. Puzzles, for example, require that the user be able to move the pieces.

There are essentially two parts to creating a basic draggable MovieClip. First, you need to tell Flash to start dragging the object—this means that the object should follow the movement of the mouse. Then, at some point, you need to tell Flash to stop dragging the object. Typically, draggable MovieClip objects do both of these things, although in some unique situations an object will only start dragging—for example, when creating a custom mouse cursor (see Chapter 21). But for the most part you will utilize both the starting and the stopping.

Telling Flash to Start Dragging a MovieClip

To start dragging a MovieClip object, all you need to do is call the startDrag() method from the MovieClip instance. In the most basic format, it might look like this:

```
mCircle.startDrag();
```

Typically, you invoke a startDrag() method within an object's onPress() event handler method. For example:

```
mCircle.onPress = function():Void {
   this.startDrag();
};
```

In the preceding code example, the MovieClip mCircle starts dragging when the user clicks the object. The object will follow the mouse relative to the point on the object at which the user clicked. For example, if the user clicks the very edge of the object, the user will drag the object from the very edge. In the majority of situations, this is exactly what you want. However, you can also tell Flash to snap the object so that the center of the object aligns with the mouse. You can do this by passing the method a single parameter value of true:

```
mCircle.onPress = function():Void {
   this.startDrag(true);
};
```

Typically, this technique is employed when creating a custom mouse cursor or other similar goal.

There is one more variation on the startDrag() method. You can tell Flash that you want the object to be draggable only within a particular area. This is particularly useful when creating sliders or any other situation in which you want to make sure the user can move the object only within a particular range. In these cases, you need to pass the method five parameters—a Boolean value indicating whether or not to snap to the center of the object, the leftmost X value of the area, the topmost Y value of the area, the rightmost X value of the area, and the bottom-most Y value of the area. All the coordinate values should be specified relative to the object's parent's coordinate space. Here is an example in which mCircle is made draggable only within a rectangle defined by 0, 0, 200, 300.

```
mCircle.onPress = function():Void {
  this.startDrag(false, 0, 0, 200, 300);
};
```

 Note   Only one object can be dragged at a time using startDrag().

Telling Flash to Stop Dragging a MovieClip

Anytime you want to stop the dragging action, simply invoke the stopDrag() method from the draggable object. For example:

```
mCircle.stopDrag();
```

The stopDrag() method does not require any parameters. It simply drops the object at the current position on the stage.

Just as the startDrag() method is typically invoked within an onPress() event handler method, the stopDrag() method is typically invoked within an onRelease() event handler method. When the user clicks the object it becomes draggable, and when the user releases the click, the object is dropped.

```
mCircle.onRelease = function():Void {
  this.stopDrag();
};
```

Checking for Overlapping

In some of your Flash movies, it is absolutely essential that you can detect when two MovieClip objects enter the same space in the X- and Y-coordinate space. For example, if you create a game, you might need to detect when a ball hits against a wall or a laser beam hits a spaceship. Other times, you simply need to see if a MovieClip object is within a certain "hotspot" space. You can do all this quite simply with the hitTest() method of any MovieClip object. The hitTest() method allows you to check for overlapping objects in two ways. In either case, the method returns a Boolean value — true if there is overlap and false if there is not overlap.

✦ You can pass the method a reference to another MovieClip object. Flash will then check to see if the object from which the method is called overlaps with the object you pass as a parameter. Here is an example of the first usage of hitTest():

```
var bOverlap:Boolean = mCircle.hitTest(mSquare);
```

 Note   When you use this technique, Flash checks to see if the bounding boxes of the two objects overlap. This means that, for example, even if the two objects are circles, they will report as overlapping at some times even when the actual circles are not overlapping.

✦ You can also call the `hitTest()` method by passing it three parameters — an X-coordinate, a Y-coordinate, and a Boolean value indicating whether you want to test on the actual shape of the object or the bounding box of the object. Here is an example of this second usage in which you check to see if the mouse is currently overlapping the object:

```
var bOverlap:Boolean = mCircle.hitTest(this._xmouse, this._ymouse, true);
```

Typically, you don't perform hit tests as a one-time operation. Instead, you normally place your `hitTest()` calls within an interval function or method so that you can continually poll to check the current status. Here is an example:

```
function checkOverlap():Void {
  if(mCircle.hitTest(mSquare)) {
    trace("The objects overlap.");
  }
}

var nOverlapInterval:Number = setInterval(checkOverlap, 100);
```

Working with Coordinate Spaces

As you already know, the coordinate spaces within nested `MovieClip` objects might not coincide with the coordinates for the parent object. This depends on the placement of the nested object. This can make it somewhat tricky when you want to compare coordinates within different coordinate spaces.

When converting between coordinate spaces, there are essentially two types of coordinate spaces — global and local. The coordinates within the `_root` object are referred to as the *global* coordinates. The coordinates within the nested `MovieClip` objects are referred to as the *local* coordinates. Using the `globalToLocal()` and `localToGlobal()` methods, you can convert between these two types of coordinates.

The `localToGlobal()` method converts local coordinates to the global equivalents. Likewise, the `globalToLocal()` method converts global coordinates to the local equivalents. In both cases, the methods each require a single parameter in the form of a point object. A *point object* is simply an object with two properties — x and y. The x property should have the value of the X-coordinate, and the y property should have the value of the Y-coordinate. Here is an example of how to create a point object:

```
var oPoint:Object = {x:30, y:60};
```

With a point object created, you can pass it to the respective method. The methods do not return any values. Instead, they convert the point object values to the global or local equivalents. Here is an example that converts the local coordinates 30,60 from the `mCircle` instance to the global equivalents:

```
var oPoint:Object = {x:30, y:60};
mCircle.localToGlobal(oPoint);
trace(oPoint.x + " " + oPoint.y);
```

By combining the `localToGlobal()` and `globalToLocal()` methods, you can convert the coordinates from one nested object's coordinate space to that of another nested object. Here is an example that converts the coordinates 30,60 from the `mCircle` object's coordinate space to the equivalent coordinates within the `mSquare` instance:

```
var oPoint:Object = {x:30, y:60};
mCircle.localToGlobal(oPoint);
mSquare.globalToLocal(oPoint);
trace(oPoint.x + " " + oPoint.y);
```

You can also use the `getBounds()` method to determine the bounding coordinates of one object within the coordinate space of another. From the first `MovieClip` object, invoke the `getBounds()` method, and pass it a single parameter — a reference to a `MovieClip` object in whose coordinate space the results should be given. The method then returns a new object containing four properties — `xMin`, `xMax`, `yMin`, and `yMax`. Here is an example that gets the boundaries of `mCircle` within the coordinate space of the `mSquare` instance:

```
var oBoundaries:Object = mCircle.getBounds(mSquare);
```

Creating Scriptable Masks

Using `setMask()`, you can assign another `MovieClip` to function as a mask for the object from which the method is invoked. Here is an example in which `mMask` is set as the mask of `mCircle`:

```
mCircle.setMask(mMask);
```

The `MovieClip` that works as the mask can contain animation (that is, shape tweens or motion tweens), and it can be controlled through ActionScript itself to create complex masks. If and when you no longer want the masked object to be masked, you can again call the `setMask()` method and pass it the `null` value. For example:

```
mCircle.setMask(null);
```

Note   A *mask* is a shape that defines the visible area for an object. For example, a `MovieClip` object containing a rectangular image can be masked so that it displays only a circular portion of that image.

Practicing Attaching and Dragging MovieClip Objects

In this exercise, you'll continue working from where you left off in the last exercise. This time you add all the `MovieClip` instances programmatically. And, instead of making the accessories show and hide when clicked, you'll make them draggable so that you can place them on the man. You'll need to have `person001.fla` available. If you didn't complete the previous exercise, you can find `person001.fla` on the web site.

1. Open `person001.fla` and save it as `person002.fla`.

2. Delete the Man layer. This will delete the layer and its contents — the `mMan` instance. Don't worry, you'll add it programmatically now.

3. Open the library. Set each symbol to export for ActionScript. Set the linkage identifiers to Hat, Glasses, Beard, Coat, Shoes, Cane, Man, and Body.

4. On the Actions layer, remove all previous code, and add the following code:

```
addArtwork();
makeHidden();
setHandlers();

function addArtwork():Void {

  // Create an empty MovieClip into which we will add all
  // the subsequent instances.
  this.createEmptyMovieClip("mMan", this.getNextHighestDepth());

  // Use attachMovie() to add instances to the mMan
  // object.
  this.mMan.attachMovie("Man",
                        "mClothedMan",
                        this.mMan.getNextHighestDepth());
  this.mMan.attachMovie("Beard",
                        "mBeard",
                        this.mMan.getNextHighestDepth());
  this.mMan.attachMovie("Cane",
                        "mCane",
                        this.mMan.getNextHighestDepth());
  this.mMan.attachMovie("Coat",
                        "mCoat",
                        this.mMan.getNextHighestDepth());
  this.mMan.attachMovie("Glasses",
                        "mGlasses",
                        this.mMan.getNextHighestDepth());
  this.mMan.attachMovie("Hat",
                        "mHat",
                        this.mMan.getNextHighestDepth());
  this.mMan.attachMovie("Shoes",
                        "mShoes",
                        this.mMan.getNextHighestDepth());
}

function makeHidden():Void {

  // Loop through all the instances in mMan.mClothedMan
  // and except for the mBody instance, set them all to
  // be invisible.
  for(var sInstance:String in mMan.mClothedMan) {
    if(sInstance == "mBody") {
     continue;
    }
    mMan.mClothedMan[sInstance]._visible = false;
  }
```

```
  }

  function setHandlers():Void {

    // Loop through all the instances in mMan and except
    // for mClothedMan make them draggable.
    for(var sInstance:String in mMan) {
      if(sInstance == "mClothedMan") {
        continue;
      }
      mMan[sInstance].onPress = function():Void {
        this.startDrag();
      };
      mMan[sInstance].onRelease = function():Void {
        this.stopDrag();
      };

      // Set all the instances placement so they appear to
      // the right of the man.
      mMan[sInstance]._x = 450;
      mMan[sInstance]._y = 200;
    }
  }
```

5. Save and test the movie.

When you test the movie, you should be able to drag and drop all the accessories. Now, take a closer look at the code.

The addArtwork() function should be fairly self-explanatory. In this function, you create a new empty MovieClip object named mMan and then use attachMovie() to create nested instances within it. The nested instances are created from the symbols you set to export previously.

Next is the makeHidden() function. You may be wondering why you would have attached an instance of the Man symbol instead of an instance of the Body symbol. After all, if you attached an instance of the Body symbol you wouldn't have to hide all the nested instances within it. This is a good point. You're going to want to have those hidden nested instances in there for the next exercise so in order to hide them (the nested instances within the mClothedMan object), this example uses a for...in statement and sets the _visible property of each to false. The only exception is the mBody instance—you want that instance to remain visible. To ensure that instance remains visible, you use an if statement to check for the current instance name, and if it is mBody, you use a continue statement to skip to the next.

```
  function makeHidden():Void {
    for(var sInstance:String in mMan.mClothedMan) {
      if(sInstance == "mBody") {
        continue;
      }
      mMan.mClothedMan[sInstance]._visible = false;
    }
  }
```

The `setHandlers()` function in this exercise shares its name with the function from the last exercise, but it is different in what it does. Again, you use a `for...in` statement — this time looping through all the nested instances of `mMan`. With the exception of the `mClothedMan` instance you assign `onPress()` and `onRelease()` methods to each such that each instance is made draggable. And, additionally, you set each instance's placement so that it appears to the right of the man.

```
function setHandlers():Void {
  for(var sInstance:String in mMan) {
    if(sInstance == "mClothedMan") {
      continue;
    }
    mMan[sInstance].onPress = function():Void {
      this.startDrag();
    };
    mMan[sInstance].onRelease = function():Void {
      this.stopDrag();
    };
    mMan[sInstance]._x = 450;
    mMan[sInstance]._y = 200;
  }
}
```

Practicing Checking for Overlaps and Loading Content

In the last exercise, you made an application in which you can drag and drop the accessories onto the cartoon man. In this exercise, you'll add some feature enhancements to that application, including the following:

✦ **Snap to** — When the user drags and drops an accessory near the correct location, the accessory will automatically snap to.

✦ **Correct location hinting** — When the accessory is dragged over the correct area, the instance will lower its alpha to 50.

✦ **Current object on top** — The current object (the object being dragged) always appears on top.

✦ **A JPEG background image** — You'll load a JPEG at runtime to use as the background.

So let's get started. Follow along with these steps:

1. Open `person002.fla` and save it as `person003.fla`. If you didn't complete the last exercise, you can find `person002.fla` on the web site.

2. Modify the code on the first frame of the main timeline as shown here (additions in bold):

```
// Declare a variable to reference the MovieClip that is
// currently being moved.
```

```
var mSelected:MovieClip;

// Declare a variable that stores whether or not an object ought
// to snap to the man.
var bSnapTo:Boolean;

// Use an interval function to continually check for overlap.
setInterval(checkOverlap, 100);

addArtwork();
makeHidden();
setHandlers();
setOverlapChecker();
loadBackground();

function addArtwork():Void {
  this.createEmptyMovieClip("mMan", this.getNextHighestDepth());
  this.mMan.attachMovie("Man",
                        "mClothedMan",
                         this.mMan.getNextHighestDepth());
  this.mMan.attachMovie("Beard",
                        "mBeard",
                         this.mMan.getNextHighestDepth());
  this.mMan.attachMovie("Cane",
                        "mCane",
                         this.mMan.getNextHighestDepth());
  this.mMan.attachMovie("Coat",
                         "mCoat",
                          this.mMan.getNextHighestDepth());
  this.mMan.attachMovie("Glasses",
                        "mGlasses",
                         this.mMan.getNextHighestDepth());
  this.mMan.attachMovie("Hat",
                        "mHat",
                         this.mMan.getNextHighestDepth());
  this.mMan.attachMovie("Shoes",
                        "mShoes",
                         this.mMan.getNextHighestDepth());
}

function makeHidden():Void {
  for(var sInstance:String in mMan.mClothedMan) {
    if(sInstance == "mBody") {
     continue;
     }
    mMan.mClothedMan[sInstance]._visible = false;
  }
}

function setHandlers():Void {
  for(var sInstance:String in mMan) {
```

```
    if(sInstance == "mClothedMan") {
      continue;
    }
    mMan[sInstance].onPress = function():Void {
      this.startDrag();

      // Set the mSelected variable to reference the object.
      mSelected = this;
    };
    mMan[sInstance].onRelease = function():Void {
      this.stopDrag();

      // Set mSelected to null so we know that
      // the object is no longer being dragged.
      mSelected = null;

      // Set the alpha back to 100 in case it wasn't
      // already.
      this._alpha = 100;

      // If the custom snapTo property is true...
      if(bSnapTo) {

        // Create a points object with the points of the
        // corresponding instance within mClothedMan.
        var oPoint = new Object();
        oPoint.x = this._parent.mClothedMan[this._name]._x;
        oPoint.y = this._parent.mClothedMan[this._name]._y;

        // Convert the points to the local points within
        // mMan (this._parent), and then move this object
        // to that location.
        this._parent.mClothedMan.localToGlobal(oPoint);
        this._parent.globalToLocal(oPoint);
        this._x = oPoint.x;
        this._y = oPoint.y;
      }
      bSnapTo = null;
    };
    mMan[sInstance]._x = 450;
    mMan[sInstance]._y = 200;
  }
}

function checkOverlap():Void {

  // If the selected object is overlapping with the
  // corresponding object within mClothedMan...
  if (mSelected.hitTest(mMan.mClothedMan[mSelected._name])) {
    bSnapTo = true;
    mSelected._alpha = 50;
```

```
    }
    else {
      bSnapTo = false;
      mSelected._alpha = 100;
    }

    // Loop through every instance in mMan...
    for(var sInstance:String in mMan) {
      if(sInstance == mSelected._name ||
          sInstance == "mClothedMan")
      {
        continue;
      }
      // If the current object overlaps with any of the
      // others, and if the instance has a lower depth,
      // change the depths.
      if(mSelected.hitTest(mMan[sInstance]) &&
          mSelected.getDepth() < mMan[sInstance].getDepth())
      {
        mSelected.swapDepths(mMan[sInstance]);
      }
    }
  }

  function loadBackground():Void {

    // Create an empty MovieClip for the background. And
    // because we're loading a JPEG, create a nested
    // MovieClip named mJPEG into which we'll load the
    // content.
    this.createEmptyMovieClip("mBackground",
                          this.getNextHighestDepth());
    this.mBackground.createEmptyMovieClip("mJPEG",
                    this.mBackground.getNextHighestDepth());

    // Create a listener object for the MovieClipLoader.
    var oListener:Object = new Object();
    oListener.onLoadComplete = function(mImage:MovieClip):Void {

      // When the JPEG loads, set the depth of mBackground
      // to 0 so that it appears below the other instances.
      var mBackground:MovieClip = mImage._parent;
      mBackground.swapDepths(0);
    };
    var mlLoader:MovieClipLoader = new MovieClipLoader();
    mlLoader.addListener(oListener);
    mlLoader.loadClip("http://www.person13.com/asb/image2.jpg",
                    mBackground.mJPEG);
  }
```

3. Save and test the movie.

When you test the movie, you should be able to drag the accessories over the man. If you drag the instances over the correct locations they should lower in transparency, and if you drop the instance it should snap to its exact location. The object you are dragging should always appear above the others. A background should load behind the rest of the content.

Optimizing Playback with Cached Bitmap Surfaces

If you had to describe the primary function of Flash, you'd probably have to say that it's a vector animation player. Flash is good at working with vectors. And vectors have many advantages. Vectors scale losslessly, and they often require much less bandwidth to transfer than analogous bitmaps. However, vectors are not without drawbacks. One of the drawbacks is that when animating complex vector shapes, Flash Player can run slowly, causing choppy playback. That is because every time a vector moves Flash redraws the shape. It doesn't merely translate pixels. It updates the vector values, recalculates how to draw it, and draws it. For simple vector shapes with just a few vectors the effect is minimal, and it is frequently faster than shifting pixels around as Flash would have to do with bitmaps. However, if a shape contains many vectors it can have a greater effect since Flash has to redraw each vector each time the shape moves. Contrast that with how Flash treats bitmaps. With bitmaps, Flash simply shifts the pixels around the stage. It doesn't have to run any calculations to determine how to redraw something. So, while it is relatively more difficult for Flash to move bitmaps than very simple vector shapes, it is relatively more difficult for Flash to move complex vector shapes than complex bitmaps.

You may be wondering how this discussion of vectors and bitmaps is relevant to movie clips and optimizing playback. Up until Flash Player 8, it wasn't particularly relevant. However, Flash Player 8 introduces a new `MovieClip` property called `cacheAsBitmap`. With the `cacheAsBitmap` property, it is possible to tell Flash to make a bitmap surface from a movie clip's vector data, and to move the movie clip as though it were a bitmap. That can be very useful when a movie clip contains complex vector shapes that you want to tween, for example. The bitmap surface looks just like the vector artwork. However, when the movie clip is moved, Flash doesn't have to redraw the vectors. Instead, it simply shifts the bitmap pixels. That can cause Flash Player to run much more smoothly in cases where you have many complex shapes animating.

The `cacheAsBitmap` property holds a Boolean value. The default value is `false`, which means that bitmap caching is off. Assigning a value of `true` causes Flash Player to treat the movie clip as a bitmap surface:

```
mClip.cacheAsBitmap = true;
```

Before you go setting `cacheAsBitmap` to true for every movie clip, however, there are a few cautions. Bitmap surface caching only optimizes playback when animating movie clips with complex vector shapes. Setting `cacheAsBitmap` to `true` for movie clips already containing bitmap data will not optimize anything. Furthermore, using bitmap surfaces for simple vector shapes will likely have the opposite effect from what you'd want. Using bitmap surfaces is a tradeoff. Bitmap surfaces are stored in memory in the player. Since simple vectors won't benefit from bitmap caching, setting `cacheAsBitmap` to true will only cause Flash Player to use more memory needlessly, which can make playback choppy. Additionally, bitmap caching works best for movie clips that have fairly static content or content that is updated infrequently. Every time the content of a movie clip changes (animations within a movie clip, for example) the bitmap surface is redrawn, using player resources. And, bitmap surfaces are redrawn every time a movie clip is rotated or scaled. So, if a movie clip is going to rotate frequently, it's unlikely that bitmap caching will optimize playback.

Let's next take a look at an example in which bitmap surface caching can be helpful. In the following exercise you'll build an animation that uses the Tween class to move six movie clips on stage. The movie clips contain complex vector shapes. With bitmap caching off, the playback is choppy. With bitmap caching enabled the playback is much smoother.

1. Open cacheAsBitmap_starter.fla from the web site, and save it as cacheAsBitmap.fla to your local disk.

2. Note that in the library there is a symbol containing complex vector artwork. The symbol is set to export with a linkage identifier of Shape.

3. Select the first keyframe of the default layer on the main timeline, and add the following ActionScript.

```actionscript
import mx.transitions.Tween;

// Define a listener object to use with the Tween objects. Each
// time a tween finishes, play it back in reverse.
var oListener:Object = new Object();
oListener.onMotionFinished = function(twObject:Tween):Void {
  twObject.yoyo();
};

var aShapeClips:Array = new Array();
var mShape:MovieClip;
var nDepth:Number;
var aTweens:Array = new Array();
var nY:Number = 0;

// Use a for statement to make 6 instances of the Shape symbol.
for(var i:Number = 0; i < 6; i++) {

  // Get the next depth, and use attachMovie() to add an
  //instance.
  nDepth = this.getNextHighestDepth();
  mShape = this.attachMovie("Shape", "mShape" + nDepth, nDepth);

  // Assign a y coordinate to the object.
  mShape._y = nY;

  // Add the movie clip to the array.
  aShapeClips.push(mShape);

  // Define a Tween object for the movie clip. Animate the _
  // x property so it moves back and forth across the stage. If i
  // is even start the  movie clip on the left. Otherwise, start
  // the movie clip on the right.
  aTweens.push(new Tween(mShape, "_x", null,
(i % 2 == 0) ? 0 : 550 - mShape._width,
(i % 2 == 0) ? 550 - mShape._width : 0,
```

```
Math.random() * 4 + 4, true));

    // Add a listener object to the tween.
    aTweens[i].addListener(oListener);

    // If i is odd increment nY;
    if(i % 2 == 1) {
      nY += 140;
    }
  }

  // Every time the user clicks the mouse toggle the cacheAsBitmap
  // property for each of the movie clips.
  function onMouseDown():Void {
    for(var i:Number = 0; i < aShapeClips.length; i++) {
      aShapeClips[i].cacheAsBitmap = !aShapeClips[i].cacheAsBitmap;
    }
  }
}
```

   4. Test the movie.

When the animation starts, the playback is likely rather choppy. If you click the mouse on the stage it will toggle the cacheAsBitmap property for each of the movie clips. One click will likely demonstrate that cacheAsBitmap can cause much smoother playback. Clicking again will toggle back to choppy playback.

Next, look at how cacheAsBitmap can have no effect or even a negative effect on playback.

   1. Open cacheAsBitmap.fla, and save it as cacheAsBitmapRotation.fla.

   2. Edit the ActionScript code, and add the following code just after defining the onMotionFinished() method for the oListener object.

```
oListener.onMotionChanged = function(twObject:Tween):Void {
  twObject.obj._rotation++;
};
```

   3. Test the movie.

The onMotionChanged() method updates the _rotation property of each movie clip each time the _x property is updated. You'll likely notice that the playback doesn't improve regardless of whether bitmap caching is toggled on or off. That's because every time the _rotation property is updated for the movie clip, it has to redraw the bitmap surface. That not only cancels any benefits that bitmap caching might have in this case, but it also requires the player to do more work by redrawing the surface.

Web Resource

We'd like to know what you thought about this chapter. Visit www.rightactionscript .com/asb/comments to fill out an online form with your comments.

Summary

✦ Use the playback methods such as `play()`, `stop()`, `gotoAndStop()`, and `gotoAndStop()` to affect movie clip timeline playback.

✦ You can programmatically add new movie clip instances using `attachMovie()`, `duplicateMovieClip()`, and `createEmptyMovieClip()`.

✦ Flash Player 8 can load SWF, JPEG, GIF, and PNG content at runtime. Use the `MovieClipLoader` class to accomplish that.

✦ Use the `getURL()` method to open URLs in a browser.

✦ Use the `startDrag()` and `stopDrag()` methods to make draggable movie clips.

✦ The `hitTest()` method lets you check if objects are overlapping.

✦ You can potentially optimize playback of complex vector artwork using the `cacheAsBitmap` property.

✦   ✦   ✦

Drawing Programmatically

✦ ✦ ✦ ✦

In This Chapter

Learning how the Drawing API enables you to draw lines, fills, and shapes programmatically with ActionScript

Creating and working with a custom DrawingUtilities class for more powerful scripted drawing

Working with the Drawing API to create fully scripted masks

Practicing using the Drawing API

✦ ✦ ✦ ✦

Macromedia introduced the ActionScript Drawing API in Flash MX, enabling you to develop Flash applications in which lines, curves, shapes, fills, and so on can be programmatically drawn. This creates a whole slew of possibilities that were not previously available. Scripting simple artwork can be an effective and efficient part of your Flash applications. In this chapter, we'll explore how you can programmatically draw everything from simple lines to shapes filled with complex gradient fills. We'll also take a look at some of the many possible uses of scripted graphics.

Introducing the Drawing API

What is referred to as the Drawing API in Flash is simply a subset of methods accessible from `MovieClip` objects. These methods enable you to draw within the object from which they are invoked. Typically, therefore, it is recommended that you create a new `MovieClip` instance for each shape you want to draw. If you recall from our discussion in Chapter 14, the `createEmptyMovieClip()` method allows you to programmatically create empty `MovieClip` objects. This is the perfect technique for creating `MovieClip` objects for use with the Drawing API.

When discussing the Drawing API, it is convenient to work with the metaphor of a pen. You can think of Flash as having an invisible pen that you can command. For example, you can tell it to move to a point without drawing a line — similar to lifting a pen off the paper to move to another point. You can also tell the pen to draw a line from its current location to another point. The Drawing API itself does not consist of many methods. In the following sections, we take a look at each of the handful of methods.

Setting a Line Style

Before you can do anything with the pen, you have to first tell it what kind of lines to draw. This is kind of like selecting among a set of different pens before drawing on a piece of paper. You want to choose the right pen for the job. Do you want a thin or thick line? What color should the line be? Each `MovieClip` object has its own pen. So, you have to set the line style for each `MovieClip` before you can draw in it. To set the line style you can use the `lineStyle()` method. This method accepts eight parameters. All but the line thickness are optional. The following lists the parameters in the order in which the method expects them.

✦ `thickness` — This numeric value can range from 0 (hairline) to 255. This value indicates how many points across the line should be. The parameter is required.

✦ `color` — This numeric value should be the color for the line. Typically, it is convenient to work with hexadecimal representation for this value, though it is not required. For example, to draw a blue line you can use the value 0x0000FF. The default value is 0x000000.

✦ `alpha` — This is a value from 0 to 100 indicating the alpha of the line. Typically, a value of 0 is used only when you want to create a filled shape that displays no outline. The default value is 100.

✦ `pixelSnapping` — New to Flash 8, this optional Boolean parameter lets you instruct Flash to snap to whole pixel values. The default value is `false`.

✦ `scaleType` — Also new to Flash 8, you can optionally specify how a line thickness scales. By default the value is normal, which means the line scales as the movie clip scales. For example, a 1-pixel line within a movie clip that is scaled to 200 percent will appear 2 pixels wide. Setting the value to vertical means it only scales if the movie clip is scaled vertically, and setting the value to horizontal means it only scales if the movie clip is scaled horizontally. Setting the value to none means the line does not scale.

✦ `endCaps` — In Flash 8 you can specify what type of end cap to apply to the line. The default is round. You can also specify square or none.

✦ `joinStyle` — In Flash 8, you can specify how lines join to one another. If two lines share a common end point, then Flash applies a join style. By default the join style is round. You can also specify none or miter, which can cause a pointed or blunted join.

✦ `miterLimit` — If you specify a miter join slyle, you can also specify a number to use as the miter limit. The miter limit specifies the number of pixels from the line joint point the join is cut off. The default value is 3, and the valid range is from 0 to 255.

Here is an example in which we create a new `MovieClip` and set the line style. We'll use a hairline, red line with 100 alpha (implicit because no value is specified).

```
this.createEmptyMovieClip("mShape", this.getNextHighestDepth());
mShape.lineStyle(0, 0xFF0000);
```

You can change the line style at any point as well. For example, you may want to draw one red line and then one green line. You'll take a look at the `lineTo()` method in more detail in a moment, but for right now, here is a simple example that demonstrates how you can change the line style.

```
this.createEmptyMovieClip("mShape", this.getNextHighestDepth());
mShape.lineStyle(0, 0xFF0000);
mShape.lineTo(100, 0);
mShape.lineStyle(0, 0x00FF00);
mShape.lineTo(100, 100);
```

The following code illustrates the pixel snapping functionality. The code draws two rectangles using almost identical parameters. The only difference is that one uses pixel snapping in the line style, and the other does not. When you test the code, you'll notice that the first rectangle has jagged lines while the second has square, smooth lines. The effect is shown in Figure 15-1.

```
this.createEmptyMovieClip("mRectangleA", this.getNextHighestDepth());
mRectangleA.lineStyle(1, 0, 100, false);
mRectangleA.lineTo(100, 0.4);
mRectangleA.lineTo(100.4, 50);
mRectangleA.lineTo(0, 50.4);
mRectangleA.lineTo(0.4, 0)

this.createEmptyMovieClip("mRectangleB", this.getNextHighestDepth());
mRectangleB.lineStyle(1, 0, 100, true);
mRectangleB.lineTo(100, 0.4);
mRectangleB.lineTo(100.4, 50);
mRectangleB.lineTo(0, 50.4);
mRectangleB.lineTo(0.4, 0);
mRectangleB._x = 200;
```

Figure 15-1: The pixel snapping parameter can cause lines to straighten.

The following code illustrates the scale type parameter. Both rectangles are scaled to 400 in the x direction. However, while the line thickness in the first rectangle scales, the line thickness in the second does not. The effect is shown in Figure 15-2.

```
this.createEmptyMovieClip("mRectangleA", this.getNextHighestDepth());
mRectangleA.lineStyle(1, 0, 100);
mRectangleA.lineTo(100, 0);
mRectangleA.lineTo(100, 50);
mRectangleA.lineTo(0, 50);
mRectangleA.lineTo(0, 0);
mRectangleA._xscale = 400;

this.createEmptyMovieClip("mRectangleB", this.getNextHighestDepth());
mRectangleB.lineStyle(1, 0, 100, false, "none");
mRectangleB.lineTo(100, 0);
mRectangleB.lineTo(100, 50);
mRectangleB.lineTo(0, 50);
mRectangleB.lineTo(0, 0);
mRectangleB._y = 100;
mRectangleB._xscale = 400;
```

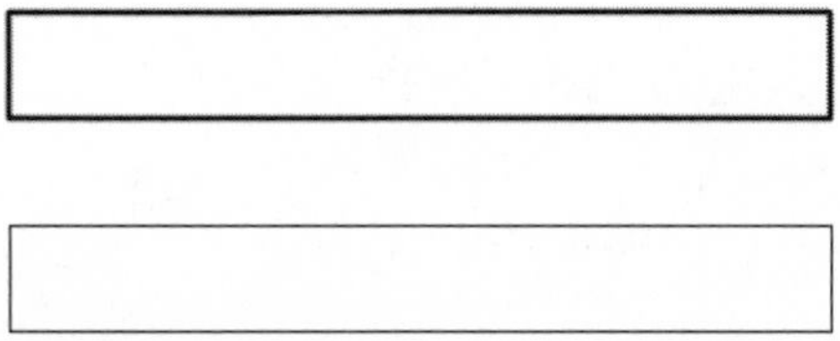

Figure 15-2: Setting the scale type parameter determines how lines scale.

The following code illustrates the types of line end caps. The effect is shown in Figure 15-3.

```
this.createEmptyMovieClip("mLineA", this.getNextHighestDepth());
mLineA._x = 100;
mLineA._y = 100;
mLineA.lineStyle(20, 0, 100, false, "none", "round");
mLineA.lineTo(100, 0);

this.createEmptyMovieClip("mLineB", this.getNextHighestDepth());
mLineB._x = 100;
mLineB._y = 150;
mLineB.lineStyle(20, 0, 100, false, "none", "square");
mLineB.lineTo(100, 0);

this.createEmptyMovieClip("mLineC", this.getNextHighestDepth());
mLineC._x = 100;
mLineC._y = 200;
mLineC.lineStyle(20, 0, 100, false, "none", "none");
mLineC.lineTo(100, 0);
```

 **Figure 15-3:** The line cap styles.

The following code illustrates the join styles and miter limits. The effect is shown in Figure 15-4.

```
this.createEmptyMovieClip("mLinesA", this.getNextHighestDepth());
mLinesA._x = 100;
mLinesA._y = 100;
mLinesA.lineStyle(20, 0, 100, false, "none", "none", "round");
mLinesA.lineTo(100, 0);
mLinesA.lineTo(0, 50);

this.createEmptyMovieClip("mLinesB", this.getNextHighestDepth());
mLinesB._x = 250;
mLinesB._y = 100;
mLinesB.lineStyle(20, 0, 100, false, "none", "none", "none");
mLinesB.lineTo(100, 0);
mLinesB.lineTo(0, 50);

this.createEmptyMovieClip("mLinesC", this.getNextHighestDepth());
mLinesC._x = 100;
mLinesC._y = 200;
mLinesC.lineStyle(20, 0, 100, false, "none", "none", "miter");
mLinesC.lineTo(100, 0);
mLinesC.lineTo(0, 50);

this.createEmptyMovieClip("mLinesD", this.getNextHighestDepth());
mLinesD._x = 250;
```

```
mLinesD._y = 200;
mLinesD.lineStyle(20, 0, 100, false, "none", "none", "miter", 10);
mLinesD.lineTo(100, 0);
mLinesD.lineTo(0, 50);
```

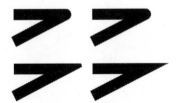

Figure 15-4: Joint styles.

Moving the Pen without Drawing

If you've ever worked with an Etch-a-Sketch, you know how limiting it is to not be able to lift the pen in order to move it without drawing a line. Fortunately, the Flash Drawing API does not have this limitation. You can use the moveTo() method to instruct the pen to move to a specific point within the MovieClip object's coordinate system without drawing a line. The moveTo() method requires two parameters — the X- and Y-coordinate values. Here is an example that creates a MovieClip object, sets the line style, and then moves the pen to 100,100 without drawing a line yet.

```
this.createEmptyMovieClip("mShape", this.getNextHighestDepth());
mShape.lineStyle(0, 0xFF0000);
mShape.moveTo(100, 100);
```

Remember, the point to which you are moving is a coordinate within the coordinate space of the movie clip.

Drawing a Straight Line

The simplest type of drawing in ActionScript is a line. You can create a straight line with the lineTo() method. The lineTo() method, like the moveTo() method, requires that you specify the X- and Y-coordinates to which you want to move the pen. The difference is that unlike moveTo(), the lineTo() method actually draws a line to that point. The line is always drawn from the current coordinate of the pen. If you have not otherwise moved the pen within a MovieClip object, the pen rests at 0,0. Once you have moved the pen using moveTo(), lineTo(), or the curveTo() method (which you'll look at in just a moment) the pen rests at the destination point you specified in the method call. The following example creates a MovieClip object, sets the line style, and then draws a line to 100,0:

```
this.createEmptyMovieClip("mShape", this.getNextHighestDepth());
mShape.lineStyle(0, 0xFF0000);
mShape.lineTo(100, 0);
```

Now that you have drawn one line, if you add another lineTo() that draws a line to 100,100, the second line will be drawn starting from 100,0 — the previous resting place for the pen.

```
mShape.lineTo(100, 100);
```

Of course, if you don't want to start drawing from 0,0, or if you want to draw a line and then draw another line that is not immediately adjacent to the first, you can use lineTo() in conjunction with moveTo(). Here is an example:

```
this.createEmptyMovieClip("mShape", this.getNextHighestDepth());
mShape.lineStyle(0, 0xFF0000);
mShape.moveTo(100, 100);
mShape.lineTo(150, 100);
mShape.moveTo(200, 100);
mShape.lineTo(250, 100);
mShape.moveTo(125, 200);
mShape.lineTo(225, 200);
```

Drawing a Curve

Okay. You've mastered drawing straight lines, and you're anxiously awaiting the next exciting drawing method. Your anticipation is not in vain. The next method looks at the curveTo() method — it's leaps and bounds more exciting than drawing simple lines. Now you can tell Flash to draw a *curved* line.

To draw a curved line, Flash needs several pieces of information — the starting point (which it already knows without you having to tell it), the destination point, and a control point. A control point is a point that is not on the curve. Rather, it is the point at which the tangents to the curve at the starting and ending points of the curve will intersect. Figure 15-5 illustrates this concept.

Figure 15-5: A curve and its control point.

The curveTo() method, therefore, requires four parameters — the X- and Y-coordinates for the control point and the X- and Y-coordinates for the destination point. Here is an example that draws a curve starting at 0,0 to 100,0. The curve has a control point of 50,100.

```
this.createEmptyMovieClip("mShape", this.getNextHighestDepth());
mShape.lineStyle(0, 0xFF0000, 100);
mShape.curveTo(50, 100, 100, 0);
```

Adding a Simple One-Color Fill

When you draw closed shapes, you can have Flash fill the shape with either a solid color or a gradient. The solid color fill is much simpler, so we'll look at that first.

The beginFill() and endFill() methods should always be used in conjunction with one another. The beginFill() method should be called just prior to the lineTo() and/or curveTo() methods that draw a closed shape. The endFill() method should be called just after those methods. The beginFill() method requires one parameter — the numeric color value you want to use to fill the shape. The endFill() method does not require any parameters. Here is an example that draws a 100 by 100 pixel square with a red outline and a yellow fill. Figure 15-6 shows the square.

```
this.createEmptyMovieClip("mShape", this.getNextHighestDepth());
mShape.lineStyle(0, 0xFF0000);
mShape.beginFill(0xFFFF00,100);
mShape.lineTo(100, 0);
mShape.lineTo(100, 100);
mShape.lineTo(0, 100);
mShape.lineTo(0, 0);
mShape.endFill();
```

Figure 15-6: A square with a fill applied using beginFill().

If you call the beginFill() method before a sequence of lineTo() and/or curveTo() methods that do not create a closed shape, Flash will automatically add a line to close the shape if possible.

```
this.createEmptyMovieClip("mShape", this.getNextHighestDepth());
mShape.lineStyle(0, 0xFF0000, 100);
mShape.beginFill(0xFFFF00,100);
mShape.curveTo(50, 100, 100, 0);
mShape.endFill();
```

Notice that the code creates only a single curve. However, if you test this code you will discover that Flash automatically adds another line to create a closed shape, as shown in Figure 15-7.

Figure 15-7: Flash will attempt to close a shape if possible.

Adding a Bitmap Fill

You can add a bitmap fill to any shape using a BitmapData object (see Chapter 18 for more details) in conjunction with the beginBitmapFill() method. The beginBitmapFill() method requires a single parameter — a BitmapData object — but accepts up to three additional parameter — a Matrix object (see Chapter 16 for more details regarding the flash.geom.Matrix class) to apply to the bitmap, whether or not to clip the bitmap (in other words, prevent the bitmap from tiling), and whether or not to apply smoothing to bitmap if it's scaled.

Let's look at an example. The following example uses a MovieClipLoader object to load a JPEG into a MovieClip instance. It then uses that MovieClip to draw the bitmap data into a BitmapData object. At that point it draws a shape, and uses the BitmapData object as a bitmap fill for the shape.

```
import flash.display.BitmapData;
import flash.geom.Matrix;

// Make a movie clip into which to draw the shape.
this.createEmptyMovieClip("mShape", 1);

// Make a movie clip into which to load the image.
this.createEmptyMovieClip("mBitmap", 2);

// Move the shape movie clip so it's visible on stage.
mShape._x = 100;
mShape._y = 200;

// Define a listener object for the MovieClipLoader instance.
var oListener:Object = new Object();

// The onLoadInit() method is called when the image has loaded into the
// movie clip.
oListener.onLoadInit = function(mClip:MovieClip):Void {

  // Define a BitmapData object with dimensions identical to the movie
  // clip with the image.
  var bmpImage:BitmapData = new BitmapData(mClip._width, mClip._height);

  // Draw the image into the BitmapData object.
  bmpImage.draw(mClip, new Matrix());

  // Set the image movie clip to invisible.
  mClip._visible = false;

  // Draw a shape, and use the BitmapData object as the bitmap fill.
  mShape.lineStyle(10);
  mShape.beginBitmapFill(bmpImage);
  mShape.curveTo(100, -50, 200, 0);
  mShape.lineTo(200, 100);
  mShape.lineTo(0, 100);
  mShape.lineTo(0, 0);
  mShape.endFill();
};

var mlBitmap:MovieClipLoader = new MovieClipLoader();
mlBitmap.addListener(oListener);
mlBitmap.loadClip("http://www.rightactionscript.com/
samplefiles/image1.jpg", mBitmap);
```

Figure 15-8 shows the bitmap fill from the preceding code.

Figure 15-8: A shape with a bitmap fill applied.

Next, check what happens when using the optional parameters with the `beginBitmapFill()` method. Using the same code as in the preceding example, update the `beginBitmapFill()` statement to the following:

```
mShape.beginBitmapFill(bmpImage, new Matrix(.1, 0, 0, .1));
```

The matrix used in the preceding line of code scales the bitmap to one-tenth. You'll notice that the scaled bitmap fill tiles within the shape, as shown in Figure 15-9.

Figure 15-9: A bitmap fill with a matrix transform applied.

If you omit the third parameter, it's the equivalent of specifying a value of true. However, if you specify false, the bitmap will not tile. Instead, the edge pixels will extend to the edges of the shape. You can see an example of that by using the following line of code in place of the previous `beginBitmapFill()` line. Figure 15-10 shows the effect.

```
mShape.beginBitmapFill(bmpImage, new Matrix(.1, 0, 0, .1), false);
```

Figure 15-10: Specifying false for the third parameter causes the bitmap not to tile.

The fourth parameter, if omitted, is the equivalent to specifying false. When the parameter is omitted or false, and if the bitmap is scaled greater than 100 percent, it may appear blocky. Use the following line of code in place of the previous `beginBitmapFill()` statement to see what that can look like.

```
mShape.beginBitmapFill(bmpImage, new Matrix(10, 0, 0, 10));
```

Then, use the following line of code to notice how it appears with smoothing.

```
mShape.beginBitmapFill(bmpImage, new Matrix(10, 0, 0, 10), true, true);
```

Working with Gradients

There are two types of gradients that you can apply using the Drawing API — gradient lines and gradient fills. Gradient lines are new to Flash Player 8, while gradient fills have been around for several versions. Each works in a very similar fashion, so once you learn one, the other will be quite simple to learn. Additionally, the `Matrix` class (see Chapter 16 for more details) provides a method, `createGradientBox()` that assists in building the necessary matrix when applying gradients. That makes your work that much simpler compared to previous versions of Flash, in which you had to construct the matrix manually.

Applying Gradients to Lines

With Flash 8, you can apply gradient styles to lines using the `lineGradientStyle()` method. The `lineGradientStyle()` method is not a substitute for the `lineStyle()` method. The `lineStyle()` method is still necessary to set the basic line style thickness parameter. However, once you've set that, you can also use the `lineGradientStyle()` method to instruct Flash to draw a line using a gradient. The method requires the following parameter data:

✦ `type` — Specifies whether the gradient is to be *linear* (the color changes gradually along a line) or *radial* (the color changes gradually from a central point and moves outward).

✦ `colors` — ActionScript expects you to specify an array of numeric color values. For linear gradients the colors gradate from left to right. For radial gradients the colors gradate from the center out.

✦ `alphas` — For each color value you must include an accompanying alpha value. Again, ActionScript expects an array for these values. Each element of the alphas array should correspond to an element of the colors array. The alpha values should be from 0 to 100.

✦ `ratios` — Flash also needs to know what ratios to use for the colors. Where along the spectrum of the gradient should Flash center each color from the colors array? Flash uses values from 0 to 255 to indicate the ratios. A value of 0 means that the corresponding color's center should be located at the far left (linear) or center (radial) of the gradient. A value of 255 indicates that the corresponding color's center should be located at the far right (linear) or outside (radial) of the gradient.

✦ `matrix` — The default gradient used by Flash is a 1 pixel by 1 pixel gradient. Obviously, that is not going to fill most lines or shapes. Therefore, Flash needs to know how to transform this unit gradient to fill the line or shape in the way that you want. In order to accomplish this, Flash uses a transformation matrix which you can construct using a Matrix object as discussed shortly.

✦ `spreadMethod` — The spread method is a string value of either `"pad"` (default), `"reflect"`, or `"repeat"`. The pad option means that if the gradient dimensions are less than those of the line or shape, it pads the remainder of the line or shape using the last color in the colors array. Reflect means that it will reverse the gradient repeatedly as necessary. For example, if the gradient gradually goes from red to blue, if necessary it will then go from blue to red. When the repeat option is selected the same gradient simply repeats as necessary.

✦ `interpolationMethod` — The interpolation method is a string value of either `"RGB"` (default) or `"linearRGB"`. If the linearRGB option is specified, the colors are distributed linearly.

✦ `focalPointRatio` — The focal point ratio can range from -1 to 1, with the default being 0. It only has an effect when the gradient type is radial, as it shifts the focus (the center of the gradient) from left (-1) to right (1) within the ellipse.

That's a lot of parameters, so a few examples will probably help. First, however, let's briefly discuss how to construct a matrix using the Matrix class. You can construct a standard Matrix object, and then use the createGradientBox() method. The createGradientBox() method accepts up to five parameters — width, height, rotation (in radians), amount to translate in the X direction, and amount to translate in the Y direction. The width and height parameters are required. The remaining parameters have default values of 0. The following code makes a Matrix object that you can use with the lineGradientStyle() method to apply a gradient that has dimensions of 200 x 100 pixels.

```
import flash.geom.Matrix;

var mxBox:Matrix = new Matrix();
mxBox.createGradientBox(200, 100);
```

Next, let's look at some examples. The following draws a shape, and applies a gradient to the line that uses a linear gradient that ranges from yellow to cyan, as shown in Figure 15-11.

```
import flash.geom.Matrix;

this.createEmptyMovieClip("mShape", 1);

mShape._x = 100;
mShape._y = 100;

// Define a matrix that will scale the gradient to 200 by 200 pixels.
var mxBox:Matrix = new Matrix();
mxBox.createGradientBox(200, 200);

// Set the line style.
mShape.lineStyle(10);

// Set the line gradient style to apply a linear gradient that goes from
// yellow to cyan with yellow at the left edge and cyan at the right
// edge.
mShape.lineGradientStyle("linear", [0xFFFF00, 0x00FFFF], [100, 100],
[0x00, 0xFF], mxBox);
mShape.curveTo(200, -100, 400, 0);
mShape.lineTo(400, 200);
mShape.lineTo(0, 200);
mShape.lineTo(0, 0);
mShape.endFill();
```

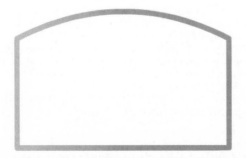

Figure 15-11: A line with a gradient applied.

You'll notice that when you test the code, the gradient is not evenly distributed across the entire shape. The cyan is at 100 percent at halfway across the shape. That is because the matrix scales the gradient to 200 x 200 pixels, but the shape is 400 pixels across. Since the default spread method is `pad`, the cyan pads the rest of the shape. Next take a look at the effects of the optional parameters. We'll start by updating the preceding code by specifying a value for the `spread` method parameter. Update the `lineGradientStyle()` line to the following:

```
mShape.lineGradientStyle("linear", [0xFFFF00, 0x00FFFF],
    [100, 100], [0x00, 0xFF], mxBox, "reflect");
```

When you do that, you'll notice that the gradient goes from yellow on the left to cyan in the middle, and then back to yellow on the right. If you use a value of `repeat` instead, the same gradient will repeat so that it will go from yellow to cyan and then yellow to cyan again.

The next parameter determines how Flash interpolates the colors as they gradate. So far, you've seen the effects of the standard interpolation algorithm. Update the `lineGradientStyle()` line as follows to use the linear interpolation algorithm. The effects are rather subtle, particularly because the gradient is applied to a 10 point line.

```
mShape.lineGradientStyle("linear", [0xFFFF00, 0x00FFFF],
    [100, 100], [0x00, 0xFF], mxBox, "reflect", "linearRGB");
```

In order that the focal point ratio parameter can have a noticeable effect, let's use a radial gradient for the next few updates to the example. If you update the `lineGradientStyle()` method as follows, it will tell Flash to use a radial grandient instead of a linear one. Notice that we're also setting the `spread` method to pad.

```
mShape.lineGradientStyle("radial", [0xFFFF00, 0x00FFFF],
    [100, 100], [0x00, 0xFF], mxBox, "pad", "linearRGB");
```

When you test the code, you'll likely see what appears to be a solid cyan line. That's because the yellow portion is located within the shape, and it radiates outward toward the cyan edges. In order to be able to see some of the yellow portion of the gradient, let's update the line style to draw a 100-point line instead of a 10-point line:

```
mShape.lineStyle(100);
```

Then, when you test the code you'll see the edges of the yellow radiating outward. Let's next adjust the focal point:

```
mShape.lineGradientStyle("radial", [0xFFFF00, 0x00FFFF],
    [100, 100], [0x00, 0xFF], mxBox, "pad", "linearRGB", 1);
```

You can set the ratio to anything from -1 to 1. Check out the effect with different values.

Applying Gradient Fills

You can apply gradient fills using the `beginGradientFill()` method. The `beginGradientFill()` method works similarly to the `beginFill()` method in that you call it just prior to drawing the shape, and you call `endFill()` once you've drawn the shape. The `beginGradientFill()` method accepts the same parameters as does `lineGradientStyle()`, so refer to the preceding section for more details about the parameters. The following code illustrates how to use the `beginGradientFill()` method. Figure 15-12 shows the effect.

```
import flash.geom.Matrix;

this.createEmptyMovieClip("mShape", 1);

mShape._x = 100;
mShape._y = 100;

var mxBox:Matrix = new Matrix();
mxBox.createGradientBox(200, 200);

mShape.lineStyle(10);
mShape.beginGradientFill("radial", [0xFFFF00, 0x00FFFF],
[100, 100], [0x00, 0xFF], mxBox, "reflect", "RGB", 1);
mShape.curveTo(200, -100, 400, 0);
mShape.lineTo(400, 200);
mShape.lineTo(0, 200);
mShape.lineTo(0, 0);
mShape.endFill();
```

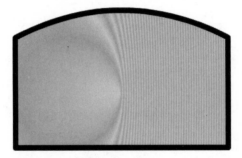

Figure 15-12: A gradient fill.

Clearing Previously Drawn Graphics

Of course, even the trusty Etch-a-Sketch allows you to clear what you have drawn so that you can draw again. The ActionScript Drawing API, not to be shamed by Etch-a-Sketch, also provides you the means by which you can clear what you have drawn. The clear() method removes all lines, curves, and fills that have been drawn within a MovieClip object:

```
mShape.clear();
```

Working with a Drawing Utilities Class

Although the Drawing API is a great foundation, it does not appear particularly robust. For example, it does not provide methods for drawing simple shapes such as rectangles, circles, and assorted, regular polygons (triangles, hexagons, and so on). To provide this kind of functionality, you'll need a custom class. On the web site you will find just such a custom class.

On The Web Site

To use the custom class, copy the DrawingUtilities.as file from the Web site to a directory in your global Flash classpath.

Getting Started with DrawingUtilities

The DrawingUtilities class is a helper class for working with the Drawing API. The class includes all the basic Drawing API functionality (lineTo(), moveTo(), and so on), but it also includes methods for drawing other kinds of shapes. And, in addition, the class has a default line style so that if you want to use a black hairline as the line style, you don't have to invoke the lineStyle() method explicitly.

In order to work with the DrawingUtilities class, you must first create an instance. The constructor for DrawingUtilities requires that you pass it a reference to the MovieClip into which it should draw. Here is an example in which you create a new MovieClip object and then create a new DrawingUtilities object to draw into that MovieClip:

```
this.createEmptyMovieClip("mShape", this.getNextHighestDepth());
var duDrawer:DrawingUtilities = new DrawingUtilities(mShape);
```

Once you've created a new DrawingUtilities instance that targets a MovieClip instance, you can invoke all the same Drawing API methods from the DrawingUtilities instance. For example:

```
this.createEmptyMovieClip("mShape", this.getNextHighestDepth());
var duDrawer:DrawingUtilities = new DrawingUtilities(mShape);
duDrawer.lineStyle(12, 0xFFFF00);
duDrawer.lineTo(100, 100);
```

Of course, if that was all you intended to do, it would be rather silly to create the DrawingUtilities instance in the first place. You might as well invoke the methods directly from the MovieClip instance. The benefits of working with a DrawingUtilities object are in being able to work with the built-in methods for creating shapes. Let's take a look at some of those methods now.

Drawing Rectangles

One of the simplest types of shapes is the rectangle. The drawRectangle() method can be invoked from a DrawingUtilities object in order to draw a rectangle within the target MovieClip instance. The method requires four parameters — the width and height of the rectangle to be drawn and the X- and Y-coordinates of that rectangle's center within the MovieClip. Here's an example:

```
import actionscriptbible.drawing.DrawingUtilities;

this.createEmptyMovieClip("mShape", this.getNextHighestDepth());
var duDrawer:DrawingUtilities = new DrawingUtilities(mShape);
duDrawer.drawRectangle(100, 150, 200, 200);
```

The preceding code will draw a rectangle outline as shown in Figure 15-13.

Figure 15-13: A shape created with drawRectangle().

If you want to fill the rectangle, all you need to do is invoke the beginFill() (or beginGradientFill()) method before calling drawRectangle() and invoke the endFill() method after calling drawRectangle():

```
import actionscriptbible.drawing.DrawingUtilities;

this.createEmptyMovieClip("mShape", this.getNextHighestDepth());
var duDrawer:DrawingUtilities = new DrawingUtilities(mShape);
duDrawer.beginFill(0xFF0000, 100);
duDrawer.drawRectangle(100, 150, 200, 200);
duDrawer.endFill();
```

Note Notice that in the preceding code examples, the lineStyle() method was not explicitly called. This is because the DrawingUtilities class uses a default line style. If you want to change the line style you can do so by invoking the lineStyle() method from the DrawingUtilities object with the same parameters as when you invoke the method from a MovieClip.

Drawing Circles

Another common shape is the circle. Drawing a good circle on your own with the Drawing API can be a bit of a challenge. But with the drawCircle() method of the DrawingUtilities class, it is as simple as a single method call. The method expects three parameters — the radius of the circle and the X- and Y-coordinates of the center of the circle. Here is an example:

```
import actionscriptbible.drawing.DrawingUtilities;

this.createEmptyMovieClip("mShape", this.getNextHighestDepth());
var duDrawer:DrawingUtilities = new DrawingUtilities(mShape);
duDrawer.beginFill(0xFF0000, 100);
duDrawer.drawCircle(100, 200, 200);
duDrawer.endFill();
```

The preceding code will draw a filled circle with a radius of 100, as illustrated in Figure 15-14.

Figure 15-14: A shape drawn with drawCircle().

Drawing Regular Polygons

Regular polygons are closed shapes in which each of the sides is equal (necessarily, there-fore, all the interior angles are equal and all the exterior angles are equal). An equilateral tri-angle is a three-sided regular polygon, and a square is a four-sided regular polygon. The `drawPolygon()` method allows you to draw a regular polygon with five parameters — the radius from center to vertex, the number of sides, the rotation in radians, and the X- and Y-coordinates of the center of the polygon. Here is an example that draws a triangle rotated by 0 (in other words, not rotated).

```
import actionscriptbible.drawing.DrawingUtilities;

this.createEmptyMovieClip("mShape", this.getNextHighestDepth());
var duDrawer:DrawingUtilities = new DrawingUtilities(mShape);
duDrawer.drawPolygon(100, 3, 0, 200, 200);
```

Figure 15-15 shows the triangle that the code will draw.

Figure 15-15: A shape drawn with drawPolygon().

Drawing Fills

The `DrawingUtilities` class also includes a rather unique method. The `drawPatternFill()` method draws a series of shapes to fill an area. The method takes a single parameters — an object with any of the properties shown in Table 15-1.

Table 15-1: Properties of the drawPatternFill() Parameter Object

Property Name	Default Value	Description
width	100	The width in pixels of the fill area.
height	100	The height of the fill area in pixels.
cols	10	The number of columns within the fill area.
x	0	The starting X-coordinate of the fill area relative to the `MovieClip` object's coordinate space.
y	0	The starting Y-coordinate of the fill area relative to the `MovieClip` object's coordinate space.
rotation	0	The amount of rotation for the shapes in radians.
offset	1	A number indicating how much each row should be offset from the adjacent rows. A value of 0 lines up all the columns.

Property Name	Default Value	Description
shape	{shape:"circle"}	An object with a shape property. The shape property can have a value of circle, square, or polygon. If the value is polygon you should also include a sides property with a numeric value of 3 or more.
fill	Undefined	If defined, this numeric value is used as the color to fill the shapes.
randomizeColor	False	A Boolean value indicating whether to randomize the colors of each of the shapes in the fill.

If you don't pass any parameter to the drawPatternFill() method, it uses all defaults. Otherwise, if you pass it an object it still uses the defaults for any properties you don't define. Here's an example that uses the default values for all the properties:

```
import actionscriptbible.drawing.DrawingUtilities;

this.createEmptyMovieClip("mFill", this.getNextHighestDepth());
var duDrawer:DrawingUtilities = new DrawingUtilities(mFill);
duDrawer.drawPatternFill();
```

The fill that it generates looks like what you see in Figure 15-16.

 Figure 15-16: The default pattern fill.

Notice that the MovieClip is automatically masked. This is a feature built into drawPatternFill(). This feature works as long as you have used getNextHighestDepth() to generate all the depths for programmatically created MovieClip, Button, and TextField objects within the same parent object as the fill MovieClip.

Here's another example that draws a pattern fill with some parameters other than the defaults:

```
import actionscriptbible.drawing.DrawingUtilities;

this.createEmptyMovieClip("mFill", this.getNextHighestDepth());
var duDrawer:DrawingUtilities = new DrawingUtilities(mFill);
var oParameters:Object = new Object();
oParameters.shape = {name: "polygon", sides:"6"};
oParameters.cols = 6;
oParameters.rotation = Math.PI/4;
oParameters.width = 300;
oParameters.height = 300;
oParameters.space = 1;
duDrawer.drawPatternFill(oParameters);
```

Figure 15-17 shows what the preceding code creates.

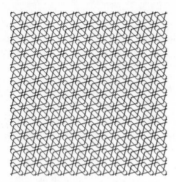

Figure 15-17: A nondefault
pattern fill.

Here's yet another example that shows how you can use the `fill` parameter to fill each of the shapes in the fill. Also, this example sets the `lineStyle()` for the `DrawingUtilities` object in order to specify the color of the lines.

```
import actionscriptbible.drawing.DrawingUtilities;

this.createEmptyMovieClip("mFill", this.getNextHighestDepth());
var duDrawer:DrawingUtilities = new DrawingUtilities(mFill);
var oParameters:Object = new Object();
oParameters.shape = {name: "polygon", sides:"3"};
oParameters.rotation = Math.PI/4;
oParameters.width = 200;
oParameters.height = 200;
oParameters.fill = 0xFF0000;
duDrawer.lineStyle(2, 0xFF00FF, 100);
duDrawer.drawPatternFill(oParameters);
```

The preceding code creates a fill, as shown in Figure 15-18.

Figure 15-18: A filled pattern.

Practicing Dynamic Masking

In Chapter 14, you had the opportunity to read about scriptable masking. But scriptable masking is only minimally useful, and only of use if you cannot dynamically create the mask itself. The Drawing API enables you to do just that. In this example, you place two `MovieClip` objects containing images on the stage. The objects will be placed such that they overlap and only the topmost image can be seen. Then, you'll use the Drawing API to draw a mask to the dimensions of the top `MovieClip` object, and you'll tell Flash to animate the mask when the stage is clicked. This creates a simple wipe transition effect between the two images. Complete the following steps:

1. Open a new Flash document, and save it to your local disk as `dynamicMask.fla`.

2. Add the following code to the first frame of the default layer of the main timeline:

```
import actionscriptbible.drawing.DrawingUtilities;

var sDirection:String = "off";
var nInterval:Number = null;

this.createEmptyMovieClip("mA", this.getNextHighestDepth());
mA.createEmptyMovieClip("mImage", 1);
mA._visible = false;
this.createEmptyMovieClip("mB", this.getNextHighestDepth());
mB.createEmptyMovieClip("mImage", 1);
mB._visible = false;
this.createEmptyMovieClip("mMask", this.getNextHighestDepth());

var oListener:Object = new Object();
oListener.onLoadInit = function(mClip:MovieClip):Void {
  if(mA._width > 0 && mB._width > 0) {
    mA._visible = true;
    mB._visible = true;
    drawMask();
  }
};

var mlImages:MovieClipLoader = new MovieClipLoader();
mlImages.addListener(oListener);
mlImages.loadClip("http://www.rightactionscript.com/
samplefiles/image1.jpg", mA.mImage);
mlImages.loadClip("http://www.rightactionscript.com/
samplefiles/image2.jpg", mB.mImage);

mA.onRelease = function():Void {
  if(nInterval == null) {
    nInterval = setInterval(slideMask, 10);
  }
};

function drawMask():Void {
```

```
      var duMaskDrawer:DrawingUtilities =
new DrawingUtilities(mMask);
      duMaskDrawer.beginFill(0, 100);
      duMaskDrawer.drawRectangle(mB._width, mB._height,
mB._width/2, mB._height/2);
      duMaskDrawer.endFill();
      mB.setMask(mMask);
   }

function slideMask():Void {
   mMask._x -= 10;
   if(sDirection == "on") {
     if(mMask._x <= 0) {
       clearInterval(nInterval);
       nInterval = null;
       mMask._x = 0;
       sDirection = "off";
     }
   }
   else {
     if(mMask._x <= -mMask._width) {
       clearInterval(nInterval);
       nInterval = null;
       mMask._x = mMask._width;
       sDirection = "on";
     }
   }
   updateAfterEvent();
}
```

3. Save the document and test the movie.

When you test the movie, you should be able to click on the stage and see a simple wipe occur between the two images. Click again and the application will wipe between the images again.

Now that you've had a chance to see the application work, take a closer look at the code.

The mA and mB MovieClip objects each have nested mImage MovieClip objects. That is necessary because the code loads images into the application at runtime. If an image is loaded into a MovieClip object some properties and methods no longer work. However, if the images are loaded into the nested mImage objects, the parent mA and mB objects still function as normal MovieClip objects. Additionally, since you cannot accurately predict which image will load before the other, we set mA and mB to invisible until the images are loaded into the player.

```
this.createEmptyMovieClip("mA", this.getNextHighestDepth());
mA.createEmptyMovieClip("mImage", 1);
mA._visible = false;
this.createEmptyMovieClip("mB", this.getNextHighestDepth());
mB.createEmptyMovieClip("mImage", 1);
mB._visible = false;
```

Next, make the MovieClip into which you'll draw the mask.

```
this.createEmptyMovieClip("mMask", this.getNextHighestDepth());
```

The listener object is used by the `MovieClipLoader` object to determine when the images have loaded into the player. Once both images have loaded into the player, both mA and mB will have nonzero dimensions. At that point set the visibility of the objects to true, and call `drawMask()`. Use the `MovieClipLoader` object to load the images into the two nested MovieClip objects.

```
var oListener:Object = new Object();
oListener.onLoadInit = function(mClip:MovieClip):Void {
  if(mA._width > 0 && mB._width > 0) {
    mA._visible = true;
    mB._visible = true;
    drawMask();
  }
};

var mlImages:MovieClipLoader = new MovieClipLoader();
mlImages.addListener(oListener);
mlImages.loadClip("http://www.rightactionscript.com/
samplefiles/image1.jpg", mA.mImage);
mlImages.loadClip("http://www.rightactionscript.com/
samplefiles/image2.jpg", mB.mImage);
```

Use an `onRelease()` event handler method to run some actions whenever the user clicks on the images. If no interval is currently running, use `setInterval()` to start a new interval that repeatedly calls `slideMask()`.

```
  mA.onRelease = function():Void {
    if(nInterval == null) {
      nInterval = setInterval(slideMask, 10);
    }
  };
```

The `drawMask()` function uses a `DrawingUtilities` object to draw a black rectangle within mMask that matches the dimensions of mB. It then sets mMask as the mask of mB.

```
function drawMask():Void {
  var duMaskDrawer:DrawingUtilities = new DrawingUtilities(mMask);
  duMaskDrawer.beginFill(0, 100);
  duMaskDrawer.drawRectangle(mB._width, mB._height, mB._width/2, mB._height/2);
  duMaskDrawer.endFill();
  mB.setMask(mMask);
}
```

The `slideMask()` function, which is called on an interval when the mouse is clicked, moves mMask to the left by 10 pixels. The mask needs to stop once it reaches a certain point. The point is determined by whether the mask is moving off of the image or over the image. The sDirection variable has a value of either off or on, and it assists in determining what action the application ought to take. If the direction is on then it means that the mask started off the image, and it is moving over (or on) the image. Therefore once the X-coordinate of mMask is less than or equal to 0, the mask ought to stop. To make sure the mask is at 0, the _x property is then assigned 0. On the other hand, if the direction is off, that means it ought to stop once the right edge of the mask is less than or equal to 0 (in more technical terms it stops when the X-coordinate is less than or equal to the negative width of the mask). At that point, the mask is then moved so the X-coordinate is to the right of the images. In either case, the value of sDirection is then reversed and the interval is cleared.

```
function slideMask():Void {
  mMask._x -= 10;
  if(sDirection == "on") {
    if(mMask._x <= 0) {
      clearInterval(nInterval);
      nInterval = null;
      mMask._x = 0;
      sDirection = "off";
    }
  }
  else {
    if(mMask._x <= -mMask._width) {
      clearInterval(nInterval);
      nInterval = null;
      mMask._x = mMask._width;
      sDirection = "on";
    }
  }
  updateAfterEvent();
}
```

Practicing Responsive Objects

In this exercise. you use the Drawing API to create a square that responds to the mouse. When the user moves the mouse near a side of the square, that side will appear to be pressed in, following the movement of the mouse. Complete the following steps:

1. Open a new Flash document, and save it as responsiveObject.fla.

2. On the first frame of the first layer add the following code:

```
import actionscriptbible.drawing.DrawingUtilities;

var aColors:Array = [0xFEEFD6, 0xEDFED6, 0xDED7FD,
0xFED6ED, 0xFFD5D5];
var nSelectedColor:Number = aColors[0];
var oSides:Object = new Object();
var oColors:Object = new Object();
var mCurrent:MovieClip;
var nInterval:Number;

oSides.mRight = {y:0, x:110, rotation:90};
oSides.mBottom = {y:100, x:0, rotation:0};
oSides.mLeft = {y:0, x:0, rotation:90};
oSides.mTop = {y:-10, x:0, rotation:0};

makeColorOptions(aColors);
makeBoxAndSides(aSides);
drawSquare();

function makeBoxAndSides():Void {
```

```
  this.createEmptyMovieClip("mShape",                        ⊃
this.getNextHighestDepth());
  mShape.createEmptyMovieClip("mBox",                        ⊃
mShape.getNextHighestDepth());
  var mSide:MovieClip;
  var duDrawer:DrawingUtilities;
  for(var sSide:String in oSides) {
    mSide = mShape.createEmptyMovieClip(sSide,               ⊃
mShape.getNextHighestDepth());
    duDrawer = new DrawingUtilities(mSide);
    duDrawer.lineStyle(0, 0, 0);
    duDrawer.beginFill(0, 0);
    duDrawer.drawRectangle(100, 10, 50, 5);
    mSide.useHandCursor = false;
    mSide.onRollOver = function():Void {
      if(mCurrent == this) {
        return;
      }
      resetSide(mCurrent);
      mCurrent = this;
      this.startDrag(true);
      nInterval = setInterval(drawSquare, 10);
    };
    resetSide(mSide);
  }
  addBoxMethod();
  drawSquare();
  mShape._x = Stage.width/2 - mShape._width/2;
  mShape._y = Stage.height/2 - mShape._height/2;
}

function resetSide(mSide:MovieClip):Void {
  mSide._y = oSides[mSide._name].y;
  mSide._x = oSides[mSide._name].x;
  mSide._rotation = oSides[mSide._name].rotation;
  mSide.stopDrag();
  clearInterval(nInterval);
}

function makeColorOptions(aColors:Array):Void {
  for(var i:Number = 0; i < aColors.length; i++) {
    mSwatch = this.createEmptyMovieClip(                     ⊃
"mColorSwatch" + i, this.getNextHighestDepth());
    oColors[mSwatch._name] = aColors[i];
    duDrawer = new DrawingUtilities(mSwatch);
    duDrawer.beginFill(aColors[i], 100);
    duDrawer.drawRectangle(15, 15, 7.5, 7.5);
    duDrawer.endFill();
    mSwatch._x = 30;
    mSwatch._y = 20 * i + 30;
    mSwatch.onRelease = function():Void {
      nSelectedColor = oColors[this._name];
      drawSquare();
    };
```

```
    }
}

function drawSquare():Void {
  var oRight:Object = {x: mShape.mRight._x - 10,
y: mShape.mRight._y};
  var oBottom:Object = {x: mShape.mBottom._x,
y: mShape.mBottom._y};
  var oLeft:Object = {x: mShape.mLeft._x, y: mShape.mLeft._y};
  var oTop:Object = {x: mShape.mTop._x, y: mShape.mTop._y + 10};
  var nMx:Number = mShape.mBox._xmouse;
  var nMy:Number = mShape.mBox._ymouse;
  switch (mCurrent._name) {
    case "mRight":
      if(nMx > 110) {
        resetSide(mCurrent);
        mCurrent = null;
      }
      if(nMx < 25) {
        nMx = 25;
      }
      else if(nMx > 100) {
        nMx = 100;
      }
      if(nMy < 25) {
        nMy = 25;
      }
      else if(nMy > 75) {
        nMy = 75;
      }
      oRight.x = 2*nMx - 100;
      oRight.y = 2*nMy - 50;
      break;
    case "mBottom":
      if(nMy > 110) {
        resetSide(mCurrent);
        mCurrent = null;
      }
      if(nMx < 25) {
        nMx = 25;
      }
      else if(nMx > 75) {
        nMx = 75;
      }
      if(nMy < 25) {
        nMy = 25;
      }
      else if(nMy > 100) {
        nMy = 100;
      }
      oBottom.x = 2*nMx - 50;
      oBottom.y = 2*nMy - 100;
      break;
```

```
    case "mLeft":
      if(nMx < -10) {
        resetSide(mCurrent);
        mCurrent = null;
      }
      if(nMx < 0) {
        nMx = 0;
      }
      else if(nMx > 75) {
        nMx = 75;
      }
      if(nMy < 25) {
        nMy = 25;
      }
      else if(nMy > 75) {
        nMy = 75;
      }
      oLeft.x = 2*nMx;
      oLeft.y = 2*nMy - (.5 * 100);
      break;
    case "mTop":
      if(nMy < -10) {
        resetSide(mCurrent);
        mCurrent = null;
      }
      if(nMx < 25) {
        nMx = 25;
      }
      else if(nMx > 75) {
        nMx = 75;
      }
      if(nMy < 0) {
        nMy = 0;
      }
      else if(nMy > 75) {
        nMy = 75;
      }
      oTop.x = 2*nMx - (.5 * 100);
      oTop.y = 2*nMy;
      break;
  }
  mShape.mBox.clear();
  mShape.mBox.lineStyle(0, 0, 100);
  mShape.mBox.beginFill(nSelectedColor, 100);
  mShape.mBox.curveTo(oTop.x, oTop.y, 100, 0);
  mShape.mBox.curveTo(oRight.x, oRight.y, 100, 100);
  mShape.mBox.curveTo(oBottom.x, oBottom.y, 0, 100);
  mShape.mBox.curveTo(oLeft.x, oLeft.y, 0, 0);
  mShape.mBox.endFill();
  updateAfterEvent();
}
```

3. Save the document as responsiveBox001.fla **and test the movie.**

When you test the movie you should initially see a large square in the center, and five smaller squares on the left side, as shown in Figure 15-19. The large square is the responsive object that will reshape according to the mouse movement. The five smaller squares allow you to select a new color for the responsive square.

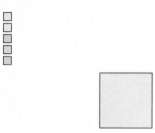

Figure 15-19: The initial appearance of responsiveBox.swf.

When you move the mouse so that it touches one of the sides of the square, you'll see that it pushes the side inward as shown in Figure 15-20.

Figure 15-20: The square responds to mouse movement.

So now that you've seen it working, the question is *how* does it work? If you make a temporary change to a single line of code, you'll be able to see how it works a little better. On or around approximately line 28 is the following line:

```
duDrawer.beginFill(0, 0);
```

Change that line of code to:

```
duDrawer.beginFill(0, 50);
```

This changes the transparency of the four previously invisible rectangles that border the sides of the box. If you test the movie now you can see these rectangles move with the mouse when you roll over them.

The four rectangles enable Flash to know when the mouse has moved near one of the sides . . . and it allows Flash to know *which* side. Once the rectangle has been rolled over, it is set as draggable, and the corresponding side of the square is redrawn to match the current mouse location.

You can set the `alpha` value back to 0. Now take a look at the code that makes this all work.

The first thing you want to do is define an array of color values. You pass this array of colors to the `makeColorOptions()` function — a function you'll examine in just a moment.

```
var aColors:Array = [0xFEEFD6, 0xEDFED6, 0xDED7FD, 0xFED6ED, 0xFFD5D5];
```

You then assign the first color value to a variable, `nSelectedColor`. This variable is used throughout to determine which color to assign to the box.

```
var nSelectedColor:Number = aColors[0];
```

The `oSides` and `oColors` objects are associative arrays that use MovieClip instance names as keys. They store data specific to the instances, and that way the data can get looked up by way of the `_name` property of an instance from within an event handler method, as you'll see shortly.

```
var oSides:Object = new Object();
var oColors:Object = new Object();
```

The `oSides` associative array has four elements — one that corresponds to each of the four sides of the square. Each element contains data that the application uses to set the default coordinates and rotation of detector MovieClips on each side.

```
oSides.mRight = {y:0, x:110, rotation:90};
oSides.mBottom = {y:100, x:0, rotation:0};
oSides.mLeft = {y:0, x:0, rotation:90};
oSides.mTop = {y:-10, x:0, rotation:0};
```

The `makeBoxAndSides` function does what it says. It makes a new MovieClip object called `mShape`, and it then defines a nested MovieClip object called `mBox`.

```
function makeBoxAndSides():Void {
  this.createEmptyMovieClip("mShape", this.getNextHighestDepth());
  mShape.createEmptyMovieClip("mBox", mShape.getNextHighestDepth());
```

Then, it loops through each of the elements of the `oSides` associative array, and it defines a detector MovieClip object into which it draws a rectangle with 0 alpha applied to the outline and fill.

```
for(var sSide:String in oSides) {
  mSide = mShape.createEmptyMovieClip(sSide, mShape.getNextHighestDepth());
  duDrawer = new DrawingUtilities(mSide);
  duDrawer.lineStyle(0, 0, 0);
  duDrawer.beginFill(0, 0);
  duDrawer.drawRectangle(100, 10, 50, 5);
  mSide.useHandCursor = false;
```

The detectors each have an `onRollOver()` event handler method that makes the object draggable, and it starts an interval that calls `drawSquare()` repeatedly.

```
    mSide.onRollOver = function():Void {
      if(mCurrent == this) {
        return;
      }
      resetSide(mCurrent);
      mCurrent = this;
      this.startDrag(true);
      nInterval = setInterval(drawSquare, 10);
    };
```

The function then calls `drawSquare()` to draw the square, and it places it in the middle of the stage.

```
drawSquare();
mShape._x = Stage.width/2 - mShape._width/2;
mShape._y = Stage.height/2 - mShape._height/2;
```

The `resetSide()` function resets the location of the specified object to the default coordinates from the `oSides` associative array. It also calls `stopDrag()` on the specified object, and it clears any existing interval.

```
function resetSide(mSide:MovieClip):Void {
  mSide._y = oSides[mSide._name].y;
  mSide._x = oSides[mSide._name].x;
  mSide._rotation = oSides[mSide._name].rotation;
  mSide.stopDrag();
  clearInterval(nInterval);
}
```

The `makeColorOptions()` function takes an array parameter, and it draws as many swatches with corresponding colors. Each swatch is assigned an `onRelease()` event handler such that when it is clicked it sets the value of `nSelectedColor` to match the corresponding color from `oColors`, and it then redraws the square.

```
function makeColorOptions(aColors:Array):Void {
  for(var i:Number = 0; i < aColors.length; i++) {
    mSwatch = this.createEmptyMovieClip(
"mColorSwatch" + i, this.getNextHighestDepth());
    oColors[mSwatch._name] = aColors[i];
    duDrawer = new DrawingUtilities(mSwatch);
    duDrawer.beginFill(aColors[i], 100);
    duDrawer.drawRectangle(15, 15, 7.5, 7.5);
    duDrawer.endFill();
    mSwatch._x = 30;
    mSwatch._y = 20 * i + 30;
    mSwatch.onRelease = function():Void {
      nSelectedColor = oColors[this._name];
      drawSquare();
    };
  }
}
```

The `drawSquare()` function does the drawing of the square repeatedly through the application. It defines four objects that have *x* and *y* properties, the values of which determine the control point for a curve that will form a straight line. These are the default settings that create a square:

```
function drawSquare():Void {
  var oRight:Object = {x: mShape.mRight._x - 10, y: mShape.mRight._y};
  var oBottom:Object = {x: mShape.mBottom._x, y: mShape.mBottom._y};
  var oLeft:Object = {x: mShape.mLeft._x, y: mShape.mLeft._y};
  var oTop:Object = {x: mShape.mTop._x, y: mShape.mTop._y + 10};
```

Then you want to get the current X- and Y-coordinates of the mouse. You'll use these values to help determine the control point for one of the curved sides if necessary:

```
var nMx:Number = mShape.mBox._xmouse;
var nMy:Number = mShape.mBox._ymouse;
```

You want to calculate a new control point if the mouse position will cause one of the sides to be curved. Which side should be curved is determined by the currently selected side rectangle. You use a `switch` statement to figure out which side is being affected (if any).

```
switch (mCurrent._name) {
```

If the right side is being affected, then you first want to see if the user has moved the mouse off to the right — away from the square. If that is the case, you'll want to reset the `mRight` rectangle:

```
if(nMx > 110) {
  resetSide(mCurrent);
  mCurrent = null;
}
```

Then, you want to set some boundaries within which the side can be pushed. If the mouse has moved beyond those boundaries, you want to set some default values:

```
if(nMx < 25) {
  nMx = 25;
}
else if(nMx > 100) {
  nMx = 100;
}
if(nMy < 25) {
  nMy = 25;
}
else if(nMy > 75) {
  nMy = 75;
}
```

This next calculation enables you to determine the control point for the curve that corresponds to the mouse location. This uses a standard Bezier formula to determine the X- and Y-coordinates of the control point.

```
oRight.x = 2*nMx - 100;
oRight.y = 2*nMy - 50;
```

Each of the other cases is similar but corresponds to a different side of the square.

Then, once all the points have been calculated, you use the Drawing API methods to draw a filled shape determined by four curves. If the mouse has not affected any points, these curves will appear as straight lines.

```
mShape.mBox.clear();
mShape.mBox.lineStyle(0, 0, 100);
mShape.mBox.beginFill(nSelectedColor, 100);
mShape.mBox.curveTo(oTop.x, oTop.y, 100, 0);
mShape.mBox.curveTo(oRight.x, oRight.y, 100, 100);
```

```
mShape.mBox.curveTo(oBottom.x, oBottom.y, 0, 100);
mShape.mBox.curveTo(oLeft.x, oLeft.y, 0, 0);
mShape.mBox.endFill();
updateAfterEvent();
```

Practicing Drawing

In this exercise, you'll create an application that allows the user to draw using either a line tool or a pencil tool. Follow along with these steps:

1. Open a new Flash document, and save it as drawingBoard.fla.

2. On the first frame of the default layer of the main timeline add the following code:

```
import actionscriptbible.drawing.DrawingUtilities;
import flash.geom.Matrix;

var mSelected:MovieClip;
var mCurrent:MovieClip;
var nInterval:Number;
var oStartPoint:Object;

this.createEmptyMovieClip("mBoard", this.getNextHighestDepth());
mBoard.createEmptyMovieClip("mBackground", 1);
mBoard.createEmptyMovieClip("mForeground", 2);

var duDrawer:DrawingUtilities =
new DrawingUtilities(mBoard.mBackground);
duDrawer.beginFill(0xFFFFFF, 100);
duDrawer.drawRectangle(400, 350, 200, 175);
duDrawer.endFill();

mBoard._x = 125;
mBoard._y = 25;

mBoard.onPress = function():Void {
  oStartPoint = {x: this._xmouse, y: this._ymouse};
  var nDepth:Number = mBoard.mForeground.getNextHighestDepth();
  mCurrent = mBoard.mForeground.createEmptyMovieClip(
"mLine" + nDepth, nDepth);
  nInterval = setInterval(draw, 10);
};

mBoard.onRelease = function():Void {
  clearInterval(nInterval);
};

var mLine:MovieClip = makeButton("mLine");
var mPen:MovieClip = makeButton("mPen");
var mEraser:MovieClip = makeButton("mEraser");
mPen._y = 50;
```

```
mEraser._y = 100;

function makeButton(sInstanceName:String):MovieClip {
  var mButton:MovieClip = this.createEmptyMovieClip(
sInstanceName, this.getNextHighestDepth());
  mButton.createEmptyMovieClip("mButton", 1);
  mButton.createEmptyMovieClip("mIcon", 2);
  drawButton(mButton.mButton);
  var duDrawer:DrawingUtilities =
new DrawingUtilities(mButton.mIcon);
  switch(sInstanceName) {
    case "mLine":
      duDrawer.lineStyle(2, 0, 100);
      duDrawer.moveTo(10, 10);
      duDrawer.lineTo(55, 30);
      break;
    case "mPen":
      duDrawer.lineStyle(2, 0, 100);
      duDrawer.moveTo(10, 10);
      duDrawer.curveTo(32.5, 50, 55, 10);
      break;
    case "mEraser":
      duDrawer.lineStyle(0, 0, 0);
      var mxBox:Matrix = new Matrix();
      mxBox.createGradientBox(40, 20);
      duDrawer.beginGradientFill("linear",
[0xFFFFFF, 0xFFFFFF], [0, 100], [0, 255], mxBox);
      duDrawer.drawRectangle(40, 20, 32.5, 20);
      duDrawer.endFill();
  }
  mButton.onPress = function():Void {
    drawButton(mLine.mButton);
    drawButton(mPen.mButton);
    if(this == mEraser) {
      for(var sItem:String in mBoard.mForeground) {
        mBoard.mForeground[sItem].removeMovieClip();
      }
    }
    drawButton(this.mButton, true);
    mSelected = this;
  };
  mButton.onRelease = function():Void {
    if(this == mEraser) {
      drawButton(this.mButton);
    }
  };
  return mButton;
}

function drawButton(mButton:MovieClip, bPressed:Boolean):Void {
  var duDrawer:DrawingUtilities = new DrawingUtilities(mButton);
```

```
      duDrawer.clear();
      duDrawer.lineStyle(0, 0, 0);
      duDrawer.beginFill(bPressed ? 0x5555FF : 0xEEEEFF, 100);
      duDrawer.drawRectangle(65, 40, 32.5, 20);
      duDrawer.endFill();
      duDrawer.beginFill(bPressed ? 0xEEEEFF : 0x5555FF, 100);
      duDrawer.drawRectangle(63, 38, 33.5, 21);
      duDrawer.endFill();
      duDrawer.beginFill(0xAAAAFF, 100);
      duDrawer.drawRectangle(61, 36, 32.5, 20);
      duDrawer.endFill();
   }

   function draw():Void {
      var duDrawer:DrawingUtilities = new DrawingUtilities(mCurrent);
      switch(mSelected) {
        case mLine:
          duDrawer.clear();
            duDrawer.moveTo(oStartPoint.x, oStartPoint.y);
            duDrawer.lineTo(mBoard._xmouse, mBoard._ymouse);
            break;
        case mPen:
            duDrawer.moveTo(oStartPoint.x, oStartPoint.y);
            duDrawer.lineTo(mBoard._xmouse, mBoard._ymouse);
            oStartPoint = {x: mBoard._xmouse, y: mBoard._ymouse};
      }
   }
```

3. Save the document and test the movie.

When you test the movie, you should be able to select either the line tool or pen tool and draw on the stage. When you want to start over, you can click the clear button to clear the canvas.

Let's take a look at the code that makes this work.

The mBoard MovieClip instance is the area within which the user can draw. The object contains two nested MovieClip objects — mBackground and mForeground. The mBackground object is simply a rectangle, while mForeground is a container for the lines that the user can draw. We use a DrawingUtilities object to draw the rectangle in mBackground.

```
this.createEmptyMovieClip("mBoard", this.getNextHighestDepth());
mBoard.createEmptyMovieClip("mBackground", 1);
mBoard.createEmptyMovieClip("mForeground", 2);

var duDrawer:DrawingUtilities = new DrawingUtilities(mBoard.mBackground);
duDrawer.beginFill(0xFFFFFF, 100);
duDrawer.drawRectangle(400, 350, 200, 175);
duDrawer.endFill();
```

When the user clicks on the drawing board area, it starts the drawing. It does so by setting the value of oStartPoint to the current mouse coordinates, adding a new MovieClip object nested within mForeground, and setting an interval at which the draw() function is called.

```
mBoard.onPress = function():Void {
  oStartPoint = {x: this._xmouse, y: this._ymouse};
  var nDepth:Number = mBoard.mForeground.getNextHighestDepth();
  mCurrent = mBoard.mForeground.createEmptyMovieClip("mLine" + nDepth, nDepth);
  nInterval = setInterval(draw, 10);
};
```

When the user releases the mouse over mBoard, clear the interval.

```
  mBoard.onRelease = function():Void {
    clearInterval(nInterval);
  };
```

Make three button MovieClip objects using the custom makeButton() function—one for each of the drawing options (line, pen, eraser).

```
  var mLine:MovieClip = makeButton("mLine");
  var mPen:MovieClip = makeButton("mPen");
  var mEraser:MovieClip = makeButton("mEraser");
  mPen._y = 50;
  mEraser._y = 100;
```

The makeButton() function makes a new MovieClip object with a unique instance name, and it adds two nested objects within it—mButton into which the button shape is drawn and mIcon into which the button's icon is drawn. It then calls the custom drawButton() function, passing it the nested mButton reference so it can draw the button shape.

```
  function makeButton(sInstanceName:String):MovieClip {
    var mButton:MovieClip = this.createEmptyMovieClip(        ↩
  sInstanceName, this.getNextHighestDepth());
    mButton.createEmptyMovieClip("mButton", 1);
    mButton.createEmptyMovieClip("mIcon", 2);
    drawButton(mButton.mButton);
```

Use a DrawingUtilities instance to draw the icon. The icon for mLine is a diagonal line, the icon for mPen is a curved line, and the icon for mEraser is a gradient-filled rectangle.

```
    var duDrawer:DrawingUtilities =                          ↩
  new DrawingUtilities(mButton.mIcon);
    switch(sInstanceName) {
      case "mLine":
        duDrawer.lineStyle(2, 0, 100);
        duDrawer.moveTo(10, 10);
        duDrawer.lineTo(55, 30);
        break;
      case "mPen":
        duDrawer.lineStyle(2, 0, 100);
        duDrawer.moveTo(10, 10);
        duDrawer.curveTo(32.5, 50, 55, 10);
        break;
      case "mEraser":
      duDrawer.lineStyle(0, 0, 0);
        var mxBox:Matrix = new Matrix();
        mxBox.createGradientBox(40, 20);
        duDrawer.beginGradientFill("linear",                 ↩
```

```
[0xFFFFFF, 0xFFFFFF], [0, 100], [0, 255], mxBox);
    duDrawer.drawRectangle(40, 20, 32.5, 20);
    duDrawer.endFill();
}
```

When the button is pressed, call drawButton() for both mLine and mPen so as to reset the visual state to the default. Then, if the instance is mEraser, call removeMovieClip() for each object nested in mBoard.mForeground. Call drawButton() with a second parameter of true to draw the button in the pressed state. Set the value of mSelected to the button MovieClip instance.

```
mButton.onPress = function():Void {
    drawButton(mLine.mButton);
    drawButton(mPen.mButton);
    if(this == mEraser) {
      for(var sItem:String in mBoard.mForeground) {
        mBoard.mForeground[sItem].removeMovieClip();
      }
    }
    drawButton(this.mButton, true);
    mSelected = this;
};
```

The onRelease() function is only necessary for the mEraser instance because it is the only one of the buttons that doesn't toggle state. When onRelease() is called for mEraser, immediately call drawButton() to redraw the button in the up state.

```
mButton.onRelease = function():Void {
    if(this == mEraser) {
      drawButton(this.mButton);
    }
};
```

The drawButton() function draws the button shape into the specified MovieClip object. The bPressed parameter determines whether it draws the up state or the pressed state. The shape consists of three overlapping rectangles — the shadow, highlight, and surface of the button. When drawn in the pressed state, the shadow and highlight are reversed.

```
function drawButton(mButton:MovieClip, bPressed:Boolean):Void {
    var duDrawer:DrawingUtilities = new DrawingUtilities(mButton);
    duDrawer.clear();
    duDrawer.lineStyle(0, 0, 0);
    duDrawer.beginFill(bPressed ? 0x5555FF : 0xEEEEFF, 100);
    duDrawer.drawRectangle(65, 40, 32.5, 20);
    duDrawer.endFill();
    duDrawer.beginFill(bPressed ? 0xEEEEFF : 0x5555FF, 100);
    duDrawer.drawRectangle(63, 38, 33.5, 21);
    duDrawer.endFill();
    duDrawer.beginFill(0xAAAAFF, 100);
    duDrawer.drawRectangle(61, 36, 32.5, 20);
    duDrawer.endFill();
}
```

The draw() function is called on an interval. The action it takes depends on the selected option. If mSelected is mLine, the function redraws the line from the start point to the current mouse coordinates. If the pen option is selected, the function does not clear the current MovieClip object, but it appends a new line, and it updates the start point to the current mouse coordinates.

```
function draw():Void {
  var duDrawer:DrawingUtilities =
new DrawingUtilities(mCurrent);
  switch(mSelected) {
    case mLine:
      duDrawer.clear();
      duDrawer.moveTo(oStartPoint.x, oStartPoint.y);
      duDrawer.lineTo(mBoard._xmouse, mBoard._ymouse);
      break;
    case mPen:
      duDrawer.moveTo(oStartPoint.x, oStartPoint.y);
      duDrawer.lineTo(mBoard._xmouse, mBoard._ymouse);
      oStartPoint = {x: mBoard._xmouse, y: mBoard._ymouse};
  }
}
```

Web Resource

We'd like to know what you thought about this chapter. Visit www.rightactionscript .com/asb/comments to fill out an online form with your comments.

Summary

✦ The Drawing API is a set of MovieClip class methods that enable you to draw lines, curves, fills, and shapes with ActionScript.

✦ Scripted drawing enables you to create highly dynamic content.

✦ By creating and working with a custom DrawingUtilities class, you can simplify drawing shapes such as circles, rectangles, and regular polygons.

✦ You can work with the Drawing API to create fully scripted masks.

✦   ✦   ✦

Transforming Colors

The `flash.geom.Transform` class lets you apply two sorts of transformations to MovieClip objects — geometric and color. A `Transform` object has a handful of properties, two of which are called `matrix` and `colorTransform`. The `matrix` property is a `Matrix` object you can use to apply geometric transforms, as discussed in the section "Working with Matrix Transforms." The `colorTransform` property is a `ColorTransform` object you can use to apply color transforms, as discussed in the section "Working with Color Transforms."

Working with Matrix Transforms

You've already seen how you can transform a display object in basic ways using properties such as x, y, width, height, and so on. However, using matrices you can apply more complex transformations — not only offsetting the coordinates, scaling, or rotating the object, but also skewing/shearing the object.

A matrix is a representation of a set of linear equations. For example, the following equation determines a line in two-dimensional space:

```
2x + 10y = 5
```

That linear equation can be written as the following matrix:

```
| 2  10  5 |
```

If you have more than one linear equation, you can group each of them into a single matrix. For example, consider the following three linear equations:

```
2x + 10y = 5
1x + 2y = 8
4x + 1y = 3
```

The preceding three equations can be written as the following matrix:

```
| 2  10 5 |
| 1   2 8 |
| 4   1 3 |
```

Since every point in a two-dimensional Cartesian system can be represented by a linear equation, matrixes work well to apply transformations. Matrix operations are frequently more efficient than their non-matrix counterparts. There is an entire branch of mathematics pertaining to working with matrices. However, even if you don't know much about matrix operations, you can still apply matrix transformation to display objects via the `flash.geom.Matrix` class.

Every display object has a `transform.matrix` property that is a `Matrix` instance specifying the transformations applied to it. The `Matrix` object represents a 3 x 3 matrix that can be denoted as follows:

```
| a  b  0 |
| c  d  0 |
| tx ty 1 |
```

In its default state, when placed at 0,0, the matrix values are as follows:

```
| 1 0 0 |
| 0 1 0 |
| 0 0 1 |
```

The default matrix is known as the *identity matrix*. Setting a display object's matrix to the identity matrix resets any transformations to the default state.

The properties of the `Matrix` class are as follows:

✦ **a**—The scale amount in the X direction. The default is 1, which means 100%. A value of 2 would scale the object in the X direction to 200%.

✦ **b**—The amount to shear the object in the Y direction. A shear in the Y direction is the amount by which the Y pixels are shifted for every corresponding X pixel value. Another way of thinking of that in more mathematical terms is the slope of the horizontal lines. For example, a Y shear of 1 would mean the horizontal lines would be at a 45-degree angle (a slope of 1). The default value is 0, which means the horizontal lines are actually horizontal.

✦ **c**—The amount to shear the object in the X direction. A shear in the X direction is similar to a shear in the Y direction, but it shifts the pixels along the X axis rather than along the Y axis. You can think of an X shear as the slope of the vertical lines. The default value is 0, which means the vertical lines are vertical.

✦ **d**—The scale amount in the Y direction. The default is 1, which means 100%.

✦ **tx**—The amount of translation in the X direction. The `tx` property defaults to 0.

✦ **ty**—The amount of translation in the Y direction. The `ty` property defaults to 0.

Obviously there is a relationship between the matrix properties and some of the basic display object properties such as x, y, width, height, xscale, yscale, and rotation. The relationship between x and y and `tx` and `ty` is direct. If the object is moved to 100,200 then the `tx` and `ty` properties of the matrix will have values of 100 and 200, respectively. Likewise, there is an obvious relationship between the width, height, xscale, and yscale properties with the a and d properties of the matrix. The relationship between the rotation property and the matrix is not quite so apparent, but it does exist. A change in the rotation property affects the a, b, c, and d properties of the matrix.

Aside from setting the properties of a `Matrix` object, you can also use some of the methods to simplify things. For example, rather than setting the `tx` and `ty` properties directly, you can use the `translate()` method, as follows:

```
// The equivalent of setting tx to 100 and ty to 200
mtxInstance.translate(100, 200);
```

And rather than setting a and d, you can call the `scale()` method:

```
// The equivalent of setting a to 3 and d to 2.
mtxInstance.scale(2, 3);
```

Using some trigonometry you can determine the proper values to assign to each of the matrix properties in order to rotate an object. However, it's much simpler to use the `rotate()` method. The `rotate()` method expects an angle in radians. If you find it more convenient to use degrees, you can convert from degrees to radians by multiplying by Math.PI/180. The following code applies a rotation of 31 degrees by converting it to radians, and passing the value to the `rotate()` method of a `Matrix` object.

```
var nRadians:Number = 31 * Math.PI / 180;
mtxInstance.rotate(nRadians);
```

Matrix methods are cumulative. Each method adds the new values to the existing values. For example, the following constructs a `Matrix`, translates it by 100 pixels to the right, then by 100 pixels to the right again. Notice that the effect is that the `Matrix` is translated y 200 pixels total rather than just 100 pixels.

```
var mtxInstance:Matrix = new Matrix();
trace(mtxInstance); // (a=1, b=0, c=0, d=1, tx=0, ty=0)
mtxInstance.translate(100, 0);
trace(mtxInstance); // (a=1, b=0, c=0, d=1, tx=100, ty=0)
mtxInstance.translate(100, 0);
trace(mtxInstance); // (a=1, b=0, c=0, d=1, tx=200, ty=0)
```

The same thing occurs with `scale()` and `rotate()`. While it may seem obvious, the effect can cause some unexpected behaviors if you accidentally assume it will work differently. That's not too difficult to do — especially when you're working with the `rotate()` method. You might want to rotate an object by Math.PI/2 (90 degrees) total. However, if you already called `rotate()` for the same Matrix object previously, then the effect might be other than what you had anticipated. And it gets particularly complex when you start applying various transformations. For example, once you've rotated, scaled, and translated a `Matrix` object, it gets particularly difficult to then rotate it to an absolute value (noncumulative).

So, what if you want to apply more than one transformation effect? In such cases you can make new Matrix objects for each transformation effect (scale, rotate, translate, shear) and combine them using the `concat()` method. The `concat()` method combines the matrices using matrix multiplication. Matrix multiplication is a noncommutative operation, which means that matrixA * matrixB is not necessarily the same as matrixB * matrixA. Therefore, when you combine matrices using the `concat()` method, it may make a difference which order you use to concatenate them.

The `concat()` method requires a `Matrix` parameter. It then multiplies the calling matrix by the parameter, and it updates the properties of the calling matrix with the product. The following code is an example in which there are two matrices that get concatenated. You can see that the effect is that the original matrix is translated by 100, 200.

```
import flash.geom.Matrix;

var mtxCumulative:Matrix = new Matrix();
trace(mtxCumulative); // (a=1, b=0, c=0, d=1, tx=0, ty=0)
var mtxRotate:Matrix = new Matrix();
```

```
mtxRotate.rotate(Math.PI/2);
// (a=6.12303176911189e-17, b=1, c=-1, d=6.12303176911189e-17, tx=0, ty=0)
trace(mtxRotate); var mtxShear:Matrix = new Matrix(1, 1, 0, 1, 0, 0);
trace(mtxShear); // (a=1, b=1, c=0, d=1, tx=0, ty=0)
mtxCumulative.concat(mtxRotate);
mtxCumulative.concat(mtxShear);
trace(mtxCumulative); // (a=6.12303176911189e-17, b=1, c=-1, d=-1, tx=0, ty=0)
```

Notice what happens when the matrices are concatenated in the other order.

```
import flash.geom.Matrix;

var mtxCumulative:Matrix = new Matrix();
trace(mtxCumulative);  // (a=1, b=0, c=0, d=1, tx=0, ty=0)
var mtxRotate:Matrix = new Matrix();
mtxRotate.rotate(Math.PI/2);
// (a=6.12303176911189e-17, b=1, c=-1, d=6.12303176911189e-17, tx=0, ty=0)
trace(mtxRotate); var mtxShear:Matrix = new Matrix(1, 1, 0, 1, 0, 0);
trace(mtxShear); // (a=1, b=1, c=0, d=1, tx=0, ty=0)
mtxCumulative.concat(mtxRotate);
mtxCumulative.concat(mtxShear);
trace(mtxCumulative); // (a=-1, b=1, c=-1, d=6.12303176911189e-17, tx=0, ty=0)
```

Using Matrix Transformations

In the following simple exercise, you'll build a SWF that uses matrices to transform four rectangles using shearing, scaling, rotation, and translation transformations.

Note   The following example assumes you've installed the `DrawingUtilities` class. If you have not, see Chapter 15 for more details.

1. Open a new Flash document, and save it as `matrixTransform.fla`.

2. Add the following code to the first keyframe on the main timeline.

```
import flash.geom.Transform;
import flash.geom.Matrix;
import actionscriptbible.drawing.DrawingUtilities;

// Define arrays of associative arrays that you can use to construct
// nested controller MovieClip objects within the rectangles.
var aControllersA:Array = [
{name: "mA_UpDown", width: 10, height: 10, x: -85, y: -45},
{name: "mA_RightLeft", width: 10, height: 10, x: -95, y: -35},
{name: "mB_UpDown", width: 10, height: 10, x: 85, y: -45},
{name: "mB_RightLeft", width: 10, height: 10, x: 95, y: -35},
{name: "mC_UpDown", width: 10, height: 10, x: -85, y: 45},
{name: "mC_RightLeft", width: 10, height: 10, x: -95, y: 35},
{name: "mD_UpDown", width: 10, height: 10, x: 85, y: 45},
{name: "mD_RightLeft", width: 10, height: 10, x: 95, y: 35}];

var aControllersB:Array = [
{name: "mRight", width: 10, height: 20, x: 95, y: 0},
{name: "mLeft", width: 10, height: 20, x: -95, y: 0},
```

```
{name: "mTop", width: 20, height: 10, x: 0, y: -45},
{name: "mBottom", width: 20, height: 10, x: 0, y: 45}];

var aControllersC:Array = [{name: "mRotate", radius: 5, x: 95, y: -45}];

var aControllersD:Array = [{name: "mTranslate", radius: 5, x: 0, y: 0}];

// Make four rectangle MovieClip objects.
this.createEmptyMovieClip("mRectangleA", this.getNextHighestDepth());
this.createEmptyMovieClip("mRectangleB", this.getNextHighestDepth());
this.createEmptyMovieClip("mRectangleC", this.getNextHighestDepth());
this.createEmptyMovieClip("mRectangleD", this.getNextHighestDepth());

// For each rectangle MovieClip object and the corresponding array
// of controller data, call the custom drawRectangle() function in order
// to draw the nested rectangle and controllers.
drawRectangle(mRectangleA, aControllersA);
mRectangleA._x = 150;
mRectangleA._y = 100;

drawRectangle(mRectangleB, aControllersB);
mRectangleB._x = 400;
mRectangleB._y = 100;

drawRectangle(mRectangleC, aControllersC);
mRectangleC._x = 150;
mRectangleC._y = 250;

drawRectangle(mRectangleD, aControllersD);
mRectangleD._x = 400;
mRectangleD._y = 250;

var nInterval:Number;

var mtxInstance:Matrix;

function drawRectangle(mRectangle:MovieClip, aControllers:Array):Void {

  // Make a nested MovieClip object within the rectangle. Then use a
  // DrawingUtilities object to draw a rectangle within that object.
  mRectangle.createEmptyMovieClip("mShape", mRectangle.getNextHighestDepth());
  var duDrawer:DrawingUtilities = new DrawingUtilities(mRectangle.mShape);
  duDrawer.beginFill(0xFFFFFF, 100);
  duDrawer.drawRectangle(200, 100);

  var mController:MovieClip;

  // Loop through each of the elements of the controllers array, and for each
  // add a nested MovieClip object, and use the data to draw the object.
  for(var i:Number = 0; i < aControllers.length; i++) {
    mController = mRectangle.createEmptyMovieClip(aControllers[i].name,     ⤶
```

```
mRectangle.getNextHighestDepth());
    mController._x = aControllers[i].x;
    mController._y = aControllers[i].y;
    duDrawer = new DrawingUtilities(mController);
    duDrawer.beginFill(0xCCCCFF, 100);

    // If the controller data has no radius property, draw a rectangle.
    // Otherwise, draw a circle.
    if(aControllers[i].radius == undefined) {
      duDrawer.drawRectangle(aControllers[i].width, aControllers[i].height);
    }
    else {
      duDrawer.drawCircle(aControllers[i].radius);
    }

    // Assign event handler methods to each controller object. In each case,
    // start an interval at which the transformRectangle() function is called
    // when the user clicks on the controller. When the user releases the mouse
    // clear the interval.
    mController.onPress = function():Void {
      nInterval = setInterval(transformRectangle, 10, this);
    };
    mController.onRelease = function():Void {
      clearInterval(nInterval);
    };
    mController.onReleaseOutside = mController.onRelease;
  }
}

// The transformRectangle() function is called repeatedly as long as
// the user is clicking on a controller. The function gets passed a
// reference to the controller, and based on that the function determines
// how to transform the parent object.
function transformRectangle(mController:MovieClip):Void {

  // The rectangle is the parent of the controller.
  var mRectangle:MovieClip = mController._parent;

  // Get the current coordinates of the rectangle so it can be reset after
  // the transformations are applied.
  var nX:Number = mRectangle._x;
  var nY:Number = mRectangle._y;

  // Get the current transform matrix of the rectangle.
  mtxInstance = mRectangle.transform.matrix;

  // Set the tx and ty properties of the matrix to 0 before applying any other
  // transformations. Otherwise the effects could appear incorrect. We'll
  // translate the matrix back after applying any other transformations.
  mtxInstance.tx = 0;
```

```
    mtxInstance.ty = 0;

    // Determine which controller is calling the function.
    switch(mController._name) {

      // In the case of the right, left, top, or bottom controllers, adjust the
      // a or d properties in order to scale the object. Don't use the scale()
      // method since the effects are cumulative. Determine the scale (1 is 100%).
      // The x scale is twice the difference from the center of the rectangle to
      // the x coordinate of the mouse divided that by the default width
      // of the rectangle. The y scale is basically the same thing, but using
      // the y coordinates and the default height of the rectangle.
      case "mRight":
        mtxInstance.a = (_xmouse - mRectangle._x) * 2 / mRectangle.mShape._width;
        break;
      case "mLeft":
        mtxInstance.a = (mRectangle._x - _xmouse) * 2 / mRectangle.mShape._width;
        break;
      case "mTop":
        mtxInstance.d = (_ymouse - mRectangle._y) * 2 / mRectangle.mShape._height;
        break;
      case "mBottom":
        mtxInstance.d = (_ymouse - mRectangle._y) * 2 / mRectangle.mShape._height;
        break;

      // The UpDown and RightLeft controllers shear the rectangle, so we'll update
      // the d and b properties of the matrix. Determine the amount to shear by
      // determining the tangent of the angle formed between the edge of the
      // rectangle and the mouse coordinate.
      case "mA_UpDown":
        mtxInstance.b = (mRectangle._y - (mRectangle.mShape._height / 2) - ↵
_ymouse) / (mRectangle.mShape._width / 2);
        break;
      case "mB_UpDown":
        mtxInstance.b = (_ymouse - mRectangle._y +↵
(mRectangle.mShape._height / 2)) / (mRectangle.mShape._width / 2);
        break;
      case "mC_UpDown":
        mtxInstance.b = (mRectangle._y + (mRectangle.mShape._height / 2) - ↵
_ymouse) / (mRectangle.mShape._width / 2);
        break;
      case "mD_UpDown":
        mtxInstance.b = (_ymouse - mRectangle._y -↵
(mRectangle.mShape._height / 2)) / (mRectangle.mShape._width / 2);
        break;
      case "mA_RightLeft":
        mtxInstance.c = (mRectangle._x - (mRectangle.mShape._width / 2) - ↵
_xmouse) / (mRectangle.mShape._height / 2);
        break;
      case "mB_RightLeft":
        mtxInstance.c = (mRectangle._x + (mRectangle.mShape._width / 2) - ↵
```

```
_xmouse) / (mRectangle.mShape._height / 2);
      break;
    case "mC_RightLeft":
      mtxInstance.c = (_xmouse - mRectangle._x +
(mRectangle.mShape._width / 2)) / (mRectangle.mShape._height / 2);
      break;
    case "mD_RightLeft":
      mtxInstance.c = (_xmouse - mRectangle._x -
(mRectangle.mShape._width / 2)) / (mRectangle.mShape._height / 2);
      break;

    // In order to rotate the matrix using the rotate() method. Determine the
    // angle using the coordinates of the mouse relative the center of the
    // rectangle as well as the coordinates of the corner of the rectangle.
    // Note that since the rotate() method is cumulative you can simply re-
    // initialize the matrix using a constructor.
    case "mRotate":
      mtxInstance = new Matrix();
      mtxInstance.rotate(-Math.atan2(_xmouse - mRectangle._x, _ymouse -
mRectangle._y) + Math.atan2(mRectangle.mRotate._x, mRectangle.mRotate._y));
      break;

    // Translate the matrix by reinitializing the matrix and then setting nX and
    // nY to the current coordinates of the mouse.
    case "mTranslate":
      mtxInstance = new Matrix();
      nX = _xmouse;
      nY = _ymouse;
      break;
    }

    // Translate the matrix to nX and nY. If the controller was anything other
    // than the translate controller then nX and nY are the coordinates of the
    // rectangle. Otherwise, nX and nY are the coordinates of the mouse.
    mtxInstance.translate(nX, nY);

    // Apply the matrix to the rectangle.
    mRectangle.transform.matrix = mtxInstance;
}
```

Working with Color Transforms

There are several ways to apply color changes to display objects — using the
transform.colorTransform property (which is an instance of the ColorTransform class)
or using a ColorMatrixFilter object. Using the transform.colorTransform property,
you can quickly apply solid color fills and tints to display objects. For more complex color
operations such as changing brightness, hue, and the like., use a ColorMatrixFilter object
as discussed in Chapter 17.

Note You can also use the `Color` class, which works somewhat similarly to `ColorTransform`. However, as of Flash Player 8 the `Color` class is deprecated.

Applying Color Transforms

The `transform.colorTransform` property of a display object is a `flash.geom.ColorTransform` object. Each display object has a default `ColorTransform` object assigned to it. You can retrieve the object already assigned to the object, make changes to it, and reassign it, or you can construct a new `ColorTransform` object, and assign that to the `transform.colorTransform` property of the display object.

When retrieving the `transform.colorTransform` property of a display object, Flash returns a copy. That means that making changes to the copy won't affect the MovieClip. You have to assign the object to the `transform.colorTransform` property again for any changes to take effect. Likewise, when you apply a `ColorTransform` object to the `transform.colorTransform` property of a `MovieClip` object, Flash applies a copy. Therefore, any updates to the object won't affect the MovieClip unless you reassign it to the `transform.colorTransform` property.

Getting and Setting the Color

The `ColorTransform` class defines a `rgb` property that lets you apply and retrieve a solid color fill. The value of the `rgb` property is an unsigned integer value ranging from 0x000000 to 0xFFFFFF. The corresponding color is then applied to every pixel of the MovieClip. The property applies a solid color fill, and not a tint. That means that any contrast of color that is visible in the actual contents of a `MovieClip` object is indistinguishable after the fill is applied. For example, if you apply a solid color fill to a object containing a rectangular photograph, the effect will be a rectangle filled with a solid color.

The following example constructs a new `ColorTransform` object, assigns a value of 0xFF0000 (red) to the `rgb` property, and then assigns the object to the `transform.colorTransform` property of a MovieClip instance named `mCircle`.

```
import flash.geom.ColorTransform;

var ctCircleColor:ColorTransform = new ColorTransform();
ctCircleColor.rgb = 0xFF0000;
mCircle.transform.colorTransform = ctCircleColor;
```

You can also retrieve the color that is currently applied to a MovieClip using the `rgb` property. The property returns the current color applied to the `ColorTransform` object (if any).

```
var ctCircleColor:ColorTransform = mCircle.transform.colorTransform;
trace(ctCircleColor.rgb);
```

However, a `ColorTransform` object does not report the color of the artwork within a `MovieClip`. It only reports on the color transform applied to the instance. For example, if a `MovieClip` instance has a yellow square within it, but no color transform applied to the instance, then the `transform.colorTransform.rgb` property will not return the number corresponding to yellow. It will return 0 because no color transformation has yet been applied.

Tinting a MovieClip

The `ColorTransform` class defines the following properties for working color transformations with more control than is possible using `rgb` property.

✦ `redMultiplier`

✦ `greenMultiplier`

✦ `blueMultiplier`

✦ `alphaMultiplier`

✦ `redOffset`

✦ `greenOffset`

✦ `blueOffset`

✦ `alphaOffset`

You can set the properties of a `ColorTransform` object using the constructor, or you can set them once the object has already been constructed. The constructor accepts from 0 to 8 parameters matching the properties in the preceding list. The order of the parameters is the same as that in which the properties appear in the preceding list. The following code constructs a new `ColorTransform` object with the default properties:

```
var ctInstance:ColorTransform = new ColorTransform();
```

Each of the multiplier properties (`redMultiplier`, `greenMultiplier`, etc.) can range from -1 to 1 and determines the percentage of the color component that is applied to each pixel. Every color can be represented by a combination of red, green, and blue. Each pixel contains a color value ranging from 0x000000 to 0xFFFFFF. In hexadecimal format (such as 0xFFFFFF) each pair of digits represents a red, green, or blue value that comprises the entire value— 0xRRGGBB. Therefore, 0xFF0000 is pure red, 0x00FF00 is pure green, and 0x0000FF is pure blue. The multiplier properties default to 1, which means that each red, green, and blue component of each pixel's color is at 1 percent. By changing the multiplier properties, you can effectively apply a tint to a display object. When the multiplier properties are changed, it doesn't remove the contrast and definition of the contents within a display object. For example, if a display object contains a photograph, applying changes to the multiplier properties will change the tint of the photograph, but the subject of the photograph will likely still be distinguishable. The following code applies a green tint (by reducing the red and blue components to 0) to a MovieClip object called `mPhotograph`.

```
mPhotograph.transform.colorTransform = new ColorTransform(0, 1, 0, 1, 0, 0, 0, 0);
```

The offset properties (`redOffset`, `greenOffset`, and so on) add and subtract to and from the red, green, blue, and alpha components of the color. The ranges for the offset properties are from -255 to 255. The default values are 0. The following applies a red tint to a `mPhotograph` by setting the `redOffset` to 255.

```
var ctPhotograph:ColorTransform = new ColorTransform();
ctPhotograph.redOffset = 255;
mPhotograph.transform.colorTransform = ctPhotograph;
```

The multiplier and offset properties of a `ColorTransform` object can work in conjunction with one another. The difference is that the multiplier properties affect the percentage of a color component already present within each pixel, whereas the offset properties add or subtract to or from the color component of the pixel. For example, if a pixel has a color of 0xFFFFFF (white) then setting the `redMultiplier` to 0 or setting the `redOffset` to -255 has the same effect. However, if the color is 0x000000 (black) then setting the `redMultiplier` property will not change the amount of red in the color. 100 percent and 0 percent of 0 are both 0. But you can set the `redOffset` to add red to the color.

Note The `rgb` property and the offset properties are interconnected. When you set the `rgb` property, it sets the offset properties. When you set the offset properties, they affect the `rgb` property. The `rgb` property is simply a more convenient way to work with the offsets.

Resetting Colors

You can reset the colors applied to a `MovieClip` object by applying a `ColorTransform` object with the default properties as follows:

```
mClip.transform.colorTransform = new ColorTransform();
```

Transforming Colors

In the following example, you'll load an image into the player, and then use a `ColorTransform` object to tint it based on the location of the mouse. Each click of the mouse will cycle through the multiplier properties (`redMultiplier`, `greenMultiplier`, `blueMultiplier`, and `alphaMultiplier`,) and each gets set to 0 as the mouse is at the far left and to 100 as the mouse is at the far right. An icon in the upper left of the screen tells you which multiplier is currently selected.

Note The following example requires the `DrawingUtilities`. If you haven't yet installed the library, consult Chapter 15.

1. Open a new Flash document, and save it as `colorTransform.fla`.

2. Add the following code to the first keyframe of the main timeline.

```
import flash.geom.ColorTransform;
import actionscriptbible.drawing.DrawingUtilities;

// Make a new MovieClip object for the image.
this.createEmptyMovieClip("mImage", this.getNextHighestDepth());

// Nest a MovieClip object within mImage in order
// to load the image into it.
mImage.createEmptyMovieClip("mHolder",                          ⊃
mImage.getNextHighestDepth());

// Make a MovieClip object for the icon.
this.createEmptyMovieClip("mMultiplierIcon",                    ⊃
this.getNextHighestDepth());

// Declare a variable for the image MovieClip' ColorTransform
```

```
// object.
var ctImage:ColorTransform;

// Use a DrawingUtilities object to draw a square in the icon
// MovieClip object.
var duDrawer:DrawingUtilities =
new DrawingUtilities(mMultiplierIcon);
duDrawer.lineStyle(0, 0, 0);
duDrawer.beginFill(0xFFFFFF, 100);
duDrawer.drawRectangle(50, 50, 25, 25);
duDrawer.endFill();

// Set the color of the icon to red since that is the
// multiplier that is selected by default.
var ctIcon:ColorTransform = new ColorTransform();
ctIcon.rgb = 0xFF0000;
mMultiplierIcon.transform.colorTransform = ctIcon;

// Define an array with the multiplier property names.
var aMultipliers:Array = ["redMultiplier", "greenMultiplier",
"blueMultiplier", "alphaMultiplier"];

// We'll use nIndex to determine which of the multipliers is
// selected.
var nIndex:Number = 0;

mImage.onPress = function():Void {

  // Each time the user clicks on mImage increment nIndex to
  // cycle through the multipliers. If nIndex is outside of
  // the range of elements in the array, reset it to 0.
  nIndex++;
  if(nIndex >= aMultipliers.length) {
    nIndex = 0;
  }

  // Update the color of the icon. Construct a ColorTransform
  // object with the multipliers and offsets set to 0 (except
  // the alpha multiplier.) The, set each of the offset
  // properties based on which multiplier is currently
  // selected.
  ctIcon = new ColorTransform(0, 0, 0, 1, 0, 0, 0, 0);
  ctIcon.redOffset = (aMultipliers[nIndex] ==
"redMultiplier") ? 255 : 0;
  ctIcon.greenOffset = (aMultipliers[nIndex] ==
"greenMultiplier") ? 255 : 0;
  ctIcon.blueOffset = (aMultipliers[nIndex] ==
"blueMultiplier") ? 255 : 0;
  ctIcon.alphaMultiplier = (aMultipliers[nIndex] ==
 "alphaMultiplier") ? .25 : 1;
  mMultiplierIcon.transform.colorTransform = ctIcon;
```

```
};

// Load the image into the player.
var mlImage:MovieClipLoader = new MovieClipLoader();
mlImage.loadClip(
"http://www.rightactionscript.com/sampleFiles/image2.jpg",
mImage.mHolder);

function onMouseMove():Void {

    // Determine the ratio of the _xmouse to the width of the
    // stage. That returns a value from 0 to 1. Then assign
    // that value to the selected multiplier property of the
    // ColorTransform object for the image MovieClip object.
    var nRatio:Number = _xmouse / 550;
    ctImage = mImage.transform.colorTransform;
    ctImage[aMultipliers[nIndex]] = nRatio;
    mImage.transform.colorTransform = ctImage;
}
```

We'd like to know what you thought about this chapter. Visit `www.rightactionscript` `.com/asb/comments` to fill out an online form with your comments.

Summary

✦ Each `MovieClip` object has a `transform` property from which you can access the `matrix` and `colorTransform` properties in order to apply transforms to the object.

✦ Using the `matrix` property, you can apply transforms such as rotation, translation, scaling, and shearing.

✦ Using the `colorTransform` property, you can apply colors and tints to `MovieClip` objects.

✦ ✦ ✦

Applying Filters

Filters are built-in effects you can apply to any display object: button, movie clip, or text field. Unlike effects in Flash MX 2004, the filters in Flash 8 are built into the player, and they use native bitmap functionality to make effects that were simply not possible in previous versions of Flash. Blur effects, for example, use technology built into Flash Player 8 to render bitmap surfaces that look much like blurs you might see in other programs such as Fireworks or Photoshop.

Applying a filter to a movie clip causes Flash Player to render a bitmap surface with the related effect. That has consequences in terms of how filters behave. As you'll recall from the discussion of bitmap caching in Chapter 14, when a movie clip is rotated or scaled, Flash redraws the bitmap surface. That means that when a movie clip is rotated, for example, the filter is reapplied to the rotated object. As you'll see later in this chapter, that can cause unexpected effects.

Many of the filters can be applied at authoring time or runtime. However, there are some filters that can only be applied at runtime, which means that you have a distinct advantage if you work with filters via code rather than at authoring time. The following filters are available.

- ✦ Bevel
- ✦ Blur
- ✦ Color matrix
- ✦ Convolution
- ✦ Displacement map
- ✦ Drop shadow
- ✦ Glow
- ✦ Gradient bevel
- ✦ Gradient glow

In this chapter, we'll look at each of the filters, and how to apply filters to display objects.

✦ ✦ ✦ ✦

In This Chapter

Understanding filters

Working with filter types

Applying filters

✦ ✦ ✦ ✦

Applying a Filter

Every MovieClip instance has a filters property. The filters property is an array of filter objects applied to the instance. If you apply a filter at authoring time, that filter object is accessible during runtime via the filters property. For example, if you apply a bevel filter to a MovieClip object named mClip during authoring time, the bevel filter object will be the first element of the filters property.

However, when you read elements from the filters array, it returns *copies* rather than references to the actual filter objects. That means that any changes you make to the properties of the filter object won't be applied to the display object automatically.

When you want to apply a filter to an object programmatically, you must assign an array of filter objects to the filters property. Not only does the filters array return copies of the filter objects, but when you read the filters property, it returns a copy of the array rather than a reference. So, it won't work to use standard array methods such as push(), and you cannot overwrite elements of the array and have the updates affect the display object automatically. If you're still uncertain of how to apply a filter object, some examples will help make things clearer. In subsequent sections, you'll learn more about each of the different types of filter classes. For the next few examples, however, we'll construct very basic filter objects. For example, the following code constructs a basic DropShadowFilter object:

```
var dsfInstance:DropShadowFilter = new DropShadowFilter();
```

Once the filter object is constructed, you can apply it to a display object by adding it as an element of an array and assigning that array to the filters property of the display object. For the following examples, we'll use array literal syntax to make an array (refer back to Chapter 7 for a refresher on arrays). Array literal syntax uses square brackets with a comma-delimited list of the array's elements. In the case of the example, the array has just one element: the DropShadowFilter object. We'll apply the drop shadow to a movie clip named mCircle:

```
mCircle.filters = [dsfInstance];
```

Not only does the filters property return copies of the filter objects when you read it, but it also applies a copy of the filter when you assign the filter object. That means that if you change a property of the filter object after you assign it to the filters array of a display object, it will have no effect on the display object. For example, DropShadowFilter objects have a distance property that determines the displacement of the shadow in pixels. The default is 4 pixels. If you set the property before assigning the object to the filters array, there will be a visible effect:

```
dsfInstance.distance = 100;
mCircle.filters = [dsfInstance];
```

However, if you change the property after assigning the object to the filters array, it won't affect the display object:

```
mCircle.filters = [dsfInstance];
dsfInstance.distance = 100;
```

If you want to reapply a filter after making changes to the properties as in the preceding example, you need to then reassign the filters array. For example, the following retrieves a filter from the filters array, makes a change to it, and reassigns the filter.

```
var dsfInstance:DropShadowFilter =
DropShadowFilter(mCircle.filters[0]);
dsfInstance.distance = 0;
mCircle.filters = [dsfInstance];
```

Adding the Bevel Filter

Bevel filters are instances of the `BevelFilter` class. `BevelFilter` instances have the following properties:

- ✦ `distance` — The offset of the bevel in pixels. The greater the number, the more pronounced the bevel. The default is 4.

- ✦ `angle` — The angle of the light source to the object in degrees. A value of 0 makes the light source directly to the left, while a value of 180 makes the light source directly to the right. The default is 45.

- ✦ `highlightColor` — The highlight color specified as an unsigned integer from 0x000000 to 0xFFFFFF. The default value is 0xFFFFFF.

- ✦ `highlightAlpha` — The alpha of the highlight. The range is from 0 to 1. The default is 1.

- ✦ `shadowColor` — The shadow color specified as an unsigned integer from 0x000000 to 0xFFFFFF. The default value is 0x000000.

- ✦ `shadowAlpha` — The alpha of the shadow. The range is from 0 to 1. The default is 1.

- ✦ `blurX` — The number of pixels to blur the bevel in the horizontal direction. The greater the number, the softer the bevel appears. The default is 4.

- ✦ `blurY` — The number of pixels to blur the bevel in the vertical direction. The greater the number, the softer the bevel appears. The default is 4.

- ✦ `strength` — The punch strength of the bevel. The greater the number, the more visible the shadow and highlight will be when the blur properties are set to greater numbers. The default is 1.

- ✦ `quality` — The number of times to run the blur. The range is from 1 to 15. The greater the number, the smoother the bevel appears. The default is 1.

- ✦ `type` — The type can be one of the `flash.filters.BitmapFilter.Type` constants: `inner`, `outer`, or `full`. The default is `inner`.

- ✦ `knockout` — Whether or not to knockout the contents of the object. The default is `false`.

The `BevelFilter` constructor accepts between 0 and 12 parameters. Parameters are in the same order they appear in the preceding list. For example, the following instantiates a `BevelFilter` object with a distance of 10 and an angle of 0:

```
var bvfInstance:BevelFilter = new BevelFilter(10, 0);
```

The following instantiates a new `BevelFilter` object with each of the 12 parameters:

```
var bvfInstance:BevelFilter = new BevelFilter(10, 0,
0xFF0000, .5, 0xCCCCCC,.5, 10, 10, 5, 15, Type.inner, true);
```

You can adjust any of the properties of a BevelFilter object once it's instantiated. The following makes a new BevelFilter object with the default settings, and then sets the type to outer:

```
var bvfInstance:BevelFilter = new BevelFilter();
bvfInstance.type = "outer";
```

Figure 17-1 shows the effect of the following code on a movie clip called mCircle.

```
import flash.filters.BevelFilter;

var bvfInstance:BevelFilter = new BevelFilter(5, 45, 0xFFCCCC,
1, 0x000000, 1, 10, 10, 5, 15, "inner");
mCircle.filters = [bvfInstance];
```

 Figure 17-1: A bevel filter applied to a circle.

Adding the Blur Filter

You can add blur effects to display objects using BlurFilter objects. The BlurFilter class has three properties:

✦ blurX —The number of pixels to blur in the x direction. The default is 4.

✦ blurY —The number of pixels to blur in the y direction. The default is 4.

✦ quality —The number of times to run the blur. The range is from 0 to 15. The default value is 1.

You can make a new BlurFilter instance using the BlurFilter constructor. The constructor accepts from 0 to 3 parameters. The parameters are in the same order as they appear in the preceding list. The following code constructs a BlurFilter instance with default settings:

```
var blfInstance:BlurFilter = new BlurFilter();
```

The following constructs a new BlurFilter instance that blurs 100 pixels in the X direction but no pixels in the Y direction. It uses a quality setting of 15 to achieve a very smooth blur.

```
var blfInstance:BlurFilter = new BlurFilter(100, 0, 15);
```

As with any other filter, you can change the properties of a BlurFilter object after it's been instantiated.

Figure 17-2 shows the effect of the following code:

```
import flash.filters.BlurFilter;

var bfInstance:BlurFilter = new BlurFilter(10, 40);
mCircle.filters = [bfInstance];
```

Figure 17-2: A blur filter applied to a circle.

Adding the Drop Shadow Filter

You can use `DropShadowFilter` objects to apply drop shadows to display objects. The class has the following properties:

- `distance` — The number of pixels from the display object to offset the shadow. The default is 4.

- `angle` — The angle of the light source in degrees where 0 is directly to the left of the object. The default value is 45.

- `color` — The color of the shadow specified as an unsigned integer from 0x000000 to 0xFFFFFF. The default value is 0x000000.

- `alpha` — The alpha of the shadow from 0 to 1. The default is 1.

- `blurX` — The amount to blur the shadow in the X direction from 0 to 255. The default is 4.

- `blurY` — The amount to blur the shadow in the Y direction from 0 to 255. The default is 4.

- `strength` — The punch strength of the shadow from 0 to 255. The default is 1.

- `quality` — The number of times to run the blur on the shadow. The range is from 0 to 15. The higher the number, the smoother the blur of the shadow will appear. The default is 1.

- `inner` — A Boolean value indicating whether or not the shadow should be applied to the inside of the object. The default value is false, which means the shadow is applied outside the object.

- `knockout` — A Boolean value indicating whether or not the original display object contents should be transparent. If true, that section of the object is transparent (the background or whatever is underneath the object is visible) and the drop shadow is visible around the edges of that area. The default value is false.

- `hideObject` — A Boolean value indicating whether or not to hide the contents of the display object. If true, the contents of the display object are hidden, and the drop shadow is visible. The default value is `false`.

The `DropShadowFilter` constructor accepts between 0 and 11 parameters. The parameters are in the order they appear in the preceding list. The following constructs a `DropShadowFilter` object with the default settings:

```
var dsfInstance:DropShadowFilter = new DropShadowFilter();
```

The following constructs a `DropShadowFilter` object with a distance of 20, an angle of 0, and a color of 0xFF0000.

```
var dsfInstance:DropShadowFilter = new DropShadowFilter(20, 0,
0xFF0000);
```

As with other filter objects, you can change the properties of a `DropShadowFilter` instance after it's constructed. The following constructs an instance with the default settings, and then changes the drop shadow to an inner shadow.

```
var dsfInstance:DropShadowFilter = new DropShadowFilter();
dsfInstance.inner = true;
```

Figure 17-3 shows the effect of the following code:

```
import flash.filters.DropShadowFilter;

var dsfInstance:DropShadowFilter = new DropShadowFilter(10, 0,
0x000000, 1, 10, 10);
mCircle.filters = [dsfInstance];
```

 Figure 17-3: A drop shadow filter applied to a circle.

Adding the Glow Filter

You can use instances of the `GlowFilter` class to apply glows to display objects. The `GlowFilter` class has the following properties:

✦ `color` — The color of the glow specified as an unsigned integer from 0x000000 to 0xFFFFFF. The default value is 0xFF0000.

✦ `alpha` — The alpha of the glow from 0 to 1. The default is 1.

✦ `blurX` — The amount to blur the glow in the X direction from 0 to 255. The default is 6.

✦ `blurY` — The amount to blur the glow in the Y direction from 0 to 255. The default is 6.

✦ `strength` — The punch strength of the shadow from 0 to 255. The default is 2.

✦ `quality` — The number of times to run the blur on the glow. The range is from 0 to 15. The higher the number, the smoother the blur of the glow will appear. The default is 1.

✦ `inner` — A Boolean value indicating whether or not the glow should be applied to the inside of the object. The default value is false, which means the glow is applied outside the object.

✦ `knockout` — A Boolean value indicating whether or not the original display object contents should be transparent. If true, that section of the object is transparent (the background or whatever is underneath the object is visible) and the glow is visible around the edges of that area. The default value is false.

The `GlowFilter` constructor accepts from 0 to 8 parameters. The parameters are in the order they appear in the preceding list. The following code constructs a `GlowFilter` object with the default settings:

```
var gfInstance:GlowFilter = new GlowFilter();
```

The following code constructs a `GlowFilter` object with a color of 0x00FFFF and an alpha of 50:

```
var gfInstance:GlowFilter = new GlowFilter(0x00FFFF, 50);
```

As with other filter objects, you can change the properties of a `GlowFilter` object after it's been constructed. The following constructs a `GlowFilter` object with default settings and then makes it an inner glow.

```
var gfInstance:GlowFilter = new GlowFilter();
gfInstance.inner = true;
```

Figure 17-4 shows the effect of the following code:

```
import flash.filters.GlowFilter;

var gfInstance:GlowFilter = new GlowFilter(0x000000, .5, 40, 20);
mCircle.filters = [gfInstance];
```

Figure 17-4: A glow filter applied to a circle.

Adding the Gradient Bevel Filter

The `GradientBevelFilter` class is much like the `BevelFilter` class, except that you can specify more control over the colors. The class defines the following properties:

✦ `distance` — The number of pixels from the edge of the display object to offset the bevel. The default is 4.

✦ `angle` — The angle of the light source in degrees where 0 is directly to the left of the object. The default value is 45.

✦ `colors` — The colors of the bevel specified as an array of an unsigned integer from 0x000000 to 0xFFFFFF.

✦ `alphas` — The alphas of the bevel specified as an array of values from 0 to 100 such that each element corresponds to an element in the colors array. The default is 100.

✦ `ratios` — The ratios to use when distributing the colors across the bevel specified as an array of values from 0 to 255. Each element of the array corresponds to an element of the colors array. Each color in the colors array blends into the next, and so each color appears at 100% at just one point in the continuum.

✦ `blurX` — The amount to blur the bevel in the x direction from 0 to 255. The default is 4.

✦ `blurY` — The amount to blur the bevel in the y direction from 0 to 255. The default is 4.

✦ `strength` — The punch strength of the bevel from 0 to 255. The default is 1.

✦ `quality` — The number of times to run the blur on the bevel. The range is from 0 to 15. The higher the number, the smoother the blur of the bevel will appear. The default is 1.

✦ type — The type can be one of the following values: inner, outer, or full. The default value is inner.

✦ knockout — A Boolean value indicating whether or not the original display object contents should be transparent. If true, that section of the object is transparent (the background or whatever is underneath the object is visible). The default value is false.

The GradientBevelFilter constructor accepts between 0 to 11 parameters. The parameters are in the order they appear in the preceding list. The following code constructs a new GradientBevelFilter with the default values:

```
var gbfInstance:GradientBevelFilter = new GradientBevelFilter();
```

However, unlike many other filter types, the GradientBevelFilter default values don't have any visible effect because the defaults for the three array parameters are undefined. Therefore, in order for there to be some visible effect, you need to somehow specify values for at least the three array parameters. The following code constructs a new GradientBevelFilter object with blue, white, and black colors:

```
var aColors:Array = [0x0000FF, 0xFFFFFF, 0xFFFFFF, 0xFFFFFF,
0x000000];
var aAlphas:Array = [100, 20, 0, 20, 100];
var aRatios:Array = [0, 255 / 4, 2 * 255 / 4, 3 * 255 / 4, 255];
var gbfInstance:GradientBevelFilter = new GradientBevelFilter(10, 45,
aColors, aAlphas, aRatios);
```

You can also construct an instance with default settings, and then assign values to the properties:

```
var gbfInstance:GradientBevelFilter = new GradientBevelFilter();
gbfInstance.colors = aColors;
gbfInstance.alphas = aAlphas;
gbfInstance.ratios = aRatios;
```

Unlike the BevelFilter type, GradientBevelFilter automatically fills the entire object with the gradient bevel. That means that the middle element(s) in the colors array fills the main contents of the object. For example, in the preceding examples the colors array has five elements. The third element is used to fill the shape of the display object inside the bevel. Normally, the alpha of the element is set to 0, as in the preceding examples.

Adding the Gradient Glow Filter

Gradient glows are applied using GradientGlowFilter objects. The properties of the GradientGlowFilter class are identical to those of GradientBevelFilter. Similarly, the GradientGlowFilter constructor accepts the parameters in the same order as the GradientBevelFilter constructor does. Refer to the preceding section for more information.

Adding the Color Matrix Filter

For basic color operations, the ColorTransform class will work. However, for more complex color transformations such as changes in color saturation, hue, and so forth, you can apply a ColorMatrixFilter.

The `ColorMatrixFilter` class has one property: matrix. The matrix property is an array that defines a 4 x 5 (four rows and five columns) grid of values, as shown here:

```
| a b c d e |
| f g h i j |
| k l m n o |
| p q r s t |
```

Note If you don't know anything about matrices, you may want to refer to the "Working with Matrix Transforms" section in Chapter 16 for a brief introduction.

The default matrix is an identity matrix, and it looks something like the following:

```
| 1 0 0 0 0 |
| 0 1 0 0 0 |
| 0 0 1 0 0 |
| 0 0 0 1 0 |
```

The default identity matrix means that no color transformation is applied. Applying the identity matrix at any point resets the colors.

Cross-Reference See Chapter 16 for a discussion of matrices and identity matrices.

The matrix is used in a matrix multiplication operation with color vectors representing the colors of the display object. The color vectors look something like the following:

```
| red   |
| green |
| blue  |
| alpha |
```

The matrix multiplication product is a new 4 x 1 matrix that represents the updated color.

```
| updated red   |
| updated green |
| updated blue  |
| updated alpha |
```

If you're not familiar with matrix multiplication, you can calculate the product vector using the following equations:

```
updated red = red * a + green * b + blue * c + alpha * d + e
updated green = red * f + green * g + blue * h + alpha * i + j
updated blue = red * k + green * l + blue * m + alpha * n + o
updated alpha = red * p + green * q + blue * r + alpha * s + t
```

There are many color transformations that you can apply using a `ColorMatrixFilter`. Some of the most common include the following:

✦ Digital negative

✦ Grayscale

✦ Saturation

✦ Tint

✦ Brightness

✦ Contrast

✦ Hue

The following sections address each of these in turn.

Applying a Digital Negative

A digital negative substitutes the complementary color for each pixel in the original. A complementary color is the color that, when paired with the original color, adds to 0xFFFFFF. You can calculate the complementary color by subtracting the red, blue, and green parts each from 255, and then compositing them. If you wanted to make those calculations, it would require quite a few lines of code in order to calculate and apply the complementary color to each pixel in a display object using conventional means. However, using a color matrix, you can apply the change in as little as one line of code. The matrix that converts a display object to its digital negative is:

```
| -1  0   0 0 255 |
|  0 -1   0 0 255 |
|  0  0  -1 0 255 |
|  0  0   0 1 0   |
```

Therefore, if you want to simply apply a digital negative effect to a display object, you can use the following ColorMatrixFilter object:

```
var cmfDigitalNegative:ColorMatrixFilter = new ColorMatrixFilter([-1,
0, 0, 0, 255, 0,-1, 0, 0, 255, 0, 0,-1, 0, 255, 0, 0, 0, 1, 0]);
```

Then, apply the filter using the filters property of the display object:

```
mPhotograph.filters = [cmfDigitalNegative];
```

Figure 17-5 shows the effect of the following code on a movie clip containing an image. The figure shows the original image on the left and the inverted image on the right.

```
import flash.filters.ColorMatrixFilter;

var cmfInstance:ColorMatrixFilter = new ColorMatrixFilter(
[-1, 0, 0, 0, 255, 0, -1, 0, 0, 255, 0, 0, -1, 0, 255, 0,
0, 0, 1, 0]);
mImage.filters = [cmfInstance];
```

Figure 17-5: A digital negative effect.

Applying a Grayscale

While areas of color images are distinguished by variations in both color values and luminance, grayscale images vary only in luminance. That means that it is possible to convert a color image to grayscale by determining the luminance at each point.

A nontechnical way of understanding luminance is as a measurement of brightness. It is possible to determine the luminance of a color by multiplying the red, green, and blue parts by constants of 0.3086, 0.6094, and 0.0820, respectively. You can use a color matrix to aid in making those calculations. Doing so simplifies things significantly. You can use the following color matrix to convert an image to grayscale:

```
| 0.3086 0.6094 0.0820 0 0 |
| 0.3086 0.6094 0.0820 0 0 |
| 0.3086 0.6094 0.0820 0 0 |
| 0      0      0      1 0 |
```

Note The NTSC standard constants to calculate luminance are 0.299, 0.587, and 0.114. However, the values 0.3086, 0.6094, and 0.0820 are more common for computer graphics.

The following code constructs a `ColorMatrixFilter` object that will convert an image to grayscale:

```
var cmfGrayscale:ColorMatrixFilter = new ColorMatrixFilter([0.3086,
0.6094, 0.0820, 0, 0, 0.3086, 0.6094, 0.0820, 0, 0, 0.3086, 0.6094,
0.0820, 0, 0, 0, 0, 0, 1, 0]);
```

Then, apply the filter using the `filters` property of the display object.

```
mPhotograph.filters = [cmfGrayscale];
```

Applying Saturation Changes

You can change the saturation of colors using a matrix that looks like the following:

```
| a b c 0 0 |
| d e f 0 0 |
| g h i 0 0 |
```

In the preceding matrix, a through i are calculated as shown in the following code, where `rw`, `gw`, and `bw` are the luminance constants discussed in the preceding section, and `level` is a saturation level generally in the range of 0 to 3.

```
a = (1 - level) * rw + level
b = (1 - level) * gw
c = (1 - level) * bw
d = (1 - level) * rw
e = (1 - level) * gw + level
f = (1 - leve) * bw
g = (1 - level) * rw
h = (1 - level) * gw
i = (1 - level) * bw
```

As you may notice, when the level is 0, the matrix formed by a through i is equivalent to the grayscale matrix. Therefore, when the saturation level is set to 0, the effect is to convert the display object to grayscale. A value of 1 for the level forms an identity matrix, so the effect is that the colors are set to the defaults. The higher the level, the more saturated the colors appear. Beyond a level of 3, the colors start to blend together so much as to make the display object's contents indistinguishable.

The following code makes a `ColorMatrixFilter` object with a matrix that increases the color saturation slightly to boost the vibrance of the colors in a MovieClip called `mPhotograph`.

```
var nRed:Number = 0.3086;
var nGreen:Number = 0.6094;
var nBlue:Number = 0.0820;
var nLevel:Number = 1.5;
var nA:Number = (1 - nLevel) * nRed + nLevel;
var nB:Number = (1 - nLevel) * nGreen;
var nC:Number = (1 - nLevel) * nBlue;
var nD:Number = (1 - nLevel) * nRed;
var nE:Number = (1 - nLevel) * nGreen + nLevel;
var nF:Number = (1 - nLevel) * nBlue;
var nG:Number = (1 - nLevel) * nRed;
var nH:Number = (1 - nLevel) * nGreen;
var nI:Number = (1 - nLevel) * nBlue + nLevel;
var aSaturation:Array = [nA, nB, nC, 0, 0,
                         nD, nE, nF, 0, 0,
                         nG, nH, nI, 0, 0,
                          0,  0,  0, 1, 0];
mPhotograph.filters = [new ColorMatrixFilter(aSaturation)];
```

Applying Tint

You can use a color matrix to apply a tint. There are two ways to apply the tint, and they correspond to the two ways of tinting via a `ColorTransform` object: multipliers and offsets. Using a `ColorMatrixFilter` object, the multipliers are the diagonal elements represented by r, g, b, and a in the following matrix.

```
| r 0 0 0 |
| 0 g 0 0 |
| 0 0 b 0 |
| 0 0 0 a |
```

The range that is typically useful for the multipliers is from -1 to 1. The following code applies a `ColorMatrixFilter` to a MovieClip (mPhotograph) such that it halves the green and blue components so that the effect is a red tint.

```
var aRedTint:Array = [1, 0, 0, 0, 0,
                      0, .5, 0, 0, 0,
                      0, 0, .5, 0, 0,
                      0, 0, 0, 1, 0];
mPhotograph.filters = [new ColorMatrixFilter(aRedTint)];
```

Changing the multipliers in a matrix that otherwise looks like an identity matrix is called *scaling* the color. That is because the effect of such a matrix is that it simply multiplies one or more of the color components (red, blue, green, or alpha).

You can also apply offsets to each of the color components via a matrix such as the following. In the following matrix r, g, b, and a represent the red, green, blue, and alpha offsets.

```
| 1 0 0 0 r |
| 0 1 0 0 g |
| 0 0 1 0 b |
| 0 0 0 1 a |
```

The range that is typically useful for offsets is from -255 to 255. The following code applies a `ColorMatrixFilter` object to a MovieClip (`mPhotograph`) such that the red component is offset by 255. That applies a strong red tint to the display object.

```
var aRedTint:Array = [1, 0, 0, 0, 255,
                      0, 1, 0, 0, 0,
                      0, 0, 1, 0, 0,
                      0, 0, 0, 1, 0];
mPhotograph.filters = [new ColorMatrixFilter(aRedTint)];
```

Of course, you can combine both multipliers and offsets in one matrix, just as you can combine multipliers and offsets in a `ColorTransform` object.

Applying Brightness

You can apply brightness effects by either scaling or offsetting the color uniformly with the red, green, and blue multipliers or offsets. The following example scales each of the red, green, and blue values uniformly with a multiplier of 2, which causes the display object to appear brighter:

```
var aBrighten:Array = [2, 0, 0, 0, 0,
                       0, 2, 0, 0, 0,
                       0, 0, 2, 0, 0,
                       0, 0, 0, 1, 0];
mPhotograph.filters = [new ColorMatrixFilter(aBrighten)];
```

Similarly, the following code brightens the display object by applying a `ColorMatrixFilter` in which the red, green, and blue offsets are uniformly adjusted:

```
var aBrighten:Array = [1, 0, 0, 0, 100,
                       0, 1, 0, 0, 100,
                       0, 0, 1, 0, 100,
                       0, 0, 0, 1, 0];
mPhotograph.filters = [new ColorMatrixFilter(aBrighten)];
```

If you combine both multiplier and offset matrices, you'll change the contrast rather than the brightness.

Applying Contrast

You can adjust the contrast of a display object by applying a `ColorMatrixFilter` object that both scales and offsets the red, green, and blue values. The Adjust Color filter available from the Property inspector at authoring time uses the `ColorMatrixFilter` class to manage the color effects, and for contrast effects it uses the following matrix ranges:

✦ Multiplier range from 0 to 11

✦ Offset range from 63.5 to -635

If you want contrast effects that match those from the `Adjust Color` filter, you can use calculations such as those in the following code. Note that you'll want to change `nContrast:`, which has a practical range from 0 to 1, to affect the amount of contrast. The closer `nContrast` is to 0, the less contrast.

```
var nContrast:Number = .5;
var nScale:Number = nContrast * 11;
var nOffset:Number = 63.5 - (nLevel * 698.5);
var aContrast:Array = [nScale, 0, 0, 0, nOffset,
                       0, nScale, 0, 0, nOffset,
                       0, 0, nScale, 0, nOffset,
                       0, 0, 0, 1, 0];
mPhotograph.filters = [new ColorMatrixFilter(aContrast)];
```

Adding the Convolution Filter

The convolution filter does not have an authoring time interface. It can only be applied at runtime. You can apply a convolution filter by way of a `ConvolutionFilter` object. The `ConvolutionFilter` class defines the following properties.

✦ `matrixX` — The number of columns in the convolution matrix.

✦ `matrixY` — The number of rows in the convolution matrix.

✦ `matrix` — An array defining the elements of the convolution matrix.

✦ `divisor` — The divisor is applied to the values calculated after the matrix has been applied. The default is 1.

✦ `bias` — The bias is a number that is added to the values after the matrix has been applied. The default is 0.

✦ `preserveAlpha` — By default, the value is true, which means that the convolution matrix is applied only to the red, green, and blue channels. If `false`, the convolution matrix is applied to the alpha channel as well.

✦ `clamp` — Convolution transformations are applied by applying a matrix transformation to all the pixels that surround each pixel. Therefore, necessarily the pixels along the edges will have to use some nonexistent values for the pixels that are off the edge of the image. By default, the value of `clamp` is set to true, which means that the edge pixels values are duplicated for those calculations. A value of `false` means that an alternate color value is used.

✦ `color` — If `clamp` is set to false, then `color` is used to specify the alternate color value.

✦ `alpha` — The alpha value corresponding to the alternate color.

Convolution matrix transforms enable advanced effects such as edge detection, embossing, and sharpening. Because the use of `ConvolutionFilter` is so specialized, we won't discuss it in too much detail. However, you may find some of the following matrices to be useful guides.

For edge detection use the following matrix.

```
| 0  1  0 |
| 1 -4  1 |
| 0  1  0 |
```

For sharpen effects use the following matrix.

```
|  0 -1  0 |
| -1  5 -1 |
|  0 -1  0 |
```

For an emboss effect use the following matrix.

```
| -2 -1  0 |
| -1  1  1 |
|  0  1  2 |
```

The following example code applies an emboss effect to `mPhotograph`.

```
mPhotograph.filters = [new ConvolutionFilter(3, 3, [-2, -1,
0, -1, 1, 1, 0, 1, 2])];
```

Adding the Displacement Map Filter

The `DisplacementMapFilter` class lets you apply distortion and texture effects to display objects. For example, using `DisplacementMapFilter`, you can apply a magnifying lens effect or make an image look like it's reflecting in a pool of rippling water. The `DisplacmentMapFilter` class has the following properties:

✦ `mapBitmap` — A `BitmapData` object (see Chapter 18) to use as the displacement map.

✦ `mapPoint` — A `flash.geom.Point` object to use to map the `BitmapData` object to a point on the coordinate space of the display object.

✦ `componentX` — A color channel to use from the `BitmapData` object in order to map to the display object in the X direction. Possible values are 1 for red, 2 for green, 4 for blue, and 8 for alpha.

✦ `componentY` — A color channel to use from the `BitmapData` object to map to the display object in the Y direction. Possible values are the same as for `componentX`.

✦ `scaleX` — The multiplier to use when scaling the displacement in the X direction. A value of 0 causes no displacement.

✦ `scaleY` — The multiplier to use when scaling the displacement in the Y direction.

✦ `mode` — How to displace pixels along the edges. When the filter is applied, part of the display object is shifted by an amount determined by the `scaleX` and `scaleY` properties. Options for mode are the `IGNORE`, `WRAP`, `CLAMP`, and `COLOR` constants from the `flash.dilters.DisplacementMapFilter.Mode` class. `IGNORE` causes the adjacent edges to repeat. `WRAP` causes the displaced pixels from the opposite edges to wrap to the other side. `CLAMP` causes the edge pixels to extend outward. `COLOR` uses a solid color.

✦ `color` — If `COLOR` is specified for mode, then the `color` property determines the color to use. The default is 0xFFFFFF.

✦ `alpha` — If `COLOR` is specified for mode, then the `alpha` property determines the alpha of the color. The default is 100.

Adding More Than One Filter

You can add more than one filter to an object by simply placing each filter object as an element in the filters array. For example, the following code applies a bevel and a drop shadow to a movie clip named `mCircle`:

```
import flash.filters.BevelFilter;
import flash.filters.DropShadowFilter;

var bvfInstance:BevelFilter = new BevelFilter();
var dsfInstance:DropShadowFilter = new DropShadowFilter();
mCircle.filters = [bvfInstance, dsfInstance];
```

The filters have cumulative effects. Each filter is applied in the order in which it appears in the array. For example, in the preceding code the bevel is applied before the drop shadow. The sequence in which the filters are applied can be important. Since the effects are cumulative, it makes a difference whether a drop shadow or a bevel filter was applied first.

In some cases, you may want to apply more than one filter to a display object, but you may not want the effects to be cumulative. For example, if you apply a glow to a display object, then a drop shadow, then the shadow will apply not only to the original shape of the display object but also to the glow. If you want the drop shadow to apply only to the original shape of the display object, you can use `duplicateMovieClip()` to make a duplicate of the original movie clip, and then apply the glow filter to one instance and the drop shadow to the other. The following code illustrates the difference. The code assumes there are two movie clips on stage at authoring time: `mCircleA` and `mCircleB`.

```
import flash.filters.DropShadowFilter;
import flash.filters.GlowFilter;
import flash.display.BitmapData;
import flash.geom.Matrix;

mCircleA.filters = [new DropShadowFilter(100),
new GlowFilter(0xFF0000, .5, 100, 100)];

mCircleB.filters = [new DropShadowFilter(100)];
var mCircleGlow:MovieClip =
mCircleB.duplicateMovieClip("mCircleGlow",
this.getNextHighestDepth());
mCircleGlow.filters = [new GlowFilter(0xFF0000, .5, 100, 100)];
```

Figure 17-6 shows the effects of the preceding code on two circle movie clips. The `mCircleA` movie clip is on the left.

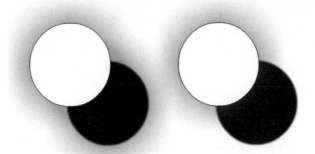

Figure 17-6: Cumulative and noncumulative filter effects.

Rotating Objects with Filters

As noted earlier in this chapter, filters are applied as bitmap surfaces. That means that anything that causes a bitmap surface to redraw will also cause the filter to be reapplied. This has implications with regard to rotation. For example, consider a circle movie clip to which a blur has been applied. The blur has a blurX property set to 40 and a blurY property set to 10. That means that the blur is taller than it is wide. As you rotate the movie clip, you'd likely expect the blur to rotate as well, so that when it is rotated 90 degrees the blur is wider than it is tall. However, because the filter is reapplied each time the object is rotated, the blur always appears taller than it is wide.

To achieve a proper rotation effect, you can use the BitmapData class (discussed in more detail in Chapter 18). With the BitmapData class, you can draw the contents of a movie clip (with filters applied) to a BitmapData object. You can then display that object in a movie clip, and rotate that movie clip. The following code illustrates how this works.

```
import flash.filters.BlurFilter;
import flash.display.BitmapData;
import flash.geom.Matrix;

var bfInstance:BlurFilter = new BlurFilter(10, 40);
mCircle.filters = [bfInstance];

var bmpCircle:BitmapData = new BitmapData(mCircle._width + 20,
mCircle._height + 80);
bmpCircle.draw(mCircle, new Matrix(1, 0, 0, 1, 10, 40));

mCircle._visible = false;

this.createEmptyMovieClip("mCircleCopy",
this.getNextHighestDepth());
mCircleCopy.attachBitmap(bmpCircle, 1);

function onMouseMove():Void {
  mCircleCopy._rotation = (_xmouse/550) * 360;
}
```

We'd like to know what you thought about this chapter. Visit `www.rightactionscript` `.com/asb/comments` to fill out an online form with your comments.

Summary

✦ Filters let you apply bitmap effects to display objects.

✦ You can apply a filter to a display object via the filters array property.

✦ Filter effects are cumulative. If you want to apply more than one filter in a noncumulative fashion, you can make duplicates of the display object and apply each filter individually.

✦ Filter effects are reapplied each time an object rotates. You can use a `BitmapData` object to apply rotating filter effects.

✦   ✦   ✦

Using the Bitmap API

Flash 8 introduces a new API for working with bitmaps. The `flash.display.BitmapData` class is the main focus with regard to bitmaps, and it has methods for getting and setting pixels, applying pixel dissolves threshold settings, applying filters, and more. In this chapter, you'll look at how to work with the new API to achieve a variety of effects.

Constructing a BitmapData Object

There are basically two ways to construct a new `BitmapData` object in ActionScript. You can use the constructor to make a new, blank `BitmapData` object with specific dimensions and background. If you have a library asset (a Bitmap symbol) from which you want to make a new `BitmapData` object, you can do that using a static method of the `BitmapData` class. In the following sections we'll look at how to use those two ways to construct BitmapData objects. No matter how you want to work with bitmaps via ActionScript, you'll need to use at least one of those ways to construct the object.

Using the Constructor Method

You can construct a new `BitmapData` object using the constructor method as part of a new statement. The constructor requires at least two parameters and allows for up to four parameters (two optional). The parameters are:

- ✦ `width` — The width of the bitmap in pixels.

- ✦ `height` — The height of the bitmap in pixels.

- ✦ `transparent` — Indicates whether or not the bitmap background is transparent. The default is true.

- ✦ `fillColor` — The color to use for the background if the background is not transparent. The value is specified as 0xAARRGGBB. The default is 0xFFFFFFFF (opaque white).

The following code constructs a new `BitmapData` object for a 500 x 200 pixel image. The background is set to transparent.

```
import flash.display.BitmapData;

var bmpRectangle:BitmapData = new BitmapData(500, 200);
```

The following code constructs the same `BitmapData` object, except the background is an opaque red.

```
import flash.display.BitmapData;

var bmpRectangle:BitmapData = new BitmapData(500, 200, false, 0xFFFF0000);
```

Note   Simply constructing a `BitmapData` object does not render it. To render the image, you have to use `MovieClip.attachBitmap()` as discussed in the section "Displaying BitmapData Images."

Loading a Library Item

You can construct a new `BitmapData` object from a bitmap library symbol using the static `BitmapData.loadBitmap()` method. For the method to work, you must have a Bitmap symbol in the library set to export for ActionScript with a valid linkage identifier. You can set the linkage identifier for a Bitmap symbol using the following steps:

1. Select the symbol in the library.

2. Right-click or Ctrl-click the symbol to open the contextual menu for the symbol, or click on the menu icon in the upper-right corner of the Library panel to open the library menu.

3. Select Linkage from the menu.

4. Check the Export for ActionScript check box. Specify a linkage identifier.

5. You can typically use the default linkage identifier that matches the symbol name. Optionally, enter a new linkage identifier.

6. Click OK.

With the symbol set to export, you can then use ActionScript to make a `BitmapData` object that uses the symbol data. The `BitmapData` class has a static method called `loadBitmap()` that requires one parameter, the linkage identifier of the symbol, and returns a new `BitmapData` object. Assuming that the Library has a Bitmap symbol set to export with a linkage identifier of image, the following code will construct a new `BitmapData` object based on that symbol:

```
import flash.display.BitmapData;

var bmpImage:BitmapData = BitmapData.loadBitmap("image");
```

Note   The preceding code does not render the image. See "Displaying BitmapData Images" for details on how to accomplish that task.

Displaying BitmapData Images

Regardless of how you construct a `BitmapData` object, it exists only in the unrendered state until you specifically instruct the player to render the data visually. You can render the data visually to a `MovieClip` object. To do so, use the `attachBitmap()` method of the `MovieClip` object. The `attachBitmap()` method requires two parameters and accepts up to four. The parameters are:

✦ bitmap—The BitmapData object.

✦ depth—The depth within the MovieClip at which to render the bitmap.

✦ pixelSnapping—One of the following strings: auto, always, never. The default is auto.

✦ smoothing—Indicates whether or not to applying smoothing to the image as it is scaled beyond 100%. The default is true.

The following code makes a new BitmapData object with an opaque purple background, and renders it to a MovieClip object:

```
import flash.display.BitmapData;

var bmpSquare:BitmapData = new BitmapData(200, 200, false, 0xFFCC00CC);
this.createEmptyMovieClip("mSquare", this.getNextHighestDepth());
mSquare.attachBitmap(bmpSquare, mSquare.getNextHighestDepth());
```

Notice that in the example we use an empty MovieClip object. Although you can attach many BitmapData objects to one MovieClip object (at unique depths), and you can nest both BitmapData renderings as well as display objects within a MovieClip object, it is generally advisable to use a new empty MovieClip for each BitmapData object you want to render.

Pixel Snapping

If a bitmap rendering is not placed at integer coordinates, you can use pixel snapping to snap it to integer coordinates. As noted in the preceding section, the attachBitmap() method lets you optionally specify a pixel snapping setting. The default, auto, means that any unscaled, unrotated bitmap rendering will snap to integer coordinates. The value of always means that the bitmap rendering will always snap to integer coordinates regardless of whether or not it is scaled or rotated. You can also specify never in order that the bitmap rendering will not snap to integer coordinates.

Note

A bitmap rendering will appear at non-integer coordinates if the parent movie clip is at non-integer coordinates.

Image Smoothing

By default, rendered bitmaps apply smoothing when they are scaled beyond 100 percent. That prevents the image from being rendered with a pixilated appearance. However, it also means that the image may appear blurry when scaled. If you prefer that Flash not apply smoothing, you can specify a value of false for the fourth parameter of the attachBitmap() method.

Working with BitmapData Properties

BitmapData objects have the following read-only properties:

✦ width—The width of the BitmapData object in pixels.

✦ height—The height of the BitmapData object in pixels.

✦ transparent—A Boolean value indicating whether or not the background is transparent.

✦ rectangle—A Rectangle object representing the dimensions of the BitmapData object for use with methods that require a Rectangle object.

The properties are read-only, so you cannot use them to make adjustments to the `BitmapData` object after it's been constructed.

Copying Images

The `BitmapData` class defines several methods for copying bitmap data from other ActionScript objects. Specifically, it defines methods for copying bitmap data from `MovieClip` objects, and it defines methods for copying bitmap data from `BitmapData` objects.

Copying from MovieClips

The `draw()` method copies every pixel from a source to the `BitmapData` object from which it is called. The source can be either a `MovieClip` or a `BitmapData` object. We'll first look at copying the pixels from a `MovieClip`.

The `draw()` method requires one parameter: the reference to the source object. However, when you are copying a `MovieClip` you can specify additional parameters. When copying a `MovieClip`, the `draw()` method accepts the following parameters:

✦ `source`—A reference to the `MovieClip` object from which to copy the pixels.

✦ `matrix`—A `Matrix` object to use to apply any transformations. The default is an identity matrix that applies no transformations.

✦ `colorTransform`—A `ColorTransform` object that adjusts the colors as the pixels are copied. By default no color transformation is applied.

✦ `blendMode`—Indicates what, if any, blend mode to apply. The blend modes are specified using the `MovieClip.BlendModeTypes` constants.

✦ `clipRectangle`—A `Rectangle` object that specifies the region of the target `BitmapData` object into which to draw the pixels. By default the `Rectangle` X and Y values are 0, and the width and height are equal to the width and height of the source data.

The following code illustrates one use of the `draw()` method. In the example, you programmatically draw a design (two concentric circles with two crossed rectangles) within a `MovieClip` object. You then make four `BitmapData` objects, and use `draw()` to draw four quadrants of the design — one quadrant per `BitmapData` object.

```
import flash.display.BitmapData;
import flash.geom.Matrix;
import flash.geom.Rectangle;
import actionscriptbible.drawing.DrawingUtilities;

// Make a MovieClip object into which to draw the design.
this.createEmptyMovieClip("mClip", this.getNextHighestDepth());

// Use a DrawingUtilities object to draw the design into the
// MovieClip. If you haven't copied DrawingUtilities to your
// classpath, refer to Chapter 15.
var duDrawer:DrawingUtilities = new DrawingUtilities(mClip);
duDrawer.drawCircle(100, 100, 100);
```

```
duDrawer.drawRectangle(150, 100, 100, 100);
duDrawer.drawRectangle(100, 150, 100, 100);
duDrawer.drawCircle(50, 100, 100);

// Make a BitmapData object with the same dimensions as the
// MovieClip. Set the background to opaque, and set the color
// to a light red. That way we can differentiate between
// the BitmapData objects when they are rendered to the stage.
var bmpA:BitmapData = new BitmapData(200, 200, false, 0xFFFFCCCC);

// Copy the pixels from mClip to the new BitmapData object.
// Only copy to the upper left quadrant.
bmpA.draw(mClip, new Matrix(), null, null, new Rectangle(0, 0, 100, 100));

// Make a MovieClip object, and render the BitmapData object.
this.createEmptyMovieClip("mClipA", this.getNextHighestDepth());
mClipA.attachBitmap(bmpA, mClipA.getNextHighestDepth());

// Make a BitmapData object for the second quadrant. Use
// a background color of light green.
var bmpB:BitmapData = new BitmapData(200, 200, false, 0xFFCCFFCC);

// Copy only to the second quadrant.
bmpB.draw(mClip, new Matrix(), null, null, new Rectangle(100, 0, 100, 100));
this.createEmptyMovieClip("mClipB", this.getNextHighestDepth());
mClipB.attachBitmap(bmpB, mClipB.getNextHighestDepth());
mClipB._x = 200;

// Make a BitmapData object for the third quadrant. Use
// a background color of light blue.
var bmpC:BitmapData = new BitmapData(200, 200, false, 0xFFCCCCFF);

// Copy only to the third quadrant.
bmpC.draw(mClip, new Matrix(), null, null, new Rectangle(0, 100, 100, 100));
this.createEmptyMovieClip("mClipC", this.getNextHighestDepth());
mClipC.attachBitmap(bmpC, mClipC.getNextHighestDepth());
mClipC._y = 200;

// Make a BitmapData object for the fourth quadrant. Use
// a background color of light yellow.
var bmpD:BitmapData = new BitmapData(200, 200, false, 0xFFFFFFCC);
bmpD.draw(mClip, new Matrix(), null, null, new Rectangle(100, 100, 100, 100));
this.createEmptyMovieClip("mClipD", this.getNextHighestDepth());
mClipD.attachBitmap(bmpD, mClipD.getNextHighestDepth());
mClipD._x = 200;
mClipD._y = 200;

// Move the mClip object to the front and center so we can see
// it along with the four quadrants.
mClip.swapDepths(this.getNextHighestDepth());
mClip._x = 100;
mClip._y = 100;
```

Figure 18-1 shows the effect.

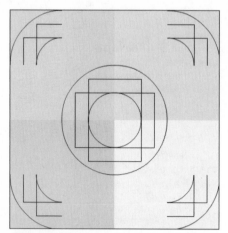

Figure 18-1: Using the draw() method to copy regions of a design from a MovieClip to BitmapData objects.

You'll likely notice in the preceding example that the quadrants are copied to the new BitmapData object with the same x and y coordinates as they appeared in the original MovieClip object. That means the new BitmapData objects have nothing drawn in the other quadrants. How about drawing the new BitmapData objects such that the object's dimensions are equal to the region you want to draw into it? That's possible too. The next example looks at how you can accomplish that by simply moving the artwork within the source MovieClip before copying. The following code is nearly identical to the preceding example. The changes are bolded, and comments are added to indicate what the changes do. The effect is shown in Figure 18-2.

```
import flash.display.BitmapData;
import flash.geom.Matrix;
import flash.geom.Rectangle;
import actionscriptbible.drawing.DrawingUtilities;

this.createEmptyMovieClip("mClip", this.getNextHighestDepth());

// Make a nested MovieClip object within mClip. Then, draw the
// design within that object. That way we can quickly move the
// nested object just before copying pixels.
mClip.createEmptyMovieClip("mDesign", mClip.getNextHighestDepth());
var duDrawer:DrawingUtilities = new DrawingUtilities(mClip.mDesign);
duDrawer.drawCircle(100, 100, 100);
duDrawer.drawRectangle(150, 100, 100, 100);
```

```
duDrawer.drawRectangle(100, 150, 100, 100);
duDrawer.drawCircle(50, 100, 100);

// In each case we're making BitmapData objects that have
// dimensions that match the quadrants.
var bmpA:BitmapData = new BitmapData(100, 100, false, 0xFFFFCCCC);
bmpA.draw(mClip, new Matrix(), null, null, new Rectangle(0, 0, 100, 100));
this.createEmptyMovieClip("mClipA", this.getNextHighestDepth());
mClipA.attachBitmap(bmpA, mClipA.getNextHighestDepth());

var bmpB:BitmapData = new BitmapData(100, 100, false, 0xFFCCFFCC);

// Before copying and pixels, move the nested MovieClip object
// so that the second quadrant is at 0,0 within the container
// object. Then, use a Rectangle that copies a 100 X 100 region
// from 0,0.
mClip.mDesign._x = -100;
bmpB.draw(mClip, new Matrix(), null, null, new Rectangle(0, 0, 100, 100));
this.createEmptyMovieClip("mClipB", this.getNextHighestDepth());
mClipB.attachBitmap(bmpB, mClipB.getNextHighestDepth());
mClipB._x = 200;

var bmpC:BitmapData = new BitmapData(100, 100, false, 0xFFCCCCFF);

// Move the nested MovieClip object such that the third
// quadrant is at 0,0.
mClip.mDesign._x = 0;
mClip.mDesign._y = -100;
bmpC.draw(mClip, new Matrix(), null, null, new Rectangle(0, 0, 100, 100));
this.createEmptyMovieClip("mClipC", this.getNextHighestDepth());
mClipC.attachBitmap(bmpC, mClipC.getNextHighestDepth());
mClipC._y = 200;

var bmpD:BitmapData = new BitmapData(100, 100, false, 0xFFFFFFCC);

// Move the nested MovieClip object such that the fourth
// quadrant is at 0,0.
mClip.mDesign._x = -100;
bmpD.draw(mClip, new Matrix(), null, null, new Rectangle(0, 0, 100, 100));
this.createEmptyMovieClip("mClipD", this.getNextHighestDepth());
mClipD.attachBitmap(bmpD, mClipD.getNextHighestDepth());
mClipD._x = 200;
mClipD._y = 200;

// Delete the mClip object. We already know what it looks like,
// and this time let's just display the four quadrants.
mClip.removeMovieClip();
```

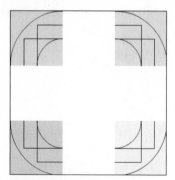

Figure 18-2: The four quadrants
drawn to BitmapData objects
with correct dimensions.

Loading BitmapData Images

Although you cannot directly make a `BitmapData` object from an external image, you can
use a `MovieClip` object as an intermediary. Using `MovieClipLoader`, you can load the image
into a `MovieClip` container. Then, you can construct a new `BitmapData` object using the
constructor, and use the `draw()` method to copy the pixels from the `MovieClip` object to
the `BitmapData` object. The following code uses the preceding technique to load an image
and draw four quadrants into four `BitmapData` objects.

```
import flash.display.BitmapData;
import flash.geom.Matrix;
import flash.geom.Rectangle;

// Make a MovieClip object and a nested object within that into
// which to load the image.
this.createEmptyMovieClip("mClip", this.getNextHighestDepth());
mClip.createEmptyMovieClip("mImage", mClip.getNextHighestDepth());

// Define a listener object for use with the MovieClipLoader
// instance.
var oListener:Object = new Object();
oListener.onLoadInit = function(mClip:MovieClip):Void {

  // When the image loads, call drawQuadrants() and then make
  // mClip invisible.
  drawQuadrants();
  mClip._visible = false;
};

// Define the MovieClipLoader object, and load the image into
// mClip.mImage.
var mlImage:MovieClipLoader = new MovieClipLoader();
mlImage.addListener(oListener);
```

```
mlImage.loadClip("http://www.person13.com/asb/image2.jpg", mClip.mImage);

function drawQuadrants():Void {

  // The width and height of the quadrants are equal to one
  // half the width and height of mClip.
  var nWidth:Number = mClip._width/2;
  var nHeight:Number = mClip._height/2;

  // As in the example from the preceding section, make four
  // BitmapData objects with widths and heights equal to the
  // dimensions of the rectangular regions you want to copy.
  // Then use draw() to copy the pixels from mClip to the
  // BitmapData objects. To draw each quadrant, move
  // mClip.mImage before drawing.
  var bmpA:BitmapData = new BitmapData(nWidth, nHeight);
  bmpA.draw(mClip, new Matrix(), null, null, new Rectangle(0, 0,  ⤵
nWidth, nHeight));
  this.createEmptyMovieClip("mClipA", this.getNextHighestDepth());
  mClipA.attachBitmap(bmpA, mClipA.getNextHighestDepth());

  var bmpB:BitmapData = new BitmapData(nWidth, nHeight);
  mClip.mImage._x = -nWidth;
  bmpB.draw(mClip, new Matrix(), null, null, new Rectangle(0, 0,  ⤵
nWidth, nHeight));
  this.createEmptyMovieClip("mClipB", this.getNextHighestDepth());
  mClipB.attachBitmap(bmpB, mClipB.getNextHighestDepth());
  mClipB._x = nWidth + 10;

  var bmpC:BitmapData = new BitmapData(nWidth, nHeight);
  mClip.mImage._x = 0;
  mClip.mImage._y = -nHeight;
  bmpC.draw(mClip, new Matrix(), null, null, new Rectangle(0, 0,  ⤵
nWidth, nHeight));
  this.createEmptyMovieClip("mClipC", this.getNextHighestDepth());
  mClipC.attachBitmap(bmpC, mClipC.getNextHighestDepth());
  mClipC._y = nHeight + 10;

  var bmpD:BitmapData = new BitmapData(nWidth, nHeight);
  mClip.mImage._x = -nWidth;
  bmpD.draw(mClip, new Matrix(), null, null, new Rectangle(0, 0,  ⤵
nWidth, nHeight));
  this.createEmptyMovieClip("mClipD", this.getNextHighestDepth());
  mClipD.attachBitmap(bmpD,mClipD.getNextHighestDepth());
  mClipD._x = nWidth + 10;
  mClipD._y = nHeight + 10;
}
```

Copying from BitmapData Objects

You can copy pixels not only from `MovieClip` instances but also from `BitmapData` objects. You can use the following methods to copy from a `BitmapData` object:

✦ `clone()` — Makes a new `BitmapData` object with an exact copy of the data of the original object.

✦ `draw()` — Works just like copying pixels from a MovieClip.

✦ `copyPixels()` — Copy a region of pixels.

✦ `copyChannel()` — Copies the red, green, blue, or alpha channel.

✦ `merge()` — Merges images.

✦ `getPixel()`/`setPixel()`/`getPixel32()`/`setPixel32()` — Get and set pixels.

Cloning a BitmapData Object

You can clone a `BitmapData` object using the `clone()` method. The method requires no parameters, and it makes a new `BitmapData` object with a copy of the data of the original:

```
var bmpClone:BitmapData = bmpOriginal.clone();
```

Drawing into a BitmapData Object

Earlier in this chapter, you learned how to use the `draw()` method to copy pixels from a `MovieClip` object to a `BitmapData` object. You can use the `draw()` method in the same way to copy pixels from one `BitmapData` object to another `BitmapData` object. If you specify only one parameter, the `draw()` method makes a copy of the data into the new `BitmapData` object:

```
bmpB.draw(bmpA);
```

When you use the `draw()` method to copy pixels from a `BitmapData` object, you can specify one additional parameter. The sixth (optional) parameter is a Boolean value that determines whether or not to smooth the image when it is scaled beyond 100 percent. The default is `false`. The following code illustrates how to use the smoothing parameter. The code loads an image, copies the pixels to a `BitmapData` object, and then copies that data to two `BitmapData` objects: one with smoothing and one without, as shown in Figure 18-3. You can see that the one on the left is pixilated, while the one on the right is smoothed.

```
import flash.display.BitmapData;
import flash.geom.Matrix;
import flash.geom.Rectangle;

// Make a MovieClip object into which to load the image.
this.createEmptyMovieClip("mClip", this.getNextHighestDepth());
mClip.createEmptyMovieClip("mImage", mClip.getNextHighestDepth());

// Define a listener object such that when the image loads it
// calls the custom copy() function and sets the MovieClip to
// invisible.
var oListener:Object = new Object();
oListener.onLoadInit = function(mClip:MovieClip):Void {
  copy();
  mClip._visible = false;
```

```
};

var mlImage:MovieClipLoader = new MovieClipLoader();
mlImage.addListener(oListener);
mlImage.loadClip("http://www.person13.com/asb/image1.jpg", mClip.mImage);

function copy():Void {

  var nWidth:Number = mClip._width;
  var nHeight:Number = mClip._height;

  // Copy the pixels from the MovieClip to a BitmapData object.
  var bmpCopy:BitmapData = new BitmapData(nWidth, nHeight);
  bmpCopy.draw(mClip, new Matrix());


  // Copy the pixels from the BitmapData object to a new
  // BitmapData object. Use the default setting for smoothing.
  var bmpA:BitmapData = new BitmapData(nWidth, nHeight);
  bmpA.draw(bmpCopy, new Matrix(10, 0, 0, 10));
  this.createEmptyMovieClip("mClipA", this.getNextHighestDepth());
  mClipA.attachBitmap(bmpA, mClipA.getNextHighestDepth());

  // Copy the pixels from the BitmapData object. Use smoothing.
  var bmpB:BitmapData = new BitmapData(nWidth, nHeight);
  bmpB.draw(bmpCopy, new Matrix(10, 0, 0, 10), null, null, null, true);
  this.createEmptyMovieClip("mClipB", this.getNextHighestDepth());
  mClipB.attachBitmap(bmpB, mClipB.getNextHighestDepth());

  // Move mClipB to the right so you can see part of both of
  // the images.
  mClipB._x = 275;

}
```

Figure 18-3: The left image has no smoothing applied, while the right does.

Copying Pixels

You can use the copyPixels() method to copy rectangular regions of a BitmapData object. From a practical perspective it is similar to the draw() method. However, the parameters are different, and the copyPixels() method allows you to copy pixels in a slightly different way. The parameters are:

✦ sourceBitmap—The BitmapData object from which you want to copy pixels.

✦ sourceRectangle—A Rectangle object specifying the region of the source bitmap you want to copy.

✦ destinationPoint—A Point object specifying the point in the destination bitmap at which you want to start placing the copied pixels.

✦ alphaBitmap—A BitmapData object from which you want to use the alpha channel. The parameter is optional. By default, the alpha channel of the source BitmapData object is used.

✦ alphaPoint—A Point object that specifies a point within the alpha BitmapData object that maps to the upper-left corner of the destination BitmapData object. The parameter is optional.

✦ mergeAlpha—A Boolean value indicating whether or not to merge the alpha channels of both the source BitmapData object and the alpha BitmapData object. If false, only the alpha BitmapData alpha channel is used. If true, both alpha channels are used. The parameter is optional.

As already stated, the copyPixels() method is often used in much the same way as the draw() method: to copy rectangular regions. The following code is a rewrite of a previous example from the "Loading BitmapData Images" section, using copyPixels() instead of draw(). While both produce the same effect, the logic is slightly different.

Note   The following code does still use draw() to copy the image data from a MovieClip object to a BitmapData object. However, it uses copyPixels() to make rectangular regions from the original bitmap.

```
import flash.display.BitmapData;
import flash.geom.Matrix;
import flash.geom.Rectangle;

// Make a MovieClip object and a nested object within that into
// which to load the image.
this.createEmptyMovieClip("mClip", this.getNextHighestDepth());
mClip.createEmptyMovieClip("mImage", mClip.getNextHighestDepth());

// Define a listener object for use with the MovieClipLoader
// instance.
var oListener:Object = new Object();
oListener.onLoadInit = function(mClip:MovieClip):Void {

  // When the image loads, call drawQuadrants() and then make
  // mClip invisible.
  drawQuadrants();
  mClip._visible = false;
```

```
};

// Define the MovieClipLoader object, and load the image into
// mClip.mImage.
var mlImage:MovieClipLoader = new MovieClipLoader();
mlImage.addListener(oListener);
mlImage.loadClip("http://www.person13.com/asb/image2.jpg", mClip.mImage);

function drawQuadrants():Void {

   // The width and height of the quadrants are equal to one
   // half the width and height of mClip.
   var nWidth:Number = mClip._width/2;
   var nHeight:Number = mClip._height/2;

   // Make a new BitmapData object, and use draw() to copy the
   // MovieClip pixels into it.
   var bmpCopy:BitmapData = new BitmapData(mClip._width, mClip._height);
   bmpCopy.draw(mClip, new Matrix());

   // Make four BitmapData objects with widths and heights equal
   // to the  dimensions of the rectangular regions you want to
   // copy.  Then use copyPixels() to copy the regions from
   // bmpCopy to the BitmapData objects.
   var bmpA:BitmapData = new BitmapData(nWidth, nHeight);
   bmpA.copyPixels(bmpCopy, new Rectangle(0, 0, nWidth, nHeight),      ⊃
new Point(0, 0));
   this.createEmptyMovieClip("mClipA", this.getNextHighestDepth());
   mClipA.attachBitmap(bmpA, mClipA.getNextHighestDepth());

   var bmpB:BitmapData = new BitmapData(nWidth, nHeight);
   bmpB.copyPixels(bmpCopy, new Rectangle(nWidth, 0, nWidth, nHeight), ⊃
new Point(0, 0));
   this.createEmptyMovieClip("mClipB", this.getNextHighestDepth());
   mClipB.attachBitmap(bmpB, mClipB.getNextHighestDepth());
   mClipB._x = nWidth + 10;

   var bmpC:BitmapData = new BitmapData(nWidth, nHeight);
   bmpC.copyPixels(bmpCopy, new Rectangle(0, nHeight, nWidth, nHeight),⊃
new Point(0, 0));
   this.createEmptyMovieClip("mClipC", this.getNextHighestDepth());
   mClipC.attachBitmap(bmpC, mClipC.getNextHighestDepth());
   mClipC._y = nHeight + 10;

   var bmpD:BitmapData = new BitmapData(nWidth, nHeight);
   bmpD.copyPixels(bmpCopy, new Rectangle(nWidth, nHeight, nWidth, nHeight), ⊃
new Point(0, 0));
   this.createEmptyMovieClip("mClipD", this.getNextHighestDepth());
   mClipD.attachBitmap(bmpD,mClipD.getNextHighestDepth());
   mClipD._x = nWidth + 10;
   mClipD._y = nHeight + 10;
}
```

Copying Channels

The `copyChannel()` method lets you copy the red, green, blue, and alpha channels from a `BitmapData` object. The parameters for `copyChannel()` are:

✦ `sourceBitmap`—The `BitmapData` object from which you want to copy pixels.

✦ `sourceRectangle`—A `Rectangle` object specifying the region of the source bitmap you want to copy.

✦ `destinationPoint`—A `Point` object specifying the point in the destination bitmap at which you want to start placing the copied pixels.

✦ `sourceChannel`—A number from the set of 1, 2, 4, and 8 representing red, green, blue, and alpha, respectively.

✦ `destinationChannel`—a number from the set of 1, 2, 4, and 8 representing red, green, blur, and alpha, respectively.

The following code is very similar to the code in the previous section. However, rather than using `copyPixels()`, the following code uses `copyChannel()`. Each of the quadrants renders only specific channels from the original image so that they appear as red, green, blue, and yellow.

```
import flash.display.BitmapData;
import flash.geom.Matrix;
import flash.geom.Point;
import flash.geom.Rectangle;

this.createEmptyMovieClip("mClip", this.getNextHighestDepth());
mClip.createEmptyMovieClip("mImage", mClip.getNextHighestDepth());

var oListener:Object = new Object();
oListener.onLoadInit = function(mClip:MovieClip):Void {
  drawQuadrants();
  mClip._visible = false;
};

var mlImage:MovieClipLoader = new MovieClipLoader();
mlImage.addListener(oListener);
mlImage.loadClip("http://www.person13.com/asb/image2.jpg", mClip.mImage);

function drawQuadrants():Void {

  var nWidth:Number = mClip._width/2;
  var nHeight:Number = mClip._height/2;

  var bmpCopy:BitmapData = new BitmapData(mClip._width, mClip._height);
  bmpCopy.draw(mClip, new Matrix());

    // Make each of the BitmapData objects with opaque black
    // backgrounds. Otherwise the colors will show up
    // incorrectly.
```

```
  var bmpA:BitmapData = new BitmapData(nWidth, nHeight, false, 0xFF000000);

  // Copy the red channel.
  bmpA.copyChannel(bmpCopy, new Rectangle(0, 0, nWidth, nHeight),      ⊃
new Point(0, 0), 1, 1);
  this.createEmptyMovieClip("mClipA", this.getNextHighestDepth());
  mClipA.attachBitmap(bmpA, mClipA.getNextHighestDepth());

  var bmpB:BitmapData = new BitmapData(nWidth, nHeight, false, 0xFF000000);

  // Copy the green channel.
  bmpB.copyChannel(bmpCopy, new Rectangle(nWidth, 0, nWidth, nHeight),   ⊃
new Point(0, 0), 2, 2);
  this.createEmptyMovieClip("mClipB", this.getNextHighestDepth());
  mClipB.attachBitmap(bmpB, mClipB.getNextHighestDepth());
  mClipB._x = nWidth + 10;

  var bmpC:BitmapData = new BitmapData(nWidth, nHeight, false, 0xFF000000);

  // Copy the blue channel.
  bmpC.copyChannel(bmpCopy, new Rectangle(0, nHeight, nWidth, nHeight),   ⊃
new Point(0, 0), 4, 4);
  this.createEmptyMovieClip("mClipC", this.getNextHighestDepth());
  mClipC.attachBitmap(bmpC, mClipC.getNextHighestDepth());
  mClipC._y = nHeight + 10;

  var bmpD:BitmapData = new BitmapData(nWidth, nHeight, false, 0xFF000000);

  // Copy both the red and green channels to make yellow.
  bmpD.copyChannel(bmpCopy, new Rectangle(nWidth, nHeight, nWidth, nHeight), ⊃
new Point(0, 0), Channel.RED, Channel.RED);
  bmpD.copyChannel(bmpCopy, new Rectangle(nWidth, nHeight, nWidth, nHeight), ⊃
new Point(0, 0), 8, 8);
  this.createEmptyMovieClip("mClipD", this.getNextHighestDepth());
  mClipD.attachBitmap(bmpD,mClipD.getNextHighestDepth());
  mClipD._x = nWidth + 10;
  mClipD._y = nHeight + 10;
}
```

Merging BitmapData Images

You can use the merge() method to merge the data from BitmapData objects. The method requires the following parameters:

✦ sourceBitmap—The BitmapData object from which you want to copy pixels.

✦ sourceRectangle—A Rectangle object specifying the region of the source bitmap you want to copy.

✦ destinationPoint—A Point object specifying the point in the destination bitmap at which you want to start placing the copied pixels.

✦ redMultiplier—The amount by which to multiply the red value of the source bitmap. The range is from 0 to 256.

✦ greenMultiplier—The amount by which to multiply the green value of the source bitmap. The range is from 0 to 256.

✦ blueMultiplier—The amount by which to multiply the blue value of the source bitmap. The range is from 0 to 256.

✦ alphaMultiplier—The amount by which to multiply the alpha value of the source bitmap. The range is from 0 to 100.

It may not immediately be obvious how you can use the multiplier parameters to achieve the effect you want. The formulas that Flash uses are:

```
red = (redSource * redMultiplier) +
(redDestination * (256: redMultiplier)) / 256

green = (greenSource * greenMultiplier) +
(greenDestination * (256: greenMultiplier)) / 256

blue= (blueSource * blueMultiplier) +
(blueDestination * (256: blueMultiplier)) / 256

alpha= (alphaSource * alphaMultiplier) +
(alphaDestination * (100: alphaMultiplier)) / 100
```

The following code loads two images, copies them to BitmapData objects, and then merges them.

```
import flash.display.BitmapData;
import flash.geom.Matrix;
import flash.geom.Point;
import flash.geom.Rectangle;

this.createEmptyMovieClip("mClipA", this.getNextHighestDepth());
mClipA.createEmptyMovieClip("mImage", mClipA.getNextHighestDepth());

this.createEmptyMovieClip("mClipB", this.getNextHighestDepth());
mClipB.createEmptyMovieClip("mImage", mClipB.getNextHighestDepth());

// Declare a variable to use in order to determine how many of
// the images have downloaded.
var nDownloaded:Number = 0;

var oListener:Object = new Object();
oListener.onLoadInit = function(mClip:MovieClip):Void {

  // Increment nDownloaded. Then, check if two images have
  // downloaded. If so, then call the mergeImages() function,
  // and make the MovieClip objects invisible.
  nDownloaded++;
  if(nDownloaded == 2) {
```

```
    mergeImages();
    mClipA._visible = false;
    mClipB._visible = false;
  }
};

var mlImage:MovieClipLoader = new MovieClipLoader();
mlImage.addListener(oListener);
mlImage.loadClip("http://www.person13.com/asb/image1.jpg", mClipA.mImage);
mlImage.loadClip("http://www.person13.com/asb/image2.jpg", mClipB.mImage);

function mergeImages():Void {

  // Copy image1 to a BitmapData object.
  var bmpCopyA:BitmapData = new BitmapData(mClipA._width, mClipA._height,  ⮌
false, 0xFF000000);
  bmpCopyA.draw(mClipA, new Matrix());

  // Copy image2 to a BitmapData object.
  var bmpCopyB:BitmapData = new BitmapData(mClipB._width, mClipB._height,  ⮌
false, 0xFF000000);
  bmpCopyB.draw(mClipB, new Matrix());

  // Merge the two BitmapData objects into one.
  var bmpMerged:BitmapData = new BitmapData(mClipB._width, mClipB._height,  ⮌
 false, 0xFF000000);
  bmpMerged.merge(bmpCopyA, new Rectangle(0, 0, bmpCopyA.width,  ⮌
bmpCopyA.height), new Point(0, 0), 256, 256, 256, 100);
  bmpMerged.merge(bmpCopyB, new Rectangle(0, 0, bmpCopyB.width,  ⮌
bmpCopyB.height), new Point(0, 0), 0, 256, 0, 100);

  this.createEmptyMovieClip("mMergedClip", this.getNextHighestDepth());
  mMergedClip.attachBitmap(bmpMerged, mMergedClip.getNextHighestDepth());

}
```

Getting and Setting Pixels

You can get and set pixels using the getPixel(), setPixel(), getPixel32(), and setPixel32() methods. The getPixel() method returns a number in the form of 0xRRGGBB for a pixel specified by X- and Y-coordinates:

```
  trace(bmpImage.getPixel(100, 100).toString(16));
```

The setPixel() method sets the color of a pixel. The parameters are the X-coordinate, the Y-coordinate, and the color as a number in the form of 0xRRGGBB:

```
  bmpImage.setPixel(100, 100, 0xRR0000);
```

The getPixel32() and setPixel32() methods work like the getPixel() and setPixel() methods. However, they work with colors in the format of 0xAARRGGBB.

Applying Color Transformations

You can use the colorTransform() method to apply color transformations to regions of a BitmapData object. The colorTransform() method requires two parameters: a Rectangle object defining the region to which to apply the color transform and a ColorTransform object to use.

Cross-Reference   Refer to Chapter 16 for more details on working with ColorTransform objects.

The following code downloads an image to the player, copies the image to a BitmapData object, and then applies four ColorTransform objects to four quadrants of the image.

```
import flash.display.BitmapData;
import flash.geom.ColorTransform;
import flash.geom.Matrix;
import flash.geom.Point;
import flash.geom.Rectangle;

this.createEmptyMovieClip("mClip", this.getNextHighestDepth());
mClip.createEmptyMovieClip("mImage", mClip.getNextHighestDepth());

var oListener:Object = new Object();
oListener.onLoadInit = function(mClip:MovieClip):Void {
  applyColorTransform();
};

var mlImage:MovieClipLoader = new MovieClipLoader();
mlImage.addListener(oListener);
mlImage.loadClip("http://www.person13.com/asb/image2.jpg", mClip.mImage);

function applyColorTransform():Void {

  var bmpCopy:BitmapData = new BitmapData(mClip._width, mClip._height);
  bmpCopy.draw(mClip, new Matrix());
  bmpCopy.colorTransform(new Rectangle(0, 0, bmpCopy.width/2,          ⤸
bmpCopy.height/2), new ColorTransform(1, 0, 0, 1, 0, 0, 0, 0));
  bmpCopy.colorTransform(new Rectangle(bmpCopy.width/2, 0,             ⤸
bmpCopy.width/2, bmpCopy.height/2), new ColorTransform(0, 1, 0, 1, 0, 0, 0, 0));
  bmpCopy.colorTransform(new Rectangle(0, bmpCopy.height/2,            ⤸
bmpCopy.width/2, bmpCopy.height/2), new ColorTransform(0, 0, 1, 1, 0, 0, 0, 0));
  bmpCopy.colorTransform(new Rectangle(bmpCopy.width/2, bmpCopy.height/2,  ⤸
bmpCopy.width/2, bmpCopy.height/2), new ColorTransform(1, 1, 0, 1, 0, 0, 0, 0));

  this.createEmptyMovieClip("mCopyClip", this.getNextHighestDepth());
  mCopyClip.attachBitmap(bmpCopy, mCopyClip.getNextHighestDepth());

}
```

Applying Fills

You can apply fills to `BitmapData` objects using the `fillRect()` and `floodFill()` methods.

Applying Rectangular Fills

You can apply fills to rectangular regions using the `fillRect()` method. The method requires two parameters: a `Rectangle` object defining the region to which to apply the fill, and a color as a number in the form of 0xAARRGGBB. The following example makes a `BitmapData` object, and then applies four fills.

```
import flash.display.BitmapData;
import flash.geom.Matrix;
import flash.geom.Point;
import flash.geom.Rectangle;

var bmpRegions:BitmapData = new BitmapData(200, 200);
bmpRegions.fillRect(new Rectangle(0, 0, 100, 100), 0xFFFF0000);
bmpRegions.fillRect(new Rectangle(100, 0, 100, 100), 0xFF00FF00);
bmpRegions.fillRect(new Rectangle(0, 100, 100, 100), 0xFF0000FF);
bmpRegions.fillRect(new Rectangle(100, 100, 100, 100), 0xFFFFFF00);
this.createEmptyMovieClip("mClip", this.getNextHighestDepth());
mClip.attachBitmap(bmpRegions, mClip.getNextHighestDepth());
```

Applying Flood Fills

Flood fills are fills that are applied to a region based on the existing color of the region. A flood fill requires a destination point. It applies a color to the destination point as well as every adjoining point that has the same color as the prefilled color of the destination point. You are likely most familiar with flood fills by way of the paint bucket tool in most drawing/painting applications (such as Flash).

You can programmatically apply flood fills to `BitmapData` objects using the `floodFill()` method. The method requires the following parameters: the X-coordinate of the destination point, the Y-coordinate of the destination point, and the color in the form of 0xAARRGGBB. The following example uses the example from the preceding section as a starting point and then adds an `onPress()` event handler method that applies a flood fill to the `BitmapData` object at the mouse coordinates.

```
import flash.display.BitmapData;
import flash.geom.Matrix;
import flash.geom.Point;
import flash.geom.Rectangle;

var bmpRegions:BitmapData = new BitmapData(200, 200);
bmpRegions.fillRect(new Rectangle(0, 0, 100, 100), 0xFFFF0000);
bmpRegions.fillRect(new Rectangle(100, 0, 100, 100), 0xFF00FF00);
bmpRegions.fillRect(new Rectangle(0, 100, 100, 100), 0xFF0000FF);
bmpRegions.fillRect(new Rectangle(100, 100, 100, 100), 0xFFFFFF00);
this.createEmptyMovieClip("mClip", this.getNextHighestDepth());
```

```
mClip.attachBitmap(bmpRegions, mClip.getNextHighestDepth());

mClip.onPress = function():Void {

  // Use the _xmouse and _ymouse properties as the coordinates,
  // and composite a color using 0xFF000000 and a random number
  // from 0 to 0xFFFFFF.
  bmpRegions.floodFill(mClip._xmouse, mClip._ymouse,
0xFF000000 | Math.random() * 0xFFFFFF);
};
```

Applying Effects

The BitmapData class has methods that let you apply effects such as replacing colors, performing pixel dissolves, and remapping the color palette.

Replacing Colors with Threshold

The threshold() method lets you replace colors within a BitmapData object using various operations. The method accepts the following parameters.

✦ sourceBitmap—The BitmapData object from which you want to copy pixels.

✦ sourceRectangle—A Rectangle object specifying the region of the source bitmap you want to copy.

✦ destinationPoint—A Point object specifying the point in the destination bitmap at which you want to start placing the copied pixels.

✦ operation—One of the following as a string: <, >, <=, >=, !=, ==.

✦ threshold—A number in the form of 0xAARRGGBB that specifies the threshold color.

✦ color—The color to use in place of anything that tests true to the threshold operation. The value is in the form of 0xAARRGGBB. The default is 0x00000000.

✦ mask—A color in the form of 0xAARRGGBB to use as a mask in the operation. The default is 0xFFFFFFFF.

✦ copySource—A Boolean value indicating whether or not to copy the source bitmap data that doesn't test true. The default is false.

Using the threshold() method you can make transition effects, two-tone contrast versions of raster graphics, and more. The operation and threshold parameters work together to determine the operation to run. For example, if you use an operation parameter of < and a threshold parameter of 0xFF00FF00, Flash will use the color value for each of the pixels in the destination object that correspond to pixels in the source object with colors "less than" green. The following example code illustrates how you can use threshold() to apply an interesting transition effect.

```
import flash.display.BitmapData;
import flash.geom.Matrix;
import flash.geom.Point;
import flash.geom.Rectangle;

this.createEmptyMovieClip("mClip", this.getNextHighestDepth());
mClip.createEmptyMovieClip("mImage", mClip.getNextHighestDepth());
```

```
var nInterval:Number;
var nThreshold:Number = 0xCCFF;
var bmpCopy:BitmapData;
var bmpThreshold:BitmapData;
var bDirection:Boolean = false;
var nColor:Number;

selectRandomColor();

var oListener:Object = new Object();
oListener.onLoadInit = function(mClip:MovieClip):Void {
  copyImage();
  nInterval = setInterval(applyThreshold, 100);
  mClip._visible = false;
};

var mlImage:MovieClipLoader = new MovieClipLoader();
mlImage.addListener(oListener);
mlImage.loadClip("http://www.person13.com/asb/image2.jpg", mClip.mImage);

function selectRandomColor():Void {
  nColor = 0xFF000000 | (Math.random() * 0xFFFFFF);
}

function copyImage():Void {
  bmpCopy = new BitmapData(mClip._width, mClip._height);
  bmpCopy.draw(mClip, new Matrix());

  bmpThreshold = bmpCopy.clone();

  this.createEmptyMovieClip("mCopy", this.getNextHighestDepth());
  mCopy.attachBitmap(bmpThreshold, mCopy.getNextHighestDepth());

}

function applyThreshold():Void {
  var nPixels:Number = bmpThreshold.threshold(bmpCopy,
new Rectangle(0, 0, bmpCopy.width, bmpCopy.height), new Point(0, 0), "<=",
0xFF000000 | nThreshold, nColor, 0xFFFFFFFF, true);
  if(bDirection) {
    nThreshold -= (nThreshold)/5;
    if(nThreshold <= 0x00CCCC) {
      bDirection = false;
      selectRandomColor();
    }
  }
  else {
    nThreshold += (0xFFFFFF - nThreshold)/5;
    if(nThreshold >= 0xFFCCCC) {
      bDirection = true;
    }
  }
}
```

Using Pixel Dissolves

The `pixelDissolve()` method does just what it says: dissolves pixels. The method accepts the following parameters:

✦ `sourceBitmap` — The *BitmapData* object from which you want to copy pixels.

✦ `sourceRectangle` — A `Rectangle` object specifying the region of the source bitmap you want to copy.

✦ `destinationPoint` — A `Point` object specifying the point in the destination bitmap at which you want to start placing the copied pixels.

✦ `randomSeed` — A random number used by the Flash Player to run the pixel dissolve. The value ought to start at 0. Subsequently, the value ought to be the value returned by the previous call to the `pixelDissolve()` method.

✦ `numberOfPixels` — The number of pixels to dissolve. The default is 1/30 of the total pixels.

✦ `fillColor` — If you specify the destination as the source bitmap, it dissolves to a solid color. You can specify the color using the `fillColor` parameter with a number in the form of 0xAARRGGBB. The default is 0x00000000.

The `pixelDissolve()` method dissolves the number of pixels specified by the `numberOfPixels` parameter from the source `BitmapData` object to the destination `BitmapData` object. It uses an algorithm to randomly select which pixels to dissolve. Therefore, it is possible that it could dissolve one or more pixels that have already been dissolved. However, the method returns a number that you can use in the next call to the method as the `randomSeed` parameter. If you do so, Flash will not dissolve a pixel that was already dissolved. That way you can ensure that every pixel will be dissolved within a specific number of calls to the method.

The following example code illustrates how to use `pixelDissolve()`. It loads two images, copies them to `BitmapData` objects, and then uses `setInterval()` and `pixelDissolve()` to continually dissolve between the two images.

```
import flash.display.BitmapData;
import flash.geom.Matrix;
import flash.geom.Point;
import flash.geom.Rectangle;

this.createEmptyMovieClip("mClipA", this.getNextHighestDepth());
mClipA.createEmptyMovieClip("mImage", mClipA.getNextHighestDepth());

this.createEmptyMovieClip("mClipB", this.getNextHighestDepth());
mClipB.createEmptyMovieClip("mImage", mClipB.getNextHighestDepth());

var nInterval:Number;
var bmpCopyA:BitmapData;
var bmpCopyB:BitmapData;
var bmpRenderer:BitmapData;
var bDirection:Boolean = false;
var nCount:Number = 0;
var nDownloaded:Number = 0;
var nRandom = 0;
```

```
var oListener:Object = new Object();
oListener.onLoadInit = function(mClip:MovieClip):Void {
  nDownloaded++;
  if(nDownloaded == 2) {
    copyImages();
    nInterval = setInterval(applyPixelDissolve, 100);
    mClipA._visible = false;
    mClipB._visible = false;
  }
};

var mlImage:MovieClipLoader = new MovieClipLoader();
mlImage.addListener(oListener);
mlImage.loadClip("http://www.person13.com/asb/image1.jpg", mClipA.mImage);
mlImage.loadClip("http://www.person13.com/asb/image2.jpg", mClipB.mImage);

function selectRandomColor():Void {
  nColor = 0xFF000000 | (Math.random() * 0xFFFFFF);
}

function copyImages():Void {
  bmpCopyA = new BitmapData(mClipA._width, mClipA._height);
  bmpCopyA.draw(mClipA, new Matrix());

  bmpCopyB = new BitmapData(mClipB._width, mClipB._height);
  bmpCopyB.draw(mClipB, new Matrix());

  bmpRenderer = bmpCopyA.clone();

  this.createEmptyMovieClip("mRenderer", this.getNextHighestDepth());
  mRenderer.attachBitmap(bmpRenderer, mRenderer.getNextHighestDepth());

}

function applyPixelDissolve():Void {
  var bmpCopy:BitmapData = (bDirection) ? bmpCopyB : bmpCopyA;
  var nPixels:Number = bmpCopy.width * bmpCopy.height / 10;
  nRandom = bmpRenderer.pixelDissolve(bmpCopy, new Rectangle(0, 0,
bmpCopy.width, bmpCopy.height), new Point(0, 0), nRandom, nPixels);
  nCount++;
  if(nCount > 10) {
    bDirection = !bDirection;
    nCount = 0;
  }
}
```

Remapping the Color Palette

You can remap the color palette of a `BitmapData` object using the `paletteMap()` method. For example, you can tell it to convert every red pixel to green and every blue pixel to yellow. The `paletteMap()` method accepts the following parameters:

✦ sourceBitmap—The BitmapData object from which you want to copy pixels.

✦ sourceRectangle—A Rectangle object specifying the region of the source bitmap you want to copy.

✦ destinationPoint—A Point object specifying the point in the destination bitmap at which you want to start placing the copied pixels.

✦ redArray—An array of 256 numbers mapping reds.

✦ greenArray—An array of 256 numbers mapping greens.

✦ blueArray—An array of 256 numbers mapping blues.

✦ alphaArray—An array of 256 numbers mapping alphas.

Each of the array parameters is optional. If they are omitted or null then the corresponding color channel map is not changed.

```
import flash.display.BitmapData;
import flash.geom.ColorTransform;
import flash.geom.Matrix;
import flash.geom.Point;
import flash.geom.Rectangle;

this.createEmptyMovieClip("mClip", this.getNextHighestDepth());
mClip.createEmptyMovieClip("mImage", mClip.getNextHighestDepth());

var oListener:Object = new Object();
oListener.onLoadInit = function(mClip:MovieClip):Void {
  applyRemap();
  mClip._visible = false;
};

var mlImage:MovieClipLoader = new MovieClipLoader();
mlImage.addListener(oListener);
mlImage.loadClip("http://www.person13.com/asb/image2.jpg", mClip.mImage);

function applyRemap():Void {
  var bmpCopy:BitmapData = new BitmapData(mClip._width, mClip._height);
  bmpCopy.draw(mClip, new Matrix());

  var aRed:Array = new Array();
  for(var i:Number = 0; i < 256; i++) {
    aRed[i] = 0xFF00FFFF | (255 - i) << 16;
  }

  var aGreen:Array = new Array();
  for(var i:Number = 0; i < 256; i++) {
    aGreen[i] = 0xFFFF00FF | (255 - i) << 8;
  }

  var aBlue:Array = new Array();
  for(var i:Number = 0; i < 256; i++) {
```

```
   aBlue[i] = 0xFFFFFF00 | (255 - i);
  }

  bmpCopy.paletteMap(bmpCopy, new Rectangle(0, 0, bmpCopy.width,
bmpCopy.height), new Point(0, 0), aRed, aGreen, aBlue);

  this.createEmptyMovieClip("mRemapped", this.getNextHighestDepth());
  mRemapped.attachBitmap(bmpCopy, mRemapped.getNextHighestDepth());
}
```

Making Noise

Noise typically refers to unintentional and random data interruptions that can cause specks or grain in images. However, there are many possible reasons that you might want to *intentionally* introduce noise. For example, you can use noise to apply texture and to apply randomness. The `noise()` and `perlinNoise()` methods let you do just that.

Adding Noise

The `noise()` function lets you apply standard noise to a `BitmapData` object. The noise is applied to the entire `BitmapData` object and is constructed by assigning a random value (within certain parameters) to each pixel. The `noise()` method accepts the following parameters:

✦ `randomSeed`—A number to use in order to generate the randomization factor.

✦ `low`—The lowest value to use for each channel (red, green, blue, and alpha). The default is 0.

✦ `high`—The highest value to use for each channel. The default is 255.

✦ `channelOptions`—Which channels to utilize. Use 1 for red, 2 for green, 4 for blue, and 8 for alpha. Combine channels by adding the numbers. For example, 5 is red and blue (1+4).

✦ `grayscale`—A Boolean value indicating whether or not to convert the noise colors to grayscale. The default is `false`.

The following code makes a `BitmapData` object. It then uses `setInterval()` and `noise()` to continually reapply random noise. The effect appears like static.

```
import flash.display.BitmapData;
import flash.geom.Matrix;
import flash.geom.Point;
import flash.geom.Rectangle;

this.createEmptyMovieClip("mClip", this.getNextHighestDepth());

var bmpNoise:BitmapData = new BitmapData(200, 200);

mClip.attachBitmap(bmpNoise, mClip.getNextHighestDepth());
```

```
setInterval(applyNoise, 10);

function applyNoise():Void {
  bmpNoise.noise(Math.random() * 10000);
}
```

The following code use the alpha channel as well as the color channels to make static that appears over an image.

```
import flash.display.BitmapData;
import flash.geom.Matrix;
import flash.geom.Point;
import flash.geom.Rectangle;

this.createEmptyMovieClip("mImage", this.getNextHighestDepth());
mImage.createEmptyMovieClip("mImageHolder", mImage.getNextHighestDepth());

this.createEmptyMovieClip("mClipA", this.getNextHighestDepth());
this.createEmptyMovieClip("mClipB", this.getNextHighestDepth());
this.createEmptyMovieClip("mClipC", this.getNextHighestDepth());
this.createEmptyMovieClip("mClipD", this.getNextHighestDepth());

var mlImage:MovieClipLoader = new MovieClipLoader();
mlImage.addListener(oListener);
mlImage.loadClip("http://www.person13.com/asb/image2.jpg", mImage.mImageHolder);

var bmpNoiseA:BitmapData = new BitmapData(200, 200);
var bmpNoiseB:BitmapData = new BitmapData(200, 200);
var bmpNoiseC:BitmapData = new BitmapData(200, 200);
var bmpNoiseD:BitmapData = new BitmapData(200, 200);

mClipA.attachBitmap(bmpNoiseA, mClipA.getNextHighestDepth());
mClipB.attachBitmap(bmpNoiseB, mClipB.getNextHighestDepth());
mClipC.attachBitmap(bmpNoiseC, mClipC.getNextHighestDepth());
mClipD.attachBitmap(bmpNoiseD, mClipD.getNextHighestDepth());

mClipB._x = 200;

mClipC._y = 200;

mClipD._x = 200;
mClipD._y = 200;

setInterval(applyNoise, 10);

function applyNoise():Void {
  bmpNoiseA.noise(Math.random() * 10000, 10, 100, 8);
  bmpNoiseB.noise(Math.random() * 10000, 10, 100, 9);
  bmpNoiseC.noise(Math.random() * 10000, 10, 100, 10);
  bmpNoiseD.noise(Math.random() * 10000, 10, 100, 12);
}
```

Adding Perlin Noise

Perlin noise is a specific type of noise named after Ken Perlin who invented the algorithm in order to make more realistic textures during the movie *TRON*. Perlin noise is not entirely random. It has a degree of randomness; however, that randomness is controllable so that you can achieve effects that have an expected texture. While standard noise is good for making graininess or static, Perlin noise is good for making textures of many types. For example, using Perlin noise you can make water, clouds, fire, and other sorts of textures that would be difficult to otherwise mimic.

The `perlinNoise()` method accepts the following parameters:

✦ `baseX` — The number of pixels in the X direction for the noise. Use the width of the `BitmapData` object as a standard of measurement. As the `baseX` decreases relative to the width of the `BitmapData` object, the effect will be a vertical zoom out.

✦ `baseY` — The number of pixels in the Y direction for the noise. Use the height of the `BitmapData` object as a standard of measurement. As the `baseY` decreases relative to the height of the `BitmapData` object, the effect will be a horizontal zoom out.

✦ `octaves` — Perlin noise layers noise. Each layer is called an octave. More octaves means greater detail. More octaves can also require more time to render. Use as few octaves as possible in order to achieve the effect you want. You can specify the number of octaves with the octaves parameter.

✦ `randomSeed` — A number the method uses to generate the randomness of the noise.

✦ `stitch` — A Boolean value indicating whether to smooth the edges of the bitmap in the event it is used as a tiling bitmap fill with the Drawing API. The default value is `false`, which means if it tiles the edges are likely to be apparent. If `stitch` is set to `true` and the image tiles, the edges aren't likely to be apparent.

✦ `fractalNoise` — A Boolean specifying whether to make fractal noise (`true`) or turbulence (`false`). The default is `false`. Fractal noise is more continuous, whereas turbulence has more gaps. Each is appropriate for various purposes.

✦ `channelOptions` — The `channelOptions` parameter works much like the `channelOptions` parameter for the `noise()` method. See the previous section for more details.

✦ `grayscale` — A Boolean indicating whether or not to make the noise grayscale. The default is `false`.

✦ `offsets` — An array of `Point` objects indicating the amount by which to offset each octave.

The `perlinNoise()` method may seem slightly difficult at first, but a few examples are likely to make it much more accessible to you. We'll use some code examples to highlight the effects of the parameters.

The following code applies Perlin noise to a 400 x 400 `BitmapData` object. Using `onMouseMove()`, the noise is updated each time the mouse moves, and the `baseX` and `baseY` values are set to the mouse coordinates, so you can see the effect of the `baseX` and `baseY` parameters.

```
import flash.display.BitmapData;

this.createEmptyMovieClip("mClip", this.getNextHighestDepth());

var bmpNoise:BitmapData = new BitmapData(400, 400, true, 0);

mClip.attachBitmap(bmpNoise, mClip.getNextHighestDepth());

function onMouseMove():Void {
  bmpNoise.perlinNoise(_xmouse, _ymouse, 1, 1, false, false);
}
```

The following code is similar to the preceding. However, rather than continually updating the baseX and baseY parameters, the code updates the octaves parameter. The number of octaves ranges from 0 when the mouse is at the far left to 10 when the mouse is on the right side.

```
import flash.display.BitmapData;

this.createEmptyMovieClip("mClip", this.getNextHighestDepth());

var bmpNoise:BitmapData = new BitmapData(400, 400, true, 0);

mClip.attachBitmap(bmpNoise, mClip.getNextHighestDepth());

function onMouseMove():Void {
  bmpNoise.perlinNoise(100, 100, _xmouse * 10 / 400, 1, false, false);
}
```

The randomSeed parameter is responsible for the randomness of the noise. The following code updates the parameter value once per second using setInterval() and Math.random().

```
import flash.display.BitmapData;

this.createEmptyMovieClip("mClip", this.getNextHighestDepth());

var bmpNoise:BitmapData = new BitmapData(400, 400, true, 0);

mClip.attachBitmap(bmpNoise, mClip.getNextHighestDepth());

setInterval(applyNoise, 1000);

function applyNoise():Void {
  bmpNoise.perlinNoise(100, 100, 1, Math.random() * 1000, false, false);
}
```

Note   The player will make different random values using the same randomSeed value if the application is reloaded. However, during the playback of an SWF the same randomSeed value will cause the same random value. The effect is that the Perlin noise will look the same if you use the same parameters during a single playback.

The following code makes a `BitmapData` object with Perlin noise, and then uses that object as a bitmap fill. Since the `stitch` parameter is `false`, the edges are visible as it tiles.

```
import flash.display.BitmapData;

this.createEmptyMovieClip("mClip", this.getNextHighestDepth());

var bmpNoise:BitmapData = new BitmapData(400, 400, true, 0);

setInterval(applyNoise, 1000);

mClip.lineStyle(0, 0, 0);
mClip.beginBitmapFill(bmpNoise);
mClip.lineTo(550, 0);
mClip.lineTo(550, 400);
mClip.lineTo(0, 400);
mClip.lineTo(0, 0);
mClip.endFill();

function applyNoise():Void {
  bmpNoise.perlinNoise(100, 100, 1, Math.random() * 10000, false, false);
}
```

However, notice what happens when you use the same code, but set the `stitch` parameter to `true`. Then the tiling looks seamless.

You can also use the preceding example code to see the effects of the `fractalNoise` parameter. Use a value of `true` instead of `false`, and you'll notice that the effect is much smoother in appearance.

The only other parameter that is likely to need much explanation is the `offsets` parameter. The `offsets` parameter can make for some neat effects such as continuous scrolling of the noise. The following code uses the `offsets` parameter to continuously scroll the texture. Note that even though the noise is continually updated, the noise does not redistribute radically. That is because the same value is used each time for the `randomSeed` parameter.

```
import flash.display.BitmapData;
import flash.geom.Point;

this.createEmptyMovieClip("mClip", this.getNextHighestDepth());

var bmpNoise:BitmapData = new BitmapData(400, 400, true, 0);

mClip.attachBitmap(bmpNoise, mClip.getNextHighestDepth());

setInterval(applyNoise, 10);

var nOffset:Number = 0;

function applyNoise():Void {
  bmpNoise.perlinNoise(100, 100, 1, 1, false, false,
  1, false, [new Point(nOffset++, 0)]);
  updateAfterEvent();
}
```

Applying Filters

You can apply filters to `BitmapData` objects as well as `MovieClip` objects. You learned about applying filters to `MovieClip` objects in Chapter 17. The same filter types work with `BitmapData` objects as well. To apply a filter to a `BitmapData` object, use the `applyFilter()` method. The `applyFilter()` method accepts the following parameters:

✦ `sourceBitmap`—The `BitmapData` object from which you want to copy pixels.

✦ `sourceRectangle`—A `Rectangle` object specifying the region of the source bitmap you want to copy.

✦ `destinationPoint`—A `Point` object specifying the point in the destination bitmap at which you want to start placing the copied pixels.

✦ `filter`—The `filter` object you want to apply.

The following code uses a `DisplacementMapFilter` object to apply a water ripple effect to an image drawn within a `BitmapData` object.

```
import flash.display.BitmapData;
import flash.display.BitmapData.Channel;
import flash.filters.DisplacementMapFilter;
import flash.geom.Matrix;
import flash.geom.Point;
import flash.geom.Rectangle;

this.createEmptyMovieClip("mClip", this.getNextHighestDepth());
mClip.createEmptyMovieClip("mImage", mClip.getNextHighestDepth());

this.createEmptyMovieClip("mRenderedClip", this.getNextHighestDepth());

var bmpNoise:BitmapData = new BitmapData(550, 400, true, 0);
var bmpImage:BitmapData;
var bmpRendered:BitmapData;

var oListener:Object = new Object();
oListener.onLoadInit = function(mClip:MovieClip):Void {
  drawImage();
  setInterval(applyFilter, 10);
  mClip._visible = false;
};

var mlImage:MovieClipLoader = new MovieClipLoader();
mlImage.addListener(oListener);
mlImage.loadClip("http://www.person13.com/asb/image2.jpg", mClip.mImage);

function drawImage():Void {
  bmpImage = new BitmapData(mClip._width, mClip._height, true, 0);
  bmpImage.draw(mClip, new Matrix());
  bmpRendered = bmpImage.clone();
  mRenderedClip.attachBitmap(bmpRendered, mClip.getNextHighestDepth());
```

```
}

function applyFilter():Void {
  bmpNoise.perlinNoise(50, 50, 10, Math.random() * 10000, false, false,    ⊃
Channel.RED | Channel.ALPHA);

  var dmfFilter:DisplacementMapFilter = new DisplacementMapFilter(bmpNoise,   ⊃
new Point(0, 0), Channel.RED, Channel.RED, 5, 5);
  bmpRendered.applyFilter(bmpImage, new Rectangle(0, 0, bmpImage.width,    ⊃
bmpImage.height), new Point(0, 0), dmfFilter);
  mRenderedClip.filters = [dmfFilter];
}
```

 Web Resource We'd like to know what you thought about this chapter. Visit `www.rightactionscript` `.com/asb/comments` to fill out an online form with your comments.

Summary

✦ You can construct new `BitmapData` objects using the `BitmapData` constructor method. Optionally, you can use the static `BitmapData.loadBitmap()` method to construct a new `BitmapData` object from a bitmap symbol exported for ActionScript.

✦ Use the `MovieClip` method `attachBitmap()`, to render a `BitmapData` object.

✦ The `draw()` method lets you copy the pixels from a `MovieClip` object to a `BitmapData` object.

✦ You can use many different methods to copy from a `BitmapData` object. Some methods copy pixel regions, while other methods copy channels or merge data.

✦ Apply color transforms using `colorTransform()`.

✦ You can use the `fillRect()` and `floodFill()` methods to apply fills to `BitmapData` objects.

✦ The `threshold()`, `pixelDissolve()`, and `paletteMap()` methods let you apply special effects.

✦ Apply noise using either the `noise()` or the `perlinNoise()` methods.

✦ Use filters with the `applyFilter()` method.

✦   ✦   ✦

Working with Text Fields and Selection

Text is an indispensable part of most Flash applications. In this chapter, you get a chance to look at the many facets of working with text within Flash. You'll read about how to create text that can be controlled with ActionScript and how to actually use the ActionScript to effect changes. You can render HTML, scroll text, embed fonts, and much more.

Closely related to text is the Selection class. You can use the Selection class to get and set *focus*. The active object on the stage, the one receiving the user's mouse and keystroke interaction, has focus. And you can also use the Selection class to get and set the selection within a TextField. That means that you can set an insert point for input text and you can retrieve the text that the user highlights. Read on in this chapter to learn about these things and more.

Understanding Types of Text

In Flash you can work with three types of text: static, dynamic, and input. Prior to learning ActionScript, you have likely used static text almost exclusively. However, although static text has its place, it is not something that you will work with when managing text in ActionScript. Static text is not scriptable or controllable in the same ways as dynamic or input text. So, let's take a closer look at the two types of text that you will be working with via ActionScript.

Dynamic Text

Dynamic text is the basic type of text that you can manage with ActionScript. With dynamic text you can display, scroll, format, resize, and even create text completely with code. That is something that you'll be sure to want to do as you start developing more Flash applications that contain greater amounts of dynamic content. For example, if you want to display updated news or features, you'll want to use dynamic text. Any text that you want to update while the application is running, whether that update occurs based on loaded data, user interaction, or any other reason, should be dynamic text.

Input Text

Input text enables a user to provide textual interaction. Input text actually includes all the same functionality as dynamic text, but it also provides the additional functionality of allowing the user to enter text values. Input text fields allow users the opportunity to do everything from entering their username and password to inputting shipping information for an e-commerce application.

Creating TextField Objects

When you create a dynamic or input text field you are actually creating a TextField object. This is important because dynamic and input text fields are instances of the TextField class, which means that you can utilize all the built-in properties and methods of the TextField class to control the instances with ActionScript code.

Obviously, before you can do anything with a TextField instance you first need to create it. In the following sections you'll get a chance to see the various ways that you can create TextField objects. Essentially, you can categorize these ways as either authoring-time creation or runtime creation. Whether you create a TextField object at authoring time or at runtime, the object is still a TextField object that can be managed in the same way as any other TextField object. So, the main consideration should be simply which technique is most appropriate given the scenario. Let's take a closer look.

Making Text at Authoring Time

Creating text at authoring time means that you are creating the text using the Text tool and drawing the TextField object on the stage. Creating text at authoring time has some advantages (over creating text at runtime) in certain situations:

✦ For a visually oriented person, it might be much more convenient to layout text created during authoring time than text created at runtime.

✦ When you create text at authoring time you can use the Property inspector to set many properties of the TextField object, and thus you don't have to necessarily write all the ActionScript code to initialize the object with those values.

If you've created static text before, you already know the basics of how to create a dynamic or input TextField object during authoring time because to create dynamic or input text, just as with static text, you should choose the Text tool and draw the shape of the new TextField object. The primary difference between creating static text or dynamic or input text is that you should select the correct type from the Text type menu before drawing the text on the stage. Therefore, after selecting the Text tool, but before drawing the TextField object, you should select the appropriate type — Dynamic Text for a dynamic TextField object or Input Text for an input text field — from the Text type menu in the Property inspector, as shown in Figure 19-1.

Note   Although you can modify the text type for a TextField object after you've drawn it, we recommend setting the type before drawing it only as a general workflow tip. It works much in the same way as drawing a shape on the stage: You can select the fill color beforehand, or you can select the shape after it's been drawn and change the fill color.

Figure 19-1: Select Dynamic Text or Input Text from the Text type menu.

Although you can change the type of a `TextField` object after you've drawn it, in many cases it is important that you make sure that either Dynamic Text or Input Text is selected *before* you draw the object. Often when you create dynamic and/or input text, you don't want to add any value to it during authoring time. Instead, you'll want to add the value at runtime (in the case of dynamic text) or allow the user to enter a value (in the case of input text). However, if you don't enter a value for static text, Flash will remove it from the stage. Dynamic and input text, on the other hand, will allow you to draw the object and not provide a value.

Once you've drawn the `TextField` object on the stage, the next step is to give the object an instance name. This is a crucial step because the instance name is the way in which you can manage the object with ActionScript. You can add the instance name by way of the Property inspector. With the `TextField` object selected on the stage, open the Property inspector and enter the value in the Instance name field just as you would do with a `Button` or `MovieClip` object. The instance name should follow the same naming rules as any other object. If you need a refresher for those naming rules, you can refer back to Chapter 3; the naming rules are the same for variables and objects.

If you've been using Flash for a while, it is possible that you have used the Flash 5 technique of assigning a variable name to text. Although Flash 8 still allows you to do so for the purposes of authoring backward-compatible applications, under no circumstances should you give text a variable name instead of an instance name if you are authoring Flash 6+ content. If you try to work with text with a variable name instead of an instance name, you will not be able to access the properties and methods that it inherits from the `TextField` class. Figure 19-2 shows the Property inspector for an example `TextField` object. Notice that on the left is the `<Instance Name>` field. That is the correct place to assign an instance name to the object. On the right, you'll see a field labeled `Var:` and in the box to the right of it you can assign a variable name to the text but only when authoring content for older player versions. Otherwise, you should not assign a value to the field labeled `Var`.

Figure 19-2: The Property inspector for a TextField object.

When you create a `TextField` object during authoring time, you can set the many of the properties with the Property inspector as well. Many of the options should be fairly self-evident and familiar to you. For example, you will likely have no difficulties understanding how to select the font face, size, color, or alignment. Some of the other options may be somewhat unfamiliar to you, and therefore this section examines them in more detail. Namely, we'll look at the line type, selectable, HTML-enabled, border, and maximum character settings. In this section, you'll learn how to modify those settings in the Property inspector. The corresponding ActionScript properties are discussed later in the chapter.

The Line type menu allows you to select from the following options:

✦ Single line—This default setting allows only one line of text to be typed into the input text. However, in the unlikely event that you need to assign text to this field using ActionScript expressions, you can use the newline operator (or \n backslash, discussed later) to force a carriage return in the field.

✦ Multiline—This setting allows several lines of text to be typed into the field and automatically wraps each line of text.

✦ Multiline no wrap—This setting allows several lines of text to be entered into the field by the user but only pressing the Enter or Return key starts a new line of text. Text does not automatically wrap if the user types beyond the length of the text field.

✦ Password—You can hide the user's input, keeping it from being displayed by using this option. Each typed character is seen as an asterisk (*), just like password fields in most other common user interfaces. However, if you access the field's value in ActionScript expressions, the actual typed characters are available. The password option is only available if the text type is input.

Immediately to the right of the Line type menu are other options that control the formatting of the editable text field. The first option, Selectable, if enabled, allows users to highlight text within a TextField object in order to copy and paste it into another field (or external document). To the right of the Selectable option is the Enable HTML option, which allows you to use HTML formatting tags within your editable TextField object when you assign the value via ActionScript. Just to the right of the HTML option is the Show border option. When enabled, this option automatically formats an input text field with a white background and black hairline border. If you do not enable the Show border option, the Flash Player displays the TextField object with a dashed outline during authoring time. This outline is not visible when you publish your movie and view it in the Flash Player.

Tip　Make sure that the text color is one that will stand out. A common mistake is to have white text on a white background. When that occurs, obviously the text will not be visible, even though it is in place. Should you notice that your text does not seem to appear, make sure that the color is set correctly.

On the right of the Property inspector is a field labeled Maximum Characters. This option allows you specify a limit to the number of characters that can be typed into the input text field. By default, it is set to zero (0), which means that an unlimited number of characters can be typed into the field.

Making Runtime Text

Runtime text refers to a TextField object that you create using ActionScript code instead of using the Text tool during authoring time. Although authoring-time text has its benefits, it does not allow you the same programmatic control that runtime text can provide. Runtime text provides such benefits as the following:

✦ Runtime text can be created based on content that is loaded from external sources such as XML files and databases.

✦ Runtime text can be created based on user interaction.

✦ When you have sequences of text you want to create, runtime text can provide a more efficient way of adding it rather than trying to add it at authoring time.

There is just one technique for creating runtime text — regardless of whether you want it to be used for input or as dynamic text. The createTextField() method can be called from any MovieClip object in order to create a new TextField object nested within it. The createTextField() method requires six parameters: instance name, depth, x, y, width, and height. So, for example, to create a new TextField object named tLabel within the current MovieClip object you could use the following code:

```
this.createTextField("tLabel", this.getNextHighestDepth(), 0, 0, 100, 20);
```

The preceding code creates the new TextField object with the next highest depth, places it at 0,0, and sizes it to 100 x 20 pixels.

New Feature

In Flash 8, the createTextField() method returns a reference to the newly created TextFIeld instance — something that you might expect given how methods such as attachMovie() and duplicateMovieClip() work. However, it is a new feature, and previous versions of the player did not return a reference to the new TextField instance.

By default, when you create a new runtime TextField object its properties are:

antiAliasType = "advanced"	multiline = false
autoSize = "none"	password = false
background = false	restrict = null
backgroundColor = 0xFFFFFF	selectable = true
border = false	sharpness = 0
borderColor = 0x000000	textColor = 0x000000
condenseWhite = false	thickness = 0
embedFonts = false	type = "dynamic"
gridFitType = "pixel"	variable = null
html = false	wordWrap = false
maxChars = null	

You'll take a look at these properties in more detail throughout this chapter.

Working with TextField Object Basics

Creating a TextField object is only the first step. After you've done that you'll surely want to work with the object by assigning new values to properties and calling methods. The following sections detail many of the types of things you can do programmatically with a TextField object.

Understanding Basic TextField Properties and Methods

The TextField class inherits some common display object properties and methods. As such, they aren't discussed in detail in this chapter. If you have questions about any of the properties and methods, refer back to Chapter 13 for a more in-depth description.

The shared properties and methods are as follows: `_accProps`, `_alpha`, `_focusrect`, `_height`, `_name`, `_parent`, `_rotation`, `_target`, `_url`, `_visible`, `_x`, `_xmouse`, `_xscale`, `_y`, `_ymouse`, `_yscale`, `tabEnabled`, `tabIndex`, and `getDepth()`.

Many of these properties can be used to change the way in which the instance appears visibly. You can use many of those properties in the same way that you would use them for a `MovieClip` or `Button` instance. For example, if you wanted to move a `TextField` object named `tLabel` to 100,100, the ActionScript would look like the following:

```
tLabel._x = 100;
tLabel._y = 100;
```

There are a few of the properties, however, that will not work in the same way with the default settings for a `TextField` object. The properties `_alpha` and `_rotation` cannot be utilized on a `TextField` object unless the font has been embedded. If you attempt to set one of those properties for a `TextField` object that does not have an embedded font, the instance will simply no longer be visible. See the section "Embedding Fonts" later in this chapter for more information on how to address such a situation.

Adding Text

Once you've created a `TextField` object, either at authoring time or at runtime, one of the things you're most likely to want to do is to give it a new text value so that it is displayed in the application. To do, this you need to assign a new string value to its `text` property. For example, if you have created a `TextField` object named `tLabel`, you can add text to be displayed in the following manner:

```
tLabel.text = "This is a label.";
```

You can then later replace the text shown in a `TextField` object by assigning a new value to the `text` property. For example:

```
tLabel.text = "This is another label.";
```

Managing Multiline Text

`TextField` objects can display single-line or multiline content. When you are working with dynamic text then you can display single-line or multiline content regardless of the setting of the object's `multiline` property. However, when using input text, it makes a difference. By default a `TextField` object is single-line, and if you want to allow the user to enter multiple lines of text, you need to set the object's `multiline` property to `true` (it's `false` by default).

```
tLabel.multiline = true;
```

Word wrapping is another consideration. When you are working with multiline text, you may want to have the text wrap to the next line when it reaches the extent of the bounding box width. To achieve that with ActionScript, you need only set the `wordWrap` property to `true`.

```
tLabel.wordWrap = true;
```

Otherwise, as long as `wordWrap` is `false` the text will continue to extend past the width of the bounding box until a line break is encountered.

Using Unicode with TextField Objects

You can specify UTF-8, UTF-16LE, or UTF-16BE encodings with text datasources that are loaded into the Flash movie at authoring time or runtime. You can also use \u escape sequences in the values of TextField object properties, such as the text and restrict properties. If you want to see a specific character's escape sequence, open the Character Map application in Microsoft Windows (for Windows XP, you can choose Start ➪ Programs ➪ Accessories ➪ System Tools ➪ Character Map).

In ActionScript, you can specify the character for a copyright symbol (U+00A9) in the text property of a text field, as shown in the following code.

```
tArticle.text = "\u00A9";
```

If you don't want to use escape sequences, you can specify UTF-8 text in a separate AS file that is referenced in an ActionScript #include directive. The following text can be found in the title_multilanguage.as file located on the book's web site. This AS file was saved from Notepad in Windows XP. Notepad, like many text editors (including TextEdit on Mac OS 9), can save UTF-8-encoded text.

```
//!-- UTF8

title_english = "Welcome to our site.";
title_japanese = "私達の場所への歓迎。";
title_chinese = "欢迎到我们的站点。";
title_arabic = "مرحبا؟إلى؟موقعنا";
```

You need to specify the //!--UTF8 description on the first line of an included AS file for Flash MX to properly interpret the encoded characters. In the Flash document, the following actions will attach the title_multilanguage.as file and set the text field named output to the title_english value.

```
#include "title_multilanguage.as"
this.createTextField("tOutput", this.getNextHighestDepth(), 25, 25, ta
150, 18);
tUutput.text = title_english;
```

You can also use UTF-8, UTF-16LE, and UTF-16BE encoding with dynamic datasources that are loaded into a Flash movie at runtime by using the LoadVars or the XML class.

You may also find the following language translation sites helpful in your experimentation with Unicode text:

✦ babelfish.altavista.com

✦ tarjim.ajeeb.com/ajeeb/default.asp?lang=1

For more information, Macromedia has prepared very detailed tutorials on Unicode for Flash MX at the following URL:

www.macromedia.com/support/flash/languages/unicode_in_flmx/

To display multiple languages on your operating system, make sure that you have installed the required language packs. For example, Japanese characters will not be displayed within a Flash movie unless you have the Japanese language pack installed on your system.

Resizing a TextField Object

Because the text in a TextField object is subject to change dynamically, you may not know the dimensions of the text during authoring time. Instead, you may want to change the dimensions based on the content.

When we discuss resizing a TextField object, we are distinguishing between resizing and scaling. If you set the _xscale and/or _yscale property for a TextField object, the text that it displays will also scale. If you want to resize a TextField object, that means you want to change the dimensions of the bounding box while maintaining the font size of the text.

The simplest type of resizing involves telling Flash to automatically resize the TextField to accommodate any text that is assigned to it. You can do that by assigning the corresponding value to the object's autoSize property. The following is a list of the possible values:

✦ none — This is the default setting, and it means that the TextField object is not resized automatically.

✦ left — This means that the object is automatically resized to the content using the upper-left corner of the TextField instance as the fixed point.

✦ right — This means that the object is automatically resized as it is with the setting of left, but it uses the upper-right corner as the fixed point instead of the left corner.

✦ center — This means that the object is automatically resized as with a setting of left or right, but it uses the upper center as the fixed point.

Note

> If you assign a Boolean value to the autoSize property, it will work. A value of true is synonymous with left and a value of false is synonymous with none. However, we encourage you to use the correct string values, especially considering ActionScript's move toward stronger typing.

To understand how the autoSize property affects resizing, it is helpful to see an example. The following code creates three TextField objects, adds text to them, and tells them to resize in different ways:

```
this.createTextField("tLabel1", this.getNextHighestDepth(), 0, 0, 0, 0);
tLabel1.text = "Label one";
tLabel1.autoSize = "left";
this.createTextField("tLabel2", this.getNextHighestDepth(), 0, 25, 0, 0);
tLabel2.text = "Label two";
tLabel2.autoSize = "right";
this.createTextField("tLabel3", this.getNextHighestDepth(), 0, 50, 0, 0);
tLabel3.text = "Label three";
tLabel3.autoSize = "center";
```

Figure 19-3 shows what the preceding code displays when tested. The vertical line is added where x is 0 to give you a reference point.

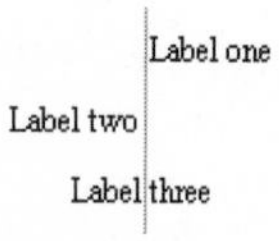

Figure 19-3: An example of three TextField objects with different autoSize values.

You can also, of course, simply assign new values to the `_width` and `_height` properties. That will cause the bounding box to resize to specific pixels widths. The `textWidth` and `textHeight` properties return the pixel width and height of the text contained within a `TextField` object and, thus, can be used for some simple resizing effects. Flash places a 2-pixel margin around the text within a `TextField` object, so when you use the `textWidth` and/or `textHeight` properties, be aware that you'll probably want to add four pixels to those values. The following code creates a `TextField` object sized to match the width of the text, but is set to a fixed 20 pixels in height:

```
this.createTextField("tSample", this.getNextHighestDepth(), 0, 0, 0, 0);
tSample.text = "This is\nsome\nsample\ntext.";
tSample._height = 20;
tSample._width = tSample.textWidth + 4;
```

The preceding example would be useful if, for example, you wanted to create a `TextField` that is a specific number of pixels in one dimension but that fits the text exactly in the other dimension. You can then use the scrolling properties to scroll the text as shown in the section "Scrolling Text" later in this chapter.

The `textWidth` and `textHeight` properties provide very simple information about the text dimensions within a `TextField` object. For more complex information, you can use the `getTextExtent()` method of a `TextFormat` object as described in Chapter 20.

Making Text Unselectable

The default setting for text is that it is selectable. That means that the user can use the mouse to highlight and copy the text as well as place the cursor within the instance for input (in the case of input text). In some situations that is preferable. For example, input text must be selectable, and if you want the user to be able to copy and paste something you should make sure that it is selectable. However, you might well want other text to be unselectable. Labels, titles, and so on, should probably be made unselectable. And when text is used within a button it should definitely be made unselectable so that it doesn't interfere with the state detection of the button.

You can change the selectable state of a `TextField` object with the `selectable` property. The default value is `true`, which means that the user can select the text. Setting the value to `false` makes the instance unselectable.

```
tLabel.selectable = false;
```

Setting Border and Background

`TextField` objects display without borders and backgrounds by default. However, you can programmatically control whether or not these items are displayed.

The `border` property defaults to `false`. If you set the value to `true`, Flash displays a hairline border around the `TextField` instance:

```
tLabel.border = true;
```

Likewise, the `background` property defaults to `false`, but if you set the property to `true`, a background fill is displayed behind the text within the `TextField` object.

```
tLabel.background = true;
```

By default, the border is black and the background is white. You can programmatically change the colors with the `borderColor` and `backgroundColor` properties. The properties expect a numeric value representing the color you want to assign to the border and/or background. The following assigns a red border color and a yellow background color to an instance named `tLabel`:

```
tLabel.borderColor = 0xFF0000;
tLabel.backgroundColor = 0xFFFF00;
```

Creating Input Text

As we mentioned earlier in this chapter, both dynamic text and input text are `TextField` objects. Flash distinguishes between the two with a single property: `type`. The `type` property can have two values: `dynamic` or `input`. The default value is `dynamic`. Setting the value to `input` makes the object an input `TextField` object that allows the user to type or paste text into it. For example, the following creates a new object named `tUsername`, and it assigns the value input to the `type` property, thus allowing for user input:

```
this.createTextField("tUsername", this.getNextHighestDepth(), 0, 0, 100, 20);
tUsername.type = "input";
```

Typically, when you create input text you'll want to make sure that the border is displayed so that the user knows where to enter the text:

```
tUsername.border = true;
```

Managing Input

When working with input text, you may want to control the text that can be input into a field. There are two ways that ActionScript enables you to exercise this control. You can assign a maximum number of characters that can be input, and you can specify which specific characters might not be input.

The `maxChars` property controls the maximum number of characters that a user can input. By default, this property has a value of `null`, which allows an unlimited number of characters to be typed into the field. Regardless of the value for this property, ActionScript code has unrestricted access to add content. This value is strictly for the amount of text allowed by the user. The following example limits the number of characters that can be input to 10 for an instance named `tUsername`:

```
tUsername.maxChars = 10;
```

The `restrict` property controls the allowable characters for a particular object. As the name implies, you can use this property to restrict the range of characters that the user can type into the field. The value for this property is a string value specifying the acceptable and/or unacceptable characters (or character ranges).

Note   Even if a field is restricted, you can still insert whatever text you want via ActionScript. The `restrict` property can prohibit users from entering undesired characters into a field.

To specify enabled characters, simply type the characters in the string value. These values are case-sensitive. The following code tells the `tArticle` field to accept only characters A, B, C, or D.

```
tArticle.restrict = "ABCD";
```

Tip

When a `TextField` object's `restrict` property specifies uppercase characters (but not lowercase) pressing the lowercase key will enter the equivalent uppercase character. Likewise, when lowercase characters are specified (but not uppercase), then pressing the uppercase key will enter the equivalent lowercase character.

You can also use a dash (-) to indicate a range of characters. The following code is another way of establishing characters A through D:

```
tArticle.restrict = "A-D";
```

You can specify several ranges in one string. The following code enables A through D, a space character, and 1 through 4:

```
tArticle.restrict = "A-D 1-4";
```

To omit or specify unacceptable characters, precede the character (or character range) with the ^ character. The following code enables all characters except 0–9 for a text field named article:

```
tArticle.restrict = "^0-9";
```

To specify one of the syntax operators used to denote ranges (-) or omissions (^), precede the operator with a backslash. The following code prevents the user from typing a minus character (-) in the `tArticle` text field. You can also use a backslash pair to denote the backslash character (\) itself as \\.

```
tArticle.restrict = "^\-";
```

Tip

You can also enable or disable Unicode characters from text fields using \u escape sequences. See the "Using Unicode with TextField Objects" sidebar earlier in this chapter.

Creating Password Text

When you are creating input fields for potentially sensitive data such as passwords, you may want to make the input field a password field. That means that rather than displaying the text that the user enters, Flash will display asterisk characters. This prevents other people who can see the screen from being able to read the data. You can make any input text field a password field simply by setting the value of its `password` property to `true`.

```
tPassword.password = true;
```

It is important to understand that a password field does nothing more than alter how the content is displayed in the application. The data that the user enters is still accessible via ActionScript as usual. This also means that using a password field does not provide any additional security or encryption functionality to your application. You should be very careful to not send sensitive data from a Flash application without encryption. That typically means using Secure Sockets Layer (SSL), another technology supported by Flash.

Web Resource

You can read more about SSL at www.netscape.com/eng/security.

Changing Text Color

There are several ways in which you can change text color:

✦ Assign a new value to the `TextField` object's `textColor` property.

✦ Use HTML and `<font>` tags.

✦ Use a `TextFormat` object.

✦ Use Cascading Style Sheets (CSS).

The `textColor` property can be used to apply a single color to all the text in a `TextField` object. All you need to do is assign a numeric value to the property. For example, the following makes all the text red in a `TextField` object named `tLabel`:

```
tLabel.textColor = 0xFF0000;
```

The HTML, `TextFormat`, and CSS options provide you with much more control over the color (as in you can apply different colors to different text) within a `TextField` object. The HTML solution is discussed in more detail in the next part of this chapter. The `TextFormat` and CSS options are discussed in Chapter 20.

Using String Hexadecimal Values in Color Properties

Many Flash developers and students learning ActionScript often ask if it's possible to convert a string value containing a hexadecimal value into a number that's recognized by ActionScript object methods and properties that require number data types, not strings. For example, you may want to use a string input by the user with the `rgb` property of a `ColorTransform` object or one of the numerous color properties of the `TextField` class. However, you cannot properly use a string of format RRGGBB or 0xRRGGBB when a number is expected. The following code will not function correctly in ActionScript:

```
tArticle.textColor = "0xFFFFFF";
```

The `textColor` property requires a number data type. Luckily, the answer is pretty simple. You can convert a string value specifying a hexadecimal value into a numeric data type by using the `parseInt()` function. The following code converts a string variable named `nHexColor` to a numeric data type for the `textColor` property of the `TextField` object:

```
var sHexColor:String = "FF0000";
article.textColor = parseInt("0x" + sHexColor);
```

The significance of this approach may not be immediately apparent. However, what if you wanted to provide an input text field to your user so that he or she could enter a hexadecimal value for a custom interface element? His or her input in the text field would be typed as string data, and you would need a way of converting this string into a number. Again, `parseInt()` can do the work for you. Another use for this process is the conversion of any loaded text values from an external datasource. For example, you may have a database of custom colors for a Flash movie. When the Flash movie loads that data, it will be typed as a string. Using the `parseInt()` function, you can convert the loaded variable's variable into a number.

Removing Text

You can remove TextField objects programmatically using the removeTextField()
method. As with the removeMovieClip() method of the MovieClip class, the
removeTextField() method only works if the depth of the object is within the removable
range. The removeTextField() method can be called from a TextField object.

```
tLabel.removeTextField();
```

Creating a Simple Notes Application

In this exercise, you get the opportunity to put into practice many of the things you've
learned thus far in the chapter. You'll create a very simple notes application in which the user
can log in and view and store notes. The notes are stored in a local shared object. For more
information on local shared objects, consult Chapter 31.

Note   This application provides a simple login process before the user can read and/or update the
notes. The primary purpose is to illustrate the various basic TextField properties in context.
You should, therefore, be made aware that the login process in this example is not secure.
The username and password in this example are stored within the SWF file, and can easily be
read by most any user. Username and password combinations, in secure applications, should
be stored externally in a repository such as a database.

   1. Open a new Flash document, and save it to your local disk as notes001.fla.

   2. Add the following ActionScript to the first frame of the main timeline code:

```
import actionscriptbible.drawing.DrawingUtilities;

var mLoginButton:MovieClip;
var mSaveButton:MovieClip;

makeLoginScreen();

// The drawButton() function makes a new MovieClip object with a nested
// label TextField object.
function drawButton(mParent:MovieClip, sLabel:String,
nWidth:Number, nHeight:Number):MovieClip {

   // Make a new MovieClip object nested in the parent object. Use a unique
   // instance name and depth.
   var nDepth:Number = mParent.getNextHighestDepth();
   var mButton:MovieClip = mParent.createEmptyMovieClip("mButton" +
nDepth, nDepth);

   // Draw a rectangle in the MovieClip object.
   var duDrawer:DrawingUtilities = new DrawingUtilities(mButton);
   duDrawer.beginFill(0xFFFFCC, 100);
   duDrawer.drawRectangle(nWidth, nHeight, nWidth/2, nHeight/2);
```

```
  duDrawer.endFill();

  // Add a TextField object to the MovieClip. Apply the label.
  var tLabel:TextField = mButton.createTextField("tLabel",
mButton.getNextHighestDepth(), 0, 0, nWidth, nHeight);
  tLabel.selectable = false;
  tLabel.text = sLabel;

  return mButton;
}

function makeLoginScreen():Void {

  // Create the TextField and MovieClip objects.
  this.createTextField("tUsername", this.getNextHighestDepth(), 100, 100,
200, 20);
  this.createTextField("tPassword", this.getNextHighestDepth(), 100, 140,
200, 20);
  this.createTextField("tMessage", this.getNextHighestDepth(),  100, 60,
200, 20);
  mLoginButton = drawButton(this, "Login", 100, 25);

  // Set the properties of the TextField objects.
  tUsername.border = true;
  tPassword.border = true;
  tUsername.type = "input";
  tPassword.type = "input";
  tPassword.password = true;
  tMessage.textColor = 0xFF0000;

  // Place the button.
  mLoginButton._x = 100;
  mLoginButton._y = 180;

  mLoginButton.onRelease = function():Void {

    // Check to see if the user has entered the correct username
    // and password. If so, call the login() function.
    // Otherwise, display
    // a message to the user and clear the values from the login
    // TextField objects.
    if(tUsername.text == "admin" && tPassword.text == "admin") {
      login();
    }
    else {
      tMessage.text = "Try again.";
      tUsername.text = "";
      tPassword.text = "";
    }
  };
```

```
}

function login():Void {

  // Remove the TextField and MovieClip objects that made up the
  // login screen.
  tUsername.removeTextField();
  tPassword.removeTextField();
  mLoginButton.removeMovieClip();

  // Create the TextField and MovieClip for the notes screen.
  this.createTextField("tNotes", this.getNextHighestDepth(), 100, 100,
350, 200);
  mSaveButton = drawButton(this, "Save", 100, 25);

  // Set the properties of the TextField object.
  tNotes.border = true;
  tNotes.type = "input";

  // Place the button.
  mSaveButton._x = 100;
  mSaveButton._y = 320;

  // Open a local shared object.
  var lsoNotes:SharedObject = SharedObject.getLocal("notes");

  // Assign the stored text, if any.
  tNotes.text = (lsoNotes.data.notes == undefined) ? "" : lsoNotes.data.notes;

  // When the user clicks and releases the button, store the
  // current notes. in the shared object.
  mSaveButton.onRelease = function():Void {
    lsoNotes.data.notes = tNotes.text;
    lsoNotes.flush();
  }
}
```

3. Test the movie.

If you attempt to log in with the incorrect username and password combination, you will see the message appear in red text. Otherwise, if you log in with the admin/admin username/password combination, you will get access to the notes screen.

Using HTML with TextField Objects

Not only can TextField objects display regular text but they can also display HTML. Flash supports only a subset of HTML tags, including the following:

✦ <a> — Flash supports only the href and target attributes of the anchor tag. That means you can use <a> to create hyperlinks in your text.

✦
 — The <br> tag creates a line break in the text.

✦ <font> — The color, face, and size attributes are supported for this tag. You can use <font> to apply simple formatting to parts of the text.

✦ <p> — The align and class attributes are supported for this tag. The align attribute aligns the text to left, right, or center. The class attribute is used with cascading style sheets, a feature that is discussed in more detail in Chapter 20.

✦ <span> — The class attribute is supported for this tag, and the tag is therefore used only in conjunction with cascading style sheets as discussed in Chapter 20.

✦ <b>, <u>, and <i> — These tags make text appear bolded, underlined, and italicized, respectively.

✦ <li> — This tag creates a list item. List items appear indented.

Flash also provides support for the <img> tag and a tag called <textformat>. The <img> tag support is discussed in more detail in the section "Embedding Content in Text." The <textformat> tag is unique to Flash, and it is more commonly utilized with of a TextFormat object. You can read more about TextFormat objects in Chapter 20.

Rendering HTML in Text

By default, Flash TextField objects render all text literally. This means that if you ask the TextField to display the following:

```
<font color="#FF0000">Red Text</font>
```

Flash displays that text literally instead of rendering the HTML and displaying only Red Text with a red color applied to it. If you want Flash to render the text in a TextField object as HTML, you need to tell it to do so. You can do that by setting the object's html property to true. For example, the following tells Flash to allow a TextField object named tTitle to render HTML:

```
tTitle.html = true;
```

Once an object is set to render HTML you should assign all HTML content to the object's htmlText property. Even though a TextField object may be set to render HTML, if you assign the value to the text property, it will still render literally. The following shows an example of some HTML content assigned to the htmlText property of tTitle.

```
tTitle.htmlText = "<b>ActionScript Bible</b>";
```

Even though you may set the html property to true for a TextField object, it will still render newline, multiple sequential spaces, and tab characters normally. As you may know, that is not how HTML is typically rendered. In HTML, for example, typically newline characters are not rendered. Line breaks are rendered only with the <br> tag. Sometimes one way is more useful, and sometimes the other way is advantageous. Flash provides you with the option to render whitespace characters (spaces, newline characters, and so on) or not when you have enabled a TextField to display HTML. The default setting is that it does render such characters. By setting the value of the condenseWhite property to false, however, you can tell Flash to disregard whitespace characters (other than single spaces) just as HTML is typically rendered in a web browser.

Inserting Special Characters into HTML Fields

Often, you may want to use text characters in HTML text fields that aren't included in the regular alphanumeric set (that is, alphabet and numbers). Although most characters outside of this set can be found as Shift key combinations on keyboards (for example, Shift+2 produces an @ symbol), you need to encode certain characters — on or off the keyboard — in order to properly use them within HTML text fields. For example, if you want to display a greater-than (>) or less-than (<) sign in an HTML text field, you won't see it if you simply type that character in an ActionScript expression. ActionScript interprets less-than and greater-than signs as the opening and closing characters (respectively) for HTML tags. Therefore, if you type a < or > character into a string value used for an HTML field, ActionScript treats the text around it as part of an HTML tag and does not display it. You can try this for yourself with the following code:

```
this.createTextField("tInfo", this.getNextHighestDepth(), 0, 0, 0, 0);
tInfo.autoSize = "left";
tInfo.html = true;
tInfo.htmlText = "< is a less than sign";
```

When you place the preceding code on the first frame of a new Flash document and test the movie, you'll see that no text is displayed.

So, to tell ActionScript that you want to display special characters literally, you need to encode the character as an *entity name* or a *decimal character reference*. You've probably seen entity names in regular HTML. The entity name for a less-than sign is <. If you insert this name in the ActionScript expression, the Flash Player properly displays the < character:

```
    tInfo.htmlText = "&lt; is a less than sign";
```

When you test your movie with the entity name instead of the literal <, you see < is the less than sign display in the movie. Many HTML entity names, such as &copy for the © symbol, do *not* work in Flash ActionScript. For these symbols, use the decimal character reference instead, as in:

```
    tInfo.htmlText = "&#169; is the copyright sign.";
```

For a list of common character entity names (or decimal character references), refer to Table 19-1.

Table 19-1: Special Characters for HTML Text Fields

Character	Name	ActionScript Value	Unicode Value
<	Less-than sign	&lt;	\u003C
>	Greater-than sign	&gt;	\u003E
"	Double quotation mark	&quot;	\u0022
&	Ampersand	&amp;	\u0026
•	Bullet	&#149;	\u2022
¶	Pilcrow sign	&#182;	\u00B6

Continued

Table 19-1 *(continued)*

Character	Name	ActionScript Value	Unicode Value
©	Copyright sign	&#169;	\u00A9
®	Registered sign	&#174;	\u00AE
™	Trademark sign	&#153;	\u2122
£	Pound sign	&#163	\u00A3
¢	Cent sign	&#162;	\u00A2
°	Degree sign	&#176;	\u00B0
÷	Division sign	&#247;	\u00F7

Caution   Some of these upper ASCII characters will not display correctly in Flash Player 6 or later if you do not set the new `System.codePage` property to the correct value. See Chapter 24 for more information. If you do not want to use a different `codePage` value, you can also use a Unicode value (as shown in Table 19-1) for consistent display in Flash Player 6 or later.

Adding Hyperlinks to Text

You can use the `<a>` tag to add hyperlinks to your text. For example, the following will create a hyperlink within a `TextField` named `tContent`:

```
tContent.html = true;
tContent.htmlText = "<a href='http://www.person13.com'>www.person13.com</a>";
```

Caution   Be sure that you are careful with your use of quotation marks. Notice that in the preceding example the inner quotation marks are single quotes so that they don't conflict with the outer quotation marks. If you prefer to use all double quotes or all single quotes then make sure to escape the inner quotes with the backslash character. You can read more about this topic in Chapter 11.

Hyperlinks in Flash text don't necessary behave like standard HTML hyperlinks. Pay particular attention to the target that you use for opening the new links. The default target for opening a hyperlink is the current browser frame. That means that if the Flash application is being played in a browser window, the current browser frame will be replaced by the new content. If you want to specify another target, you can use a target attribute in the `<a>` tag. For example, the following will open the link in a new browser window:

```
tContent.htmlText = "<a href='http://www.person13.com'          ⊃
target='_blank'>www.person13.com</a>";
```

You'll also notice that unlike most web browsers, Flash does not render hyperlinks in such a way that they stand apart from the rest of the text. If you are accustomed to using web browsers to view HTML then you are probably familiar with how hyperlinks are typically underlined and blue (or purple if they've been visited). Because Flash doesn't distinguish hyperlink text in any visual way you may want to add some simple formatting to help the user

Troubleshooting the htmlText Property

You may experience problems if you successively invoke the `htmlText` property for a given `TextField` object. If you add HTML-formatted text to existing HTML text in a text field, a line break occurs at the new addition because a `<P>` tag is automatically inserted around the new additions. For example, the following code creates two separate lines of text in a multiline text field — even though no `<BR>`, `<P>`, or `\r` is indicated:

```
this.createTextField("tArticle", this.getNextHighestDepth(), 25, 35, 300,
100);
tArticle.html = true;
tArticle.multiline = true;
tArticle.wordWrap = true;
tArticle.htmlText = "<B>Bold text</B>";
tArticle.htmlText += "<I>Italic text</I>";
```

To avoid unwanted line breaks, you can set the `htmlText` property once, or store the current content into a new `String` variable and set the `htmlText` to that new variable. This latter solution is shown in the following code.

```
this.createTextField("tArticle", this.getNextHighestDepth(),            ⊃
25, 35, 300, 100);
tArticle.html = true;
tArticle.multiline = true;
tArticle.wordWrap = true;
var sTempHTML:String = "<B>Bold text</B>";
sTempHTML += "<I>Italic text</I>";
tArticle.htmlText = sTempHTML;
```

Another problem with `htmlText` can occur if you use the `htmlText` property in looping code, such as a `for` or `while` loop. If you need to process multiple items for insertion into a text field, the Flash Player can more efficiently render text as HTML if there is only one execution of the `htmlText` property. Here's an example of code that could potentially slow down the Flash Player. A text field is inserted into a `for` loop that cycles 50 times, adding HTML-formatted text with each pass:

```
this.createTextField("tArticle", this.getNextHighestDepth(), 25, 35, 300,
100);
tArticle.html = true;
tArticle.multiline = true;
tArticle.wordWrap = true;
trace(getTimer());
for(var i:Number = 0; i < 100; i++) {
   tArticle.htmlText += "<b>item</b><br>";
}
trace(getTimer());
```

Continued

Continued

If you insert this code into an empty Flash document, the second `trace()` action will take quite some time to display in the Output panel. Although the actual difference between the value reported before and the value reported after the `for` statement will vary; our tests have shown values ranging from three seconds to seven seconds. Next take a look at how you can make a slight change to the code that dramatically changes the execution time:

```
this.createTextField("tArticle", this.getNextHighestDepth(),
25, 35, 300, 100);
tArticle.html = true;
tArticle.multiline = true;
tArticle.wordWrap = true;
trace(getTimer());
var sTempHTML:String = "";
for(var i:Number = 0; i < 100; i++) {
  sTempHTML += "<b>item</b><br>";
}
tArticle.htmlText = sTempHTML;
trace(getTimer());
```

The preceding code will likely take less than 150 milliseconds to run. That's quite a difference!

know that the text is a link. For example, the addition of a `<font>` and `<u>` tag can format the linked text just as it might show up in a web browser:

```
tContent.htmlText = "<font color='#0000FF'><u>
<a href='http://www.person13.com'
target='_blank'>www.person13.com</a></u></font>";
```

Adding Mail Links

Flash supports several other `href` directives, including the `mailto` directive. The `mailto` directive allows you to open a new email message to an email address.

Note

A `mailto` directive in Flash text behaves just like a `mailto` directive in a regular HTML web page. When the user clicks the link, a new email message opens in the user's default email application, such as Microsoft Outlook (or Outlook Express). The user needs to actually send the email though; the `mailto` directive simply opens the new email window with a predefined "to" field (and, optionally, the subject and body fields).

To do that, simply use an `<a>` tag as shown in the preceding section, but use a `mailto` directive followed by a colon and the email address to which you want to have the new message sent. For example:

```
tContent.htmlText = "<a href="mailto:joey@person13.com">send email</a>";
```

Calling JavaScript Functions

If your Flash application is playing within a web browser that supports JavaScript, you can call JavaScript functions using the `javascript` directive within an `<a>` tag. We recommend that you also enclose all the JavaScript calls within the `void()` operator so that no other windows are opened. The following shows how you can add a simple link that pops open a JavaScript alert:

```
tContent.htmlText = "<a href=\"javascript:void(alert(          ⤵
'This is a message from Flash'));\">click this text</a>";
```

Of course, you can also use the `javascript` directive to call custom JavaScript functions you have defined within the hosting HTML page.

You can find more details about which browsers support which functionality by viewing the page at www.macromedia.com/support/flash/ts/documents/browser_support_matrix.htm.

If you are authoring to Flash Player 8 consider using the new `ExternalInterface` **class discussed in Chapter 38.**

Calling ActionScript Functions from Text

One feature not well known but often quite useful is the ability to call ActionScript functions from text. The `asfunction` directive can be used within an `<a>` tag to call an ActionScript function. This functionality allows to you add much more interactivity to your text.

The `asfunction` **syntax is:**

```
asfunction:functionName[,param1...,paramN]
```

There should be no spaces between the directive, colon, function name, commas, or parameters. The only permissible spaces in the syntax are spaces within the parameter values.

Here's an example that calls the `trace()` statement and passes it a value of `a message`:

```
tContent.htmlText = "<a href='asfunction:trace,a message'>click this text</a>";
```

You can also use the `asfunction` **directive to call custom functions. For example:**

```
tContent.htmlText = "<a href='asfunction:changeTextColor'>          ⤵
    click to change color</a>";
function changeTextColor():Void {
  tContent.textColor = Math.random() * 255 * 255 * 255;
}
```

It is also worth mentioning that you can use the `asfunction` directive with static text. You can enter the `asfunction` directive in the URL link field in the Property inspector for static text. For example:

```
asfunction:trace,a message from static text
```

Embedding Content in Text

When publishing to Flash 7 or 8, you can embed content in HTML `TextField` objects. The embedded content can be an external image or SWF or a Movie Clip symbol with a linkage identifier. Before discussing this feature, we should mention that at the time of this writing it is inconsistent at best. Although you are, of course, welcome to try using the feature, be forewarned that our tests have shown that there are a great many factors that seem to affect how it works — if it even works at all under some circumstances. If you try to embed multiple content items in the text, they may overlap such that one or more might not seem to be there. And when creating `TextField` objects programmatically and attempting to add embedded content prior to any text, we've noticed it simply doesn't work. You should check the Macromedia web site for any player updates that may fix these issues.

With all that said, let's take a look at how the feature is at least supposed to work. The HTML `<img>` tag allows you to embed an image within a standard HTML document. Flash extends upon that functionality slightly by allowing you to use an `<img>` tag within an HTML-enabled `TextField` object to display not only images, but also SWF content and Movie Clip symbol content. For example, you can use the following code to display an image in a `TextField` object:

```
this.createTextField("tContent", this.getNextHighestDepth(), 0, 0, 200, 200);
tContent.border = true;
tContent.html = true;
tContent.htmlText = "A picture of a lake: <img width='180'
   height='120' src='http://www.person13.com/asb/image2.jpg'>";
```

Notice from the preceding example that the Flash support for the `<img>` tag includes the `width` and `height` attributes. The complete list of supported attributes is as follows:

✦ `width`—The width, in pixels, at which to display the content.

✦ `height`—The height, in pixels, at which to display the content.

✦ `src`—The URL or linkage identifier for the content. If you are specifying a URL, it can be an absolute or relative URL. Alternatively, you can also display `MovieClip` content added from a symbol in the library with a linkage identifier.

✦ `align`—The horizontal alignment of the content within the `TextField` object. You can align left (default), right, or center.

✦ `hspace`—The number of pixels that space the content in the vertical direction. The default value is 8.

✦ `vspace`—The number of pixels that space the content in the horizontal direction. The default value is 8.

✦ `id`—An identifier for the content that you can use to target the embedded content with ActionScript.

Note that when you load graphical content into a `TextField` object it loads asynchronously. That means that the `TextField` initializes based on textual content. Therefore, once the graphical content loads the `TextField` might not reinitialize. For example, when you load an image into a `TextField` object with `autoSize` set to `true`, the object will not properly resize to accommodate the loaded image (although our tests show that it will resize in the vertical direction). Additionally, we have noticed that you cannot have an `<img>` tag as the first content within a `TextField` object created at runtime. In such cases the `<img>` tag is seemingly ignored. That issue does not seem to be the case for authoring-time objects.

Note   All of the preceding statements are true at the time of this writing. We encourage you to check for player updates, which may potentially correct some of the issues with embedded graphical content in `TextField` objects.

In the list of supported ⟨img⟩ tag attributes you will notice that Flash supports an attribute named id. The attribute can be used to target the graphical content that is nested within the TextField. The content is loaded into a nested MovieClip object with the instance name specified by the id attribute. That means that you can use any of the properties and methods of the MovieClip class with the embedded content. For example, you might want to instruct a loaded SWF to stop or play or check the load progress of an image and tell the TextField to resize once the content has loaded and initialized. For example:

```
this.createTextField("tContent", this.getNextHighestDepth(), 0, 0, 200, 200);
tContent.html = true;
tContent.htmlText = "A picture of a lake: <img id='mImage'
  width='180' height='120' align='center' vspace='0' hspace='0'
  src='http://www.person13.com/asb/image2.jpg'>";

// Define a function that checks for the load progress of the image.
function checkLoad():Void {
  var nLoaded:Number = tContent.mImage.getBytesLoaded();
  var nTotal:Number = tContent.mImage.getBytesTotal();

  // If the content has loaded and initialized, tell the TextField
  // to resize and clear the interval.
  if(nLoaded/nTotal >= 1 && tContent.mImage._width > 0) {
    tContent.autoSize = "left";
    clearInterval(nInterval);
  }
}

// Set an interval that calls the checkLoad() function at approximately 100
// millisecond intervals.
var nInterval:Number = setInterval(checkLoad, 100);
```

When you implement the preceding code, you should be aware of two things:

✦ If you display the border in the TextField object, the border will not resize correctly.

✦ You must create the TextField object such that its initial dimensions are large enough to accommodate the loaded content. Otherwise, it will crop the loaded content.

Creating an HTML-Based Information Viewer

In this section, you use some of the HTML concepts you learned in the previous sections to create an application that allows the user to select a topic from an index and view more information about that topic in an HTML-enabled TextField object.

1. Open a new Flash document, and save it as informationViewer001.fla.

2. Add the following code to the first frame of the main timeline:

```
function createTextFields():Void {

  // Create the two TextField objects.
  this.createTextField("tIndex", this.getNextHighestDepth(),50,100,100,200);
```

```
    this.createTextField("tContent", this.getNextHighestDepth(),200,100,200,200);

    // Set the properties of tIndex.
    tIndex.selectable = false;
    tIndex.border = true;
    tIndex.html = true;
    tIndex.multiline = true;
    tIndex.wordWrap = true;

    // Create the HTML text for the index, and then assign it to
    // the object's htmlText property.
    var sIndex:String = "Click on one of the following links:<br>";
    sIndex += "<li><a href='asfunction:viewSection,text'>text</a></li>";
    sIndex += "<li><a href='asfunction:viewSection,html'>html</a></li>";
    sIndex += "<li><a href='asfunction:viewSection,scrolling'>scrolling</a></li>";
    tIndex.htmlText = sIndex;

    // Set the properties for tContent.
    tContent.selectable = false;
    tContent.border = true;
    tContent.html = true;
    tContent.multiline = true;
    tContent.wordWrap = true;
}

function viewSection(sSection:String):Void {

    // Determine which content to display based on which selection
    // was clicked.
    switch (sSection) {
        case "text":
            tContent.htmlText = "This is the section about text.";
            break;
        case "html":
            tContent.htmlText = "HTML allows you to <font
                color='#FF0000'>colorize</font> text";
            break;
        case "scrolling":
            tContent.htmlText = "Read more about scrolling in the next part
                of the chapter.";
    }
}

createTextFields();
```

3. Test the movie.

Scrolling Text

The text within a text field can be scrolled both horizontally and vertically with ActionScript. The TextField scrolling properties come into play whenever the amount of text that you assign to a text field exceeds the actual space available in the viewable portion of the field. For example, if you have 10 lines of text, but have a text field with a height of only 5 lines, you'll need to adjust the scroll property in order to view the remaining five lines of text. Each line of text in a text field has an index number. This index number is 1-based, meaning that the first line is index 1. Figure 19-4 illustrates how programmatic scrolling works with TextField objects.

Line index

scroll	1	Amendment I
	2	
	3	Congress shall make no law respecting an establishment of
	4	religion, or prohibiting the free exercise thereof; or abridging
	5	the freedom of speech, or of the press; or the right of the
	6	people peaceably to assemble, and to petition the
	7	Government for a redress of grievances.
	8	
	9	
	10	Amendment II
	11	
	12	A well regulated Militia, being necessary to the security of a
	13	free State, the right of the people to keep and bear Arms,
maxscroll 1	14	shall not be infringed.
2	15	
3	16	
4	17	Amendment III
bottomScroll 5	18	
6	19	No Soldier shall, in time of peace be quartered in any house,
7	20	without the consent of the Owner, nor in time of war, but in
8	21	a manner to be prescribed by law.
9	22	
10	23	
11	24	Amendment IV
12	25	
13	26	The right of the people to be secure in their persons,
14	27	houses, papers, and effects, against unreasonable searches
15	28	and seizures, shall not be violated, and no Warrants shall
16	29	issue, but upon probable cause, supported by Oath or
17	30	affirmation, and particularly describing the place to be
18	31	searched, and the persons or things to be seized.

Figure 19-4: This text field has been assigned content that has 31 lines, yet the viewable portion of the field has only 18 lines.

Scrolling Text Vertically

The scroll property of a text field controls which line index of a text field's content is currently at the top of the actual viewable portion of the field. This property is a read-write property, which means you can assign a new value to it to cause the text to scroll vertically. When you assign a text value to a TextField object with ActionScript, the text context is automatically indexed as it "fills" the text field. The example shown in Figure 19-4 has 31 lines of text content, but the field displaying the content has only 18 viewable lines. However, the number of content lines is *not* equivalent to the number of scroll values — you'll see why in the maxscroll property description.

To scroll the content of a field upward, add to the scroll property. The following code will advance the text within a text field named tArticle by one line with each click of mScrollUp.

```
mScrollUp.onRelease = function():Void {
  tArticle.scroll++;
}
```

To scroll the content of a field downward (the text moves from top to bottom), subtract from the scroll property. The following code will retreat the text back by one line with each click of the button:

```
mScrollDown.onRelease = function():Void {
  tArticle.scroll--;
}
```

As the text advances or retreats within the field, the scroll property will update to reflect the index value currently visible at the top of the field.

Note   You can use the scroll property with Flash 4 and 5 text fields. Target the Var name of an editable text field to use the scroll property.

The bottomScroll property returns the index number for the text currently displayed in the last viewable line of the TextField object. Unlike the scroll property, the bottomScroll is read-only; you cannot change the position of the text content with bottomScroll. For the example shown in Figure 19-4, the range of possible values for bottomScroll is 18 through 31.

The maxscroll property, as the name implies, is the maximum scroll value that a TextField object can return. This property is read-only, and unless you dynamically add or subtract actual text from a TextField object, the maxscroll value is fixed. You cannot scroll beyond the maxscroll value, nor can you scroll to negative values within text fields.

As you add to the scroll property, the text field will stop advancing as soon as the last line of the text content is displayed at the very bottom of the text field. In the example shown in Figure 19-4, the last line of text is line 31, and the text field is 18 lines high. Eighteen lines up from line 31 is line 14. Line 14 is the maximum scroll value for this content in this particular text field. This value is the same value that the maxscroll property will return for this text field. The maxscroll property can be calculated manually in the following way:

```
maxscroll = total number of lines - viewable number of lines in text field + 1
```

Note   The maxscroll property is available via the Var name of editable text fields in Flash 4 and 5 movies.

Scrolling Text Horizontally

ActionScript also offers the capability to scroll text field content horizontally. Unlike the previous scrolling methods, hscroll and maxhscroll use pixel units — not line index numbers.

The hscroll property is a read-write property that retrieves or sets the current horizontal scroll position (in pixels) of the TextField object. When a TextField object is initialized with default values, the value of hscroll is 0. If you increase the value of hscroll, the text within the TextField object moves from right to left. If you decrease the value of hscroll, the text moves from left to right. The value of hscroll cannot be set below 0. The following code placed on the main timeline creates a TextField object containing text that scrolls from right to left by 10 pixels whenever the stage of the Flash movie is clicked.

```
_this.createTextField("tDisplay", 1, 25, 25, 30, 300);
tDisplay.text = "Hello, how are you? This text scrolls with each mouse click.";

this.onMouseDown = function(){
    tDisplay.hscroll += 10;
};
```

The read-only property maxhscroll returns the maximum hscroll value of the text field. Like maxscroll, this property returns the maximum offset of the text within the text field. The value of hscroll cannot be set beyond the value of maxhscroll. The value of maxhscroll depends on the amount of text that cannot be displayed within the visible area of the text field. As you add text to an individual line within a field, the value of maxhscroll increases.

Scrolling Text with Scrollbars

The UIScrollBar component is useful for scrolling text as well. Although we'll discuss the component in more detail within Chapter 28, we'll discuss some of the text scrolling-specific functionality in this section.

As with other components (read Chapter 29 for more details), you can add instances of the UIScrollBar component either at authoring time by dragging instances from the Components panel or at runtime by way of the createObject() or createClassObject() method. When you use a UIScrollBar component with an authoring-time, multiline dynamic, or input TextField object you can drag and drop the component instance onto the TextField object, and the UIScrollBar object will automatically snap to the TextField object, setting the necessary parameters so that it will scroll the text. In order for the feature to work, you must make sure that object snapping is on. Figures 19-5 and 19-6 show a UIScrollBar instance being dragged over a TextField object on stage. When the component is dropped on the TextField object, it snaps to the side.

Figure 19-5: Dragging a UIScrollBar instance over a TextField object.

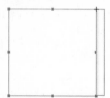

Figure 19-6: The UIScrollBar object snaps to the TextField object.

As you can see, the `UIScrollBar` object aligns itself to the side near which it was dropped and sets the width and height of the instance. It also sets the `_targetInstanceName` property of the component instance to that of the `TextField` object. That is the property that determines which `TextField` the `UIScrollBar` instance scrolls. If the `TextField` hasn't yet been named, Flash automatically assigns an instance name to it, and uses that instance name for the `_targetInstanceName` property as well. If you change the `TextField` instance name later, you'll want to change the `_targetInstanceName` property value of the `UIScrollBar` instance as well. When a `UIScrollBar` instance snaps to a `TextField` object it also sets the horizontal property accordingly. If it snaps to the top or bottom of the `TextField`, it sets the horizontal property to `true`, which means it scrolls the text horizontally.

If you add a `UIScrollBar` object programmatically, you have to set the target `TextField` object programmatically as well using the `setScrollTarget()` method. And you'll also likely want to programmatically move the component and set the dimensions with the `move()` and `setSize()` methods. The following code illustrates how it works. For the code to work you must have the `UIScrollBar` component in the library, which you can accomplish by adding an instance to the stage, and then deleting it.

```
import mx.controls.UIScrollBar;

// Make the TextField object. Set the type to input.
this.createTextField("tField", this.getNextHighestDepth(),
100, 100, 200, 200);
tField.type = "input";
tField.border = true;
tField.multiline = true;
tField.wordWrap = true;

// Make the UIScrollBar instance.
this.createClassObject(UIScrollBar, "csbScroller",
this.getNextHighestDepth());

// Set the scroll target.
csbScroller.setScrollTarget(tField);

// Set the dimensions of the UIScrollBar, and move
// it to the right of the TextField.
csbScroller.setSize(csbScroller.width, tField._height);
csbScroller.move(tField._x + tField._width, tField._y);
```

You can also set the horizontal property of the `UIScrollBar` to specify how it ought to scroll the text. A value of `true` scrolls the text horizontally. The text scrolls vertically if the value is `false`.

Note   You can also use the `TextArea` component to scroll text. You can read more about the `TextArea` component in Chapter 28.

Scrolling by Pixels

As you've already seen, when you scroll text by way of the `scroll` property or when you scroll text horizontally with a `UIScrollBar` instance, the text scrolls by lines. If you want to scroll by pixels (which yields a smoother scrolling effect) you can approach it in several ways.

When you want to scroll text by pixels, you place the `TextField` within a `MovieClip` object. One approach to scrolling text by pixels is to then mask the `MovieClip` and continuously update the _x or _y property. The following code illustrates that technique.

```
import actionscriptbible.drawing.DrawingUtilities;

// Make the MovieClip object. Then nest the TextField within the MovieClip.
this.createEmptyMovieClip("mTextClip", this.getNextHighestDepth());
var tField:TextField = mTextClip.createTextField("tField",
mTextClip.getNextHighestDepth(), 0, 0, 200, 200);
tField.multiline = true;
tField.wordWrap = true;

// Note that the width of the TextField is set to 200 when instantiated with the
// preceding code. Therefore, setting autoSize to left will cause the TextField
// to maintain the 200 pixel width, but it will adapt the height to match the
// text.
tField.autoSize = "left";

var duDrawer:DrawingUtilities;

// Draw a 200 X 200 rectangle, and use it as the mask for mTextClip.
this.createEmptyMovieClip("mMask", this.getNextHighestDepth());
duDrawer = new DrawingUtilities(mMask);
duDrawer.beginFill(0xFFFFFF, 100);
duDrawer.drawRectangle(200, 200, 100, 100);
duDrawer.endFill();
mMask._x = mTextClip._x;
mMask._y = mTextClip._y;
mTextClip.setMask(mMask);

// Use a LoadVars object to load text. You can read more about LoadVars in
// Chapter 33.
var lvText:LoadVars = new LoadVars();
lvText.onData = function(sText:String):Void {
  tField.text = sText;
};
lvText.load("http://www.person13.com/asb/lorem_ipsum.txt");

// Make two MovieClip objects to use as buttons to scroll the text. In each draw
// a rectangle and a triangle. In mScrollUp the triangle points upward. In
// mScrollDown the triangle points downward.
```

```
this.createEmptyMovieClip("mScrollUp", this.getNextHighestDepth());
duDrawer = new DrawingUtilities(mScrollUp);
duDrawer.beginFill(0xFFFFFF, 100);
duDrawer.drawRectangle(20, 20, 10, 10);
duDrawer.endFill();
duDrawer.drawPolygon(5, 3, Math.PI / 6, 10, 10);

this.createEmptyMovieClip("mScrollDown", this.getNextHighestDepth());
duDrawer = new DrawingUtilities(mScrollDown);
duDrawer.beginFill(0xFFFFFF, 100);
duDrawer.drawRectangle(20, 20, 10, 10);
duDrawer.endFill();
duDrawer.drawPolygon(5, 3, -Math.PI / 6, 10, 10);

// Move the button clips to the right side of mTextClip.
mScrollUp._x = mTextClip._x + tField._width;
mScrollUp._y = mTextClip._y;
mScrollDown._x = mScrollUp._x;
mScrollDown._y = mTextClip._y + 200 - 20;

var nInterval:Number;

// When the buttons are pressed start an interval that calls scroll(). When the
// buttons are released, clear the interval.
mScrollUp.onPress = function():Void {
  nInterval = setInterval(scroll, 10, 1);
};

mScrollUp.onRelease = function():Void {
  clearInterval(nInterval);
};

mScrollUp.onReleaseOutside = mScrollUp.onRelease;

mScrollDown.onPress = function():Void {
  nInterval = setInterval(scroll, 10, -1);
};

mScrollDown.onRelease = function():Void {
  clearInterval(nInterval);
};

mScrollDown.onReleaseOutside = mScrollDown.onRelease;

function scroll(nScrollAmount:Number):Void {

  // Update the _y property of mTextClip. Increment by 1 or -1 depending on
  // which button was pressed.
  mTextClip._y += nScrollAmount;

  // Check if the MovieClip has moved so the edge of the text is at the edge of
```

```
  // the mask. If so, clear the interval.
  if(mTextClip._y > 0) {
    clearInterval(nInterval);
    mTextClip._y = 0;
  }
  if(mTextClip._y < -mTextClip._height + 200) {
    clearInterval(nInterval);
    mTextClip._y = -mTextClip._height + 200;
  }
}
```

The alternative, if publishing to Flash 8, is to use the `scrollRect` property of the `MovieClip` object. You can read more about the `scrollRect` property in Chapter 14. Using `scrollRect` has several potential advantages. One advantage is that it automatically masks the `MovieClip` object. Additionally, if you are embedding fonts it is possible that using `scrollRect` will scroll the text more smoothly. The following code is very similar to the preceding code, but it utilizes `scrollRect`. The changes are shown in bold.

```
import flash.geom.Rectangle;
import actionscriptbible.drawing.DrawingUtilities;

this.createEmptyMovieClip("mTextClip", this.getNextHighestDepth());
var tField:TextField = mTextClip.createTextField("tField",
mTextClip.getNextHighestDepth(), 0, 0, 200, 200);
tField.multiline = true;
tField.wordWrap = true;
tField.autoSize = "left";

// Set the initial scrollRect property value to a Rectangle scrolled to 0,0.
mTextClip.scrollRect = new Rectangle(0, 0, 200, 200);

var duDrawer:DrawingUtilities;

var lvText:LoadVars = new LoadVars();
lvText.onData = function(sText:String):Void {
  tField.text = sText.substring(0, 1000);
};
lvText.load("http://www.person13.com/asb/lorem_ipsum.txt");

this.createEmptyMovieClip("mScrollUp", this.getNextHighestDepth());
duDrawer = new DrawingUtilities(mScrollUp);
duDrawer.beginFill(0xFFFFFF, 100);
duDrawer.drawRectangle(20, 20, 10, 10);
duDrawer.endFill();
duDrawer.drawPolygon(5, 3, Math.PI / 6, 10, 10);

this.createEmptyMovieClip("mScrollDown", this.getNextHighestDepth());
duDrawer = new DrawingUtilities(mScrollDown);
duDrawer.beginFill(0xFFFFFF, 100);
duDrawer.drawRectangle(20, 20, 10, 10);
duDrawer.endFill();
```

```
duDrawer.drawPolygon(5, 3, -Math.PI / 6, 10, 10);

mScrollUp._x = mTextClip._x + tField._width;
mScrollUp._y = mTextClip._y;
mScrollDown._x = mScrollUp._x;
mScrollDown._y = mTextClip._y + 200 - 20;

var nInterval:Number;

mScrollUp.onPress = function():Void {
  nInterval = setInterval(scroll, 10, 1);
};

mScrollUp.onRelease = function():Void {
  clearInterval(nInterval);
};

mScrollUp.onReleaseOutside = mScrollUp.onRelease;

mScrollDown.onPress = function():Void {
  nInterval = setInterval(scroll, 10, -1);
};

mScrollDown.onRelease = function():Void {
  clearInterval(nInterval);
};

mScrollDown.onReleaseOutside = mScrollDown.onRelease;

function scroll(nScrollAmount:Number):Void {
  // Retrieve the current scrollRect value.
  var rctText:Rectangle = mTextClip.scrollRect;

  // Update the y property of the Rectangle.
  rctText.y += -nScrollAmount;

  // Check if the Rectangle would scroll the text out of bounds. If so, clear
  // the interval. Otherwise, assign the updated Rectangle object to the
  // scrollRect property.
  if(rctText.y < 0) {
    clearInterval(nInterval);
  }
  else if(rctText.y > mTextClip.tField._height - 200) {
    clearInterval(nInterval);
  }
  else {
    mTextClip.scrollRect = rctText;
  }
}
```

Using Events for Text Fields

ActionScript defines several event handlers for editable text fields. These event handlers can execute code whenever the user interacts with a text field in the movie. You can specify an anonymous or named function for each of these handlers.

Detecting Text Changes

The onChanged() event handler method detects any text changes initiated by the user within the object. If the user is adding text to a field via the keyboard, this handler is invoked when the user presses the key, not when it is released.

Caution

The onChanged() handler method does not detect changes to a text field made via ActionScript. In other words, if you change the contents of a TextField object using the text or htmlText property, the onChanged() handler method is not called.

The following code sends a trace() message to the Output panel whenever text is added to a TextField object named tComments in Test Movie mode:

```
this.createTextField("tComments", 1, 25, 25, 100, 20);
tComments.border = true;
tComments.type = "input";
tComments.onChanged = function():Void {
  trace("Text within comments field = " + tComments.text);
};
```

Tip

If you need to define several functions to be executed with a specific TextField object's onChanged() handler method, you can create several listener objects for the TextField object. Each listener object can have its own onChanged() handler. You learn about listeners for the TextField object in the "Adding Listeners to TextField Objects" section of this chapter.

Detecting Focus Changes

When focus is moved to a TextField object by means of user interaction (that is, the user clicks on the TextField object or moves focus to it by way of the Tab key), Flash calls that object's onSetFocus() event handler method. The method is passed a parameter indicating the previous object that held focus (if any existed). The following code displays a trace() action in the Output panel when the movie is in Test Movie mode. If the user clicks in either of the two fields, the trace() action indicates which field received focus. If a previous field was focused, the onSetFocus() method also reports that object's name.

```
this.createTextField("tMessageOne", this.getNextHighestDepth(), 25,25,200,20);
this.createTextField("tMessageTwo", this.getNextHighestDepth(), 250,25,200,20);
tMessageOne.border = true;
tMessageTwo.border = true;
tMessageOne.text = "message one";
tMessageTwo.text = "message two";

tMessageOne.onSetFocus = function(oPrevFocus:Object):Void {
```

```
  trace(this._name + " is now focused.");
  if(tPrevFocus._name != null){
    trace(tPrevFocus._name + " no longer has focus.");
  }
};

tMessageTwo.onSetFocus = function(oPrevFocus:Object):Void {
  trace(this._name + " is now focused.");
  if(tPrevFocus._name != null){
    trace(tPrevFocus._name + " no longer has focus.");
  }
};
```

In contrast, when the focus shifts away from a `TextField` due to user interaction, Flash calls the `onKillFocus()` method of the object. This handler is passed a reference to the object that receives the new focus. If focus leaves the field and is not directed to a new object, the parameter is equal to `null`. The following code sends a `trace()` action to the Output panel in Test Movie mode when the `onKillFocus()` handler method is invoked. If you click inside the `tMessage` text field and then click outside of it, the handler is invoked. The `obj` argument represents the object (if any) that receives the new focus.

```
this.createTextField("tMessage", this.getNextHighestDepth(), 25, 25, 200, 20);
tMessage.text = "You have a message waiting.";
tMessage.border = true;
tMessage.onKillFocus = function(oNewFocus:Object):Void {
  trace(this._name + " is no longer focused.");
  trace(oNewFocus._name + " is now focused.");
};
```

Detecting Scrolling

The `onScroller()` handler method detects when the `TextField` object's scroll properties change. Among other uses, this handler can advance the `scroll` property of a `TextField` to always make sure that the last line of text is displayed at the bottom of the field. The following code creates a mouse listener that adds text to the message field when the user clicks and then releases the mouse. When the text in the message field exceeds the number of lines visible in the field, the `onScroller()` handler method is invoked, setting the `scroll` property equal to the value of the `maxscroll` property:

```
this.createTextField("tMessage", this.getNextHighestDepth(), 25, 25, 200, 100);
tMessage.border = true;
tMessage.multiline = true;
tMessage.wordWrap = true;

var nCount:Number = 0;

tMessage.text = "You have " + nCount + " message(s) waiting.\n";

tMessage.onScroller = function():Void {
  this.scroll = this.maxscroll;
};

oAddTextListener = new Object();
```

```
oAddTextListener.onMouseUp = function():Void {
   nCount++;
   tMessage.text += "You have " + nCount + " message(s) waiting.\n";;
};
Mouse.addListener(oAddTextListener);
```

Adding Listeners to TextField Objects

TextField objects can use listeners that detect changes to the text content or scroll properties. The methods that you define for the listeners behave identically to the methods by the
same names discussed in the previous section. The primary difference between onChanged()
and onScroller() as listener object methods and TextField methods is that you can create
several listener objects for the same text field — each listener can have its own onChanged()
and onScroller() handlers.

Detecting Text Changes

The onChanged() method of a listener object works identically to the onChanged() method
for a TextField object except that it is passed a parameter that the event handler method
is not — a reference to the TextField that dispatched the event. To use the onChanged()
method with a listener object, first define the listener object. The listener can be of many
types, the simplest of which is an Object object. Then, register the listener with the
TextField object via the addListener() method.

The following code creates two TextField objects. The first is an input field that allows the
user to enter text. A listener object's onChanged() method is called each time the user modifies the value in the first field, and it updates the second to display the reverse text:

```
this.createTextField("tInput", this.getNextHighestDepth(), 25, 25, 200, 200);
this.createTextField("tCopy", this.getNextHighestDepth(), 250, 25, 200, 200);
tInput.border = true;
tCopy.border = true;
tInput.type = "input";
var oListener:Object = new Object();
oListener.onChanged = function(tDispatcher:TextField):Void {
   var sText:String = tDispatcher.text;
   var aText:Array = sText.split("");
   aText.reverse();
   sText = aText.join("");
   tCopy.text = sText;
};
tInput.addListener(oListener);
```

Detecting Scrolling

The onScrolled() method for a listener object detects changes to the scroll properties of
a TextField object. Just as with the onChanged() method, you should defined the method for
a listener object and then register the listener with the TextField using the addListener()
method. Also, the listener onScrolled() method is passed a parameter that references the
TextField object that dispatched the event.

Working with Fonts

The following sections look at some of the ways you can work with fonts in Flash.

Embedding Fonts

One nice feature of Flash movies on the Web is the fact that you can consistently view artwork and fonts with any version of the Flash Player. Font embedding is usually the most overlooked optimization step in Flash deployment. If you're not careful, you can add a substantial file size to your Flash movies (SWF files) by embedding entire fonts.

Aside from just allowing text to look the way you want it to look, embedded fonts actually enable your TextField objects to do some things that they wouldn't otherwise do. For example, as mentioned, a TextField object that uses device fonts (nonembedded fonts) cannot be rotated nor can you change the alpha. But once you embed the font, you can do both of these things.

Static Text

Whenever you create static text in a movie, Flash automatically embeds the specific characters that you typed into the field. Because static text cannot change dynamically, Flash embeds only the characters you actually type into the field on the stage. However, if you want to disable font embedding for static text, you can choose the Use Device Fonts option in the Property inspector when you have selected the static text on the stage. This prevents the font characters from being embedded in the Flash movie (SWF file) and displays the font selected in the Property inspector *only* if the user has that exact font installed on his or her system. Otherwise, a generic system font is substituted in its place.

Authoring Time Dynamic and Input Text

By default, Flash does not embed fonts for dynamic and input text. Therefore, if you want to ensure that the proper font is used you need to explicitly tell Flash to embed the font. You can do that by selecting the TextField object and clicking the Embed button in the Property inspector. Figure 19-7 shows the Character Embedding dialog box.

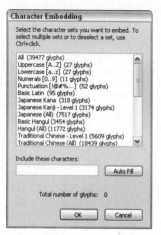

Figure 19-7: The Character Embedding dialog box has specific font-embedding features for editable text fields.

The default setting, as you can see, is to embed no characters. However, by choosing the Specify Ranges option you can select any combination of the preset ranges. Or, you can opt to specify a custom set of characters in the Include These Characters field. The more characters you include, the larger the file size.

If you need to embed only a limited set of characters, type the desired character(s) into the Include These Characters field. Note that for some fonts you actually need to embed a space character (that is, insert an empty space by pressing the spacebar in this field).

Tip Many Flash developers like to include Internet URLs in dynamic and input text fields. Make sure that you enable the @ (for email) and the &, =, +, and - (for script queries) characters in the character option described previously if you intend to display such URLs to the user in your Flash movie.

Following is a list of common behaviors for some of the font embedding options:

✦ If you enable only one case (lowercase or uppercase) the nonembedded case is displayed as the embedded case. For example, if you embed lowercase characters and the user types an uppercase A, a lowercase a is displayed in the field.

✦ If you try to assign nonembedded characters to an editable text field via an ActionScript expression (either through a Var name or the text property of the TextField object), the character does not display in the text field. However, the variable or text property still retains the value prescribed in the expression until the user focuses the text or until the variable is given a new value with a new ActionScript expression.

✦ The Property inspector's font style buttons, Bold and Italic, also influence the file size and visual appearance of the text field in the Flash movie (SWF file). The first character of any editable field determines the color, style, and point size of the entire field. If you want to control specific formatting within individual sections of the same text field, we recommend that you use the HTML option of editable text fields. This issue (working with HTML and TextField objects) is discussed earlier in the chapter.

✦ If you enable several different fields to embed different subsets of the same font face, all the fields can use each other's embedded characters. For example, if one editable text field has lowercase letters of Verdana, and another field has uppercase letters of Verdana enabled, both fields can use upper- and lowercase characters. These fields do *not* need to coexist on the same frame (or timeline) in order for this effect to work.

✦ You must use embedding options for any editable text field that will be masked by a Mask Layer or nested within a MovieClip instance that is transformed with settings in the Transform panel or the Color menu of the Property inspector for symbol instances. The Flash Player rendering engine needs to have the outlines of any characters embedded in the Flash movie (SWF file) to perform these visual effects.

✦ You cannot access embedded fonts in one Flash movie (SWF file) from another Flash movie (SWF file). For example, if you enable lowercase Verdana characters in a TextField object of your initial Flash movie and embed uppercase Verdana characters in a TextField object of another Flash movie that is loaded into the initial Flash movie, you cannot interchangeably use the lowercase and uppercase characters between the two movies. In order to share an embedded font across several Flash movies, you need to create font symbols in shared libraries and link them to your text fields.

Runtime Text

When you create a `TextField` object at runtime, the only way to embed fonts is program-matically. There are two ways you can do this. The first way is to create an authoring-time `TextField` instance (that is, create an input or dynamic text field with the Text tool) that embeds the font, and then tell your runtime instances to use that same font. The second way is to use a font symbol. We'll take a look at each way.

Using an Authoring-Time TextField's Font

Perhaps the simplest way to programmatically use an embedded font is to embed the font first with an authoring-time `TextField`. You can create a single dynamic `TextField` object offstage, and embed the characters you want to use. The advantage of embedding fonts with an authoring-time `TextField` is that not only that it is somewhat simpler to implement, but it also enables you to have more control over what characters are embedded. Use the following steps to programmatically use fonts embedded in an authoring-time `TextField`:

1. Create an authoring-time `TextField` offstage. You can give the instance and name or not, and you can add text to it or not. Because you will not necessarily be using the `TextField` for any other purposes, those things are not particularly pertinent.

2. Embed the characters of the font you want to use in the authoring-time `TextField` by following the instructions in the section "Authoring-Time Dynamic and Input Text."

3. Create the runtime text using the `createTextField()` method.

4. Set the `embedFonts` property of the `TextField` to `true`.

5. Create a `TextFormat` object.

6. Assign the embedded font name to the `TextFormat` object's `font` property.

7. Assign the `TextFormat` object to the `TextField` using the `setTextFormat()` method.

We haven't yet discussed font symbols or the `TextFormat` class. You can read more about each of those topics in detail in Chapter 20. However, you'll get the basic information you need to know in this section.

You've just read the generalized instructions. Let's practice with a specific example:

1. Create a new dynamic `TextField` object at authoring time. Place the object offstage; you don't need to give it an instance name.

2. Select Verdana from the Font menu, and then open the Character Options dialog box for the `TextField`, and embed the Uppercase Letters. Then click OK.

3. Add the following code to the first frame of the main timeline:

```
this.createTextField("tLabel", this.getNextHighestDepth(),
    100, 100, 100, 20);
tLabel.text = "abcdefg";
```

4. Test the movie. You should see the text appear in the default serif font. You're testing the movie just to confirm that the text is, in fact, displayed before you set it to embed the font.

5. Append the following code after the code you added in Step 3:

```
tLabel.embedFonts = true;

var tfFormatter:TextFormat = new TextFormat();
tfFormatter.font = "Verdana";

tLabel.setTextFormat(tfFormatter);
```

6. Test the movie again. You should not see any text this time, because you have embedded the uppercase characters only for the Verdana font.

7. Open the Character Options dialog box for the authoring-time `TextField` once again. Set it to embed the lowercase letters instead.

8. Test the movie again. This time, you should see the text display in the Verdana font.

Using a Font Symbol

You can also embed a font using a Font symbol. On one hand, a font symbol allows you to use shared libraries and may be preferable in some situations. On the other hand, a font symbol requires that you embed the entire font. So, if you are using only a few characters, you may want to use an authoring-time `TextField` to embed just those specific characters.

The following are the basic steps for using a Font symbol:

1. Create a font symbol in the library, and set the symbol to export for ActionScript.

2. Set the `embedFonts` property for the `TextField` object to `true`.

3. Create a `TextFormat` object and assign the linkage identifier for the font symbol to the `TextFormat` object's `font` property.

4. Assign the `TextFormat` object to the `TextField`.

Let's take a closer look at some of the preceding steps with the following example.

1. Open the library and select the New Font from the library's menu.

2. In the Font Symbol Properties dialog box, give the symbol a name and select the font you want to embed.

3. After you've created the symbol, open the symbol's linkage settings, check the Export for ActionScript option, and give the symbol a linkage identifier.

The `embedFonts` property for a `TextField` object defaults to `false`. By setting the property to `true` you tell Flash to use only the specified embedded font (which you specify in the next step with a `TextFormat` object). If Flash is unable to find the specified embedded font then no text will display in that field.

```
tLabel.embedFonts = true;
```

To create a `TextFormat` object that uses the embedded font and assign the object to the `TextField`, complete the following steps:

1. Create a new `TextFormat` object with the constructor:

```
var tfFormatter:TextFormat = new TextFormat();
```

2. Assign the linkage identifier name to the `TextFormat` object's `font` property. For example, if you created a font symbol with linkage identifier `ArialEmbeddedFont`:

```
tfFormatter.font = "ArialEmbeddedFont";
```

3. Assign the `TextFormat` object to the `TextField` object with the `setTextFormat()` method:

```
tLabel.setTextFormat(tfFormatter);
```

Using Faux Bold and Italic Styles with Embedded Fonts

If you would like to use faux bold or italic style with an embedded font, you can select either option (or both options) in the Font Symbol Properties dialog box. However, each of these options creates specific font outlines to be generated and exported with your Flash movie (SWF file). For example, if you select the Bold check box for the Verdana font, you used in the last exercise, you can use only the following `TextFormat` object properties with your text fields. (Note that you can name your `TextFormat` object differently — you don't have to use the name `tfStyle`.)

```
var tfStyle:TextFormat = new TextFormat();
tfStyle.font = "Verdana";
tfStyle.bold = true;
tfStyle.size = 12;
tComments.setTextFormat(tfStyle);
```

If you omit the `bold` property, the text does not display in the `TextField` object. Likewise, if you select both the Bold and Italic check boxes in the Font Properties dialog box, you can use that font only if you have the `bold` and `italic` properties set to `true`.

```
var tfStyle:TextFormat = new TextFormat();
tfStyle.font = "Verdana";
tfStyle.bold = true;
tfStyle.italic = true;
tfStyle.size = 12;
tComments.setTextFormat(tfStyle);
```

If you want the option to use normal, faux bold, or faux italic styles, you need to create three separate font symbols in the Library panel — one for each style. If you want to use faux bold and faux italic together, you need to add a fourth font symbol that has both the Bold and Italic options selected. Remember, each font symbol must be set to export with the Flash movie (SWF file) to be used with ActionScript. Embedding so many fonts may be impractical for the file size requirements for your Flash movie. Make sure that you need to use these styles before you decide to include them.

Remember, as well, that these styles are *faux* bold and *faux* italic, meaning Flash makes a "best guess" at what a font should look like as bold or italic as it creates the outlines to be exported with the Flash movie. Most professional font faces have individual font files for these styles, such as Futura Oblique (oblique is another term used for italic) or Futura Bold. Instead of using faux bold or faux italic, you may want to embed an original font face designed for bold or italic formatting.

To minimize the added file size (in bytes) of font outlines in the final Flash movies, you may want to explore the use of Macromedia Fontographer to create custom font files that have only the characters you need to use with text fields in your specific project. Flash MX does not offer any font subset options for font symbols as it does for regular dynamic or input text fields in the Character Options dialog box (accessible from the Property inspector).

Using Flash Device Fonts

You can also opt to use three different font faces with unique Flash names. These fonts are listed at the very top (Windows) or very bottom (Macintosh) of the Font menu in the Property inspector. Alternatively, you can find them listed at the top of the Text ➪ Font menu in both Windows and Macintosh versions of Flash:

✦ `_sans` — This font choice uses the system's default sans serif font for displaying text in the specified field. A sans serif (meaning "without serif") typeface has of rounded corners on all characters — you usually don't find ornamental edges on sans serif typefaces. On Windows, the default sans serif font is Arial. On Macintosh, it's Helvetica. Sans serif typefaces are often called Gothic typefaces.

✦ `_serif` — This font choice uses the system's default serif font for displaying text in the specified field. A serif is a fine line used to complete the edges of characters in a typeface. The typeface used for this book is a serif font — notice the edges of characters such as *F* and *D* compared to the same letters as they appear in this section's title, which is a sans serif typeface The default system serif font on Windows is Times New Roman. On the Macintosh, it is Times.

✦ `_typewriter` — This font choice uses the system's default monospaced typeface for displaying text in the specified field. A monospaced typeface uses the same width for every character in the typeface. Most fonts are not monospaced — for example, the width required for a *W* is much greater than that required for *I*. On Windows, the default monospaced typeface is Courier New. On Macintosh, it is Courier.

When you use these device fonts, you do not want to use any of the font embedding controls in the Property inspector for the Text tool. Device fonts are commonly used to reduce the file size of Flash movies (SWF files) when an exact typeface is unnecessary for text within the movie. For example, although you may want to make sure that your company's logo uses the same typeface that you use in printed materials and signage, you may not need to use that font for a Flash form in which users type their contact information.

Caution Device fonts do not display text in editable text fields that are governed by Mask layers or that are transformed. For example, if you rotate a `TextField` object using a device font, you do not see any text displayed. Any changes in the Transform panel or the Color menu of the Property inspector for that instance render the text invisible.

Inserting Special Characters into Editable Text Fields

Some characters require special syntax in order to be displayed within an ActionScript-defined editable text field. For example, if you want to use ActionScript to set the value of a `TextField` object, you need to know how to insert carriage returns, quotation marks, and tabs into the string expression. Following is a list of special formatting characters you can use within ActionScript-assigned text. Most of them are *backslash pairs,* a term used by several scripting languages for special characters. Backslash pairs are always written *inline,* meaning that they are specified within the string itself. Backslash pairs are also called escape sequences.

✦ `newline, \n, \r` — `newline` is a Flash-specific operator that forces a carriage return within an editable text field. The `newline` operator is not used within the string expression. However, the backslash pair `\n` or `\r`, which always insert a carriage return, are written as part of the string expression.

✦ `\\` — If you need to insert a backslash character (\) into an editable text field via ActionScript, this backslash pair does it for you.

✦ \t — This backslash pair inserts a Tab character into the field. This is actually something you *can't* do manually within an editable text field.

✦ \" — This pair inserts a double-quotation mark character within a string.

✦ \' — This pair inserts a single quotation mark into the string used for the editable text field.

Note   Although their use may be isolated and rare, you can use other escape sequences, such as \b for a backspace character or \f for a form-feed character. Also, you can specify bytes in octal (\000–\377), hexadecimal (\x00–\xFF), or a 16-bit Unicode character in hexadecimal (\u0000–\uFFFF).

To use these special formatting sequences, simply place them in the string expression that you write for the editable text field. For example, if you created a `TextField` instance named `tArticle` and created an action on frame 1 of the current timeline as follows:

```
tArticle.text = "Part I" + newline + "This is how it began.";
```

this code displays the text in the field like this:

```
Part I
This is how it began.
```

You could also write this code with the following syntax:

```
tArticle.text = "Part I\rThis is how it began.";
```

Even though this syntax appears to create one term, `I\rThis`, ActionScript interprets the backslash pair correctly and displays the text in the field as follows:

```
Part I
This is how it began.
```

Caution   These sequences should not be typed into the actual editable text field on the Flash stage. You use these sequences only in ActionScript.

Working with Advanced Anti-Aliasing

Flash Player 8 has a new text engine, and you if you publish to Flash 8, you can use advanced anti-aliasing features. When you set a text field to use advanced anti-aliasing, you can specify how the text is rendered to the pixel grid, you can manage sharpness, and you can adjust the thickness of fonts.

Setting the Anti-Aliasing Type

You can set the anti-aliasing type of a `TextField` object using the `antiAliasType` property. The property has two valid values — `normal` and `advanced`. The `normal` setting is the traditional type of anti-aliasing. With the `normal` setting, you cannot use the `gridFitType`, `sharpness`, and `thickness` properties described in the following sections. The `advanced` settings only work when you set the `antiAliasType` property to `advanced`.

Setting `antiAliasType` to `advanced` only works if the font is embedded. If you have not embedded the font, the setting will have no visible effect. If the font is embedded, the `advanced` settings typically works well for smaller font sizes. As the font gets smaller, it can be less legible. By using advanced anti-aliasing settings, you can adjust the font to make it more readable. The default settings of the `advanced` settings typically make smaller fonts more legible even without any further adjustment, as is illustrated by the following example. The example requires that you've embedded Times New Roman using the dynamic text field technique. Each time you click on the stage, the text's `antiAliasType` property toggles between `normal` and `advanced`.

```
this.createTextField("tField", this.getNextHighestDepth(), 0, 0, 550, 400);
tField.wordWrap = true;
tField.multiline = true;
tField.selectable = false;

// Embed the font.
tField.embedFonts = true;

tField.antiAliasType = "advanced";

// Use a TextFormat object to specify the font and to make the font size
// 10 point.
var tfFormatter:TextFormat = new TextFormat();
tfFormatter.font = "Times New Roman";
tfFormatter.size = 10;

// Load the text.
var lvText:LoadVars = new LoadVars();
lvText.onData = function(sText:String):Void {
  tField.text = sText;
  tField.setTextFormat(tfFormatter);
};
lvText.load("http://www.person13.com/asb/lorem_ipsum.txt");

// Each time the user clicks on the stage, toggle the antiAliasType value.
function onMouseDown():Void {
  tField.antiAliasType = (tField.antiAliasType == "normal") ?
"advanced" : "normal";
  trace(tField.antiAliasType);
}
```

Setting the Grid Fit Type

The `gridFitType` property lets you specify how the text ought to be rendered relative to the pixels on the monitor. The property has the following possible string values:

✦ `none` — When the value is set to `none`, the fonts are not snapped to the pixel grid. Typically, at smaller point sizes fonts will look blurrier when `gridFitType` is set to `none`.

✦ `pixel` — When the value is set to `pixel`, Flash snaps vertical and horizontal lines within the font to whole pixels. That can cause the text to appear more legible at smaller point sizes when the text is left-aligned. If the text is not left-aligned it will not necessarily look any more legible.

✦ `subpixel` — The `subpixel` setting is for LCD displays. LCD displays have red, green, and blue subpixels for each pixel. Flash will snap vertical and horizontal lines to subpixels.

The following code illustrates the effects of the `gridFitType` property. Much of the code is similar to the example in the preceding section. The changes are bolded.

```
this.createTextField("tField", this.getNextHighestDepth(), 0, 0, 550, 400);
tField.wordWrap = true;
tField.multiline = true;
tField.selectable = false;
tField.embedFonts = true;
tField.antiAliasType = "advanced";

var tfFormatter:TextFormat = new TextFormat();
tfFormatter.font = "Times New Roman";
tfFormatter.size = 10;

var lvText:LoadVars = new LoadVars();
lvText.onData = function(sText:String):Void {
  tField.text = sText;
  tField.setTextFormat(tfFormatter);
};
lvText.load("http://www.person13.com/asb/lorem_ipsum.txt");

function onMouseDown():Void {
  // Set the gridFitType property.
  switch(tField.gridFitType) {
    case "none":
      tField.gridFitType = "pixel";
      break;
    case "pixel":
      tField.gridFitType = "subpixel";
      break;
    case "subpixel":
      tField.gridFitType = "none";
      break;
  }
  trace(tField.gridFitType);
}
```

Setting Sharpness

The sharpness property determines the blurriness of the edges of the font. The range of values is from -400 (blurriest) to 400 (sharpest). The following example illustrates the effect. As with the other examples in this section, the following example requires that the Times New Roman font is embedded. The code is similar to the preceding example, and the changes are bolded.

```
this.createTextField("tField", this.getNextHighestDepth(), 0, 0, 550, 400);
tField.wordWrap = true;
tField.multiline = true;
tField.selectable = false;
tField.embedFonts = true;
tField.antiAliasType = "advanced";

var tfFormatter:TextFormat = new TextFormat();
tfFormatter.font = "Times New Roman";
```

```
tfFormatter.size = 10;

var lvText:LoadVars = new LoadVars();
lvText.onData = function(sText:String):Void {
  tField.text = sText;
  tField.setTextFormat(tfFormatter);
};
lvText.load("http://www.person13.com/asb/lorem_ipsum.txt");

function onMouseDown():Void {
  // Increment the sharpness by 40. If the sharpness is greater than 400 then
  // jump to -400.
  tField.sharpness += 40;
  if(tField.sharpness > 400) {
    tField.sharpness = -400;
  }
  trace(tField.sharpness);
}
```

Setting the Thickness of a Font

The thickness property determines the width of the edges of the font. The valid range is from -200 (least thick) to 200 (thickest). The following example is much like the previous examples in this section, and uses much of the same code. AS with the other examples, you must embed Times New Roman for the code to work. Changes from the previous example are bolded.

```
this.createTextField("tField", this.getNextHighestDepth(), 0, 0, 550, 400);
tField.wordWrap = true;
tField.multiline = true;
tField.selectable = false;
tField.embedFonts = true;
tField.antiAliasType = "advanced";

var tfFormatter:TextFormat = new TextFormat();
tfFormatter.font = "Times New Roman";
tfFormatter.size = 10;

var lvText:LoadVars = new LoadVars();
lvText.onData = function(sText:String):Void {
  tField.text = sText;
  tField.setTextFormat(tfFormatter);
};
lvText.load("http://www.rightactionscript.com/samplefiles/lorem_ipsum.txt");

function onMouseDown():Void {
  // Increment the thickness property by 20. If it is greater than 200 then
  // cycle to -200;
  tField.thickness += 20;
  if(tField.thickness > 200) {
    tField.thickness = -200;
  }
  trace(tField.thickness);
}
```

Creating a Random Letter Displayer

In this exercise, you'll create an interesting effect that fades letters in and out randomly across the stage. Because the effect relies on modifying the _alpha property value of the TextField objects, you'll need to embed the font.

1. Open a new Flash document and save it as randomLetters.fla.

2. Rename the default layer as Embedded Font, and add a new layer named actions.

3. Using the Text tool, add an authoring-time dynamic TextField object offstage on the Embedded Font layer.

4. With the TextField object selected, use the drop-down list to change the font to Verdana and then click the Character button in the Property inspector to open the Character Embedding dialog box.

5. Choose the Specify Ranges option, and enter the value abcdef in the Include These Characters field.

6. Click OK to exit the Character Options dialog box.

7. Add the following code to the first frame of the actions layer.

```
// Create the array of letters.
var aLetters:Array = ["a", "b", "c", "d", "e", "f"];

// Set the interval at which a new letter should be displayed.
var nDisplayInterval:Number = setInterval(this, "displayLetter", 1);

// Define an associative array to store data about each letter.
var oLetters:Object = new Object();

function displayLetter():Void {

  // Create a random integer to yield one of the indices from the
  // aLetters array.
  var nRandomIndex:Number = Math.floor(Math.random() * aLetters.length);

  // Create random numbers to use for the x and y coordinates of
  // the letter TextField.
  var nRandomX:Number = Math.random() * 550;
  var nRandomY:Number = Math.random() * 400;

  // Get the next available depth.
  var nDepth:Number = this.getNextHighestDepth();

  // Create a new TextField object at the random x and y
  // coordinates.
  var tLetter:TextField = this.createTextField("tLetter" + nDepth,
nDepth, nRandomX, nRandomY, 0, 0);

  // Set the autoSize and text properties so the random letter
  // displays.
```

```
tLetter.autoSize = "left";

// Set the text.
tLetter.text = aLetters[nRandomIndex];

// Initialize the _alpha property to 0.
tLetter._alpha = 0;

// Tell Flash to embed the font for the TextField.
tLetter.embedFonts = true;

// Define a new object into which to store some data for the letter.
var oLetter:Object = new Object();

// Assign the object to the oLetters associative array using the instance name
// of the TextField object as the key.
oLetters[tLetter._name] = oLetter;

// Set a element called fadeDirection that determines
// the increment by which the alpha will change. And set the
// alpha to 0 initially.
oLetter.fadeDirection = 5;

// Define an element that references the TextField.
oLetter.letterField = tLetter;

// Create a TextFormat object that tells Flash to use the
// Verdana font and set the size to 15.
var tfFormatter:TextFormat = new TextFormat();
tfFormatter.font = "Verdana";
tfFormatter.size = 15;

// Assign the TextFormat to the TextField.
tLetter.setTextFormat(tfFormatter);

// Set an interval at which the letter will fade in and out. Assign the ID
// to a property of the oLetter object so we can clear it later. Pass the
// alphaFade() function a reference to the oLetter object.
oLetter.interval = setInterval(alphaFade, 10, oLetter);
}

function alphaFade(oLetter:Object):Void {

// Retrieve the TextField object reference.
var tLetter:TextField = oLetter.letterField;

// Increment the letter TextField's alpha.
tLetter._alpha += oLetter.fadeDirection;

// Check to see if the letter has faded in completely. If so
// set the fadeDirection property to -5 so that the TextField
```

```
// starts to fade out. Otherwise, if the letter has faded out
// completely clear the interval and remove the TextField.
if(oLetter.fadeDirection > 0 && tLetter._alpha >= 100) {
  oLetter.fadeDirection = -5;
}
else if(oLetter.fadeDirection < 0 && tLetter._alpha <= 0) {
  clearInterval(oLetter.interval);
  delete oLetters[tLetter._name];
  tLetter.removeTextField();
}

// Make sure to update the screen.
updateAfterEvent();
}
```

   8. Test the movie.

Understanding the Selection Class

The `Selection` class can help you control focus and selection within your Flash application. `TextField`, `MovieClip`, and `Button` objects can receive focus, but selection only applies to `TextField` objects. You take a closer look at focus and selection in the following sections.

The methods of the `Selection` class are static. That means that you do not need to instantiate the class. Instead, you should call all methods directly from the class itself.

Working with Focus

Focus is a term used in many scripting languages to describe which part of the application is active and responds to the keyboard. For example, with web browser windows, the foreground window is usually the focused one, meaning that actions such as keyboard input are received by that window, and not another. The same thing applies to Flash applications. A `Button`, `MovieClip`, or `TextField` object can receive focus within Flash. For example, when a user uses the mouse to click within a `TextField` instance, she brings focus to that instance. Once the object has focus, the user can enter text.

Determining Focus

The `getFocus()` method returns the full path (as a string) to the currently focused `TextField`, `Button`, or `MovieClip` object. If there isn't any object with focus, a `null` value is returned. For example, if a text field named `tUsername` on the main timeline is active, `Selection.getFocus()` returns `_level0.tUsername` as a string. Usually, this method is used to assign a value to a variable that stores the path information. You'll see this usage in later examples.

Note   If a `TextField` object has both a variable and an instance name assigned, `getFocus()` returns the path with the instance name. If only a variable name is specified, `getFocus()` returns the path with the variable name.

Setting Focus

The setFocus() method brings the focus to the object specified as the parameter. The parameter should be the path (relative or absolute) as a string to a MovieClip, Button, or TextField object. If the object to which you are bringing focus is a TextField object, then Flash will also display the I-beam cursor within that instance.

The following example creates a new TextField object and brings focus to it:

```
this.createTextField("tUsername", this.getNextHighestDepth(), 25, 25, 150, 20);
tUsername.border = true;
tUsername.type = "input";
Selection.setFocus("tUsername");
```

Listening for Focus Changes

You can add listener objects to the Selection class to be notified when focus changes occur. To add a listener object, use the Selection.addListener() method. For example, the following registers a new listener named oListener:

```
Selection.addListener(oListener);
```

And to remove a listener, use the Selection.removeListener() method:

```
Selection.removeListener(oListener);
```

When focus changes occur, the Selection class notifies all registered listeners and calls their onSetFocus() method. The onSetFocus() method is automatically passed two parameters — a reference to the object that previously had focus and the object that has just received focus. The following is an example:

```
var oFocusListener:Object = new Object();
oFocusListener.onSetFocus = function(oPrevFocus:Object, oNewFocus:Object):Void {
  trace("Current focus = " + oNewFocus);
  trace("Previous focus = " + oPrevFocus);
};
Selection.addListener(oFocusListener);
```

Working with Selection

A *selection* is the range of characters within a TextField object that is highlighted. Anytime you click and highlight characters within text, you make a selection. You can also make a selection programmatically, as you'll see in just a moment. In input text, you can also insert the I-beam cursor at any position within the field. This position is known as the *caret*. With ActionScript and the Selection class, you can retrieve the current value of the caret's position, the current position value of the beginning of a selection, and the position value of the end of a selection. You can also use ActionScript to enable automated selections (or highlights) within a text field.

Note   All methods of the Selection class work with zero-based indices.

Note that all of the `Selection` class's methods for working with the selection and caret do not require you to specify the `TextField` object for which you wish to set or retrieve the selection. Because there can be only one selection made at a time, the `TextField` object that currently has focus is automatically used. As you have already learned, a `TextField` object can receive focus by user interaction or by programmatic means.

Getting the Current Selection

A selection has a beginning and an ending point that are given by the respective indices within the focused `TextField`. To retrieve the indices you can use the `Selection.getBeginIndex()` and `Selection.getEndIndex()` methods.

The `Selection.getBeginIndex()` method returns the starting index of a selection. If there is no selection, the method returns -1. The `Selection.getEndIndex()` method returns the index of the position immediately after the last character of the selection. If there is no selection when this method is called, the method returns -1.

You can test these methods with the following code:

```
this.createTextField("tOutput", this.getNextHighestDepth(), 100, 100, 200, 200);
tOutput.border = true;
tOutput.multiline = true;
tOutput.wordWrap = true;
tOutput.text = "The Selection class enables you to retrieve the selected     ⊃
   text programmatically.";
this.onMouseUp = function():Void {
  trace(Selection.getBeginIndex() + " " + Selection.getEndIndex());
};
```

When you test the preceding code, highlight some of the text, and release the mouse click, the beginning and ending indices of the selection are displayed in the Output panel.

Often you are likely to use the selection indices in conjunction with the `substring()` and/or `substr()` methods of the `String` class. For example, the following code is a slight variation (changes shown in bold) on the previous code in which the current selection is displayed in the Output panel instead of just the indices:

```
this.createTextField("tOutput", this.getNextHighestDepth(), 100, 100, 200, 200);
tOutput.border = true;
tOutput.multiline = true;
tOutput.wordWrap = true;
tOutput.text = "The Selection class enables you to retrieve the selected     ⊃
   text programmatically.";
this.onMouseUp = function():Void {
  trace(tOutput.text.substring(Selection.getBeginIndex(),               ⊃
   Selection.getEndIndex()));
};
```

Setting the Selection

In addition to retrieving the selection, you can also programmatically set the selection by calling the `Selection.setSelection()` method. The method requires two parameters — integers specifying the beginning and ending indices. The beginning index is the index of the first character in the selection, and the ending index is the index just following the last character.

Often, the `Selection.setSelection()` method is used in conjunction with the `Selection.setFocus()` method. Remember that the `Selection.setSelection()` is applied to the `TextField` that currently has focus, so it is generally the case that you will want to programmatically bring focus to the `TextField` first. The following code creates a `TextField` object; when you click and release the mouse, the word "set" is highlighted.

```
this.createTextField("tOutput", this.getNextHighestDepth(), 100, 100, 200, 200);
tOutput.border = true;
tOutput.multiline = true;
tOutput.wordWrap = true;
tOutput.selectable = false;
tOutput.text = "The Selection class also enables you to set the selected ↩
  text programmatically.";
this.onMouseUp = function():Void {
  Selection.setFocus("tOutput");
  Selection.setSelection(40, 43);
};
```

Working with the Caret

You can get and set the caret within a `TextField` object programmatically as well. The `getCaretIndex()` method returns the current index of the I-beam cursor. If there is no active I-beam cursor, this method returns -1.

You can set the caret with the `setSelection()` method. Just set the beginning and ending indices to the same value.

Replacing Selected Text

This `replaceSel()` method of the `TextField` class replaces the active selection with the value specified as the method's parameter. Because a selection must be the current focus in order for this method to work, you will likely use this method in combination with listeners attached to either the `Mouse` or `Selection` object.

Note   Remember that you cannot have focus in two places at once. In other words, you can't use the `replaceSel()` method to enable a user to select some text and then click a button or other user interface element to change the text — as soon as the user clicks the button, the selection (and focus) on the text field is lost.

The following code replaces the selected text (or index) within a `TextField` object named `tArticle` with the contents of a field named `tWord`. The replacement occurs whenever the user clicks and releases the mouse and focus is on the `tArticle` field.

```
this.createTextField("tArticle", this.getNextHighestDepth(), 100, 25, 200, 100);
this.createTextField("tWord", this.getNextHighestDepth(), 25, 25, 50, 20);
tArticle.border = true;
tWord.border = true;
tWord.type = "input";
tArticle.text = "This is some text in a text field.";
var oListener:Object = new Object();
oListener.onMouseUp = function(){
  if(Selection.getFocus().indexOf("tArticle") != -1){
```

```
    tArticle.replaceSel(tWord.text);
    Selection.setFocus(null);
  }
};
Mouse.addListener(oListener);
```

Working with Tab Order

When working with `TextField` objects, you may want to consider how focus is brought to them via the Tab key. Standard computing practices allow the user to change focus using the Tab key, and by default `TextField` objects are enabled to accept focus in that way. You can, however, enable and disable that functionality as well as specify the order in which `TextField` objects should receive focus when the Tab key is pressed.

Enabling and Disabling Tab-Initiated Focus

You can use the `tabEnabled` property to determine whether pressing the Tab key can bring focus to the text. By default the property is `true`, meaning that the instance can receive focus initiated by pressing the Tab key. Typically, input text should be Tab-enabled. But dynamic text likely should not be Tab-enabled.

Changing Tab Order

The `tabIndex` property allows you to determine the order in which objects are accessed with the Tab key. Any positive integer can be used for the value of the `tabIndex` property. Lower numbers are accessed in ascending order — an object with a `tabIndex` value of 1 is the first object that will be focused before an object with a `tabIndex` value of 2. As soon as you've assigned a `tabIndex` value to any object currently visible on the stage, the Tab order is determined solely by the `tabIndex` values for the visible objects. If an object does not have a `tabIndex` property value, it is not included in the sequence.

The following code creates three input `TextField` objects. The `tEmail` and `tPostalCode` objects are assigned `tabIndex` property values, whereas the `tComments` object is not. If you test the code, you'll see that you can use the Tab key to change focus between `tEmail` and `tPostalCode`. However, to bring focus to the `tComments` field you have to click in the field.

```
this.createTextField("tEmail", 1, 25, 35, 100, 20);
tEmail.border = true;
tEmail.type = "input";
tEmail.tabIndex = 1;

this.createTextField("tPostalCode", 2, 150, 35, 200, 20);
tPostalCode.border = true;
tPostalCode.type = "input";
tPostalCode.tabIndex = 2;

this.createTextField("tComments", 3, 25, 75, 325, 200);
tComments.border = true;
tComments.type = "input";
```

If you append the following line of code to the preceding, you can see that by setting the tabIndex property for tComments, tComments is included in the sequence:

```
tComments.tabIndex = 3;
```

Cross-Reference

TextField, MovieClip, and Button objects have the tabIndex property. For more information, read the coverage of tabIndex in Chapter 13.

Web Resource

We'd like to know what you thought about this chapter. Visit www.rightactionscript .com/asb/comments to fill out an online form with your comments.

Summary

✦ Text in Flash is classified as static, dynamic, or input. Dynamic text and input text are the types of text you'll work with when using ActionScript.

✦ You can create TextField objects at authoring time using the Text tool or at runtime using the createTextField() method.

✦ Using the basic properties of the TextField class, you can control the aspects of an object such as the text that is displayed, word wrapping, text color, and more.

✦ Flash text can render some HTML tags, enabling you to add formatting and hyperlinks and even to embed content.

✦ You can scroll text vertically and horizontally using the built-in scrolling properties.

✦ Focus refers to the active portion of an application. You can get and set focus within a Flash application using the Selection.getFocus() and Selection.setFocus() methods.

✦ The Selection class also enables you to get and set the selected text within the focused TextField object.

✦ Using the tabEnabled and tabIndex properties you can determine how the Tab key affects focus within the application.

✦ ✦ ✦

Formatting Text

In the preceding chapter, you learned all about working with text with ActionScript. In this chapter, you'll look at how you can use ActionScript to then format that text. Although you have already seen how you could use HTML to apply some basic formatting to your text, this chapter discusses how you can apply more detailed formatting using the TextFormat and StyleSheet classes.

Working with TextFormat

You can use the TextFormat class to apply formatting to TextField objects' contents for Flash 6+ applications. The TextFormat class enables you to specify the following formatting options:

✦ Alignment

✦ Margins

✦ Indentation

✦ Block indentation

✦ Tab stops

✦ Line spacing (called "leading")

✦ Bolded text

✦ Italicized text

✦ Underlined text

✦ Bullet points

✦ Text color

✦ Font face

✦ Font size

✦ Hyperlinks and target windows

You can adjust the formatting options for part or all of the content of a TextField object.

Creating a TextFormat Object

One of the obvious things that you need to do before you can apply any formatting is create the TextFormat object that you'll use. You can create a TextFormat object with the constructor. The most common way is to call the constructor with no parameters. For example:

```
var tfFormatter:TextFormat = new TextFormat();
```

Once you've defined a TextFormat object in the preceding manner, you can define the values for its properties as discussed in subsequent sections.

The TextFormat constructor also enables you to define some of the object's properties as you create the object. Frankly, this option is rarely used because it is difficult to remember the parameter order and because you must specify all 13 parameters to use it. However, if you find it useful, you can create a TextFormat object in the following way:

```
var tfFormatter:TextFormat = new TextFormat(font, size,
color, bold, italic, underline, url, target, align,
leftMargin, rightMargin, indent, leading);
```

If you prefer not to assign a specific value, you can use null. The following code creates a tfTitle object that uses Verdana font face at 15 point. The text is centered and underlined. The text is blue, and it links to http://www.person13.com/asb web site. It uses default margins, indentation, and leading settings.

```
var tfTitle:TextFormat = new TextFormat("Verdana", 15,
0x0000FF, null, null, true, "http://www.person13.com/asb",
"_blank", "center", null, null, null, null);
```

As you can see, that syntax can be somewhat cumbersome because you have to remember the correct order for the parameters. You might prefer the following syntax in order to accomplish the same thing:

```
var tfTitle:TextFormat = new TextFormat();
tfTitle.font = "Verdana";
tfTitle.size = 15;
tfTitle.color = 0x0000FF;
tfTitle.align = "center";
tfTitle.underline = true;
tfTitle.url = "http://www.person13.com/asb";
tfTitle.target = "_blank";
```

Also notice that you cannot specify block indentation and tab stops in the constructor. You must specify those values as properties. You can modify the properties of a TextFormat object subsequent to instantiating it regardless of which constructor you use.

Assigning Formatting to a TextField Object

Once you have created a TextFormat object, the next step is to apply that formatting to a TextField object's contents. You can accomplish that with the setTextFormat() method of the TextField object to which you want to add the formatting. Using the setTextFormat() method you can add formatting to the entire contents, a single character, or a range of characters. Let's take a look at these options:

✦ `setTextFormat(TextFormat object)` — This usage applies the properties of the specified `TextFormat` object to the entire contents of the `TextField` object from which the methods are called.

✦ `setTextFormat(index, TextFormat object)` — This syntax applies the `TextFormat` object properties to a specific character within the field. Each character is numerically indexed starting at 0. So, to apply the formatting to the first character, you use the value of 0 for the first parameter.

✦ `setTextFormat(beginIndex, endIndex, TextFormat object)` — This syntax applies the `TextFormat` object properties to a specific range of characters within the field.

Now that you've had a chance to see the theory, let's take a look at a few practical examples that use the `setTextFormat()` method in various ways.

First, the following code creates a `TextField` object, displays some text within it, and applies bold formatting to the entire text:

```
this.createTextField("tOutput", this.getNextHighestDepth(), 100, 100, 100, 20);
tOutput.text = "Formatted text";
var tfFormatter:TextFormat = new TextFormat();
tfFormatter.bold = true;
tOutput.setTextFormat(tfFormatter);
```

If you change the last line of code as follows, the bold formatting is applied only to the first letter:

```
tOutput.setTextFormat(0, tfFormatter);
```

And if you change the last line again to the following code, the bold formatting is applied only to the second word:

```
tOutput.setTextFormat(10, 14, tfFormatter);
```

The formatting that you apply to the `TextField` object is removed if and when you change the value of the object's `text` property. That means you need to reapply the formatting when you change the text content programmatically. For example:

```
this.createTextField("tOutput", this.getNextHighestDepth(), 100, 100, 100, 20);
tOutput.text = "Formatted text";
var tfFormatter:TextFormat = new TextFormat();
tfFormatter.bold = true;
tOutput.setTextFormat(tfFormatter);
tOutput.text = "New text";
tOutput.setTextFormat(tfFormatter);
```

It is also very important to note that changes you make to the `TextFormat` object are not applied to the `TextField` object until you reapply the `TextFormat` to the `TextField`. For example, the following code causes the text to appear bolded but not underlined:

```
this.createTextField("tOutput", this.getNextHighestDepth(), 100, 100, 100, 20);
tOutput.text = "Formatted text";
var tfFormatter:TextFormat = new TextFormat();
tfFormatter.bold = true;
tOutput.setTextFormat(tfFormatter);
tfFormatter.underline = true;
```

In order to get the underline setting to take effect, you need to call the `setTextFormat()` method again to reapply the formatting:

```
this.createTextField("tOutput", this.getNextHighestDepth(), 100, 100, 100, 20);
tOutput.text = "Formatted text";
var tfFormatter:TextFormat = new TextFormat();
tfFormatter.bold = true;
tOutput.setTextFormat(tfFormatter);
tfFormatter.underline = true;
tOutput.setTextFormat(tfFormatter);
```

Obviously, the preceding example, as is, is not something you would encounter in an actual application. Instead, you simply set the bold and underline properties prior to calling the `setTextFormat()` method the first time. However, consider the scenario in which the bold and underline properties are updated via user interaction. Each time the user changes the setting, you need to reapply the formatting.

The `setTextFormat()` method works only for text that is assigned programmatically. However, it will not apply formatting to new text as the user is entering it. Instead, you use the `setNewTextFormat()` method to tell Flash what formatting to apply to any new text that the user enters. Unlike `setTextFormat()`, the `setNewTextFormat()` method has only one usage syntax. You need only pass it the reference to the `TextFormat` object. You don't need to specify any indices because the formatting with `setNewTextFormat()` is applied only to new text entered by the user at the end of any existing text.

The following shows an example that creates an input `TextField` object and applies formatting so that any user-input text is bolded:

```
this.createTextField("tInput", this.getNextHighestDepth(), 100, 100, 100, 20);
tInput.type = "input";
tInput.border = true;
var tfFormatter:TextFormat = new TextFormat();
tfFormatter.bold = true;
tInput.setNewTextFormat(tfFormatter);
```

Understanding Formatting Properties

The `TextFormat` class has 16 properties that you can use to apply various formatting to `TextField` object content. The following sections detail each of these properties.

Additionally, on the web site is `TextFormattingExample.fla`, a Flash document that allows you to change many of the formatting properties of some text to see the effects.

align

You can use the `align` property to place the text relative to the right and left edges of the `TextField` object's bounding box. The property can have the following values:

✦ `left` — This value places the text such that the left side of the text is against the left side of bounding box.

✦ `right` — This value places the text such that the right side of the text is against the right side of the bounding box.

✦ center — This value places the text such that the center of the text is aligned with the center of the bounding box.

✦ justify — New in Flash Player 8, you can use a value of justify so that the text fits the width of each line, adjusting spacing per line as necessary.

✦ null — The null value is the default value and it resolves to the same thing as a value of left.

The following code creates text aligned to the center.

```
this.createTextField("tContent", this.getNextHighestDepth(),
                     100, 100, 200, 200);
tContent.multiline = true;
tContent.border = true;
tContent.wordWrap = true;
tContent.text = "center-aligned text";
var tfFormatter:TextFormat = new TextFormat();
tfFormatter.align = "center";
tContent.setTextFormat(tfFormatter);
```

blockIndent

The blockIndent property has an effect on text only when the text is aligned left. In that case, the blockIndent property indents the entire block of text inward relative to the left margin. The value should be a number indicating the points value by which you want to indent the text.

Note   The blockIndent property indents the entire block of text. To indent just the first line of text in a paragraph, use the indent property instead.

The following code creates text that is indented as a block:

```
this.createTextField("tContent", this.getNextHighestDepth(),100, 100, 200, 200);
tContent.multiline = true;
tContent.border = true;
tContent.wordWrap = true;
tContent.text = "a few lines\nof text\nthat are indented\nas a block";
var tfFormatter:TextFormat = new TextFormat();
tfFormatter.blockIndent = 10;
tContent.setTextFormat(tfFormatter);
```

bold

The bold property applies faux bold formatting to the targeted text. To turn bold formatting on, use a Boolean value of true. To turn bold off, use a Boolean value of false. By default, this property is defined with a null value, which produces the same effect as false.

bullet

The bullet property adds a bullet character (•) in front of the text if the property's value is set to true. You can turn off bullet formatting by assigning a false value to the property. By default, this property has a value of null. The font face used for the bullet character is the same as that defined for other text in the TextFormat object (via the font property, discussed later). The bullet points are placed 19 pixels from the left margin of the field, affected only by the left margin settings. (Properties such as `blockIndent` don't have an effect when bullet points are used.) The bulleted text is spaced 15 pixels to the right of the bullet point.

> **Caution**
>
> The built-in spacing provided for bullets remains the same, regardless of font size. Be careful if you are using bullets with large sizes, such as 72 pt. The bullet can appear too close to the actual text. In this case, you might want to avoid the `bullet` property and simply specify a bullet character in the expression used for the `text` or `htmlText` property of the `TextField` object.

The following code displays a list of bulleted text:

```
this.createTextField("tContent", this.getNextHighestDepth(),100, 100, 200, 200);
tContent.multiline = true;
tContent.border = true;
tContent.wordWrap = true;
tContent.text = "a\nb\nc\nd";
var tfFormatter:TextFormat = new TextFormat();
tfFormatter.bullet = true;
tContent.setTextFormat(tfFormatter);
```

color

As the name implies, the `color` property controls the font color of the targeted text. The value for this property should be numeric. The following code displays red text:

```
this.createTextField("tContent", this.getNextHighestDepth(),100, 100, 200, 200);
tContent.multiline = true;
tContent.border = true;
tContent.wordWrap = true;
tContent.text = "red text";
var tfFormatter:TextFormat = new TextFormat();
tfFormatter.color = 0xFF0000;
tContent.setTextFormat(tfFormatter);
```

> **Caution**
>
> Do not attempt to use string values (such as `"0xFF0000"`) with the `color` property. If you have a string representation of a hexadecimal value that you want to use with the `color` property, convert the string expression into a number value using the `parseInt()` function.

font

The `font` property controls the font face used for the text. This property uses a string value, indicating the name of the font. The name that you use can depend on how you are working with the font in Flash. If you are not embedding the font or if you have embedded the font using an authoring-time `TextField` object, use the name of the font as it displayed in the Font menu of the Property inspector. If you have embedded the font, but you did so using a Font symbol, use the Font symbol's linkage identifier.

By default, the `font` property has a value of `null`, which results in the default font being used. The font face can be applied only if the user has the font installed on his/her system or if the font has been embedded or shared with the Flash movie.

The following code displays the text formatted with the Verdana font face:

```
this.createTextField("tContent", this.getNextHighestDepth(),100, 100, 200, 200);
tContent.multiline = true;
tContent.border = true;
tContent.wordWrap = true;
tContent.text = "Verdana text";
var tfFormatter:TextFormat = new TextFormat();
tfFormatter.font = "Verdana";
tContent.setTextFormat(tfFormatter);
```

Cross-Reference For more information on the use of embedded fonts with `TextField` and `TextFormat` objects, refer to Chapter 19.

You might want to use the `TextField.getFontList()` method in conjunction with the `font` property of a `TextFormat` object. The `TextField.getFontList()` method is a static method that returns an array of the fonts available on the client computer.

Web Resource For an example of how to use the `TextField.getFontList()` method to allow the user to select a font, see the example file called `TextFormattingExample.fla` on the web site.

indent

The `indent` property controls the spacing applied from the left margin to the first line of text within a paragraph. A *paragraph* is defined as any text that precedes a carriage return (such as `\r`). This property uses pixel units. The default value is `null`. The following code indents the text by 10 pixels:

```
this.createTextField("tContent", this.getNextHighestDepth(),100, 100, 200, 200);
tContent.multiline = true;
tContent.border = true;
tContent.wordWrap = true;
tContent.text = "When you have several lines of text, ";
tContent.text += "and you have set the indent value to a positive ";
tContent.text += "integer, the first line will appear indented.";
var tfFormatter:TextFormat = new TextFormat();
tfFormatter.indent = 10;
tContent.setTextFormat(tfFormatter);
```

italic

The `italic` property controls whether the targeted text uses faux italic formatting. If the property is set to `true`, the text appears in italic. If the property is set to `false`, the text appears normal. By default, this property has a value of `null`, which achieves the same effect as a value of `false`.

leading

The `leading` property controls the spacing inserted between each line of text. The values for this property are pixel-based. By default, the value of this property is `null`. You cannot programmatically set the leading value to be a negative number.

The following code inserts 10 pixels of space between each line of text:

```
this.createTextField("tContent", this.getNextHighestDepth(),100, 100, 200, 200);
tContent.multiline = true;
tContent.border = true;
tContent.wordWrap = true;
tContent.text = "When you have several lines of text, ";
tContent.text += "and you have set the leading value to a positive ";
tContent.text += "integer, the spacing between the lines changes."
var tfFormatter:TextFormat = new TextFormat();
tfFormatter.leading = 10;
tContent.setTextFormat(tfFormatter);
```

leftMargin

The `leftMargin` property determines the spacing (in pixels) inserted between the text and the left border of the `TextField` object. By default, the value of this property is `null`, which achieves the same effect as a value of 0. The following code creates a left margin of 10 pixels.

```
this.createTextField("tContent", this.getNextHighestDepth(),100, 100, 200, 200);
tContent.multiline = true;
tContent.border = true;
tContent.wordWrap = true;
tContent.text = "Left margin";
var tfFormatter:TextFormat = new TextFormat();
tfFormatter.leftMargin = 10;
tContent.setTextFormat(tfFormatter);
```

The `blockIndent` and `leftMargin` properties affect the text offset on the left side in a cumulative manner.

rightMargin

The `rightMargin` property controls the spacing (in pixels) inserted between the text and the right border of the `TextField` object. By default, the value of this property is `null`.

The following code illustrates the effect of the `rightMargin` property:

```
this.createTextField("tContent", this.getNextHighestDepth(),100, 100, 200, 200);
tContent.multiline = true;
tContent.border = true;
tContent.wordWrap = true;
tContent.text = "Right margin text that wraps to the next line";
var tfFormatter:TextFormat = new TextFormat();
tfFormatter.rightMargin = 10;
tContent.setTextFormat(tfFormatter);
```

size

The `size` property determines the size (in points) of the text. Remember that when a value is given in points it will display differently depending on the font face used. Therefore, the actual pixel size for two font faces can differ even if the point size is the same.

The following code creates text that displays with a point size of 20:

```
this.createTextField("tContent", this.getNextHighestDepth(),100, 100, 200, 200);
tContent.multiline = true;
tContent.border = true;
tContent.wordWrap = true;
tContent.text = "Some text";
var tfFormatter:TextFormat = new TextFormat();
tfFormatter.size = 20;
tContent.setTextFormat(tfFormatter);
```

tabStops

The `tabStops` property defines a custom array specifying the values used by tabs within the text. The first element of the array specifies the spacing (in points) to use for the first tab character in succession. The second element specifies the spacing to use for the second tab character in succession, and so on. The value of the last element in the array is used for all subsequent tab characters. For example, if the `tabStops` array has three elements — 10, 20, 50 — and four tab characters are used in succession, a value of 50 is used.

The default value for `tabStops` is null. When the property has a value of `null`, the default value of four points is used between each successive tab character. However, using the `tabStops` property you can specify how ordered tabs are spaced within text.

For example, you can create a `TextFormat` object that uses a tab spacing of 10 pixels for the first tab, a tab spacing of 50 pixels for the second tab (in succession), and a tab spacing of 150 pixels for the third tab. The following code does just that:

```
this.createTextField("tContent", this.getNextHighestDepth(),100, 100, 200, 200);
tContent.multiline = true;
tContent.border = true;
tContent.wordWrap = true;
tContent.text = "\ta\n";
tContent.text += "\t\tb\n";
tContent.text += "\t\t\tc";
var tfFormatter:TextFormat = new TextFormat();
tfFormatter.tabStops = [10, 50, 150];
tfFormatter.align = "left";
tContent.setTextFormat(tfFormatter);
```

It is important to understand that the values in the `tabStop` array determine the pixels from the edge of the `TextField`, not between each tab. That means that the values in the array are not cumulative but are absolute values. In other words, in the preceding code, the third tab is 150 pixels from the left edge of the `TextField`, not 210 (which would be the sum of 10, 50, and 150).

target

The `target` property works in conjunction with the `url` property (discussed later in this section). You can specify a string value for the `target` property that indicates the name of the browser window (or frame) where the URL specified in the `url` property should appear. You can use the predefined target values of "_blank" (new empty browser window), "_self" (the current frame or window), "_parent" (the parent frame or window), or "_top" (the outermost frame or window), or you can use a custom browser window or frame name (as assigned in the HTML document or JavaScript). If you use the `url` property without specifying a value for the `target` property, the URL loads into the current frame or window ("_self").

underline

The underline property can add an underline to text. When this property is set to true, an underline appears with the text. When it is set to false, any underlines are removed. By default, the value of this property is null, which has the same effect as a value of false.

Tip You might want to use the underline property to indicate text that is linked to URLs (see the url property, discussed next).

url

The url property allows you to add a hyperlink to text. The Flash Player does not provide any immediate indication that the url property is in use for a given range of text — you may want to change the color and add an underline to the affected text to make the link more apparent to the user. However, the mouse pointer automatically changes to the hand icon when the mouse rolls over the linked text.

In order to use the url property, you must make sure that the html property is set to true for the TextField. Otherwise, the hyperlink is not applied properly.

The following code applies a hyperlink to a portion of the text:

```
this.createTextField("tContent", this.getNextHighestDepth(),100, 100, 200, 200);
tContent.multiline = true;
tContent.border = true;
tContent.wordWrap = true;
tContent.text = "Visit the Web site";
tContent.html = true;
var tfFormatter:TextFormat = new TextFormat();
tfFormatter.url = "http://www.person13.com/asb";
tfFormatter.target = "_blank";
tfFormatter.underline = true;
tContent.setTextFormat(10, 18, tfFormatter);
```

Tip You can specify asfunction code as the value of the url property. The asfunction directive invokes ActionScript functions when the linked text is clicked. You can read more about asfunction in Chapter 19.

Determining Text Metrics

In many cases, you can allow for Flash to handle the text metrics issues automatically. For example, you might want to just allow Flash to automatically resize the TextField to match the text, or you can employ various other techniques. However, when you want to have exacting control that allows you to better determine the dimensions of the text, you can use the TextFormat class's getTextExtent() method. The method returns the text metrics for a string of text as it would appear given the formatting options.

The text metric information that getTextExtent() returns is in the form of an object with the following properties:

✦ ascent — The number of pixels above the baseline for the line of text.

✦ descent — The number of pixels below the baseline for the line of text.

✦ width — The width of the text.

✦ height — The height of the text.

✦ textFieldWidth — The width required for a TextField to display the text.

✦ textFieldHeight — The height required for a TextField to display the text.

The textFieldWidth and textFieldHeight properties differ from the width and height properties by four pixels. The reason is that TextField objects have a 2-pixel margin between the border and the text.

When you call the getTextExtent() method, you have two options. First, you can pass it a single parameter — the string of text for which you want to get the metrics. For example:

```
var oMetrics:Object = tfFormatter.getTextExtent("Some text");
```

Flash then calculates the metrics for the text, assuming that the text will not wrap in the text field. Therefore, the number of lines of text is based on newline characters only.

If you are authoring to Flash Player 7 or higher, you can also pass the getTextExtent() method a second parameter indicating the pixel count at which you want to wrap the text. For example:

```
var oMetrics:Object = tfFormatter.getTextExtent("Some text", 10);
```

With the second parameter, Flash calculates the metrics based on the assumption that the text should wrap at the specified width.

The following example uses the returned text metrics to size the TextField object.

```
var sCopy:String = "This is the copy to fit in the TextField.";
var tfFormatter:TextFormat = new TextFormat();
tfFormatter.bold = true;
tfFormatter.font = "Verdana";
var oTextMetrics:Object = tfFormatter.getTextExtent(sCopy);
this.createTextField("tContent", this.getNextHighestDepth(), 100, 100,
    oTextMetrics.textFieldWidth, oTextMetrics.textFieldHeight);
tContent.border = true;
tContent.text = sCopy;
tContent.setTextFormat(tfFormatter);
```

Getting the TextFormat

You can retrieve the TextFormat object for a TextField or selection within the text. This enables you to make modifications to the current formatting without having to keep track of the formatting in another way.

The getTextFormat() method of the TextField object returns a TextFormat object containing the formatting properties of the text within the field. You can use this method with three types of syntax, similarly to how there are three types of syntax for the setTextFormat() method:

✦ getTextFormat() — If you omit an argument for this method, the returned TextFormat object contains the formatting properties for all of the text in the field. If there are mixed formats in the field, the returned property value for the mixed format will be null. For example, if the first line uses Times New Roman and the second line uses Courier New as the font face, the font property of the returned TextFormat object will be null.

✦ `getTextFormat(index)` — You can retrieve the formatting characteristics of a specific character within a text field by using an index argument with the method. This index is 0-based, which means that the first character in the field has an index of 0, the second character has an index of 1, and so on.

✦ `getTextFormat(beginIndex, endIndex)` — This version of the method allows you to retrieve the formatting properties for a specific range of text within the field. The `beginIndex` value is the starting position in the content, whereas the `endIndex` value is the index of the last position in the range. If there are mixed values for any given property in the range of text, that property's value will be `null`.

For an example of how to use `getTextFormat()`, look at the `TextFormattingExample.fla` file on the web site.

The `getNewTextFormat()` method returns a `TextFormat` object describing the properties of text that will be added to an input field by the user. It does not require any parameters because it does not target existing text within a field. You can test the properties of the object returned by the `getNewTextFormat()` method to make sure that new text receives the proper formatting.

Working with Cascading Style Sheets

Flash Player 7+ supports Cascading Style Sheets (CSS) for HTML- or XML-formatted text. First, this section discusses some of the basics of what CSS is, how it works, and what properties are supported in Flash. Then, it takes a look at how to create a `TextField.StyleSheet` object in ActionScript so that you can start working with CSS. Once you have created a `StyleSheet` object, you have the choice of either creating the style sheet using ActionScript or loading the CSS from an external file — both methods are covered here.

If you're not already familiar with CSS, you might want to consult a good resource such as the W3Schools online tutorial at `www.w3schools.com/css`. Even if you're not familiar with CSS, you can still benefit from the general overview in the following sections.

Understanding CSS

CSS allows you to define a set of rules that Flash will use to format text. CSS was originally created for the purposes of formatting HTML in web browsers. The original HTML specification was fairly simple and had to do with creating academic papers. Thus, it was not designed to support complex formatting. To accommodate the formatting needs, new tags such as `<font>` were introduced. However, these tags managed to make coding HTML more complicated, and they made it very difficult to change formatting. CSS was developed primarily to separate the essential content from the rules that determine how that content is displayed.

You can define essentially two types of styles — those that are automatically applied to a tag and special classes that can be explicitly applied to a tag. Because CSS defines a specification for formatting, you can save a lot of time when trying to format your text. By defining a style for the `<p>` tag, for example, all content within `<p>` tags are styled in that fashion. If you later want to change the style, you need change it in only one place. CSS also saves you time in another way. It is called *Cascading* Style Sheets because the rules that you define can be inherited. Nested tags automatically inherit the rules applied to a parent tag, unless they are overridden. That means that if you apply a style to the `<p>` tag, any nested `<a>` tag contents also automatically inherit that style. You'll see some examples of that in a bit.

You can apply CSS to both HTML and XML. That means that you can even apply styles to unrecognized HTML tags. For example, Flash does not recognize the `<html>`, `<title>`, or `<body>` tags, to name but a few standard HTML elements. If you load an HTML document for display within Flash, you can potentially end up with some unwanted results because the contents of, for example, the `<title>` tag might display in a way other than what you intended. Using CSS, you can define a style for the `<title>` tag that either formats the content in a way you want or hides the contents from display.

Flash currently supports only a subset of the standard CSS properties. Table 20-1 shows the supported properties.

Table 20-1: Supported CSS Properties

Standard CSS Property	ActionScript CSS Property	Description
Color	color	The color of the text. The value should be a hexadecimal representation of the color given as a string, and the first character should be a pound sign (#) because the color values are specified in HTML. For example: #FF0000.
Display	display	This property determines how the text should display. The value should be a string. The default value of block means that a line break is placed before and after the text. A value of inline means that no line breaks are inserted. A value of none causes the text to be invisible.
font-family	fontFamily	This property can be used to specify the font face used. You can use any of the same values you can use with the TextFormat class's font property.
font-size	fontSize	The font size can be specified numerically. To support standard CSS values, the value can also be a string such as 12pt. Only the numeric portion is interpreted, and Flash supports only points, so even if the value is specified in pixels Flash will use points.
font-style	fontStyle	This property can be set to normal or italic. If it is set to italic, the faux italic is applied to the text.
font-weight	fontWeight	This property can be set to normal or bold. If it is set to bold, the faux bold is applied to the text.
margin-left	marginLeft	This property can be a numeric value indicating the number of pixels on the left margin. As with the fontSize property, the value can be a string such as 20px. Flash uses only pixel values for margins, so even if the value is specified in points the margin is calculated in pixels.

Continued

Table 20-1 *(continued)*

Standard CSS Property	ActionScript CSS Property	Description
margin-right	marginRight	This property operates in the same way as the marginLeft property, but the value is used to determine the right margin, not the left.
text-align	textAlign	This property determines how the text aligns in the field. You can specify values of left, right, or center.
text-decoration	textDecoration	This property can be set to normal or underline. If you set the property to underline, the text is underlined.
text-indent	textIndent	This property determines how the text is indented. The value can be numeric or a string as with the font size and margin properties. Regardless of the units specified, Flash calculates the indentation in pixels.

Creating a StyleSheet Object

Regardless of whether you are going to create the style sheet information with ActionScript or by loading an external file, you first need to create a StyleSheet object. To create a StyleSheet object, use the constructor as follows:

```
var cssStyles:TextField.StyleSheet = new TextField.StyleSheet();
```

Adding Styles with ActionScript

You can add new styles to a style sheet using several techniques. The first one we discuss is the setStyle() method; it allows you to programmatically add one new style at a time. The method takes two parameters — the name of the style as a string and an object representing the style. The following adds a new style for <p> tags to a StyleSheet object named cssStyles. The style tells Flash to display the text within <p> tags using the _sans font face.

```
cssStyles.setStyle("p", {fontFamily: "_sans"});
```

The preceding example causes all text within <p> tags to display using the _sans font face when the StyleSheet object is applied to a TextField object. Because the name of the style matches the name of a tag, it is used automatically to format the tag's contents. You can also create style classes that have to be explicitly applied to a tag instance. In order to do so, the style name should start with a dot. The following defines a style class named emphasized:

```
cssStyles.setStyle(".emphasized", {fontWeight: "bold",
  textDecoration: "underline"});
```

The preceding style class is applied to the contents of a tag only when the tag explicitly specifies that it should be by way of the class attribute. When you apply the class in this way, make sure that you do not include the dot at the beginning of the name. The dot is used only to distinguish the style classes from the intrinsic tag styles in the style sheet. The following HTML text example shows how the emphasized class can be applied to some text:

```
<p class="emphasized">This text is emphasized</p>
```

In the preceding case, the text would be rendered with both the _sans font face and the bolded and underlined formatting.

You can also define styles in ActionScript by using the parseCSS() method to parse a CSS string. The parseCSS() method accepts a CSS definition as a string, and it parses it and applies it to the style sheet. The following is an example:

```
cssStyles.parseCSS("html{font-family: _typewriter;}");
```

Applying Styles to Text

Once you've defined a StyleSheet object, you can apply it to a TextField object by assigning it to the object's styleSheet property. For example, the following assigns cssStyles to the styleSheet property of a TextField named tContent:

```
tContent.styleSheet = cssStyles;
```

The styles defined in the StyleSheet object are then applied to any HTML text that is assigned to the TextField object. The only catch is that you must assign the value of the styleSheet property *before* you assign the HTML text. The following example defines a simple StyleSheet object and applies those styles to a TextField object.

```
var cssStyles:TextField.StyleSheet = new TextField.StyleSheet();
cssStyles.setStyle("a", {textDecoration: "underline", color: "#0000FF"});
this.createTextField("tOutput", this.getNextHighestDepth(), 0, 0, 100, 100);
tOutput.border = true;
tOutput.html = true;
tOutput.styleSheet = cssStyles;
tOutput.htmlText = "<a href='http://www.person13.com/asb'>Web site</a>";
```

Notice that the styleSheet assignment is before the htmlText assignment in the preceding example code. If you were to reverse those two lines, the style would not be applied.

Formatting an HTML Article with CSS

In this exercise, you load HTML text from an external file using the LoadVars class, display the content in a TextField object, and use CSS to format it. Complete the following steps:

1. On the web site, find css.html. The document contains a simple HTML-formatted article. Copy the file to your local disk.

2. Open a new Flash document and save it as css001.fla to the same directory as you saved the css.html file.

3. Add the following code to the first frame of the default layer of the main timeline.

```
// Create the new StyleSheet object.
var cssStyles:TextField.StyleSheet = new TextField.StyleSheet();

// Define the styles.
```

```
cssStyles.setStyle("html", {fontFamily: "_sans"});
cssStyles.setStyle("title", {fontWeight: "bold",
textDecoration: "underline", textAlign: "center", fontSize: 10});
cssStyles.setStyle(".code", {marginLeft: 15, fontFamily: "_typewriter"});
cssStyles.setStyle("h1", {fontWeight: "bold"});
cssStyles.setStyle("a", {textDecoration: "underline", color: "#0000FF"});
cssStyles.setStyle("a:hover", {color: "#AAAAFF"});
cssStyles.setStyle("a:active", {color: "#FF00FF"});

// Create the TextField object.
this.createTextField("tOutput", this.getNextHighestDepth(), 0, 0, 550, 400);

// Set the properties of the TextField object such that it
// auto-sizes, renders as HTML, handles multiple lines
// of text with word wrap, and condenses whitespace.
tOutput.autoSize = "left";
tOutput.selectable = false;
tOutput.html = true;
tOutput.multiline = true;
tOutput.wordWrap = true;
tOutput.condenseWhite = true;

// Apply the style sheet to the TextField object.
tOutput.styleSheet = cssStyles;

// Define a LoadVars object for loading the HTML.
var lvHTML:LoadVars = new LoadVars();

// When the data loads, assign the value to the htmlText
// property of the TextField object.
lvHTML.onData = function(sData:String):Void {
  tOutput.htmlText = sData;
};

// Tell Flash to load the HTML.
lvHTML.load("css.html");
```

4. Test the movie. You should see the HTML rendered with the formatting you defined using CSS.

Loading External CSS

One of the really nice features of the Flash support for CSS is that you can load an external CSS file. That means that you can define a single CSS file shared between your HTML *and* Flash documents.

To load an external CSS file, use the load() method of the StyleSheet object into which you want the styles to be parsed. Then, as when loading any other kind of external content (using XML, LoadVars, and so on) you should define an onLoad() method that will automatically be called when Flash has loaded and parsed the CSS. Within the onLoad() method, you should assign the StyleSheet to the styleSheet property of the TextField object, and you should assign the HTML text to the TextField object. And just as with the onLoad() method of other ActionScript classes such as XML and LoadVars, the onLoad() method for a StyleSheet object is passed a Boolean parameter indicating whether the CSS loaded successfully.

The following example loads CSS from a file named styles.css into a StyleSheet object named cssStyles. When the CSS is loaded and parsed, it is applied to a TextField object named tContent.

```
cssStyles.onLoad = function(bSuccess:Boolean):Void {
  if(bSuccess) {
    tOutput.styleSheet = this;
    tOutput.htmlText = "<p>Some text</p>";
  }
};
```

Formatting HTML with CSS Loaded from an External File

In the last exercise, you applied formatting to HTML using CSS that you defined within ActionScript. In this exercise, you apply the same formatting but using CSS that you load from an external file.

1. On the web site, you'll find a file called styles.css. Copy the file to your local disk in the same directory to which you have previously saved css.html and css001.fla. You might want to open styles.css to see how the styles are defined and compare that with how you previously had defined the styles within the FLA file.

2. Open a new Flash document and save it as css002.fla. Save it to the same directory as you saved css.html and styles.css.

3. Add the following code to the first frame of the default layer of the main timeline.

```
// Create the StyleSheet object.
var cssStyles:TextField.StyleSheet = new TextField.StyleSheet();

// Create the TextField object.
this.createTextField("tOutput", this.getNextHighestDepth(), 0, 0, 550, 400);

// Set the properties of the TextField object as before.
tOutput.autoSize = "left";
tOutput.selectable = false;
tOutput.html = true;
tOutput.multiline = true;
tOutput.wordWrap = true;
tOutput.condenseWhite = true;

// Define a LoadVars object to load the HTML.
var lvHTML:LoadVars = new LoadVars();

// When the HTML loads, assign it to the htmlText
// property of the TextField object.
lvHTML.onData = function(sData:String):Void {
```

```
  tOutput.htmlText = sData;
};

// Define an onLoad() method for the StyleSheet. When
// the CSS loads, assign the StyleSheet object to the
// styleSheet property of the TextField object and then
// tell Flash to load the HTML.
cssStyles.onLoad = function(bSuccess:Boolean):Void {
  if(bSuccess) {
    tOutput.styleSheet = this;
    lvHTML.load("css.html");
  }
};

// Tell Flash to load the CSS from the external file.
cssStyles.load("styles.css");
```

4. Test the movie. The formatting should be the same as in the previous exercise.

We'd like to know what you thought about this chapter. Visit `www.rightactionscript` `.com/asb/comments` to fill out an online form with your comments.

Summary

✦ ActionScript provides you with several ways to format text, including the `TextFormat` class and the `TextField.StyleSheet` class.

✦ The `TextFormat` class enables you to apply styles to text within a `TextField` object. You can apply the styles to the entire contents, a single character, or a range of characters.

✦ The `TextFormat` class includes properties for affecting everything from text color, indentation, and font face to hyperlinks.

✦ Cascading Style Sheets (CSS) is a technology that was developed to efficiently apply formatting to HTML text in a web browser. Flash supports a subset of the standard CSS properties, allowing you to apply CSS to HTML and XML text in Flash.

✦ You can define CSS styles in Flash using the `setStyle()` or `parseCSS()` methods, or you can load CSS styles from an external file.

✦ When you apply CSS to a `TextField`, you must do so *before* you assign the text to which you want the styles applied.

✦   ✦   ✦

Scripting
Player Control

Managing Mouse and Key Interactivity

The `Mouse` and `Key` classes are two static classes that you can use to work with two of the standard user input interfaces — the mouse and keyboard. With these static classes, you simply call the class by its name and invoke one of its methods or properties:

```
Mouse.hide();
```

The preceding line hides the user's mouse cursor icon. Since there is only one mouse or keyboard device at a time on the average computer, it is not necessary to make instances of either class as you might with classes such as `Array` or `MovieClip`. In the following sections, you learn more about the following classes:

✦ `Mouse` — This class controls the display of the mouse cursor icon. Together with the `MovieClip` class and methods, you can create custom mouse cursors with the `Mouse` class.

✦ `Key` — You can determine which key(s) a user types using this class. Among other uses, the `Key` class can enable your scripts to nudge graphics on the stage using the arrow keys, to create keyboard shortcuts to other sections of the Flash movie, or to guide the user with Flash forms and data entry using the Tab key.

Using the Mouse Class to Control the Cursor

Have you ever wanted to get rid of the regular white or black mouse cursor icon or use a different cursor icon for `Button` instances? The `Mouse` class has the power to not only turn off the default cursor icon but to also affix a new graphic to the mouse cursor.

Using the `Mouse` class, you can control the visibility of the standard and `rollOver` cursor icons. However, Input text fields and selectable Dynamic text fields always display the I-beam cursor when the mouse enters the area of the text field, regardless of the `Mouse` class's settings. In the next section, you learn the methods of the `Mouse` class that control the cursor's appearance.

Note For those readers familiar with Macromedia Director and Lingo programming, there are no cursor codes in ActionScript.

Hiding the Mouse Cursor

The `Mouse.hide()` method does exactly that — it hides the mouse cursor icon, globally throughout the entire Flash movie. When this method is invoked, the mouse cursor continues to be invisible until the `show()` method of the `Mouse` class is invoked.

Note The I-beam cursor that appears over selectable text is not hidden when the `Mouse.hide()` method is invoked. You cannot hide this cursor type in a Flash movie.

Revealing the Mouse Cursor

The `Mouse.show()` method makes the mouse cursor icon reappear for all default mouse icon states (that is, standard and `rollOver` mouse icons). The mouse cursor remains visible until a `hide()` method is invoked.

Note The `hide()` and `show()` methods do not control the appearance of the mouse cursor when the cursor moves outside of the area allocated to the Flash Player and the movie.

Working with Mouse Listeners

In ActionScript, you can assign a listener object to the `Mouse` class. A listener object must have specific event handler methods that are called when the corresponding events occur. The Mouse listener event handler methods correspond to three of the MovieClip event handler methods — `onMouseDown()`, `onMouseUp()`, and `onMouseMove()`. Given that you can use `MovieClip` event handler methods to detect the same events, you may wonder what reason you might have to use Mouse listeners instead of simply using `MovieClip` objects. There are two main reasons:

✦ If an event is not logically associated with a particular `MovieClip` object, it is a better programming practice to use a listener object. From an architectural standpoint, it simply makes more sense.

✦ Sometimes, you may want to build a class that responds to the mouse, but the class is neither a `MovieClip` subclass nor does it have any `MovieClip` properties.

Listener objects can be any object for which you can define one or more of the event handler methods. Typically that means that a Mouse listener object is either an `Object` instance or an instance of a custom class for which you have defined the event handler method(s).

Detecting a Mouse Down Event

The `onMouseDown()` method can define a function to occur whenever the mouse button is clicked *anywhere* within the stage. Specifically, this method detects a press of the mouse button — the first downward stroke on the mouse button. The following code creates a listener object named `oMouseListener` and uses a `trace()` action to display a message in the Output panel when the mouse is clicked:

```
var oMouseListener:Object = new Object();
oMouseListener.onMouseDown = function():Void {
   trace("The mouse button has been pressed.");
};
Mouse.addListener(oMouseListener);
```

The act of defining a listener and an onMouseDown() method, however, does not actually enable the code within the method. The listener needs to be enabled with the addListener() method, as illustrated in the preceding example. The addListener() method is described in a moment.

> **Note** With two- (or more) button mouse devices, usually only left-button mouse clicks can be detected with this handler. Some middle-button mouse clicks might also be detected. If you have a specific mouse device, be sure to test your Flash movie with it.

Detecting a Mouse Up Event

The onMouseUp() method defines a function that occurs whenever the mouse button is released within the space of the Flash movie. The return motion of the mouse button after a click is considered the release. The following code creates a listener named oMouseListener and displays a message to the Output panel:

```
var oMouseListener:Object = new Object();
oMouseListener.onMouseUp = function():Void {
    trace("The mouse button has been released.");
};
Mouse.addListener(oMouseListener);
```

As in the previous section, the listener is not enabled until it is initiated with the addListener() method.

Detecting Mouse Movement

The onMouseMove() method defines a function that occurs when any vertical or horizontal movement of the mouse is detected within the space of the Flash movie. The following code creates a listener named oMouseListener and displays a message to the Output panel:

```
var oMouseListener:Object = new Object();
oMouseListener.onMouseMove = function():Void {
    trace("The mouse pointer is moving.");
};
Mouse.addListener(oMouseListener);
```

This listener is not enabled until it is initiated with the addListener() method, as shown in the example.

> **Caution** So far, all the Mouse listener methods perform nearly the same as the MovieClip event handler methods. However, onMouseMove() has one major disadvantage when used as a Mouse listener: the updateAfterEvent() function will not execute. Refer to the sidebar "onMouseMove() and updateAfterEvent()" in this chapter.

Monitoring the Scroll Wheel Activity (Windows Only)

Flash Player 7+ for Windows adds the capability to capture events sent by the scroll wheel of a user's mouse. The onMouseWheel() method of a listener can be used for this event. The method receives two parameters: delta and scrollTarget. A listener using this method can be constructed in the following way:

```
var oMouseListener:Object = new Object();
oMouseListener.onMouseWheel = function(nDelta:Number, mTarget:MovieClip):Void {
    trace(">> onMouseWheel >>");
```

```
    trace("\t        delta:\t" + nDelta);
    trace("\tscrollTarget:\t" + mTarget);
};
Mouse.addListener(oMouseListener);
```

Note   In this code, `trace()` actions can be built to display more meaningful and visually structured information in the Output panel. The `\t` backslash pairs indicate a tab insertion. Therefore, when the `onMouseWheel()` method is invoked, the Output panel displays the following:

```
    >> onMouseWheel >>
                delta:   3
         scrollTarget:  mTarget
```

The `delta` value specifies how many lines each scroll "click" should scroll. This value is usually between 1 and 3 lines and is a hardware setting in the user's system Control Panel for the mouse device. You can use this value to adjust the scroll property of a `TextField` object, increase values displayed in a text field, or move an object on the stage (to name just a few examples).

Note   A downward wheel stroke returns a negative `delta` value, whereas an upward stroke returns a positive `delta` value.

The `scrollTarget` returns the object reference to the topmost `MovieClip` object that is underneath the current position of the mouse cursor when the wheel movement occurs.

Later in this chapter, you build an example that uses this new event handler.

Tip   Several Flash UI components already use the `onMouseWheel()` handler, such as the `TextArea`, `ComboBox`, and `List` components.

Assigning a Listener to the Mouse Class

After you have created a listener with methods for the `Mouse` class, you can enable the listener by using the `addListener()` method of the `Mouse` class. You can enable the listener immediately after the definition of the listener (as the following code demonstrates) or enable it later in the Flash movie (for example, within a `Button` or `MovieClip` handler):

```
var oMouseListener:Object = new Object;
oMouseListener.onMouseMove = function(){
    trace("The mouse pointer is moving.");
};
Mouse.addListener(oMouseListener);
```

You can also define multiple methods per listener, as the following code demonstrates:

```
var oMouseListener:Object = new Object();
oMouseListener.onMouseMove = function():Void {
    trace("The mouse pointer is moving.");
};
oMouseListener.onMouseUp = function():Void {
    trace("The mouse button has been released.");
};
```

```
oMouseListener.onMouseDown = function():Void {
   trace("The mouse button has been pressed.");
};
Mouse.addListener(oMouseListener);
```

In this code sample, the same listener, oMouseListener, has three separate methods defined. All of them are passed to the Mouse class with one addListener() method.

Tip You can also define separate listeners (for example, oMouseListener1, oMouseListener2, and so on) that run different actions. You can then add (or remove) each one at different times to the Mouse class. This is true for all classes that use listeners.

Deleting an Active Listener from the Mouse Class

With the Mouse.removeListener() method, you can remove an active listener from the Mouse class. Note that this method does not actually delete the listener object from the Flash movie—it simply deletes the listener from the callback list of the Mouse class. When a listener is removed, the methods assigned to the listener will no longer be invoked when the event occurs. In the following code, a listener named oMouseListener is removed from the Mouse class:

```
Mouse.removeListener(oMouseListener);
```

If you would like to reinitiate the listener, specify the listener in a subsequent addListener() method of the Mouse class.

Showing and Hiding the Mouse Cursor

In this exercise, you learn how to use the hide() and show() methods of the Mouse class. When the mouse enters the area of a MovieClip instance, we'll tell Flash to execute the hide() method of the Mouse class. When the mouse leaves the area of the MovieClip instance, the show() method is invoked. To capture the user's act of moving his or her mouse icon within the Flash movie, you use a Mouse listener object with the onMouseMove() event handler method.

1. Open a new Flash document, and save it as mouseHideShow.fla.

2. Select frame 1 of the default layer of the main timeline, and open the Actions panel (F9). Add the following code to the Script pane:

```
// Add a new MovieClip into which you'll load the image.
this.createEmptyMovieClip("mEarth", this.getNextHighestDepth());
mEarth.createEmptyMovieClip("mImage",                              ⤶
mEarth.getNextHighestDepth());

// Place the MovieClip instance at the center of the stage.
mEarth._x = 275;
mEarth._y = 200;

// Declare a variable to which we can assign the radius of the
// image (it's circular) once it's loaded.
var mRadius:Number;

// Define a listener object to use with the MovieClipLoader
```

```
// instance.
var oLoaderListener:Object = new Object();
oLoaderListener.onLoadInit = function(mClip:MovieClip):Void {

  // When the image loads mClip refers to the nested mImage
  // MovieClip object. Use the following code to center it within
  // the parent object.
  mClip._x = -mClip._width/2;
  mClip._y = -mClip._height/2;

  // If the parent MovieClip is mEarth (in a subsequent version
  // of the application there will be more than one MovieClip)
  // then determine the radius.
  if(mClip._parent == mEarth) {
    nRadius = mClip._height/2;
  }
};

// Use a MovieClipLoader object to load the image into
// mEarth.mImage.
var mlImages:MovieClipLoader = new MovieClipLoader();
mlImages.addListener(oLoaderListener);
mlImages.loadClip("http://www.rightactionscript.com/
samplefiles/EarthImage.png",
mEarth.mImage);

// Use a Mouse listener object to detect when the mouse moves.
var oMouseListener:Object = new Object();
oMouseListener.onMouseMove = function():Void {

  // Use the Pythagorean theorem to determine if the mouse is
  // over the image or not. If so, hide the cursor. Otherwise,
  // show the cursor.
  if (Math.sqrt(Math.pow(mEarth._xmouse, 2) +
Math.pow(mEarth._ymouse, 2)) < nRadius) {
    Mouse.hide();
  }
  else {
    Mouse.show();
  }
};
Mouse.addListener(oMouseListener);
```

3. Save the Flash document and test it. Move the mouse cursor over the mEarth instance, and the cursor disappears. When you move the mouse cursor out of the mEarth instance, the mouse cursor reappears.

In the next section, you learn how to attach a custom graphic to the mouse cursor, so the user has some visual indication of the mouse's position on the screen.

If you execute more than one `show()` (or `hide()`) method in succession, the mouse icon's appearance does not reflect any changes. Unlike alpha effects, the process of showing or hiding a mouse produces no cumulative effects. Although the `_alpha` property of `MovieClip` instances can exceed 100 percent (or fall below 0 percent), the visibility of the mouse cursor is not affected by multiple `hide()` or `show()` executions. Therefore, if you execute the `hide()` method twice, you do not need to execute the `show()` method twice to "undo" the effect.

Attaching a Custom Graphic to the Cursor

Now that you've learned how to show and hide the mouse cursor, you can take your mouse moves to the next step. In this section, you learn how to use a custom cursor icon. Actually, you can't attach anything to the mouse cursor itself. Rather, you can use a `MovieClip` object, and set the instance's X- and Y-coordinates (as `_x` and `_y` properties, respectively) to match those of the mouse cursor. Even if the mouse cursor is not visible, it still has readable properties, such as `_xmouse` and `_ymouse`.

Although you can use `startDrag()` to make the new "cursor" follow the hidden default icon, it's generally better to use the `MovieClip.onMouseMove()` event handler method and update the `_x` and `_y` properties. That's because you can only make one object draggable at a time using `startDrag()`. Because you presumably want the custom cursor to move with the mouse at all times, it works better to use `onMouseMove()` than `startDrag()` because otherwise the custom cursor would stop moving if you called `startDrag()` for any other `MovieClip` object. The following code illustrates the basics of using a custom cursor.

```
import actionscriptbible.drawing.DrawingUtilities;

// Make the cursor MovieClip.
this.createEmptyMovieClip("mCursor", this.getNextHighestDepth());

// Add the artwork to the MovieClip. In this example, draw a
// triangle.
var duDrawer:DrawingUtilities = new DrawingUtilities(mCursor);
duDrawer.beginFill(0xFFFFFF, 100);
duDrawer.drawPolygon(10, 3, 0, 0, 0);
duDrawer.endFill();

// Hide the standard cursor.
Mouse.hide();

// Use an onMouseMove() event handler method to update the _x
// and _y properties of the cursor MovieClip.
mCursor.onMouseMove = function():Void {
  this._x = _xmouse;
  this._y = _ymouse;
};
```

Of course, as you add other display objects, you'll have to manage the depths so that the cursor appears above other display objects. The following code illustrates what happens otherwise. Note that it is the same code as the previous example, but with the addition of a text field. When the mouse moves in the same coordinate space as the text field, the custom cursor disappears behind the text field.

```
import actionscriptbible.drawing.DrawingUtilities;

this.createEmptyMovieClip("mCursor", this.getNextHighestDepth());

var duDrawer:DrawingUtilities = new DrawingUtilities(mCursor);
duDrawer.beginFill(0xFFFFFF, 100);
duDrawer.drawPolygon(10, 3, 0, 0, 0);
duDrawer.endFill();

Mouse.hide();

mCursor.onMouseMove = function():Void {
  this._x = _xmouse;
  this._y = _ymouse;
};

this.createTextField("tField", this.getNextHighestDepth(), 100, 100, 200, 200);
tField.border = true;
tField.wordWrap = true;
tField.multiline = true;
tField.background = true;
tField.selectable = false;

var lvText:LoadVars = new LoadVars();
lvText.onData = function(sText:String):Void {
  tField.text = sText.substring(0, 1000);
};
lvText.load("http://www.rightactionscript.com/samplefiles/lorem_ipsum.txt");
```

You can correct this in several ways. One is to make the custom cursor only after any other display objects have been added. That way when you call `getNextHighestDepth()`, the depth will be greater than any other depths used by display objects on the stage. Another option is to add just two `MovieClip` objects to the root container — one as a container for every other display object, and the other for the cursor. That way, so long as you assign the cursor object a greater depth than the container object, any other display object will appear below the cursor (since they are nested within the container object). Optionally, you can use the `swapDepths()` method to move the custom cursor to the next highest depth after adding any new display object. The preceding code will work properly if you add the following line of code after making the text field:

```
mCursor.swapDepths(this.getNextHighestDepth());
```

Let's build a simple example that uses a custom cursor. We'll use `mouseHideShow.fla` (from the previous exercise) as the starting point for the new example.

1. Open the `mouseHideShow.fla` file in Flash 8. Save it as `mouseCustomCursor.fla`.

2. Update the code to the following. Changes are bolded.

```
this.createEmptyMovieClip("mEarth", this.getNextHighestDepth());
mEarth.createEmptyMovieClip("mImage", mEarth.getNextHighestDepth());
this.createEmptyMovieClip("mMoon", this.getNextHighestDepth());
mMoon.createEmptyMovieClip("mImage", mMoon.getNextHighestDepth());

mEarth._x = 275;
```

```actionscript
mEarth._y = 200;

var mRadius:Number;

var oLoaderListener:Object = new Object();
oLoaderListener.onLoadInit = function(mClip:MovieClip):Void {
  mClip._x = -mClip._width/2;
  mClip._y = -mClip._height/2;
  if(mClip._parent == mEarth) {
    nRadius = mClip._height/2;
  }
};

var mlImages:MovieClipLoader = new MovieClipLoader();
mlImages.addListener(oLoaderListener);
mlImages.loadClip("http://www.rightactionscript.com/
samplefiles/EarthImage.png", mEarth.mImage);
mlImages.loadClip("http://www.rightactionscript.com/
samplefiles/MoonImage.png", mMoon.mImage);

var oMouseListener:Object = new Object();
oMouseListener.onMouseMove = function():Void {
  if (Math.sqrt(Math.pow(mEarth._xmouse, 2) +
Math.pow(mEarth._ymouse, 2)) < nRadius) {
    Mouse.hide();
  }
  else {
    Mouse.show();
  }
  mMoon._x = _xmouse;
  mMoon._y = _ymouse;
};
Mouse.addListener(oMouseListener);
```

3. After you have added the code in Step 2, save your Flash document as `mouseCustomCursor`

Using updateAfterEvent() for Mouse Moves

You might have noticed that the moon's movement in the last section wasn't quite fluid. If you moved the mouse fast enough, you would have noticed that the position of the mMoon instance wasn't updated at the same speed you were moving the mouse. Unless told to do otherwise, Flash movies update the screen only at the rate set in the Document Properties dialog box (Modify ➪ Document). In the example, the frame rate was already set to 12fps. Try setting your Flash movie's frame rate to 1fps, and test the movement of the mMoon instance. You'll likely notice that it appears choppier than before. To improve this situation, you could use an incredibly fast frame rate, such as 20 or 30fps, but many older computers can't keep up with this frame rate.

In Flash 5, Macromedia introduced the updateAfterEvent() function, which enables you to refresh or update the screen display as soon as an event has finished executing—even if that happens to occur between normal frame intervals. The updateAfterEvent() function can be used in the following situations:

✦ Within functions defined for the MovieClip class's onMouseMove(), onMouseUp(), onMouseDown(), onKeyDown(), or onKeyUp() methods

✦ Within onClipEvent() handlers for the MovieClip class, for the following events: mouseMove, mouseDown, mouseUp, keyDown, or keyUp

✦ Within functions invoked by the setInterval() function

Caution

The updateAfterEvent() function does not work with the onMouseMove() method of a Mouse listener. See the "onMouseMove() and updateAfterEvent()" sidebar.

onMouseMove() and updateAfterEvent()

As discussed in the coverage of the Mouse class, the onMouseMove() method of a listener cannot use the updateAfterEvent() function. Therefore, if you need to control the movement of graphics in tandem with the movement of the mouse, you should use the onMouseMove() method of the MovieClip class. To illustrate this difference, you can create the following example:

1. In a new Flash document, rename Layer 1 as mCircle.

2. On frame 1 of the circle layer, draw a small circle with the Oval tool.

3. Convert the artwork to a MovieClip symbol named circleClip.

4. In the Property inspector, name the instance mCircle in the *<Instance Name>* field.

5. Create a new layer named Actions. On frame 1 of this layer, insert the following code:

```
var oMouseListener:Object = {};
oMouseListener.onMouseMove = function():Void {
   mCircle._x = _root._xmouse;
   mCircle._y = _root._ymouse;
   updateAfterEvent();
};
Mouse.addListener(oMouseListener);
```

This code uses the onMouseMove() method of the Mouse listener.

6. Save the Flash document as updateAfterEvent_problem.fla and test it. As you move the mouse pointer, notice the sluggish movement of the circle instance.

7. Go back to frame 1 of the actions layer, and comment all the code you inserted in Step 5. Your code should resemble the following:

```
/*
var oMouseListener:Object = {};
oMouseListener.onMouseMove = function():Void {
   mCircle._x = _root._xmouse;
   mCircle._y = _root._ymouse;
   updateAfterEvent();
};
Mouse.addListener(oMouseListener);
*/
```

8. After the closing comment code (*/), insert the following:

```
mCircle.onMouseMove = function():Void {
    this._x = _root._xmouse;
    this._y = _root._ymouse;
    updateAfterEvent();
};
```

This code uses the same actions as the listener, except that the actions are applied to the mCircle instance with the onMouseMove() method of the MovieClip class.

9. Save the document and test the movie. As you move the mouse pointer, the mCircle instance will fluidly follow the mouse pointer.

As this example demonstrates, you cannot accomplish smooth movement with the onMouseMove() method of a Mouse listener. Use the onMouseMove() method of the Mouse listener only for tasks that do not require smooth graphic display or movement.

With the following steps, you add an updateAfterEvent() function to the Flash movie you created in the last section:

1. If you changed the frame rate from its original value of 12fps, set it back to 12fps in the Document Properties dialog box (Modify ⇨ Document).

2. Select frame 1 of the actions layer, and open the Actions panel. Just before the close of the last curly brace for the onMouseMove() handler, type the following code:

```
updateAfterEvent();
```

3. Save your Flash document and test it. Notice how much smoother the moon's movement is? The updateAfterEvent() allows the screen to refresh independently of the movie's frame rate. To test this effect, change the movie's frame rate to 1fps in the Document Properties dialog box (Modify ⇨ Document) and retest the Flash movie. The moon's movement is just as smooth as it was at 12fps.

You'll look at other uses of updateAfterEvent() in the following section on the Key class.

Cross-Reference For more information on updateAfterEvent(), read the coverage of the setInterval() function in Chapter 4.

Detecting Key Events with the Key Class

Using the Key class, you can detect when a certain key is pressed, and do something in your Flash movie as a result. For example, you can enable the user to use the left and right arrow keys to go to different keyframes. You can create virtual keyboards in a Flash movie that show a graphic of the key being pressed as the user presses the physical key on the keyboard. In the following sections, you'll see several examples utilizing the Key class.

Tip The Buttons Library (Window ⇨ Other Panels ⇨ Common Libraries ⇨ Buttons) now has a Key Buttons folder featuring common keyboard graphics. Also, in the Component Buttons folder of that Library, you will find a keyboard button component that will display a custom character assigned in the Property inspector.

Property and Method Overview of the Key Class

The Key class also has six methods and two event handlers to enable enhanced keyboard functionality within your Flash movies:

✦ getAscii() — This method returns the decimal ASCII value of the current key pressed. For example, if you press the R key, Key.getAscii() returns 82. This method does not accept any arguments.

✦ getCode() — To retrieve the virtual key code value of the current key pressed, you can invoke the getCode() method. Remember that the virtual key code is usually the same for both uppercase and lowercase values. Therefore, if you press the R key, Key.getCode() returns the same value as the previous example: 82.

✦ isDown(keycode) — If you want to determine whether a specific key is being pressed, you can use the isDown() method of the Key class. The isDown() method returns a Boolean value (that is, true or false). You should specify a virtual key code as the argument for the isDown() method. For example, you can determine whether the user is holding down the P key by using Key.isDown(80).

✦ isToggled(keycode) — You can determine whether either the Num Lock or Caps Lock key is enabled with the isToggled() method. You can specify the values as either key code values or as Key constants — Key.isToggled(Key.CAPSLOCK) or Key.isToggled(20) return true if the Caps Lock key is enabled (that is, toggled).

✦ addListener(listener) — You can create a Key listener that has an onKeyDown() and/or onKeyUp() method defined. The process for assigning the listener to the Key class is the same as that for the Mouse class, as discussed prior to this section:

```
var oKeyListener:Object = new Object();
oKeyListener.onKeyDown = function():Void {
    if(Key.isDown(Key.LEFT)){
        trace("The left arrow key has been pressed.");
    }
};
Key.addListener(oKeyListener);
```

You'll look at examples of Key listeners later in this chapter.

• Listener.onKeyDown() — This method of a listener enables you to detect when any key is pressed. More specifically, this method detects the downward stroke on any key.

• Listener.onKeyUp() — This method of a listener enables you to detect when a key has been released. The release action is the upward stroke of any key.

✦ removeListener(listener) — As with other static classes such as Stage and Mouse, any listener that has been added to the class can be removed with the removeListener() method. You need to specify the object name of the listener to be removed.

Detecting Key Events

Utilizing the Key class, you can enable applications with the capability to detect key events. The Key class detects when a key event has occurred, and it then sends a message notifying any listeners. Listeners were described earlier in this chapter, so you might want to review the discussion in the section titled "Assigning a Listener to the Mouse Class."

As you will see in later sections of this chapter, ActionScript logic (in the form of `if` and `else` statements) is necessary to detect *specific* keypresses. For now, you will focus on understanding the basic operation of a `Key` listener. Key listener objects can define two methods to handle key events — `onKeyDown()` and `onKeyUp()`. The following code executes a `trace()` action when the user presses any key:

```
var oKeyListener:Object = new Object();
oKeyListener.onKeyDown = function():Void {
    trace("A key has been pressed.");
};
Key.addListener(oKeyListener);
```

Likewise, the `onKeyUp()` method can detect when any key has been released, as in the following:

```
var oKeyListener:Object = new Object();
oKeyListener.onKeyUp = function():Void {
    trace("A key has been released.");
};
Key.addListener (oKeyListener);
```

You can add both methods to the same `Key` listener. In the next section, you continue to explore the dynamics of key events with `Key` listeners.

Determining Which Key Is Causing the Event

After you know how to enable Flash movies to receive key events, you can start to add more interactive navigation and usability options to your Flash movies. However, in order to work properly your Flash applications need to know which key is causing the event. Did the user press the uppercase Q key? The Enter key? In the following sections, you look at the ways in which you can detect which key or keys are causing the key events.

Using getCode() and Key Constants

The `Key.getCode()` method returns the key code of the key that was most recently pressed. What are key codes? There are many ways to refer to keys on the keyboard: ASCII, EBCDIC (Extended Binary-Coded Decimal Interchange Code), and Unicode are only a few. With ActionScript, you can use Macromedia's virtual key codes, which are distilled values derived from the ASCII character codes, or the traditional and more comprehensive ASCII character codes themselves.

> **Note**   All ASCII codes in ActionScript are decimal-based.

Although each character on the keyboard has a unique ASCII value, the virtual key set uses one numeric value to refer to both the uppercase and lowercase equivalents of a given character. As a general rule, the virtual key code is the uppercase ASCII value for most characters. For example, the ASCII code for a lowercase *a* is 97, but the virtual key code is 65. However, the ASCII code and virtual key code for an uppercase A is the same value: 65.

The `Key` class has 18 properties (or constants), all of which are key names to commonly used keys for interactivity (see Table 21-1). Usually, you need to know the key code value for the key you want to detect, but Macromedia's engineers provided a simple way to refer to the codes of keys used most commonly (such as the arrow, Page Up, and Page Down keys).

Table 21-1: Key Class Constants

Grouping	Constant	Uses/Notes
Direction	Key.LEFT Key.RIGHT Key.UP Key.DOWN	The arrow keys are commonly used to move objects in a Flash movie.
Modifiers	Key.CONTROL Key.SHIFT Key.CAPSLOCK Key.ESCAPE	Key.CONTROL represents either the Control or ⌘ key in the Macintosh version of Flash Player 6 or later.
Document keys	Key.INSERT Key.DELETEKEY Key.HOME Key.END Key.PGUP (Page Up) Key.PGDN (Page Down)	These keys navigate pages of text, as several lines in one editable text field.
White space	Key.SPACE (Spacebar) Key.BACKSPACE Key.TAB Key.ENTER	The Enter key is commonly used to enable a Send, Submit, or Search button.

Using the getCode() method and properties of the Key class, you can specifically enable the right arrow key to initiate some code, as illustrated in the following example. In the following code, the trace() statement only is called when the right arrow key is pressed:

```
var oKeyListener:Object = new Object();
oKeyListener.onKeyDown = function():Void {
  if(Key.getCode() == Key.RIGHT){
    trace("You pressed the right arrow key.");
  }
};
Key.addListener(oKeyListener);
```

Remember that Key.getCode() returns the current virtual key code value for the key(s) being detected by the key event. In this example, you want to compare the current key's value to a reference (or absolute) value — the right arrow key. Because ActionScript has a Key constant called Key.RIGHT for the right arrow key, you can refer to that value in your comparison. You can also write the code as follows:

```
var oKeyListener:Object = new Object();
oKeyListener.onKeyDown = function():Void {
  if(Key.getCode() == 39){
    trace("You pressed the right arrow key.");
  }
};
Key.addListener(oKeyListener);
```

Here, you refer to the actual key code for the key rather than using the constant. The right arrow key has a virtual key code of 39. Of course, it's much simpler to remember or read a key's Key constant (if it has one, such as Key.RIGHT) instead of the numeric assignment for each key.

Determining Alphanumeric Key Values

In the preceding section, you learned how to detect events for specific keys using getCode(). You also learned how to use the Key constants for commonly utilized keys. However, suppose that you want to enable the p key to start playback of the Flash movie. Because there is no Key.P constant automatically available, you can do one of two things: look up the virtual key code value for the letter P and use it in your getCode() comparison or let ActionScript look up the ASCII key code value and then use that in a getAscii() comparison. The former is less convenient than the latter. Furthermore, the former technique only works when you can compare the key event to a specific key such as when you want to check if the user has pressed the p key. However, only the latter works when the comparison key is also variable.

In the preceding section, you learned how to use the getCode() method for determining which key was pressed. The getCode() method returns the key code of the last key that was pressed. The getAscii() method returns the ASCII value of the last key that was pressed. Every key on the keyboard has a key code. For example, the Ctrl and Shift keys have key codes. However, only the alphanumeric (and punctuation) keys have ASCII values. That means you cannot rely on the ASCII value to tell you if the user pressed the Ctrl key. However, working with the ASCII values has several advantages when working with alphanumeric keys. Unlike key codes, which use the same value for a key regardless of whether or not additional keys are pressed (such as Shift+A), the ASCII values are unique for each character. That means that the ASCII value for a and A are unique. Additionally, using ASCII values you can devise a simple way to check for key presses even when the comparison key is variable. To do so, use the String method toCharCode() to convert a string to the ASCII equivalent. The following simple example uses the described technique to detect when the user has pressed a lowercase p.

```
var oKeyListener:Object = new Object();
oKeyListener.onKeyDown = function():Void {
  if(Key.getAscii() == new String("p").charCodeAt(0)) {
    trace("You pressed the lowercase p.");
  }
  else {
    trace("You did not press the lowercase p.");
  }
};
Key.addListener(oKeyListener);
```

You can accomplish essentially the same thing in a slightly different manner using the String.fromCharCode() method to convert the ASCII code of the pressed key to the string equivalent and compare that with the string. For example, the preceding code can be rewritten as follows:

```
var oKeyListener:Object = new Object();
oKeyListener.onKeyDown = function():Void {
  if(String.fromCharCode(Key.getAscii()) == "p") {
    trace("You pressed the lowercase p.");
  }
  else {
```

```
    trace("You did not press the lowercase p.");
  }
};
Key.addListener(oKeyListener);
```

One advantage of the latter is that it allows you to more simply detect keys in a case-insensitive manner. You can simply apply the `toUpperCase()` or `toLowerCase()` method to the value returned by `String.fromCharCode()`. The following detects either uppercase or lowercase p.

```
var oKeyListener:Object = new Object();
oKeyListener.onKeyDown = function():Void {
  if(String.fromCharCode(Key.getAscii()).toUpperCase() == "P") {
    trace("You pressed the p key.");
  }
  else {
    trace("You did not press the p key.");
  }
};
Key.addListener(oKeyListener);
```

Note that the `onKeyDown()` method is called when pressing Shift. Therefore, in the preceding example, if you type an uppercase P the Output panel will display the following sequence — the first corresponding to pressing the Shift key.

```
You did not press the p key.
You pressed the p key.
```

As mentioned, using `getAscii()` lets you compare keys even when the comparison key is variable. The following simple example illustrates that. In the code, you use a function to update the character displayed in a text field each time the user pressed a key. When the user presses a key, the code checks if the key the user pressed matches the character displayed in the text field, and it displays either `true` or `false` in the Output panel.

```
this.createTextField("tField", this.getNextHighestDepth(), 0, 0, 200,
25);
randomCharacter();

var oKeyListener:Object = new Object();
oKeyListener.onKeyDown = function():Void {
  trace((Key.getAscii() == tField.text.charCodeAt(0)));
  randomCharacter();
};
Key.addListener(oKeyListener);

function randomCharacter():Void {
  tField.text = String.fromCharCode(Math.round(Math.random() * 26) +
97);
}
```

Nudging a MovieClip Object with the Arrow Key

In this section, you create a movie that enables the user to move an image of the moon by using all four arrow keys.

1. Open a new Flash document, and save it as keyMover001.fla.

2. Select frame 1 of the default layer, and open the Actions panel. In the Script pane, add the following code:

```
// Make the movie clip into which to load the image.
this.createEmptyMovieClip("mMoon", this.getNextHighestDepth());
mMoon.createEmptyMovieClip("mImage",
mMoon.getNextHighestDepth());

// Define a listener object to use with the MovieClipLoader
// object. When the image loads into the movie clip, center it.
var oLoaderListener:Object = new Object();
oLoaderListener.onLoadInit = function(mClip:MovieClip):Void {
  mClip._x = -mClip._width/2;
  mClip._y = -mClip._height/2;
};

// Load the image into the movie clip.
var mlImage:MovieClipLoader = new MovieClipLoader();
mlImage.addListener(oLoaderListener);
mlImage.loadClip("http://www.rightactionscript.com/
samplefiles/MoonImage.png", mMoon.mImage);

// Define a key listener object such that when the user presses a
// key Flash calls moveMoon().
var oKeyListener:Object = new Object();
oKeyListener.onKeyDown = function():Void {
  moveMoon();
};
Key.addListener(oKeyListener);

function moveMoon():Void {

  // Check if one of the arrow keys has been pressed. If so, move
  // the moon in the corresponding direction.
  if(Key.getCode() == Key.RIGHT) {
    mMoon._x += 10;
  }
  if(Key.getCode() == Key.LEFT) {
    mMoon._x -= 10;
  }
  if(Key.getCode() == Key.UP) {
    mMoon._y -= 10;
  }
  if(Key.getCode() == Key.DOWN) {
    mMoon._y += 10;
  }
}
```

3. Save your Flash document and test it.

Now you know how to enable arrow keys in order to move `MovieClip` objects. If you want to pursue this example further, please read the following section. Otherwise, continue to later sections for other `Key` class examples.

Dealing with Key Repeater Settings

In its current state, the `mMoon` object from the preceding example moves repeatedly due to a feature of your operating system and the keyboard: the key repeat rate. To see the effect of the key repeat rate on your Flash movie, do one of the following (depending on your operating system):

    ✦ **Windows** — Open the Control Panel (Start ⇨ Settings ⇨ Control Panel), and double-click the Keyboard icon. In the Keyboard Properties dialog box (shown in Figure 21-1), change the Repeat rate setting to a new value (that is, if it's currently set to Fast, change it to Slow, or vice versa).

    ✦ **Macintosh OS X** — Open the System Preferences (Apple Menu ⇨ System Preferences), and click the Keyboard icon. In the Keyboard dialog box (shown in Figure 21-2), change the Key Repeat Rate setting to a new value.

If you test the example from the preceding section again with the new key repeat rate settings, you'll likely notice that the moon moves faster or slower than before.

You can also change the key repeat delay in your Keyboard Control Panel, which affects the amount of time required to wait before the OS actually starts to repeat the keypress. Because the key repeat rate (and delay) are user settings and not controlled by the Flash player, you might not want to rely on the key event to control the movement rate of the `mMoon` object. One alternative procedure is to use `setInterval()` to both detect which key is being pressed *and* control the rate at which the `_x` and `_y` properties are updated. Basically, when the key listener's `onKeyDown()` method is called, you want to set an interval using `setInterval()`. Then, when the `onKeyUp()` method is called, you want to clear the interval.

Figure 21-1: Windows XP Keyboard Properties Control Panel.

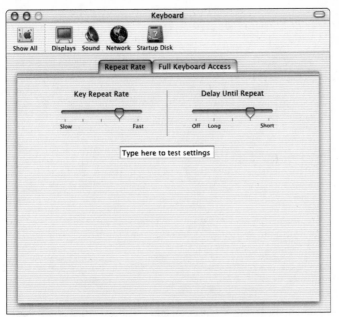

Figure 21-2: Macintosh OS X Keyboard Control Panel.

1. Open the `keyMover001.fla` document that you created in the last section.

2. Select frame 1 of the default layer, and open the Actions panel. Update the code as follows. The updates are shown in bold.

```
this.createEmptyMovieClip("mMoon", this.getNextHighestDepth());
mMoon.createEmptyMovieClip("mImage",
mMoon.getNextHighestDepth());

var oLoaderListener:Object = new Object();
oLoaderListener.onLoadInit = function(mClip:MovieClip):Void {
  mClip._x = -mClip._width/2;
  mClip._y = -mClip._height/2;
};

var mlImage:MovieClipLoader = new MovieClipLoader();
mlImage.addListener(oLoaderListener);
mlImage.loadClip("MoonImage.png", mMoon.mImage);

var nInterval:Number;

var oKeyListener:Object = new Object();
oKeyListener.onKeyDown = function():Void {
  if(nInterval == null) {
    nInterval = setInterval(moveMoon, 50);
  }
```

```
};
oKeyListener.onKeyUp = function():Void {
  clearInterval(nInterval);
  nInterval = null;
};
Key.addListener(oKeyListener);

function moveMoon():Void {
  if(Key.getCode() == Key.RIGHT) {
    mMoon._x += 10;
  }
  if(Key.getCode() == Key.LEFT) {
    mMoon._x -= 10;
  }
  if(Key.getCode() == Key.UP) {
    mMoon._y -= 10;
  }
  if(Key.getCode() == Key.DOWN) {
    mMoon._y += 10;
  }
  updateAfterEvent();
}
```

3. Save your Flash document as `keyMover002.fla`, and test the movie (Ctrl+Enter or ⌘+Enter).

Notice that when you test the movie with the updated code, there is no delay before the moon starts moving after pressing a key. Furthermore, note that the rate at which the moon moves is consistent regardless of what the key repeat settings are.

Detecting Keypress Combinations

In the preceding examples you may have noticed that if you press two arrow keys at the same time the movie clip object moves only in one of the directions. For example, if you press and hold the right arrow key, the object moves to the right. If, while holding the right arrow key, you press and hold the up arrow key, the object will start to move upward, but it will cease to move to the right. However, if you check the code, you'll see that since the `moveMoon()` function uses a series of `if` statements without `else if` clauses, the reason for the behavior is due to the functionality of `Key.getCode()`, and it is not caused by a structural issue with the code.

The `Key.getCode()` and `Key.getAscii()` methods return the key code or ASCII code of the most recent key that was pressed. That means that using `Key.getCode()` or `Key.getAscii()`, you cannot directly determine whether or not a combination of keys is pressed. However, the `Key.isDown()` method allows you to check if a key is currently pressed. It will return `true` if the key is pressed and `false` otherwise. Utilizing the `Key.isDown()` method, you can determine if a combination of keys is pressed. The method requires one parameter — the key code of the key for which you want to check if the key is currently pressed. The following code displays `true` in the Output panel if the Shift key is pressed.

```
trace(Key.isDown(Key.SHIFT));
```

The following code checks if the Shift key, the Ctrl key, and the J key are pressed.

```
trace(Key.isDown(new String("J").charCodeAt(0)) &&
Key.isDown(Key.CONTROL) && Key.isDown(Key.SHIFT));
```

The following exercise builds from the preceding exercise, enabling the movie clip to move in diagonal directions by utilizing `Key.isDown()`.

1. Open keyMover002.fla from the preceding exercise, and save it as keyMover003.fla.

2. Update the code on the first frame as follows. The updates are bolded.

```
this.createEmptyMovieClip("mMoon", this.getNextHighestDepth());
mMoon.createEmptyMovieClip("mImage",
mMoon.getNextHighestDepth());

var oLoaderListener:Object = new Object();
oLoaderListener.onLoadInit = function(mClip:MovieClip):Void {
  mClip._x = -mClip._width/2;
  mClip._y = -mClip._height/2;
};

var mlImage:MovieClipLoader = new MovieClipLoader();
mlImage.addListener(oLoaderListener);
mlImage.loadClip("http://www.rightactionscript.com/
samplefiles/MoonImage.png", mMoon.mImage);

var nInterval:Number;

var oKeyListener:Object = new Object();
oKeyListener.onKeyDown = function():Void {
  if(nInterval == null) {
    nInterval = setInterval(moveMoon, 50);
  }
};
oKeyListener.onKeyUp = function():Void {
  clearInterval(nInterval);
  nInterval = null;
};
Key.addListener(oKeyListener);

function moveMoon():Void {
  if(Key.isDown(Key.RIGHT)) {
    mMoon._x += 10;
  }
  if(Key.isDown(Key.LEFT)) {
    mMoon._x -= 10;
  }
  if(Key.isDown(Key.UP)) {
    mMoon._y -= 10;
  }
  if(Key.isDown(Key.DOWN)) {
    mMoon._y += 10;
  }
  updateAfterEvent();
}
```

3. Test the movie. Press and hold two arrow keys (for example, the right and up arrow keys) at the same time.

We'd like to know what you thought about this chapter. Visit `www.rightactionscript` `.com/asb/comments` to fill out an online form with your comments.

Summary

✦ The `Mouse` class enables you to hide and show the default mouse cursor icons used by the Flash Player.

✦ You can create custom mouse cursors by hiding the default cursor and instructing a `MovieClip` object to follow the mouse.

✦ The `Mouse` class can use listener objects that detect mouse clicks, mouse movement, and mouse scroll wheel activity.

✦ The `Key` class can be used to gather information about key events initiated by the user.

✦ The `Key` object has 18 built constants (or properties) for keys that are commonly used in application, such as the arrow keys, the Enter key, and the Spacebar.

✦ The `getCode()` method of the `Key` class returns the virtual key code of the pressed key. The virtual key code values used by ActionScript are a subset of the standard, decimal-based ASCII code system.

✦ The `getAscii()` method of the `Key` object returns the decimal ASCII code of the pressed key.

✦ The `isDown()` method checks if a specified key is currently pressed, and it is helpful in determining if key combinations are pressed.

✦ `Key` listener objects can work in tandem with `setInterval()` functions to monitor keypress activity.

✦   ✦   ✦

Working with the Stage

◆ ◆ ◆ ◆

In This Chapter

Controlling how a movie scales and aligns

Detecting the width and height of a Flash movie

Dynamically placing movie elements in the Flash Player space

◆ ◆ ◆ ◆

When Flash Player 6 was released, ActionScript added a new Stage class to the language. The Stage class represents the physical space occupied by the Flash movie's stage or the area occupied by the Flash Player. (This difference is discussed later in the chapter.) This class has only one instance at any time in the Flash movie and is, therefore, a *static* class.

Controlling the Movie's Stage

Unlike many ActionScript classes that are instantiated, the Stage class is always controlled directly through the Stage class reference, and it is not instantiated. For example, the following code illustrates how to access the scaleMode property of the Stage class:

```
Stage.scaleMode = "noScale";
```

In this code example, the scaleMode property of the Stage class is set to "noScale". Of course, you need to understand just what scaleMode and the other properties of the Stage class are. Take a look.

Understanding the Viewing Area

Before we discuss the properties of the Stage class, it will likely be helpful for you to better understand how the viewing area of a Flash movie works. To do this, we'll create a few simple Flash movies.

1. Create a new Flash document and open the Document Properties dialog box (Ctrl+J or ⌘+J). Specify a document width of 400 pixels, a height of 300 pixels, and a green background color. Rename Layer 1 movie area, draw a 400 × 300 black stroked box with a white fill, and center it on the stage.

2. Now, create a new layer named static text. On this layer, use the Text tool to add the words movie area to the top-left corner of the stage.

3. Open the Publish Settings dialog box (File ➾ Publish Settings) and click the HTML tab. For this test, use the Flash Only template, and leave the Dimensions set to Match Movie. In the

Scale menu, leave the Default (Show all) option selected. Save the Flash document as `showAll_match.fla`. Choose File ➪ Publish Preview ➪ Default – (HTML) to view the Flash movie in a web browser. Try resizing the browser window. Notice that the Flash movie does not scale, nor does it center on the page.

4. Go back to the Flash document and open the Publish Settings dialog box again. In the HTML tab, change the Dimensions to Percent, and leave the Width and Height fields set to the new 100 percent values. Save your Flash document as `showAll_percent.fla`, and publish preview the HTML document. This time, when you resize the web browser window, notice that the Flash movie scales to fill the browser window. However, the movie area is never cropped — the green background fills either the left and right or top and bottom sides of the browser window.

5. Go back to the Flash document and change the Scale option to No Border. Save your Flash document as `noBorder_percent.fla` and publish preview the HTML document. Now, as you resize the document, the Flash movie scales to fill the entire window at the expense of cropping either the horizontal or vertical dimensions of the movie area.

6. Return to the Flash document and change the Scale option to Exact fit. Save your Flash document as `exactFit_percent.fla`, and publish preview the HTML document. The Flash movie will scale to fill the browser window, and the artwork will be stretched or distorted to fill the entire window.

7. Now, change the Scale option to No scale. Save the Flash document as `noScale_percent.fla`, and publish preview the HTML document. The Flash movie does not scale as you resize the browser window. However, the Flash movie stays centered in the window at 100 percent scale. If you size the window smaller than the original dimensions of the Flash movie, the movie area will be cropped.

8. Finally, test the Flash Alignment options in the HTML tab. So far, each of the previous examples aligned the movie area to the vertical and horizontal center of the window. Go back to the HTML tab, choose Left in the Horizontal menu, and select Top in the Vertical menu — leaving the Scale menu set to No scale. Save your Flash document as `noScale_percent_lt.fla`, and publish preview the HTML document. As you size the browser window, the Flash movie remains at 100 percent and stays fixed in the top-left corner of the window. Although you cannot visibly detect it, the Flash Player area is still expanding to the full area of the browser window.

The important point to remember with these examples is that the Flash Player, when set to use a dimension such as 100 percent for width and height, expands the area of the movie area or the stage. Scale all, No border, and Exact fit scale the movie area to fill the area prescribed by the dimensions. No scale, however, expands the viewing area of the Flash Player to fill the browser window, even though the scale of the Flash movie remains 100 percent. Keep this in mind as you explore the properties and methods of the Stage class in the following sections.

Note If the Flash movie is assigned to a viewing area (in the Dimensions settings) that's the same size as the movie itself, you will not notice any difference with the scale option.

All of the scale options you just used are available in the Stage class's scaleMode property. The following sections define the properties of the Stage class.

Changing the Scale Behavior with Stage.scaleMode

The `scaleMode` property of the `Stage` class controls how the Flash movie will fill the viewing area for the Flash movie (SWF file). Four string values are recognized by the `scaleMode` property. You will apply each of these values into a working Flash document later in this chapter.

✦ `showAll` — This is the default value of the `scaleMode` property. This option fits the entire Flash movie into the area defined by the dimension attributes in the HTML document. The original aspect ratio of the Flash movie will not be distorted. However, borders can appear on two sides of the Flash movie.

✦ `noBorder` — This value forces the Flash movie to fill the area defined by the dimension attributes without leaving borders To accomplish this borderless effect, the Flash movie's aspect ratio is not distorted or stretched. However, this value may crop two sides of the Flash movie.

✦ `exactFit` — This value stretches the Flash movie to fill the entire area defined by the dimension attributes. Severe distortion or stretching of the Flash movie occurs if the dimensions do not match those defined in the Document Properties dialog box.

✦ `noScale` — When `scaleMode` uses this value, the size of the Flash movie's stage stays fixed at the dimensions prescribed by the Document Properties dialog box. As such, elements within the movie always stay at 100 percent of their original size as you placed or created them in the Flash document.

Controlling the Movie's Alignment with Stage.align

The `align` property controls how the Flash movie is positioned within the area assigned to the Flash Player. In the tests at the beginning of this chapter, you saw how the left and top alignment settings in the Publish Settings dialog box positioned a `noScale` Flash movie in the top-left corner of the browser window. The `align` property works with the same values as Publish Settings, using the string values shown in Table 22-1. The following code sets the Flash movie to display in the top-left corner of the dimensions allocated to the Flash Player:

```
Stage.align = "LT";
```

Tip　Any string value other than the values shown in Table 22-1 resets the alignment to the center of the Flash Player area. For example, `Stage.align = "ZZ";` aligns the movie to the default center position. However, we recommend that you use `"CC"` as a value to align along the center of the horizontal and vertical axes.

Table 22-1: Values for the align Property of the Stage Class

Alignment	Value	Alignment	Value
Left center	`"L"`	Left top	`"LT"`
Right center	`"R"`	Left bottom	`"LB"`
Top center	`"T"`	Right top	`"RT"`
Bottom center	`"B"`	Right bottom	`"RB"`

Reporting the Movie's Width with Stage.width

The width property of the Stage class enables you to access the pixel value currently used for the width of the Flash movie or the Flash Player area. As you will see later, the width property can return the width value entered in the Document Properties dialog box, or it can return the width of the current area allocated to the Flash Player. This property is read-only. You cannot set the width of the movie or Flash Player area with this property. In the following code, the value of the width property is displayed in a TextField object named tMovieWidth:

```
tMovieWidth.text = Stage.width;
```

Reporting the Movie's Height with Stage.height

This property retrieves the height (in pixels) currently used by the Flash movie or the Flash Player area. Like the width property, the height property returns the height value entered in the Document Properties dialog box or the height of the current area allocated to the Flash Player. In the rest of this chapter, you learn how to use this property with a Flash document. In the following code, the value of the height property is displayed in a TextField object named tMovieHeight:

```
tMovieHeight.text = Stage.height;
```

Working with scaleMode

In this exercise, you'll work with the scaleMode of a Flash movie. You'll add a text field that displays the dimensions of the stage, and use four text fields with links to affect Stage.scaleMode.

1. Open a new Flash document, and save it as stageScaleMode.fla.

2. Set the dimensions of the document to 200 x 400.

3. Add the following code to the first keyframe of the default layer.

```
import actionscriptbible.drawing.DrawingUtilities;

// Make a movie clip object, and draw a rectangle so that it's
// possible to see the borders of the stage. Draw a rectangle
// that is 199 by 399 so that it is just one pixel less than the
// stage dimensions in either direction. That way the right and
// bottom edges are visible even when the movie is scaled to
// exactFit.
this.createEmptyMovieClip("mBackground",
this.getNextHighestDepth());
var duDrawer:DrawingUtilities =
new DrawingUtilities(mBackground);
duDrawer.drawRectangle(199, 399, 100, 200);

// Make a text field to display the dimensions.
this.createTextField("tDimensions", this.getNextHighestDepth(),
0, 0, 200, 25);

// Make text fields for the scale mode links.
this.createTextField("tNoScale", this.getNextHighestDepth(), 0,
40, 200, 25);
```

```
this.createTextField("tShowAll", this.getNextHighestDepth(), 0,
75, 200, 25);
this.createTextField("tNoBorder", this.getNextHighestDepth(), 0,
110, 200, 25);
this.createTextField("tExactFit", this.getNextHighestDepth(), 0,
145, 200, 25);

// Set the scale mode link text fields to render HTML so the
// asfunction code will work.
tNoScale.html = true;
tShowAll.html = true;
tNoBorder.html = true;
tExactFit.html = true;

// Set the text fields to be non-selectable.
tNoScale.selectable = true;
tShowAll.selectable = true;
tNoBorder.selectable = true;
tExactFit.selectable = true;

// In each link text field use an <a href> tag to apply a link
// that uses asfunction to call the setScaleMode() function. In
// each case the link passes the function a parameter specifying
// the scale mode.
tNoScale.htmlText = "<a href='asfunction:setScaleMode,        ⤶
noScale'>No Scale</a>";
tShowAll.htmlText = "<a href='asfunction:setScaleMode,        ⤶
showAll'>Show All</a>";
tNoBorder.htmlText = "<a href='asfunction:setScaleMode,       ⤶
noBorder'>No Border</a>";
tExactFit.htmlText = "<a href='asfunction:setScaleMode,       ⤶
exactFit'>Exact Fit</a>";

updateDimensionsDisplay();

function updateDimensionsDisplay():Void {
  tDimensions.text = Stage.width + " " + Stage.height;
}

function setScaleMode(sMode:String):Void {
  Stage.scaleMode = sMode;
  updateDimensionsDisplay();
}
```

4. Open the Publish Settings.

5. If not already selected by default, select Flash and HTML from the Types list in the Formats tab.

6. Select the HTML tab.

7. Select Percent from the Dimensions menu. (See Figure 22-1.)

8. Set the Width and Height to 100×100.

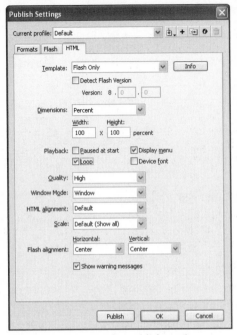

Figure 22-1: Setting the Publish Settings.

9. Click Publish.

10. Click OK.

11. Locate `stageScaleMode.html` in the same directory as the Flash document.

12. Edit `stageScaleMode.html`. The standard HTML templates specify XHTML doctype declarations. However, the documents don't validate properly, and that will cause some browsers (notably Mozilla-based browsers such as Netscape and Firefox) to display the Flash Player so that it is cut off. Delete the doctype declaration, and other related tags from the document. The code ought to look like the following.

```
<html>
<head>
<title>stageScaleMode</title>
</head>
<body bgcolor="#ffffff">
<object classid="clsid:d27cdb6e-ae6d-11cf-96b8-444553540000"
codebase="http://fpdownload.macromedia.com/pub/shockwave/cabs/fla
sh/swflash.cab#version=8,0,0,0" width="100%" height="100%"
id="stageScaleMode" align="middle">
<param name="allowScriptAccess" value="sameDomain" />
<param name="movie" value="stageScaleMode.swf" /><param
name="quality" value="high" /><param name="bgcolor"
value="#ffffff" /><embed src="stageScaleMode.swf" quality="high"
```

```
bgcolor="#ffffff" width="100%" height="100%" name="ScaleMode"
align="middle" allowScriptAccess="sameDomain"
type="application/x-shockwave-flash"
pluginspage="http://www.macromedia.com/go/getflashplayer" />
</object>
</body>
</html>
```

13. Save the HTML document, and run it in the browser.

When you click on the links, the movie updates the scale mode. As you click on each link, you can see how the scale modes affect the display of the movie. Note that only noScale causes the player to report the dimensions of the player. Otherwise, it reports the dimensions set in the document properties.

Working with the Movie's Alignment

In this exercise, you'll build alignment functionality into the application from the preceding exercise. The updated version will have a text field of links that allow the user to align the contents to the left, right, top, bottom, center, or any combination thereof.

1. Open stageScaleMode.fla, and save it as stageScaleModeAlign.fla.

2. Edit the ActionScript as follows. Changes are bolded.

```
import actionscriptbible.drawing.DrawingUtilities;

this.createEmptyMovieClip("mBackground",
this.getNextHighestDepth());
var duDrawer:DrawingUtilities =                           ↰
new DrawingUtilities(mBackground);
duDrawer.drawRectangle(199, 399, 100, 200);

this.createTextField("tDimensions", this.getNextHighestDepth(),
0, 0, 200, 25);
this.createTextField("tNoScale", this.getNextHighestDepth(), 0,
40, 200, 25);
this.createTextField("tShowAll", this.getNextHighestDepth(), 0,
75, 200, 25);
this.createTextField("tNoBorder", this.getNextHighestDepth(), 0,
110, 200, 25);
this.createTextField("tExactFit", this.getNextHighestDepth(), 0,
145, 200, 25);
this.createTextField("tAlign", this.getNextHighestDepth(), 0,
180, 200, 25);

tNoScale.html = true;
tShowAll.html = true;
tNoBorder.html = true;
tExactFit.html = true;
tAlign.html = true;

tNoScale.selectable = true;
```

```
tShowAll.selectable = true;
tNoBorder.selectable = true;
tExactFit.selectable = true;
tAlign.selectable = true;

tNoScale.htmlText = "<a href='asfunction:setScaleMode,        ↩
noScale'>No Scale</a>";
tShowAll.htmlText = "<a href='asfunction:setScaleMode,        ↩
showAll'>Show All</a>";
tNoBorder.htmlText = "<a href='asfunction:setScaleMode,       ↩
noBorder'>No Border</a>";
tExactFit.htmlText = "<a href='asfunction:setScaleMode,       ↩
exactFit'>Exact Fit</a>";
tAlign.htmlText = "<a href='asfunction:setAlign,L'>L</a>      ↩
 <a href='asfunction:setAlign,R'>R</a>                  ↩
 <a href='asfunction:setAlign,T'>T</a>                  ↩
 <a href='asfunction:setAlign,B'>B</a>                  ↩
 <a href='asfunction:setAlign,LT'>LT</a>                ↩
 <a href='asfunction:setAlign,LB'>LB</a>                ↩
 <a href='asfunction:setAlign,RT'>RT</a>                ↩
 <a href='asfunction:setAlign,RB'>RB</a>                ↩
 <a href='asfunction:setAlign,CC'>CC</a>";

updateDimensionsDisplay();

function updateDimensionsDisplay():Void {
  tDimensions.text = Stage.width + " " + Stage.height;
}

function setScaleMode(sMode:String):Void {
  Stage.scaleMode = sMode;
  updateDimensionsDisplay();
}

function setAlign(sAlign:String):Void {
  Stage.align = sAlign;
}
```

3. Save the document, and test the movie.

4. Make a copy of `stageScaleMode.html`, and name it `stageScaleModeAlign.html`.

5. Edit `stageScalemodeAlign.html`, and update every reference to `stageScaleMode.swf` to `stageScaleModeAling.swf`.

6. Test `stageScaleModeAlign.html` in the browser.

When you click on the align options, the contents should align accordingly in the player.

Detecting a New Player Size

The `Stage` class lets you register listener objects to detect when the player size has be updated. The listener object can define an `onResize()` method that tells the Flash movie what to do when the movie's dimensions are changed. The listener object can be an instance of the `Object` class or you can define a custom class that listens for events from the `Stage` class. The following constructs a new `Object` instance to use as a Stage listener:

```
var oStageListener:Object = new Object();
```

You can assign any name to this object, but it must then be assigned an `onResize()` method in order to work. For example, if you want to trace the new `Stage.width` and `Stage.height` values of a `noScale` Flash movie, you can define the following method for the `oStageListener` created previously:

```
oStageListener.onResize = function():Void {
  trace("Width = " + Stage.width);
  trace("Height = " + Stage.height);
};
```

After the object and method are defined, you can register the listener by using the `addListener()` method of the `Stage` class, which is described next.

Applying a Listener with Stage.addListener()

This method takes a predefined listener object and adds it to the callback list for the `Stage` class. Essentially, this means that any time the event handler(s) defined in the listener object are detected, the `Stage` class responds by executing the function defined for the event handler. Because there is only one listener method, `onResize()`, for the `Stage` class, the only event that can be detected and assigned to the `Stage` class via `addListener()` is the act of resizing the window containing the Flash movie. To detect the act of resizing the window, you need to add the listener object:

```
Stage.addListener(oStageListener);
```

This code takes the `oStageListener` (and the `onResize()` method defined within it) and adds it to the `Stage` class. When the window containing the Flash movie is resized, the functions within the `onResize()` handler execute.

Tip   You can add multiple listener objects to a given class. For example, you can create two objects that have unique `onResize()` methods. You can then selectively add or remove these objects to or from the `Stage` class.

Unregistering a Listener with Stage.removeListener()

This method removes a listener object from the `Stage` class. The only argument necessary for this method is the reference to the listener object — you do not need to delete the actual object itself. After a listener is removed, the listener method(s) stop responding to future events. The following code removes an object named `oStageListener` that has an `onResize()` handler defined:

```
Stage.removeListener(oStageListener);
```

In the next section, you learn how to apply a listener object to the `Stage` class.

Controlling Placement of Elements According to Stage Size

In the following exercise, you'll use a listener object to update the display of the stage dimensions as they change.

1. Open `stageScaleModeAlign.fla`, **and save it as** `stageListener.fla`.

2. Edit the ActionScript as follows. The changes are bolded.

```
import actionscriptbible.drawing.DrawingUtilities;

this.createEmptyMovieClip("mBackground",
this.getNextHighestDepth());
var duDrawer:DrawingUtilities =
new DrawingUtilities(mBackground);
duDrawer.drawRectangle(199, 399, 100, 200);

this.createTextField("tDimensions", this.getNextHighestDepth(),
0, 0, 200, 25);
this.createTextField("tNoScale", this.getNextHighestDepth(), 0,
40, 200, 25);
this.createTextField("tShowAll", this.getNextHighestDepth(), 0,
75, 200, 25);
this.createTextField("tNoBorder", this.getNextHighestDepth(), 0,
110, 200, 25);
this.createTextField("tExactFit", this.getNextHighestDepth(), 0,
145, 200, 25);
this.createTextField("tAlign", this.getNextHighestDepth(), 0,
180, 200, 25);

tNoScale.html = true;
tShowAll.html = true;
tNoBorder.html = true;
tExactFit.html = true;
tAlign.html = true;

tNoScale.selectable = true;
tShowAll.selectable = true;
tNoBorder.selectable = true;
tExactFit.selectable = true;
tAlign.selectable = true;

tNoScale.htmlText = "<a href='asfunction:setScaleMode,
noScale'>No Scale</a>";
tShowAll.htmlText = "<a href='asfunction:setScaleMode,
showAll'>Show All</a>";
tNoBorder.htmlText = "<a href='asfunction:setScaleMode,
noBorder'>No Border</a>";
tExactFit.htmlText = "<a href='asfunction:setScaleMode,
exactFit'>Exact Fit</a>";
tAlign.htmlText = "<a href='asfunction:setAlign,L'>L</a>
 <a href='asfunction:setAlign,R'>R</a>
 <a href='asfunction:setAlign,T'>T</a>
 <a href='asfunction:setAlign,B'>B</a>
 <a href='asfunction:setAlign,LT'>LT</a>
 <a href='asfunction:setAlign,LB'>LB</a>
```

```
 <a href='asfunction:setAlign,RT'>RT</a>
 <a href='asfunction:setAlign,RB'>RB</a>
 <a href='asfunction:setAlign,CC'>CC</a>";

var oStageListener:Object = new Object();
oStageListener.onResize = function():Void {
  updateDimensionsDisplay();
};
Stage.addListener(oStageListener);

updateDimensionsDisplay();

function updateDimensionsDisplay():Void {
  tDimensions.text = Stage.width + " " + Stage.height;
}

function setScaleMode(sMode:String):Void {
  Stage.scaleMode = sMode;
  updateDimensionsDisplay();
}

function setAlign(sAlign:String):Void {
  Stage.align = sAlign;
}
```

3. Save the document, and test the movie.

4. Make a copy of `stageScaleModeAlign.html`, **and save it as** `stageListener.html`.

5. Edit `stageListener.html`, **and update any reference to** `stageScaleModeAlign.swf` to `stageListener.swf`.

6. Test `stageListener.html` in the browser.

As long as `noScale` is selected, you can resize the browser window, and you'll see that the text field display is updated accordingly.

 We'd like to know what you thought about this chapter. Visit `www.rightactionscript .com/asb/comments` to fill out an online form with your comments.

Summary

✦ Use the HTML options in the Publish Settings dialog box to understand the principles of dimensions, scale, and alignment before you attempt to use the `Stage` class and its properties and methods.

✦ The `Stage` class has five properties: `scaleMode`, `align`, `width`, `height`, and `showMenu`.

✦ The `Stage` class can utilize listener objects that have an `onResize()` handler defined.

✦ ✦ ✦

Using Context Menus

Context menus are the menus that appear when the user right-clicks or Ctrl-clicks on the player or on an object within the player. The menu that appears is determined by where the user has clicked, hence the *context* of context menu. For example, when a user opens the default Flash Player context menu, there are standard options relevant to the Flash Player such as zoom or player settings. However, when the user opens the context menu for a text field, the menu has options relevant to a text field such as copying and pasting. In this chapter, you learn how to programmatically work with context menus using ActionScript.

Controlling the Standard Flash Player Context Menu Display

With the `Stage.showMenu` property, you can control the user's access to the right-click (or Control-click on Mac) menu options of the Flash Player plug-in or stand-alone projector. `Stage.showMenu` is a Boolean property: a value of `true` enables the right-click menu, and a value of `false` disables the right-click menu.

By default, this property has a value of `true`. With this setting, the user will see the menu shown in Figure 23-1 upon right-clicking the Flash Player movie area in the browser plug-in or stand-alone projector. The following code enables the built-in menu. It is also the default value, so unless you've assigned a value of `false` to the property, the value is already `true`.

```
Stage.showMenu = true;
```

Figure 23-1: The Flash Player standard context menu.

If the value is set to `false`, the user cannot access the playback control items in the context menu. The restricted player menu is shown in Figure 23-2. The following code disables the standard options in the built-in menu:

```
Stage.showMenu = false;
```

Figure 23-2: The Flash Player restricted context menu.

The `Stage.showMenu` property does not let you remove the standard context menu entirely. In fact, the Flash player has no native functionality that allows you to remove the entire context menu.

Using the ContextMenu Class

ActionScript gives you the power to control the menu items that are displayed in Flash Player 7+ context menu. If you refer to Figures 23-1 and 23-2, you can see the menu control that the `Stage` class offers. Remember, you access this menu by right-clicking (or Control-clicking on Mac) the stage area of the Flash Player. With the `ContextMenu` class, not only can you control the built-in menu items such as Zoom, Play, and Rewind, but you can also add your own custom menu items, complete with caption names and custom ActionScript callback handlers. In this section, you learn how to precisely enable (or disable) built-in and custom menu items.

The `ContextMenu` class can be used to attach specific context menus to display objects. Based on the previous paragraph, you might be wondering what the `ContextMenu` class offers over the `Stage.showMenu` property. If you can turn off the player's menu with `Stage.showMenu`, why do you need the `ContextMenu` class? The answer is twofold:

✦ With the `ContextMenu` class, you can *selectively* disable built-in player menu items with various items in your Flash movie. For example, if you want the built-in player menu items (Play, Zoom, Rewind, and so on) available in most areas of the movie but want those same items disabled on a specific piece of artwork (such a `MovieClip` object) in the movie, you can create a `ContextMenu` instance and assign it to that artwork.

✦ You can control your own custom menu items for the player's menu with the `ContextMenu` class. The `Stage` class does not enable you to control, add, or remove specific items in the menu.

As you learn in the following sections, the general steps for using the `ContextMenu` class are:

1. Make a new instance of the `ContextMenu` class using the constructor.

2. Define the properties of the `ContextMenu` instance's built-in items using the `ContextMenu.builtInItems` property (optional).

3. Add your own menu items to the `ContextMenu` instance using one or more instances of the `ContextMenuItem` class (optional).

4. Define the event handler methods for the `ContextMenu` instance and/or `ContextMenuItem` instances (optional).

5. Assign the `ContextMenu` instance to a `MovieClip`, `Button`, or `TextField` instance, using the new `menu` property of those classes.

Controlling Flash Player's Built-in Menu

The `builtInItems` property of the `ContextMenu` class controls the display of the Flash Player's default context menu items, as shown in Figure 23-2. The `builtInItems` property contains the subproperties described in Table 23-1. These subproperties can be set to `true` (display) or `false` (hide). By default, all properties have a value of `true`.

Table 23-1: Properties of the ContextMenu.builtInItems Property

Property	Displayed Name	Description
save	Save	This menu item is available only in the Macromedia Shockmachine application and a special AOL-only version of the Flash Player. In these environments, the Save item enables you to save a copy of the Flash movie (a SWF file).
zoom	Zoom In Zoom Out 100% Show All	These menu items enable the user to change the scale of the entire Flash movie. The `zoom` property controls all of the menu items related to the view.
quality	Quality	This menu item enables the user to control the anti-aliasing of artwork within the movie. The `quality` property controls the Quality menu item and the Low, Medium, and High submenu items.
play	Play	This menu item enables the user to initiate a `play()` command on the main timeline (_level0) of the Flash movie. This menu item is available only if there is more than one frame on the main timeline.
loop	Loop	This menu item determines whether playback of the Flash movie's main timeline (_level0) will repeat when the last frame is reached. This menu item is available only if there is more than one frame on the main timeline.
rewind	Rewind	This menu item enables the user to go back to the first frame of the Flash movie's main timeline (_level0). This menu item is available only if there is more than one frame on the main timeline.
forward_back	Forward Back	These menu items are equivalent to issuing `nextFrame()` and `prevFrame()` actions, respectively, on the Flash movie's main timeline (_level0). These menu items are available only if there is more than one frame on the main timeline.
print	Print	This menu item enables the user to print the current frame of the Flash movie.

If you want to disable all of these properties (thus hiding all of these menu items), you can use the `hideBuiltInItems()` method of the `ContextMenu` class.

In the following steps, you practice various uses of the `builtInItems` property.

1. Open a new Flash document, and save it as `contextMenuBuiltInItems.fla`.

2. Select frame 1 of the default layer, and open the Actions panel. Add the following code:

```
var cmMovie:ContextMenu = new ContextMenu();
cmMovie.builtInItems.zoom = false;
cmMovie.builtInItems.print = false;
this.menu = cmMovie;
```

This code adds a new `ContextMenu` instance named `cmMovie` (line 1). In lines 2 and 3, the `zoom` and `print` properties of the `builtInItems` property are set to `false`. In line 4, the `cmMovie` menu is then assigned to the main timeline (`this`), using the `MovieClip` class's `menu` property.

Note   You can apply the same `ContextMenu` instance to multiple objects in your Flash movie.

3. Save your Flash document and test it. When you right-click (or Control-click on the Mac) the movie's stage area, only the Quality and Settings items should be enabled. The Zoom controls and the Print item will not be displayed (or enabled).

Note   The Settings and About Flash Player 8 menu items are always displayed in any context menu. You cannot disable these menu items. If you are using the Debug version of the Flash Player, you will also always see the Debugger menu item.

4. Go back to frame 1 of the actions layer and change your code to the following:

```
var cmMovie:ContextMenu = new ContextMenu();
// cmMovie.builtInItems.zoom = false;
// cmMovie.builtInItems.print = false;
cmMovie.hideBuiltInItems();
this.menu = cmMovie;
```

Here, you use the `hideBuiltItItems()` method to disable and hide all of the default context menu items shown in Table 23-1.

5. Save your document as `contextMenuHideBuiltInItems.fla` and test it. When you right-click (or Control-click on the Mac) the stage, you should see only the Settings (and Debugger) menu items. If you test the movie in a Web browser, you should also see the About Flash Player 8 menu item.

Building Custom Menu Items with the ContextMenuItem Class

If you want to add a new customized menu item to the Flash Player's context menu, you can use the `ContextMenuItem` class to define the item's name and functionality. When you need a custom menu item, do the following:

1. Create a `ContextMenu` instance, as described in the earlier exercise.

2. Create a new `ContextMenuItem` instance.

3. Define the name of the menu item (the `caption` property) and the event handler function for the item. The callback handler is invoked when the user selects the item from the menu.

4. Add the `ContextMenuItem` instance to the `ContextMenu` instance's `customItems` array. The `customItems` property is a built-in array of the `ContextMenu` class. Anytime you create a new `ContexMenu` instance, the `customItems` array is initially empty.

5. Assign the `ContextMenu` instance to the menu property of a `MovieClip`, `Button`, or `TextField` instance in your Flash movie.

Constructing a ContextMenuItem Object

You can instantiate a new `ContextMenuItem` object using the constructor as part of a new statement. The constructor accepts up to five parameters:

✦ `caption` — A string to use as the label for the menu item.

✦ `onSelect` — A reference to a function that Flash will automatically call when the menu item is selected.

✦ `seperatorBefore` — A Boolean value indicating whether or not to display a line before the menu item. The default value is `false`.

✦ `enabled` — A Boolean value indicating whether or not to enable the menu option by default. The default value is `true`.

✦ `visible` — A Boolean value indicating whether or not the menu option is visible by default. The default value is `true`.

The `caption` and `onSelect` parameters are required. The remaining parameters are optional.

```
var cmiA:ContextMenuItem = new ContextMenuItem("Menu Item", onMenuSelect);
```

You can change each of the settings via corresponding properties once the item has been constructed. For more details regarding the `onSelect` parameter, read the next section.

Handling Menu Item Select Events

When the user selects a custom context menu item, Flash calls the function that has been associated with the corresponding `ContextMenuItem` instance. You can associate the function with the menu item using the second parameter of the constructor. Additionally, you can update the setting at any point by assigning a new function reference to the `onSelect` property of the `ContextMenuItem` instance. The function reference can be assigned indirectly, or you can use an anonymous function as follows:

```
cmiA.onSelect = function(oDisplayObject:Object,
cmiInstance:ContextMenuItem):Void {
  trace("menu item selected");
};
```

As you can see in the preceding example, the `onSelect()` event handler method is passed two parameters — a reference to the display object (movie clip, button, or text field) to which the parent context menu is associated, and a reference to the `ContextMenuItem` instance that dispatched the event. The parameters are passed to the function regardless of how it was assigned to the `onSelect` property of the menu item (via the constructor or assigned to the `onSelect` property after the object was constructed).

Placing Menu Item Separators

Menu item separators are lines that can appear above any item in the menu. Menu item separators help to group related menu items for the user. By default, custom menu items do not have menu item separators above them. However, you can specify that an item have a separator using the separatorBefore property. You can set the property via a parameter passed to the constructor, or you can set the value at any point after the object has been constructed by using the separatorBefore property. The property requires a Boolean value. The following code places a menu item separator before cmiA:

```
cmiA.separatorBefore = true;
```

Enabling Menu Items

By default, menu items are enabled. That means that they appear in black text, and they are selectable by the user. However, there are legitimate reasons to temporarily disable a menu item. For example, you may have menus items that let the user start and stop a timer. If the timer is already started, the user doesn't need to have the option to start the timer. Likewise, if the timer is stopped, the user doesn't need to have the option to stop the timer. You can disable and re-enable menu items using the enabled property. (You can initialize a menu item's enabled mode with the corresponding parameter in the constructor.) When a menu item is disabled it still appears in the context menu. However, it appears gray rather than black, and it is not selectable by the user.

Toggling Menu Item Visibility

You can toggle the visibility of menu items. In some applications, the use cases dictate that menu items ought to be temporarily removed from the context menu rather than simply disabled. In such cases you can use the visible property.

Adding a Background Selector Feature to a Flash Movie

In the following exercise, you build a simple Flash application that lets the user select a background image using the context menu. Complete the following steps:

1. Open a new Flash document, and save it as contextMenuBackgroundSelector.fla.

2. Select the first keyframe on the default layer, open the Actions panel, and add the following code.

```
// Make a new movie clip into which we'll place the background.
var mBackground:MovieClip =
this.createEmptyMovieClip("mBackground",
this.getNextHighestDepth());

initialize();

// Add a nested movie clip into which the image will load.
mBackground.createEmptyMovieClip("mImage",
mBackground.getNextHighestDepth());

// Place a text field within the movie clip in order to display a
// message to the user when the application starts.
var tMessage:TextField =
mBackground.mImage.createTextField("tMessage",
```

```
mBackground.mImage.getNextHighestDepth(), 0, 0, 0, 0);
tMessage.autoSize = "center";
tMessage.selectable = false;
tMessage.text = "Right-click/Control-click to select
a background.";

// Place the text field at the center of the stage.
tMessage._x = Stage.width/2 - tMessage._width/2;
tMessage._y = Stage.height/2 - tMessage._height/2;

// Make a MovieClipLoader object in order to load the
// backgrounds.
var mlBackgroundImage:MovieClipLoader = new MovieClipLoader();

// Make a new ContextMenu object, and tell it to hide the built-
// in items.
var cmMain:ContextMenu = new ContextMenu();
cmMain.hideBuiltInItems();

// Make the ContextMenuItem objects.
var cmiBackground1:ContextMenuItem =
new ContextMenuItem("Background 1", onBackgroundSelect);

// Make cmiBackground2 a copy of cmiBackground1, then change the
// caption.
var cmiBackground2:ContextMenuItem = cmiBackground1.copy();
cmiBackground2.caption = "Background 2";

// Make cmiReset so that it has a line before it in the menu and
// it is disabled by default.
var cmiReset:ContextMenuItem =
new ContextMenuItem("Reset Background", initialize, true, false);

// Add the menu items to the context menu.
cmMain.customItems.push(cmiBackground1);
cmMain.customItems.push(cmiBackground2);

cmMain.customItems.push(cmiReset);

// Assign the ContextMenu object to the menu property of the main
// movie clip.
this.menu = cmMain;

// The onBackgroundSelect() function is called as the event
// handler method when the menu items are selected.
function onBackgroundSelect(mTarget:MovieClip,
cmiSelected:ContextMenuItem):Void {
  if(cmiSelected == cmiBackground1) {
    mlBackgroundImage.loadClip(
"http://www.rightactionscript.com/samplefiles/image1.jpg",
mBackground.mImage);
```

```
      cmiBackground2.enabled = true;
    }
    else {
      mlBackgroundImage.loadClip(
"http://www.rightactionscript.com/samplefiles/image2.jpg",
mBackground.mImage);
      cmiBackground1.enabled = true;
    }
    cmiReset.enabled = true;
    cmiSelected.enabled = false;
}

function initialize():Void {

    // Make a movie clip nested within mBackground. We'll load the
    // background into mImage. Make mImage at depth 1 so that it
    // overwrites the movie clip if it was previously instantiated.
    mBackground.createEmptyMovieClip("mImage", 1);

    // Make a text field to display a message to the user.
    var tMessage:TextField =
    mBackground.mImage.createTextField("tMessage",
    mBackground.mImage.getNextHighestDepth(), 0, 0, 0, 0);
    tMessage.autoSize = "center";
    tMessage.selectable = false;
    tMessage.text = "Right-click/Control-click to select
    a background.";
    tMessage._x = Stage.width/2 - tMessage._width/2;
    tMessage._y = Stage.height/2 - tMessage._height/2;
    cmiReset.enabled = false;
    cmiBackground1.enabled = true;
    cmiBackground2.enabled = true;
}
```

3. Save the Flash document, and test the movie.

When you right-click/Control-click on the stage, you get an option to select one of the two backgrounds.

 We'd like to know what you thought about this chapter. Visit `www.rightactionscript` `.com/asb/comments` to fill out an online form with your comments.

Summary

✦ Using the `ContextMenu` and `ContextMenuItem` classes, you can control and customize the Flash Player's context menu. This feature enables you to add shortcuts and enhanced features to your movie's elements.

✦   ✦   ✦

Understanding the Capabilities and Security Objects

◆ ◆ ◆ ◆

In This Chapter

Working with top-level System class properties, methods, and events

Determining client system and player capabilities

Using the System.security object to allow cross-domain access to SWF content

◆ ◆ ◆ ◆

The System class is a static class that aggregates functionality and data at the Flash Player level. The System class itself provides you with some rather disparate methods and properties, as well as an event-handler method. In addition, it provides you with access to a capabilities object and a security object as well as the IME class. The capabilities object returns information about the system on which the player is running. The security object provides you with the capability to allow cross-domain access to the SWF. The IME class lets you more effectively work with the operating system's input method editor (IME) for non-ASCII text (for example, Japanese or Korean). This chapter looks at each of these topics in more detail.

The System class may seem like a rather strange assortment of things. This chapter categorizes the discussion of the class as follows:

- ◆ Properties, methods, and event-handler methods accessed directly from the System class
- ◆ The System.capabilities object
- ◆ The System.security object
- ◆ The System.IME class

Using the Top-Level System Functionality

The System class provides you with a motley crew of two methods, two properties (not including the capabilities and security object references), and one event-handler method. Without further ado, let's look at each of these items.

Setting the Clipboard Contents

If you are authoring to Flash Player 7+, you can use the `System.setClipboard()` method to assign a string value to the user's system Clipboard. The Clipboard is where content is normally placed when the user selects and copies some text. When the user chooses to paste text, the contents of the Clipboard are pasted into the focused area of the current application. However, using the `System.setClipboard()` method, you can programmatically replace the contents of the Clipboard without the user having to copy any text. The following example replaces the current Clipboard contents with a string: `Flash 8`.

```
System.setClipboard("Flash 8");
```

Showing the Flash Player Settings

The Flash Player has a Flash Player Settings panel, which you might not be familiar with. The panel opens in three ways:

✦ You can open the panel by right-clicking/Control-clicking in the Flash Player and selecting Settings.

✦ The panel automatically opens in certain circumstances. For example, if the application is attempting to access the user's camera and/or microphone, the panel opens to ask the user to approve or decline the request.

✦ You can programmatically open the panel using the `System.showSettings()` method.

The Flash Player Settings panel has four tabbed sections. Figure 24-1 shows the panel opened to the Local Storage section. In addition, there are the Privacy, Microphone, and Camera sections.

Figure 24-1: The Flash Player Settings panel has four sections; this is one.

The `System.showSettings()` method can be called with or without a parameter. If you call the method without a parameter, the panel opens to the section to which it had last been opened. However, you can also specify the section to which you want it to open by passing the method a numeric parameter. Here are the valid values:

✦ 0: Privacy

✦ 1: Local Storage

✦ 2: Microphone

✦ 3: Camera

For example, the following code tells Flash to open the panel to the Local Storage section.

```
System.showSettings(1);
```

Determining How Local Settings and Data Are Saved

The Flash Player saves some data locally to the client computer. For example, it can save information about whether or not the user has granted access to a microphone and/or camera. Local shared object data is stored to the client computer as well. These types of information are stored by domain. That means that the local settings and the local shared object data can be set for each domain without having to worry about conflicts.

However, in Flash Player 7, the changes to the sandbox security model spilled over into how local data is stored. By default, Flash Player stores Flash 7 and 8 local content by exact domain. That means that, for example, `www.somedomain.com` and `staging.somedomain.com` are treated as two different domains by which local data can be stored. You can use the `System.exactSettings` property to specify whether you want Flash to use the default behavior and save the data by the full, exact domain or save data by *superdomain* (for example, `www.flashsupport.com` and `beta.flashsupport.com` share the superdomain of `flashsupport.com`), as Flash 6 content was saved. The default value for `System.exactSettings` is `true`. If you set the value to `false`, content is saved by superdomain. That means that Flash will save local data from `www.somedomain.com` and `staging.somedomain.com` both under the same superdomain, called simply `somedomain.com`.

If you do want to set `System.exactSettings` to `false`, you must do so before any local settings are accessed within the application. Therefore, you should typically set `System.exactSettings` on the first line of the first frame of the application if you want to set it to `false`. If you want to allow the default behavior, you don't need to do anything with the property.

Using Code Pages

Since Flash Player 6, Flash has supported Unicode. That means that it is much easier to display international and specialized text content to users than in previous versions. Earlier player versions did not support Unicode and instead rendered text using the code page of the user's operating system. That meant that the user had to have the same code page as the one used to author the text. Therefore, if the authoring system used a code page for the Japanese character set, the content would not correctly display on a system using the code page for English. Unicode text, on the other hand, can be correctly rendered without having to rely on the operating system's code page.

Because Flash Player 6 and higher support Unicode, you likely don't need to worry about the `System.useCodePage` property. As long as you are authoring content for these most recent players, just make sure that any text you load is saved as Unicode and it will be displayed properly. However, if you want to have the text rendered based on the user's code page, you can set the `System.userCodePage` property to `true` (it is `false` by default).

Creating a Catch-All Status Handler

The `Camera`, `Microphone`, `NetStream`, `LocalConnection`, and `SharedObject` classes all have `onStatus()` event-handler methods to handle status messages. Each of these status handlers works in the same way. When a status message is returned, the `onStatus()` method of the relevant class is called and passed a parameter that contains information about the status. Typically, you define the `onStatus()` method for a specific object. For example, you might attempt to create a local shared object named `lsoData`, and define an `onStatus()` method for that object in the following manner:

```
var lsoData:SharedObject = SharedObject.getLocal("settings");
lsoData.onStatus = function(oData:Object):Void {
  if(oData.code = "SharedObject.Flush.Failed") {
    // Display a message to the user.
    tOutput.text = "Failed to save data to local shared object.";
  }
};
```

However, if the `onStatus()` method is not defined for an object, and a status event is received, Flash will next look for a `System.onStatus()` method. The `System.onStatus()` method can be used as a catch-all for handling status events. You must define the `System.onStatus()` method. For example:

```
System.onStatus = function(oData:Object):Void {
  trace("status event received");
};
```

Determining the Client Computer's Capabilities

The `System.capabilities` object provides you with information about the computer running the Flash Player on the client. This type of information is particularly useful when you are authoring content that is to be played back on a variety of devices. You can use the information from the `capabilities` object to determine what content to load and how to display it. The following sections look at some of the information that the `System.capabilities` object can provide.

The `System.capabilities` object has a property named `serverString`. The `serverString` property contains URL-encoded name-value pairs such as the following:

```
A=t&SA=t&SV=t&EV=t&MP3=t&AE=t&VE=t&ACC=f&PR=t&SP=t&SB=f&DEB=
t&V=WIN%207%2C0%2C14%2C0&M=Macromedia%20Windows&R=1024x768&DP=
72&COL=color&AR=1.0&OS=Windows%20XP&L=en&PT=External&AVD=f&LFD=
f&WD=f
```

The `serverString` value is parsed by Flash and used to automatically populate the other properties that you'll see in the following sections. For example, in the preceding `serverString` example value, you can see a parameter named V with a value of `WIN%207%2C0%2C14%2C0`. That value is used to populate the `version` property with a value of `WIN 7,0,14,0`. Although you can work directly with the `serverString` value, you'll likely find the values that have been parsed into the other properties to be much more convenient.

Getting Audio and Video Capabilities

The `System.capabilities` object can return a lot of information about the audio and video capabilities on the client computer. Table 24-1 lists the audio- and video-related properties of the `System.capabilities` object.

Table 24-1: Audio and Video Capabilities

Property	Description	Example	Minimum Player Version
avHardwareDisable	A Boolean value indicating whether the client computer's microphone and camera are enabled or disabled.	true	7
hasAudio	A Boolean value indicating whether the client computer has the hardware to play back audio. Does not detect whether the speakers are connected or turned on. Simply indicates hardware capabilities.	true	6
hasAudioEncoder	A Boolean value indicating whether the client computer has the capability to encode an audio stream. An audio stream is most frequently the sound from a microphone.	true	6
hasEmbeddedVideo	A Boolean value indicating whether the client computer can display embedded video.	true	6
hasMP3	A Boolean value indicating whether the client computer has the capability to decode MP3 sounds.	true	6
hasScreenBroadcast	A Boolean value indicating whether the client computer has the capability to broadcast the user's screen. Broadcasting the screen is a live video feature that requires Flash Communication Server.	true	6
hasScreenPlayback	A Boolean value indicating whether the client computer has the capability to play back a live screen broadcast.	true	6
hasStreamingAudio	A Boolean value indicating whether the client computer has the capability to play streaming audio.	true	6
hasStreamingVideo	A Boolean value indicating whether the client computer has the capability to play streaming video.	true	6
hasVideoEncoder	A Boolean value indicating whether the client computer has the capability to encode a video stream. Most often, the video stream is from a Web camera.	true	6

The audio and video capabilities properties can be useful when building applications that run on various environments. For example, if the client computer does not have audio capabilities, you likely will not want to have the user load audio content. Audio content can often be some of the most bandwidth-intensive content in an application, and you don't want to have users download that content if they cannot even play it. Therefore, using the hasAudio property, you can download the audio only if the users can play it. For example:

```
if(System.capabilities.hasAudio) {
  this.createEmptyMovieClip("mSoundHolder", this.getNextHighestDepth());
  var sndAudio:Sound = new Sound(mSoundHolder);
  sndAudio.onLoad = function():Void {
    this.start();
  };
  sndAudio.load("audio.mp3");
}
```

The other audio and video capabilities properties can be used similarly to optimize your application.

Determining Versions

The System.capabilities object provides information about player and operating system versions. Table 24-2 shows these properties.

Table 24-2: Version Properties

Property	Description	Example	Minimum Player Version
os	A string indicating the operating system on the client computer.	Windows XP	6
version	A string indicating the player version, including revision number.	WIN 7,0,14,0	6
manufacturer	A string indicating the manufacturer of the player.	Macromedia Windows	6
language	A string indicating the language used by the client computer. The value is composed of a lowercase two-character language code from ISO 639-1. Optionally, the value can be further specified using an uppercase two-character country code from ISO 3166.	en	6
isDebugger	A Boolean value indicating whether the player is the debugger version.	true	6
hasAccessibility	A Boolean value indicating whether the player can communicate with accessibility software.	true	6r65 (Player 6, revision 65)

Property	Description	Example	Minimum Player Version
hasPrinting	A Boolean value indicating whether the player supports printing.	true	6
playerType	A string indicating the player type. The value is one of the following: StandAlone, External, ActiveX, or PlugIn.	StandAlone	7
localFile ReadDisable	A Boolean value indicating whether the player has access to read content from the local file system.	true	7

Determining versions can be potentially useful in a variety of situations. Some features are known to work incorrectly or unpredictably on some operating systems, for example. By detecting the operating system, you can help ensure that you can properly handle such occurrences.

Determining the language used by the client computer can assist you in providing multilingual content. For example, you might have text stored in external files — perhaps one file per language. You can then use the language property to determine which text to load and ultimately display to the users. The following code demonstrates how that might work:

```
var lvText:LoadVars = new LoadVars();
lvText.onData = function(sText):Void {
  tContent.text = sText;
};
switch (System.capabilities.language) {
  case "es":
    lvText.load("copy_spanish.txt");
    break;
  case "ja":
    lvText.load("copy_japanese.txt");
    break;
  default:
    lvText.load("copy_english.txt");
}
```

Web Resource   For more information on ISO 639-1 codes, see www.loc.gov/standards/iso639-2/ englangn.html.

Getting Screen and Resolution Information

The screen and resolution information properties provided by the System.capabilities object are listed in Table 24-3. You can use these properties to ensure that you are displaying the proper content in an optimized format for the viewer's display.

Table 24-3: Screen and Resolution Properties

Property	Description	Example	Minimum Player Version
pixelAspectRatio	A number indicating the pixel aspect ratio. Most desktop systems report 1. Other devices can have different aspect ratios.	1	6
screenColor	A Boolean value indicating whether the screen supports color.	true	6
screenDPI	A number indicating the dots per inch of the screen.	72	6
screenResolutionX	A number indicating the horizontal resolution of the screen.	1024	6
screenResolutionY	A number indicating the vertical resolution of the screen.	768	6

As an example of how you might use some of these properties, consider a scenario in which you have published several versions of your application to the same URL. Each version is intended for a different device (because these various devices have very different resolutions). The following code shows how you can use the screenResolutionX and screenResolutionY properties to detect the type of device and display the correct version.

```
var nScreenWidth:Number = System.capabilities.screenResolutionX;
var nScreenHeight:Number = System.capabilities.screenResolutionY;

if (nScreenWidth >= 640 && nScreenHeight >= 480) {
  // Direct probable desktop users to the main movie.
  this.gotoAndStop("mainmovie");
} else if (nScreenWidth == 640 && nScreenHeight == 200) {
  // Load fullscreen Nokia movie which is 640x200.
  this.getURL("nokia_full.swf", "_blank");
} else if (nScreenWidth == 463 && nScreenHeight == 200) {
  // Load regular Nokia movie which is 463x200.
  this.getURL("nokia_reg.swf", "_blank");
} else {
  // Catch-all for all other possible resolutions. Just
  // direct them to the desktop user content.
  this.gotoAndStop("mainmovie");
}
```

Working with Player Security When Loading SWF Content

The Flash Player has sandbox security that prevents an SWF on one domain from loading and then having access to the data within or the properties and methods of the loaded SWF. The security model changed somewhat between Flash Player 6 and Flash Player 7, and again very slightly from Flash Player 7 to Flash Player 8. Previously, Flash Player 6 disallowed access only between two completely different superdomains, but allowed access between two different subdomains and/or protocols within the same superdomain. For example, Flash Player 6 would allow a Flash application at `https://secure.somedomain.com` to load and have access to an SWF at `http://www.somedomain.com`. In Flash Player 7, the domains must match exactly — including subdomain and protocol.

Although the default security restrictions prevent you from being able to fully load SWF content across domains, subdomains, and protocols, the `System.security` object enables you to modify some settings that will allow you to grant access to an SWF. The `allowDomain()` and `allowInsecureDomain()` methods provide you with the necessary functionality.

If you want to specify that another domain and/or subdomain (using the same protocol) should be able to load and use the data from an SWF file, you should use the `allowDomain()` method. The method should be placed within the first frame of the SWF that you want to load. It allows you to specify a list of parameters indicating locations from which you want the SWF to be accessible. The parameters should be string values, and they can be in the following formats:

- ✦ `domainName` (for example, `www.rightactionscript.com`)

- ✦ `protocol://domainName` (for example, `http://www.flashsupport.com`)

- ✦ `protocol://IPAddress` (for example, `http://123.456.78.9`)

Because the Flash Player 7+ model differs slightly from the Flash Player 6 model, the use of the `allowDomain()` method is slightly different. For example, previously the following code would allow any SWF in the `flashsupport.com` domain to load the SWF and have access to its data:

```
System.security.allowDomain("flashsupport.com");
```

However, with the Flash Player 7+ model, the preceding code allows access from SWF files being served from `flashsupport.com`, but not from `www.flashsupport.com`, `beta.flashsupport.com`, and so on. With Flash Player 7+, you must supply the complete domain name, including subdomain. Therefore, if you want to allow access from both `flashsupport.com` and `www.flashsupport.com`, your code needs to look like the following:

```
System.security.allowDomain("flashsupport.com", "www.flashsupport.com");
```

Although it presents a security risk, you might want to sometimes grant access for an application running over regular HTTP to load and have access to an SWF being served from HTTPS. To accomplish that, you cannot simply use the `allowDomain()` method. Instead, you need to use the `allowInsecureDomain()` method. Otherwise, the two methods operate similarly. You can specify one or more domains to which you want to grant access as parameters for the `allowInsecureDomain()` method:

```
System.security.allowInsecureDomain("flashsupport.com", "www.flashsupport.com");
```

By default, each domain restricts access to its content such that only Flash movies on the same exact domain can send and load it. However, you can create a `crossdomain.xml` file for the domain that specifies what domains and IP addresses can have access.

The file itself is an XML file in which the root element is a `<cross-domain-policy>` tag. Nested within the root element can be zero or more `<allow-access-from>` tags. The `<allow-access-from>` tag has a `domain` attribute specifying the allowed domain or IP address. If you are specifying a domain name, you can use the * as a wildcard. Here is an example policy file:

```
<?xml version="1.0"?>
<cross-domain-policy>
  <allow-access-from domain="*.themakers.com" />
  <allow-access-from domain="*.person13.com" />
</cross-domain-policy>
```

The preceding example file allows any requesting SWF served from `themakers.com` or `person13.com` to access the resources on the domain on which the file is located. The requesting movie can be served from `www.person13.com`, `testing.person13.com`, `www2`
`.themakers.com`, or `www.themakers.com`, to give just a few examples. However, if a movie served from `www.anotherdomain.com` makes a request for a resource on the server, the request is denied.

 Note   The wildcard character does not work with IP addresses.

By default, the policy file must be placed in the root directory for the domain. That is, `crossdomain.xml` must exist such that it is accessible at, for example, `http://www`
`.yourdomain.com/crossdomain.xml`. Flash Player 7 up through 7.0.14.0 looks only in the root path of the domain for which the request is being made for a file called `crossdomain.xml`. That policy file then defines the policy for the entire domain. For example, if a Flash application uses `LoadVars` to make a request to `http://www.yourdomain.com/scripts/`
`script.php`, Flash will look for a file at `http://www.yourdomain.com/crossdomain.xml`. However, there are several issues with that. One issue is that the policy file defines the policy for the entire domain, and using the default model you cannot define different policies for different paths (that is, a policy for `http://www.yourdomain.com/a/` and a policy for `http://`
`www.yourdomain.com/b/`). Another issue relates to persistent socket connections via XMLSocket. By default the Flash Player checks for a policy file called `crossdomain.xml` on port 80 (the standard HTTP port) of the same domain for which the XMLSocket connection is being requested. That requires that a web server is running in addition to the socket server in such cases. Both of these issues are managed by the `System.security.loadPolicyFile()` method in Flash Player 7.0.19.0+. The `loadPolicyFile()` method requires one parameter: a string specifying the URL to the policy file. Using the `loadPolicyFile()` method, you can load policy files from specific locations, and you can even request policy files from socket servers. The following code requests a policy file called `flashpolicies.xml` from `http://www.yourdomain.com/a/`:

```
System.security.loadPolicyFile("http://www.yourdomain.com/a/
flashpolicies.xml");
```

The preceding policy file then applies to any requests from the Flash movie to any resources within `http:///www.yourdomain.com/a/` and subdirectories. That means that if the Flash movie then makes a `LoadVars` request to `http://www.yourdomain.com/a/scripts/`
`script.php`, the preceding policy file applies. However, requests to `http://www.yourdomain`
`.com/b/scripts/script.php` would not utilize the policy file because it is requesting a resource outside the path. It would then check to see if there was a policy file that had been loaded that applied to the requested resource. If not, it would check for a policy file located at `http://www.yourdomain.com/crossdomain.xml`.

If you want to make a policy file request from a socket server, you can specify the `xmlsocket` protocol when making the `loadPolicyFile` request. The format is as follows.

```
System.security.loadPolicyFile("xmlsocket://domain:port");
```

For example, if you want to request a policy file from a socket server running at `www` `.yourdomain.com` on port 100, you use the following line of code:

```
System.security.loadPolicyFile("xmlsocket://www.yourdomain.com:100");
```

When the Flash Player connects to the socket server it sends the following XML packet:

```
<policy-file-request />
```

The packet is followed by a null byte. The server must be configured to listen for that request and then return the policy file as an XML string. The policy file is identical to a standard policy file except that in addition to specifying domains it must also specify ports using the `to-ports` attribute. The ports can be specified as a comma-delimited string, you can specify ranges using a dash, and you can use the * wildcard. The following policy file grants permission to ports 80 and 100 through 110 to Flash movies making requests from `www.person13.com`. It also grants permission to any port to Flash movies making requests from `examples` `.person13.com`.

```
<cross-domain-policy>
  <allow-access-from domain="www.person13.com" to-ports="80,100-110" />
  <allow-access-from domain="examples.person13.com" to-ports="*" />
</cross-domain-policy>
```

Using the IME

IME stands for *input method editor*, an application utilized by a computer's operating system to input non-Latin characters using a standard Latin character keyboard. If you work primarily with applications that use standard Latin characters you may not utilize the IME. But if you build or utilize applications that require the user be able to input Japanese, Chinese, Thai, or Korean characters, for example, the IME is something you'll want to be able to utilize. Flash applications are no exception. If you are building Flash applications for an audience that needs to be able to input Japanese characters, for example, you need to integrate the application with the IME as well as possible. That's where the `System.IME` class can assist.

The `System.IME` class is new to Flash Player 8. It's a static class, meaning the properties and methods are called directly from the class. In the following sections we'll discuss how to accomplish the following:

✦ Determine whether the user has the IME installed on the computer.

✦ Determine whether the IME is enabled or not, and toggle the enabled status.

✦ Specify a conversion mode.

✦ Convert strings.

Checking for the IME

Before the user can use the IME, he has to have installed it on the computer. If the user hasn't installed the IME you probably want to alert him. Flash Player 8 lets you determine whether the IME is installed quite simply via the `System.capabilities.hasIME` property. The property returns `true` if the IME is installed and `false` otherwise.

Enabling the IME

If the IME is installed, you next want to check that it's enabled. You can determine if the IME is enabled using the `System.IME.getEnabled()` method, which returns `true` or `false`.

```
trace(System.IME.getEnabled());
```

If you want to set the enabled state you can do so using the `setEnabled()` method. The method requires a Boolean parameter. The following code enables the IME.

```
System.IME.setEnabled(true);
```

Setting the Conversion Mode

The IME can work in different conversion modes depending on what character sets are installed for the operating system. For an operating system with Latin and Chinese characters installed, for example, the IME can convert to alphabetic/numeric characters or to Chinese characters. If the system has Japanese characters installed then the IME can convert to hiragana or katakana. With most operating systems, you can get and set the conversion mode of the IME directly from Flash Player 8. For OS X, you can only get and set conversion modes for Japanese from Flash, and for Macintosh classic the Flash Player does not set conversion modes. In those cases where the Flash Player does not set the conversion modes, the user is responsible for setting conversion mode manually.

The System.IME class has the following constants that you can use when getting and setting the conversion mode: `ALPHANUMERIC_FULL`, `ALPHANUMERIC_HALF`, `CHINESE`, `JAPANESE_HIRAGANA`, `JAPANESE_KATAKANA_FULL`, `JAPANESE_KATAKANA_HALF`, `KOREAN`, `UNKNOWN`. You can use the `System.IME.getConversionMode()` method to retrieve the current conversion mode. You can set the conversion mode using `setConversionMode()`.

Converting Strings

You can convert strings using Flash Player and the IME. From the Flash Player, you can set a string to convert and send it to the IME. Then, Flash Player can use a listener to get notified when the IME sends the converted string.

You can set the string you want to convert using the `System.IME.setCompositionString()` method. The method requires a string parameter. The following is an example:

```
System.IME.setCompositionString("ii desu nee");
```

Next, you call the `doConversion()` method to send the string to the IME. The method does not require any parameters:

```
System.IME.doConversion();
```

Assuming that the IME is properly enabled and configured, it will then run the editor, and it will give the user the option to adjust or accept the converted string. If the user accepts the string, an event is sent back to Flash Player. If you want Flash to get notified you have to utilize a listener object. The listener object must have a method called `onIMEComposition()`. The method is automatically called when the IME responds. The method is passed a string parameter — the converted string. The following defines a listener object that assigns the converted string to a text field:

```
var oIMEListener:Object = new Object();
oIMEListener.onIMEComposition = function(sMessage:String):Void {
  tField.text = sMessage;
};
```

You can register listener objects with the IME class using the static `addListener()` method:

```
System.IME.addListener(oIMEListener);
```

You can also unregister listener objects using `removeListener()`:

```
System.IME.removeListener(oIMEListener);
```

Web Resource

We'd like to know what you thought about this chapter. Visit `www.rightactionscript .com/asb/comments` to fill out an online form with your comments.

Summary

+ The `System` class is a static class that aggregates many properties and methods, including the `capabilities` and `security` objects.

+ The top-level properties, methods, and events of the `System` class include properties for determining code page use and domain-name matching, methods for setting the Clipboard contents and opening the Flash Player Settings panel, and an event-handler method for handling status messages issued by various other classes.

+ The `capabilities` object reports information about the client computer system and player, including information about the operating system, player version, and various player capabilities ranging from accessibility to audio, to language.

+ The `security` object provides you with the capability to have one SWF grant access so that other SWFs on other domains, subdomains, and protocols can load the SWF and have access to its data.

+ You can use the new `IME` class to manage input of non-Latin-based characters.

✦   ✦   ✦

Printing

In this chapter, you learn how to manage the printing of Flash content using the `PrintJob` class. With ActionScript, you can control what portions of your movie are printable, and you can even specify the way those portions print.

Note This chapter does not cover the now deprecated `print()` and `printAsBitmap()` functions. These functions are compatible with Flash Player 4, 5, and 6.

Why Print from Flash?

Even though you don't need to print everything, some things are still better printed, such as driving maps (until everyone has mobile devices with GPS units), coupons, and purchase receipts. In this section, you explore some printing features that work with Flash movies.

Most web browsers simply can't print *any* plug-in content. Some browsers print a gray area where the plug-in content should be, or they leave it empty. Therefore, if you do want to print from the Flash Player plug-in, you should use ActionScript's `PrintJob` class to do the work. You'll learn the specifics of the `PrintJob` class later in this chapter.

It can be difficult to predict how regular HTML web pages print, even with traditional layouts without plug-in content. Each browser defines page margins differently, and prints unique header and footer information. Have you ever gone to a web site that offers driving directions, and printed a map that just barely bled off the edge of the printed version? You can avoid frustrating situations such as this by using the print capabilities of Flash Player, which gives you a greater degree of control of the printable area of your movie's content. You can define what area of the stage prints for each frame, if necessary. More importantly, though, you can control the relationship of the Flash movie's stage size to the printed size.

Of course, you also have the normal benefits of using Flash for any type of output, whether it is for the computer screen or the printed page:

> ✦ **Embedded fonts**—Although many web pages use the same web fonts, such as Verdana or Georgia, you can design Flash movies that use whatever fonts you want your visitors to see. These fonts can be used on printed output from Flash movies as well.

✦ **Easy and precise layout tools**—You can create Flash artwork and elements very easily; and place the content without using frames, tables, and DHTML layers.

✦ **Incredibly small file sizes**—Compared to equivalent Acrobat PDF files or HTML pages, Flash movies with graphics and text intended for print can download very quickly. The native vector format of Flash movies makes them ideal for printing anything with logo and branding elements.

Given the preceding points, there is the radical notion that Flash movies can be a reasonable substitute for Adobe Acrobat PDF documents. Seem far-fetched? Well, with embedded fonts and precision layout, Flash movies can offer many of the same features that PDF documents do. However, PDF files still offer some advantages. The following list details some of the benefits of PDF files. If Flash movies offer a similar benefit then that is listed as well.

✦ PDF files are an industry standard for printable documents on the Web. Just about every major company on the Web, from Macromedia to Sony, provides downloadable and printable information in the PDF format. However, with FlashPaper technology (http://www.macromedia.com/software/flashpaper) it's possible to deploy SWF-based printable documents. Flash Player is all that is required to view FlashPaper documents, and Flash Player generally takes less time to start than Acrobat Reader.

✦ PDF files have a more standardized structure than Flash movies. For example, PDF files can have a table of contents (Bookmarks) that does not require the content developer to invent his or her own system of indexing. Creating an index of a printable Flash movie involves much more time and planning.

✦ Some search engines such as Google.com can index (and therefore search) the content of PDF files on the Web. As of this writing, such services for Flash movies are not as developed.

✦ Several web sites (including this book's publisher) use server-side technology that can convert PDF documents to HTML pages on the fly. Because PDF files have a standard structure, these server-side applications to render HTML layouts are very similar to the PDF original. The Adobe Document Server is just one of several applications that create such HTML documents from PDF files. However, it's worth noting that one of the reasons for converting PDF files to HTML is for the benefit of readers without Acrobat Reader or for those that don't want to wait for Acrobat Reader to start. Since Flash-based documents require Flash Player, it's far more likely that a reader will be able to view the document in the Flash format, and Flash Player start time is minimal. Furthermore, the Acrobat Reader application and plug-in are much larger downloads (in excess of 8MB!) than the Flash Player plug-in. So, even if a reader doesn't have Flash Player, it's not too difficult to download and install when compared with Acrobat Reader.

✦ PDF files can be encrypted and password-protected. There's currently no similar option for SWF-based documents.

✦ The full version of Adobe Acrobat installs the Acrobat PDFWriter or Distiller printer driver, which enables you to print just about any document (for example, Microsoft Word documents) to a PDF file. FlashPaper lets you convert any document to an SWF.

While Flash movies aren't appropriate for every printing scenario, they are often the best option. As noted in some of the preceding points, FlashPaper technology can convert documents to Flash movies. FlashPaper documents have built-in printing capabilities. As such, there's no need to add any additional ActionScript code to enable printing. However, for standard, non-FlashPaper Flash movies you'll have to write some ActionScript code to manage printing. Let's take a look at the ActionScript PrintJob class next.

Controlling Printer Output from Flash

With the `PrintJob` class, you can define how pages are constructed and sent to the printer. This section describes each of the methods and properties of the `PrintJob` class, collectively known as the `PrintJob` API (*application programming interface*), and explains how each works. If you want to see the `PrintJob` API in action, continue to the section "Adding Print Functionality to Applications" as well.

Introducing the PrintJob Class

On the surface, there isn't too much to the `PrintJob` class. In fact, there are only three methods for the class. To create a new instance of the `PrintJob` class, you use the constructor in a `new` statement:

```
var pjOutput:PrintJob = new PrintJob();
```

You do not specify any parameters with the constructor. Once you have a `PrintJob` object, you initiate the three methods of the object, in the following order:

✦ `start()` — This method opens the Print dialog box on the user's operating system. If the user clicks the Print (or OK) button in the Print dialog box, the method returns a `true` value. If the user cancels the dialog box, the method returns a `false` value. You should use the other two methods only if the `start()` method returns a `true` value.

✦ `addPage()` — This method tells the `PrintJob` object which `MovieClip` object to print from your Flash movie. You can invoke several `addPage()` methods. Each method call will add one page to the printer's output. This method uses several complex arguments, which are discussed in the following sections.

✦ `send()` — This method finalizes the output and sends the data to the printer's spooler.

Once you have sent the output to the printer with the `send()` method, it's usually a good idea to delete the `PrintJob` object. Let's take a closer look at the `start()` and `addPage()` methods.

Starting a Print Request

The `start()` method does two things: it prompts the user to accept or cancel the print request, and it enables the Flash movie to retrieve the user's print settings. When you call the `start()` method, Flash opens a new print dialog box that asks the user to click OK or Cancel. It also lets the user adjust the settings, such as the printer to which to send the document, the page size, and page orientation.

The following properties are set on the `PrintJob` object if the user clicks OK to a print dialog box initiated from a Flash movie. Some of the properties use a unit of measurement called a *point,* abbreviated as *pt.* There are 72 points to 1 inch.

✦ `paperHeight` — This property returns the height (in points) of the paper size that the user has selected. For example, if the user has selected a paper size of 8.5" × 11", `paperHeight` returns a value of 792 points (11" × 72 pt/inch = 792 pt).

✦ `paperWidth` — This property returns the width (in points) of the paper size that the user has selected. Using the previous example, an 8.5" × 11" paper size returns a `paperWidth` value of 612 points.

✦ pageHeight — Perhaps the more useful of the height-based properties, the pageHeight property returns the height (in points) of actual printable area. Most printers can print to only a certain portion of the paper size, leaving a margin around the edges of the paper. For example, on an 8.5" × 11" piece of paper, most printers can print only an area sized 8.17" × 10.67". If you are trying to size output to the page, you should use this property over paperHeight.

✦ pageWidth — As mentioned with the pageHeight property, this property is likely to be more useful to you than the paperWidth property. This property returns the width (in points) of the actual printable area on the paper.

Note

The datatype of all width and height properties is Number.

✦ orientation — This property returns a string value of either portrait or landscape, based on the user's setting in the Print dialog box. The width and height properties will simply flip-flop from one orientation to the next.

The start() method is synchronous. That means that it effectively pauses Flash until the user clicks the OK or Cancel button in the print dialog.

Note

You must have a print driver installed to print from Flash or any other application. If you don't have a printer you can still install a print driver to print to a file. There are many commercial and even free drivers that print to a file.

Determining the Print Target and Its Formatting Options

Perhaps the most difficult aspect of Flash printing involves using the addPage() method. The addPage() method uses the following syntax, where pjOutput represents a PrintJob instance:

```
pjOutput.addPage(mTarget, oPrintArea, oPrintOptions, nFrame);
```

The parameters are as follows:

✦ target — The MovieClip object that you want to print. You can also pass a Level number to print. For example, passing the number 0 prints the main timeline (_root) of Level 0. This parameter is required.

✦ print area — An Object instance whose properties determine the margins of the printable target. This parameter is optional; if it is omitted or incorrectly specified, the entire area of the target clip (or Level) is printed. The Object instance, if specified, must contain all four of the following properties:

  • xMin — The top-left coordinate of the left margin

  • xMax — The top-right coordinate of the right margin

  • yMin — The bottom-left coordinate of the left margin

  • yMax — The bottom-right coordinate of the right margin

Note

The print area's coordinates are determined from the registration point of the target timeline you are printing.

✦ **print options**—An `Object` instance that determines how the target's contents are sent to the printer. By default, all contents are sent as vector artwork. This parameter is optional. The `Object` instance has only one property, `printAsBitmap`. This property uses a `Boolean` value. If the property is set to `true`, the artwork is rendered as a bitmap and then sent to the printer. If the property is set to `false`, the artwork is rendered in vectors and then sent to the printer. See the sections titled "Printing Targets as Vectors" and "Printing Targets as Bitmaps" for more information.

✦ **frame**—The frame number of the target clip (or Level) to print. If you want to print a specific frame of the target, you can use this optional parameter. If you omit this parameter, the current frame of the target is printed. Note that any ActionScript code on the specified frame will not be executed. Thus, if you have any code that you want to affect the look of your printed target, you should make sure that code is invoked before using the `addPage()` method.

You apply these parameters in later examples of this chapter. In the next sections, you learn more specifics of the `addPage()` parameters and how they affect the printed output from the Flash movie.

Printing Targets as Vectors

The `printAsBitmap` property of the print options parameter for the `addPage()` method should be set to `false` strictly when you are printing the following vector artwork elements in a `MovieClip` object or Level, including the main timeline (`_root`):

✦ Text contained within Static, Dynamic, or Input text fields.

✦ Artwork created with Flash tools, or imported from an illustration application such as Macromedia FreeHand or Adobe Illustrator.

✦ Symbol instances *without* any alpha, brightness, tint, or advanced color effects. If you've used the Color menu options in the Property inspector for an instance, you've automatically ruled out using `printAsBitmap` set to `false`. (This rule also applies to instances that have been manipulated with the `Color` object in ActionScript code.)

If your Flash content is limited to these considerations, you can safely set `printAsBitmap` to `false` to print high-quality output. If the output is directed to a high-quality printer, all lines and artwork print "clean," with very smooth edges.

Caution

Any alpha or color settings for symbol instances or artwork are ignored when the `printAsBitmap` property is set to `false`. Bitmap images also print with more aliasing (that is, rough, pixelated edges) if `printAsBitmap` is set to `false`. When set to `false`, `printAsBitmap` also fills alpha channels of any bitmap images with solid white.

Printing Targets as Bitmaps

The `printAsBitmap` property should be set to `true` when you are using a variety of sources for your artwork and content. If you have a Flash movie with a mixture of the elements listed in the previous section *and* the following items, you should set `printAsBitmap` to `true` in the `addPage()` method:

✦ Symbol instances using alpha, brightness, tint, or advanced color effects. If you have used the Property inspector or a `Color` object in ActionScript to modify the appearance of a symbol instance, you should set `printAsBitmap` to `true`.

✦ Artwork or symbol instances containing imported bitmap images. Although bitmap images can be printed with `printAsBitmap` set to `false`, they appear sharper when printed with the `printAsBitmap` set to `true`. More important, bitmap images with alpha channels print correctly if the transparent areas of the alpha channel overlap other artwork.

What happens to vector artwork (including text) that is printed with the `printAsBitmap` property set to `true`? The `true` setting still prints vector artwork, but it won't be as crisp as artwork outputted with the `false` setting. However, you might find the differences between true and false settings with vector artwork negligible—if you're ever in doubt, test your specific artwork with both settings and compare the output. The `true` setting is usually the safest bet if you are using bitmap images and any alpha or color effects.

Note

Colors with alpha settings in the Color Mixer panel used as fills or strokes print perfectly fine with the `true` setting but not with the `false` setting.

Printing Issues with Flash: Color, Grayscale, and PostScript

Although this book focuses on the development side of Flash movies, you want to make sure that your artwork prints reasonably well on a wide range of printers. Not everyone has a high-quality color inkjet or laser printer connected to her or his computer. Given this, you want to test your Flash movie output to a couple of different printers or ask another associate to test the output on his or her printer. The artwork might not have the same contrast ratios when converted to grayscale.

How can you help correct the problem of not-so-great-looking black-and-white print output from a color original? You can try two things to help alleviate poor grayscale translations of colored artwork: Choose colors that have greater tint variation, or make "hidden" grayscale equivalents of artwork directly in Flash. For the former method, as an example; don't use red and green colors that are close in lightness or brightness values. Rather, choose a darkly tinted red and a lightly tinted green. For the latter method, create a separate Movie Clip symbol of a grayscale version of the artwork. Just duplicate its symbol in the Library, and use the Paint Bucket and Ink Bottle tools to quickly fill with grayscale colors.

Finally, make sure that you test your printed output on both PostScript and non-PostScript printers. According to Macromedia, the Flash Player's print functionality supports both types of printers, but non-PostScript printers convert vectors to bitmaps. Not all non-PostScript printers do an excellent job of converting vector graphics to bitmap graphics (known as *ripping*, from the term RIP, which stands for *raster image processing*). Therefore, you might decide to let Flash do such image conversions by setting the `printAsBitmap` property to `true` (in the `oPrintOptions` parameter of the `PrintJob.addPage()` method). Again, you should test your content with both types of printers. Most laser printers have PostScript language interpreters, whereas most inkjet printers need additional software such as iProof Systems' PowerRIP software (available as demo software at `www.iproofsystems.com`) to properly render PostScript graphics.

Controlling the Printable Area of the Target

Perhaps the most difficult concept to grasp with the addPage() method is how the target is sized to the printed page. Unlike the deprecated print() and printAsBitmap() functions from previous releases of Flash, Flash Player 7, and higher now output absolute print sizes. Using a conversion formula, you can determine how large your target will print on the printer's paper:

```
1 pixel = 1 point = 1/72 inch
```

Therefore, if you have a MovieClip object containing a 400 × 400 pixel square, that artwork will print at roughly 5.5" × 5.5" on the printed page. You can keep this formula in mind if you're planning to print on standard page sizes such as 8.5" × 11" — as long as your target's size uses the same aspect ratio (roughly 1:1.3), your target can be resized to fill the page.

Potential Issues with the Flash Printed Output

Watch out for the two following pitfalls with the addPage() method parameters, which can cause unpredictable or undesirable output from a printer:

✦ **Device fonts** — If at all possible, avoid using device fonts with the printed output. Make sure all text is embedded for each text field used for printable content. Text that uses device fonts will print — however, if you have several elements in addition to device font text, the device text may not properly align with other elements on the page.

✦ **Background colors** — If you are using a dark background color in the Document Properties dialog box (Modify ➪ Document) for your Flash document, make sure you add a white, filled rectangle behind your printable content within the targeted MovieClip instance.

Be sure to check your movies for these problems before you test your printed output from a Flash movie.

Adding Print Functionality to Applications

In the following exercise, you'll add printing functionality to Flash applications.

1. Copy lorem_ipsum.txt from the web site to a directory on your local disk.

2. Open a new Flash document, and save it as printing001.fla.

3. Add the following code to the first keyframe of the default layer:

```
var tfFormatter:TextFormat = new TextFormat();
tfFormatter.size = 15;

// Make a movie clip within which to nest the text field.
this.createEmptyMovieClip("mToPrint",
this.getNextHighestDepth());

// Add the text field.
var tField:TextField = mToPrint.createTextField(
"tLoremIpsum", mToPrint.getNextHighestDepth(), 0, 0, 400, 0);
```

```
tField.multiline = true;
tField.wordWrap = true;
tField.autoSize = "left";

// Define a LoadVars object in order to load the text from
// lorem_ipsum.txt.
var lvLoremIpsum:LoadVars = new LoadVars();

// When the text is loaded, assign it to the text field, and
// apply the formatting.
lvLoremIpsum.onData = function(sText:String):Void {
  tField.text = sText;
  tField.setTextFormat(tfFormatter);
};
lvLoremIpsum.load("lorem_ipsum.txt");

// Make a text field button that calls startPrint() when clicked.
var tPrintButton:TextField = this.createTextField(        ⊃
"tPrintButton", this.getNextHighestDepth(), 440, 0, 0, 0);
tPrintButton.autoSize = "left";
tPrintButton.border = true;
tPrintButton.selectable = false;
tPrintButton.html = true;
tPrintButton.htmlText =                                    ⊃
"<a href='asfunction:startPrint'>Print</a>";

function startPrint():Void {  var pjLoremIpsum:PrintJob =   ⊃
new PrintJob();

    // The start() method returns true if the user clicks OK. In
    // that case, add a page, and send the print request.
  if(pjLoremIpsum.start()) {
    pjLoremIpsum.addPage(mToPrint);
    pjLoremIpsum.send();
  }
  delete pjLoremIpsum;
}
```

4. Test the movie.

When you click the print button and click OK in the print dialog box, one page will print. That one page will be the first page of text. The following example shows a way to print the entire text.

1. Open printing001.fla, and save it as printing002.fla.

2. Edit the code on frame 1 as follows. The changes are bolded.

```
var tfFormatter:TextFormat = new TextFormat();
tfFormatter.size = 15;

this.createEmptyMovieClip("mToPrint",                      ⊃
this.getNextHighestDepth());
```

```
    var tField:TextField = mToPrint.createTextField(                ⊃
    "tLoremIpsum", mToPrint.getNextHighestDepth(), 0, 0, 400, 0);
    tField.multiline = true;
    tField.wordWrap = true;
    tField.autoSize = "left";

    var lvLoremIpsum:LoadVars = new LoadVars();
    lvLoremIpsum.onData = function(sText:String):Void {
      tField.text = sText;
      tField.setTextFormat(tfFormatter);
    };
    lvLoremIpsum.load("lorem_ipsum.txt");

    var tPrintButton:TextField = this.createTextField(              ⊃
    "tPrintButton", this.getNextHighestDepth(), 440, 0, 0, 0);
    tPrintButton.autoSize = "left";
    tPrintButton.border = true;
    tPrintButton.selectable = false;
    tPrintButton.html = true;
    tPrintButton.htmlText =                                         ⊃
    "<a href='asfunction:startPrint'>Print</a>";

    function startPrint():Void {
      var pjLoremIpsum:PrintJob = new PrintJob();
      if(pjLoremIpsum.start()) {

        // Scale the text field so it fits to the page height.
        tField._yscale = 100 * pjLoremIpsum.pageHeight /            ⊃
    tField._height;
        tField._xscale = tField._yscale;
        pjLoremIpsum.addPage(mToPrint);
        pjLoremIpsum.send();

        // Scale the text back to 100%.
        tField._xscale = 100;
        tField._yscale = 100;
      }
      delete pjLoremIpsum;
    }
```

Note that when you print from the movie this time, it prints the entire text on one page. The text is scaled down. It fits on one page, but it's not legible. In the next example, rather than scale the text, we'll set the width of the text so that it will print at the same width of the page.

1. Open printing002.fla, and save it as printing003.fla.

2. Edit the code on frame 1. The changes are bolded.

```
    var tfFormatter:TextFormat = new TextFormat();
    tfFormatter.size = 15;

    this.createEmptyMovieClip("mToPrint",                           ⊃
```

```
this.getNextHighestDepth());
var tField:TextField = mToPrint.createTextField(
"tLoremIpsum", mToPrint.getNextHighestDepth(), 0, 0, 400, 0);
tField.multiline = true;
tField.wordWrap = true;
tField.autoSize = "left";

var lvLoremIpsum:LoadVars = new LoadVars();
lvLoremIpsum.onData = function(sText:String):Void {
  tField.text = sText;
  tField.setTextFormat(tfFormatter);
};
lvLoremIpsum.load("lorem_ipsum.txt");

var tPrintButton:TextField = this.createTextField(
"tPrintButton", this.getNextHighestDepth(), 440, 0, 0, 0);
tPrintButton.autoSize = "left";
tPrintButton.border = true;
tPrintButton.selectable = false;
tPrintButton.html = true;
tPrintButton.htmlText =
"<a href='asfunction:startPrint'>Print</a>";

function startPrint():Void {
  var pjLoremIpsum:PrintJob = new PrintJob();
  if(pjLoremIpsum.start()) {

    // Set the _width property equal to the pageWidth.
    tField._width = pjLoremIpsum.pageWidth;

    pjLoremIpsum.addPage(mToPrint);
    pjLoremIpsum.send();

    // Set the width back to 400.
    tField._width = 400;
  }
  delete pjLoremIpsum;
}
```

This time the text prints legibly so that it fits to the width of the page. However, it still only prints one page. Next we'll look at how to print the text over many pages.

1. Open printing003.fla, and save it as printing004.fla.

2. Edit the code on frame 1. The changes are bolded.

```
var tfFormatter:TextFormat = new TextFormat();
tfFormatter.size = 15;

this.createEmptyMovieClip("mToPrint",
this.getNextHighestDepth());
var tField:TextField = mToPrint.createTextField(
```

```
"tLoremIpsum", mToPrint.getNextHighestDepth(), 0, 0, 400, 0);
tField.multiline = true;
tField.wordWrap = true;
tField.autoSize = "left";

var lvLoremIpsum:LoadVars = new LoadVars();
lvLoremIpsum.onData = function(sText:String):Void {
  tField.text = sText;
  tField.setTextFormat(tfFormatter);
};
lvLoremIpsum.load("lorem_ipsum.txt");

var tPrintButton:TextField = this.createTextField(           ⊃
"tPrintButton", this.getNextHighestDepth(), 440, 0, 0, 0);
tPrintButton.autoSize = "left";
tPrintButton.border = true;
tPrintButton.selectable = false;
tPrintButton.html = true;
tPrintButton.htmlText =                                      ⊃
"<a href='asfunction:startPrint'>Print</a>";

function startPrint():Void {
  var pjLoremIpsum:PrintJob = new PrintJob();
  if(pjLoremIpsum.start()) {

    tField._width = pjLoremIpsum.pageWidth;

    // Determine how many pages by dividing the text field height
    // by the page height.
    var nPages:Number = tField._height / pjLoremIpsum.pageHeight;

    // Use a for statement to add each page.
    for(var i:Number = 0; i < nPages; i++) {

      // Add the pages using the second parameter to specify the
      // region to print for each page.
      pjLoremIpsum.addPage(mToPrint, {xMin: 0,                ⊃
yMin: pjLoremIpsum.pageHeight * i, xMax: tField._width,      ⊃
yMax: pjLoremIpsum.pageHeight * (i + 1)});
    }
    pjLoremIpsum.send();
    tField._width = 400;
  }
  delete pjLoremIpsum;
}
```

When you test printing this time, the program will print as many pages as necessary to output the entire text. Although it's a marked improvement over the first few stages, there is still one major issue with how the text is printing. You'll notice that the page breaks can occur in the middle of a line of text such that the top of a line of text can appear on one page, and the bottom of that line of text appears on the next page.

We'd like to know what you thought about this chapter. Visit www.rightactionscript .com/asb/comments to fill out an online form with your comments.

Summary

✦ You can print many useful items from Flash movies, such as purchase receipts, artwork, and product catalogs or datasheets.

✦ The PrintJob class has all of the methods and properties necessary to print Flash content.

✦ The addPage() method of the PrintJob class enables you to control which MovieClip object (or Level) is printed and how it should be printed.

✦ Avoid the use of device fonts or dark background colors for Flash content that you intend to print.

✦ You might want to give your users the option of confirming an interaction that will send output to the printer. This confirmation dialog box can contain information about how many pages will be printed.

✦ You can print content that is temporarily added to the movie's stage with the MovieClip.attachMovie() method. This technique can be useful to print material formatted differently from what the user sees on the stage, such as printing a black-and-white version of a color graphic.

✦   ✦   ✦

Working with Media

Programming Sound

S ince Flash 5, developers have had the capability to dynamically manage sound resources using ActionScript. If you've worked with sounds in Flash at authoring time, you likely know that you can place sound resources on keyframes. Using ActionScript, the resources may or may not be placed on keyframes in the Flash timeline. It's possible for ActionScript to attach the sound resource to the Flash movie at runtime. You can even load MP3 sounds from files external to the Flash movie. In this chapter, you learn how to access the Sound class's properties and methods in order to create efficient sound loading and playback in a Flash movie.

Tip　In Flash Player 6 or later, external MP3 files can be loaded into Flash movies at runtime. You no longer need to embed a sound file into a Flash movie (SWF file) to play it. You learn about this and other features of the Sound class throughout this chapter.

An Introduction to the Sound Class

In ActionScript, you use the Sound class to manage sound resources — whether loading MP3s, setting the volume, or checking the playback time. A Sound object is actually comprised of three elements that work together to initiate and control a sound resource in the Flash movie:

✦ A sound file imported into the movie's Library or a sound file downloaded separately as an MP3 file at runtime.

✦ A Sound instance created with the Sound constructor.

✦ A MovieClip object (or timeline) that stores the attached or loaded sound file. The movie clip is the container for the sound resource, and every management function is proxied through the movie clip by way of the Sound object that targets it.

Creating a New Sound Object

As with most intrinsic ActionScript classes, Sound objects require a constructor to create a new instance of the class. To create a new Sound object, you need the following constructor.

```
var sndInstance:Sound = new Sound(mInstance);
```

CHAPTER

In This Chapter

Understanding Sound objects and MovieClip object targets

Controlling sound properties

Loading MP3 files at runtime

Adding a volume slider

Using the mouse position with the setTransform() method

In the preceding line of code, sndInstance is the name for the specific Sound object you're creating, and mInstance is the movie clip within which you want the sound resource stored.

The following ActionScript represents a new Sound object named sndTrack that creates a holder for an actual sound (from the Library or an external MP3 file) on a MovieClip named mSoundHolder.

```
var sndTrack:Sound = new Sound(mSoundHolder);
```

Understanding Sound Resources and Timelines

Although not strictly necessary, it's generally advisable to use one movie clip per sound. You can store many sounds in one movie clip. However, as we'll see, doing so has drawbacks.

Technically, the MovieClip object reference is an optional argument for the Sound constructor. If you omit the argument, the Sound object stores the sound resource on the _level0 timeline (that is, Level 0). The following code creates a Sound object that targets _level0:

```
var sndTrack:Sound = new Sound();
```

If you are controlling only one sound with ActionScript in your movie (or if you're *not* using the action in a loaded SWF file), omitting the MovieClip object reference might not cause any difficulties. However, if you start to create multiple Sound objects *without* unique MovieClip objects to contain the sound resources, you will run into troubles. Here is an example of several Sound objects with the same target movie clip (_level0).

```
var sndOne:Sound = new Sound();
var sndTwo:Sound = new Sound();
```

The structure in the preceding example does not allow each sound resource to be stored in its own container. As a result, if you try to control one Sound object, the other sound resources will respond as well. In other words, setting the volume of sndOne will effectively set the volume of sndTwo as well. In the world of ActionScript, allocating the proper resources to each code element can ensure independence of the associated objects. In order to maintain complete control over each sound resource that is used by each Sound object, make sure you create a unique MovieClip object to hold each sound resource.

It's frequently useful to make new movie clips using the createEmptyMovieClip() method. The following code makes two new Sound objects, each with unique movie clip targets.

```
this.createEmptyMovieClip("mSoundHolderOne", this.getNextHighestDepth());
this.createEmptyMovieClip("mSoundHolderTwo", this.getNextHighestDepth());
var sndOne:Sound = new Sound(mSoundHolderOne);
var sndTwo:Sound = new Sound(mSoundHolderTwo);
```

Now that you understand how Sound objects store and reference loaded sound assets, you will learn how to use ActionScript to control a Sound object after it has been initialized.

Scripting Audio with the Sound Class

The Sound class enables you to play audio from the movie's Library or from an external MP3 file. Prior to the Sound class's introduction to ActionScript, all audio had to be manually added to a Flash timeline on a specific keyframe, and if you wanted to adjust the volume, pan, or looping you had to do that at authoring time. Now, you can manage sounds with ActionScript — from loading sounds programmatically to controlling the volume, pan, looping, and playback of a sound in a Flash movie.

There are four basic steps to use a Sound object in a Flash movie:

1. Set an audio file to export from the Library, or create a separate MP3 file.

2. Make a new Sound object.

3. Attach (or load) the audio file to the Sound object.

4. Control the playback, volume, pan, and looping of the sound.

In the following sections, you learn the properties and methods of the Sound class and create some Flash movies that use it.

Loading Methods of the Sound Class

The following methods can be used to load or monitor the loading of a sound resource into a Sound object. These methods are presented in the order in which they are commonly used:

1. Attach or load a sound into a Sound object.

2. Monitor the download of the sound resource (optional — applies only to loaded sounds, not attached sounds).

3. Execute a function when the sound resource is done loading (optional — applies only to loaded sounds, not attached sounds).

Using an Exported Sound from the Library

The Sound.attachSound() method enables you to link a sound in the movie's Library to a Sound object in the movie. The only parameter for the method is a string value that refers to the sound asset's linkage identifier. To set a sound's linkage identifier, right-click/Control-click the sound in the Library panel, and select Linkage. In the Linkage Properties dialog box that appears, select Export for ActionScript and assign a name in the Identifier field.

Tip   When you select the Export for ActionScript check box, the Linkage Properties dialog box automatically fills the Identifier field with the asset's Library name. Flash also allows you to specify a separate frame in which the sound asset is "stored" in the Flash movie. By default, the Export in First Frame check box is selected, meaning that the entire sound resource must download into the Flash Player before the movie can play frame 1. If you clear this check box, you must manually insert the sound somewhere else in your Flash movie, on a keyframe as an event sound. You can also view Linkage identifier names in the Library panel — extend the panel's width to reveal the Linkage column information.

The following code creates a Sound object named sndTrack and attaches a sound with the identifier name of backgroundSound to the object:

```
this.createEmptyMovieClip("mSoundTrackHolder", this.getNextHighestDepth());
var sndTrack:Sound = new Sound(mSoundTrackHolder);
sndTrack.attachSound("backgroundSound");
```

Calling the attachSound() method does not cause the sound to start to playback. It simply associates the sound resource with the Sound object. You'll learn how to playback a sound in a subsequent section.

Loading an MP3 File with Sound.loadSound()

Flash Player 6 or later can use the loadSound() method to load MP3 files into Flash movies at runtime. Although the attachSound() method works with sound files that have been imported into the Flash document (FLA file) and exported with the Flash movie, the loadSound() method loads an external MP3 file directly into Flash Player 6 or later, into virtual memory and the browser's cache.

Note If you need to create Sound objects that are compatible with Flash Player 5, use the attachSound() method with linked symbols in the movie's Library. Flash Player 5 cannot use the loadSound() method.

This method has two arguments — the URL of the MP3 file, and a Boolean value indicating whether to play back the MP3 as a progressive download (true) or only after the entire sound has loaded into the player (false). The URL for the MP3 file can be a valid http:// or ftp:// address, or a relative path to the MP3 file. The following code loads an MP3 file from the www.rightactionscript.com web server:

```
var sndTrack:Sound = new Sound();
sndTrack.loadSound("http://www.rightactionscript.com/samplefiles/sample.mp3",
true);
```

You can also use a relative URL. The following code loads an MP3 file located in the same directory as the SWF file:

```
var sndTrack:Sound = new Sound();
sndTrack.loadSound("sample.mp3", true);
```

Caution The ftp:// URL addresses work only when the Flash movie is played in a web browser. The stand-alone player (or the Test Movie mode) cannot load MP3 files that use FTP.

The second argument of the loadSound() method specifies whether the sound resource is a progressive download or event sound. A progressive download sound will play as it downloads into the Flash Player. An event sound, conversely, must fully download into the Flash Player before playback can begin. To treat the sound resource as a progressive download sound, use a value of true. For an event sound, use a value of false. The following code establishes a progressive download sound that will play the sample.mp3 file as soon as enough bytes from the file have loaded into the Flash Player:

```
var sndTrack:Sound = new Sound();
sndTrack.loadSound("sample.mp3", true);
```

Caution The Macromedia documentation refers to progressive download sounds as *streaming*. However, that is misleading on at least two accounts. Flash Player cannot stream sounds by itself — only with the assistance of a server-side technology such as Flash Communication Server. Streaming means that sounds are not cached, and this has significant implications for digital rights management. Furthermore, streaming sounds can buffer and start playback from any point, whereas progressive download sounds download linearly, and they can only start playback from a point that has already downloaded. It's also misleading to use the term "streaming" in this context because of the association with *Stream* sounds in Flash movies. Stream sounds (which can be set in the Property inspector for a given keyframe) can force the Flash Player to drop frames in order to synchronize playback of a sound with animation on the timeline. Progressive download sounds do not control the frame rate of the Flash movie in this manner. Most important, once a progressive download sound begins playback, you can only stop the sound — you *cannot* use the start() method of the Sound object on streaming sounds. Nor can you pause streaming sounds with a controller interface.

To make an event sound, change the true value to false:

```
var sndTrack:Sound = new Sound();
sndTrack.loadSound("sample.mp3", false);
```

Event sounds will not play until the entire MP3 file has downloaded and a start() method is executed with the Sound object. The start() method is discussed later in this chapter.

Cross-Reference

The onLoad() event handler for Sound objects can detect if the URL for an MP3 file is invalid. onLoad() can also be used to start playback of an event sound loaded into a Sound object. This event handler is discussed in the "Determining When an MP3 Has Fully Loaded" section of this chapter.

Determining How Many Bytes of an MP3 File Have Loaded

The getBytesLoaded() method returns the number of bytes from an MP3 file that are being downloaded via the loadSound() method. You can use this method to check the loading progress of an MP3 file. The following code puts the current bytes loaded into a TextField object named tProgress.

```
var sndTrack:Sound = new Sound();
sndTrack.loadSound("http://www.rightactionscript.com/samplefiles/sample.mp3",
true);
this.createTextField("tProgress", 1, 10, 10, 100, 20);
tProgress.border = true;
var nProgressID:Number = setInterval(updateProgress, 100);

function updateProgress():Void {
  tProgress.text = sndTrack.getBytesLoaded();
}
```

Here, the setInterval() function calls a function once every 100 milliseconds, updating the text property of the tProgress text field with the current bytes loaded of the sndTrack object.

Getting the Total File Size of the MP3 File

The getBytesTotal() method returns the file size (in bytes) of an MP3 file that is being downloaded into a Sound object with the loadSound() method. Combined with the getBytesLoaded() method, you can determine the percent loaded of the MP3 file. The following code is an update to the code from the previous section.

```
var sndTrack:Sound = new Sound();
sndTrack.loadSound("http://www.rightactionscript.com/mp3/sample.mp3", true);
this.createTextField("tProgress", 1, 10, 10, 100, 20);
tProgress.border = true;
var nProgressID:Number = setInterval(updateProgress, 100);

function updateProgress():Void {
  var nPercent:Number = Math.round(sndTrack.getBytesLoaded() /
  sndTrack.getBytesTotal() * 100);
  tProgress.text = nPercent + "%";
}
```

This code calculates a nPercent variable within displays the value in the tProgress text field.

Note   The loadSound(), onLoad(), getBytesLoaded(), and getBytesTotal() methods are *not* available for Sound objects in Flash Player 5 or earlier movies.

Determining When an MP3 Has Fully Loaded

The onLoad() event handler can be defined for a Sound object to indicate when an MP3 file has finished downloading into Flash Player 6 or later. This handler executes a callback function that tells the movie what to do when either a load operation has completed or a load operation has failed. The method uses a Boolean argument, indicating the status of the load operation. If the load was successful, a true value is passed to the callback function. If the load failed (due to an invalid URL or incompatible sound file), the callback function is passed a false value. The following code executes a trace() action when an Event sound has finished loading, and starts playback of the sound:

```
var sndTrack:Sound = new Sound();
sndTrack.onLoad = function(bSuccess:Boolean):Void {
  if(bSuccess){
    trace("the sound has finished loading");
    this.start();
  } else {
    trace("there was an error occurred with loading");
  }
};
sndTrack.loadSound("http://www.rightactionscript.com/samplefiles/sample.mp3",
false);
```

Managing Playback

Once a sound resource has been attached or loaded into a Sound object, you can control playback of the sound with the methods described in this section.

Note   All of the methods in this grouping, except the onSoundComplete() event handler, are compatible with Flash Player 5 or later movies. onSoundComplete() requires Flash Player 6 or later, and the onID3() method discussed later in the chapter requires Flash Player 7 or later.

Playing a Sound with Sound.start()

The Sound.start() method plays a specific Sound object. There are two optional parameters for this method that allow you to specify a nonzero offset and a number of times to loop the sound.

The offset parameter determines the "in" point of the sound in seconds. For example, if you have a 10-second sound and you want to skip the first four seconds of the sound, you supply the number 4 as the offset parameter.

The looping parameter sets the number of times you want to play the sound. If you decide to use the parameter, you must also supply a value for the offset parameter (use 0 if you want to start the sound at its beginning). A looping parameter of 0 or 1 produces the same result: The sound plays once. If you specify a value of 2, the sound plays twice in a row. If you use a nonzero offset then each time the sound loops it starts at the specified offset, not at the start of the sound. The following code would make a new Sound object, attach a sound named backgroundSound, and play it four times — skipping the first two seconds of the sound:

```
this.createEmptyMovieClip("mSoundTrackHolder",
this.getNextHighestDepth());
var sndTrack:Sound = new Sound(mSoundTrackHolder);
sndTrack.attachSound("backgroundSound");
sndTrack.start(2, 4);
```

Note   You cannot specify an "out" point for a Sound object with the start() method. The out point is the place within the sound where playback stops (or loops back to the in point where playback begins). Unless you are repurposing the same sound file for several uses, we recommend that you trim your sound files in a sound editor application (such as Sony's Sound Forge or Bias Peak) before you import the sound into Flash MX 2004. That way, when you set a sound to export (or download an MP3 file), the entire sound will be included (or downloaded) in your Flash movie (SWF file), regardless of where you specify it to start playing in your ActionScript code. You can, however, use the position property of the Sound class and the setInterval() function to detect when a sound reaches a specific time in playback.

Stopping a Sound with Sound.stop()

The stop() method halts the sound's playback. There are no parameters for this method, just as with the stop() method of the MovieClip object.

Caution   This is *not* a pause feature. If you use the stop() method and later issue a start() method for the same Sound object, the sound will start from the beginning (or from its offset value, if one is supplied). However, using the position property of the Sound object, you can pause an attached sound or a loaded event sound.

Pausing a Sound

Although the Sound class doesn't have a method specifically for pausing and resuming a sound, you can accomplish the effect using the stop() and start() methods in conjunction with the position property. The stop() method stops the sound and effectively resets the playhead to the beginning. The start() method, by default, starts the sound from the beginning. However, as you learned, the start() method lets you optionally specify the offset from which to start the playback. If you retrieve the playhead position just before the sound is stopped, you can restart the sound at the same place.

The position property returns the playhead position in milliseconds from the beginning of the sound. When you want to pause a sound, assign the value of the position property to a variable just before calling stop().

```
var nResumeMilliseconds:Number = sndTrack.position;
sndTrack.stop();
```

Then, when you want to resume the sound, simply call the start() method with an offset parameter. Note that the offset parameter is specified in seconds, not milliseconds. That means you need to convert the milliseconds returned by the position property to seconds by dividing by 1,000.

```
sndTrack.start(nResumeMiliseconds/1000);
```

Detecting When a Sound Finishes

The onSoundComplete() event handler defines a callback function to be executed when a Sound object has finished playing. The onSoundComplete() method can be used for many purposes—updating a status message to automatically start a new song in an MP3 playlist. The following code updates a message text field when a sound has finished playing:

```
var sndTrack:Sound = new Sound();
sndTrack.onSoundComplete = function():Void {
  tMessage.text = "the sound has finished playing";
};
this.createTextField("tMessage", 1, 10, 10, 200, 20);
tMessage.border = true;
var sUrl:String = "http://www.rightactionscript.com/mp3/sample.mp3";
sndTrack.loadSound(sUrl, true);
```

Retrieving the Sound's Length

The duration property of the Sound class enables you to determine the length of a sound resource loaded into the Flash Player. The value is returned in milliseconds (1 second = 1,000 milliseconds). The duration property is a read-only property, meaning that you cannot set it to a new value—every sound resource has a definite length. The only way you can change the duration of a sound resource is to alter the actual sound file in a sound editing application.

Tip   You can, however, loop a sound resource, which enables the sound to play for longer periods of time. See the description of the start() method in the "Playing a Sound with Sound.start()" section earlier in this chapter.

The following code displays the length of a sound resource in the Output panel.

```
this.createEmptyMovieClip("mCarHornHolder", this.getNextHighestDepth());
var sndTrack:Sound = new Sound(mCarHornHolder);
sndTrack.attachSound("carHorn");
trace("carHorn is " + sndTrack.duration + " milliseconds in length.");
trace("carHorn is " + (sndTrack.duration/1000) + " seconds in length.");
```

Retrieving the Sound's Current Time

The position property of the Sound class returns the current playback time (in milliseconds). For example, if a 10-second sound has played back from 3 seconds, the position property returns 3,000. The following code creates and plays a Sound object, and creates a Mouse listener that enables a mouse click anywhere in the movie to display the current position value (in seconds) in the Output panel:

```
this.createEmptyMovieClip("mSoundTrackHolder", this.getNextHighestDepth());
var sndTrack:Sound = new Sound(mSoundTrackHolder);
sndTrack.attachSound("soundtrack");
sndTrack.start();
function onMouseDown():Void {
  trace("Current position:\t" + (sndTrack.position/1000) + " seconds");
};
```

Cross-Reference   For more information on the Mouse listeners, refer to Chapter 21.

Looped sounds return a value relative to the native length of the sound resource. For example, if you loop a 10-second sound three times, the position property always returns values between 0 and 10,000.

Reading an MP3 File's ID3 Tags

You can use the id3 property of a Sound object to retrieve information about an MP3 file loaded into the Sound object. ID3 tags contain information about the MP3 file. You can read these tags after the ID3 information has loaded or after the MP3 file has loaded.

You can use the onID3() handler of the Sound class to determine when the ID3 header information of an MP3 file has loaded. ID3 tags are stored at the very beginning of an MP3 file. As such, you can access the ID3 tag information before the sound is ready for playback. The following code creates a text field named tMessage, displaying all of the ID3 tags available in the loaded MP3 file:

```
var sndTrack:Sound = new Sound();
sndTrack.onID3 = function():Void {
    tMessage.htmlText += "---- ID3 tags ----\n";
    for (var i:String in this.id3) {
        tMessage.htmlText += "<b>" + i + "</b> : " + this.id3[i] + "\n";
    }
};
this.createTextField("tMessage", 1, 10, 10, 500, 300);
tMessage.border = true;
tMessage.html = true;
tMessage.multiline = true;
tMessage.wordWrap = true;
var sUrl:String = "http://www.rightactionscript.com/samplefiles/sample.mp3";
sndTrack.loadSound(sUrl, true);
```

Note   The onID3() handler is actually called twice if both ID3 v1.0 and v2.0 (or later) tags are stored in the MP3 file, once for each set of tags.

ID3 information can be stored as ID3 1.0 or ID3 2.0 (or later). If your MP3 file uses ID3 1.0 tags, you can use the following properties in ActionScript:

✦ Sound.id3.comment

✦ Sound.id3.album

✦ Sound.id3.genre

✦ Sound.id3.songname

✦ Sound.id3.artist

✦ Sound.id3.track

✦ Sound.id3.year

For example, the following code shows the MP3's song name, as stored in an ID3 v1.0 tag, in a TextField instance named tDisplay:

```
this.createEmptyMovieClip("mCarHornHolder", this.getNextHighestDepth());
var sndTrack:Sound = new Sound(mSoundTrackHolder);
sndTrack.onID3 = function(){
```

```
   createTextField("tDisplay", 1, 20, 20, 300, 30);
   tDisplay.text = "Title: " + this.id3.songname;
};
sndTrack.loadSound("sample.mp3", true);
```

If your MP3 file uses ID3 v2.0 (or later) tags, many ID3 tags are available; they are too numerous to list here. The following are some common ones:

- ✦ Sound.id3.COMM (**comment**)

- ✦ Sound.id3.TALB (**album**)

- ✦ Sound.id3.TCON (**genre**)

- ✦ Sound.id3.TIT2 (**songname**)

- ✦ Sound.id3.TPE1 (**artist**)

- ✦ Sound.id3.TRCK (**track number**)

- ✦ Sound.id3.TYER (**year**)

You can find the complete specification for all ID3 v2.0 tag names at www.id3.org/id3v2.3.0. html#sec4. Using the previous example of reading ID3 v1.0 tags, you simply need to modify the name of the id3 property you want to use for ID3 v2.0 (or later) tags. Note that your MP3 file must contain these tags in order for the Flash Player to read them:

```
var sndInstance:Sound = new Sound(this);
sndInstance.onID3 = function():Void {
   createTextField("tDisplay", 1, 20, 20, 300, 30);
   tDisplay.text = "Title: " + this.id3.TIT2;
};
sndInstance.loadSound("atmospheres_1.mp3", true);
```

Tip Flash Player 7+ automatically copies the values of ID3 v1.0 tags to their ID3 v2.0 equivalents. Given this, you should be able to consistently use ID3 v2.0 references in your ActionScript code, provided that an equivalent ID3 v1.0 tag exists in your loaded MP3 file.

Applying Sound Transforms

Once you understand the basic loading and playback methods and event handlers of the Sound class, you're ready to learn the methods that enable control over the volume and balance of the sound output.

Note All of the methods in this grouping are compatible with Flash Player 5 or later movies.

Controlling the Volume

To control the volume of your sound, you can call the setVolume() method of the Sound class. The percentage argument is a value in the 0–100 range, where 0 represents no volume (silence), and 100 represents full volume (the default volume of the sound). However, you can specify values higher than 100. Note that increasing the volume beyond 100 percent creates cutouts in your sound quality — any sound levels that are beyond 150 percent will start to crackle. The following syntax sets a Sound object named sndTrack to a volume of 50 percent:

```
sndTrack.setVolume(50);
```

Note
Be aware that the setVolume() method does not control the actual volume setting on the computer's speakers, or the system volume. This method simply controls the sound output of the specific Flash sound you are controlling.

The Sound.getVolume() method retrieves the current volume level of a specified Sound object. No argument is required for this method. You can create sound fades using the getVolume() method. The following code tells the sndTrack object to fade from 0 to 100.

```
var sndTrack:Sound = new Sound();
sndTrack.attachSound("bgSound");
sndTrack.start();
sndTrack.setVolume(0);
var nInterval:Number = setInterval(fadeSound, 100);

function fadeSound():Void{
  if(sndTrack.getVolume() < 100){
    sndTrack.setVolume(sndTrack.getVolume() + 10);
  } else {
    clearInterval(nInterval);
  }
}
```

Controlling the Balance

The setPan() method works like a balance knob on your stereo system. The method uses a parameter, which is a number in the range of –100 to 100, where negative values favor the left channel (or speaker), and positive values favor the right channel (or speaker). A value of 0 distributes the current volume equally to both channels.

The Sound.getPan() method retrieves the current pan value of the specified Sound object. You can use this method to create panning sounds that fade from left to right, or vice versa.

The setTransform() method is the most advanced method of the Sound class. The setTransform() method of the Sound class provides precision volume distribution over the left and right channels. A transform object is necessary to pass the volume properties to the Sound object. The transform object has four properties, each using a value in the range of 0 to 100:

✦ **ll** — This value designates what portion of the original left channel should actually be heard in the left channel. A value of 100 retains the original output of the left channel, whereas 0 silences the original output of the left channel.

✦ **lr** — This value controls what portion of the original right channel will be heard in the left channel. A value of 100 plays the full output of the right channel in the left channel, whereas 0 silences any applied output of the right channel in the left channel.

✦ **rr** — This value specifies how much of the original right channel should actually be heard in the right channel. A value of 100 plays the full output of the right channel, whereas 0 silences the original output of the right channel.

✦ **rl** — This value controls what portion of the original left channel will be played in the right channel. A value of 100 plays the full output of the left channel in the right channel, whereas 0 silences any applied output of the left channel in the right channel.

Note
You can use values higher than 100, just as you can with the setVolume() method of the Sound class. However, levels above 100 will likely distort the quality of the sound.

Any time you create a new Sound object, it has the following properties: $ll = 100$, $lr = 0$, $rr = 100$, and $rl = 0$. However, the following example shows how to play both channels in the left speaker.

```
this.createEmptyMovieClip("mSoundTrackHolder", this.getNextHighestDepth());
var sndTrack:Sound = new Sound(mSoundTrackHolder);

// Attach a sound from the library
sndTrack.attachSound("backgroundSound");

// Play the sound
sndTrack.start();

// Make a new transform object
var oSoundLeft:Object = new Object();

// Let the left channel to play 100% in the left speaker
oSoundLeft.ll = 100;

// Assign 100% of the right channel to play in the left speaker
oSoundLeft.lr = 100;

// Silence the right channel in the right speaker
oSoundLeft.rr = 0;

// Silence the left channel in the right speaker
oSoundLeft.rl = 0;

// Apply the transformObject to the Sound object
sndTrack.setTransform(oSoundLeft);
```

You can also create a transform object and assign its properties using object literal notation:

```
var oSoundLeft:Object = { ll: 100, lr: 100, rr: 0, rl: 0};
```

Why would you want so much control over your Sound objects? For the most part, setTransform() is most useful for Flash movies that incorporate stereo sounds. Later in this chapter, you learn how to play two separate sounds, one in each speaker. As the user moves the mouse to the left of the screen, the sound in the left speaker will start to take over the right channel as well. When the mouse moves to the right of the screen, the sound in the right speaker will start to take over the left speaker.

The getTransform() method retrieves the properties of a Sound object that was previously altered with setTransform(). There is no argument for this method. The method returns properties that can be applied to a new object. For example, the following code returns the current properties for a Sound object named sndTrack and stores those properties in an Object instance named oCurrentTransform:

```
var oCurrentTransform:Object = sndTrack.getTransform();
```

You can then use oCurrentTransform in a future use of setTransform(). If you had a user interface that enabled the user to control sound settings, you could store them temporarily in an object such as oCurrentTransform. The user could then continue to experiment with different sound properties. Later, if the user wanted to revert to the previously saved sound properties, you could add the following code to a button instance (labeled Reset or something similar):

```
btnReset.onRelease = function():Void {
  sndTrack.setTransform(oCurrentTransform);
};
```

Another use of getTransform() is to apply one sound's properties to another Sound object:

```
// Retrieve the values of one sound
var oCurrentTransform:Object = sndTrackOne.getTransform();

// Apply the values to another sound
sndTrackTwo.setTransform(oCurrentTransform);
```

In the following sections, you will apply your knowledge of the Sound class to some practical examples.

Attaching and Managing Playback of a Sound

In the following exercise, you'll build a simple application that attaches a sound that is exported in the SWF. It then lets the user manage the playback of the sound with start/stop and pause/resume buttons.

1. Open a new Flash document, and save it as soundAttachSound.fla.

2. Import a sound into the library by selecting File ➪ Import ➪ Import to Library. You can import any sound resource you want. However, it's recommended that you import sample.mp3, which you can find on the web site.

3. Select the Sound symbol in the Library, and open the Linkage settings.

4. Check the Export for ActionScript option.

5. Set the linkage identifier to sample.

6. Click the OK button.

7. Select the first keyframe of the default layer of the main timeline, and open the Actions panel. Then add the following code:

```
// Make a holder movie clip.
this.createEmptyMovieClip("mSoundTrackHolder",        ⊃
this.getNextHighestDepth());

// Declare a variable to keep track of the playback position
// if the user clicks the pause button.
var nResumeSeconds:Number;

// Make a new Sound object targeting the movie clip.
var sndTrack:Sound = new Sound(mSoundTrackHolder);

// Attach the sound exported with the linkage identifier of
// sample.
```

```
sndTrack.attachSound("sample");

// Define an onSoundComplete() method for the Sound object
// such that when the sound plays to the end it displays a
// message to the user and resets the buttons to the default
// states.
sndTrack.onSoundComplete = function():Void {
  tMessage.text = "The MP3 file has finished playing";
  setButtonState("start");
  setButtonState("pause");
};

// Make a text field to display messages to the user.
var tMessage:TextField = makeHTMLText(20, 50, 350, 20);

// Make text fields that have links with asfunction directives
// applied so that they work like buttons. One button starts and
// stops the sound, and the other pauses and resumes the sound.
var tStartStop:TextField = makeTextButton(20, 110);
var tPauseResume:TextField = makeTextButton(100, 110);

// Set the default states of the text field buttons.
setButtonState("start");
setButtonState("pause");

// Make text fields with asfunction directives.
function makeTextButton(nX:Number, nY:Number,
sLabel:String, sFunction:String, aParameters:Array):TextField {

  // Make the text field.
var tTextButton:TextField = makeHTMLText(nX, nY,
null, null, true);

// If a label has been specified, assign a link to the htmlText//
property. The link uses asfunction to call a function when
// clicked.
  if(sLabel != undefined) {
    tTextButton.htmlText = "<a href='asfunction:" + sFunction + "," +
aParameters + "'>" + sLabel + "</a>";
  }
  return tTextButton;
}

// Make a text field with the html property set to true.
function makeHTMLText(nX:Number, nY:Number, nWidth:Number,
nHeight:Number, bBorder:Boolean, bInput:Boolean,
bMultiline:Boolean):TextField {

  // Make the new text field.
  var nDepth:Number = this.getNextHighestDepth();
  var tHTMLField:TextField = this.createTextField("tHTMLText"
+ nDepth, nDepth, nX, nY, nWidth, nHeight);
```

```
// If no width was defined then set the text field to auto-size
// from the left.
  if(nWidth == null) {
    tHTMLField.autoSize = "left";
}
  tHTMLField.border = bBorder;
  if(bInput) {
    tHTMLField.type = "input";
  }
  tHTMLField.multiline = bMultiline;
  tHTMLField.html = true;
  return tHTMLField;
}

// The togglePlayback() function gets called when the user clicks
// on one of the text field buttons via asfunction.
function togglePlayback(sCommand:String):Void {

  // Affect the sound according to the parameter value. In each
  // case toggle the button state. (If the button was set to
  // "stop" previously, toggle it to "start", for example.)
  if(sCommand == "start") {
    sndTrack.start();
    setButtonState("stop");
  }
  else if(sCommand == "stop") {
    sndTrack.stop();
    setButtonState("start");
  }
  else if(sCommand == "pause") {
    nResumeSeconds = sndTrack.position / 1000;
    sndTrack.stop();
    setButtonState("resume");
  }
  else if(sCommand == "resume") {
    sndTrack.start(nResumeSeconds);
    setButtonState("pause");
  }
}

// Update the link and label for the text field buttons.
function setButtonState(sCommand:String):Void {
  if(sCommand == "stop" || sCommand == "start") {
    tStartStop.htmlText = "<a href='asfunction:          ⊃
togglePlayback," +sCommand + "'>" + sCommand + "</a>";
  }
  else {
    tPauseResume.htmlText = "<a href='asfunction:         ⊃
togglePlayback," + sCommand + "'>" + sCommand + "</a>";
  }
}
```

When you test the movie, it ought to display two buttons with default labels of start and pause. Click on the start button, and it will start the playback of the sound, and the button will toggle to the stop state. While the sound is playing you can pause it. With the sound paused you can resume the sound.

Loading MP3 Sounds

In this exercise, you'll modify the previous application slightly so that it loads an MP3 rather than attaching a sound.

1. Open `soundAttachSound.fla`, and save it as `soundLoadSound.fla`.

2. Delete the Sound symbol from the Library.

3. Edit the ActionScript on frame 1 by deleting the following line of code:

   ```
   sndTrack.attachSound("sample");
   ```

4. Add new code as follows (new code is bolded).

   ```
   this.createEmptyMovieClip("mSoundTrackHolder",
   this.getNextHighestDepth());

   var nResumeSeconds:Number;
   var nProgressInterval:Number;

   var sndTrack:Sound = new Sound(mSoundTrackHolder);

   // When the sound loads (or if the sound does not load) display
   // the appropriate message to the user, clear the interval, and
   // set the pause/resume button state to the default pause state.
   sndTrack.onLoad = function(bSuccess:Boolean):Void {
     if (bSuccess) {
       tMessage.text = "The MP3 file has downloaded";
     }
     else {
       tMessage.text = "Invalid URL";
     }
     clearInterval(nProgressInterval);
     setButtonState("pause");
   };

   sndTrack.onSoundComplete = function():Void {
     tMessage.text = "The MP3 file has finished playing";
     setButtonState("start");
     setButtonState("pause");
   };

   // Define a new input text field.
   var tURL:TextField = makeHTMLText(20, 20, 350, 20, true, true);

   // Specify default text as a message to the user.
   tURL.text = "<url to sound>";

   // When the text field gets focus, if the text is the default
   ```

```
// message, delete it.
tURL.onSetFocus = function():Void {
  if(tURL.text == "<url to sound>") {
    tURL.text = "";
  }
};

var tMessage:TextField = makeHTMLText(20, 50, 350, 20);

var tStartStop:TextField = makeTextButton(20, 110);
var tPauseResume:TextField = makeTextButton(100, 110);

setButtonState("start");
setButtonState("pause");

// Add two new text field buttons for downloading the sound as a
// progressive download and as an event sound.
var tLoadSoundProgressive:TextField = makeTextButton(20, 80,
"load progressive sound", "loadMP3", ["progressive"]);
var tLoadSoundEvent:TextField =
makeTextButton(tLoadSoundProgressive._width + 20 + 10, 80,
"load event sound", "loadMP3", ["event"]);

function makeTextButton(nX:Number, nY:Number, sLabel:String,
sFunction:String, aParameters:Array):TextField {
  var tTextButton:TextField = makeHTMLText(nX, nY, null,
null, true);
  if(sLabel != undefined) {
    tTextButton.htmlText = "<a href='asfunction:" +
sFunction + "," + aParameters + "'>" + sLabel + "</a>";
  }
  return tTextButton;
}

function makeHTMLText(nX:Number, nY:Number, nWidth:Number,
nHeight:Number, bBorder:Boolean, bInput:Boolean,
bMultiline:Boolean):TextField {
  var nDepth:Number = this.getNextHighestDepth();
  var tHTMLField:TextField = this.createTextField(
"tHTMLText" + nDepth, nDepth, nX, nY, nWidth, nHeight);
  if(nWidth == null) {
    tHTMLField.autoSize = "left";
  }
  tHTMLField.border = bBorder;
  if(bInput) {
    tHTMLField.type = "input";
  }
  tHTMLField.multiline = bMultiline;
  tHTMLField.html = true;
  return tHTMLField;
}

function togglePlayback(sCommand:String):Void {
```

```
if(sCommand == "start") {
  sndTrack.start();
  setButtonState("stop");
}
else if(sCommand == "stop") {
  sndTrack.stop();
  setButtonState("start");
}
else if(sCommand == "pause") {
  nResumeSeconds = sndTrack.position / 1000;
  sndTrack.stop();
  setButtonState("resume");
}
else if(sCommand == "resume") {
  sndTrack.start(nResumeSeconds);
  setButtonState("pause");
}
}

function setButtonState(sCommand:String):Void {
  if(sCommand == "stop" || sCommand == "start") {
    tStartStop.htmlText = "<a href='asfunction:
toggePlayback," + sCommand + "'>" + sCommand + "</a>";
  }
  else {
    tPauseResume.htmlText = "<a href='asfunction:
togglePlayback," + sCommand + "'>" + sCommand + "</a>";
  }
}

// The loadMP3() function gets called when the user clicks one of
// the load sound text field buttons. The function simply calls
// the loadSound() method of the Sound object, and it starts an
// interval that checks the download progress.
function loadMP3(sType:String):Void {
  sndTrack.loadSound(tURL.text,
sType == "progressive" ? true : false);
  nProgressInterval = setInterval(checkProgress, 100);
  setButtonState(sType == "progressive" ? "stop" : "start");
}

// Monitor the download progress, and display the percent to the
// user.
function checkProgress():Void {
  var nLoadedBytes:Number = sndTrack.getBytesLoaded();
  var nTotalBytes:Number = sndTrack.getBytesTotal();
  var nPercent:Number = Math.round((nLoadedBytes/
nTotalBytes) * 100);
  tMessage.text = nPercent + "% of the sound has downloaded";
}
```

When you test the movie, you ought to have the option to enter a URL to a MP3 file. You can use a URL to any valid MP3 file. You can copy `sample.mp3` from the web site to the same location as the Flash document, and then use `sample.mp3` as the URL. Optionally, you can specify `http://www.rightactionscript.com/samplefiles/sample.mp3`.

Managing Volume and Pan

In the following exercise, you'll build volume and pan management functionality into the application from the previous section.

1. Open `soundLoadSound.fla`, and save it as `soundVolumePan.fla`.

2. Edit the ActionScript as follows. The new code is bolded.

```
this.createEmptyMovieClip("mSoundTrackHolder",
this.getNextHighestDepth());

var nResumeSeconds:Number;
var nProgressInterval:Number;

var sndTrack:Sound = new Sound(mSoundTrackHolder);

sndTrack.onLoad = function(bSuccess:Boolean):Void {
  if (bSuccess) {
    tMessage.text = "The MP3 file has downloaded";
  }
  else {
    tMessage.text = "Invalid URL";
  }
  clearInterval(nProgressInterval);
  setButtonState("pause");
};

sndTrack.onSoundComplete = function():Void {
  tMessage.text = "The MP3 file has finished playing";
  setButtonState("start");
  setButtonState("pause");
};

var tURL:TextField = makeHTMLText(20, 20, 350, 20, true, true);
tURL.text = "<url to sound>";
tURL.onSetFocus = function():Void {
  if(tURL.text == "<url to sound>") {
    tURL.text = "";
  }
};

var tMessage:TextField = makeHTMLText(20, 50, 350, 20);

var tStartStop:TextField = makeTextButton(20, 110);
var tPauseResume:TextField = makeTextButton(100, 110);
```

```
setButtonState("start");
setButtonState("pause");

var tLoadSoundProgressive:TextField = makeTextButton(20,
80, "load progressive sound", "loadMP3", ["progressive"]);
var tLoadSoundEvent:TextField =
makeTextButton(tLoadSoundProgressive._width + 20 + 10, 80,
"load event sound", "loadMP3", ["event"]);

// Define three text fields - a minus button, a label, and a plus
// button. In the case of the minus and plus buttons, link them
// so they call the setSoundVolume() function. The minus button
// passes a value of -10 in order to decrement the volume by 10,
// and the plus button passes a value of 10.
var tVolumeMinus:TextField = makeTextButton(400, 50, " - ",
"setSoundVolume", ["-10"]);
var tVolumeLabel:TextField = makeTextButton(
tVolumeMinus._width + tVolumeMinus._x + 5, 50, "volume");
var tVolumePlus:TextField = makeTextButton(
tVolumeLabel._width + tVolumeLabel._x + 5, 50, " + ",
"setSoundVolume", ["10"]);

// As with the preceding lines of code, the following adds three
// text fields. They are almost identical to the preceding text
// fields except that they are for pan rather than volume.
var tPanMinus:TextField = makeTextButton(400, 80, " - ",
"setSoundPan", ["-10"]);
var tPanLabel:TextField = makeTextButton(
tPanMinus._width + tPanMinus._x + 5, 80, "pan");
var tPanPlus:TextField = makeTextButton(
tPanLabel._width + tPanLabel._x + 5, 80, " + ",
"setSoundPan", ["10"]);

function makeTextButton(nX:Number, nY:Number, sLabel:String,
sFunction:String, aParameters:Array):TextField {
  var tTextButton:TextField = makeHTMLText(nX, nY, null,
null, true);
  if(sLabel != undefined) {
    tTextButton.htmlText = "<a href='asfunction:" +
sFunction + "," + aParameters + "'>" + sLabel + "</a>";
  }
  return tTextButton;
}

function makeHTMLText(nX:Number, nY:Number, nWidth:Number,
nHeight:Number, bBorder:Boolean, bInput:Boolean,
bMultiline:Boolean):TextField {
  var nDepth:Number = this.getNextHighestDepth();
  var tHTMLField:TextField = this.createTextField(
"tHTMLText" + nDepth, nDepth, nX, nY, nWidth, nHeight);
```

```
    if(nWidth == null) {
      tHTMLField.autoSize = "left";
    }
    tHTMLField.border = bBorder;
    if(bInput) {
      tHTMLField.type = "input";
    }
    tHTMLField.multiline = bMultiline;
    tHTMLField.html = true;
    return tHTMLField;
}

function togglePlayback(sCommand:String):Void {
  if(sCommand == "start") {
    sndTrack.start();
    setButtonState("stop");
  }
  else if(sCommand == "stop") {
    sndTrack.stop();
    setButtonState("start");
  }
  else if(sCommand == "pause") {
    nResumeSeconds = sndTrack.position / 1000;
    sndTrack.stop();
    setButtonState("resume");
  }
  else if(sCommand == "resume") {
    sndTrack.start(nResumeSeconds);
    setButtonState("pause");
  }
}

function setButtonState(sCommand:String):Void {
  if(sCommand == "stop" || sCommand == "start") {
    tStartStop.htmlText = "<a href='asfunction:
togglePlayback," + sCommand + "'>" + sCommand + "</a>";
  }
  else {
    tPauseResume.htmlText = "<a href='asfunction:
togglePlayback," + sCommand + "'>" + sCommand + "</a>";
  }
}

function loadMP3(sType:String):Void {
  sndTrack.loadSound(tURL.text, sType == "progressive"
? true : false);
  nProgressInterval = setInterval(checkProgress, 100);
  setButtonState(sType == "progressive" ? "stop" : "start");
}

function checkProgress():Void {
```

```
   var nLoadedBytes:Number = sndTrack.getBytesLoaded();
   var nTotalBytes:Number = sndTrack.getBytesTotal();
   var nPercent:Number = Math.round((nLoadedBytes/
nTotalBytes) * 100);
   tMessage.text = nPercent + "% of the sound has downloaded";
}

// Update the volume.
function setSoundVolume(sIncrement:String):Void {

// Since asfunction parameters are typed as String, convert the
// string to a number.
var nIncrement:Number = Number(sIncrement);

// Increment (or decrement) the volume.
   sndTrack.setVolume(sndTrack.getVolume() + nIncrement);
   tMessage.text = "Setting volume to " + sndTrack.getVolume();
}

// The following function works almost identically to
// setSoundVolume().
function setSoundPan(sIncrement:String):Void {
   var nIncrement:Number = Number(sIncrement);
   sndTrack.setPan(sndTrack.getPan() + nIncrement);
   tMessage.text = "Setting pan to " + sndTrack.getPan();
}
```

When you test the movie, it functions much as before. However, with the new functionality you can adjust the volume and pan of the sound during playback.

Working with ID3 Data

In the following exercise, you'll build on the previous exercise, adding ID3 tag functionality.

1. Open soundVolumePan.fla, and save it as soundID3.fla.

2. Edit the ActionScript code as follows. The new code is bolded.

```
this.createEmptyMovieClip("mSoundTrackHolder",
this.getNextHighestDepth());

var nResumeSeconds:Number;
var nProgressInterval:Number;

var sndTrack:Sound = new Sound(mSoundTrackHolder);

sndTrack.onLoad = function(bSuccess:Boolean):Void {
   if (bSuccess) {
     tMessage.text = "The MP3 file has downloaded";
   }
   else {
```

```
      tMessage.text = "Invalid URL";
    }
    clearInterval(nProgressInterval);
    setButtonState("pause");
};

sndTrack.onSoundComplete = function():Void {
  tMessage.text = "The MP3 file has finished playing";
  setButtonState("start");
  setButtonState("pause");
};

// When the sound downloads, display the ID3 tag data in a text
// field called tID3.
sndTrack.onID3 = function():Void {
  tID3.htmlText = "<b>artist</b> " + this.id3.artist + "<br />";
  tID3.htmlText += "<b>album</b> " + this.id3.album + "<br />";
  tID3.htmlText += "<b>song</b> " + this.id3.songname + "<br />";
  tID3.htmlText += "<b>year</b> " + this.id3.year + "<br />";
  tID3.htmlText += "<b>comment</b> " + this.id3.comment +       ⊃
"<br />";
};

var tURL:TextField = makeHTMLText(20, 20, 350, 20, true, true);
tURL.text = "<url to sound>";
tURL.onSetFocus = function():Void {
  if(tURL.text == "<url to sound>") {
    tURL.text = "";
  }
};

var tMessage:TextField = makeHTMLText(20, 50, 350, 20);

var tStartStop:TextField = makeTextButton(20, 110);
var tPauseResume:TextField = makeTextButton(100, 110);

setButtonState("start");
setButtonState("pause");

var tLoadSoundProgressive:TextField = makeTextButton(20, 80,    ⊃
"load progressive sound", "loadMP3", ["progressive"]);
var tLoadSoundEvent:TextField =                                 ⊋
makeTextButton(tLoadSoundProgressive._width + 20 + 10, 80,      ⊃
"load event sound", "loadMP3", ["event"]);

var tVolumeMinus:TextField = makeTextButton(400, 50, " - ",     ⊃
"setSoundVolume", ["-10"]);
var tVolumeLabel:TextField = makeTextButton(                    ⊃
tVolumeMinus._width + tVolumeMinus._x + 5, 50, "volume");
var tVolumePlus:TextField = makeTextButton(                     ⊋
tVolumeLabel._width + tVolumeLabel._x + 5, 50, " + ",
```

```
                  "setSoundVolume", ["10"]);

                  var tPanMinus:TextField = makeTextButton(400, 80, " - ",
                  "setSoundPan", ["-10"]);
                  var tPanLabel:TextField = makeTextButton(
                  tPanMinus._width + tPanMinus._x + 5, 80, "pan");
                  var tPanPlus:TextField = makeTextButton(
                  tPanLabel._width + tPanLabel._x + 5, 80, " + ",
                  "setSoundPan", ["10"]);

                  // Make the text field for displaying the ID3 tags.
                  var tID3:TextField = makeHTMLText(20, 140, null, null,
                  false, false, true);

                  function makeTextButton(nX:Number, nY:Number, sLabel:String,
                  sFunction:String, aParameters:Array):TextField {
                    var tTextButton:TextField = makeHTMLText(nX, nY, null, null, true);
                    if(sLabel != undefined) {
                      tTextButton.htmlText = "<a href='asfunction:" +
                  sFunction + "," + aParameters + "'>" + sLabel + "</a>";
                    }
                    return tTextButton;
                  }

                  function makeHTMLText(nX:Number, nY:Number, nWidth:Number,
                  nHeight:Number, bBorder:Boolean, bInput:Boolean,
                  bMultiline:Boolean):TextField {
                    var nDepth:Number = this.getNextHighestDepth();
                    var tHTMLField:TextField = this.createTextField(
                  "tHTMLText" + nDepth, nDepth, nX, nY, nWidth, nHeight);
                    if(nWidth == null) {
                      tHTMLField.autoSize = "left";
                    }
                    tHTMLField.border = bBorder;
                    if(bInput) {
                      tHTMLField.type = "input";
                    }
                    tHTMLField.multiline = bMultiline;
                    tHTMLField.html = true;
                    return tHTMLField;
                  }

                  function setSoundVolume(sIncrement:String):Void {
                    var nIncrement:Number = Number(sIncrement);
                    sndTrack.setVolume(sndTrack.getVolume() + nIncrement);
                    tMessage.text = "Setting volume to " + sndTrack.getVolume();
                  }

                  function setSoundPan(sIncrement:String):Void {
                    var nIncrement:Number = Number(sIncrement);
                    sndTrack.setPan(sndTrack.getPan() + nIncrement);
```

```
    tMessage.text = "Setting pan to " + sndTrack.getPan();
}

function togglePlayback(sCommand:String):Void {
  if(sCommand == "start") {
    sndTrack.start();
    setButtonState("stop");
  }
  else if(sCommand == "stop") {
    sndTrack.stop();
    setButtonState("start");
  }
  else if(sCommand == "pause") {
    nResumeSeconds = sndTrack.position / 1000;
    sndTrack.stop();
    setButtonState("resume");
  }
  else if(sCommand == "resume") {
    sndTrack.start(nResumeSeconds);
    setButtonState("pause");
  }
}

function setButtonState(sCommand:String):Void {
  if(sCommand == "stop" || sCommand == "start") {
    tStartStop.htmlText = "<a href='asfunction:            ⤵
togglePlayback," + sCommand + "'>" + sCommand + "</a>";
  }
  else {
    tPauseResume.htmlText = "<a href='asfunction:          ⤵
togglePlayback," + sCommand + "'>" + sCommand + "</a>";
  }
}

function loadMP3(sType:String):Void {
  sndTrack.loadSound(tURL.text, sType == "progressive"       ⤵
? true : false);
  nProgressInterval = setInterval(checkProgress, 100);
  setButtonState(sType == "progressive" ? "stop" : "start");
}

function checkProgress():Void {
  var nLoadedBytes:Number = sndTrack.getBytesLoaded();
  var nTotalBytes:Number = sndTrack.getBytesTotal();
  var nPercent:Number = Math.round((nLoadedBytes/            ⤵
nTotalBytes) * 100);
  tMessage.text = nPercent + "% of the sound has downloaded";
}
```

For the preceding code to work properly, you must use a MP3 file with ID3 tags. If you use the sample.mp3 file from the online version at http://www.rightactionscript.com/samplefiles/sample.mp3, the application ought to display the ID3 data when the sound downloads.

We'd like to know what you thought about this chapter. Visit `www.rightactionscript` `.com/asb/comments` to fill out an online form with your comments.

Summary

✦ The constructor for the `Sound` class uses the `new` operator. Each instance of the `Sound` class should be constructed in the following syntax: `var sndName:Sound = new Sound(mcTarget);`.

✦ `Sound` objects marry sounds from the movie's Library or an external MP3 file to a specific timeline in the movie by using the `attachSound()` or `loadSound()` method, respectively, of the `Sound` class.

✦ The `start()` and `stop()` methods are used to play or halt `Sound` objects, respectively.

✦ The `setVolume()` and `getVolume()` methods control or retrieve the loudness of a specific `Sound` object, respectively.

✦ The `setPan()` and `getPan()` methods work with the balance (that is, the volume distribution between the left and right speakers) of a specific `Sound` object.

✦ The `setTransform()` and `getTransform()` methods of the `Sound` class enable you to precisely control left and right channel output in the actual left and right speakers of the computer system.

✦ There are three properties of the `Sound` class: `duration`, `position`, and `id3`. The `loadSound()` method is used to download MP3 files into the Flash Player at runtime, and the `onLoad()`, `onSoundComplete()`, and `onID3()` event handlers enhance the playback control of Sound objects.

✦   ✦   ✦

Managing Video

When Flash Player 6 first introduced video playback, you had to use either embedded video within a Flash movie (SWF file) or use Flash Communication Server to deliver the Flash Video file (FLV) to the Flash movie. Since Flash Player 7, it is possible to use progressive download playback of FLV files, which doesn't require any additional software. In this chapter, you learn how to load FLV files into a Flash movie using the `NetStream` class. You learn how to use a `Video` object to display the visual portion of the `NetStream` output as well.

Working with Flash Video Files

In this section, you learn how to make a FLV file from an existing digital video file. You also learn the different ways in which you can access a Flash Video file in a Flash movie. Later in this chapter, you learn how to load the FLV file into a movie using ActionScript.

Making an FLV File with the Flash Video Encoder

If you're using Flash Professional then you already have the Flash Video Encoder installed. By default Flash Video Encoder is installed in a directory called Flash 8 Video Encoder that is placed in the Macromedia directory in the default location for program files. For example, on Windows the application is installed at `C:\Program Files\Macromedia\Flash 8 Video Encoder`.

Once you've started the Flash Video Encoder, you can add a video file to the queue to encode by clicking the Add button on the right side of the window. That will bring up a dialog that prompts you to select the video file you want to code. The Flash Video Encoder can encode quite a few video formats — Active Streaming Format (`.asf`), AVI, DV Stream, QuickTime, MPEG, MPEG-4, and Windows Media. Using the dialog, you can add one or more video files to encode.

For each video in the queue, you can apply settings by selecting the video from the queue list and pressing the Settings button. The settings dialog box lets you specify an output file name. Otherwise, the new file name is the same as the source file name, but with the `.flv` file extension. You can also select from a list of presets that allow you to encode for Flash 7 or Flash 8 and with different bitrates. Optionally, you can click on the Show Advanced Settings button, and then modify the encoding settings in more detail.

Note Flash Player 8 can play back video with the new On2 VP6 codec. Flash Player 7 and Flash Player 8 can playback video with the older Sorenson Spark codec. If you want to encode video for Flash Player 7, use the Spark codec. If you are encoding video for Flash Player 8, use the VP6 codec since you'll notice an improvement in video quality.

You can also trim the video using the in and out point slider controls on the video preview in the upper right portion of the dialog box. The advanced settings also let you add cue points and crop the video.

Once you've added the videos to the queue and applied the correct settings, simply click the Start Queue button to start the encoding.

Note There are additional encoding utilities available. As of this writing On2 has an FLV encoding utility that uses 2-pass encoding instead of 1-pass encoding like the Flash Video Encoder.

Using RTMP to Access FLV Files

Flash Video (FLV) files were originally designed to be streamed in real time from Macromedia Flash Communication Server. This media server technology can serve audio/video streams to multiple users simultaneously, record audio/video streams from a user's Webcam, edit together videos on the fly, and much more. Flash Communication Server uses a proprietary protocol called RTMP, or Real Time Messaging Protocol, to connect Flash movies (SWF files) to Flash Communication Server applications. When Flash Video (FLV) files are streamed with Flash Communication Server, the FLV file is never stored locally in the browser's cache folder — only the current frames being played are stored in the Flash Player's buffer.

The following list provides reasons why you might want to use a Flash Communication Server to deliver audio/video streams (from your FLV files):

✦ **Flash Player compatibility** — If you use Flash Communication Server to deliver FLV files, you can reach a wider market. You need only Flash Player 6 or later to view audio/video streams from Flash Communication Server, rather than using Flash Player 7+ for HTTP-loaded FLV files.

✦ **Digital Rights Management (DRM)** — If you have a business client that is protective of its content, the use of Flash Communication Server can make it harder for users to copy audio/video content. FLV files are stored in a protected area of the server and can be delivered by the Flash Communication Server only. When viewed by a user, the FLV file is never downloaded in its entirety, nor is it stored as a local file in the browser's cache.

✦ **True streaming** — With Flash Communication Server, the user will be able to begin watching the video sooner, and the video can begin playback at any point within the FLV file. The user does not have to wait until the entire stream has downloaded up to the point that is requested.

✦ **Minimize bandwidth consumption** — Regardless of a Flash Video file's length (or duration), Flash Communication Server serves only what the user is currently watching. Therefore, if you have a 45-minute video file but the user wants to watch only 5 minutes, your server's connection will not be burdened with sending the entire video file to the user.

✦ **Extended options** — With Flash Communication Server, you can record ActionScript data to a stream (FLV file), retrieve a stream's length (in seconds), and make new copies of the stream (with different in/out points) on the server.

However, there's always a cost for such things. The following list covers some of these drawbacks:

✦ **Licensing** — You have to purchase a license for Flash Communication Server. Licensing costs vary depending on your connection and user needs.

✦ **Learning curve** — You have to learn how to build and script Flash movies and Flash Communication Server applications to work with real-time streams.

✦ **Port and protocol restrictions** — If your target audience is using a computer that's behind a tight firewall or proxy server, Flash movies (SWF files) might be unable to connect to a Flash Communication Server for viewing audio/video streams.

✦ **Server installation** — You need to install and maintain Flash Communication Server independently of your web server. Although you can have a web server and the Flash Communication Server software running on the same computer, you'll likely want to purchase a dedicated machine for serving and connecting clients with Flash Communication Server.

 For more production information on Flash Communication Server, refer to Macromedia's site at www.macromedia.com/software/flashcom.

Using HTTP to Access FLV Files

If you don't want to use Flash Communication Server to deliver FLV files to your audience, you're in luck. Flash Player 7+ enables Flash movies (SWF files) to directly load FLV files at runtime, over a standard HTTP (Hypertext Transfer Protocol) connection. HTTP is the same protocol used to view regular web pages and content. You simply upload your FLV file to your web server, point your Flash movie to the FLV file's location, and viewers can watch progressive download FLV content. The following list provides some reasons why you might want to deliver FLV files over HTTP:

✦ **Cost effective** — If you're making Flash content for the Web, you already have a web server that you can use to deliver FLV files.

✦ **Easy to implement** — Once you learn how to load an FLV file into a Flash movie with ActionScript (as discussed in the next section), you do not need to learn a new server-side language to serve the video file (as Flash Communication may require, depending on the complexity of your application).

However, there are some drawbacks, including the following:

✦ **Potential bandwidth overhead** — When you load an FLV file from a web server, the entire file is downloaded to the user's machine. It doesn't matter if the user watches only a portion of it — once a web server receives a request for a resource, it can deliver only the whole resource, not just a portion of it.

Note When you serve an FLV file over HTTP, you are not technically streaming the content into the Flash movie. Media assets served over HTTP are progressive downloads — although it's possible to begin playback before the entire file has downloaded, you can't prematurely pause the downloading process. Once it's started, the only way to stop it is to exit your web browser and/or Flash movie.

✦ **Digital Rights Management (DRM)** — Because the FLV is delivered over HTTP, it must be a public location. Users can potentially load and save the FLV separately from your Flash movie (SWF file), or they can search the browser cache for the FLV file.

Regardless of which protocol or server technology you use to deliver FLV files, keep the following points in mind:

✦ Audio/video content is rarely a small download for the user. Serving audio/video content can rack up bandwidth charges on your server hosting account.

✦ Make sure that you have the rights to showcase the audio/video content. If you didn't shoot or record the content yourself, chances are that you'll need to obtain written consent to use the material on your own site.

✦ Don't use HTTP solely because it's perceived to be less of a financial hit. Thoroughly analyze the requirements for the audio/video content usage, and provide an overview of HTTP versus RTMP concerns to your business client.

Loading FLV Files into a Flash Movie

After you make an FLV file, you're ready to load it into a Flash movie (SWF file). Although you can load FLV content without displaying it, most frequently you'll want to use a `Video` object to render the video. You can then use a `NetStream` object to load the FLV content, and associate the data with the `Video` object. The next few sections discuss how to accomplish that.

Adding a Video Object

The `Video` class defines a class of objects that can display the video portion of FLV content. The `Video` class does not let you build a new instance using a constructor. Instead, you must add a new Video symbol to the library, and then add an instance of the Video symbol to the stage. You can add a Video symbol to the library by selecting the New Video option from the library menu. The default type for a Video symbol is called Video (ActionScript-controlled), and that is the type that you want when using FLV files.

Once you've added a Video symbol to the library, you can add an instance to the stage. Simply drag an instance from the library to the stage as you would a movie clip. And, as with a movie clip, assign an instance name to a `Video` object via the Property inspector.

You cannot assign a linkage identifier to a Video symbol. That means that you cannot directly attach a `Video` object at runtime. However, you can make a Movie Clip symbol with a nested `Video` object, and you can then set the Movie Clip symbol to export for ActionScript with a linkage identifier. You can then use `attachMovie()` to add instances of the movie clip at runtime. That will indirectly add new `Video` objects as well since each new movie clip instance will have a nested `Video` object.

Building an HTTP Connection to an FLV File

To playback progressive download FLV files, you need to do the following:

1. Construct a new `NetConnection` object. The NetConnection constructor doesn't require any parameters.

   ```
   var ncFLVConnection:NetConnection = new NetConnection();
   ```

2. Call the `connect()` method for the `NetConnection` object. The `connect()` method is normally used when connecting to a Flash Communication Server application. In those

cases, you pass the method the URL of the application. For progressive download video, specify `null`:

```
ncFLVConnection.connect(null);
```

3. Construct a new `NetStream` object that is linked to the `NetConnection` object. Use the `NetStream` constructor in a `new` statement, and pass the `NetConnection` object to the constructor:

```
var nsVideo:NetStream = new NetStream(ncFLVConnection);
```

4. Call the `play()` method of the `NetStream` object, specifying the URL to the FLV file:

```
nsVideo.play("video.flv");
```

Displaying the NetStream Data in a Video Object

Once you've added a `Video` object and used the `NetConnection` and `NetStream` classes to start the playback of the FLV video, you next need to tell Flash how to display the video. You can do that by way of the `attachVideo()` method of the `Video` class. The `attachVideo()` method requires one parameter — a reference to the `NetStream` object:

```
vFLVDisplay.attachVideo(nsVideo);
```

Checking Status Messages from the NetStream Class

The `NetStream` class has an `onStatus()` event handler, which can be used to monitor the activity occurring on the `NetStream` instance. A `NetStream` object gets notified as events such as buffering, starting, and stopping occur. The `onStatus()` method gets passed one parameter. That parameter is an associative array with a property called `code`. The `code` property contains a string value that indicates what event has just occurred.

✦ When a stream begins to play, the `onStatus()` handler receives a `code` property of `NetStream.Play.Start`.

✦ When enough of the FLV file has downloaded into the Flash Player's buffer, the `NetStream.Buffer.Full` message is sent to the `onStatus()` handler.

✦ When the stream playback reaches the end of the FLV file, the `code` property `NetStream.Play.Stop` is sent to the `onStatus()` handler.

✦ When all of the stream data has emptied from the Flash Player's buffer, the `code` property of `NetStream.Buffer.Empty` is sent to the `onStatus()` handler.

✦ For FLV files served over HTTP, there is also a `code` property of `NetStream.Play.StreamNotFound`. This value is returned to the `onStatus()` handler if the URL is invalid. This message can also occur if the Flash Player does not have a working Internet connection.

There are other code values for FLV files served over an RTMP connection to a Flash Communication Server application, such as NetStream.Pause.Notify.

Note   All code values are a `String` datatype. For a full listing of code values, see the *Client-Side Communication ActionScript Dictionary* PDF on Macromedia's site at `www.macromedia.com/support/flashcom/documentation.html`.

Tip   You can create a System.onStatus() handler to catch NetStream events. If you do not assign an onStatus() handler to a NetStream instance, the Flash Player will pass the message along to a System.onStatus() handler:

The following is an example of an onStatus() method definition for a NetStream object called nsVideo.

```
nsVideo.onStatus = function(oData:Object):Void {
  trace(oData.code);
};
```

Retrieving Metadata

FLV files contain metadata that Flash Player retrieves when the FLV starts to download. The metadata contains an array of data. Arguably the most useful datum of the metadata is the duration of the FLV. The NetStream class doesn't define a property that tells you what the total playback time of the FLV is. However, you can retrieve the duration from the metadata for the FLV. As you'll see, the duration is critical if you want the user to be able to scrub the playback or if you want to display accurate playback progress.

When the metadata is read from an FLV, the onMetaData() event handler method is called for the NetStream object playing back the FLV. The onMetaData() method is passed one parameter—an associative array. The keys of the associative array are the metadata. The duration metadatum is stored with a key of duration.

```
nsVideo.onMetaData = function(oMetaData:Object):Void {
  trace(oMetaData.duration);
};
```

Scripting Basic Controls for a NetStream Object

The NetStream object you use to start the playback of an FLV is responsible for managing the playback throughout. You already learned about the play() method, which starts the playback of an FLV. The NetStream class also lets you pause and resume, fast forward and rewind, and stop the playback of the video.

Pausing FLV Playback

The pause() method lets you instruct the video playback to pause and resume. The pause() method, without any parameters, toggles the playback of the video.

```
// Pause a playing video, or resume a paused video.
nsVideo.pause();
```

Optionally, you can pass the method a Boolean value. A value of true pauses the video if it's playing back, and it does nothing if the video is already paused. Likewise, a value of false causes the video to resume if it is paused, and it does nothing if the video is already playing back.

```
nsVideo.pause(true);
```

Jumping to Specific Points

The seek() method lets you jump to a specific point in a video. The method requires one parameter — a number specifying the number of seconds to which to jump. For example, the following tells Flash Player to jump to 40.4 seconds from the start of the FLV:

```
nsVideo.seek(40.4);
```

You cannot jump to a point in the video that has not yet downloaded.

Stopping the Video

If you want to stop a video, first determine whether you want to stop the download or simply pause the video. If you want to stop the download, call the close() method from the NetStream object:

```
nsVideo.close();
```

The close() method will stop the playback of the video and will cause Flash Player to delete the local version of the FLV. At that point, if you want to play the video again Flash Player will have to start downloading the FLV again.

If you want to stop the playback of the video and move the playhead to the beginning of the FLV, but you want the FLV to continue to download in the background, then pause the video, and use the seek() method to jump to 0:

```
nsVideo.pause(true);
nsVideo.seek(0);
```

Displaying Playback Progress

To display playback progress, you can use the time property of the NetStream object that is playing back the FLV. The time property reports, in seconds, the current playback time of the video. The following code uses an interval to repeatedly display the playback time of a NetStream object in the Output panel:

```
setInterval(displayTime, 1000);
function displayTime():Void {
  trace(nsVideo.time);
}
```

Often, you'll want to display the playback time relative to the duration of the playback. For example, you might want to display something like the following to the user to tell them that the playback time is 2 minutes and 3 seconds out of a total 4 minutes running time:

```
2:03 of 4:00
```

As mentioned previously, the NetStream class does not define a duration property, but it does retrieve duration metadata. You can use the duration metadata to determine the total running time of a video.

Configuring Video Dimensions

A Video object has default dimensions of 160×120. You can set the dimensions either at authoring time via the Property inspector or at runtime using the _width and _height properties. The dimensions of a Video object determine the dimensions at which the video will be played back. For example, if a video is encoded at 320×240 but the Video object is 160×120, the video will play back at 160×120.

If the dimensions of the video are unknown at authoring time, and you want the Video object to playback the video at the encoded dimensions, you can use the width and height metadata values to adjust the dimensions of the Video object at runtime. The following onMetaData() event handler method assigns the new width and height to the _width and _height properties of the Video object.

```
nsVideo.onMetaData = function(oMetaData:Object):Void {
  vFLV._width = oMetaData.width;
  vFLV._height = oMetaData.height;
};
```

Building a FLV Playback Application

In the following exercise, you'll build an application that can playback an FLV video. It uses controls to let the user play, pause, and stop the video. The playback progress is displayed using a progress bar.

1. Copy video.flv from the web site to your local disk.

2. Open video_starter.fla from the web site, and save it as video.fla on your local disk in the same directory to which you copied video.flv.

3. Notice that a Video symbol has already been added to the library, an instance to the stage, and several movie clips have also been added. Note the instance names of each — vFLV (Video object), mProgress, mPlay, mPause, and mStop. Note also that nested within mProgress is a movie clip called mPercent.

4. Select the first keyframe of the Actions layer, and add the following code:

```
var ncVideo:NetConnection = new NetConnection();
ncVideo.connect(null);

var nsVideo:NetStream = new NetStream(ncVideo);
nsVideo.play("video.flv");

vFLV.attachVideo(nsVideo);

var nDuration:Number = 0;

nsVideo.onMetaData = function(oMetaData:Object):Void {
  nDuration = oMetaData.duration;
};

mPlay.onPress = function():Void {
```

```
    nsVideo.pause(false);
  };

  mPause.onPress = function():Void {
    nsVideo.pause(true);
  };

  mStop.onPress = function():Void {
    nsVideo.pause(true);
    nsVideo.seek(0);
  };

  setInterval(updateProgress, 100);

  function updateProgress():Void {
    var nPercent:Number = 100 * nsVideo.time / nDuration;
    mProgress.mPercent._xscale = nPercent;
  }
```

When you test the movie, the video will start playing back immediately. The progress bar will update to show how much of the video has played back. The controls will let you pause, resume, and stop the video.

Adding Captions

You can add captions to FLV files directly in several ways. While the Flash Video Encoder allows you to add captions (they are called *cue points* in the Flash Video Encoder), it does not let you edit existing captions in an FLV file. Furthermore, the interface for adding captions/cue points in the Flash Video Encoder is not very user-friendly. Therefore, we don't recommend using the Flash Video Encoder to add captions to FLV files. Rather, we recommend that you use a utility such as Captionate. Captionate is a commercial application available for purchase from www.captionate.com.

When you use Captionate to add captions to an FLV, it encodes them into the file. Then, the FLV dispatches events that the NetStream object can handle with an onCaption() method. The onCaption() method is passed a string specifying the value of the caption text.

```
  nsVideo.onCaption = function(sCaption:String):Void {
    trace(sCaption);
  };
```

In the following exercise, you'll use an FLV with embedded captions and display those captions in a text field.

1. Copy video_captions.flv from the web site to the same directory where you copied video.flv from the previous exercise.

2. Open video.fla, and edit the ActionScript code as follows (at which point you can save it as video_captions.fla). Changes are bolded.

```
  this.createTextField("tCaptions", this.getNextHighestDepth(),     ↩
  vFLV._x + 180, vFLV._y, 200, 0);
  tCaptions.autoSize = "left";
```

```
tCaptions.multiline = true;
tCaptions.wordWrap = true;

var ncVideo:NetConnection = new NetConnection();
ncVideo.connect(null);

var nsVideo:NetStream = new NetStream(ncVideo);
nsVideo.play("video_captions.flv");

vFLV.attachVideo(nsVideo);

var nDuration:Number = 0;

nsVideo.onMetaData = function(oMetaData:Object):Void {
  nDuration = oMetaData.duration;
};

nsVideo.onCaption = function(sCaption:String):Void {
  tCaptions.text = sCaption;
};

mPlay.onPress = function():Void {
  nsVideo.pause(false);
};
mPause.onPress = function():Void {
  nsVideo.pause(true);
};
mStop.onPress = function():Void {
  nsVideo.pause(true);
  nsVideo.seek(0);
};

setInterval(updateProgress, 100);

function updateProgress():Void {
  var nPercent:Number = 100 * nsVideo.time / nDuration;
  mProgress.mPercent._xscale = nPercent;
}
```

When you test the movie, the video will play back as before. However, this time the captions that are embedded in the FLV will play back as well.

We'd like to know what you thought about this chapter. Visit www.rightactionscript .com/asb/comments to fill out an online form with your comments.

Summary

✦ Flash Video (FLV) files can be played in Flash Players 6 or higher. If you're using Flash Communication Server, FLV files can be streamed to Flash Player 6 or higher. If you're loading FLV files over HTTP, the Flash movie must be a Flash Player 7 or higher SWF file viewed in Flash Player 7 or higher.

✦ The NetStream class works in conjunction with the NetConnection and Video classes. A Video object displays the visual portion of a NetStream instance playing an FLV file.

✦ The onStatus() handler of a NetStream instance receives an information object with a code property. The code property specifies which particular event is occurring on a NetStream instance.

✦ Use onMetaData() to read the metadata from an FLV file.

✦ You can use the play(), pause(), and seek() methods of the NetStream class to control the playback of an FLV file. You can also use the time property of the NetStream class to report the current playback time of the FLV file, and the duration metadatum to determine the total playback time.

✦   ✦   ✦

Using Components

Using UI Components

Components are, in simplistic terms, particular types of Movie Clip symbols that can perform a large array of specialized tasks in your Flash applications. Once you have created an instance of a component, you can set various parameters via the Component Inspector panel and you can even perform complex operations via the component's programmatic interface of properties, methods, and events (also called the API). By allowing for interaction both by a graphical user interface and a programmatic interface, components are designed to appeal to both programmers and nonprogrammers alike.

The possibilities for components are really limitless. As you'll see in Chapter 30, you have the option to build your own components (or, of course, download and install others' components). But for the purposes of this chapter, you're going to look specifically at the built-in user interface components that are included with Flash 8.

Introducing the Components Panel

When you want to work with components you will, almost inevitably, need to open the Components panel. In the default panel layout the Components panel can be found to the right side of the stage along with the Color Mixer and assorted other panels. The panel might be collapsed, and so you might need to click the panel's title bar to expand it. If you don't see the Components panel, you can open it by pressing Ctrl+F7 or ⌘+F7, or by choosing Window ⇨ Development Panels ⇨ Components. Figure 28-1 shows what the Components panel looks like in Flash 8 Professional (with the Data and Media Components menus collapsed). Flash 8 Basic contains a subset of the components shown in Figure 28-1.

Figure 28-1: The Flash 8 Professional Components panel.

Adding New Component Instances

There are a few ways you can add new component instances to your Flash document:

✦ Add instances by dragging and dropping at authoring time

✦ Add instances dynamically at runtime with ActionScript

Adding instances at authoring time means you can drag an instance from the Components panel onto the stage. This copies the component symbol into the Flash document's library, and also creates an instance on the stage.

To add instances at runtime, you first need to add the symbol to the library. To do this, drag an instance from the Components panel onto the stage as though creating an authoring time instance. Then, you should delete the instance from the stage. The symbol will remain in the library. Once the symbol is in the library, you can add new instances programmatically using one of two methods:

✦ Using `createObject()`

✦ Using `createClassObject()`

The `createObject()` method is identical to the `attachMovie()` method (see Chapter 14 for more information on `attachMovie()`). The linkage identifier for each component matches the symbol name (that is, the linkage identifier for the Button component is `Button`). Here's an example that adds a `Button` component instance with ActionScript:

```
this.createObject("Button", "cbtSubmit", this.getNextHighestDepth());
```

The createClassObject() method is very similar to the createObject() method except that instead of the first parameter indicating the symbol's linkage identifier, it should be a reference to the component's class. Most of the component classes are in the mx.controls package. Here is an example that adds a Button component instance with the createClassObject() method.

```
this.createClassObject(mx.controls.Button, "cbtSubmit",
this.getNextHighestDepth());
```

Both the createObject() and createClassObject() methods allow you to specify a fourth, optional parameter in the form of an initialization object. The initialization object for these methods works just as the initialization object for duplicateMovieClip() and attachMovie() (see Chapter 14 for more information on initialization objects).

Naming Component Instances

When naming component instances, we suggest that you use the prefixes shown in Table 28-1. These prefixes all begin with the letter *c* to indicate a component. (These suggestions are made only for the purposes of helping you to adopt good coding practices. The prefixes do not offer special functionality or features not otherwise available. But using the prefixes helps you to organize your code and makes your code more readable.)

Table 28-1: Component Instance Name Prefixes

Component	Prefix
Accordian	cac
Alert	ca
Button	cbt
CheckBox	cch
ComboBox	ccb
DataGrid	cdg
DateChooser	cdc
DateField	cdf
Label	clbl
List	cl
Loader	cld
Menu	cm
MenuBar	cmb
NumericStepper	cns
ProgressBar	cpb
RadioButton	crb

Continued

Table 28-1 *(continued)*

Component	Prefix
ScrollPane	csp
TextArea	cta
TextInput	cti
Tree	ctr
UIScrollBar	csb
Window	cw

Setting Component Parameters

There are basically two ways you can set a component's parameters. Which way you set the parameters, depends, in part, on how you have created the instance. If you create the instance at authoring time, you can set the parameters either with the Component Inspector panel or with the API. If, however, you create the instance programmatically, you can set the parameters only via the API.

Working with the Component Inspector Panel

The Component Inspector panel allows you to change the properties for a component instance that was instantiated during authoring time. Figure 28-2 shows what the Component Inspector panel looks like for a Button component instance in Flash 8 Professional. (The Bindings and Schema tabs are available only in the Professional version.)

Figure 28-2: The Component Inspector panel for a Button instance (in Flash 8 Professional).

In the Parameters tab, you have options for all the available parameters for the selected component instance. In the case of a Button component instance there are parameters such as icon, label, and labelPlacement. (You'll look at the parameters for each component type in subsequent sections.) Changing the values of the parameters in the Component Inspector panel can affect the view of the component on the stage if live preview is on. You can turn on live preview by selecting Control ➪ Enable Live Preview.

Note You can also set some component parameters via the Property inspector. However, the Component Inspector panel allows you to set all the available parameters, not just a subset.

Working with the Component APIs

Each component has its own API (application programming interface — in this case, the *application* being the component you are working with), composed of methods, properties, and events. In the preceding section, you saw how to modify the parameters of a component using the Component Inspector panel. However, you can use that technique to configure component instances only during authoring time. That means that you can use it only to affect components created during authoring time, and also that you can use it to initialize the settings only of an authoring-time component instance.

Working with the API has several advantages:

✦ You can set the parameters for component instances that have been created during runtime.

✦ The API allows you to control much more than you can control with the Component Inspector panel. For example, you can use the API to set listeners for an instance.

✦ You can set parameters in response to events that take place during runtime. For example, you can load some data via an XML object (or LoadVars or Flash Remoting) and when the data loads, you can assign that data to the component (perhaps a database query that returns all the U.S. state names in order to populate a ComboBox component).

All the parameters in the Component Inspector panel are properties of a component instance. Therefore, as a simple example, you can programmatically create a Button component instance and set the label with the following code:

```
this.createObject("Button", "cbtSubmit", 1);
cbtSubmit.label = "Submit";
```

Or, you can even use an init object in your call to createObject() to accomplish the preceding in one line of code:

```
this.createObject("Button", "cbtSubmit", 1, {label: "Submit"});
```

Understanding the Fundamental UI Component APIs

All the User Interface components are based on the same set of parent classes, one of which is UIObject. The UIObject class provides some common functionality for all components. Additionally, each component class has been initialized by the UIEventDispatcher class in order to dispatch events to listener objects. The following sections look at listener objects, the common component functionality and then each of the component APIs.

Working with Listener Objects

Each component dispatches events. For example, when the user clicks a Button component instance, that instance dispatches a click event. It's up to you to set up something to handle that event. There are several options for how to handle these events, but the technique that we advocate is the *listener object* technique.

A listener object can be any instance of any dynamic class. For example, a listener object can be an instance of the `Object` class or the `MovieClip` class. You must do two things so that the listener object can handle component instance events:

✦ Define a method for the object that corresponds to the event for which you want it to listen. For example, if you want the object to be able to listen for a Button component's click event, you should define a `click()` method for the listener object. All events are dispatched with an event object, so the method can/should accept a parameter. The event objects are instances of the `Object` class that have a `target` property that is a reference to the component instance that dispatched the event, and a `type` property that specifies the type of event that was dispatched (some event objects might contain other properties as well).

```
var oListener:Object = new Object();
oListener.click = function(oEvent:Object):Void {
  // Displays the path to the component that
  // dispatched the event.
  trace(oEvent.target);
};
```

✦ Add the object to the component instances list of listeners by calling the `addEventListener()` method. The `addEventListener()` method requires two parameters — the name of the event as a string and a reference to the listener object.

```
cbtSubmit.addEventListener("click", oListener);
```

A single listener object can listen for more than one event. And the same listener object can listen for events from multiple component instances. For example, if `cbtSubmit` and `cbtReset` are both `Button` component instances, the following code allows the same listener to handle both click and unload events for both component instances:

```
var oListener:Object = new Object();
oListener.click = function(oEvent:Object):Void {
  if(oEvent.target._name == "cbtSubmit") {
    trace("submit clicked");
  }
  else {
    trace("reset clicked");
  }
};
oListener.unload = function(oEvent:Object):Void {
  if(oEvent.target._name == "cbtSubmit") {
    trace("submit unloaded");
  }
  else {
    trace("reset unloaded");
  }
};
cbtSubmit.addEventListener("click", oListener);
cbtSubmit.addEventListener("unload", oListener);
cbtReset.addEventListener("click", oListener);
cbtReset.addEventListener("unload", oListener);
```

Working with Common Component Functionality

Each type of component inherits some common functionality from the superclass UIObject. Rather than discuss each of the common pieces of functionality separately for each component, let's take a look at the common functionality first.

Creating and Removing Component Instances

You can use the createObject() and createClassObject() methods (see discussion of these methods earlier in this chapter) to create new instances of a component at runtime. These methods can be called from any MovieClip instance as well as component instances, and they create the new instance nested within the object from which they are called. For example, the following code, called from the main timeline, creates a new Button instance nested within the main timeline:

```
this.createObject("Button", "cbtSubmit", this.getNextHighestDepth());
```

To remove a component instance, use the destroyObject() method. This method should be invoked from the parent object, and it requires that you specify the name of the instance to remove as a string parameter. For example, to remove an instance named cbtSubmit from the current timeline, use the following code:

```
this.destroyObject("cbtSubmit");
```

When you create a new instance, the component dispatches both a load and a draw event. When you remove the instance an unload event is dispatched.

Moving Component Instances

You can move a component instance in several ways. Because components are subclasses of MovieClip, they inherit the standard MovieClip properties and methods, including _x and _y. Therefore, you can move a component instance with the _x and _y properties. However, it is advantageous to utilize the UIObject move() method instead. The move() method takes two parameters — the X- and Y-coordinates to which to move the instance. But not only does the method move the instance, it also dispatches a move event.

```
cbtSubmit.move(25, 70);
```

Components also have read-only x and y parameters that report the same values as the _x and _y properties. Although in their current form reading the values of x and y offers no real advantages over reading the values of _x and _y, it is possible that future versions may leverage the component architecture in some way such that x and y might provide some benefit over _x and _y. For that reason we recommend that you use x and y.

Resizing Component Instances

You can resize a component instance in several ways. You can resize it by setting either pixels or percentages.

To resize a component instance by setting exact pixel dimensions, you can use the setSize() method. The setSize() method requires two parameters — the width and the height for the component in pixels.

```
cbtSubmit.setSize(200, 22);
```

The height and width properties are read-only properties that report the current dimensions of a component instance. If, in the preceding example, you wanted to set the width of the component to 200 pixels, but you wanted to keep the current height, you could use the following code instead:

```
cbtSubmit.setSize(200, cbtSubmit.height);
```

You should not use the _width and _height properties inherited from MovieClip unless you want the component instance to appear distorted. They will not resize the instances as you want.

When you call the setSize() method, the component dispatches a resize event.

You can also resize a component instance by percentages using the scaleX and scaleY properties. These properties determine the scale factors in the X and Y directions by which the component instance should be scaled. A value of 100 means that the instance should be scaled to 100 percent of the width and/or height. In other words, setting the scaleX and scaleY properties to 100 will cause the component to appear at either the default dimensions or at whatever dimensions you set with setSize(). Or, for example, a value of 200 will cause the instance to be scaled to twice the dimension in the given direction.

When an instance is scaled, it does not dispatch any events.

Looking at the Standard Form UI Components

The first group of components you'll look at is the form UI components included in both the basic and professional versions of Flash 8. These components include all the basic controls you need to create standard user input forms.

Working with Button Components

Button components are likely to be one of the most commonly used components in your application. When you use the majority of the other components, you will use them in combination with a Button component instance. Fortunately, the Button component is one of the simplest components as well. Button instances can be used for many purposes, including as submit buttons, reset buttons, buttons that toggle states, and so on. Figure 28-3 shows a Button instance with a label of Submit.

Figure 28-3: A Button component instance.

Handling Button Clicks

When the user clicks a Button component instance, a click event is dispatched. You can set a listener object to handle the click event with a click() method.

```
this.createObject("Button", "cbtSubmit", this.getNextHighestDepth());
var oListener:Object = new Object();
oListener.click = function(oEvent:Object):Void {
  trace(oEvent.target._name + " was just clicked");
};
cbtSubmit.addEventListener("click", oListener);
```

Caution Do not use button event handler methods with `Button` component instances. If you attempt to assign an `onPress()` or `onRelease()` event handler method, for example, to a `Button` component instance, you will get unexpected behavior.

Setting Label and Icon

You can customize the label for a `Button` component instance by setting the `label` property. For example:

```
cbtSubmit.label = "Submit";
```

You can also, optionally, display a graphic in the component instance by assigning a value to the instance's `icon` property. The value of the `icon` property should be the linkage identifier of a symbol in the library. For example, if you have a symbol in the library with a linkage identifier of `SmileySymbol`, you can display that artwork on the `Button` component instance as follows:

```
cbtSubmit.icon = "SmileySymbol";
```

If you add a graphic to the instance, you can also determine the relative placement of the graphic and the label text. By default, the label appears to the left of the graphic. You can explicitly tell Flash to place the text to the left, right, top, or bottom of the graphic by assigning that value, as a string, to the `labelPlacement` property of the component instance.

```
cbtSubmit.labelPlacement = "right";
```

Changing Button Type

`Button` component instances can act like standard push buttons that are clicked and released with each press. That is the default behavior. However, you can also choose to have the instance act as a toggle. That means that when the `Button` instance is pressed, the state changes from deselected to selected or from selected to deselected. In order to achieve this, all you need to do is set the instance's `toggle` property to `true`:

```
cbtSubmit.toggle = true;
```

And, of course, if you want to explicitly tell Flash that the instance should act like a standard push button again, you can set the `toggle` property to `false`:

```
cbtSubmit.toggle = false;
```

If, and only if, the `toggle` property is `true`, can you also tell Flash whether or not the instance should be selected (pressed in). Setting the `selected` property to `true` sets the instance to the selected state, and setting the `selected` property to `false` sets the instance to the deselected state:

```
cbtSubmit.selected = true;
```

Working with Label Components

The `Label` component enables you to quickly and simply add labels to your applications. Labels can be used for many purposes, but one of the most common uses of the `Label` component is to add labels to instances of components or groups of components. The `Label` component is quite simple. It doesn't have any methods or events. It has only a handful of configurable properties.

You can set the value that displays in the `Label` instance by setting its `text` property:

```
clblDescription.text = "Description";
```

You can set a `Label` instance such that it can display HTML by setting its `html` property to `true`. When you set the instance to display HTML, the CSS formatting will no longer apply.

```
clblDescription.html = true;
clblDescription.text = "<font color='#FF0000'>Description</font>";
```

The `autoSize` property of a `Label` component instance can have the following string values:

✦ `none` — This is the default value, and it means that the instance is not resized to fit the text.

✦ `right` — This means that the instance will be resized to automatically fit the text, and the right and top sides of the instance stay fixed and the left and bottom are adjusted as necessary.

✦ `left` — This means that the instance will be resized and that the left and top sides are fixed and the right and bottom sides will be adjusted as necessary.

✦ `center` — This means the instance will be resized and that the top-center point will stay fixed, while the label will adjust as necessary downward and to the right and left.

Working with TextInput Components

The `TextInput` component is very similar to an input `TextField`. The differences are that it provides a look that is consistent with the rest of the components and that it is built on the component architecture so that it provides the same basic functionality as other components. Figure 28-4 shows an example of a basic `TextInput` instance.

Figure 28-4: A TextInput component instance.

Setting and Getting the Text Value

The default state for a `TextInput` instance is that it is editable. That means that the user can edit the text using the keyboard. You can explicitly make a `TextInput` instance either editable or not by setting the `editable` property to `true` or `false`.

You can get and set the value of a `TextInput` instance by using the `text` property:

```
ctiPostalCode.text = "12345";
```

The `length` property returns the number of characters in the input text:

```
trace(ctiPostalCode.length);
```

Restricting Input Characters

You can allow or disallow specific characters for a `TextInput` instance. For example, for a `TextInput` field that asks the user for a telephone number, you might want to allow only numbers and spaces. You can use the restrict property to define an allowable and/or disallowable character set. For example:

```
ctiPhone.restrict = "0123456789 ";
```

The preceding code tells Flash to allow the user to enter only numbers and the space character. You can also use ranges of characters by specifying the starting character in the range, a dash, and then the ending character in the range. For example, the preceding code can be simplified as follows:

```
ctiPhone.restrict = "0-9 ";
```

If you want to allow the user to enter a dash, you need to remember to escape the character in the string. For example, it might seem, at first, that you should be able to add the dash to the string as with any other character:

```
ctiPhone.restrict = "0-9 -";  // Will not work
```

However, when you look at the string as Flash will try to interpret it, you may notice that Flash will think that the dash is indicating a range of characters. Instead, you have to escape the dash character so that Flash interprets it literally instead of with its special meaning to indicate a range of characters. If you recall from the discussion in Chapter 11, you can use the backslash character to escape as part of an escape sequence. Therefore, the next guess is usually to try the following:

```
ctiPhone.restrict = "0-9 \-";  // Still will not work
```

Although that is a good guess, it is still not quite correct. The backslash character *will* escape the dash within the string. However, you want the slash itself to be escaped as well so that the correct string value (including a literal backslash) is interpreted by the TextInput instance. If all of that is too confusing, just suffice it to say that when you want to escape a dash in a restrict string, you need to place two backslashes before it. The following is the corrected example:

```
ctiPhone.restrict = "0-9 \\-";
```

Table 28-2 gives you a few more examples of escape sequences you can use with the restrict property value.

Table 28-2: Escape Sequences

Value to Allow the User to Enter	Normal String Escape Sequence	Value to Use for the restrict Property	Example
^	\^	\\^	To allow emc^2 ctiInput.restrict = "emc\\^2";
-	\-	\\-	To allow 1-800- ctiInput.restrict = "\\-018";
\	\\	\\\\	To allow C:\ ctiInput.restrict = "C:\\\\";

You can also tell Flash what characters to *disallow* by using the ^ character at the beginning of the restrict string. All the characters and ranges that follow are disallowed. For example, the following disallows all upper- and lowercase alphabetic characters:

```
ctiSampleInput.restrict = "^a-zA-Z";
```

As with the dash, if you want to have the ^ character interpreted literally, you need to escape it by preceding it with two backslashes:ctiSampleInput.restrict = "\\^"; // Allows only the ^.

If you want to allow or disallow a literal backslash, you need to escape that character as well. In order to escape a backslash, you need to enter four backslashes:

```
ctiSampleInput.restrict = "\\\\";  // Allows only the \
```

By default, the `restrict` property has an `undefined` value. A value of `undefined`, `null`, or an empty string allows all characters.

Setting the Maximum Number of Characters

You can set a `TextInput` field to allow only a certain number of characters. For example, if you have a `TextInput` instance that asks the user for a short version of a U.S. ZIP code, you might want to set the maximum number of characters to five. You can set the maximum number of characters with the `maxChars` property:

```
ctiZip.maxChars = 5;
```

The default value is `null`, and if you set the value back to `null` then the maximum limit is removed.

Making a Password TextInput

The default setting for a `TextInput` instance displays the text as the user enters it. In some cases, you want to hide the entered text from view. For example, when the user types in a password you don't want to display that so that any person passing by can see the value. In such a case you want to set the instance to password mode. In password mode only the * (asterisk) character is displayed, but the actual value is stored programmatically in the `text` property. You can set a `TextInput` instance to password mode by setting the `password` property to `true`.

```
ctiPassword.password = true;
```

Figure 28-5 shows an example of a `TextInput` instance in password mode.

Figure 28-5: A TextInput instance in password mode displays only asterisks.

Handling TextInput Events

`TextInput` components dispatch the following events:

✦ `change` — When the value of the instance changes through user action (not when changed programmatically).

✦ `enter` — When the instance has focus and the user presses the Enter key.

Working with TextArea Components

The `TextArea` component is similar to an HTML `textarea` control. It is an area for text input that has built-in vertical and horizontal scrollbars. Figure 28-6 shows an example of a `TextArea` instance.

Figure 28-6: A TextArea component instance.

TextArea components share several similarities to TextInput components. You can get and set the text value of a TextArea instance with the text property in the same way as with a TextInput instance. You can also make a TextArea instance editable or not by using the editable property. You can set the allowable and disallowable characters for a TextArea using the restrict property, and set a TextArea instance to password mode with the password property, just as with a TextInput instance.

Wrapping Text

By default, word wrapping is activated in TextArea instances. This means that if a word runs over the width of the instance, the word is moved to the next line of displayed text. You can control whether or not an instance wraps text by setting the value of the wordWrap property. The default value is true. You can turn off wrapping by setting the value to false.

Controlling Scrollbars

The default setting for a TextArea is such that the scrollbars appear only when necessary. If no text runs off the viewable area, the scrollbars are not visible. When the text runs off the viewable area in the vertical direction, a vertical scrollbar appears. Likewise, when the text runs off the viewable area in the horizontal direction, a horizontal scrollbar appears. You can change these settings with the vScrollPolicy and hScrollPolicy properties. Each accepts the following string values:

✦ on — This means the scrollbar is always visible, regardless of whether it is needed.

✦ off — This means the scrollbar never appears, even when the text runs off the viewable area.

✦ auto — This is the default value that displays the scrollbar when appropriate.

If wordWrap is set to true (the default setting), the horizontal scrollbar will never be visible. This is so even if the hScrollPolicy is set to on.

Handling TextArea Events

TextArea component instances dispatch a change event when the text is changed by user action. This event is not dispatched when the value is changed programmatically.

Working with CheckBox Components

CheckBox component instances are most often used in forms to allow users to select between yes/no or true/false for a particular option. Sometimes a single CheckBox instance is used, for example when prompting a user to accept licensing conditions for an application or whether or not to opt into a mailing list. In other cases, a group of CheckBox instances is used to allow a user to select from a list of related options. For example, a form might prompt a user to select his favorite music genres from a list. Each genre might be represented by a CheckBox instance. The user can then select to check or uncheck each one. Figure 28-7 shows such an example.

Figure 28-7: A group of CheckBox component instances.

Setting CheckBox Label and Label Placement

You can programmatically assign a new label to a CheckBox instance using the label property:

```
cchOptIn.label = "Opt In";
```

Note   The label will be cut off if you attempt to add text beyond the bounding box of the component instance.

The default placement for a label is to the right of the actual check box. You can tell Flash to move the label to the left, right, top, or bottom by assigning the corresponding value, as a string, to the labelPlacement property:

```
cchOptIn.labelPlacement = "left";
```

Getting and Setting the Checked State

The default state for a CheckBox instance is to be unchecked. You can get or set the state with the selected property. A value of true means the instance is checked. A value of false means the instance is unchecked.

```
cchOptIn.selected = true;
```

Handling CheckBox Clicks

When a user clicks a CheckBox instance, either to check or uncheck it, the instance dispatches a click event. You can handle that event with a click() method on the listener object:

```
var oListener:Object = new Object();
oListener.click = function(oEvent:Object):Void {
  trace(oEvent.target._name + " was just clicked");
};
cchOptIn.addEventListener("click", oListener);
```

Working with RadioButton Components

RadioButton component instances and CheckBox component instances can be used for very similar purposes. However, whereas a group of CheckBox component instances can allow a user to select multiple options, a group of RadioButton instances is formally grouped as a RadioButtonGroup instance, and the user can select only one value from the group. Figure 28-8 shows an example of a group of RadioButton instances.

Figure 28-8: A group of RadioButton component instances.

You can set the label and label placement for a `RadioButton` instance in the same way that you set the label and label placement for a `CheckBox` instance. See the `CheckBox` discussion for more details.

Setting RadioButton Data

Each `RadioButton` instance must have both a label and a data value. The data value is hidden from the user, but it is what is used programmatically. You can set the data value by assigning a value to the `data` property.

```
crbAmidetrous.data = "ambi";
```

Setting the Selected State

You can set the selected state of a `RadioButton` instance with the selected property. If you set the property to `true`, the instance is selected.

```
crbAmbidextrous.selected = true;
```

If any other instance in the group was previously selected, that instance is deselected.

Grouping RadioButton Instances

Very rarely is a single `RadioButton` instance used in isolation. Instead, `RadioButton` instances are generally used in groups, whereby only one value at a time can be selected. Flash needs a way of knowing which instances are grouped together. This is especially true when there is more than one set of radio button groups on the form (for example, male and female). The `groupName` property determines how instances are grouped. All instances with the same `groupName` value belong to the same group. The value of `groupName` must be a string. When you assign a value to an instance's `groupName` property, Flash checks to see if the group has already been created. If so, it adds the instance to the group. If not, Flash first creates a new `RadioButtonGroup` object. The `RadioButtonGroup` object is created within the same scope as the `RadioButton` instance, and its name is the name assigned to the `groupName` property. For example, the following code creates a new `RadioButtonGroup` object named `crbgHandedness`, and adds the `crbAmbidextrous` instance to that group:

```
crbAmbidetrous.groupName = "crbgHandedness";
```

Getting Selected Values

You can retrieve the selected value from a `RadioButtonGroup` with the `selectedData` property. This property returns the value of the data property for the selected `RadioButton` instance in the given `RadioButtonGroup`:

```
trace(crbgHandedness.selectedData);
```

The `selection` property, on the other hand, returns a reference to the selected `RadioButton` instance from the group.

Handling Click Events

Both `RadioButton` instances and `RadioButtonGroup` objects dispatch click events when the user makes a selection. You can, therefore, assign a listener either to the group or to each instance. In most cases, if you need to handle the click events it would be most appropriate to assign the listener to the group.

```
var oListener:Object = new Object();
oListener.click = function(oEvent:Object):Void {
  trace(oEvent.target.selectedData);
};
crbgHandedness.addEventListener("click", oListener);
```

Working with ComboBox Components

The `ComboBox` is also often referred to as a drop-down menu. Like `RadioButtonGroups`, `ComboBox` instances are useful for presenting users with a set of options from which they can select only one. However, a `ComboBox` can contain a large range of values (incorporating a scrollbar if necessary), which means it takes up less space on stage compared to `RadioButtonGroups` and can sometimes be preferable for that reason. Figure 28-9 shows an example of a `ComboBox` instance that has been opened and from which a value is being selected.

Figure 28-9: A ComboBox instance.

Adding Items to a ComboBox Instance

When you first create a `ComboBox` instance, it contains no values:

```
this.createObject("ComboBox", "ccbCities", this.getNextHighestDepth());
```

Therefore, it is up to you to add new items to the list. There are several ways you can go about this.

Adding Items One at a Time

You can add new items one at a time using the `addItem()` method. The `addItem()` method appends a new items to the list. There are three basic variations on how to can call the `addItem()` method. First, you can call the method with a single parameter:

```
ccbCities.addItem("Chicago");
```

Generally, this first approach is not recommended, however. Each item in a `ComboBox` has both a label and a data value. The label is what is displayed to the user. But the data can be different from the label. For example, if the values were retrieved from a database, the data may be an ID from the database that corresponds to the label. In such cases, it is preferable to work with the ID programmatically while displaying the label to the user. When you pass only one parameter to the `addItem()` method, the item has only a label value, and the data value is left undefined. It is better, typically, to assign both a label and data value, even if they are the same value. You can assign a data value by passing a second parameter to the `addItem()` method:

```
ccbCities.addItem("Chicago", 54);
```

You can also call the `addItem()` method by passing it a single object parameter in which the object has a `label` and a `data` property:

```
ccbCities.addItem({label: "Chicago", data: 54});
```

The `addItem()` method always appends the item to the end of the current list. If you want to insert a new item into the list at a specific index, you can use the `addItemAt()` method instead. The `addItemAt()` method requires that you tell it at what index you want it to insert the new value. The items in a `ComboBox` are indexed starting with 0, so if you specify a value of 0 the new item will be added to the beginning of the list. All subsequent items are shifted by one. When you call the `addItemAt()` method you have two options. First, as with the `addItem()` method, you can specify the label value.

```
ccbCities.addItemAt(1, "St. Louis");
```

Or, the preferred way is to specify both the label and data values:

```
ccbCities.addItemAt(1, "St. Louis", 33);
```

Whereas the `addItemAt()` method inserts a new item, shifting all subsequent items by one index, the `replaceItemAt()` method adds a new item in place of the current item at the same index. As with `addItem()` and `addItemAt()`, when you call the `replaceItemAt()` method you can specify either just the label value or both the label and data values.

```
ccbCities.replaceItemAt(0, "Los Angeles", 81);
```

Adding Items as a Group

You can also add items to a `ComboBox` instance as a group. The `dataProvider` property allows you to assign it a value of either an array or any object that implements the `DataProvider` interface.

You can use an array of strings to assign a group of labels to a `ComboBox` instance. For example:

```
ccbCities.dataProvider = ["Chicago", "Los Angeles", "New York", "St. Louis];
```

However, that approach is akin to setting only the label value when calling `addItem()`. Instead, you can set both the label and data values by using an array of objects in which each object has both a label and a data property.

```
ccbCities.dataProvider = [{label: "Chicago", data: 54},
{label: "Los Angeles", data: 81}, {label: "New York",
data: 27}, {label: "St. Louis", data: 33});
```

Additionally, if your data provider array contains objects that do not contain a `label` property, you can still use the array to populate the `ComboBox`. If you set the instance's `labelField` property to the corresponding property name, it will use that property instead of looking for a `label` property. For example:

```
ccbCities.labelField = "cityName";
ccbCities.dataProvider = [{cityName: "Chicago", data: 54},
{cityName: "Los Angeles", data: 81},
{cityName: "New York", data: 27},
{cityName: "St. Louis", data: 33}];
```

In some cases, you might want to combine multiple properties from each object in the array in order to make the label. For example, if each object in the data provider array has `cityName`, `estYear`, and `data` properties, you might want to display both the city name and the year the city was established in the label. You can achieve this by assigning a function to the `labelFunction` property of the `ComboBox` instance. Flash automatically passes the function each object element from the data provider array, and it should return the label to use. For example:

```
ccbCities.labelFunction = function(oElement:Object):String {
  var sLabel:String = oElement.cityName + " (" +
oElement.estYear + ")";
  return sLabel;
};
```

Typically, working with the `dataProvider` property is most useful when you are working with datasets and recordsets returned by various types of service calls via, for example, Flash Remoting.

Getting the Number of Items

The `length` property returns the number of items in a `ComboBox` instance:

```
trace(ccbCities.length);
```

Removing Items from ComboBox Instances

You can remove items from a `ComboBox` instance one at a time with the `removeItemAt()` method. The method takes a parameter indicating the index of the item to remove:

```
ccbCities.removeItemAt(0);
```

If you want to remove all the items from a `ComboBox` instance, you can use the `removeAll()` method:

```
ccbCities.removeAll();
```

Making Editable ComboBox Instances

The default behavior of a `ComboBox` instance is that the user must select from one of the predefined values. You can, however, make the instance editable so that the user can enter a value by typing it with the keyboard. When you set the `editable` property to `true`, the selected value is editable. The user can still select from the list of values. But in addition, if she wants, she can type a value in place of that.

Getting Items and Values from ComboBox Instances

There are several approaches to getting items from a `ComboBox` instance. First, you can use the `getItemAt()` method to return an item given an index. For example, if you want to get the first item from a `ComboBox` instance:

```
var oItem:Object = ccbCities.getItemAt(0);
```

The `getItemAt()` method returns an object that corresponds to the value that was originally assigned to the item in the list. If you assigned the value with `addItem()`, `addItemAt()`, `replaceItemAt()`, or with a data provider in which the label field property was named `label`, the object returned by `getItemAt()` has a `label` and `data` property.

If you want to get the selected item, you can use the `selectedItem` property. Like `getItemAt()`, the `selectedItem` property returns an object with `label` and `data` properties (unless the `labelField` property was set to another value than `label`).

```
trace(ccbCities.selectedItem.label);
```

You can also retrieve the index of the selected item with the `selectedIndex` property:

```
trace(ccbCities.selectedIndex);
```

More often than not, you want to simply retrieve the selected value. The `value` property returns the selected value for a `ComboBox` instance. The value that it returns depends on the behavior and qualities of the instance:

✦ If the instance is a standard, noneditable instance and the selected item has both a label and a data property, `value` returns the data for the selected item.

✦ If the instance is a standard, noneditable instance and the selected item has only a label property, `value` returns the label for the selected item.

✦ If the instance is editable, `value` returns the value that the user has typed or the label of the selected item.

Opening and Closing ComboBox Instances

The `open()` and `close()` methods allow you to programmatically open and close `ComboBox` instances. These methods are not frequently used because the opening and closing of an instance is normally triggered by user interaction.

You can also set the maximum number of rows that should be displayed in a `ComboBox` when open. The default value is 5. You can assign any reasonable numeric value of one or more to the instance's `rowCount` property to affect this change. If the instance contains more items than the `rowCount` value, the list becomes scrollable.

```
ccbCities.rowCount = 2;
```

Figure 28-10 shows an example of a `ComboBox` instance in which the `rowCount` is set to 2 and the list is scrollable.

Figure 28-10: A ComboBox instance in which the list is scrollable.

Working with the Drop-Down List

The portion of a `ComboBox` instance that drops down is actually a `List` component instance. You can access the `List` instance with the `ComboBox` instance's `dropdown` property. You don't need to worry about working with the nested `List` instance directly in most cases because the `ComboBox` API provides all the basic interfaces you need. For example, the `ComboBox` methods and properties for adding items indirectly add items to the nested `List` instance. You can, however, work with the nested `List` instance to produce advanced effects. For example, you can add icons next to the `List` items if you work with the `List` instance directly via the `dropdown` reference. Or, you can use the sorting methods built into the `List` class. See the `List` component discussion for more details on some of the advanced options available to `List` instances.

Handling ComboBox Events

`ComboBox` instances dispatch the following events:

✦ change — When a value is selected or entered by the user. If the user enters a value into an editable instance, the event is dispatched with each keystroke.

✦ open — The instance begins to open.

✦ close — The instance begins to close.

✦ enter — The instance has focus and the user presses the Enter key.

✦ itemRollOver — When the user rolls over an item in the list.

✦ itemRollOut — When the user rolls out of an item in the list.

✦ scroll — When the user scrolls the item list.

Working with List Components

The List component is similar to the ComboBox in that it allows the user to select from a menu. Unlike the ComboBox, however, the List component allows the user to view multiple items at a time, and if it is set to accept multiple selections, the user can even select more than one item from the list. List instances can be used in place of ComboBox instances in situations in which you want to display more than one value to the user at a time. Alternatively, if you set a List to allow multiple selections, a List can be used in place of a group of CheckBox instances because it allows for the same basic type of selection. Figure 28-11 shows a List instance.

Figure 28-11: A List instance.

Adding Items to a List Instance

You can add items to a List instance in the same ways that you can add items to a ComboBox instance. See the discussion for ComboBox for more details.

Sorting Items in a List Instance

You can sort the items in a List instance using the sortItems() or sortItemsBy() method. The sortItems() method works just like the sort() method of the Array class. You must pass it a reference to a sorter function. A sorter function is a function that is passed two items from the list. Within the function you should return –1 if the first item should be sorted first, 0 if the order should not be changed, or 1 if the second item should be sorted first. For example:

```
this.createObject("List", "clVehicles",
this.getNextHighestDepth());
clVehicles.dataProvider = [{label: "Cart", data: 0},
{label: "Boat", data: 1}, {label: "Airplane", data: 2},
{label: "Automobile", data: 3}, {label: "Bicycle", data: 4}];
var fSorter:Function = function(a, b):Object {
  if(a.label < b.label) {
```

```
      return -1;
   }
   else if(a.label > b.label) {
      return 1;
   }
   else {
      return 0;
   }
};
clVehicles.sortItems(fSorter);
```

The sortItems() method is really more applicable in more complex sorting scenarios. In a simple sorting scenario in which you want to alphabetically sort on a single property of each item, you will likely find the sortItemsBy() method a simpler option. The sortItemsBy() method takes two parameters — the name of the property/field on which to sort and a value of either ASC or DESC indicating whether to sort in ascending or descending order.

```
clVehicles.sortItemsBy("label", "ASC");
```

Removing Items from a List Instance

You can remove items from a List in the same ways that you can remove items from a ComboBox instance. See the discussion for ComboBox for more details.

Allowing Multiple Selections

The default behavior for a List is that it allows the user to select only one item at a time. However, you can allow the user to select multiple values by setting the multipleSelection property to true. When the multipleSelection property is set to true the user can select more than one item by holding the Ctrl key or the ⌘ key and clicking multiple values. Or, the user can select a range by selecting the first item in the range, holding Shift, and selecting the last item in the range. Figure 28-12 shows an example of a List instance that allows multiple selections.

Figure 28-12: A multiple selection list.

Getting Items and Values from a List Instance

You can retrieve an item from a List instance given the index with the getItemAt() method just as with a ComboBox. Additionally, when a list is set to allow the user to select only one item at a time, you can retrieve the selected item and selected index in the same way as with a ComboBox — with the selectedItem and selectedIndex properties. If the List is set to allow for multiple selections, you should retrieve the selected items with the selectedItems property. This property returns an array of the selected items. Likewise, the selectedIndices property returns an array of the selected indices.

Adding Icons to List Items

You can add icons next to items in a list. The icon must exist as a MovieClip symbol set to export with a linkage identifier. You can then specify a property for each object corresponding to each item of the list such that the property value is the linkage identifier of the icon MovieClip symbol. You then need to set the value of the List instance's iconField property so that it indicates the name of the property/field that specifies the icon symbol. For example, let's say that you have three MovieClip symbols in the library with linkage identifiers of SmileyOneSymbol, SmileyTwoSymbol, and SmileyThreeSymbol. You can then define the data provider for a List instance as follows:

```
clUsers.dataProvider = [{label: "luv2Code", data: 8721,
icon: "SmileyOneSymbol"}, {label: "eyeAS", data: 231,
icon: "SmileyTwoSymbol"}, {label: "as2master", data: 987,
icon: "SmileyOneSymbol"}, {label: "scrtcdr", data: 567,
icon: "SmileyThreeSymbol"}, {label: "varguy", data: 3456,
icon: "SmileyTwoSymbol"}];
```

You then need to tell Flash to use the icon property/field to obtain the value for each item's icon.

```
clUsers.iconField = "icon";
```

Note   The name of the icon field/property need not be icon.

Figure 28-13 shows how the List instance would appear.

Figure 28-13: A list with icons.

You also have the option to use a function to determine which icon to use. For example, you might want to display an icon next to each user that you looked up in your database. Within the database table you might have a field named userType in which you differentiate between 30 types of users. However, for the purposes of displaying the users with icons, you want to group some of those variations together. Perhaps, for example, 10 of the different user types between which you differentiate in the database can be considered, for the purposes of display, middle management. Using a function to determine the icon to use allows you to put in place some logic instead of relying on a one-to-one relationship between some field in the data provider and the icon symbols. In such a case, you should assign a function to the List instance's iconFunction property. The function is automatically passed an object representing each item, and it should return a string indicating the linkage identifier of the icon symbol to use for that item.

```
clEmployees.iconFunction = function(oItem:Object):String {
  if(oItem.userType >= 0 && oItem.userType < 10) {
    return "StaffIconSymbol";
  }
  else if(oItem.userType >= 10 && oItem.userType < 20) {
```

```
    return "MdlMngIconSymbol";
  }
  else {
    return "UpperMngIconSymbol";
  }
};
```

Handling List Events

List component instances dispatch the following events (see the event descriptions under the discussion of ComboBox).

+ ✦ change

+ ✦ itemRollOver

+ ✦ itemRollOut

+ ✦ scroll

Working with NumericStepper Components

The NumericStepper component allows the user to select from a range of numbers by either scrolling through the list of values or by entering the value using the keyboard. NumericStepper instances are commonly used when you want to allow the user to select a numeric value, but you want to exercise some control over the options. For example, you might want to prompt a user for a whole number from 0 to 10, a multiple of 5 from –100 to 100, or a value with one decimal place from 0 to 1. The NumericStepper makes this process simple. Figure 28-14 shows an example of a NumericStepper.

 Figure 28-14: A NumericStepper component instance.

Setting the Range of Optional Values

The default range for a NumericStepper instance is from 0 to 10 in increments of 1. You can modify these settings, however. The minimum and maximum properties allow you access to the minimum and maximum values in the range, inclusive. So, for example, to adjust the range from 50 to 100 you could use the following code:

```
cnsVolume.minimum = 50;
cnsVolume.maximum = 100;
```

You can access the increment between steps with the stepSize property. For example, if you want to set the instance to increment by 5 instead of 1, you could use the following code:

```
cnsVolume.stepSize = 5;
```

Note The stepSize property seems to work such that the possible values will be increments of the stepSize starting from 0. You cannot use the technique to get the NumericStepper to count only odd numbers, for example. If you set the stepSize to 2 and initialize the value of the NumericStepper to 1, the next highest value that will display is 2 (followed by 4, 6, 8, and so on).

Working with NumericStepper Values

You can read or write the current value of a NumericStepper by using the value property. For example, to set the value to 75 use the following code:

cnsVolume.value = 75;

Each NumericStepper instance also provides two read-only properties that return the previous and next values. These properties are named previousValue and nextValue, respectively. They return the same value as if you were to subtract or add the stepSize to the current value, but they save you the extra work.

Note　　The previousValue and nextValue properties will report undefined if the next or previous value is out of range.

Handling Change Events

NumericStepper instances dispatch change events when the user changes the value. You can handle the event by defining a change() method for a listener object.

Looking at the Standard Content Display Management Components

The next group of components you'll look at involve content display management. This group includes components for scrolling content, placing content in windows, loading content, and monitoring loading progress.

Working with ScrollPane Components

The ScrollPane component allows you to scroll the display of content. This is particularly useful when you want to manage a lot of content in a not-so-big space. For example, you might want to display a long form on a single screen. In order to show the entire form at once, you'd have to set the dimensions of the Flash movie to very large. Instead, however, you can place the form within a ScrollPane instance. Figure 28-15 shows an example of this.

animal type:	dog
	cat
	gorilla
	fox
	elephant
how many:	0
	☐ Are you sure?

Figure 28-15: A form in a ScrollPane component instance.

Adding Content to a ScrollPane

You can add two types of content to a `ScrollPane` instances: content from a `MovieClip` symbol or content from an external SWF or JPEG. In either case, you tell Flash where to find the content by assigning a value to the `ScrollPane` instance's `contentPath` property. The value should be a string, and it can be one of the three following types:

✦ **A linkage identifier** — Use this type when you want to add a `MovieClip` symbol's content to a `ScrollPane` instance. The `MovieClip` symbol must be set to export and must have a linkage identifier.

```
cspFormPane.contentPath = "FormSymbol";
```

✦ **A relative URL** — Use this type when you want to add content to a `ScrollPane` that resides in an external file accessible from a relative location to the loading movie.

```
cspImagePane.contentPath = "image.jpg";
```

✦ **An absolute URL** — Use this type when you want to add content from an external file accessible from another server or domain.

```
cspMoviePane.contentPath =                                      ⊃
"http://www.person13.com/asb/movie.swf";
```

 Note   Flash will first look for a symbol in the library with the linkage identifier matching the value of the `ScrollPane`'s `contentPath` property. If it does not find such a symbol, it will next look for the content as though the `contentPath` value is a URL.

The content aligns within the `ScrollPane` as follows:

✦ Content from `MovieClip` symbols aligns so that 0,0 within the `MovieClip` coordinate space aligns to the upper-left corner of the `ScrollPane`.

✦ Loaded SWF content aligns so that the upper-left corner of the SWF (the upper-left corner of the stage of the loaded SWF) is aligned to the upper-left corner of the `ScrollPane`.

✦ Loaded JPEG content aligns the upper-left corner to the upper-left corner of the `ScrollPane`.

Once you have added content to a `ScrollPane` instance, you can reference the actual content of the `ScrollPane` instance by using the `content` property. This property returns a reference to the nested `MovieClip` instance into which all content is placed. This is very useful if you need to programmatically interface with the content. For example, you might want to change the content somehow by modifying some text values or by retrieving form control values.

 Note   The `content` property will not return a reference to the content `MovieClip` until the content has completely loaded.

Scrolling Content Programmatically

Typically, the default settings for a `ScrollPane` will suffice when it comes to scrolling. The scrollbars appear and disappear as needed, and the user can scroll the content by clicking and dragging the scrollbar thumb bars. In some cases, however, you might need more control over the scrolling.

As with the TextArea component, the ScrollPane component manages the scrollbars by hiding and showing them as needed. You can tell Flash how to hide and show the scrollbars with the vScrollPolicy (for the vertical scrollbar) and the hScrollPolicy (for the horizontal scrollbar) properties. These properties both have a default value of auto, which means that the scrollbars automatically hide and show. You can also tell Flash to always show the scrollbars by setting the properties to on, or you can tell Flash to always hide the scrollbars by setting the properties to off.

The vLineScrollSize and hLineScrollSize properties control the number of pixels that the ScrollPane scrolls when the user clicks the scrollbar arrows. The default setting is 5. You can adjust the settings by simply assigning a new numeric value to one or both of the properties. Likewise, the vPageScrollSize and hPageScrollSize properties determine the number of pixels that the ScrollPane scrolls when the user pages the scrollbars by clicking on the tracks. The default setting is 20.

The vPosition and hPosition determine the scroll position in the vertical and horizontal directions. The value of 0 for each of the properties sets the content so that it is in the original, default position within the ScrollPane. You can set the values by assigning new numeric values indicating how many pixels to scroll.

You can also tell Flash to allow the user to scroll the content by clicking on the content and dragging. By default this functionality is disabled, but you can enable it by setting the scrollDrag property to true. This functionality should be used when the content does not detect any mouse activity (such as Button controls, and so on).

Refreshing the ScrollPane

Sometimes the content within a ScrollPane changes dynamically. For example, a form might add or remove particular controls based on the value that a user selects in another control. Such changes can sometimes affect the dimensions of the content, which in turn can affect how the content fits within the ScrollPane. You can call the refreshPane() method to tell Flash to automatically refresh the ScrollPane to fit the contents.

Handling ScrollPane Events

ScrollPane instances dispatch the following events:

✦ scroll — When the content is scrolled by the user.

✦ progress — When there is load progress for external content.

✦ complete — When the external content has loaded.

When you handle the progress event, you might also find the following methods useful:

✦ getBytesLoaded() — Returns the number of bytes loaded.

✦ getBytesTotal() — Returns the number of total bytes for the loading content.

Working with Window Components

The Window component allows you to add content to a rectangular window with a title bar. Window instances are draggable, and you can optionally add a close button to them. Window instances are not resized when the borders are dragged. They also do not have shader functionality (meaning the Window instance will not collapse its display when you double-click the title bar). Figure 28-16 shows an example of a Window instance.

Figure 28-16: A Window component instance.

Adding Content to Window Instances

You can add content to `Window` instances in exactly the same way as you add content to `ScrollPane` instances. And you can add the same types of content as well. Set the `contentPath` property to the `MovieClip` symbol linkage identifier or the URL to the SWF or JPEG you want to load. For further discussion of this issue, see the `ScrollPane` section.

Also, as with the `ScrollPane` component, you can access the content of a `Window` with the `content` property.

Setting the Title of a Window

You can set a `Window` instance's title with the `title` property. Simply assign a new string value to the property as shown here:

```
cwImageWindow.title = "Lake";
```

Adding a Close Button

By default, `Window` instances do not have close buttons. You can add a close button by setting the `closeButton` property to `true` (and you can remove a close button by setting the property to `false`).

```
cwImageWindow.closeButton = true;
```

The close button does not automatically close the Window instance when clicked, however. Instead, it dispatches a click event. You then need to set up a listener to handle the click event and close the `Window` instance from which the click event was dispatched. For example:

```
var oListener:Object = new Object();
oListener.click = function(oEvent:Object):Void {
  oEvent.target.visible = false;
};
cwImageWindow.addEventListener("click", oListener);
```

The preceding code simply sets the `Window` instance's visibility to `false`. If you want to actually remove the Window, use the following code instead:

```
var oListener:Object = new Object();
oListener.click = function(oEvent:Object):Void {
  oEvent.target._parent.destroyObject(oEvent.target._name);
};
cwImageWindow.addEventListener("click", oListener);
```

Note　When you add components to the library. it can cause `getNextHighestDepth()` to return very high numbers. When you attach display objects (such as components) at those very high depths, Flash Player cannot programmatically remove them. That will cause `destroyObject()` to fail silently. As a workaround, you can use `swapDepths()` to move the component to a lower depth just before calling `destroyObject()`.

Creating Pop-Up Window Instances

You can use the `PopUpManager` class to create and remove pop-up `Window` instances. One of the nice features of the `PopUpManager` class is that it allows you to create modal `Window` instances. A modal instance automatically disables all other instances on the screen until it has been closed. This is good for displaying important messages to the user or for prompting the user for essential information.

The `PopUpManager` class is in the `mx.managers` package, and so when you work with it in your Flash application you might want to first import the class. Otherwise, you will have to specify the entire path to the class each time you reference it in your code. To import the class, use the following `import` statement:

```
import mx.managers.PopUpManager;
```

The `PopUpManager` methods also require that you specify the class name for the type of component you want to pop-up. In this case, it is the `Window` class. Again, rather than having to specify the fully qualified class name each time, you may find it more convenient to import the `Window` class (which is in the `mx.controls` package). You can import the `Window` class with the following `import` statement:

```
import mx.controls.Window;
```

To create a new pop-up you can call the static method `createPopUp()`. The `createPopUp()` method requires at least three parameters — a reference to the `MovieClip` (or component) instance into which you want to add the pop-up, a reference to the class (in this case, `Window`) for the pop-up, and a Boolean indicating whether the pop-up should be modal. You can also pass the `createPopUp()` method an `init` object (see Chapter 14 for more information on `init` objects). There is also a fifth, optional parameter that allows you to specify whether or not events occur when the user clicks outside the pop-up, but it is seldom used, and so we will not discuss it here. The `createPopUp()` method returns a reference to the new `Window` that is created. Here's an example that creates a new pop-up with content from a `MovieClip` symbol with linkage identifier `MessageSymbol`.

```
import mx.containers.Window;
import mx.managers.PopUpManager;
var cwMessage:MovieClip = PopUpManager.createPopUp(this,
mx.containers.Window, true, {contentPath: "MessageSymbol",
closeButton: true});
```

Note　For the preceding example to work, you need to make sure you have copied the `Window` component to your library. Additionally, the `PopUpManager.createPopUp()` method returns a reference to the newly created component instance, but as a `MovieClip` datatype. If you want to declare the variable as the correct datatype, you need to cast the return value from the method, as shown here:

```
var cwMessage:Window =
Window(PopUpManager.createPopUp(this,
mx.containers.Window, true, {contentPath:
"MessageSymbol", closeButton: true}));
```

When you want to remove a modal pop-up, it is important that you use the `deletePopUp()` method instead of `destroyObject()`. If you use `destroyObject()`,the modal state is not removed. The `deletePopUp()` method can be called directly from the pop-up instance, and it removes both the instance and the modal state (re-enabling all the other instances).

```
var oListener:Object = new Object();
oListener.click = function(oEvent:Object):Void {
  oEvent.target.deletePopUp();
};
cwMessage.addEventListener("click", oListener);
```

Working with Loader Components

The `Loader` component is useful when you want to load external SWF or JPEG content, but you don't want it to be framed as with the `ScrollPane` and `Window` components. For example, if you are creating a photo gallery or a product catalog in which you need to dynamically load images, the `Loader` component is a perfect choice.

Loading Content

Once you have created a `Loader` instance, you can load content by assigning the relative or absolute URL to the instance's `contentPath` property.

```
cldImage.contentPath =
"http://www.rightactionscript.com/samplefiles/image2.jpg";
```

By default, the content begins loading as soon as the value is assigned to the `contentPath` property. However, you can also tell the `Loader` instance to defer the loading by first setting the `autoLoad` property to `false` (the default value is `true`). Then, you can explicitly initialize the loading by calling the `load()` method.

Once the content has loaded you can get a reference to it by using the `Loader` instance's `content` property.

Sizing the Content

The `scaleContent` property determines whether the content should scale to fit within the `Loader` component instance. The default value is `true`, meaning the content will scale. By setting the `scaleContent` property to `false` you can tell Flash to keep the original dimensions of the content. Keeping `scaleContent` set to `true` is a convenient way to ensure a consistent dimension among loaded content.

Handling Loader Events

`Loader` component instances dispatch two events:

  ✦ `progress`—When there is load progress

  ✦ `complete`—When the content has completely loaded

When handling progress events, the following parameters are passed to the listener's `progress()` method:

✦ `bytesLoaded`—The number of bytes that have loaded

✦ `bytesTotal`—The total number of bytes

✦ `percentLoaded`—The percentage that has loaded

Working with ProgressBar Components

The `ProgressBar` component can monitor the download progress of external content into the following:

✦ `MovieClip` instances

✦ `Window` instances

✦ `ScrollPane` instances

✦ `Loader` instances

The progress bar displays the progress, as shown in Figure 28-17.

Figure 28-17: A ProgressBar component instance.

Assigning Content to Monitor

You need to tell `ProgressBar` components what loading content to monitor. You can achieve this by setting the `source` property. The `source` property value should be a string indicating the name of the `MovieClip` or component instance for which you want to monitor the load progress. For example, the following code tells a `ProgressBar` instance named `cpbMonitorImage` to monitor the load progress of the content from a `Loader` instance named `cldImage`:

```
cpbMonitorImage.source = "cldImage";
```

You can also use a path as part of the `source` string. For example:

```
cpbMonitorImage.source = "this.cldImage";
```

The `ProgressBar` instance can monitor the load progress in several ways, or *modes*. You can set the mode for a `ProgressBar` by assigning a value to the `mode` property. The default value for `mode` is `event`. The `event` mode works with `Loader` instances. Otherwise, set the `mode` to `polled`.

```
cpbMonitorWindomContent.mode = "polled";
```

Setting the ProgressBar Label

The `ProgressBar` label is the text that accompanies the actual progress bar. The default placement of the label is underneath the progress bar. You can set the label to the right, left, top, or bottom (default) by assigning those values (as strings) to the instance's `labelPlacement` property.

```
cpbMonitorImage.labelPlacement = "top";
```

The default label displays the following text:

```
LOADING percent loaded%
```

You can assign a new value to the label property of a `ProgressBar` component instance if you want to display a different value. There are three placeholders that you can use in the label string:

✦ `%1` — The amount loaded

✦ `%2` — The total amount

✦ `%3` — The percent loaded

If you want to display a literal percent sign (%), you need to escape it with another percent sign. For example, the following is the default label string:

```
LOADING %3%%
```

Notice that the `%3` is replaced by the percent loaded, and the double percent sign shows a single percent sign in the actual label.

Here's an example of how you can assign a label string that displays the bytes loaded, the total bytes, and the percent loaded:

```
cpbMonitorImage.label = "%1 of %2 bytes (%3%%) loaded";
```

By default, the `%1` and `%2` placeholders display the values in bytes. You can also set a conversion value by which the values are divided. To accomplish this, assign a numeric value to the conversion property. For example, if you want `%1` and `%2` to display kilobytes instead of bytes, set conversion to 1,024 (there are 1,024 bytes in a kilobyte).

```
cpbMonitorImage.conversion = 1024;
cpbMonitorImage.label = "%1 of %2 KB (%3%%) loaded";
```

Setting the Fill Direction

The default value for the `direction` property is `right`. This causes the progress bar to fill from left to right. If you set the value to `left` the progress bar will fill from right to left.

```
cpbMonitorImage.direction = "left";
```

Handling ProgressBar Events

`ProgressBar` instances dispatch the following events:

✦ `progress` — When there is load progress

✦ `complete` — When the content has completely loaded

When handling progress events, you might find it useful to work with the `percentComplete` property of the `ProgressBar`. The `percentComplete` property returns the percentage that has loaded.

Looking at the Professional UI Components

In addition to the standard components, Flash 8 includes a handful of additional components. The following sections take a look at each of these components.

Working with Accordion Components

The Accordion component allows you to manage multiple pieces of content on the stage by placing them into sliding segments. Each segment has a title bar, and when a user clicks on a segment's title bar, that segment opens and the others collapse. Figure 28-18 shows an example of an Accordion component instance.

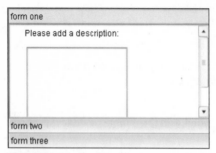

Figure 28-18: An Accordion component instance.

Adding Segments to an Accordion

By default, an Accordion instance has no segments. You can add segments with the createSegment() method. The createSegment() method requires at least three parameters. The first parameter can be either a reference to a component class or a string specifying the linkage identifier for the content of the segment. The second parameter is the name to give to the new instance (the content instance is accessible as a property of the Accordion instance). The third parameter is a string specifying the label for the segment title bar. You can also, optionally, specify a fourth parameter indicating the linkage identifier for a symbol to use as an icon in the segment's title bar.

```
cacForms.createSegment("FormOneSymbol", "formOne", "form one");
```

In the preceding example the new segment has an instance name of formOne. You can reference the segment as cacForms.formOne.

In Figure 28-18, the first segment contains a ScrollPane instance. You can achieve this by adding a ScrollPane instance as the segment and then adding the content to the ScrollPane.

```
cacForms.createSegment(mx.controls.ScrollPane, "formOne", "form one");
cacForms.formOne.contentPath = "FormOneSymbol";
```

When you add a ScrollPane to a segment, normally you will want to size the ScrollPane so that it fits exactly within the segment. You can calculate the dimensions as follows:

   ✦ ScrollPane width should be the width of the Accordion.

   ✦ ScrollPane height should be the total height of the Accordion minus the number of segments in the Accordion times 21.5. The value 21.5 is the height of a title bar.

Here's an example of how you can resize the ScrollPane nested as formOne:

```
cacForms.formOne.setSize(cacForms.width,
cacForms.height - (21.5 * cacForms.numChildren));
```

The numChildren property returns the number of segments in an Accordion.

Getting Selected Segments

You can get a reference to the selected Accordion segment with the selectedChild property. Alternatively, you can also retrieve the index of the selected segment with the selectedIndex property. You can also get a reference to a segment based on the index with the getChildAt() method.

Handling Change Events

Accordion instances dispatch change events when a segment is opened.

Working with the Alert Component

The Alert component is static. You should not create instances of the Alert component. Instead, copy the component to the library, import the class, and then use static properties and methods to open alert windows. Figure 28-19 shows an example of an alert window.

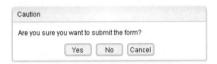

Figure 28-19: An alert window.

Opening an Alert Window

To work with alert windows, you need to make sure you have first added the component to the library. You can do this by dragging the component from the Components panel onto the stage, and then deleting it from the stage. The symbol remains in the library.

When you are working with alert windows, you access constants and static methods from the Alert class, which is in the mx.controls package. Therefore, you will find it convenient to import the class rather than having to type the fully qualified class name each time. You can import the class with the following import statement:

```
import mx.controls.Alert;
```

To open an alert window, you can then call the static method show(). The show() method allows you to specify from one to seven parameters. In the simplest form you need only specify the message to display. When you specify only the message, the alert window has no title and displays an OK button.

```
Alert.show("Welcome");
```

Figure 28-20 shows the alert window that corresponds to the preceding code.

Figure 28-20: A simple alert window.

You can optionally specify a title for the alert window with a second parameter. For example:

```
Alert.show("Welcome", "Greeting");
```

The Alert class has several constants that you can use as flags for the third parameter. The constants are:

✦ **Alert.YES** — Displays the YES button.

✦ **Alert.NO** — Displays the NO button.

✦ **Alert.CANCEL** — Displays the CANCEL button.

✦ **Alert.OK** — Displays the OK button.

✦ **Alert.NONMODAL** — Makes the window non-modal (it is modal by default).

You can use any combination of these constants with the bitwise OR operator (|). Here is an example that displays both an OK and a CANCEL button.

```
Alert.show("Welcome", "Greeting", Alert.OK|Alert.CANCEL);
```

And if you want to make that same window non-modal, you can use the following code:

```
Alert.show("Welcome", "Greeting", Alert.YES|Alert.NO|Alert.NONMODAL);
```

Listening for Alert Events

When the user clicks one of the Alert buttons, the alert window dispatches a click event. Unlike other, nonstatic components, you do not add a listener to an alert window with the addEventListener() method because there is no instance from which to call the method. Instead, you can set an alert window's listener object when you call the show() method by passing a reference to the listener object as the fifth parameter. Here is an example:

```
import mx.controls.Alert;
var oListener:Object = new Object();
oListener.click = function(oEvent:Object):Void {
  trace(oEvent.target._name);
};
mx.controls.Alert.show("Welcome", "Greeting",
Alert.YES|Alert.NO, this, oListener);
```

Typically, when you handle Alert click events you'll want to know which button the user clicked. The Event object passed to the click() method contains a detail property that holds the value of the button that was clicked. For example:

```
oListener.click = function(oEvent:Object):Void {
  switch (oEvent.detail) {
    case Alert.YES:
      trace("User clicked YES");
      break;
    case Alert.NO:
      trace("User clicked NO");
      break;
    case Alert.CANCEL:
      trace("User clicked CANCEL");
      break;
    case Alert.OK:
      trace("User clicked OK");
  }
};
```

Adding Icons to Alert Windows

You can add an icon to the left of the alert message text by specifying a sixth parameter that indicates the linkage identifier for the symbol that contains the artwork for the icon. For example, if you have a symbol that is set to export with a linkage identifier of Icon, the following code will display that symbol's artwork to the left of the text Welcome:

```
import mx.controls.Alert;
mx.controls.Alert.show("Welcome", "Greeting",
Alert.YES|Alert.NO, this, null, "Icon");
```

Setting the Default Button

You can specify which of the Alert buttons should be activated when the user presses the Enter key. You can do so with the seventh parameter you can pass to the show() method. The value should be one of the Alert constants that you used to tell Flash which buttons should be displayed. The following example sets the Yes button as the default in an alert with both a YES and NO button.

```
import mx.controls.Alert;
mx.controls.Alert.show("Welcome", "Greeting",
Alert.YES|Alert.NO, null, null, Alert.YES);
```

Setting the Button Properties

In most cases, the default button settings will suffice. However, you have the option to change the properties of the buttons by assigning new values to the following static properties:

✦ Alert.buttonHeight and Alert.buttonWidth — These properties determine the height and width of the alert window buttons. The values are in pixels.

✦ Alert.cancelLabel, Alert.okLabel, Alert.noLabel, and Alert.yesLabel — These properties determine the labels on the various button types. They simply give you the option of applying different labels.

Working with DataGrid Components

The DataGrid component enables you to present data in a table/grid-like format, as shown in Figure 28-21. Most often, DataGrid component instances are used to display data retrieved from a Web service, by way of one of the other data components, or by Flash Remoting.

Component	Availability
Alert	Professional
Button	Standard
ComboBox	Standard
Loader	Standard
Menu	Professional
NumericStepper	Standard
ProgressBar	Standard
Tree	Professional

Figure 28-21: A DataGrid component instance.

Adding New Columns to a DataGrid Instance

Once you've defined a new `DataGrid` instance, the first step is to tell Flash what columns you want it to display in the grid. There are two basic ways you can accomplish this. The first way is the simpler of the two. You can assign an array of column names to the instance's `columnNames` property.

```
cdgComponents.columnNames = ["Component", "Availability"];
```

In simple cases the preceding will work just fine. But when you want to afford more control over the columns and the data they display, you need to first create `DataGridColumn` objects and then add those objects to the `DataGrid` instance. The `DataGridColumn` is in the `mx.controls.gridclasses` package, so you will probably find it helpful to first import the class with the following `import` statement:

```
import mx.controls.gridclasses.DataGridColumn;
```

Then, you can create a new `DataGridColumn` instance using the constructor. The constructor requires that you pass it a string specifying the column name:

```
var dgcAvailability:DataGridColumn = new DataGridColumn("Availability");
```

Once you have defined a `DataGridColumn` object, you can add it to the `DataGrid` instance with the `addColumn()` or `addColumnAt()` methods. The `addColumn()` method requires you pass it the `DataGridColumn` object, and it appends the column to the `DataGrid` instance:

```
cdgComponents.addColumn(dgcAvailability);
```

The `addColumnAt()` method requires you pass it an index and a reference to the `DataGridColumn` object. Instead of merely appending the column, the `addColumnAt()` method inserts the column at the specified index, shifting any other columns over by one. The first column index is 0.

```
var dgcComponent:DataGridColumn = new DataGridColumn("Component");
cdgComponents.addColumnAt(0, dgcComponent);
```

As an alternative to instantiating the `DataGridColumn` objects via the `DataGridColumn` constructor, you can also simply set the `columnNames` property and then retrieve the `DataGridColumn` objects with the `DataGrid getColumnAt()` method. The `getColumnAt()` method returns a reference to the `DataGridColumn` at a specified index.

```
cdgComponents.columnNames = ["Component", "Availability"];
var dgcComponent:DataGridColumn = cdgComponents.getColumnAt(0);
```

Adding Data to a DataGrid Instance

A `DataGrid` without data would be, well, a `DataGrid` without data. So, typically the next step after adding columns to your `DataGrid` instance is to add data. There are several ways you can add data. You can add rows to a grid one at a time with the `addItem()` and `addItemAt()` methods. The `addItem()` method appends the new row to the end of the current data. You should pass the method an object containing the data you want to display. In the most basic approach, this means that the object should have properties whose names match the column names. For example, if a `DataGrid` named `cdgComponents` has columns named `Component` and `Availability`, the object you pass to `addItem()` should also have properties with those same names. For example:

```
cdgComponents.addItem({Component: "DataGrid", Availability: "Professional"});
```

The addItemAt() method works in basically the same way, but you need also specify the index at which you want Flash to insert the new row. The first index is 0.

```
cdgComponents.addItemAt(0, {Component: "Alert", Availability: "Professional"});
```

You can also use data providers with a DataGrid very similarly to how you can use data providers with a List or ComboBox. In the simplest case, the data provider should have field names that correspond to the column names of the DataGrid. Or, if the data provider is an array of objects, each object should have properties corresponding to the column names of the DataGrid. For example:

```
var aDataProvider:Array = [{Component: "Alert",
Availability: "Professional"}, {Component: "Button",
Availability: "Standard"}, {Component: "ComboBox",
Availability: "Standard"}];
```

You can assign a data provider to a DataGrid using the dataProvider property:

```
cdgComponents.dataProvider = aDataProvider;
```

In some cases, the data provider might not have field names that correspond to the column names in the DataGrid. For example, a recordset might contain fields including firstName and lastName. The DataGrid, on the other hand, might have a column named Full Name. In such a case, you must make sure you created the Full Name column using the DataGridColumn constructor. You can then assign a function to the DataGridColumn object's labelFunction property. This function will be used by Flash to determine what value to display in the column. The function is automatically passed each item/record from the data provider, and it should return the value that should be displayed. For example:

```
var cdgFullName:DataGridColumn = new DataGridColumn("Full Name");
dgcFullName.labelFunction = new function(oItem:Object):String {
  return (oItem.firstName + " " + oItem.lastName);
};
```

Removing Data from a DataGrid Instance

You can remove data from a DataGrid instance either one item at a time or by removing all the data at once. To remove a single row from the DataGrid use the removeItemAt() method and pass it the index of the row to remove. To remove all rows you can use the removeAll() method.

You can also remove columns either one at a time or all at once. The removeColumnAt() method removes a column given the index. The removeAllColumns() method removes all columns.

Managing Sorting

DataGrid data can be user sortable. The default is that the data is sortable. This means that when the user clicks the column header, that column sorts the data. The first time the user sorts by a column the data is sorted in ascending order. Subsequent sorts alternate between descending and ascending.

You can disable sorting on the entire DataGrid by setting sortableColumns to false. You can re-enable sorting by setting sortableColumns to true. By default, all the columns are sortable. Therefore, by default, the value of the DataGrid instance's sortableColumns property determines whether the columns are sortable. However, you can also set each column to be sortable or not by setting the sortable property on the DataGridColumn to true or false.

Affecting Column Spacing

There are two ways you can affect the spacing of the columns in a DataGrid instance. If you simply want to have the columns evenly spaced, you can call the spaceColumnsEqually() method from the DataGrid instance.

```
cdgComponents.spaceColumnsEqually();
```

Alternatively, if you want to afford more control over the width of each column, you can set the width property of the columns. For example:

```
cdgComponents.getColumnAt(0).width = 100;
```

Additionally, by default each of the columns can be resized by the user. The user can click the mouse between each of the headers and drag the columns to resize them. You can choose to disable this resizing feature either for the entire DataGrid instance or for individual columns. You can disable or re-enable resizing for the entire instance by setting the resizableColumns property. The default value is true. Setting the value to false disables resizing for the entire instance. You can also set resizing options on each of the columns by setting the column resizable property to true or false.

Making a DataGrid Editable

By default, the data in a DataGrid is read-only. However, you can allow the user to edit the data by setting the DataGrid instance's editable property to true (and you can reset the instance so that it is noneditable by setting the editable property to false). You can also set particular columns so that they are editable or not. By default, if you enable editing for the DataGrid instance, all of the columns are editable. You can explicitly enable or disable editing for each column by setting the column's editable property.

When a DataGrid is editable, you can bring focus to a particular cell by setting the focusedCell property. The focusedCell property value should be an object with two integer properties — columnIndex and itemIndex. These values indicate which cell should receive focus. For example, you can make an instance named cdgComponents editable and bring focus to the first cell of the first item as follows:

```
cdgComponents.editable = true;
cdfComponents.focusedCell = {columnIndex:0, rowIndex:0};
```

Setting Scroll Properties of a DataGrid

The DataGrid has all the same scroll properties of the List component. See the discussion of how to set the scroll properties of a List for more details.

Allowing Multiple Selections

The default setting for a DataGrid is that it allows for a single selection. You can also enable multiple selections for a DataGrid instance by setting the multipleSelection property to true. This property is inherited from the List component. See the discussion of List for more information.

Getting Selected Items

You can get the selected item or items (for a multiple selection-enabled DataGrid) with the selectedItem and selectedItems properties, respectively. You can also get the indices for selected items with the selectedIndex (single selection) or selectedIndices (multiple selection) properties. See the List discussion for more details.

Handling DataGrid Events

DataGrid component instances dispatch the following events:

✦ cellPress—When the user clicks a cell in the DataGrid (mouse down)

✦ cellEdit—When the user edits a cell and then presses Enter or Tab

✦ cellFocusIn—When the user brings focus to an editable cell

✦ cellFocusOut—When the user moves focus from an editable cell

✦ change—When the user selects a new item

✦ columnStretch—When the user resizes the columns

✦ headerPress—When the user clicks one of the column headers

In all but the columnStretch and headerPress events, the Event object passed to the handler method contains columnIndex and rowIndex properties that contain information about the cell related to the event. The columnStretch and headerPress Event objects contain columnIndex properties.

Working with DateChooser Components

The DateChooser component allows the users to select a date from a calendar interface, as shown in Figure 28-22.

Figure 28-22: A DateChooser component instance.

Configuring the Appearance of the DataChooser

There are several configurable properties of a DateChooser component instance that allow you to affect the appearance. These include properties that set the labels for both the days of the week and the months as well as the order in which the days appear within the calendar. By default, the labels for the days of the week are S, M, T, W, T, F, and S. As you can see in Figure 28-22, the labels were slightly altered in that the label for Thursday is *Th* rather than the standard *T*. You can assign new values to the dayNames property as an array of strings. The order of the labels should always be from Sunday to Saturday. For example:

```
cdcCalendar.dayNames = ["S", "M", "T", "W", "Th", "F", "S"];
```

Also, by default, the first day of the week that is displayed in the calendar is Sunday. However, as you see in Figure 28-22, you can alter which day of the week displays first. The firstDayOfWeek property determines which days should be displayed first. The possible values are from 0 (Sunday) to 6 (Saturday). To set the DateChooser instance to display Monday first as in Figure 28-22, use the following code:

```
cdcCalendar.firstDayOfWeek = 1;
```

You can also adjust the labels that display for the months. The `monthNames` property contains an array of month labels starting with January. You can change the values by assigning a new array of labels to the `monthNames` property.

Setting Current Display

By default, a `DateChooser` instance displays the current month and year. You can tell the instance to display any month and year with the `displayedMonth` and `displayedYear` properties. The `displayedMonth` property can be any integer from 0 (January) to 11 (December), and the `displayedYear` property can be any integer indicating the full year you want to display. The following code displays February of 2004.

```
cdcCalendar.displayedMonth = 1;
cdcCalendar.displayedYear = 2004;
```

Additionally, the default setting for a `DateChooser` instance is such that when the current month and year are displayed, the current date is highlighted. The `showToday` property determines this behavior. The default setting is `true`. If you set the property to `false` then the current date is not highlighted.

Setting Selectable and Nonselectable Ranges and Days

You can enable and disable particular days and ranges within a `DateChooser` instance. You can disable particular days of the week by assigning a value to the `disabledDays` property. The `disabledDays` property value should be an array with up to seven integer values in which the valid values are from 0 to 7. For example, the following disables all Sundays and Saturdays.

```
cdcCalendar.disabledDays = [0, 6];
```

You can also disable specific dates and date ranges by assigning a value to the `disabledRanges` property. The `disabledRanges` property value should be an array containing one or both of the following types of elements:

✦ `Date` objects indicating the specific dates to disable

✦ Associative arrays (`Object` objects) with a `rangeStart` and/or `rangeEnd` property — both of which should be `Date` objects:

   • If an associative array specifies only the `rangeStart` property, all dates after (and including) that value are disabled.

   • If an associative array specifies only the `rangeEnd` property, all dates before (and including) that value are disabled.

   • If an associative array specifies both the `rangeStart` and `rangeEnd` properties, the entire range from (including) the starting value up through (and including) the ending value is disabled.

Here's an example that displays February of 2007 and disables the 5th of the month, the 10th through the 15th, and then everything from the 23rd and after.

```
cdcCalendar.displayedMonth = 1;
cdcCalendar.displayedYear = 2007;
cdcCalendar.disabledRanges = [new Date(2007, 1, 5),
{rangeStart: new Date(2007, 1, 10), rangeEnd:
new Date(2007, 1, 15)}, {rangeStart: new Date(2007, 1, 23)}];
```

You can also specify dates and ranges that you want to enable rather than disable. Telling Flash to enable a range and/or dates has the opposite effect of disabling ranges. Any nonenabled dates and ranges are then automatically disabled. The `selectableRanges` property accepts the same type of value as the `disabledRanges` property, but it enables those dates and ranges rather than disabling them.

Getting and Setting the Selected Date

You can get and/or set the selected date within a `DateChooser` instance using the `selectedDate` property. The value of the `selectedDate` property is a `Date` object. You can programmatically select a date by assigning a `Date` object to the property. For example, if you want to select February 1, 2007, you can use the following code:

```
cdcCalendar.selectedDate = new Date(2007, 1, 1);
```

Handling DateChooser Events

`DateChooser` component instances dispatch the following events:

✦ **change** — When the user selects a date

✦ **scroll** — When the user scrolls the months

Working with DateField Components

The `DateField` component combines the functionality of a `DateChooser` and a `TextInput`. It allows users to select a date and have that date displayed in an efficient manner. Figure 28-23 shows a `DateField` instance in which a date has been selected.

Figure 28-23: A DateField component instance with selected date value.

Figure 28-24 shows a `DateField` component with the opened `DateChooser` that allows the users to select the date.

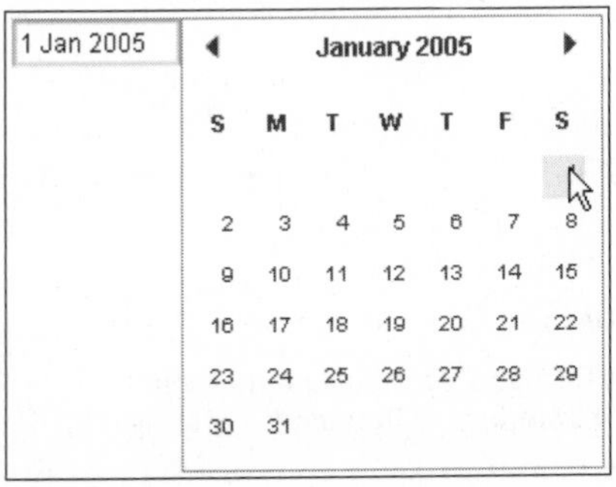

Figure 28-24: A DateField component instance with the nested DateChooser opened.

Configuring a DateField Instance

The DateField component has all the same properties as the DateChooser component. That means you can set the day names, month names, first day of week, displayed month and year, and so on. See the DateChooser discussion for more details.

You can also access the nested DateChooser instance with the pullDown property. However, because the DateChooser properties affect the nested DateChooser indirectly, there really is no reason for you to access the pullDown property in most scenarios.

Displaying the Selected Value

By default, the selected value displays in the TextInput portion of the instance in the following format: DD MM YYYY. You can tell Flash how to display the value differently if you want by assigning a formatting function to the instance's dateFormatter property. The function is passed the selected date (a Date object) as a parameter, and it should return a string that formats the date as you want it to display. For example:

```
cdfPurchaseDate.dateFormatter = function(dSelected:Date):String {
  var sFormatted:String = "";
  sFormatted += String(dSelected.getDate());
  sFormatted += "/" + String(dSelected.getMonth() + 1);
  sFormatted += "/" + String(dSelected.getFullYear());
  return sFormatted;
};
```

Getting and Setting the Selected Value

Just as with the DateChooser, you can get and set the value of a DateField with the selectedDate property. See the DateChooser discussion for more details.

Opening and Closing a DateField Instance

Typically, there is little reason to programmatically control the open and close state of a DateField instance. This is because the instance is typically opened when the user clicks it and it is closed when the user selects a date from the nested DateChooser. However, you can programmatically open and close the instance with the open() and close() methods.

Handling DateField Events

DateField components dispatch the same events as DateChooser. In addition, they also dispatch open events when the instances are opened and close events when the instances are closed.

Working with Menu Components

The Menu component allows you to add menu systems to your Flash applications. Typically, these Menu instances are associated with Button component instances, as shown in Figure 28-25.

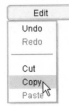

Figure 28-25: A Menu component instance associated with a Button component instance.

Creating Menu Instances

You *can* create `Menu` instances by dragging them onto the stage and naming them via the Property inspector. However, due to the way in which `Menu` component instances work, it is generally much more practical to create the instances programmatically. Unlike other types of UI components, you don't need to create the instances with `createObject()` or `createClassObject()`. Instead, the `Menu` class has a static method called `createMenu()` that creates a new `Menu` instance and returns a reference to that new instance.

Note   Menus don't display by default. You'll have to called the `show()` method for the menu to display on stage. See the section "Showing and Hiding Menu Instances" for more details.

There are two things you should consider prior to trying to instantiate a `Menu` component, however. First, as with all other components, you need to make sure that it has been added to the library. The only way to accomplish this is to first drag an instance from the Components panel onto the stage, and then to delete the instance from the stage. The component symbol is copied to the library, and it remains there even after the instance is deleted from the stage. Second, as with all the other UI components, the `Menu` class is within the `mx.controls` package. Therefore, you will likely find it helpful to first import the class. That allows you to reference the class without having to type in the fully qualified name each time. You can import the `Menu` class as follows:

```
import mx.controls.Menu;
```

You can then create a new `Menu` instance by calling `Menu.createMenu()`. If you pass the method no parameters, it creates a new, empty `Menu` instance on `_root`:

```
var cmEdit:Menu = Menu.createMenu();
```

If you want to create the `Menu` instance nested within another `MovieClip`, you can specify the path to the parent `MovieClip` as the first parameter to the `createMenu()` method.

```
var cmEdit:Menu = Menu.createMenu(mcMenuHolder);
```

Populating Menu Instances

There are several ways you can populate `Menu` instances. Although there are variations, these ways can be categorized into two groups:

✦ Populating `Menu` instances with init objects

✦ Populating `Menu` instances with `XMLNode` objects (menu data providers)

Working with init Objects

The `Menu init` objects are `Object` objects with the following possible properties:

✦ `label` — The item's label that should appear in the menu.

✦ `type` — The type of item. Possible values include:

- `normal` (default value if none specified)
- `separator`
- `check`
- `radio`

✦ `icon` — The linkage identifier for a symbol to use as an icon. This is available only for normal items.

✦ `instanceName` — A name that you can use to reference the item as a property of the `Menu` instance.

✦ `groupName` — The name of a radio group. This applies only when the type is set to `radio`.

✦ `selected` — Whether to display the item as selected. This applies to radio and check items only.

✦ `enabled` — Whether the item should be selectable. If set to `true`, the value is selectable. If set to `false`, the item is grayed out and unselectable.

You can add items using `init` objects with the `addMenuItem()` and `addMenuItemAt()` methods. The `addMenuItem()` method appends the new item to the end of the current items:

```
cmEdit.addMenuItem({label: "cut", instanceName: "cut"});
```

The `addMenuItemAt()` method adds a new item at a specific index. The first item in the menu has an index of 0.

```
cmEdit.addMenuItemAt(0, {label: "copy", instanceName: "copy"});
```

If you want to add submenus, you need to first create the main `Menu` item that will open the submenu. The `addMenuItem()` and `addMenuItemAt()` methods both return a reference to the newly created item. You haven't needed to work with that reference thus far, but when adding submenu items it is convenient. You can simply set the type of the return value as `Object`:

```
var oMenuItem:Object = cmEdit.addMenuItem({label: "edit
options", instanceName: "editOptions"});
```

You can then use the same `addMenuItem()` and `addMenuItemAt()` methods to add nested items to the submenu:

```
oMenuItem.addMenuItem({label: "copy", instanceName: "copy"});
oMenuItem.addMenuItem({label: "paste", instanceName: "paste"});
```

Working with Menu Data Providers

A menu data provider is an `XMLNode` object containing the data to populate the `Menu` or a `Menu` item. The actual element names within the XML data are not important. The structure and the attributes of the elements are what's important. Each item element can have any of the same attributes as the init object properties. For example, the following is an element that represents a normal Menu item:

```
<menuitem label="paste" instanceName="paste" enabled="false" />
```

If you nest elements within another element, the nested elements appear in a submenu:

```
<submenu>
  <menuitem label="open" instanceName="open" />
  <menuitem label="close" instanceName="close" />
</submenu>
```

You can work with menu data providers in several ways. You can use menu data providers as parameters for the addMenuItem() and addMenuItemAt() methods instead of init objects. For example:

```
import mx.controls.Menu;
var sMenuData:String = "<menuitem label='copy' instanceName='copy' />";
var cmEdit:Menu = Menu.createMenu();
cmEdit.addMenuItem(new XML(sMenuData));
```

In the preceding example, it might seem like a lot of extra work just to add a single item to the Menu. And, in fact, it is. You can accomplish the same task with an init object with less code. But for adding submenus you might find the menu data provider/addMenuItem() (or addMenuItemAt()) technique a little simpler. For example:

```
import mx.controls.Menu;
var sMenuData:String = "<submenu label='edit options'>
<menuitem label='copy' instanceName='copy' />
<menuitem label='paste' instanceName='paste' /></submenu>";
var cmEdit:Menu = Menu.createMenu();
cmEdit.addMenuItem(new XML(sMenuData));
```

The preceding code adds a submenu with two elements. For those who are comfortable with XML, the preceding syntax might be simpler than working with multiple addMenuItem() calls, as in the previous section.

The addMenuItem() and addMenuItemAt() method variations for working with menu data providers are moderately useful for initially populating a menu (we'll see how they can be used to modify values). However, the menu data provider is most powerful when used to populate the entire menu at once. There are two ways you can populate an entire menu with a menu data provider. The first is to pass the menu data provider as the second parameter to the createMenu() method when first creating the menu. For example:

```
mx.controls.Menu;
var sMenuData:String = "<menuitem label='undo'
instanceName='undo /><menuitem label='redo'
instanceName='redo' enabled='false' /><menuitem
type='separator' /><submenu label='edit options'
instanceName='editOptions'><menuitem label='copy'
instanceName='copy' /><menuitem label='paste'
instanceName='paste' /></submenu>";
var cmEdit:Menu = Menu.createMenu(this, new XML(sMenuData));
```

You can also assign a menu data provider to the menu instance's `dataProvider` property. So, the preceding code can be rewritten as:

```
import mx.controls.Menu;
var sMenuData:String = "<menuitem label='undo'
instanceName='undo' /><menuitem label='redo'
instanceName='redo' enabled='false' /><menuitem
type='separator' /><submenu label='edit options'
instanceName='editOptions'><menuitem label='copy'
instanceName='copy' /><menuitem label='paste'
instanceName='paste' /></submenu>";
var cmEdit:Menu = Menu.createMenu();
cmEdit.dataProvider = new XML(sMenuData);
```

Of course, one of the main benefits of working with a menu data provider is that you can define the menus in external XML documents or from XML generated from database data, and so on. For example, you can define an external XML document with the following code:

```
<menu>
  <menuitem label='undo' instanceName='undo' />
  <menuitem label='redo' instanceName='redo' enabled='false' />
  <menuitem type='separator' />
  <submenu label='edit options' instanceName='editOptions'>
    <menuitem label='copy' instanceName='copy' />
    <menuitem label='paste' instanceName='paste' enabled='false' />
  </submenu>
</menu>
```

Then, you can load the XML data into your Flash movie and use it to populate a menu as follows:

```
import mx.controls.Menu;
var cmEdit:Menu = Menu.createMenu();
var xmlMenuData:XML = new XML();
xmlMenuData.onLoad = function():Void {
  cmEdit.dataProvider = this.firstChild;
};
xmlMenuData.ignoreWhite = true;
xmlMenuData.load("menu.xml");
```

Notice that the data in the XML file has a root element of `<menu>` to ensure that it is well formed (well-formed XML data has a single root element per document). When the data is loaded, the `firstChild` of the `XML` object is assigned to the `dataProvider` instead of the `XML` object itself.

Removing Items

You can remove menu items with the following three methods:

✦ `removeMenuItem()` — This method requires you pass it a reference to one of the items. You can get references to menu items in several ways, as you'll see in subsequent sections. Alternatively, if this method is invoked directly from a menu item, it requires no parameters, and it removes the item from which it is called.

✦ `removeMenuItemAt()` — This method removes an item given the index.

✦ `removeAll()` — This methods removes all items in a menu or menu item.

Showing and Hiding Menu Instances

Up this point you've seen how to create Menu instances, but not how to actually show them. The default setting for a menu is that it is hidden. You can show a menu by calling the show() method. The show() method requires two parameters — the X- and Y-coordinates at which to display the menu. For example, the following code will show a menu at 100,100.

```
cmEdit.show(100, 100);
```

Most often, Menu instances are associated with Button component instances such that they are displayed when the button has been clicked. Therefore, you typically call the show() method to display the menu just above or below the Button instance. For example:

```
var oListener:Object = new Object();
oListener.menu = cmEdit;
oListener.click = function(oEvent:Object):Void {
  var nX:Number = oEvent.target.x;
  var nY:Number = oEvent.target.y + oEvent.target.height;
  this.menu.show(nX, nY);
};
cbtEdit.addEventListener("click", oListener);
```

By default Menu instances disappear once a selection has been made. Therefore, you don't often need to programmatically hide the instance. However, should you want to, you can hide the menu with the hide() method.

```
cmEdit.hide();
```

Handling Menu Events

Menu component instances dispatch the following events:

- ✦ menuShow—Dispatched when the instance is shown.
- ✦ menuHide—Dispatched when the instance is hidden.
- ✦ rollOver—Dispatched when the user rolls over an item.
- ✦ rollOut—Dispatched when the user rolls out of an item.
- ✦ change—Dispatched when the user selects an item.

The rollOver, rollOut, and change Event objects include an additional property not included in the menuShow and menuHide Event objects. The property, called menuItem, is a reference to the menu item that initiated the event.

Changing Items

You can alter menu items in two ways — setting the enabled state or selected state. Regardless of what kind of changes you want to make to a menu item, however, you first need to get a reference to the menu item. If you are making the changes within an event handler method such as rollOver(), rollOut(), or change(), the Event object's menuItem property is a reference to the menu item that initialized the event. If, within an event handler method, you want to get a reference to a menu item other than the item that initialized the event, you can obtain the reference as one of the nested items of the Menu instance that is referenced by the Event object's target property.

There are essentially two ways to get a reference to a menu item from a Menu instance (or from a nested menu item). You can use the getMenuItemAt() method to get an item by index. Or, you can get a reference by name if you gave the menu item an instance name when you created it. (You can give an item an instance name via the instanceName property/attribute.)

Each menu item is an instance of the MenuDataProvider class. The MenuDataProvider class looks very much like the XMLNode class. In fact, it has the same properties such as attributes and childNodes.

If you want to set the enabled or selected state of a menu item, the best way to do that is to use the setMenuItemEnabled() or setMenuItemSelected() methods. These methods set the state and then also automatically update the view. Both methods require you pass them a reference to the menu item, and then a Boolean value indicating the state to which you want to set the item. For example, the following disables a Menu item with an instance name of undo:

```
cmEdit.setMenuItemEnabled(cmEdit.undo, false);
```

The following example shows how you can create a Button and Menu item such that the paste option of the Menu item is enabled following the copy option being selected. Then, once paste is selected, it becomes disabled again.

```
import mx.controls.Menu;
var cmEdit = Menu.createMenu();
var xmlMenuData:XML = new XML();
xmlMenuData.onLoad = function():Void {
  cmEdit.dataProvider = this.firstChild;
};
xmlMenuData.ignoreWhite = true;
xmlMenuData.load("menu.xml");

// Create the listener object.
var oListener:Object = new Object();

// Assign a reference to the Menu so that the handler methods
// can address the Menu.
oListener.menu = cmEdit;

// Handle change events from the Menu.
oListener.change = function(oEvent:Object):Void {

  // If the selected item's label is copy, enable the paste
  // Menu item.
  if(oEvent.menuItem.attributes.label == "copy") {
    oEvent.target.setMenuItemEnabled(oEvent.target.paste, true);
  }

  // If the selected item's label is paste, disable the paste
  // Menu item.
  if(oEvent.menuItem.attributes.label == "paste") {
    oEvent.target.setMenuItemEnabled( oEvent.target.paste,
false);
  }
```

```
  };

  // Handle click events from the Button to show the menu
  // when the user clicks on the Button.
  oListener.click = function(oEvent:Object):Void {
    var nX:Number = oEvent.target.x;
    var nY:Number = oEvent.target.y + oEvent.target.height;
    this.menu.show(nX, nY);
  };

  // Add the listener to the Menu.
  cmEdit.addEventListener("change", oListener);

  // Create the Button instance and add the listener to it.
  this.createObject("Button", "cbtEdit",
  this.getNextHighestDepth(), {label: "Edit"});
  cbtEdit.addEventListener("click", oListener);
```

Working with MenuBar Components

The MenuBar component allows you to conveniently create a group of nested Menu instances. The MenuBar component is similar to the menu bar of a standard desktop application. Figure 28-26 shows an example:

Figure 28-26: A MenuBar component instance.

Adding Menus to a MenuBar

You can add menus to a MenuBar component in several ways. You can add menus without any items with the addMenu() method by passing it a single parameter — the label for the menu. For example:

```
  cmbMenus.addMenu("Edit");
```

You can then add items to the menu at a later point. The menu is a Menu component instance, and you can retrieve a reference to it with the getMenuAt() method if you know the index. You can then modify the items of the Menu instance as with any Menu instance.

```
  var cmEdit:mx.contols.Menu = cmbMenus.getMenuAt(0);
  cmEdit.dataProvider = xnEditData;
```

Optionally, you can add a menu and populate the menu at the same time by passing the addMenu() method a menu data provider as the second parameter. For example:

```
  cmbMenus.addMenu("Edit", xnEditData);
```

The addMenuAt() method also allows you to insert new menus at specific indices. You can create a new menu without items at a specific index as follows:

```
cmbMenus.addMenuAt(0, "Help");
```

And you can add a new menu at a specific index and populate that menu as shown in this example:

```
cmbMenus.addMenu(0, "Help", xnHelpData);
```

You can also set a MenuBar instance's data provider to populate the entire MenuBar at once by assigning an XMLNode object to the instance's dataProvider property. The data provider structure for a MenuBar is similar to the data provider structure for a Menu data provider. Each menu should be its own element in the top level of the data provider. The menu elements should have label attributes that define the label as it will appear in the MenuBar. Then, nested within each menu element should be the menu's contents. The following shows an example of the XML document that can be used to create the MenuBar.

```
<menus>
  <menu label='Edit'>
    <menuitem label='undo' instanceName='undo' />
    <menuitem label='redo' instanceName='redo' enabled='false' />
    <menuitem type='separator' />
    <submenu label='edit options' instanceName='editOptions'>
      <menuitem label='copy' instanceName='copy' />
      <menuitem label='paste' instanceName='paste' />
    </submenu>
  </menu>
  <menu label='Window'>
    <menuitem label='control panel' instanceName='control panel' />
    <menuitem label='color panel' instanceName='color panel'/>
  </menu>
  <menu label='Help'>
    <menuitem label='about' instanceName='about' />
  </menu>
</menus>
```

The following code can be used to load the XML from the preceding code and populate a MenuBar instance:

```
var xmlMenuData:XML = new XML();
xmlMenuData.onLoad = function(){
  cmbMenus.dataProvider = this.firstChild;
};
xmlMenuData.ignoreWhite = true;
xmlMenuData.load("menubar.xml");
```

Removing Menus

You can remove menus from a MenuBar instance with the removeMenuAt() method if you know the index:

```
cmbMenus.removeMenuAt(0);
```

Enabling and Disabling Menus

By default, all menus in a `MenuBar` are enabled. You can explicitly enable or disable the menus at specific indices with the `setMenuEnabledAt()` method. The method requires you pass it the index of the menu and a Boolean indicating whether to enable (`true`) or disable (`false`) the menu.

You can also retrieve the enabled state of a menu with the `getMenuEnabledAt()` method. The `getMenuEnabledAt()` method requires only the index of the menu.

Handling MenuBar Events

`MenuBar` component instances dispatch the same events as `Menu` components. They dispatch `change`, `menuShow`, `menuHide`, `rollOver`, and `rollOut` events. In each case the event objects have the same properties as the `Menu` event object counterparts.

Working with Tree Components

The `Tree` component enables you to add controls to your applications that display contents as folders and nested items. The folders and subfolders are expandable and collapsible. The effect is something similar to the interface by which many people navigate through their own computer's directory system. Figure 28-27 shows an example of a `Tree` component instance.

Figure 28-27: A Tree component instance.

Adding Items to a Tree

All items within a `Tree` instance are either branching (folders) or nonbranching. For the most part Flash takes care of making the items the appropriate type. Generally, all you need to do is add a new item by providing the label and data values. The label value is what is displayed in the tree, and the data value is hidden from view but used programmatically. You can add new items in several ways. The `addTreeNode()` and `addTreeNodeAt()` methods enable you to append or insert a new item by providing the label and data values as parameters. For example, the following code appends a new item named *Photos* and then inserts an item named *Documents* just before it.

```
ctr.addTreeNode("Photos", "photos");
ctr.addTreeNodeAt(0, "Documents", "docs");
```

Both methods return a reference to the newly created node. This is convenient for when you want to add nested items. You can call the `addTreeNode()` and `addTreeNodeAt()` methods on tree nodes as well to add nested items. For example:

```
var oDocsNode:Object = ctr.addTreeNodeAt(0, "Documents", "docs");
oDocsNode.addTreeNode("resume.doc", "resume.doc");
oDocsNode.addTreeNode("addresses.doc", "addresses.doc");
oDocsNode.addTreeNode("report.doc", "report.doc");
```

You can also add items to a tree by passing tree data providers to the addTreeNode() and addTreeNodeAt() methods. A tree data provider is similar to a menu data provider in that it can be any XMLNode object. The names of the XML elements are not relevant, but the structure and attributes of the elements are. Each element in the XML represents a node in the Tree. The XML element should have a label attribute and a data attribute. If an XML element contains nested elements, that element represents a folder in the Tree. Here's an example that adds a folder node to the tree in which are two nested items.

```
var sTreeData:String = "<node label='Photos' data='photos'>
<node label='sun.jpg' data='sun.jpg' /><node
label='moon.jpg' data='moon.jpg' /></node>";
var xmlTreeData:XML = new XML(sTreeData);
ctrDirectory.addTreeNode(xmlTreeData.firstChild);
```

You can also, of course, set the data provider for the entire Tree instance. Simply assign the XMLNode data to the instance's dataProvider property. Typically, when assigning the data provider for the entire Tree the data is loaded from an external source. The following shows a sample XML document's data that can be loaded and used to populate a Tree instance.

```
<tree>
  <node label='Documents' data='docs'>
    <node label='resume.doc' data='resume.doc' />
    <node label='addresses.doc' data='addresses.doc' />
    <node label='report.doc' data='report.doc' />
  </node>
  <node label='Photos' data='photos'>
    <node label='sun.jpg' data='sun.jpg' />
    <node label='moon.jpg' data='moon.jpg' />
  </node>
</tree>
```

The XML data from the preceding code can be loaded into a Flash application and used to populate a tree, as shown with the following code:

```
var xmlTreeData:XML = new XML();
xmlTreeData.onLoad = function(){
  ctrDirectory.dataProvider = this.firstChild;
};
xmlTreeData.ignoreWhite = true;
xmlTreeData.load("tree.xml");
```

Notice that the XML data is placed within a root element <tree>. This is just so that the XML is well formed. Because of the extra node, when the data has been loaded into Flash, you must assign the firstChild value to the Tree instance's dataProvider.

Setting Selection Mode

The default setting for a Tree instance is a single selection. That means a user can select only one item at a time. You can set the Tree instance to allow the user to make multiple selections by setting the multipleSelection property to true. Or, to explicitly reset a Tree instance to single selection mode, set the multipleSelection property to false.

Getting Items

You can retrieve references to items (nodes) in several ways. You can retrieve nodes by using the order in which they appear within the `Tree` instance's data provider. This way returns nodes regardless of whether they are visible or the order in which they are displayed (remember, the visible display order can vary depending on which nodes are expanded or collapsed). The `getTreeNodeAt()` method returns a reference to a node based on its index within the data provider. In Figure 28-27 the `Tree` instance's second node is always the *Photos* node regardless of whether any of the nodes are expanded or collapsed. You can retrieve that node as follows:

```
var oPhotosNode:Object = ctrDirectory.getTreeNodeAt(1);
```

You can retrieve nested items in the same way by calling the `getTreeNodeat()` method from any node object. For example, the following code first retrieves the Documents node and then retrieves the `resume.doc` item.

```
var oDocsNode:Object = ctrDirectory.getTreeNodeAt(0);
var oResumeDoc:Object = oDocsNode.getTreeNodeAt(0);
```

You can also retrieve nodes by display index. A node's display index can change based on which nodes are expanded and/or collapsed. You can retrieve a node's display index with the `getDisplayIndex()` method. For example:

```
var nPhotosDispInd:Number = ctrDirectory.getDisplayIndex(oPhotosNode);
```

Remember, however, that the display index will change. So, if you retrieve a node's display index, you cannot rely on the node still having the same display index later on.

If, on the other hand, you want to get the node currently displayed at a given index, you can use the `getNodeDisplayedAt()` method.

```
var oNode:Object = ctrDirectory.getNodeDisplayedAt(3);
```

You can retrieve the selected node or nodes (if set to multiple select) with the `selectedNode` and `selectedNodes` properties, respectively.

Setting Item Type

For the most part, Flash takes care of setting the Tree node types — either branching or nonbranching. If a node contains any items, it is automatically made branching (meaning that it displays a folder icon and can be expanded and collapsed). The only cases in which you are likely to need to explicitly set the type of a node is when you want to display an empty branching node. If a node contains no items, of course, Flash assumes it is nonbranching, but you can set the branching status with the `setIsBranch()` method. The `setIsBranch()` method requires you pass it the node object and a Boolean indicating whether the node should branch (`true`) or not (`false`).

```
var oNode:Object = ctrDirectory.addTreeNode("System", "sys");
ctrDirectory.setIsBranch(oNode, true);
```

You can also retrieve the current branching type of a node with the `getIsBranch()` method. The `getIsBranch()` method requires you pass it the node for which you want to get the value.

```
trace(ctrDirectory.getIsBranch(oNode));
```

Opening and Closing Nodes

Typically, there are few reasons to programmatically open and close nodes. This is because nodes are opened and closed through user interaction. However, there are a few reasons you might want to programmatically control whether nodes are opened or closed. For example, you might want to store the state of a Tree instance's nodes, and then when the user runs the Flash application again you can initialize the states of the nodes to how they were when the user last ran the application. You can set the opened or closed state of a node using the setIsOpen() method. The method requires that you provide a reference to the node to open or close it and a Boolean indicating whether to open (true) or close (false) the node.

```
ctrDirectory.setIsOpen(oPhotos, true);
```

Optionally, you can also specify a third parameter indicating whether to animate the opening or closing of the node. A value of true will cause the node to animate open or closed, whereas a value of false or undefined (specifying no value) will cause the node to immediately jump to the opened or closed state:

```
ctrDirectory.setIsOpen(oPhotos, true, true);
```

You can also get the current opened or closed status of a node with the getIsOpen() method:

```
trace(ctrDirectory.getIsOpen(oPhotos));
```

Using Custom Icons

You can assign a custom icon for each tree node if you don't want to use the default icons. Use the setIcon() method to set the icon for a node. The method requires at least two parameters — the node and the symbol linkage identifier for the icon to use:

```
ctrDirectory.setIcon(oNode, "TreeNodeIconSymbol");
```

If the node is a branching node, you can also specify a second symbol linkage identifier to use when the node is in the opened state:

```
ctrDirectory.setIcon(oNode, "ClosedIconSymbol", "OpenIconSymbol");
```

Removing Items

You can remove items from a Tree instance with one of three methods. The removeTreeNode() method removes a node given a node reference as the parameters:

```
ctrDirectory.removeTreeNode(oNode);
```

The removeTreeNodeAt() method removes a node at a given index:

```
ctrDirectory.removeTreeNodeAt(2);
```

The removeAll() method removes all nodes:

```
ctrDirectory.removeAll();
```

As with adding nodes, you can remove nodes from other nodes as well. For example:

```
ctrDirectory.getTreeNodeAt(0).removeTreeNodeAt(0);
```

Scrolling Tree Instances

You can programmatically control the scrolling of a Tree instance in several ways. First, as with List component instances, you can set the horizontal and vertical scrolling policies using the hScrollPolicy and vScrollPolicy properties.

You can horizontally scroll a Tree instance with the hPosition property. See the discussion of the hPosition for List for more details.

To vertically scroll a Tree instance, use the firstVisibleNode property. The node value assigned to the firstVisibleNode property is the first node visible at the top of the Tree instance.

Handling Tree Events

Tree components dispatch the change, scroll, itemRollOver, and itemRollOut events just as with List components. In addition, Tree components dispatch the following events:

✦ nodeOpen—Dispatched when a user opens a node

✦ nodeClose—Dispatched when a user closes a node

The change, nodeOpen, and nodeClose Event objects contain a node property that references the node that caused the event to dispatch.

Web Resource We'd like to know what you thought about this chapter. Visit www.rightactionscript .com/asb/comments to fill out an online form with your comments.

Summary

✦ The Flash 8 User Interface components provide many prebuilt controls. You can control the component instances extensively with the APIs, enabling you to provide a rich user interface to your Flash applications.

✦ You can find the UI components in the Components panel. Create instances at authoring time by dragging them from the Components panel onto the stage. Or, add the components to your library, and create the instances programmatically.

✦ The components discussed in this chapter are all built on the same architecture. This means that they share many of the same properties, methods, and events.

✦ Listener objects are objects that can handle events dispatched by components.

✦ In addition to the shared API, each component type includes its own collection of properties, methods, and events that allows you to programmatically control instances.

✦　　✦　　✦

Styling UI Components

In Chapter 28, you learned about the basics of working with the v2 UI components — from creating instances to programmatically configuring and controlling those instances. This chapter looks at two additional related themes. First, you'll look at setting styles for components in your application. Then you'll examine how to manage focus with components.

Working with Component Styles

Similar to nested Movie Clips, the v2 component instance's style exists in a treelike structure, whereby child styles can override the parent or group styles that they belong to. You can set v2 component styles in the following ways:

✦ Set a style for the component instance.

✦ Create a style object and apply it to one or more component instances.

✦ Create a style object that applies to an entire component class and all its instances.

✦ Set a global style that applies to all component instances.

Because you can apply styles in so many places simultaneously, but have only one style applied at a time to any given instance, Flash uses the following rules to determine which style to apply:

1. Flash looks for a style applied to the component instance. If the particular style type is defined explicitly for the component instance, Flash uses that value and doesn't continue looking for that particular style anywhere else. For example, if the `color` style is defined for a `Button` instance, Flash uses the color value defined for that instance.

2. Flash next looks for styles defined by a style object that has been applied to the instance. If a style is found in the style object, that value is used. For example, if the same `Button` instance from Step 1 does not have the `fontFamily` style defined for the instance, it will next look to the style object for the instance, if one is defined. If that style object has a `fontFamily` style defined, that value is used for the component instance.

3. If a particular style is not defined for the component instance or the style object assigned to the instance, Flash next looks to see whether a style object has been defined for the component instance's class. If so, and if the style is defined for the class's style object, that value is used by the component instance. For example, if the Button class style object has been defined, and fontSize style has not been set for either the instance or the instance's style object for a Button component instance, Flash uses the value defined in the Button class style object.

4. The last place that Flash looks for style values is in the global style object. If a style is not defined anywhere else, Flash uses the global style value.

Introducing UI Component Styles

Each of the UI components accepts a different grouping of styles. Tables 29-1 and 29-2 list the standard and professional components, respectively, and the styles they accept. Table 29-3 explains the supported styles in detail.

Table 29-1: Supported Styles for Standard UI Components

Style	cbt	cch	ccb	clbl	cl	cns	cpb	crb	csp	cta	cti	cw
alternatingRowColors			✓		✓							
backgroundColor			✓		✓							
borderColor			✓		✓							
borderStyle			✓		✓							✓
color	✓	✓	✓	✓	✓	✓	✓	✓		✓	✓	
defaultIcon			✓		✓							
disabledColor	✓	✓	✓			✓	✓	✓				
embedFonts										✓	✓	
fontFamily	✓	✓	✓	✓	✓	✓	✓	✓		✓	✓	
fontSize	✓	✓	✓	✓	✓	✓	✓	✓		✓	✓	
fontStyle	✓	✓	✓	✓	✓	✓	✓	✓		✓	✓	
fontWeight	✓	✓	✓	✓	✓	✓	✓			✓	✓	
openDuration			✓									
openEasing			✓									
rollOverColor			✓		✓							
selectionColor			✓		✓							
selectionDisabledColor			✓		✓							
selectionDuration			✓		✓							
selectionEasing			✓		✓							
textAlign			✓	✓	✓	✓				✓	✓	

Style	cbt	cch	ccb	clbl	cl	cns	cpb	crb	csp	cta	cti	cw
textDecoration		✓	✓	✓	✓	✓	✓			✓	✓	
textRollOverColor			✓		✓							
textSelectedColor			✓		✓							
ThemeColor	✓	✓	✓		✓	✓	✓	✓	✓			✓
UseRollOver			✓		✓							

Here's the key to the column headers in Table 29-1:

- cbt — Button
- cch — CheckBox
- ccb — ComboBox
- clbl — Label
- cl — List
- cns — NumericStepper
- cpb — ProgressBar
- crb — RadioButton
- csp — ScrollPane
- cta — TextArea
- cti — TextInput
- cw — Window

Table 29-2: Supported Styles for Professional UI Components

Style	cdc	cdf	cm	cmb	ctr	cdg	ca	cac
alternatingRowColors			✓	✓	✓	✓		
backgroundColor	✓	✓						✓
BorderColor		✓						✓
BorderStyle		✓						✓
buttonStyleDeclaration							✓	
Color	✓	✓	✓	✓	✓	✓	✓	✓
DisabledColor	✓	✓	✓	✓	✓	✓	✓	✓
EmbedFonts								
FontFamily	✓	✓	✓	✓	✓	✓	✓	✓

Continued

Table 29-2 *(continued)*

Style	cdc	cdf	cm	cmb	ctr	cdg	ca	cac
FontSize		✓	✓	✓	✓	✓	✓	✓
FontStyle	✓	✓	✓	✓	✓	✓	✓	✓
FontWeight		✓	✓	✓	✓	✓	✓	✓
HeaderHeight								✓
messageStyleDeclaration							✓	
OpenDuration					✓			✓
OpenEasing								✓
RollOverColor	✓	✓	✓	✓	✓	✓		
selectionColor			✓	✓	✓	✓		
selectionDisabledColor					✓	✓		
selectionDuration					✓	✓		
selectionEasing					✓	✓		
TextAlign		✓	✓	✓	✓	✓		
textDecoration	✓	✓	✓	✓	✓	✓	✓	✓
textRollOverColor					✓	✓		
textSelectedColor					✓	✓		
ThemeColor	✓	✓	✓	✓	✓	✓	✓	✓
titleStyleDeclaration							✓	
UseRollOver					✓	✓		

Here's the key to the column headers for Table 29-2:

✦ cdc—DateChooser

✦ cdf—DateField

✦ cm—Menu

✦ cmb—MenuBar

✦ ctr—Tree

✦ cdg—DataGrid

✦ ca—Alert

✦ cac—Accordion

Table 29-3: Descriptions of Supported Styles

Style	Description
alternatingRowColors	An array of two or more numeric or predefined string values indicating the colors for the rows in a List instance or other components that have a nested list (such as ComboBox and Tree).
backgroundColor	The color used for the background of the component.
BorderColor	The color of the component's border. If the border is 3-D, this value is used to color the portion that defaults to black. If the border is 2-D, this value is used for the colored portion of the border (as opposed to the shaded portion).
BorderStyle	Can be inset (component appears to be recessed), outset (component appears embossed), solid (single, solid line), or none.
Color	The color of the text.
DefaultIcon	The linkage identifier to use as the default icon in a list or another component that uses a nested list.
DisabledColor	The color for text when it is within a disabled selection or when the component is disabled.
EmbedFonts	The name of the font symbol linkage identifier to embed.
FontFamily	The name of the font family to use (for example, _serif, Arial, Courier, Courier New, and so on).
FontSize	The point size for the font.
FontStyle	Can be normal or italic.
FontWeight	Can be normal or bold.
OpenDuration	The number of milliseconds for an item with subelements to open.
OpenEasing	A reference to one of the easing methods defined within the mx.transitions.easing package of classes. The classes include Back, Bounce, Elastic, Regular, and Strong. Each class has the following methods: easeIn, easeOut, and easeInOut. There is also a None class with an easeNone method. A complete example of a possible openEasing style values is mx.transitions.easing.Bounce.easeInOut.
RollOverColor	The color of a row's highlight when the mouse rolls over it.
selectionColor	The color of a selected row.
selectionDisabledColor	The color of an item that is disabled.
selectionDuration	The number of milliseconds for a selection's highlight to appear or disappear.

Continued

Table 29-3 *(continued)*

Style	Description
selectionEasing	A reference to one of the easing methods. The options are the same as those for openEasing.
TextAlign	Can be right, left, or center.
textDecoration	Can be normal or underline.
textRollOverColor	The color of text when the mouse is over it.
textSelectedColor	The color of text when it is selected.
ThemeColor	The color of the theme applied to the entire component. Some aspects of a themeColor setting can be overwritten by other styles.
UseRollOver	Can be true or false. If it's true, mousing over a selection highlights it. If it's false, no highlighting appears when a selection is moused over.
buttonStyleDeclaration	A style object for the nested button within an Alert instance.
titleStyleDeclaration	A style object for the title within an Alert instance.
messageStyleDeclaration	A style object for the message within an Alert instance.

Working with Colors

Several styles assign color values to particular parts of component instances. Some examples are color, borderColor, backgroundColor, themeColor, disabledColor, rollOverColor, selectionColor, and selectionDisabledColor. When you assign values to these styles, you have several options:

✦ **Use a numeric value** — Typically for colors, you use hexadecimal representation, although it is not required. For example, to assign a red color to one of the styles you can use the value 0xFF0000.

✦ **Use one of the predefined color strings** — These color strings are shown in Table 29-4, and they work only with component styles (meaning that you cannot use these values for Color objects, for example).

✦ **Use other options** — For the themeColor style, you can also use one of these three additional string values: haloGreen, haloBlue, and haloOrange.

Table 29-4: Style Color String Values

Color String	Numeric Value
Black	0x000000
Blue	0x0000FF
Cyan	0x00FFFF
Green	0x00FF00
Magenta	0xFF00FF
Red	0xFF0000
White	0xFFFFFF
Yellow	0xFFFF00

Setting Instance Styles

You can set the styles for a component instance using the `setStyle()` method directly from the instance. This is most appropriate when you want to make changes to the styles for a single instance when the styles for that instance should appear differently from other component instances in the application. For example, if you want to set the `textDecoration` style for just one `List` instance, you can accomplish that by calling `setStyle()` from that instance.

The `setStyle()` method requires two parameters — the name of the style as a string and the value for that style. For example, the following code sets the value for the color style of a component instance named `clData`:

```
clData.setStyle("color", "red");
```

Although you can call the `setStyle()` method on an instance multiple times in order to set multiple styles, typically you will find it is a better approach to use a style object, as discussed in the next section.

Setting Instance Styles with a Style Object

A style object is an instance of the `mx.styles.CSSStyleDeclaration` class. You can use a style object to create a set of styles that can be applied to multiple instances. In addition to the benefit of being able to apply a style object to multiple component instances, there is the additional benefit of being able to assign the style values as properties of the style object rather than having to repeatedly use `setStyle()`.

The first step when working with a style object it to instantiate it. The object must be assigned as a new property of the `_global.styles` object. Here's an example that creates a new style object named `customStyle`:

```
_global.styles.customStyle = new mx.styles.CSSStyleDeclaration();
```

Note   The name used for the custom style object in the preceding example (`customStyle`) is not a reserved word with special meaning in Flash. You could just as well call the object `styleForComponents`, `formOneStyle`, and so on.

If you are going to create multiple style objects in your application, you might also find it convenient to first import the `CSSStyleDeclaration` class. Then you don't have to use the fully qualified class name (that is, `mx.styles.CSSStyleDeclaration`) each time you create a new style object. For example:

```
import mx.styles.CSSStyleDeclaration;
_global.styles.customStyle = new CSSStyleDeclaration();
```

Once you've defined the style object, you can assign styles as properties. For example:

```
_global.styles.customStyle.color = "red";
_global.styles.customStyle.fontFamily = "_serif";
_global.styles.customStyle.textDecoration = "italic";
```

The remaining step is to then apply that style object to one or more component instances. You can achieve this by calling `setStyle()` from the instances and setting a style named `styleName`, so that its value matches the name of the new style object:

```
clData.setStyle("styleName", "customStyle");
```

Setting Class Styles

You can create a style object on the `_global.styles` object such that the style object's name matches the class name for one of the UI components, and all instances of that class will automatically apply the style object settings. For example, if you create a `_global.styles.Button` style object, all `Button` component instances automatically apply those style settings. Here's an example:

```
import mx.styles.CSSStyleDeclaration;
_global.styles.Button = new CSSStyleDeclaration();
_global.styles.Button.setStyle("color", "red");
```

With the preceding example, all `Button` instances automatically have red text (unless instance styles or styles applied to the instance with a style object override that setting). You'll notice that the `setStyle()` method is used to assign the style value. You can also use the property syntax such as:

```
_global.styles.Button.color = 0xFF0000;
```

However, nested items within the component instance will not inherit the styles this way, unless you use `setStyle()`. This won't show up in a `Button` component, necessarily, but you'll see it with other types of components such as, for example, `ComboBox` instances. The `ComboBox` drop-down is a nested `List` component. If you assign the color style value for a `ComboBox` style class using property syntax, you'll see that the items in the drop-down do not inherit the value. But if you use `setStyle()`, the items are colored appropriately.

The technique of creating a class style object will work with almost all of the component classes. However, the following classes will not allow you to set a class style object: `List`, `DataGrid`, `Tree`, and `Menu`. With some of those classes, setting a class style object simply has no effect. With others, setting a class style object actually breaks all instances of the component. Instead, you can set a class style for all the aforementioned classes (as a group) by assigning style values to the `_global.styles.ScrollSelectList` style object. The `ScrollSelectList` style object already exists, and so you should not reinstantiate it. Instead, just assign the new values to the appropriate styles. For example:

```
_global.styles.ScrollSelectList.setStyle("color", "red");
```

The preceding code causes the text color to change to red for all `List`, `DataGrid`, `Tree`, and `Menu` instances.

Setting Global Styles

You can apply styles globally such that all component instances will apply the same styles (unless overridden by class style objects, style objects applied to the instances, or styles applied to the instances directly). The global style object is already instantiated for you, and it is accessible as `_global.style`.

Caution   Notice that the global style object is named in the singular form, style, and not the plural form, styles. The `_global.styles` object is a container for class and custom style objects as detailed in the preceding sections. The global style object, `_global.style`, is different, so be careful to make sure you are using the correct object references because the difference of a single "s" will cause unexpected results.

The `_global.style` object is a `CSSStyleDeclaration` instance on which you can set the style properties just like any other style object with which you've worked thus far. For example:

```
_global.style.setStyle("color", "red");
```

Setting the global color style to red causes all components to display with red text. Applying style settings to the global style object is a good way to create a uniform, styled appearance in your application.

Practicing Applying Styles

In this exercise, you create a simple form using a few of the standard UI components. You then use ActionScript to apply style changes to the components — some global, some as a class style object, some as a custom style object applied to a component instance, and one directly on a component instance.

1. Open a new Flash document, and save it as `applyingStyles001.fla`.

2. Open the Components panel, and drag one instance each of the following components onto the stage: `ComboBox`, `List`, and `Button`. Name these instances `ccbRegion`, `clProducts`, and `cbtSubmit`, respectively.

3. Drag two instances of the `Label` component onto the stage, naming them `clblRegion` and `clblProducts`.

4. Arrange the instances on the stage as shown in Figure 29-1, with `clblRegion` matching up with `ccbRegion`, and `clblProducts` matching up with `clProducts`.

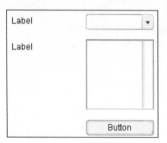

Figure 29-1: The arrangement of the component instances on the stage.

5. Rename the default layer to Form, and add a new layer named Actions.

6. Add the following ActionScript code to the first frame of the Actions layer:

```
import mx.styles.CSSStyleDeclaration;
import mx.transitions.easing.Back;
global.style.setStyle("color", 0xED5A0C);
global.style.setStyle("themeColor", "haloOrange");
global.style.setStyle("textSelectedColor", 0x9C3C07);
global.style.setStyle("textRollOverColor", 0xC54A0A);
global.styles.Label = new CSSStyleDeclaration();
global.styles.Label.setStyle("color", "red");
global.styles.openStyle = new CSSStyleDeclaration();
global.styles.openStyle.setStyle("openEasing", Back.easeInOut);
global.styles.openStyle.setStyle("openDuration", 2000);
ccbRegion.setStyle("styleName", "openStyle");
cbtSubmit.setStyle("themeColor", 0xFDFCCA);
ccbRegion.dataProvider = [{label: "North", data:1},
{label:"South", data: 2}, {label:"East", data: 3},
{label:"West", data: 4}];
clProducts.dataProvider = [{label: "Flash", data: "f"},
{label: "Dreamweaver", data: "dw"}, {label: "Fireworks",
data: "fw"}, {label: "ColdFusion", data: "cf"}];
clblRegion.text = "Region:";
clblProducts.text = "Products:";
cbtSubmit.label = "Submit";
```

7. Test the movie. The form should look something like Figure 29-2. When you open and close the ComboBox, you should notice that it takes two seconds and that it does a slight bounce.

Figure 29-2: The form when testing the movie.

Let's take a closer look at the code.

First, you import some of the classes you are going to use so you don't have to use the fully qualified names within the rest of the code. This just makes the code easier to read and can save some typing in the long run.

```
import mx.styles.CSSStyleDeclaration;
import mx.transitions.easing.Back;
```

Next, you set some global styles. You set the global color to a light orange, the theme color to haloOrange, the selected color to a dark orange, and the rollover color to a medium orange.

```
_global.style.setStyle("color", 0xED5A0C);
_global.style.setStyle("themeColor", "haloOrange");
_global.style.setStyle("textSelectedColor", 0x9C3C07);
_global.style.setStyle("textRollOverColor", 0xC54A0A);
```

Then you create a class style object for the Label class. You set the color style to red for all Label instances. Because the class styles override global styles, all the Label instances have red text instead of orange text.

```
_global.styles.Label = new CSSStyleDeclaration();
_global.styles.Label.setStyle("color", "red");
```

Next, you create a custom style object named openStyle, and define the open easing and open duration values for it. Then you apply that custom style object to the ccbRegion ComboBox instance:

```
_global.styles.openStyle = new CSSStyleDeclaration();
_global.styles.openStyle.setStyle("openEasing", Back.easeInOut);
_global.styles.openStyle.setStyle("openDuration", 2000);
ccbRegion.setStyle("styleName", "openStyle");
```

You then set the theme color for the Button instance to be yellow instead of using the haloOrange theme color. Because this style is applied directly to the instance, it will override the global setting:

```
cbtSubmit.setStyle("themeColor", 0xFDFCCA);
```

Subsequently, you simply populate the form with values.

Cross-Reference If you have questions about this part of the code, you might want to refer to Chapter 28, which discusses each of the components in detail, including how to set their properties.

```
ccbRegion.dataProvider = [{label: "North", data:1},
{label:"South", data: 2}, {label:"East", data: 3},
{label:"West", data: 4}];
clProducts.dataProvider = [{{label: "Flash", data: "f"},
{label: "Dreamweaver", data: "dw"}, {label: "Fireworks",
data: "fw"}, {label: "ColdFusion", data: "cf"}];
clblRegion.text = "Region:";
clblProducts.text = "Products:";
cbtSubmit.label = "Submit";
```

Managing Focus

When you use the UI components to create forms in your application, one of the things you'll want to be able to do is manage the focus using ActionScript. There are two basic things you want to be able to accomplish:

✦ Controlling the order in which focus changes between component instances when the users press the Tab key

✦ Setting the focus programmatically

The FocusManager class helps you to accomplish both of these tasks. The FocusManager class also assists you in handling keyboard events for the entire form. For example, you can define a Button instance that serves as the default button for the form. Therefore, if the users press the Enter key at any point, the Button instance will dispatch a click event.

Creating a FocusManager Instance

As long as you have added at least one UI component to your Flash application either at authoring time or at runtime, Flash automatically creates an instance of the FocusManager class for you on _root. That means that you should not need to instantiate your own FocusManager object. The name of the auto-generated object is focusManager, the same name as the class, but with a lowercase "f" at the beginning.

Assigning Tab Order

Standard desktop and HTML Web applications enable users to shift focus between form controls by pressing the Tab key. The same functionality is available in applications developed using Flash 8. It is remarkably simple to achieve as well. Each component instance has a tabIndex property. You can set the numeric index value for each component instance that determines the order in which they will receive focus when the users press the Tab key. If you don't want a particular instance to be able to receive focus, simply don't set a tabIndex property value for that instance. Here's an example in which the tabIndex properties for several component instances are assigned:

```
clProducts.tabIndex = 1;
ccbRegion.tabIndex = 2;
cbtSubmit.tabIndex = 3;
```

In the preceding example, if focus is brought to the clProducts instance and the user presses the Tab key, the focus will next move to the ccbRegion instance. If the user presses the Tab key again, the focus shifts to the cbtSubmit instances. Subsequent Tab key presses will cycle through the three component instances again. You should also note that the indices need not necessarily be contiguous. The following example achieves the same effect as the preceding code, assuming no other components have been assigned tabIndex values between the values assigned as follows:

```
clProducts.tabIndex = 6;
ccbRegion.tabIndex = 20;
cbtSubmit.tabIndex = 37;
```

Whereas the Tab key moves focus to the next component instance, pressing Shift+Tab moves focus to the previous instance.

The FocusManager class will automatically take care of managing the changes in focus as long as you have set the tabIndex for the component instances. The FocusManager class is fairly responsive to changes that occur within the application. For example, the user might use the Tab key to shift focus between component instances and then decide to use the mouse to bring focus to another component instance. The FocusManager class knows to then use that new component instance's tabIndex value as the current value. That ensures that when the user next presses the Tab key, the focus will shift to the component that is next in sequence, and that it will not jump out of order. Additionally, if a component instance's visible property is set to false, the FocusManager class will skip over that instance.

If you want to get the value of the next index to which focus will be given, you can access it with the nextTabIndex property of the FocusManager instance:

```
trace(focusManager.nextTabIndex);
```

Setting Focus Programmatically

You can also set the focus programmatically by calling the setFocus() method from any component instance. Doing so will automatically bring focus to the instance from which the method is called. It will also tell the FocusManager instance to update its current index to the tabIndex for the component instance from which setFocus() was called. One important point to note is that setFocus() does *not* bring a focus indicator around the component to which focus is given. The focus indicator appears around a component instance only when focus is shifted to it by the Tab key.

```
cbtSubmit.setFocus();
```

You can also get a reference to the instance with focus by calling the getFocus() method from any component instance:

```
trace(cbtSubmit.getFocus());
```

The FocusManager class also has setFocus() and getFocus() methods, and at times you might find that working with these methods is more appropriate than calling the setFocus() and getFocus() methods from the component instances directly. The getFocus() method doesn't require any parameters, whether invoked from a component instance or from a FocusManager instance. The setFocus() method, however, requires a parameter when invoked from a FocusManager instance (although not when invoked from a component instance). The reason is that obviously the setFocus() method, when invoked from a FocusManager instance, needs to know to which component instance you want to bring focus. Therefore, when you call setFocus() from the focusManager object, pass it a reference to the component to which you want to shift focus:

```
focusManager.setFocus(cbtSubmit);
```

Setting Default Buttons

Another nice feature of the FocusManager class is that it enables you to define a Button instance that will handle any Enter key presses while the user is filling out a form. This allows the user to fill out some or all of the form and then submit the form without having to actually click the button or bring focus to the button by tabbing to it. This is a feature of standard HTML forms that FocusManager enables within your Flash forms as well. In order to define a default button, you need only to assign a reference to that button to the defaultPushButton property of the FocusManager instance. For example:

```
focusManager.defaultPushButton = cbtSubmit;
```

Once you've assigned the default Button instance, that Button instance dispatches a click event to all of its listener objects when the user presses the Enter key. The effect is the same as if the user had clicked the button.

You can disable a default button by setting the defaultPushButtonEnabled property of the FocusManager instance to false. This is useful when you want to enable the button only after the user has, for example, filled out required information. You can re-enable the default button by then setting defaultPushButtonEnabled to true.

You can programmatically send a command from the FocusManager instance to the default button, telling the button to dispatch a click event. To achieve that, you can call the sendDefaultPushButtonEvent() method from the FocusManager instance.

We'd like to know what you thought about this chapter. Visit www.rightactionscript .com/asb.comments to fill out an online form with your comments.

Summary

✦ The components come with a set of predefined styles that allow you to programmatically change the appearance of the instances on the stage.

✦ You can assign component styles in four ways: globally, to the component class, with a style object, or directly to the instance.

✦ You can manage focus of component instances using the FocusManager class. An instance named focusManager is automatically created for you when you use a component.

✦ With FocusManager, you can set a default Button instance for the application.

✦   ✦   ✦

Creating Custom Components

Components are a powerful part of Flash, providing many benefits, including:

✦ **Simplicity** — Simple interfaces make them accessible to programmers and nonprogrammers alike.

✦ **Extensibility** — This means you can build upon existing components to create new and more complex/specified types.

✦ **Reusability** — Rather than reinventing the proverbial wheel with each application, you can simply drag and drop components.

✦ **Encapsulation** — All the code is hidden from view, saving you from having to hassle with the hows and wherefores of a component.

In this chapter, you learn how to create your own custom components, both from scratch and by building upon the existing v2 component architecture.

Understanding Component Anatomy

Components are, simply put, fancy Movie Clips. That is, of course, something of an oversimplification, but it is accurate in its essence and should help you to understand that components need not be overwhelming. With this in mind, take a look at the parts that make up a very basic component:

✦ **An ActionScript 2.0 class** — The class must extend `MovieClip` either directly or indirectly.

✦ **A MovieClip symbol** — Each component must have a Movie Clip symbol with which to associate the class:

  • The `MovieClip` symbol must be set to Export for ActionScript, have a linkage identifier, and must have the fully qualified class name specified within the AS 2.0 Class field of the Linkage settings.

  • The `MovieClip` symbol must have a component definition. The class must be specified in the component definition as well as in the linkage settings.

To create a very basic component, follow these steps:

1. Create the component's `MovieClip` symbol as well as any additional `MovieClip` symbols that contain elements used within the component.

2. Create a new ActionScript 2.0 class for the component. The class should define all the functionality for the component. You'll take a closer look at this step in the exercises in this chapter.

3. Within the linkage settings for the main component `MovieClip` symbol, assign it the corresponding ActionScript 2.0 class in the AS2.0 Class field. The name should be the fully qualified name of the class.

4. Set the ActionScript 2.0 class in the Component Definition settings as well. The value in the Component Definition settings' AS 2.0 Class field should match the value in the Linkage settings AS2.0 Class field.

5. Export the Compiled Clip (for testing while building the component) and then eventually the SWC file. The SWC file is a compiled and distributable version of your component. It provides several benefits when you are working with components. First, it zips up all the necessary component elements into a single file. Second, because it is precompiled, it makes the movie export faster when the component is used within another Flash document.

Don't worry if any of those steps sound unfamiliar to you. The next section clarifies all these steps with an exercise in which you create a custom component.

Making Your First Component

In this section, you create a new UI component from scratch. You'll notice that in the basic set of components there is no component that provides the slider control functionality. So, now is your chance to create such a component. Throughout the rest of the chapter, you build upon this foundation as you learn how to create more and more-sophisticated components.

1. Create a new directory on your computer called `SliderComponents`. Because there will be several versions of the component, save them in several nested directories within `SliderComponents`.

2. Create a new directory within `SliderComponents`. Name the directory `Slider001`.

3. Within `Slider001`, create a directory called `actionscriptbible`. This directory is used as part of the ActionScript 2.0 class package.

4. Within the `actionscriptbible` directory, create a new directory named `components`. Again, this directory is used as part of the package for the ActionScript 2.0 class.

5. Open a new Flash document, and save it as `Slider.fla` in Slider001.

6. Create a new `MovieClip` symbol named Slider. This will be the main component `MovieClip` symbol.

7. Open a new ActionScript file to write the ActionScript 2.0 class. If you are using Flash Professional, you can open a new ActionScript file in the Flash application. Otherwise, you will need to open a new (plain) text document in your favorite editor.

8. Add the following code to the new ActionScript file:

```
// Declare the class with the name Slider. The class is in
// the actionscriptbible.components package. The class should
// extend MovieClip.
class actionscriptbible.components.Slider extends MovieClip {

// The Slider component consists of a thumb bar and a track
// along which the thumb bar moves.
  private var _mThumbBar:MovieClip;
  private var _mTrack:MovieClip;

  // Define a private property to store the current value of
  // the slider. The value ranges from 0 to 100.
  private var _nValue:Number;

// The component uses a listener object to detect when the
// mouse moves.
  private var _oMouseListener:Object;

// The component uses the following two properties to determine
// the width and height of the component instance.
  private var _nWidth:Number;
  private var _nHeight:Number;

  // Define a getter method so that _nValue is publicly
  // accessible as a property named value.
  public function get value():Number {
    return _nValue;
  }

  // Define a constructor. The constructor is
  // automatically called when a new instance of the
  // component is created.
  public function Slider() {

    // Define default values for the width and height.
    _nWidth = 200;
    _nHeight = 10;

    // Initialize _nValue to 0.
    if(_nValue == undefined) {
      _nValue = 0;
    }


    // Make the movie clips for the thumb bar and track.
    _mTrack = createEmptyMovieClip("_mTrack",
getNextHighestDepth());
    _mThumbBar = createEmptyMovieClip("_mThumbBar",
getNextHighestDepth());

    // Draw the component.
```

```
        draw();

        // Define the listener object so that when a mouse move event
        // is detected, it calls the update() method of the Slider
        // instance.
        _oMouseListener = new Object();
        _oMouseListener.onMouseMove = mx.utils.Delegate.create(          ⏎
this, update);

        // Define onPress() and onRelease() methods for the
        // mThumbbar MovieClip object.
        _mThumbBar.onPress = mx.utils.Delegate.create(                   ⏎
this, onPressThumbBar);
        _mThumbBar.onRelease = mx.utils.Delegate.create(                 ⏎
this, onReleaseThumbBar);
        _mThumbBar.onReleaseOutside = _mThumbBar.onRelease;
    }

private function draw():Void {

    // Clear any previously-drawn content.
    _mThumbBar.clear();
    _mTrack.clear();

    // Draw a thumb bar that is 5 pixels wide and as tall as
    // specified by _nHeight.
    _mThumbBar.lineStyle(0, 0, 0);
    _mThumbBar.beginFill(0, 100);
    _mThumbBar.lineTo(5, 0);
    _mThumbBar.lineTo(5, _nHeight);
    _mThumbBar.lineTo(0, _nHeight);
    _mThumbBar.lineTo(0, 0);
    _mThumbBar.endFill();

    // Draw a track that is as wide as specified by _nWidth and
    // 10 pixels tall.
    _mTrack.lineStyle(0, 0, 100);
    _mTrack.lineTo(_nWidth, 0);
    _mTrack.lineTo(_nWidth, 5);
    _mTrack.lineTo(0, 5);
    _mTrack.lineTo(0, 0);

    // Place the track so that it is vertically centered.
    _mTrack._y = _height/2 - 2.5;
    }

    private function onPressThumbBar():Void {

    // When the user presses on the object make it
    // draggable within the specified range.
    _mThumbBar.startDrag(false, 0, 0, _mTrack._width -               ⏎
```

```
_mThumbBar._width + .5, 0);

     // Tell the component to start detecting mouse move events.
     Mouse.addListener(_oMouseListener);
   }

   private function onReleaseThumbBar():Void {

     // When the user releases the thumb bar, tell Flash
     // to stop dragging it.
     _mThumbBar.stopDrag();

     // Tell the component to stop detecting mouse move events.
     Mouse.removeListener(_oMouseListener);
     update();
   }

   // The update () method is called when the mouse moved as
   // long as the thumb bar is pressed. It simply updates
   // _nValue to reflect the current x coordinate of the
   // thumb bar.
   private function update():Void {
     _nValue = Math.round((_mThumbBar._x)/             ⤳
(_mTrack._width + .5 - _mThumbBar._width) * 100);
   }


 }
```

 9. Save the ActionScript file as `Slider.as`. You should save the file to the
 `actionscriptbible/components` directory that you created in Steps 3 and 4.

10. Return to `Slider.fla` and open the library.

11. Select the Slider MovieClip symbol and open the Linkage properties.

12. Select the Export for ActionScript box.

13. For the linkage identifier enter the name `Slider`.

14. In the AS 2.0 Class field, enter the fully qualified name of the `Slider` class:
`actionscriptbible.components.Slider`.

15. Click the OK button in the Linkage Properties dialog box.

16. Add an instance of the Slider component to the stage. Give it an instance name of
`sldExample`.

17. Add a new layer named Actions.

18. Add the following code to the first frame of the Actions layer:

```
setInterval(checkValue, 100);

function checkValue():Void {
  trace(sldExample.value);
}
```

The preceding code simply demonstrates that the `value` property of the `Slider` instance reports an updated value repeatedly.

19. Test the movie. You should see the value from the `Slider` instance displayed in the Output panel. As you drag the thumb bar, you will see the value change.

You have just created your first component. Obviously, there are still some ways in which you can build upon the `Slider` component. In subsequent exercises throughout this chapter, you'll be doing just that.

Working with Component Metadata

Flash allows you to specify some special component metadata tags in your external ActionScript 2.0 component classes. The metadata is used by Flash during authoring time to allow for different types of interaction between the component instance and the Flash authoring environment. There are seven metadata keywords: `Inspectable`, `InspectableList`, `Event`, `Bindable`, `ChangeEvent`, `ComponentTask`, and `IconFile`. Of those seven, this chapter takes a closer look at three — `Inspectable`, `InspectableList`, and `IconFile`. The remaining tags are outside the scope of this book.

Tip   Metadata tags allow you to specify special information about your ActionScript class files. That information can then be interpreted by Flash to provide some additional functionality within the authoring environment.

Understanding Metadata Tag Use

The metadata tags are always enclosed in square brackets, and they should never be followed by a semicolon. For example:

```
[Inspectable]
```

In some cases, the metadata tags can accept some additional parameterized data called *attributes*. In those cases, the extra data should be enclosed in parentheses following the metadata tag name. For example:

```
[Inspectable(defaultValue="red")]
```

Metadata tags are bound to the next line of ActionScript code. Different tags should be bound to different class elements. For example, as you'll see, `InspectableList` metadata tags should be bound to the class itself. Other metadata tags should be bound to class members. You look at some specific examples in the next few sections.

Using Inspectable

The `Inspectable` metadata tag tells Flash that a particular class member should be included in the parameters list within the Component Inspector panel. This is very important if you want users to be able to configure the component instances without having to use the ActionScript API.

You can associate an `Inspectable` tag with a public property or a public getter or setter method by placing the tag on the line just preceding the member declaration. Here is a very simple example:

```
[Inspectable]
public var value:Number;
```

In the preceding example, the parameter named `value` will show up in the Component Inspector parameters list.

More often than not, you want to specify some attributes for an `Inspectable` tag. The following list explains the more commonly used attributes for the `Inspectable` tag:

✦ **name** — By default, Flash displays the property name in the parameters list. If you want to specify a custom display name, you can do so with the `name` attribute.

✦ **type** — Specifies the data type for the parameter. By default, Flash assumes the data type of the property that is being made inspectable.

✦ **defaultValue** — The default value to use.

✦ **enumeration** — A list of possible values for the parameter.

Using InspectableList

The `InspectableList` tag allows you to list a subset of all the possible inspectable properties that you want to actually display to the user in the Component Inspector panel. The use of this tag might not be readily obvious. After all, why would you mark some properties as inspectable only to then remove them from the list of displayed parameters? The key to remember is that some component classes extend other components. In such a case, you might not necessarily want to display all the inspectable properties from the superclass for instances of the subclass. Therefore, you can use `InspectableList` to indicate which parameters to display so that not all the inherited inspectable properties are included. The `InspectableList` tag requires that you specify a list of the property names that should be included. For example:

```
[InspectableList("value","velocity")]
```

The `InspectableList` tag should be associated with the class itself, so you should place it on the line preceding the class declaration:

```
[InspectableList("wingspan","velocity")]
class Bird {
```

Using IconFile

The `IconFile` tag tells Flash what image file it should use to display next to the component in the Component panel and in the library as well. Without the `IconFile` tag, Flash uses the default component icon.

The image must follow these specifications:

✦ Must be saved in PNG format.

✦ Must be 18 by 18 pixels.

✦ Must be saved in the same directory as the FLA in which the component symbol is saved. When you export the SWC file, Flash will look for the image in that directory.

The `IconFile` tag should be associated with the class. Here is an example:

```
[IconFile("bird.png")]
class Bird {
```

Using Metatags with the Slider Component

In the following exercise, you build a new version of the Slider component from the previous exercise. The updated version will use an `Inspectable` metatag to let nonprogrammers assign a value to the component without any ActionScript.

1. Make a copy of the `Slider001` directory and its contents. Call the new directory `Slider002`. The files referred to in the rest of this exercise are from the new `Slider002` directory and its subdirectories.

2. Edit `Slider.as`, modifying the code as follows. The changes are bolded.

```
class actionscriptbible.components.Slider extends MovieClip {

  private var _mThumbBar:MovieClip;
  private var _mTrack:MovieClip;
  private var _nValue:Number;
  private var _oMouseListener:Object;
  private var _nWidth:Number;
  private var _nHeight:Number;

  public function get value():Number {
    return _nValue;
  }

  // Add a setter method for the value property. Use an
  // Inspectable metatag so that the property is accessible via
  // the Component Inspector panel at authoring time.
  [Inspectable(defaultValue=100)]
  public function set value(nValue:Number):Void {

    // Make sure the value is not outside the range of 0 to 100.
    if(nValue > 100) {
      nValue = 100;
    }
    else if(nValue < 0) {
      nValue = 0;
    }

    // Assign the new value to _nValue;
    _nValue = nValue;

    // Update the x-coordinate of the thumb bar.
    _mThumbBar._x = _nValue / 100 *
(_nWidth + .5 - _mThumbBar._width);
  }
```

```
public function Slider() {

  _nWidth = 200;
  _nHeight = 10;

  if(_nValue == undefined) {
    _nValue = 0;
  }

  _mTrack = createEmptyMovieClip("_mTrack",                    ⊃
getNextHighestDepth());
  _mThumbBar = createEmptyMovieClip("_mThumbBar",             ⊃
getNextHighestDepth());

  draw();

  _oMouseListener = new Object();
  _oMouseListener.onMouseMove = mx.utils.Delegate.create(     ⊃
this, update);

  _mThumbBar.onPress = mx.utils.Delegate.create(              ⊃
this, onPressThumbBar);
  _mThumbBar.onRelease = mx.utils.Delegate.create(            ⊃
this, onReleaseThumbBar);
  _mThumbBar.onReleaseOutside = _mThumbBar.onRelease;
}

private function draw():Void {
  _mThumbBar.clear();
  _mTrack.clear();
  _mThumbBar.lineStyle(0, 0, 0);
  _mThumbBar.beginFill(0, 100);
  _mThumbBar.lineTo(5, 0);
  _mThumbBar.lineTo(5, _nHeight);
  _mThumbBar.lineTo(0, _nHeight);
  _mThumbBar.lineTo(0, 0);
  _mThumbBar.endFill();
  _mTrack.lineStyle(0, 0, 100);
  _mTrack.lineTo(_nWidth, 0);
  _mTrack.lineTo(_nWidth, 5);
  _mTrack.lineTo(0, 5);
  _mTrack.lineTo(0, 0);
  _mTrack._y = _height/2 - 2.5;

  // Set the value property (the setter), which causes the
  // thumb bar's _x property to get updated.
  value = _nValue;
}

private function onPressThumbBar():Void {
  _mThumbBar.startDrag(false, 0, 0,                            ⊃
```

```
_mTrack._width - _mThumbBar._width + .5, 0);
   Mouse.addListener(_oMouseListener);
 }

 private function onReleaseThumbBar():Void {
   _mThumbBar.stopDrag();
   Mouse.removeListener(_oMouseListener);
   update();
 }

 private function update():Void {
   _nValue = Math.round((_mThumbBar._x)/
(_mTrack._width + .5 - _mThumbBar._width) * 100);
 }

}
```

3. Open `Slider.fla`.

4. Select the Slider symbol in the library, and open the Component Definition settings from the library menu.

5. Set the ActionScript 2.0 class for the symbol within the Component Definition dialog box to `actionscriptbible.components.Slider`.

6. Click the OK button.

7. Select the Slider instance on stage.

8. Open the Component Inspector panel, and edit the `value` parameter.

When you test the movie, the slider value ought to reflect the value you assigned it in the Component Inspector panel. For example, if you assigned it a value of 50, the thumb bar ought to appear in the middle of the track.

Dispatching Events

One of the things you'll likely want to be able to do with components is have them dispatch events. For example, with the `Slider` component, it would be particularly useful if it would dispatch an event each time the value changes. That way you don't have to continually poll it to get the value, but you can add a listener that is alerted when the value changes. That is just one of a plethora of scenarios in which you are likely to want to have a component dispatch events.

You can configure a component class to dispatch events fairly simply using the `EventDispatcher` class. The `EventDispatcher` class is in the `mx.events` package, and it has a static method called `initialize()` that configures a class to dispatch events. All you need to do is to call the `initialize()` method from within the component class's constructor method and pass it a value of `this`. For example:

```
public function Slider() {
  mx.events.EventDispatcher.initialize(this);
  // ...Additional constructor code...
}
```

With that one piece of code, the class automatically inherits all the necessary properties and methods to be able to accept listeners and dispatch events to those listeners.

The `EventDispatcher.initialize()` method adds methods to the class prototype. It does so at runtime. That means the methods aren't defined within the ActionScript 2.0 class file or any of the classes from which it inherits. If you want to reference or call those methods without compiler errors, you need to tell the compiler not to throw an error. You can accomplish that by declaring properties with the datatype set to `Function`. There are two public methods, `addEventListener()` and `removeEventListener()`, and one private method, `dispatchEvent()`. The following code will tell the compiler that the methods are okay:

```
public var addEventListener:Function;
public var removeEventListener:Function;
private var dispatchEvent:Function;
```

Once the class is configured for dispatching events, you can dispatch an event from any other method using the `dispatchEvent()` method that it automatically "inherits." The `dispatchEvent()` method takes a single parameter — an object with the necessary event properties such as `type` and `target`. When called, the method then dispatches that object to all listeners:

```
dispatchEvent({type: "change", target: this});
```

Dispatching Events from the Slider Component

In this exercise, you build a new version of the Slider component from the previous exercise. In this updated version, the component dispatches events notifying listeners when the value has changed. That's more efficient than having to constantly poll the component.

1. Make a copy of the `Slider002` directory and its contents. Call the new directory `Slider003`. The files referred to in the rest of this exercise are from the new `Slider003` directory and its subdirectories.

2. Edit `Slider.as`, and make the changes to the code as shown in bold. (Only the first and last parts of the code are shown. The rest remains unchanged.)

```
class actionscriptbible.components.Slider extends MovieClip {

  private var _mThumbBar:MovieClip;
  private var _mTrack:MovieClip;
  private var _nValue:Number;
  private var _oMouseListener:Object;
  private var _nWidth:Number;
  private var _nHeight:Number;

  public var addEventListener:Function;
  public var removeEventListener:Function;
  private var dispatchEvent:Function;

  public function get value():Number {
    return _nValue;
  }

  [Inspectable(defaultValue=100)]
```

```
  public function set value(nValue:Number):Void {
    if(nValue > 100) {
      nValue = 100;
    }
    else if(nValue < 0) {
      nValue = 0;
    }
    _nValue = nValue;
    _mThumbBar._x = _nValue / 100 *
(_nWidth + .5 - _mThumbBar._width);
  }

  public function Slider() {

    _nWidth = 200;
    _nHeight = 10;

    mx.events.EventDispatcher.initialize(this);

          /*
          The middle code remains unchanged.
          */

  private function update():Void {
    _nValue = Math.round((_mThumbBar._x)/(_mTrack._width + .5 -
_mThumbBar._width) * 100);
    dispatchEvent({type: "change", target: this});
  }
```

3. Open Slider.fla, delete the ActionScript on the first keyframe of the Actions layer, and add the following code.

```
sldExample.addEventListener("change", this);

function change(oEvent:Object):Void {
  trace(sldExample.value);
}
```

When you test the movie, you'll notice that it only displays the value in the Output panel when the value changes.

Working with Compiled Components

Compiled components have several advantages:

✦ Compiled components don't add much to the compile time of the Flash document in which they are used, at least relative to the uncompiled versions.

✦ Compiled components have automatic live preview functionality. *Live preview* is the feature by which the component shows up in the authoring environment as it will look in the exported SWF.

✦ Compiled components are simpler to distribute because there are fewer symbols.

✦ Compiled components don't clutter the library of the Flash document in which they are used.

Compiling Clips

Typically, when you compile a component you export an SWC file, as you'll read in the next section. However, when you are working on components it's fairly inconvenient to have to export an SWC file, copy the file to a subdirectory of the `Components` directory, reload the Components panel, and copy an instance of the component from the Components panel into a new Flash document. It's much more convenient to simply convert the movie clip symbol associated with the component class into a new compiled clip for testing purposes. You can do so by selecting the movie clip symbol in the library, and then selecting the Covert to Compiled Clip option from the library menu. That will leave the movie clip symbol as it is so that it is still editable. It will add a new compiled clip symbol to the library, and it will convert instances on the stage to instance of the compiled clip. Compiled clip instances will have live preview enabled and otherwise behave much like compiled components.

Exporting SWC Files

SWC files are the compiled, distributable versions of components. You can install an SWC so that it is displayed in the Components panel. Exporting SWC files is as simple as converting symbols to compiled clips. Simply select the movie clip symbol in the library, and select Export SWC File from the library menu.

Using Live Preview

Live preview is a feature by which components can have SWF files associated with them so that the component instances display in the Flash authoring environment much as they would in the exported SWF. While it's possible to make a custom live preview SWF and associate it with a component, it is much simpler to let Flash handle that task. When you convert to a compiled clip or export an SWC, Flash automatically makes the live preview SWF and bundles it with the compiled component.

In order for live preview to work, however, you must have some artwork on the first frame of the component movie clip symbol. Live preview will only render the area of the component masked by the content on frame 1 of the symbol. Even if everything in the component is drawn or added with code, you must place some authoring time content on frame 1 of the symbol to act as a mask for the live preview.

In many cases, the artwork on frame 1 is there for the live preview mask, but you don't want it to get rendered at runtime. Therefore, by convention we place an instance of a rectangular movie clip on frame 1. We give that instance an instance name, and within the component class we can make it invisible within the component constructor. That way it makes sure the live preview mask works, but it isn't rendered at runtime.

Setting the Dimensions of a Component

Up to this point, the Slider component examples have not had any authoring time artwork. That is, just an empty movie clip instance shows up on the stage at authoring time, and it's not until runtime that you can see the component. However, once live preview is enabled there will be an authoring time preview. That means it will be possible to set the dimensions of the component using the Property inspector or the Free Transform tool.

When the dimensions are set at authoring time, you'll want those changes to be reflected at runtime. However, you typically don't want those transforms to be applied as linear scale transforms. That is, if you use the Property inspector to set the width of a Slider component instance to 400 rather than the default of 200, you want it to show up at runtime as 400 pixels wide, but not simply stretched. Instead, you'd probably expect the track to be drawn 400 pixels wide, while the thumb bar remains the normal dimensions.

Any authoring time transforms are applied as scale transforms — basically updating the _xscale and _yscale properties of the instance. That means that by default, authoring-time transforms will cause the component to look squished or stretched. If you don't want the component to appear stretched or squished, you can set the _xscale and _yscale properties to 100 (default) in the component class constructor method. However, that also means that the dimensions of the component will be the default rather than the dimensions set at authoring time. In order to correctly set the dimensions, you need to set the _xscale and _yscale properties to 100, but before that you can read the _width and _height properties and assign those values to variables you can use to draw the component to the proper dimensions. For example, consider the Slider component example. The default dimensions are 200 × 10. If the instance is transformed at authoring time to 400 × 10, then in the constructor you can read the _width and _height properties to retrieve those values, assigning them to variables or properties:

```
_nWidth = _width;
_nHeight = _height;
```

Then, after reading the _width and _height properties, you can set the _xscale and _yscale properties to 100:

```
_xscale = 100;
_yscale = 100;
```

That causes the component to be reset back to the default dimensions with no scale transform applied.

Next, you can tell the component to draw itself using the values recorded from the transformed dimensions. That way even though no scale transforms are applied, the component can draw itself as 400 × 10.

There's one more issue related to setting dimensions of a component. When the dimensions are set for the live preview SWF at authoring time (when a transform is applied via the Property inspector or the Free Transform tool), Flash looks for a specific method called setSize(). If that method is implemented in the component class, it is called. The setSize() method is passed two parameters: the width and the height to which the instance was transformed. Typically, in the setSize() method implementation, you tell the component to redraw itself. That way the live preview will transform correctly.

Adding Live Preview to the Slider Component

In this exercise you add live preview functionality to the Slider component.

1. Make a copy of the Slider003 directory and its contents. Call the new directory Slider004. The files referred to in the rest of this exercise are from the new Slider004 directory and its subdirectories.

2. Edit Slider.fla.

3. Create a new `MovieClip` symbol. Call it ComponentBox.

4. Edit the ComponentBox symbol, and using the Rectangle tool, draw a 200×10 rectangle with the upper-left corner at 0,0. The fill and line colors and styles are up to you because they won't be visible to the user.

5. Edit the Slider symbol.

6. Drag an instance of ComponentBox into Slider on the first frame at 0,0. Give it an instance name of _mComponentBox.

7. Edit `Slider.as` as follows. The changes are bolded.

```
class actionscriptbible.components.Slider extends MovieClip {

  private var _mThumbBar:MovieClip;
  private var _mTrack:MovieClip;
  private var _nValue:Number;
  private var _oMouseListener:Object;
  private var _nWidth:Number;
  private var _nHeight:Number;

// Declare _mComponentBox so the compiler doesn't thrown an
// error.
  private var _mComponentBox:MovieClip;

  public var addEventListener:Function;
  public var removeEventListener:Function;
  private var dispatchEvent:Function;

  public function get value():Number {
    return _nValue;
  }

  [Inspectable(defaultValue=100)]
  public function set value(nValue:Number):Void {
    if(nValue > 100) {
      nValue = 100;
    }
    else if(nValue < 0) {
      nValue = 0;
    }
    _nValue = nValue;
    _mThumbBar._x = _nValue / 100 *
(_nWidth + .5 - _mThumbBar._width);
  }

  public function Slider() {

    // Set _nWidth and _nHeight to the width and height of the
    // instance. By default that is 200 X 10. But if the user
    // changed the dimensions at authoring time, then the _width
    // and _height properties will reflect that.
```

```
    _nWidth = _width;
    _nHeight = _height;

    _xscale = 100;
    _yscale = 100;

    // Set the _width and _height of _mComponentBox to 0, and
    // make it invisible so it's not rendered at runtime.
    _mComponentBox._width = 0;
    _mComponentBox._height = 0;
    _mComponentBox._visible = false;

    mx.events.EventDispatcher.initialize(this);

    if(_nValue == undefined) {
      _nValue = 0;
    }

    _mTrack = createEmptyMovieClip("_mTrack",                    ⊃
getNextHighestDepth());
    _mThumbBar = createEmptyMovieClip("_mThumbBar",              ⊃
getNextHighestDepth());

    draw();

    _oMouseListener = new Object();
    _oMouseListener.onMouseMove = mx.utils.Delegate.create(      ⊃
this, update);

    _mThumbBar.onPress = mx.utils.Delegate.create(              ⊃
this, onPressThumbBar);
    _mThumbBar.onRelease = mx.utils.Delegate.create(            ⊃
this, onReleaseThumbBar);
    _mThumbBar.onReleaseOutside = _mThumbBar.onRelease;
  }

  private function draw():Void {
    _mThumbBar.clear();
    _mTrack.clear();
    _mThumbBar.lineStyle(0, 0, 0);
    _mThumbBar.beginFill(0, 100);
    _mThumbBar.lineTo(5, 0);
    _mThumbBar.lineTo(5, _nHeight);
    _mThumbBar.lineTo(0, _nHeight);
    _mThumbBar.lineTo(0, 0);
    _mThumbBar.endFill();
    _mTrack.lineStyle(0, 0, 100);
    _mTrack.lineTo(_nWidth, 0);
    _mTrack.lineTo(_nWidth, 5);
    _mTrack.lineTo(0, 5);
    _mTrack.lineTo(0, 0);
    _mTrack._y = _height/2 - 2.5;
    value = _nValue;
```

```
    }

    private function onPressThumbBar():Void {
        _mThumbBar.startDrag(false, 0, 0,
_mTrack._width - _mThumbBar._width + .5, 0);
        Mouse.addListener(_oMouseListener);
    }

    private function onReleaseThumbBar():Void {
        _mThumbBar.stopDrag();
        Mouse.removeListener(_oMouseListener);
        update();
    }

    private function update():Void {
        _nValue = Math.round((_mThumbBar._x)/
(_mTrack._width + .5 - _mThumbBar._width) * 100);
        dispatchEvent({type: "change", target: this});
    }

    public function setSize(nWidth:Number, nHeight:Number):Void {
        _nWidth = nWidth;
        _nHeight = nHeight;
        draw();
    }

}
```

8. In the Flash document, select the Slider symbol, and convert it to a compiled clip.

When you convert the symbol to a compiled clip, it will automatically add a new symbol called Slider SWF to the library, and it will make sldExample an instance of that new compiled clip. You ought to then see the live preview. If you change the value parameter in the Component Inspector panel, the live preview will reflect the new value.

Distributing and Installing Components

You can install components so that they show up in the Components panel. You can also distribute components so they install via the Extension Manager. The following sections show how that works.

Installing Components

Installing components is fairly simple. Export the SWC file to a subdirectory of the Components directory of Flash. The Components directory is in the following location:

```
Windows: C:\Documents and Settings\[Username]\Local Settings\Application
Data\Macromedia\Flash 8\en\Configuration\Components
```

For a component to show up in the Components panel, you must install the SWC in a subdirectory of the Components directory. The name of the subdirectory is the name of the folder within which the component will appear in the panel.

You can export the SWC file directory to the subdirectory of the `Components` directory, or you can use an MXP and the Extension Manager to install it there automatically. (MXP files are discussed in the next section.)

If Flash is running when you install a component, the component may not show up in the Components panel. You can either restart Flash, or you can simply select Reload from the Components panel menu.

Using the Extension Manager

The Extension Manager is a free application from Macromedia that manages any extensions (including components) for Macromedia products such as Flash, Dreamweaver, Fireworks, and the like. The Extension Manager can automatically run MXP files. MXP files are compressed archives that contain the extension to install along with any auxiliary and descriptor files.

You can also use the Extension Manager to make MXP files from a descriptor file called an MXI file. The MXI file uses an XML-based language to describe the extension. In the case of components, the extension is an SWC file. The MXI markup lets you specify many settings. At a minimum, however, you need to specify some basic descriptor data (type of extension, install location) and the extension files (the SWC files). You can read more about writing MXI files at `http://download.macromedia.com/pub/exchange/mxi_file_format.pdf`. However, for the purposes of building simple MXP files that will install Flash components, you can use an SWF utility at `http://www.rightactionscript.com/components/mxiutility.html`. The utility has a form that prompts you for the basic data for the MXI. It automatically generates the MXI code in the pane on the right. You can then copy and paste that code into a new text file on your computer. Name that file with the `.mxi` file extension.

The MXI file ought to be saved to the same location as the SWC file(s). If the Extension Manager is installed it ought to be configured to handle MXI files. If you double-click on the MXI file, it will run the Extension Manager, and you will be prompted to save a new MXP file — the archive format that you can distribute. Once you've saved the MXP file, you can double-click it, and the Extension Manager will automatically install the component.

 We'd like to know what you thought about this chapter. Visit `www.rightactionscript` `.com/asb/comments` to fill out an online form with your comments.

Summary

✦ Components are subclasses of the `MovieClip` class, either directly or indirectly.

✦ Component classes must be defined in external AS files and then associated with a `MovieClip` symbol.

✦ To build a component that utilizes the v2 UI component architecture, the class should extend `UIObject` or `UIComponent`, either directly or indirectly.

✦ You can dispatch events from your custom components by first initializing the class to do so.

✦ Component metadata can tell the Flash application about the component. Metadata can provide information about parameters to display, component icons, and more.

✦   ✦   ✦

Managing Data

Using Shared Objects

The SharedObject class allows you to store and retrieve persistent data on a client computer outside the player. That means that the data is then accessible to Flash later. You can use shared objects to store user preferences, to store application states (so the user can return to the same point later), and for many other purposes.

Saving Data with Shared Objects

One feature that is essential to applications of all kinds is the capability to save settings to the client machine. Almost every application on your computer has settings and preferences that you can modify to suit your needs. Flash itself has many preferences that allow you to customize your application in the way that you like it best. And when you modify an application's preferences, they are generally saved so that those settings are remembered the next time you open the program. Having the capability to modify preferences would not do much good if the data could not be saved. For many applications, these preferences are saved in text files within the application's installation on your computer. For traditional Web applications, such settings are saved in *cookies* (text files stored on the client computer that are managed by the browser).

ActionScript includes a class of objects called SharedObject. The SharedObject class actually provides two types of functionality — local shared objects and remote shared objects. A local shared object allows you to store and retrieve data on a client computer. This chapter covers local shared objects: Unless otherwise specified, each reference to a shared object or SharedObject instance in this chapter refers to a local shared object. Remote shared objects are one way in which your Flash application can interact with a FlashCom server. Remote shared objects are beyond the scope of this book.

A Little Bit of History

Most programs you run on your computer need only a single set of preferences (per user, that is) because the programs run only one application each, for the most part. But with Flash applications, the story is a little different. The Flash Player can have its own preferences for the player application itself. But because the player can run many applications (SWF files), you need to be able to save persistent data for each of those applications. For example, if a Flash application asks a user whether she wants to view an English version or a Spanish version, it is extremely useful to be able to save that selection so that the user doesn't have to select again next time she visits the site. Another example is one in which the Flash application is a movie that is a long presentation; if the user closes the player and then opens the movie again, it would be useful for the movie to be able to resume where it left off. The same player could play many other movies with different kinds of needs. Through the use of local shared objects, movies can create many different named pieces of persistent data saved to the client machine.

Understanding Local Shared Object Anatomy

A local shared object can refer to any one of several parts or can refer to the whole of those parts. The data for a local shared object is saved to a file on the client computer. For security purposes, the Flash movie's interface to this file is exclusively by way of the `SharedObject` class in ActionScript. This ensures that local shared objects are safe for the user and cannot be used maliciously.

In addition to the local file, a shared object also consists of a `SharedObject` instance in ActionScript. The instance provides the programmatic interface to the file. So a *local shared object* can refer to the file, the ActionScript instance, or both. Typically, the intended usage should be clear from the context.

Creating a Local Shared Object

The process for creating a new local shared object and opening a previously created local shared object is the same. The static method `getLocal()` opens a local shared object with the specified name if it can find one. Otherwise, it creates a new local shared object on the client. The method requires at least one parameter — the name of the local shared object file. And the method returns a new `SharedObject` instance that provides the programmatic interface to the local shared object file. Here is an example:

```
var lsoPreferences:SharedObject = SharedObject.getLocal("userPreferences");
```

The preceding example tells Flash to look for a local shared object file named `userPreferences` (the file extension for these files is `.lso`, but you don't include that as part of the parameter). If Flash finds this file, it opens it. Otherwise, Flash creates a new file with this name. In either case, Flash then creates a new `SharedObject` instance that interfaces with the file, and assigns that instance to a variable named `lsoPreferences`. You need to know the name of the file on the client computer only when creating or opening the file with the `getLocal()` method. From that point forward you need only to reference the `SharedObject` instance (in this example, `lsoPreferences`) in order to have an interface to that file.

Setting Values within the Shared Object

After you have successfully created a `SharedObject` instance, you can start to assign values to it that you want saved for later use. Each `SharedObject` instance has a `data` property. The `data` property is itself an object to which you can define properties that will be saved to the local shared object file. Properties assigned to the `SharedObject` object itself will not be saved to the client computer, only properties assigned to the object's `data` property. Here's an example that sets some values that will be stored to the file:

```
var lsoPreferences:SharedObject = SharedObject.getLocal("userPreferences");
lsoPreferences.data.backgroundColor = "red";
lsoPreferences.data.name = "A Reader";
lsoPreferences.data.title = "Yippee!";
```

You can add as many properties to data as you want. Furthermore, you can assign not only primitive datatypes, but also many types of objects to the `data` property so that they can be saved to the client computer for later retrieval. For example, the following is valid:

```
lsoPreferences.data.companyInfo = {name: "Widget Factory",                      ⊃
location: "New York"};
lsoPreferences.data.lastLogin = new Date();
```

Although you can save many types of objects to a local shared object, you cannot save all types. For example, you cannot save `MovieClip`, `Button`, `TextField`, `SharedObject`, or `Function` types, to name just a few.

Saving the Shared Object to the Client

After you have created a `SharedObject` and added values to it, the next step is to save the shared object to the client computer. This can be the easiest step in the whole process. You don't need to do anything, as a matter of fact. The Flash movie automatically attempts to save the shared object to the client computer when the `SharedObject` instance is deleted. This occurs under four conditions: when the player closes, when the movie is closed or replaced in the player, when the object is deleted using a `delete` statement, or when the object is garbage-collected after it falls out of scope. In any case, after you have created a `SharedObject` object, there will be an attempt to save the local shared object automatically. It is not, however, typically a best practice to rely on the automatic saving feature. Instead, you should explicitly tell Flash to save the data.

The `flush()` method allows you to save the shared object without the `SharedObject` object being deleted. Using the `flush()` method offers some serious advantages over the other, more passive approaches to saving the shared object. One advantage is that you can be assured that Flash attempts to save the data. There are some circumstances in which Flash might not actually save the data if you rely on the automatic saving features. When you call `flush()` you avoid that problem.

Another of the advantages of the `flush()` method has to do with file size considerations. Every shared object occupies a certain amount of disk space. By default, the Flash Player is set to accept all shared objects for a domain (more about domains later in this chapter), up to a total of 100KB. Users can configure their own players to accept shared objects for each domain totaling greater or less disk space. By right-clicking or ⌘-clicking on the Flash Player, you can choose settings to bring up the Macromedia Flash Player Settings dialog box (see Figure 31-1). The second tab in the dialog box, Local Storage, allows you to move a slider to choose from None, 10KB, 100KB, 1MB, 10MB, or Unlimited. Choosing 10KB through 10MB allows Flash movies to save all shared objects, up to a total of the selected disk space. Selecting Unlimited allows for shared objects to be saved as long as disk space is available. As soon as the total disk space allotted has been exceeded, the player prompts you (see Figure 31-2) for any shared objects that are being saved by a `flush()` call. Therefore, if the settings are configured with the slider set to None, you will be prompted for every attempted shared object saved with a `flush()` call.

Figure 31-1: The Macromedia Flash Player Settings dialog box allows you to specify how much disk space shared objects can use.

Figure 31-2: The dialog box prompts the user to allow or deny saving a shared object that will exceed the allotted disk space.

If you rely on a means other than `flush()` to save a shared object, the object will be saved only if it does not exceed the limit imposed by the user's player settings. Therefore, if saving the shared object is critical, you should use `flush()`. Here's an example:

```
var lsoPreferences:SharedObject = SharedObject.getLocal("userPreferences");
lsoPreferences.data.backgroundColor = "red";
lsoPreferences.data.name = "A Reader";
lsoPreferences.data.title = "Yippee!";
lsoPreferences.flush();
```

Even though you add the properties to the data object, you should still call the `flush()` method directly from the `SharedObject` instance.

But there are two more considerations you might take into account when saving the shared object. First, ask yourself whether the shared object is likely to grow in size over time. If the answer is yes, you might want to try to foresee how large the object is likely to get. For example, a local shared object file might start out at under 1KB. But if that shared object might potentially grow to 1MB in the future, you might want to allot that much space to it from the beginning. Otherwise, the users could possibly be prompted to accept the increase each time the object increases. You can specify a parameter in the `flush()` method that will set aside a certain amount of disk space for the object, whether it uses it all or not. The parameter is given in bytes. So, to set aside 1MB of space for the `lsoPreferences` shared object, you could use the following line of code (1,024 bytes in a KB and 1,024KB in a MB):

```
lsoPreferences.flush(1024 * 1024);
```

You can use the `getSize()` method to determine the size of the shared object at any point. It returns the size of the shared object in bytes:

```
trace(lsoPreferences.getSize());
```

The second consideration when saving a shared object is to test whether the object was actually saved. There are three ways that a shared object will not be saved. The first way is when the user has checked the Never ask again check box in the player settings. If this is checked, no shared objects are ever saved and the user is never prompted. The second is if the user has selected Unlimited from the player settings (by moving the slider to the far right), but there is not enough available disk space. This is an unlikely but possible occurrence. And the third way in which an object might not be saved is if the user is prompted but chooses to deny access to save the local shared object.

The flush() method actually returns a value to help you determine the status of the attempted save. It can return true, false, or "pending". If the value is true, the user has enough disk space allotted already, and the object was saved without prompting. If it is false, one of the first two conditions under which an object is not saved occurred. And if it is "pending", the user has been prompted about whether to allow the shared object to be saved. If the result is true, there is no problem. If the result is false, on the other hand, you might want to alert the user that the movie attempted to save some data, but failed. For example:

```
var bFlushStatus:Boolean = lsoPreferences.flush();
if(!bFlushStatus){
  tAlertMessage.text = "Please check your player settings to make sure you";
  tAlertMessage.text += "allow data to be saved to your computer.";
}
```

If the user has checked Never in the player settings, you might want to suggest the user change these settings and offer a button that opens the settings dialog box:

```
mSettings.onRelease = function(){
  System.showSettings(1);  // Open settings dialogue box.
};
```

Cross-Reference   You can learn more about the System object, including the showSettings() method, in Chapter 24.

If the flush() method returns "pending", it means that the user has been prompted to accept or deny the shared object. You might want to determine what the user selects. To do this, you need to set up an onStatus() event handler method for the SharedObject instance. The onStatus() method, if defined, is invoked for a SharedObject object after the user has selected either to accept or deny the shared object. Flash automatically passes the method a parameter. The parameter is an object with a code property having a value of either SharedObject.Flush.Failed (if the user chose to deny the shared object) or SharedObject.Flush.Success (if the user chose to accept the shared object). Here's an example of an onStatus() method definition for a SharedObject instance named lsoPreferences:

```
lsoPreferences.onStatus = function(oStatus:Object):Void {
  if(oStatus.code == "SharedObject.Flush.Failed") {
    trace("denied");
  }
  if(oStatus.code == "SharedObject.Flush.Success") {
    trace("saved it");
  }
};
```

Retrieving the Data

After you have created a shared object on the client computer, you will, of course, want to be able to retrieve it for use later. And actually, you already know how to do this because retrieving and creating are done with the same method: getLocal(). If the getLocal()

method finds an existing shared object with the name specified, it loads that shared object data into the `SharedObject` instance. Otherwise, the new shared object file is created and the `SharedObject` instance interfaces with it. Earlier in this chapter, you saw an example in which you created a new local shared object file named `userPreferences`. If that file already exists on the client's computer then the same code will open the file.

```
var lsoPreferences:SharedObject = SharedObject.getLocal("userPreferences");
```

It is a good idea to check to see whether the object already existed. If it existed, there will be at least one property in the `data` object. One way to test is as follows:

```
var bExists:Boolean = false;
for(item in lsoPreferences.data){
  bExists = true;
  break;
}
if(bExists) {
  trace("loaded shared object");
}
```

Conflicts, Domains, and Paths

As you have been learning about shared objects, you may have wondered about possible name conflicts between shared objects. For instance, what would happen if you made a Flash movie that used a shared object file named `userPreferences`, someone else made a movie using a shared object filed named `userPreferences`, and both were run on the same computer? Will there be a conflict? Will one overwrite the other? These are good questions. The answer is that if the Flash movies run on different domains (`themakers.com` and `person13.com`, for example), there would be no conflict. This is because all shared objects are saved under the domain from which the movie was run. Additionally, there is a local domain under which all shared objects that run locally (in a projector or stand-alone player) on your computer are saved.

Additionally, all shared objects are stored according to the path to the movie on the domain. For example, the movies `http://www.mydomain.com/A.swf` and `http://www.mydomain.com/flash/B.swf` will save the shared objects to different paths by default, and so each can create a shared object with the same name without a conflict between them.

This brings up an interesting discussion, however, about whether shared objects created by one movie can be accessible to another (see Table 25-1). Shared objects created by movies with the same domain and path are always accessible to one another. Shared objects created by movies with different domains are never accessible to one another. And shared objects created by movies with the same domain but different paths are accessible to one another if the path to the shared object is specified in the `getLocal()` method and is accessible to both movies. The `getLocal()` method accepts a second optional parameter after the shared object name that gives the path to the object.

Table 25-1: Accessibility of Shared Objects

	Same Domain	Different Domain
Same Path	Always	Never
Different Path	Sometimes	Never

For instance, if the two movies are on the same domain but with different paths, such as `http://www.mydomain.com/A.swf` and `http://www.mydomain.com/flash/B.swf`, shared objects created or opened in `A.swf` are opened with a default path of `/`, and shared objects created or opened in `B.swf` are opened with a default path of `/flash/`. The `A.swf` can access shared objects only with a path of `/` but `B.swf` can access shared objects with either the `/` or `/flash/` path. Likewise, if there was another movie at `http://www.mydomain.com/flash/moreflash/C.swf`, it would be able to access shared objects with paths of `/`, `/flash/`, or `/flash/moreflash/`. Therefore, if you want to have shared objects accessible to multiple movies on the same domain, you must make sure that the path of the shared object is accessible to all the movies. In this case, if you want the shared object to be accessible to all the movies you should make sure to create the shared object with a path of `/`. Then you also need to make sure that you specify this path each time you access the shared object as well. This would look something like:

```
var lsoInstance:SharedObject = SharedObject.getLocal("data", "/");
```

Remembering States with Shared Objects

In this exercise, you create a Flash application with randomly colored squares. The user can move the squares around on the stage by dragging them with the mouse. By way of a local shared object, Flash will remember the colors and coordinates of the squares so that when the application is run again it will have the same look as when it was last closed. Additionally, the application will have a reset button that allows the user to reset the squares to the original coordinates and assign new, random colors.

1. Open a new Flash document and save it as `blocks001.fla`.

2. On the first frame of the default layer of the main timeline, add the following code:

```
import actionscriptbible.drawing.DrawingUtilities;

// Get or make the local shared object.
var lsoBlocks:SharedObject = SharedObject.getLocal("blocks");

// Determine whether the shared object was previously saved or if
// it's new. The coordinates property is a custom property added
// by the code once the object is made, and so if it already
// exists then the shared object is not new.
var bExist:Boolean = (lsoBlocks.data.coordinates != undefined);

// Make 49 blocks (7 rows of 7.)
makeBlocks(49);

// If the shared object already existed place the blocks at their
// previous coordinates. Otherwise, initialize the coordinates
// and colors properties.
if(bExist) {
  placeBlocks(lsoBlocks);
}
else {
  lsoBlocks.data.coordinates = new Object();
```

```
        lsoBlocks.data.colors = new Array();
    }

  makeResetButton();


  function makeBlocks(nBlocks:Number):Void {
    var mBlock:MovieClip;
    var duDrawer:DrawingUtilities;
    var nColumn:Number = 0;
    var nRow:Number = 0;
    var nColor:Number;

    // Make a MovieClip object into which to draw the blocks.
    this.createEmptyMovieClip("mHolder",                           ⤶
  this.getNextHighestDepth());

    for(var i:Number = 0; i < nBlocks; i++) {

      // If a color was previously defined, retrieve it. Otherwise,
      // make a new random number and assign it to the colors array
      // within the shared object so it can be retrieved next time.
      if(lsoBlocks.data.colors[i] != undefined) {
        nColor = lsoBlocks.data.colors[i];
      }
      else {
        nColor = Math.random() * 0xFFFFFF;
        lsoBlocks.data.colors[i] = nColor;
      }

      // Make a MovieClip into which to draw the block.
      mBlock = mHolder.createEmptyMovieClip("mBlock" + i,          ⤶
  mHolder.getNextHighestDepth());

      // Draw a square with the fill color specified by nColor.
      duDrawer = new DrawingUtilities(mBlock);
      duDrawer.beginFill(nColor, 100);
      duDrawer.drawRectangle(35, 35, 15, 15);

      // Place the block in the grid.
      mBlock._x = nColumn * 40 + 50;
      mBlock._y = nRow * 40 + 50;
      nRow++;
      if(nRow > 6) {
        nRow = 0;
        nColumn++;
      }

      // Make the block draggable.
      mBlock.onPress = function():Void {
        this.swapDepths(this._parent.getNextHighestDepth());
```

```
      this.startDrag();
    };

    // When the block is dropped, assign the coordinates to the
    // corresponding element of the shared object coordinates
    // associative array.
    mBlock.onRelease = function():Void {
      this.stopDrag();
      lsoBlocks.data.coordinates[this._name] = {x: this._x,      ⤴
y: this._y};
      lsoBlocks.flush();
    };
  }
  lsoBlocks.flush();
}

function placeBlocks(lsoBlocksParam):Void {
  var oItem:Object;

  // Loop through each element of the coordinates associative
  // array.
  for(var sItem:String in lsoBlocks.data.coordinates) {
    oItem = lsoBlocksParam.data.coordinates[sItem];
    if(oItem != undefined) {

      // Place the corresponding block MovieClip object at the
      // coordinates stored in the array.
      mHolder[sItem]._x = oItem.x;
      mHolder[sItem]._y = oItem.y;
    }
  }
}

function makeResetButton():Void {

  // Make a MovieClip with a rectangle and a TextField that says
  // reset.
  this.createEmptyMovieClip("mReset",                            ⤴
this.getNextHighestDepth());
  mReset.createEmptyMovieClip("mBackground",                     ⤴
mReset.getNextHighestDepth());
  var duDrawer:DrawingUtilities =                                ⤴
new DrawingUtilities(mReset.mBackground);
  duDrawer.beginFill(0xFFFFFF, 100);
  duDrawer.drawRectangle(50, 20, 25, 10);
  duDrawer.endFill();
  mReset.createTextField("tLabel", mReset.getNextHighestDepth(),
0, 0, 50, 20);
  mReset.tLabel.text = "reset";
  mReset.tLabel.selectable = false;
  var tfFormatter:TextFormat = new TextFormat();
```

```
tfFormatter.align = "center";
mReset.tLabel.setTextFormat(tfFormatter);

// When the reset button is pressed, reinitialize the
// coordinates associative array and the colors array in the
// shared object. Remove the blocks, and redraw 49 new blocks.
mReset.onRelease = function():Void {
  lsoBlocks.data.coordinates = new Object();
  lsoBlocks.data.colors = new Array();
  mHolder.removeMovieClip();
  makeBlocks(49);
};
}
```

3. Save the document and test the movie.

4. Move some of the blocks to various locations on the stage.

5. Close the movie (the SWF file) and test the movie again. You should see the blocks in the same locations where you had previously moved them.

Web Resource

We'd like to know what you thought about this chapter. Visit `www.rightactionscript.com/asb/comments` to fill out an online form with your comments.

Summary

✦ Local shared objects allow for the creation of locally persistent data on the client computer. This is useful for saving Flash movie data that can be used the next time the movie is played.

✦ Shared objects are saved when the `SharedObject` object is deleted or when the `flush()` method is called. Calling `flush()` allows for the user to be prompted if the file cannot be saved automatically.

✦   ✦   ✦

Understanding LocalConnection Objects

The LocalConnection class allows for any movie in any player to communicate with any other movie in any other player on the same computer without needing any complicated JavaScript or other workaround solutions. The LocalConnection class doesn't care whether the movies are being run from the same domain. It doesn't care if they are being run from the same browser. All that is required is that the movies are running on the same computer and that one is set up to broadcast messages and the other is set up to listen for messages. This is useful in many scenarios. For example, an application deployed on the Web could consist of several SWF files that need to work in conjunction with one another. Using LocalConnection, the SWFs can communicate. LocalConnection also enables sophisticated logging such as the NetConnection Debugger panel used with Flash Remoting. There are many possibilities with LocalConnection. In this chapter, you'll learn how to work with the LocalConnection class.

Creating a Sending Movie

There are essentially two types of movies related to LocalConnection communication. The first of these is the *sending* movie. Sending can be accomplished in as few as two steps. The first step is obviously to create a LocalConnection object. The LocalConnection constructor requires no parameters, so you can create an object like this:

```
var lcSender:LocalConnection = new LocalConnection();
```

After you have created the object, you need only to call the send() method in order to send to a receiving movie. At a minimum, the send() method requires two parameters — the name of the connection over which you wish to send and the name of the method you want to invoke in the receiving movie. The name of the connection is a name you get to make up, but it must match the name of the connection over which the receiving movie is listening. Here is an example in which a LocalConnection object broadcasts a message over a connection named aConnection. The method invoked is named someMethod:

```
var lcSender:LocalConnection = new LocalConnection();
lcSender.send("aConnection", "someMethod");
```

Sending Parameters

You can send parameters to the receiving movie's method in addition to just calling the method. Any parameters that are added to the send() method after the required two (connection name and method name) are sent to the receiving movie's method as parameters. For example, this example shows how three parameters can be sent to the someMethod method:

```
var lcSender:LocalConnection = new LocalConnection();
lcSender.send("aConnection", "someMethod", true, "two", 3);
```

In addition to primitive datatypes, objects and arrays can be sent as parameters:

```
var lcSender:LocalConnection = new LocalConnection();
var oValues:Object = {a: "one", b: "two", c: "three"};
var aValues:Array = [1,2,3,4,5];
lcSender.send("aConnection", "someMethod", oValues, aValues);
```

Checking the Status of a Send

Every time a send() method is invoked, the object's onStatus() method is invoked if it has been defined. Flash automatically passes an object parameter to the onStatus() method. The parameter has a level property with one of two values: "status" or "error". If the value is "status", the send was successful. It does not necessarily mean that the method on the receiving end was successfully invoked. It merely means that the send was successful. If the value is "error", the send failed.

```
lcSender.onStatus = function(oStatus:Object):Void {
  trace(oStatus.level);
};
```

Creating a Receiving Movie

The receiving movie is slightly more complex than the sending movie, but not by much. There are only three steps in the simplest receiving movie:

1. Create a new LocalConnection object.

2. Define the method that will get called by the sending movie.

3. Instruct the movie to listen for messages on a particular connection.

The first step is the same as the first step in the sending movie, replacing lcSender with lcReceiver:

```
var lcReceiver:LocalConnection = new LocalConnection();
```

The second step merely defines the method for that LocalConnection object that will be called by the sending movie:

```
lcReceiver.methodName = function():Void {
  // Method body goes here.
};
```

And the last step is accomplished by the `connect()` method, which is invoked from the `LocalConnection` object you have created with a parameter of the name of the connection on which the movie should listen:

```
lcReceiver.connect(connectionName);
```

Here's an example that puts all three steps together:

```
var lcReceiver:LocalConnection = new LocalConnection();
lcReceiver.someMethod = function(){
  trace("method called");
}
lcReceiver.connect("aConnection");
```

Notice that the method name must match the method name that is passed as the second parameter of the `send()` method in the sending movie. And the connection name for the `connect()` method must match the connection name passed as the first parameter of the `send()` method of the sending movie.

Here's another example of a receiving `LocalConnection` object in which the method accepts three parameters.

```
var lcReceiver:LocalConnection = new LocalConnection();
lcReceiver.someMethod = function(a:Boolean, b:String, c:Number){
  trace(a);
  trace(b);
  trace(c);
}
lcReceiver.connect("aConnection");
```

The receiving movie continues to listen on a connection after the `connect()` method has been called, unless you instruct it not to. You can close a connection simply by calling the `close()` method from the `LocalConnection` object. For example:

```
lcReceiver.close();
```

Confirming Receipt

The `onStatus()` method can be used to determine whether a `send()` method call failed to connect to another movie. This can be useful. But it does not offer a way to know whether the method was successfully invoked on the receiving end. You can accomplish this by having the receiving movie communicate back to the sending movie. In this scenario, both movies must be set up for sending *and* receiving.

Here is an example. First, the code in the sending movie:

```
var lcSender:LocalConnection = new LocalConnection();
lcSender.send("aConnection", "someMethod", "confirmMethod");
lcSender.confirmMethod = function():Void {
  trace("the send was received");
};
lcSender.connect("bConnection");
```

And then, the code in the receiving movie:

```
var lcReceiver:LocalConnection = new LocalConnection();
lcReceiver.someMethod = function(sConfirmer:String){
  trace("method called");
  this.send("bConnection", sConfirmer);
}
lcReceiver.connect("aConnection");
```

Sending and Receiving across Domains

By default, `LocalConnection` objects attempt to communicate to the same domain. That is, if a sending movie is being run from `www.person13.com`, it defaults to broadcasting to other movies on `www.person13.com`. With just a few changes, however, you can configure movies to send and receive messages across domains so that, for example, a movie on `www.person13.com` can send to `www.themakers.com`.

The Sending Movie

The sending movie requires only one modification to send to another domain. The first parameter of the `send()` method (the connection name) can be modified in one of two ways. Either you can prefix the domain to which the command is to be sent, or you can use a connection name that starts with an underscore. Each works in a similar, but slightly different manner.

When a connection name neither prepends a domain nor starts with an underscore, Flash automatically converts the connection name to `localDomain:connection`. The domain is always the superdomain—the domain minus the subdomain such as www. For example, if the following is run from `www.person13.com`, Flash automatically converts the connection name to `person13.com:aConnection`.

```
lcSender.send("aConnection", "someMethod");
```

If we know we want to send the call to a Flash movie running from `www.joeylott.com`, we can prefix the connection name with `joeylott.com` as follows.

```
lcSender.send("joeylott.com:aConnection", "someMethod");
```

The preceding works well when you want to send only to Flash movies running on a specific domain. However, if you want to send the calls to movies running on any domain, it won't work. In those cases, you can use a connection name that starts with an underscore. If the connection name starts with an underscore, Flash doesn't automatically prefix the domain. The following will send to any Flash movie from any domain as long as it is listening on `_aConnection`:

```
lcSender.send("_aConnection", "someMethod");
```

The Receiving Movie

The receiving movie also requires a few modifications if you want it to receive calls from sending movies in different domains. Unlike the sending movie, you cannot prefix the connection name of a receiving movie with a different domain. Unless the connection name starts with an underscore, Flash automatically prepends the receiving movie's domain to the connection name, and you cannot tell it to do otherwise. For example, if the receiving movie is running from `www.person13.com`, the following connection is interpreted by Flash as `person13.com:aConnection`:

```
lcReceiver.connect("aConnection");
```

As long as the sending movie is either running from `www.person13.com` as well or the sending movie has a connection name of `person13.com:aConnection`, the calls will get picked up by the receiving movie in such a case. If the sending movie uses a connection name with an underscore as the first character, the receiving movie must also use the same connection name with the starting underscore.

However, just because the receiving movie receives the call, that doesn't mean it will then necessarily do what it was instructed by the sending movie. By default, the movie may receive calls, but it *accepts* calls only from the local domain. You can also allow other domains using the `allowDomain()` method.

When a receiving movie receives a communication from a sending movie, the `allowDomain()` method, if defined, is automatically invoked. The method is automatically passed a parameter naming the domain of the sending movie. You can then determine whether the sending domain is in a list of allowed domains and return `true` or `false`. If `allowDomain()` returns `true`, the method specified by the sending movie is called. If `allowDomain()` returns `false`, the method is not called. Here is a simple way to allow all domains:

```
lcReceiver.allowDomain = function(sDomain:String):Boolean {
  return true;
};
```

Of course, as was already stated, allowing all domains to send to your movie could prove to be a bad idea because it allows for anyone to send to your movie. So, a better idea is to check to make sure the sending movie is in a domain from a "whitelist." This example shows an `allowDomain()` method that allows connections only from `themakers.com`.

```
lcReceiver.allowDomain = function(sDomain:String):Boolean {
  return (senderDomain == "themakers.com");
};
```

You can easily allow connections from multiple domains. For example:

```
lcReceiver.allowDomain = function(sDomain:String):Boolean {
  return (sDomain == "person13.com" || sDomain == "themakers.com");
};
```

Additionally, `LocalConnection` objects have a method that returns the domain of the current movie. This can be useful for allowing the local domain to send in addition to others. The `domain()` method requires no parameters and returns a string of the current movie's domain:

```
lcReceiver.allowDomain = function(sDomain:String):Boolean {
  return (sDomain == "person13.com" ||
sDomain == "themakers.com" ||
sDomain == this.domain());
};
```

Figure 32-1 is a diagram that illustrates which sending and receiving movie combinations will work.

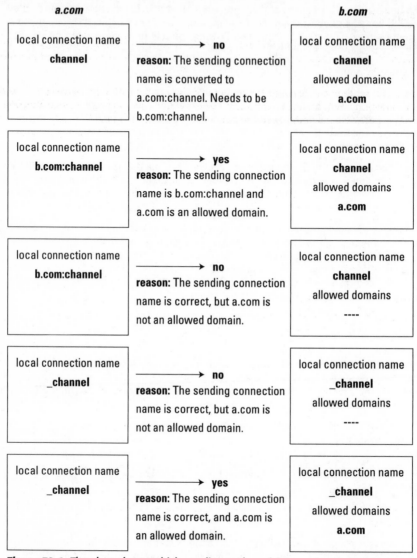

a.com		b.com
local connection name **channel**	⟶ **no** reason: The sending connection name is converted to a.com:channel. Needs to be b.com:channel.	local connection name **channel** allowed domains **a.com**
local connection name **b.com:channel**	⟶ **yes** reason: The sending connection name is b.com:channel and a.com is an allowed domain.	local connection name **channel** allowed domains **a.com**
local connection name **b.com:channel**	⟶ **no** reason: The sending connection name is correct, but a.com is not an allowed domain.	local connection name **channel** allowed domains ----
local connection name **_channel**	⟶ **no** reason: The sending connection name is correct, but a.com is not an allowed domain.	local connection name **_channel** allowed domains ----
local connection name **_channel**	⟶ **yes** reason: The sending connection name is correct, and a.com is an allowed domain.	local connection name **_channel** allowed domains **a.com**

Figure 32-1: The chart shows which sending and receiving movie parameters will work.

Web Resource We'd like to know what you thought about this chapter. Visit `www.rightactionscript.com/asb/comments` to fill out an online form with your comments.

Summary

✦ Flash movies can communicate with other Flash movies with the `LocalConnection` class of objects. `LocalConnection` allows a sending movie to call a method in a receiving movie.

✦ By default, the `LocalConnection` object allows connections only between movies on the same domain. However, with some changes in the sending and receiving movies, communication can occur between movies on different domains.

✦   ✦   ✦

Programming with the XML and LoadVars Classes

In this chapter, you learn about transferring data in and out of Flash movies using XML objects and LoadVars objects. You learn how to create the objects, load data, and send data.

If you don't know what XML is, this chapter also covers the basics from technical specifications to uses. By the end of this chapter, you should have a firm understanding of what XML is and how to work with XML data in Flash.

Working with XML

XML, which stands for Extensible Markup Language, is one of the standards for sharing and exchanging data. If you plan to do any work in which your Flash movie interacts with a web server, chances are good that sooner or later you are going to want to be able to parse and work with XML data. In fact, XML is an integral part of many of the emerging technologies in the Internet industry. For example, the Web services trend utilizes XML. Flash itself uses XML for many aspects — from custom tools and behaviors to the contents of the Action toolbox.

To effectively work with XML in Flash, you need to familiarize yourself with the XML class. On one hand, because you will likely be importing XML data into your Flash movie, the XML class offers methods for parsing through an imported XML document. On the other hand, there are occasions in which you will want to send XML data out of the Flash movie to another application. And using the XML class you can actually define a new XML document within your Flash movie.

There are a great many things for which you can use XML in your Flash applications — everything from using news streams, user management, content listings, and even chat rooms. But first you need to understand what XML is — how it is structured and what the rules are. There are plenty of books out there on XML. There are books with more pages than this one that are dedicated entirely to the subject, so it is not our intention to cover all there is to know about XML. But in the next few sections, you learn the basics you need to get up and running.

XML's Origins

If you are familiar with HTML, XML will look very familiar to you. That's because they are actually a lot like cousins. HTML, which stands for HyperText Markup Language, was developed using a very large and complex metalanguage named SGML, or Standard Generalized Markup Language. Metalanguages are languages used for creating other languages. The SGML specification is a massive document that includes syntaxes for handling a wide variety of data types and formats, and involves some fairly esoteric rules. For the kind of basic markup required to render the simple text content of web pages, the SGML standard presents an unnecessarily steep learning curve. So, HTML was developed as a simpler subset of SGML.

However, HTML served a very specific purpose. It was originally intended for formatting academic physics articles. But, as you well know, HTML quickly became the vehicle for much more than just physics documents. HTML became the way to display all kinds of content on the Web. The difficulty is that HTML is a poor way of organizing and sharing data. So in 1996, a team was formed to bring SGML to the Web.

The initial efforts of the team resulted in an awareness that SGML was far too huge for use on the Web. So, the next step was to create a new language that satisfied the requirements that had been set forth. The product was XML, a scaled-down version of SGML that met the need for simplicity while retaining the necessary features of SGML — namely, extensibility and the capability to give meaningful context to data.

One of the primary differences between HTML and XML is that HTML is not extensible. This means that HTML is limited to a set of predefined tags. On the other hand, XML has infinite possibilities for tags. In fact, the tags are invented entirely by the author of the document.

The other big distinction between HTML and XML is that the purpose of XML tags is to give meaningful *context* to the data they contain, whereas HTML is largely about *presentation* of that data. For instance, the following code in HTML will display the data in a particular way, but does not lend any particular meaning or significance to that data:

```
<h1>This is an example of HTML</h1>
```

On the other hand, tags in XML are used to provide semantic markup — to indicate the meaning of content. In fact, XML has nothing to do with the presentation of data. XML is only about organizing data and giving context to that data. The following example of XML code uses an arbitrarily named tag to give meaning to the data it contains:

```
<author>Joey Lott</author>
```

As XML emerged in 1998, it began to attract a lot of attention. And although it was initially intended as a way to bring SGML to the Web, it was clear that the applications of this data format were far-reaching. You will see XML being used all over the place, not just on the Web.

Uses of XML

Now that you know a little about the origins and the structure of XML, it is time to take a look at what XML is really designed for. As you've already seen, the purpose of XML is simply to present data in a meaningful and structured way. XML has nothing to do with the presentation of that data, in contrast with its cousin HTML. The idea is simply to have a universal format for sharing and storing data.

✦ **Exchanging Data** — Today there is an ever-increasing number of gadgets, gizmos, and devices that send and receive data. Computers, cell phones, PDAs, and many more are all demanding data. But that data needs to be shared by many platforms. News services, for example, must be able to provide current headlines to dozens or maybe even hundreds of platforms. There are a dizzying number of protocols and languages and architectures out there. Despite the fears of some that a technology giant will successfully create a monopoly in the market, there are still many thriving, competing options out there. So, what is a company such as a news service to do? There is no way to force everyone to use the same platform. So the idea is to instead create a format that is platform-independent. That is what XML is.

XML has quickly become the standard by which data is shared among platforms. All that is required is that an XML *parser* (the part of a program that can interpret XML data) be written for the platform that is receiving that data. And now, even Flash has an XML parser. That means that in no time, you too can be sending and receiving XML data.

✦ **Storing Data** — Another great use of XML is simply to store data. Application, environment, and user preferences can be stored in this format for easy processing each time the parameters need to be used. For instance, you might want to store a user's data in XML format for easy retrieval. You could always store it in some other format, but then you might well have to write your own parser. If you use XML, the parsing is handled for you.

Writing Well-Formed XML

Now that you have an idea of what XML is, you need to know what it looks like. XML leaves a lot of control to the author, but it still must conform to some basic rules. XML that conforms to these rules is called *well formed*. Making sure that your XML documents are well formed is important. HTML can afford to be more forgiving because HTML is interpreted by only a few applications, namely Netscape, Internet Explorer, Mozilla Firefox, and other web browser applications. So, as long as those applications can make sense of the HTML, no matter how jumbled, everything is okay. But remember, one of the beautiful things about XML is that it is so portable. With so many potential parsers of your XML document, it is far better to make sure that your document adheres to the rules than to try and make sure all the parsers can overlook its errors.

There are many rules for writing well-formed XML. Not all of these are necessarily important to Flash's implementation, and so they are outside of the scope of this book. But there are several elements that you must be aware of when working with well-formed XML with ActionScript:

✦ **An XML declaration** — A tag that gives some basic information about the XML version being used.

✦ **Tags** — The basic elements of an XML document must be correctly authored and matched.

✦ **Attributes** — Tags can contain attributes that provide additional information.

✦ **DTD** — The Document Type Definition defines a set of rules for the XML document.

XML Declaration

The very first thing that must appear in a well-formed XML document is the declaration. The declaration should look like this:

```
<?xml version="1.0"?>
```

This tag describes the version of the document. This will become much more important as newer versions are released.

The ActionScript XML class actually doesn't have problems dealing with documents without this declaration. However, you should likely include this declaration in your documents because it might be needed by another application trying to use the document.

Tags

As was mentioned previously, the tags in XML are completely arbitrary and up to the author of the document. Tags in HTML are limited to a predefined set such as the following table data and bold tags:

```
<td></td>
<b></b>
```

However, tags in XML can be anything you want. For example, the following are perfectly valid tags in XML:

```
<star></star>
<car></car>
<books></books>
```

The purpose of tags in XML is to describe the data they contain. But although you have a lot of leeway in determining the names of your tags, you have to follow some very specific (but simple) rules for formatting them.

First of all, all tags must be closed. This is in contrast to HTML, in which closing tags is often optional. For example, the following HTML will likely still render properly in most browsers even though there are no closing tags:

```
<head>
this is the heading
<body>
this is the body
```

But XML is not so easygoing about it. You must close the tags. To convert the tags from the HTML example into legal tags in XML, it would look like this:

```
<head>this is the heading</head>
<body>this is the body</body>
```

XML allows you to use a shortcut to open and close a tag in one go if there is no data for that tag. This is useful for tags that contain no nested tags or data, but rather contain only attributes (see the next section for more information on attributes) or exist just to satisfy the DTD (see the section on DTD for more information on this subject). You can write the following opening and closing tag pair:

```
<car></car>
```

like this:

```
<car />
```

The next important rule when it comes to tags in XML is that they must be properly nested. In HTML, you can improperly nest tags and get away with it:

```
<b><font color="red">this is some text</b></font>
```

But this simply doesn't work in XML. You must make sure that nested tags are closed first. The HTML example is written in well-formed XML like this:

```
<b><font color="red">this is some text</font></b>
```

Additionally, it is important to note that all well-formed XML documents have only one main tag, known as the root element or root node. All other tags (elements, nodes) must be nested within the root element.

```
<?xml version="1.0"?>
<people>
  <person>
    <name>Jerry</name>
  </person>
</people>
```

In this example, the root element is `people`.

Note   The ActionScript XML parser treats both tags and text as nodes. To distinguish between the types of nodes, there is a property for each node: 1 for an element (a tag) and 3 for a text node.

Attributes

In the previous examples borrowed from HTML was a tag that looked like this:

```
<font color="red">Some Text Here</font>
```

The name of the tag in this example is `font`. But this tag has something else besides just a name. It also has what is called an *attribute*. The attribute in this example is `color`. Often, whether to use attributes or nested tags is simply a matter of preference. For example, the following XML tags:

```
<book>
  <author>Mark Twain</author>
  <title>Huckleberry Finn</title>
</book>
```

can be written in one tag using attributes:

```
<book author="Mark Twain" title="Huckleberry Finn">
```

And both attributes and nested tags can be used together. For example:

```
<article publication="Daily News">
  <title>How to Use ActionScript to Better Your Life</title>
  <body>
```

```
      This is the body of the article. Blah Blah Blah.
   </body>
</article>
```

The decision to use attributes or nested tags, or both, is often just a matter of personal preference. You might find that one way works best for you in a particular situation.

DTD

ActionScript's XML parser is what's known as a *non-validating parser*. This means that it does not make sure the XML document it is parsing adheres to its own rules. But any good XML document has a set of rules known as a DTD, or Document Type Definition. Because ActionScript's XML parser is non-validating, it will be completely forgiving if your XML document does not adhere to its own DTD. This is good in the sense that it is very flexible. It can be a downside, however, if you are not careful that your XML document is correctly authored according to its DTD.

Note   A DTD is a set of rules used by validating XML parsers to ensure that an XML document is well formed. XML is commonly utilized as a protocol for sharing data between applications that know little to nothing about one another. Therefore, one application cannot necessarily know what another application will send it. But the DTD can tell the application whether or not the XML follows its own rules. As already stated, Flash Player's XML parser is non-validating, so Flash cannot do much with a DTD. However, you can compose a DTD and send it to another application via Flash Player's XML class.

Because ActionScript does not pay attention to the DTD when parsing the document, this chapter does not spend much time on it. However, it is still a good idea to know what the DTD is and what it looks like. You will want to know how to create a DTD for the XML documents you create and export from Flash to other applications.

There are two types of DTDs. One is stored in a file separate from the XML document. This chapter does not discuss that kind because it is not relevant to the discussion of XML with regard to Flash and ActionScript. The second kind of DTD is part of the XML document itself.

All internal DTDs typically follow the document declaration. The DTD is enclosed within a single tag:

```
<!DOCTYPE rootNodeName[
...DTD tags...
]>
```

So if the root node were named library, the DTD would look something like this:

```
<!DOCTYPE library[
...DTD tags...
]>
```

Within this tag are the rest of the tags that define the structure of the XML document. These tags can get very involved, so this section covers only the basics.

The following code shows an example of an XML document with an internal DTD.

```
<?xml version="1.0"?>
<!DOCTYPE library
   <!ELEMENT library  (book)>
```

```
        <!ELEMENT book    (author, title)>
        <!ELEMENT author  (#PCDATA)>
        <!ELEMENT title   (#PCDATA)>
    ]>
    <library>
    <book>
    <author>Mark Twain</author>
    <title>Huckleberry Finn</title>
    </book>
    </library>
```

As you can see, the `<!ELEMENT>` tag defines an element within the XML document. In this example, the first element, `library`, has a nested element, `book`. The next tag defines that nested `book` element as having two nested elements: `author` and `title`. Each of the next two `<!ELEMENT>` tags define the tags as containing `PCDATA`, which stands for parsed character data. In other words, these tags contain important data that the parser should read.

Using XML Objects

Anytime you want to work with XML data in ActionScript, you must first instantiate an `XML` object. To do so, you need only to call the `XML` constructor function in a `new` statement:

```
    var xmlData:XML = new XML();
```

This creates an empty `XML` object, which you can use to load data from an external source, or which you can use to create and export your own XML document within Flash. However, if you are planning to create your own XML document, most of the time it is easier to first create a string containing the value of the XML document and then pass that parameter to the `XML` constructor, like this:

```
    var sXml:String = "<?xml version=\"1.0\"?><test>great</test>";
    var xmlData:XML = new XML(sXml);
```

An alternative to this technique of populating an `XML` object is to use the `parseXML()` method. This method takes a single argument: an XML string to be parsed into the object. Any existing tree in the object is lost and replaced with the XML tree resulting from the parsing of the specified string:

```
    var sXml:String = "<blah></blah>";
    var xmlData:XML = new XML();
    xmlData.parseXML(sXml);
```

As you look at this example, the use of the `parseXML()` method might not be immediately clear. In fact, if it does the same thing as simply passing the string to the constructor, why use the method at all? There are a few good reasons why you might want to use the method.

First, if you have an existing `XML` object and you want to replace the existing XML tree in the object with the result of a parsed string, using `parseXML()` is a good idea. Otherwise, you have to delete the object and create a new one.

The second good reason for using `parseXML()` is when you want to set the `ignoreWhite` property to `true`. (The `ignoreWhite` property is covered later in this chapter.) Setting the property to `true` after the string has been parsed does no good. But in order to have an object for which to set the property, you must first call the constructor. In this case, you would definitely want to use the parseXML() method:

```
var sXml:String = "\n\n<blah>\n\n</blah>"; // contains newlines
var xmlData:XML = new XML();
xmlData.ignoreWhite = true;
xmlData.parseXML(sXml);
```

If there is an error parsing a string (or parsing a loaded document), the object's status property is automatically set to indicate what kind of error occurred. Table 33-1 shows the possible values for the status property.

Table 33-1: Values for the status Property

Value	Meaning
0	Successfully parsed
-2	Error in CDATA section
-3	Error with XML declaration
-4	Error with DTD
-5	Error with comment
-6	Error with element (tag)
-7	Out of memory (file is probably too big)
-8	Error with attribute
-9	Starting tag with no ending tag
-10	Ending tag with no starting tag

The following code demonstrates how the status property can help indicate what kind of error occurred in parsing:

```
var sXml:String = "<aTag>some value";
var xmlVal:XML = new XML();
xmlVal.parseXML(sXml);
trace(xmlVal.status);
```

In this example, the Output panel displays the following:

```
-9
```

This indicates that there is a missing ending tag somewhere in the string being parsed. And, indeed, there is. If you fix the following string by adding the closing tag, the status property is set to 0 to indicate that the parse was successful:

```
var sXml:String = "<aTag>some value</a>";
var xmlVal:XML = new XML();
xmlVal.parseXML(sXml);
trace(xmlVal.status);
```

Traversing the XML Tree

Once an XML object has been created, you will want to be able to extract the data from it. Using the properties of the XML object, you can read the data in the object's hierarchy by traversing the data tree and then reading the values of elements and attributes.

Reading the XML Declaration and the DTD

The xmlDecl and docTypeDecl properties allow you access to the XML declaration and the DTD, respectively. You can read these properties as in the following example:

```
var sXml:String = "<?xml version=\"1.0\"?>
<!DOCTYPE library[<!ELEMENT book (#PCDATA)>]>";
var xmlVal:XML = new XML(sXml);
trace(xmlVal.xmlDecl);
trace(xmlVal.docTypeDecl);
```

This example outputs the following to the Output panel:

```
<?xml version="1.0"?>
<!DOCTYPE library[<!ELEMENT book(#PCDATA)>]>
```

Understanding the XMLnode Class

The XMLnode class is the superclass to the XML class, but more importantly, it is the class definition for all elements of an XML object. In the next section, you learn about reading the child nodes of an XML object. Each child node is an XMLnode instance. The XMLnode class and the XML class have the same methods and properties, with a few exceptions.

The XMLnode class does not include the loaded, status, contentType, or ignoreWhite properties. Nor does it include the load(), send(), or sendAndLoad() methods. The reason for this is that XMLnode objects never send or load data, but XML objects do.

In almost every case, it is not important to know that a child node of an XML object is an XMLnode object instead of an XML object. After all, you probably never will try to load data into a child node. It *does* make a difference, however, when you want to work with an XML object recursively.

Reading Child Nodes

You have seen that XML documents are built according to a hierarchy, in which elements are nested within other elements. This hierarchy is often called the *document tree*. Nested elements are called the *children* or *child elements* of a *parent element*.

Note

The firstChild, lastChild, nextSibling, previousSibling, and childNodes properties are all read-only properties. This means that you can use them to read the existing data in an XML object, but you cannot use them to set values and establish new relationships within the object. There are methods presented later in this chapter that are used for doing that.

When you are stepping through the hierarchy of your XML object or traversing the document tree, it is most useful to be able to retrieve the child nodes of a parent element. For instance, if the current element you are working with is the book element in the following XML snippet

```
<book>
  <author>Mark Twain</author>
  <title>Huckleberry Finn</title>
</book>
```

you would likely want to read the names and values of its child nodes. One way to do this is to use the `firstChild` or `lastChild` properties, and then step through all the child nodes by accessing the `nextSibling` or `previousSibling` properties of the child elements. (Sibling elements are simply other elements within the same hierarchy in the tree and that are nested within the same parent element.)

Continuing the same example, the `firstChild` property of the `book` element is a reference to the `author` node. Likewise, the `lastChild` property of the `book` element is a reference to the `Huckleberry Finn` text node. Remember, both tags and text elements are nodes in the ActionScript XML parser.

The `firstChild` property of an `XML` object that has been parsed from a string or document without any additional spaces or a DTD is the root node. When there are spaces in the string or a document before the root node, or if the string or document contains a DTD, the `firstChild` of the object might not always be the root node. Later in this chapter, you see how to outline a way to handle this uncertainty.

```
var sXml:String = "<book><author>Mark Twain</author>
<title>Huckleberry Finn</title></book>";
var xmlVal:XML = new XML(sXml);
var xnRootNode:XMLNode = xmlVal.firstChild;  // <book />
var xnAuthorTag:XMLNode = xnRootNode.firstChild;  // <author />
var xnAuthor:XMLNode = xnAuthorTag.firstChild;  // Mark Twain
var xnTitleTag:XMLNode = xnAuthorTag.nextSibling;  // <title />
var xnTitle:XMLNode = xnTitleTag.firstChild;  // Huckleberry Finn
```

You can also access the `title` tag directly from its parent node, `book`, as the `lastChild` property of the parent object:

```
xnTitleTag = xnRootNode.lastChild;
```

In that case, you can reference the `author` node relative to the `xnTitleTag` object as the `previousSibling` property of the `xnTitleTag` object:

```
xnAuthorTag = xnTitleTag.previousSibling;
```

Also, notice that as was mentioned previously, text nodes are treated as children of the elements that give them context. In this case, the text nodes with the values of `Mark Twain` and `Huckleberry Finn` are the `firstChild` (and, as it turns out also the `lastChild`) properties of the `xnAuthorTag` and `xnTitleTag` objects, respectively.

The `childNodes` property is a collection, or an array, of references to all the child nodes of an `XML` object. This is an alternative to using the `firstChild` and `nextSibling` approach for traversing an XML tree. The following code shows how to use the `childNodes` property to create an array of `XMLnode` objects, each being a child of a parent node.

```
var sXml:String = "<?xml version=\"1.0\"?>
<cars><car><make>Honda</make><model>Accord</model>
<year>1985</year></car></cars>"
var xmlVal:XML = new XML(sXml);
var xnRootNode:XMLNode = xmlVal.firstChild;  // <cars>
var xnCar:XMLNode = rootNode.firstChild;  // <car>
var aChildren:Array = car.childNodes;  // child nodes of <car>
for(var i:Number = 0; i < aChildren.length; i++){
 trace(aChildren[i].toString());
}
```

This example writes the following to the Output panel:

```
<make>Honda</make>
<model>Accord</model>
<year>1985</year>
```

Each element of the array created by the childNodes property is an XMLNode object, and you can therefore access the methods and properties of those objects, as well. You can also access the firstChild properties to display the text node values. The for loop is rewritten like this:

```
for(var i:Number = 0; i < aChildren.length; i++){
 trace(aChildren[i].firstChild.toString());
}
```

And the result in the Output panel is as follows:

```
Honda
Accord
1985
```

When you are working with an element, you might simply want to check to see whether it has child elements before doing anything else with it. You can test to see whether an element has child nodes by invoking the hasChildNodes() method from the element. It returns true if child nodes exist, and false if there are no child nodes:

```
if(xmlVal.firstChild.hasChildNodes()){
    trace("the root element has children!");
}
```

Caution

This section demonstrates very simplified examples of working with an XML object by using the firstChild, lastChild, nextSibling, and previousSibling properties. These examples assume that you are already certain of the formatting of the string or document that is being parsed into the XML object. On many occasions, you will want to perform additional checks to verify the data you are working with. This includes removing whitespace nodes and the like to eliminate the possibility of offsetting your results. These issues are examined more closely later in this chapter.

Reading Parent Nodes

Every element has exactly one parent node, with the exception of the main element, or root element (which has no parent node). This is different from child nodes. A single node can have many child nodes, and, therefore, there are a handful of different properties for XML objects to access these child nodes. But with only one parent node per element, there is need for only one property to access that parent node. The parentNode property is a reference to an element's parent. If the node has no parent (that is, it is the root element), the property is null.

```
<book>
  <author>Mark Twain</author>
  <title>Huckleberry Finn</title>
</book>
```

For example, in the previous XML snippet, the `author` and `title` elements have the same `parentNode` property value of `book`.

This property is not immediately as useful in traversing the XML tree as the child and sibling properties. But it is a useful method for determining the relationship between two nodes:

```
if(xnOne.parentNode == xnTwo.parentNode){
  trace("the nodes are siblings!");
}
```

Reading Element Attributes

In many XML documents, you will have elements with attributes. Remember, an attribute is a parameter within the tag. For instance, `color` is an attribute of the `crayon` element in this XML tag:

```
<crayon color="blue"/>
```

In the example used to demonstrate the `childNodes` property, we used an `XML` object made from a string with lots of nested tags. A more nicely formatted version of that XML text looks like this:

```
<?xml version=\"1.0\"?>
<cars>
  <car>
    <make>Honda</make>
    <model>Accord</model>
    <year>1985</year>
  </car>
</cars>
```

However, you can easily enough rewrite this so that the `car` tag uses attributes to define the same data:

```
<car make="Honda" model="Accord" year="1985"/>
```

Just as you can create a collection of child nodes using the `childNodes` property, you can create a collection of attributes for a given element with the `attributes` property. The difference is that the collection that `childNodes` creates is an indexed array. The `attributes` collection is an associative array. The following is the example from the previous section that was rewritten to use attributes and the `attributes` property to create a collection.

```
var sXml:String = "<?xml version=\"1.0\"?><cars>
<car make=\"Honda\" model=\"Accord\" year=\"1985\"/></cars>"
var xmlVal:XML = new XML(sXml);
var xnRoot:XMLNode = xmlVal.firstChild;  // <cars>
var xnCarTag:XMLNode = xnRoot.firstChild;  // <car>
var oAttribs:Object = xnCarTag.attributes;  // attribs of <car>
for(var sAttrib:String in oAttribs){
  trace(sAttrib + ":" + oAttribs[sAttrib]);
}
```

This example writes the following to the Output panel:

```
make:Honda
model:Accord
year:1985
```

Notice that, because the `attributes` property is an associative array, a `for in` loop is used instead of a regular `for` loop.

Reading Element Information

All tags and text are considered to be nodes in XML. Thus, there are two *types* of nodes that can be parsed into an XML object: tags (or tag elements) and text. Each of these types has an ID. Tag elements have an ID of 1, whereas text nodes have an ID of 3. Every XMLNode object has a `nodeType` property that reveals what type of node you are dealing with. The following code shows a few examples of reading the `nodeType` property for different elements.

```
var sXml:String = "<book><author>Mark Twain</author>
<title>Huckleberry Finn</title></book>";
var xmlVal:XML = new XML(sXml);
var xnRoot:XMLNode = xmlVal.firstChild;
trace(xnRoot.nodeType);
var xnAuthorTag:XMLNode = xnRoot.firstChild;
trace(xnAuthorTag.nodeType);
var xnAuthorName:XMLNode = xnAuthorTag.firstChild;
trace(xnAuthorName.nodeType);
```

It writes the following to the Output panel:

```
1
1
3
```

Note   Whitespace nodes such as carriage returns and other special characters are treated as text nodes (`nodeType` of 3).

When a node has a `nodeType` value of 1, the `nodeName` has the value of the tag name. For instance, the following code appended to the preceding code:

```
trace(xnRoot.nodeName);
trace(xnAuthorTag.nodeName);
```

writes the following to the Output panel:

```
book
author
```

However, when a node has a `nodeType` value of 3, the `nodeName` has a `null` value:

```
trace(xnAuthorName.nodeName);
```

and results in the following in the Output panel:

```
null
```

So, how do you retrieve the value of a text node? There is yet another property of XMLnode objects that contains the value of the text node. Therefore, this property is `null` for all objects with a `nodeType` of 1. For objects with a `nodeType` of 3, the `nodeValue` contains the text value of the node:

```
trace(xnAuthorName.nodeValue);
```

which results in the following in the Output panel:

```
Mark Twain
```

Building a Document Tree

You can construct your own XML objects and build their document trees within ActionScript based on environment and user data. You have seen how to use the constructor function and the parseXML() method to parse a string into the object's document tree. But it can also be convenient to be able to build the document tree node by node. The methods of the XML object enable you to do exactly this, as explained in the following sections.

Writing the XML Declaration and DTD

The xmlDecl and docTypeDecl properties are read-write properties, and you can, therefore, use these properties to set the values of either the XML declaration or the DTD:

```
var xmlVal:XML = new XML();
xmlVal.xmlDecl = "<?xml version=\"1.0\"?>";
xmlVal.docTypeDecl = "\"<!DOCTYPE library[<!ELEMENT book (#PCDATA)>]>";
```

Creating Nodes

Once you've created a new XML object, you next want to create one or more new nodes to add to its document tree. You'll recall that all nodes are instances of the XMLNode class. Therefore, in order to create these nodes you can use the XMLNode constructor. The XMLNode constructor allows you to create either tag nodes or text nodes by specifying the type ID of 1 or 3, respectively. The following shows an example of each:

```
var xnNewElement:XMLNode = new XMLNode(1, "author");
var xnNewTextNode:XMLNode = new XMLNode(3, "Mark Twain");
```

That's all there is to it. You now have a new element, <author>, assigned to the variable xnNewElement. And you have a new text node, Mark Twain, assigned to the variable xnNewTextNode. The only catch is that the nodes don't have any parent, children, or siblings. In other words, the nodes do not have a location in the data tree within the XML object. To assign a location, you need to use either the appendChild() or the insertBefore() methods.

The appendChild() and insertBefore() methods do pretty much just what their names suggest. The appendChild() method adds the specified XMLNode instance to the end of the current child nodes of the object from which it is called. The appendChild() method is essential because you need it in order to create the root node within an XML object. The following code shows an example of this.

```
var xmlBook:XML = new XML();
var xnRoot:XMLNode = new XMLNode(1, "book");
xmlBook.appendChild(xnRoot);
trace(xmlBook.toString());  // Displays: <book />
```

The insertBefore() method also inserts an XMLNode object as a child node of the object from which it is called. But instead of appending it to the end of the child node list, the node is inserted just before the node that is referenced as the second parameter of the method. The following code shows an example that uses both appendChild and insertBefore() to populate an XML object.

```
var xmlBook:XML = new XML();
var xnRoot:XMLNode = new XMLNode(1, "book");
var xnAuthorTag:XMLNode = new XMLNode(1, "author");
```

```
var xnAuthorName:XMLNode = new XMLNode(3, "Mark Twain");
var xnTitleTag:XMLNode = new XMLNode(1, "title");
var xnTitle:XMLNode = new XMLNode(3, "Huckleberry Finn");
xmlBook.appendChild(xnRoot);
xnRoot.appendChild(xnAuthorTag);
xnRoot.insertBefore(xnTitleTag, xnAuthorTag);
xnAuthorTag.appendChild(xnAuthorName);
xnTitleTag.appendChild(xnTitle);
trace(xmlBook.toString());
```

This example constructs the XML object and then writes the following to the Output panel:

```
<book><title>Huckleberry Finn</title><author>Mark Twain</author></book>
```

Creating Attributes

Every XMLNode object has an attributes property that is an associative array of the object's attributes. The property is read-write, meaning that you can use the property to add attributes and update values for a node. In this section, you learn how to add attributes to an element.

The preceding section demonstrated how to create a new element. Once the element is created, you can add attributes by adding array elements to the attributes property. The following code demonstrates how to add three attributes (a, b, and c) to the element created in the previous section:

```
xnNewElement.attributes.a = "attribute a";
xnNewElement.attributes.b = "attribute b";
xnNewElement.attributes.c = "attribute c";
```

You can also choose to write the same thing as the follows:

```
xnNewElement.attributes["a"] = "attribute a";
xnNewElement.attributes["b"] = "attribute b";
xnNewElement.attributes["c"] = "attribute c";
```

If you were to then view the string value of the following element:

```
trace(xnNewElement.toString());
```

you would see that it looks like this:

```
<firstElement c="attribute c" b="attribute b" a="attribute a" />
```

Cloning Nodes

There are occasions when you want to make copies of an XML or XMLNode object or parts of the data from the object. You can use the cloneNode() method to do exactly this. The following code illustrates how to use cloneNode().

```
var xmlBook:XML = new XML("<book><author>Mark Twain</author>    ↵
<title>Huckleberry Finn</title></book>");
var xmlCopy:XML = new XML();
var xnRootCopy:XMLNode = xmlBook.firstChild.cloneNode();
xmlCopy.appendChild(xnRootCopy);
trace(xmlCopy.toString());
```

This results in the following being written to the Output panel:

```
<book />
```

You might have expected it to have copied all the child nodes of the root element from `xmlVal`. But the method does not clone all the child nodes recursively by default. You must specify in a parameter passed to the `cloneNode()` method. The parameter can be `false` for no recursive cloning or `true` for recursive cloning:

```
var xmlCopy:XML = new XML();
var xnRootCopy:XMLNode = xmlBook.firstChild.cloneNode(true);
xmlCopy.appendChild(xnRootCopy);
trace(xmlCopy.toString());
```

Now the Output panel will display the following:

```
<book><title>Huckleberry Finn</title><author>Mark Twain</author></book>
```

Removing Nodes

Opposite the methods for creating nodes is `removeNode()`. This method's name pretty much says it all. Invoke the method from the node you want to remove. It takes no parameters:

```
// removes root element and all children
xmlVal.firstChild.removeNode();
```

Loading and Sending XML

One of the powerful characteristics of XML is that it is a platform-independent means of sharing data. Although you can use XML effectively strictly within the confines of your Flash movie, an intended use of the `XML` object is to be able to load XML data in from external sources, as well as send XML data to external sources. Doing so enables you to create sophisticated applications that can call upon external applications to perform specific tasks. For example, many e-commerce web applications rely on shipping-and-handling calculations being performed by the servers of the shipping company they use. Often, this data is transmitted between the servers by means of XML. Using an `XML` object and sending and loading that data allow you to incorporate systems that draw upon the databases and resources of other applications.

Loading XML

Using `parseXML()` works well for parsing XML strings existing within ActionScript already. If you want to use this same method for XML documents outside of your Flash movie, you have to go through a slightly more involved process to first load the string into your movie. But the `load()` method takes care of everything for you. The `load()` method loads an XML document from an external source into your Flash movie and parses it to create the XML tree for your `XML` object.

The `load()` method takes a single parameter: the URL (as a string) to the XML document you want to load. The following code shows an `XML` object that loads a document called `data.xml` from the same directory as the movie that is playing.

```
var xmlVal:XML = new XML();
xmlVal.load("data.xml");
```

The reference can also be a full URL. Remember that the Flash movie runs on the client computer and has no access to the server's local file system. For example, if the movie is playing at www.person13.com, the `load()` method call might look like this:

```
xmlVal.load("http://www.person13.com/data.xml");
```

This raises an important point when working with loading XML documents into Flash. By default, ActionScript allows you to load XML documents only from the same domain as the movie that is playing. This is for security reasons. Obviously, this has implications in Flash movies. How can you then share data with external sources that are on remote servers? For possible solutions, see the section "Sharing Data Across Domains" later in this chapter.

Note   External XML data does not necessarily have to come from a static XML file with an XML extension. In fact, you can call a CGI, JSP, or other kind of script or program that generates dynamic XML data.

Receiving Loaded Data

XML loads asynchronously. This means that the load() method initiates the loading, but it does not wait until the entire XML document has loaded before going to the next line of code. Otherwise a Flash application could hang on an XML load() command for seconds or even minutes depending on the amount of data and the connection. Instead, the XML data loads in the background as the rest of the application continues. Therefore, you need a way to be able to handle the data once it has been loaded. Fortunately, the onLoad() method of the XML object is invoked when the data has been loaded and the data has been parsed into the XML tree. All you need to do is define the method with the actions that you want it to complete once the data has loaded, and Flash takes care of calling it at the appropriate time.

When Flash calls the onLoad() method of an XML object, it passes it a Boolean parameter indicating whether the data was successfully loaded and parsed. Also, of course, within the method definition, you can refer to the XML object with the this keyword. The following code shows an example of a very simple onLoad() method.

```
xmlVal.onLoad = function(bSuccess:Boolean):Void {
  if (bSuccess){
   trace(this.toString());
  }
  else{
   trace("document failed to load or parse.");
  }
};
```

In this example, the function checks to see whether bSuccess is true. If it is, that means the document was loaded and parsed, and the function uses the trace() function to write the XML to the Output panel. If the document failed to load, the function writes an error message to the Output panel.

Monitoring Load Progress

In some cases, you might want to monitor the progress of loading XML. The getBytesLoaded() and getBytesTotal() methods return the loaded and total bytes for the loading XML data. You can use setInterval() to set up a polling system that continually checks to see what the progress is. For example:

```
function checkXMLProgess(xmlObj:XML):Void {
  var nLoaded:Number = xmlObj.getBytesLoaded();
  var nTotal:Number = xmlObj.getBytesTotal();
  var nPercentage:Number = 0;
  if(nTotal > 0) {
```

```
    nPercentage = nLoaded/nTotal * 100;
  }
  tProgress.text = nPercentage + "% has loaded";
  if(nPercentage == 100) {
    clearInterval(nProgInterval);
  }
}

var nProgInterval:Number = setInterval(checkXMLProgress, 100, xmlVal);
```

Sending XML Data

Sending XML data can be, of course, just as important as loading XML data. And, often sending and loading are used in combination. There are two methods for sending XML data. The send() method will convert the XML object's data to an XML string and send it to the specified URL. The sendAndLoad() method, as the name suggests, will do the same thing as the send() method, but it also waits for a response from the server and loads that data back into Flash.

The send() method requires at least one parameter — a string specifying the URL to which you wish to send the XML data. For example:

```
xmlData.send("xmlSubmitter.cgi");
```

The send() method also allows you to specify a browser window into which you'd like to load the server response. For example, the following sends the XML data to the server and then displays the response in a new browser window:

```
xmlData.send("xmlSubmitter.cgi", "_blank");
```

The sendAndLoad() method requires two parameters. The first parameter is the URL to which you want to send the data. The second parameter is the XML object you want to have handle the response. The response XML object should have an onLoad() event handler method defined.

```
xmlData.sendAndLoad("xmlSubmitter.cgi", xmlLoader);
```

Setting Request Headers

By default, when your invoke the send() or sendAndLoad() methods, the data is sent with a set of default request headers. For example, the default Content-Type header is "application/x-www-form-urlform-encoded". Even though the header would suggest that the content being sent is URL-encoded, the fact is that it is not. The default value is set in this manner to make the data compatible with common application servers (Cold Fusion, ASP, and so on). However, you may find that the Content-Type header needs to be changed for it to be compatible (depending on which application server you are sending your data to). You might also want to add your own request headers.

You can set the request headers with the addRequestHeader() method. You should call this method *before* sending the data. If you want to set one header, you can call the method in the following format:

```
xmlObj.addRequestHeader(headerName, headerValue);
```

For example, you can set the Content-Type request header to text/xml as follows:

```
xmlVal.addRequestHeader("Content-Type", "text/xml");
```

If you want to set multiple headers at the same time, you can pass the method a single parameter. The parameter should be in the form of an array in which the elements alternate between header name and header value.

```
xmlObj.addRequestHeader([headerName, headerValue,
    headerName, headerValue, ...]);
```

Note   You can also use the `contentType` property to set the Content-Type header. For example:

```
xmlVal.contentType = "text/xml";
```

Dealing with Whitespace

You have learned how the ActionScript XML parser parses whitespace nodes (including tabs, carriage returns, and newlines) in an XML document as text nodes. This can be problematic when you are trying to work with the data because it can produce all kinds of unexpected nodes. Fortunately, you can use the `ignoreWhite` property to remedy this problem.

All XML objects default to `ignoreWhite` being `false`. This means that all XML objects parse whitespace nodes into the XML object by default. However, if you set the property to `true`, whitespace nodes are discarded during parsing. This does not mean that any text node with whitespace in it is discarded; it means that any text node that is *only* whitespace is discarded. Because the whitespace nodes are discarded during the parsing of the document or string into the object's data tree, the `ignoreWhite` property must be set to `true` *before* any parsing takes place in which you want whitespace nodes to be discarded.

Loading and Sending Data with LoadVars

The LoadVars class enables you to send and load variables in your Flash applications. The API for sending and loading with the LoadVars class is very similar to the API for sending and loading with the XML class. The difference between LoadVars and XML objects is simply that an XML object works with XML data and the LoadVars class works with name-value pairs.

Creating a LoadVars Object

You must create a LoadVars object before you can do anything with the class. The way to create an object is simply to call the constructor function in a new statement. The function requires no parameters:

```
var lvData:LoadVars = new LoadVars();
```

Loading Data

Loading data using LoadVars objects works very similarly to loading data using XML objects. The first step is to create the object. Next, you call the load() method from the object, passing it a parameter specifying the URL where the loaded data can be found. As with XML objects, the loading process is asynchronous, so you can define an onLoad() method that's called when the data has been loaded (or failed to load).

The data that can be processed by the LoadVars object must be in URLEncoded, name-value pair format. In other words, each name and value should be separated by an equals sign (=), each name-value pair should be separated by an ampersand (&), and non-alphanumeric characters should be escaped. For example, perhaps you want to load data into Flash concerning the book *Huckleberry Finn* by Mark Twain. The data should appear in the following format.

```
title=Huckleberry%20Finn&author=Mark%20Twain
```

The data can be stored in a text file or can be generated by a server-side script. But either way, the data must be returned in this same format.

The following code shows an example of using a `LoadVars` object to load data from a text file and then display the results in the Output panel.

```
var lvData:LoadVars = new LoadVars();
lvData.load("bookResult.txt");
lvData.onLoad = function(bSuccess:Boolean):Void {
  if(bSuccess){
    trace(this.title);
    trace(this.author);
  }
};
```

Assuming that the content of `bookResult.txt` is the Huckleberry Finn example, the Output panel then displays the following:

```
Huckleberry Finn
Mark Twain
```

There are two important things to point out in this example about how `LoadVars` objects work. First, each name-value pair in the loaded data is automatically converted into a property of the `LoadVars` object from which the `load()` method was called. In this example, therefore, once the data is loaded, the `lvData` LoadVars object has two new properties: `title` and `author`. The second important thing to notice is that escaped characters are automatically unescaped. In this example, the spaces in the values were escaped and replaced with %20 in the loaded data. However, without having to directly invoke the `unescape()` function, the values are automatically unescaped.

Like `XML` objects, `LoadVars` objects have the `getBytesLoaded()` and `getBytesTotal()` methods to provide you with a means of determining how much data has been received by the movie so far.

Sending Data

Again, like `XML` objects, data can be sent using a `LoadVars` object with either the `send()` or `sendAndLoad()` method. Each method works by sending all the custom properties (variables) of the object to a URL specified as a parameter. In both methods, the variables are sent via `POST` unless otherwise specified.

The `send()` method requires only one parameter: the URL to which the variables should be sent. For example, you could use a `LoadVars` object to send a user's responses to a survey to the server.

```
var lvData:LoadVars = new LoadVars();
lvData.favoriteColor = "red";
lvData.favoriteSong = "Row, Row, Row Your Boat";
lvData.favoriteCar = "Ford Model T";
lvData.send("http://www.myserver.com/cgi-bin/surveyResults.cgi");
```

You can also choose to specify two other optional parameters when using the `send()` method: the target browser window for the results of the send and the HTTP `send` method. If the target parameter is omitted or set to `null`, no results are displayed. You might want to specify a target if you are sending to a CGI script, for instance, that generates some HTML that you want to display. (See the `XML` object `send()` method description for more specifics on using a target.) And, as we already mentioned, the `send()` method uses the `POST` method to send the variables, unless otherwise specified. If the server-side script expects the data to be sent using `GET`, you can specify that as the third parameter. Here is an example of the `send()` method call from the preceding code, modified so that the variables are sent using `GET`, and the results are displayed in a new browser window:

```
lvData.send("http://www.myserver.com/cgi-bin/surveyResults.cgi",
            "_blank", "GET");
```

The `sendAndLoad()` method works very similarly to the `XML` object `sendAndLoad()` method. It requires two parameters: the URL to which to send the variables and the `LoadVars` object to which the results should be loaded. As with the `send()` method, you can also specify a third, optional parameter for the HTTP method used to send the variables. The following code shows the results of a request loaded into another `LoadVars` object and processed by that object's `onLoad()` method.

```
var lvData:LoadVars = new LoadVars();
var lvReceived:LoadVars = new LoadVars();
lvData.favoriteColor = "red";
lvData.favoriteSong = "Red Roses for a Blue Lady";
lvData.favoriteCar = "Ford Model T";
lvData.sendAndLoad("http://www.myserver.com/cgi-bin/surveyResults.cgi",
                   lvReceived);
lvReceived.onLoad = function(bSuccess:Boolean):Void {
  if(success){
    trace(this.responseMessage);
    trace(this.processTime);
  }
};
```

Also like `XML` objects, `LoadVars` objects have a `addRequestHeader()` method. The method allows you to set request headers before sending data. For example, by default, the Content-Type header has a value of `application/x-www-urlform-encoded`, but if the script to which the data is being sent requires a different content type, you can set the header to that value with `addRequestHeader()`. See the discussion of the `XML` class's `addRequestHeader()` method for more details.

Sharing Data across Domains

Flash movies have built-in security that restricts access to send or load content from any source that is on a different domain from where the Flash movie is playing. With Flash Player 7 and higher, the domains must match exactly, including protocol and port. In other words, a movie playing at `http://www.themakers.com` can load any data from the same domain, but it cannot load data from `http://www.person13.com`, and it cannot even load data from `http://data.themakers.com`. This can be problematic. You might want an SWF file running on one domain to be able to send and load data on another domain. You have three options:

✦ **Create a crossdomain.xml policy file**—This requires that you have access to the domain from which you want to load data or to which you want to send data. If you do have access to that domain, this is the suggested technique.

✦ **Set up DNS aliasing**—This is not a likely candidate for most. It involves a certain level of expertise and access that many folks do not have. The idea is that on the DNS servers that your server uses, you can set up an alias to a remote server so that it appears to be in the same domain. This topic is beyond the scope of this book and is not covered here.

✦ **Use a proxy script**—This is probably the option that will be available to most users. You can use a proxy script that will reside on the same domain as your Flash movie, and simply relay the data between the Flash movie and the remote domain.

Configuring a Policy File

You can read more about configuring a policy file in Chapter 24.

Working with a Proxy Script

You can write your own proxy scripts if you have the knowledge and the desire, or you can use the ones included on the web site. You can write a script using any language that you want. If you want to write a proxy script using PHP, take a look at `www.flash-db.com` for a tutorial on this very subject.

On The Web Site

You will find two proxy scripts on the web site that accompanies this book. One is written in ColdFusion (`proxy.cfm`) and the other is written in Perl (`proxy.cgi`, written by Arun Bhalla). Both of these scripts are provided to you as is. You are free to use them and modify them as you desire.

The basic idea with the proxy script is that your ActionScript code remains pretty much the same (just a few minor changes), except that your `sendAndLoad()` method calls the proxy script instead of the script or content on the remote domain. The proxy scripts included on the web site require that you specify the location of the remote resource as a parameter to the script. The parameter name should be `location`. Also, you can optionally pass the script a parameter named `httpmethod` that specifies either `GET` or `POST` for how the rest of the parameters should be passed to the remote resource.

If you use the proxy script to send or load with an `XML` object, you should append the `location` and optionally the `httpmethod` parameters to the proxy script URL as a query string, as shown here:

```
var xmlVal:XML = new XML();
xmlVal.load("http://www.localserver.com/proxy.cfm?location= ⏎
http://www.remoteserver.com/somedoc.xml");
```

When you use the proxy script to request a remote resource with a `LoadVars` object, you should always use the `sendAndLoad()` method, whether simply sending or also loading. You should then add `location` and optionally `httpmethod` properties to the `LoadVars` object. Here is an example:

```
var lvData = new LoadVars();
var lvReceiver = new LoadVars();
```

```
lvData.a = 1;
lvData.b = 2;
lvData.c = 3;
lvData.location = "http://www.remoteserver.com/testProxy.cfm";
lvData.httpmethod = "GET";
lvData.sendAndLoad("http://www.localserver.com/proxy.cfm", lvReceiver);
lvReceiver.onLoad = function():Void {
  for(var item:String in this) {
    trace(item + ": " + this[item]);
  }
};
```

You can still specify an HTTP method parameter when calling the `sendAndLoad()` method. However, the value you specify for the `sendAndLoad()` parameter affects only how the parameters are sent to the proxy script, not how the proxy script sends the parameters to the remote resource.

We'd like to know what you thought about this chapter. Visit `www.rightactionscript` `.com/asb/comments` to fill out an online form with your comments.

Summary

✦ XML (Extensible Markup Language) is a language with user-defined tags that give context to data. You can use XML to store and transfer data in a platform-independent format while still retaining both the values as well as the significance of those values in a universally understood structure.

✦ XML looks similar to HTML in structure, but more strictly enforces rules by which the language must be structured. XML that adheres to the rules is known as *well-formed* XML.

✦ Using the `XML` object, you can use ActionScript to create, send, load, and parse XML documents.

✦ `LoadVars` offers an alternative to the `MovieClip` object `loadVariables()` method. `LoadVars` is advantageous because, among other things, it allows for an `onLoad()` method that is called when data is loaded.

✦ `LoadVars` and `XML` objects send and load data in the same ways. Each allows you to define an `onLoad()` method that is called automatically when the data is loaded. The difference between the `LoadVars` and `XML` objects is in the format of the data that they handle. `XML` objects handle XML data, and `LoadVars` objects handle data in name-value pairs.

✦ ✦ ✦

Using Persistent Socket Communications

In the previous chapter, you saw what you can do with XML data in your Flash movies using XML objects. In this chapter, you learn how to use the XMLSocket class to create persistent channels of communication by which you can transfer your XML data (as well as non-XML data) to and from a server. You can use it to create applications that require constant, low-latency communication between client and server, such as chat programs and multiplayer games.

The XMLSocket class allows you to create persistent connections with a server. These connections are called *sockets*. You can then send and receive XML data across this communication channel. To understand why this is advantageous, you first need to understand the alternative model.

Ways of Transmitting Data

In order to understand the XMLSocket class, it is important to understand where it fits into the context of data transfer with Flash. There are two protocols by which data is transmitted using Flash: Data can be sent by using HTTP or by using sockets. In this section, you learn about both, and how they operate differently.

Transmitting Data via HTTP

HTTP (Hypertext Transport Protocol) is used to transfer much of Web data. The model is a simple one — a client such as a web browser connects to a remote server and makes a request. The server then returns the requested data, if found, and the connection is closed. This model works great for most Web applications such as HTML pages. It is quite efficient to open only a channel and send data when necessary, such as when a user clicks a link. But this model is not very good for creating low-latency applications such as a multi-player game.

The difficulty with using HTTP for an application such as a multiplayer game is that such an application requires that the client make very frequent requests to always have updated information about player positions and scores. This is not only inefficient, but it simply doesn't work well. A lag of only a few seconds can throw off important calculations. Perhaps this model works for a game of online chess. But when creating an action game, a few seconds can make a big difference.

Every technique for creating client-server interactivity that you have learned so far in this book uses HTTP. This includes sending and loading data using XML objects as well as LoadVars objects. And, in fact, even Flash Remoting, a technology you learn about in Chapter 36, uses HTTP. So, if Flash is to be able to create low-latency client-server applications, there has to be another solution.

Transmitting Data via Sockets

The answer to the problem of using HTTP for communication is simply to avoid it altogether. Instead, you can use TCP (Transmission Control Protocol) directly to send data as a stream across an open channel between the client and server. HTTP is an application-layer protocol that is actually built on top of TCP. Most Internet protocols are developed on top of TCP, as a matter of fact. For example, FTP (File Transfer Protocol) is an application-layer protocol built on top of TCP for file transmission. Bypassing the higher-level protocols such as HTTP enables lower-level (more) access to the functionality of TCP.

This type of communication (TCP) is implemented today in many computer (Internet) applications (such as instant messenger programs) in order to maintain a persistent connection between a client and a server. You can think of it as operating in much the same the way that a telephone works. One end initiates the call. After the other end has received the call, the connection remains until the conversation is over.

The fundamental component of this type of communication is what is called a *socket*. A socket is a basic software representation of a point for network communication. That means that there is a physical point on the computer through which data is sent and received, and the socket provides a way to control that point through code. You can create a connection between two sockets over which data can be sent. This is the general idea behind the use of the XMLSocket class in ActionScript. You can create a connection between a socket on the client computer and the server computer that will persist. Thus, any time data is sent from the client, it is received on the server and vice versa because each is listening for any data being transmitted across the socket connection.

There are several different interface types when it comes to sockets. But the only kind you will be working with when it comes to ActionScript is the *stream socket,* which means that a connection must first be established; then data can be sent, and received in the order it was sent. The connection remains alive until it is instructed to close.

The Socket End Points

Every socket connection has two end points: the server and the client. Again, this is similar to the telephone model whereby a client telephone must connect to a switchboard. Each of the two points performs slightly different tasks. The client socket can connect only to a server socket and send and receive data over that connection. The server, however, can (and most often should) accept multiple client connections, and serves as a hub through which data is relayed appropriately.

Note It is important to understand that two Flash movies running on two different machines have no native ability to communicate with one another. Sometimes people will naturally assume that this is a possibility, but in order for this to be able to happen there must be additional infrastructure. This chapter describes how to do this using XMLSocket objects with a socket server.

The Server

The trick to working with sockets with ActionScript is not on the ActionScript side of things at all. In fact, the XMLSocket class is relatively simple and straightforward. The most difficult part of working with sockets with ActionScript is setting up the server side of things.

When we refer to a client and a server in this discussion on sockets, we are referring to the computer that instantiates the connection and the sending of data as the client, and the computer that receives and processes the data as the server. In reality, they are simply two ends of a communication channel. And in fact, because computers have thousands of sockets, the client and the server applications can even reside on the same machine.

Discussions in this book always refer to the Flash component as the client. Multiple Flash movies are thought of as multiple clients, and as you will see, working to develop clients is easy in ActionScript. Most of the work is taken care of already by the XMLSocket class. However, when it comes to developing the server application, your job is not quite so easy. You have many options available for creating a server application. You can write the application in any number of languages, from C to Perl to PHP. If you know about socket programming (or you want to learn), you can develop your own socket server. For most developers, however, there is little reason to reinvent the wheel, so to speak. There are a number of socket servers that have already been developed. Table 34-1 shows a partial list of some of the available socket servers. Some of the listed servers are available for enterprise-level applications, and some are intended for fewer users.

Table 34-1: Example Socket Servers

Server Name	Language	URL
Unity Socket Server	Java	www.moock.org/unity/
FlashSock	Java	http://sourceforge.net/projects/flashsock/
MultiServer	Java	www.shovemedia.com/multiserver/
Swocket	Python	swocket.sourceforge.net/
FlashNow	C	www.nowcentral.com/

Note If you develop your own socket server, you need to know that all data sent to the server is terminated by the zero byte ("\u0000").

Socket Security

Most computers place restrictions on port numbers below 1024 because most of these ports are commonly used for serving Web content (HTTP on port 80), FTP (21), Telnet (23), Mail (25), and other typical services that might run on a computer. To prevent hackers from tampering with these services, most server machines already prevent socket connections to these ports. However, regardless of the computer configuration, the XMLSocket object attempts to make a socket connection only to ports 1024 and up.

Another restriction that ActionScript places on the XMLSocket object is that it can only connect to computers within its own domain. Therefore, if you are serving your SWF file from yourserver .com, and you try to connect to a socket on myserver.com, it should fail. This restriction exists only for movies that are being played in the web browser versions of the player. For stand-alone Flash movies, you can connect to any server on which an application is running to allow for a socket connection.

On The Web Site

On the web site accompanying this book you'll find a socket server that you can use for the exercise in this chapter. You are also welcome to use the server for your own personal projects. This server has been provided as-is by Steve Nowicki. You can find out more about the specifications for the server at http://sourceforge.net/projects/flashsock/. Instructions for installing the server are provided in the exercise later in this chapter.

The Client

For your purposes in this book, the client is always the Flash movie or movies you create that use the XMLSocket class to connect to a server. But clients can be developed using all kinds of technologies other than Flash as well. A client sends out a request for a connection, and if available, the server creates the link. The server is identified by an address such as an IP address or a domain name. The client's connection request is sent to the address, and if there is a server listening for socket connection requests on the specified port, a connection is made (see Figure 34-1).

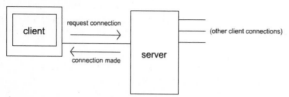

Figure 34-1: Client-server interaction.

Working with XMLSocket Objects in Flash Clients

If you use a socket server that has been developed by another party, or if you have already developed your own, the majority of your work in working with socket connections and Flash will be with XMLSocket objects in your Flash movies. Fortunately, XMLSocket objects are really very simple. Because the functionality of XMLSocket objects is very specific — creating a channel between two sockets and then sending and receiving data across that channel — there is very little to learn when it comes to working with sockets in Flash.

You can create multiple socket connections in a single Flash movie. For instance, you might want to create a socket connection to a server that handles data for a chat application, and you might want to connect to another server that handles data for a news ticker application all within the same movie. For each connection that you want to make, you need to first create the instance of the XMLSocket class.

An XMLSocket object must be instantiated using the constructor method in a new statement:

```
var xsConnection:XMLSocket = new XMLSocket();
```

The constructor takes no parameters. After the object is created, you can attempt to make a connection, and send and receive data over that socket connection. However, if you don't first invoke the appropriate methods, the object does not create any default socket connection.

Creating a Socket Connection to the Server

The first thing you want to do after you have created an XMLSocket object is attempt to create a socket connection to a server. The method to do this is connect(), which takes two parameters (the server name or address as a string, and the port number as a number) and returns a Boolean value indicating whether Flash was able to connect to the server (this does not indicate that a socket connection was yet made). If null is provided as the value for the first parameter, the connection attempt is made to localhost.

```
var bConnected:Boolean = xsConnection.connect("myserver.com", 1234);
```

Caution   Although the null value *should* cause the connection to be made to the local computer, some people have reported problems getting this to work. In the event that this happens to you, simply change the value to 127.0.0.1 or localhost (unless you have modified these values on your computer) and it should work. If it does not, perhaps you should check to make sure that there is not another problem with your ActionScript code.

The connect() method is asynchronous. That means that it does not wait for the actual socket connection before moving on to the next line of ActionScript code. Therefore, there is an event handler method that handles the connect events. The onConnect() method of an XMLSocket object is called once a socket connection is either made successfully or fails. The method is passed a Boolean value indicating whether the socket connection was made.

```
var xsConnection:XMLSocket = new XMLSocket();
var bConnected:Boolean = xsConnection.connect("myserver.com", 1234);
xsConnection.onConnect = function(bSuccess:Boolean):Void {
  if(bSuccess){
    trace("connected");
  }
  else{
    trace("no connection");
  }
}
```

Sending and Receiving Data

XMLSocket objects create bidirectional (or full-duplex) connections. This means that data can be both sent and received. Therefore, there are methods for handling both tasks.

First, if you want to send data across your socket connection, you can use the send() method. This method takes a single parameter: the data you want to send. Typically, you'll want to send XML data.

```
xsConnection.send(new XML("<test />"));
```

On one hand, calling the send() method from an XMLSocket object is all you need to do to send data across a socket connection after it has been established for that object.

On the other hand, if you want to receive data from the server, you need to create a function to process that data. Any XMLSocket object with an established socket connection automatically listens for any incoming data from the server at all times. When your Flash client receives data, you have two choices of methods to handle the receipt: onXML() and onData(). In previous versions of Flash, there were some ActionScript techniques that were considered perfectly okay that are no longer really proper. And due to some of those changes, the onXML() method is not as useful as it was in previous versions of Flash. Therefore, we recommend that you always use the onData() method.

When data is received by the XMLSocket object, the onData() method is automatically invoked and passed the data as a parameter. The data is always a string. If you want to convert it to XML, you should create a new XML object, set the object's ignoreWhite property to true, and then use the parseXML() method to parse the string into the XML object. For example:

```
xsConnection.onData = function(sData:String):Void {
  var xmlData:XML = new XML();
  xmlData.ignoreWhite = true;
  xmlData.parseXML(sData);
  // Rest of method definition...
};
```

Closing a Socket Connection

Finally, there needs to be a way to close a socket connection between the client and server with a command from the client. To do this, you simply need to call the close() method of your XMLSocket object. After the method is called, it attempts to close the connection to the server. When the connection is successfully closed, the onClose() method is automatically called. As you may have guessed, if you want something to actually happen when the connection is closed, you need to overload the function. Here is a sample of code that closes the connection and then tells the timeline to play:

```
xsConnection.onClose = function():Void {
  play();
}
xsConnection.close();
```

Creating a Chat Client

In this exercise, you create a simple chat application that allows multiple users to connect and chat with one another in real time just like many instant messaging programs. The instructions are in three parts: "Installing the Java Runtime Environment," "Installing the Socket Server," and "Setting Up the Client."

Installing the Java Runtime Environment

To run the socket server on your machine, you'll need to have the Sun Java Runtime Environment (JRE) installed. If you are working on Macintosh OS X, you already have the JRE installed on your system. If you plan to run the socket server on another platform, such as Linux or Solaris, you can find instructions for installing on these operating systems on the `java.sun.com` web site. If you're using Windows follow these instructions:

1. Go to the Sun JRE 1.4.2 download page at `http://java.sun.com/j2se/1.4.2/download.html`.

2. Click the download link in the JRE column for the Windows installation of J2SE v 1.4.2 (there may be an additional revision number) and save the installation file.

3. Once the installation file is downloaded, run it and follow the instructions.

4. You'll need to add the `lib` directory that was just installed to your Windows classpath. To do that, follow these steps:

   a. Open the System Properties dialog box by right-clicking My Computer and choosing Properties.

   b. Choose the Advanced tab.

   c. Click the Environment Variables button.

   d. In the Environment Variables dialog box that opens, look for a `CLASSPATH` variable in the System variables list in the lower portion of the box.

   e. If you find that a `CLASSPATH` variable already exists, select it and click the Edit button. Otherwise, click the New button.

   f. If you are creating a new variable, give it a name of `CLASSPATH`; otherwise, the field will be grayed out if you are editing.

   g. If there is a previous value, add a semicolon to the end and then append the new value to the existing value. Otherwise just add the new value. The new value is the path to the `lib` directory in the JRE installation. You'll have to check on your computer to verify the correct path, but it will be something like `C:\jre1.4.2\lib`.

   h. Click OK in both the Environment Variables and System Properties dialog boxes.

Installing the Socket Server

To set up the socket server on your computer, complete the following steps:

1. Copy the entire `socketServer` directory and all its contents from the web site to a location on your computer. Because Java does not always handle spaces in paths well, it is often best to copy the directory to a location that will not contain any spaces in the path. For example, `C:\socketServer` is probably better than `C:\Program Files\socketServer`.

2. Open the `socketServer` directory, and if you are using Windows, run the `runServer.bat` file. If you are in OS X, run the `runitem.sh` file. This will start the server.

Note   The version of the socket server on the web site is compiled and has the BAT and SH files. If you download the SouceForge version, you'll likely be responsible for compiling it and running the server from a command line without the BAT or SH files.

Setting Up the Client

The Flash client consists of two ActionScript 2.0 classes and one FLA file. The FLA file includes several of the v2 UI components. Therefore, if you are not yet familiar with the components, and if you find any of the usage of the components confusing, you might want to consult Chapter 28.

For the purposes of this application, the socket server accepts XML packets in the following formats:

```
<msg><type>signon</type>
<to container="user">SYS</to><content>Username</content></msg>

<msg><type>chat</type>
<to container="user">all</to><content>
<from>Username</from><chat>message</chat></content></msg>
```

And the server sends packets such as the following:

```
<msg><type>userlistupdate</type>
<to container="group">all</to><content><users>
<user>Username1</user><user>Username2</user></users>
</content></msg>

<msg><type>signonsuccess</type>
<to container="user">Username</to><content /></msg>

<msg><type>chat</type>
<to container="user">chat</to><content>
<from>Username</from><chat>message</chat></content></msg>
```

To create the Flash client, complete the following steps:

1. Open a new ActionScript file.

2. In the ActionScript file, add the following code to define the class for incoming messages from the server:

```
class IncomingMessage {

    private var _xmlData:XMLNode;
```

```
    private var _sMessageType:String;
    private var _sFromUser:String;
    private var _sChatText:String;
    private var _aUsers:Array;

    // Define the getter methods for the properties.
    function get messageType():String {
      return _sMessageType;
    }
    function get users():Array {
      return _aUsers;
    }
    function get fromUser():String {
      return _sFromUser;
    }
    function get chatText():String {
      return _sChatText;
    }

    function IncomingMessage(xmlData:XML) {

      // Extract the values from the XML packet.
      _xmlData = xmlData.firstChild;
      _sMessageType = _xmlData.firstChild.firstChild.nodeValue;

      // Depending on the message type, extract the
      // appropriate values.
      switch(_sMessageType) {
        case "chat":
          var aContentNodes:Array = _
xmlData.childNodes[2].childNodes;
          _sFromUser = aContentNodes[0].firstChild.nodeValue;
          _sChatText =
unescape(aContentNodes[1].firstChild.nodeValue);
          break;
        case "userlistupdate":
          var aUserNodes:Array =
xmlData.childNodes[2].firstChild.childNodes;
          _aUsers = new Array();
          for(var i:Number = 0; i < aUserNodes.length; i++) {
            _aUsers.push(aUserNodes[i].firstChild.nodeValue);
          }
          break;
      }
    }

  }
```

3. Save the file as IncomingMessage.as.

4. Open a new ActionScript file.

5. Add the following code to the new ActionScript file to define the class for outgoing messages:

```
class OutgoingMessage {
  private var _xmlData:XML;

  public function get message():XML {
    return _xmlData;
  }

  // Construct the message based on the type, username, and
  // message.
  function OutgoingMessage(sType:String, sUsername:String,
sMessage:String) {
    if(sType == "chat") {
      _xmlData = new XML(makeChatXML(sUsername, sMessage));
    }
    if(sType == "login") {
      _xmlData = new XML(makeLoginXML(sUsername));
    }
  }

  private function makeChatXML(sUsername:String,
sChatText:String):String {
    var sXMLString:String = "<msg><type>chat</type>
<to container=\"user\">all</to><content><from>" +
sUsername + "</from><chat>" + escape(sChatText) +
"</chat></content></msg>";
    return sXMLString;
  }

  private function makeLoginXML(sUsername:String):String {
    return "<msg><type>signon</type>
<to container=\"user\">SYS</to><content>" +
sUsername + "</content></msg>";
  }

}
```

6. Save the ActionScript file as `OutgoingMessage.as` to the same directory where you saved `IncomingMessage.as`.

7. Open a new Flash document, and save it as `chatClient001.fla` to the same directory where you saved the two class files.

8. Rename the default layer to Logged In Form. Create two new layers named Log In Form and Actions.

9. On the Log In Form layer add the following:

    a. A `TextInput` instance named `ctiMessage`. Resize the instance to 200 pixels or so.

    b. A second `TextInput` instance named `ctiUsername`. Place this instance so that it is lower than the `ctiMessage` instance.

    c. A `Button` component instance named `cbtLogin`. Place the `Button` instance to the right of `ctiUsername`. The layout should appear similar to what you see in Figure 34-2.

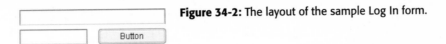

Figure 34-2: The layout of the sample Log In form.

10. Hide the Log In Form layer by clicking the Show/Hide column in the layer so that the red "X" appears.

11. In the Logged In Form, add the following:

   - A `TextArea` component instance named `ctaChatDisplay`. Resize the instance to 300 by 300.

   - A second `TextArea` component instance named `ctaInput`. Resize the instance to 300 by 60, and place it just lower than `ctaChatDisplay`.

   - A `List` instance named `clUserList`. Resize the instance to 150 by 300, and place it to the right of `ctaChatDisplay`.

   - A `Button` instance named `cbtSend`. Place the instance to the right of `ctaInput`. The layout should appear as shown in Figure 34-3.

Figure 34-3: The layout of the Logged In Form layer.

12. Add the following ActionScript code to the Actions layer:

```
var xsTransferrer:XMLSocket = new XMLSocket();
var sCurrentScreen = "login";
initSocketConnection(xsTransferrer);
showLoginScreen();
initializeScreens();

// The showLoginScreen() and showChatScreen() methods show
// and hide the component instances appropriately so as to
// give the effect of switching between two screens.
function showLoginScreen():Void {
  ctiMessage.visible = true;
  ctiUsername.visible = true;
  cbtLogin.visible = true;
  ctaChatDisplay.visible = false;
  ctaInput.visible = false;
  clUserList.visible = false;
```

```
      cbtSend.visible = false;
      sCurrentScreen = "login";
    }
    function showChatScreen():Void {
      ctiMessage.visible = false;
      ctiUsername.visible = false;
      cbtLogin.visible = false;
      ctaChatDisplay.visible = true;
      ctaInput.visible = true;
      clUserList.visible = true;
      cbtSend.visible = true;
      sCurrentScreen = "chat";
    }


    // The showConnectedMessage() method shows the appropriate
    // message indicating whether or not the client was able to
    // make a socket connection.
    function showConnectedMessage(bDidConnect:Boolean):Void {
      if(bDidConnect) {
        ctiMessage.text = "connected...please enter a username";
      }
      else {
        ctiMessage.text = "error connecting to server";
      }
    }


    // If the connection is lost, then return to the login
    // screen and try to reconnect.
    function showDisconnectedMessage():Void {
      showLoginScreen();
      ctiMessage.text = "...trying to reconnect...";
      ctiUsername.text = "";
      xsTransferrer.connect("localhost", 2001);
    }


    function initSocketConnection(xsSocket:XMLSocket):Void {

      // Define the onData() method for the XMLSocket object.
      xsSocket.onData = function(sData:String):Void {

        // Parse the string data into an XML object, then pass
        // that XML to the IncomingMessage constructor.
        var xmlData:XML = new XML();
        xmlData.ignoreWhite = true;
        xmlData.parseXML(sData);
        var imData:IncomingMessage = new IncomingMessage(xmlData);

        // Depending on the message type, perform the
        // appropriate actions.
        switch(imData.messageType) {
          case "signonsuccess":
```

```
          showChatScreen();
          break;
        case "userlistupdate":
          clUserList.dataProvider = imData.users;
          break;
        case "chat":
          ctaChatDisplay.text += imData.fromUser +
": " + imData.chatText + newline;
          ctaChatDisplay.vPosition = ctaChatDisplay.maxVPosition;
        default:
      }
    };

    // When the connection is made (or not), call the
    // function to show the appropriate message.
    xsSocket.onConnect = function(bDidConnect:Boolean):Void {
      showConnectedMessage(bDidConnect);
    };

    // When the connection is closed, show the disconnected
    // message.
    xsSocket.onClose = function():Void {
      showDisconnectedMessage();
    };

    // Connect to the server.
    xsSocket.connect("localhost", 2001);
}

function initializeScreens():Void {
    ctaChatDisplay.html = true;
    cbtLogin.label = "Log In";
    cbtSend.label = "Send";

    // Create a listener object to listen for when the
    // user logs in.
    var oLoginListener:Object = new Object();
    oLoginListener.form = this;
    oLoginListener.socket = xsTransferrer;
    oLoginListener.click = function(oEvent:Object):Void {

      // If the user has typed in a user name, create an
      // outgoing message and then send that to the server.
      if(this.form.ctiUsername.text != "") {
        var omLogin:OutgoingMessage = new OutgoingMessage("login",
                                  this.form.ctiUsername.text);
        this.socket.send(omLogin.message);
      }
    };

    // If the user presses Enter, also trigger the click
```

```
            // event.
            oLoginListener.onKeyDown = function():Void {
              if(Key.getCode() == Key.ENTER &&
        this.form.sCurrentScreen == "login") {
                this.click();
              }
            };
            cbtLogin.addEventListener("click", oLoginListener);
            Key.addListener(oLoginListener);

            // Create a listener object for the chat screen's Button.
            var oChatListener:Object = new Object();
            oChatListener.form = this;
            oChatListener.socket = xsTransferrer;
            oChatListener.click = function(oEvent:Object):Void {

              // If the user has typed something into the input then
              // create an outgoing message and send it to the
              // server.
              if(this.form.ctaInput.text != "") {
                var omhat:OutgoingMessage = new OutgoingMessage("chat",
                                         this.form.ctiUsername.text,
                                         this.form.ctaInput.text);
                this.socket.send(omhat.message);
                this.form.ctaInput.text = "";
              }
            };

            // Like on the login screen, if the user presses the
            // Enter key, trigger the click event.
            oChatListener.onKeyDown = function():Void {
              if(Key.getCode() == Key.ENTER &&
        this.form.sCurrentScreen == "chat") {
                this.click();
              }
            };
            cbtSend.addEventListener("click", oChatListener);
            Key.addListener(oChatListener);
        }
```

13. Export the SWF file.

14. Test the application by opening the SWF file in several players, logging in, and sending messages.

We'd like to know what you thought about this chapter. Visit `www.rightactionscript .com/asb/comments` to fill out an online form with your comments.

Summary

✦ Much of Web data is transferred via HTTP. Although this works just fine in most situations, it has large drawbacks in situations that require low latency. For these scenarios, such as multiplayer games and chat applications, timing is important, and a lower-level protocol can be used — TCP.

✦ TCP enables you to create socket connections between clients and servers. Socket connections are persistent connections that exist between numbered software interfaces on the client and server application hosts. Because a single machine can have many sockets, a client and host can reside on the same machine.

✦ ActionScript enables you, as a developer, to create socket connections from a Flash client to a server application, such as the socket server provided on the web site that accompanies this book. You can create these connections using an XMLSocket object.

✦ You must create a connection before you can transmit or receive any data over sockets. Use the connect() method to create this connection. You are restricted for security reasons to connections to ports greater than 1023 and to computers in the same subdomain. The onConnect() method is called when a connection is made or is rejected.

✦ You can send any type of data that can be converted to a string across a socket connection from within Flash to a server application. You use the send() method to send the data and the onData() and/or onXML() methods to receive data across the socket.

✦ You can close a connection with the close() method, and after a connection has been closed (whether on the client end or on the server end), the onClose() method is called.

✦　　✦　　✦

Using Web Services

Flash 8 provides a `WebService` class written in ActionScript (that is, it's not native to Flash Player) that lets you work with SOAP Web services from Flash. The `WebService` class is included with both Flash 8 Basic and Flash 8 Professional. Flash 8 Professional also has a set of data components including a `WebServiceConnector` component that allows you to connect to Web services from your Flash applications. Although the `WebServiceConnector` component may seem simpler initially, it is not as flexible as the `WebService` class, and it is more difficult to build into most applications. The `WebServiceConnector` component uses the `WebService` class as the underlying "engine," so there is nothing in terms of basic Web service functionality that the `WebServiceConnector` component can do that the `WebService` class cannot. Therefore, in this chapter we'll look at how to work with the lower-level `WebService` class directly.

Note   The `WebService` class is also available in Flash MX 2004.

Working with Web Services

A *Web service* is a way of distributing functionality across the Internet. It means that an application running on one server can allow other applications on other servers to utilize some type of functionality that it provides without having to reinvent it locally. Some Web services are private and some are public.

Web Resource   There are many Web services publicly available. You can look at Web service lists on sites such as `www.xmethods.net` to find Web services that might meet your application's needs. For example, you may want to access a Web service that returns the current weather conditions given a location. Or you might want to use a Web service to perform a search on a popular site such as Amazon.com. Google provides a Web service that allows you to perform Web searches. The possibilities are far too numerous to list.

Web services must describe themselves using WSDL, or Web Service Document Language. The WSDL is typically published to the Web, and then the requesting application targets that WSDL document. The document provides the requesting application with all the information it needs, such as how to access the actual service, the methods available, and the types of permissible request and response messages. The Web service then uses HTTP to transfer request and response packets over the Web. The requesting message tells the Web service what method to call and what parameters to pass to it.

Then, once the operation has finished, the Web service sends a response message back that contains the return data. Web services can use several XML variations for the request and response messages, but many Web services use something known as SOAP (Simple Object Access Protocol). Most of the time you don't have to concern yourself with the details of the message format because in most languages the serialization and deserialization of the messages is handled behind the scenes. When you use the WebService class (either through code or via the WebServiceConnector component), Flash will handle all the SOAP messages for you automatically.

Note The WebService class uses the built-in XML class to send and load messages. Therefore, you can expect the messages to be typically many times the size of a Flash Remoting AMF packet. That means that in terms of message size, Flash Remoting is many times as efficient as using the WebService class.

Calling Web Services with WebService

The WebService class is not included as part of the standard ActionScript library of class files. Instead, it is tucked away in an SWC that you must add to the library of your Flash document. You can locate the SWC by selecting Window ➪ Common Libraries ➪ Classes. This opens the Classes common library, in which you can find WebServiceClasses. Just copy the WebServiceClasses SWC from the Classes library to the library of your Flash document.

Once you've included the WebServiceClasses SWC, you can work with the WebService class in your application. The class is in the mx.services package, so you might want to import the class to make your code more readable:

```
import mx.services.WebService;
```

Each WebService method call will return a new PendingCall object, so you can import the PendingCall class as well. It's in the mx.services package:

```
import mx.services.PendingCall;
```

You then create a WebService object by calling the constructor and passing it the URL to the WSDL as a parameter. For example:

```
var sWSDLURL:String =
"http://www.xmethods.net/sd/2001/CurrencyExchangeService.wsdl";
var wsExchangeRate:WebService = new WebService(sWSDLURL);
```

You can call the Web service method directly from the WebService object. For example:

```
var pcResponse:PendingCall = wsExchangeRate.getRate("United States", "Canada");
```

Notice that when you call a Web service method in this way, it returns a new PendingCall object, which can handle the responses from the server. You can define two methods for the callback object to handle the two types of responses. The onResult() method is called when a successful response is returned from the Web service method. The returned value is automatically passed to the onResult() method as a parameter. The onFault() method is called when an error occurred.

```
pcResponse.onResult = function(nRate):Void {
  trace(nRate);
};
```

```
pcResponse.onFault = function():Void {
  trace("an error occurred");
};
```

Taking a Flash Survey

In the following exercise, you have the opportunity to work with the `WebService` class. You'll build a simple application that calls methods of a FlashSurvey Web service. The user can take the survey, and they can retrieve the results of the survey.

The FlashSurvey Web service is published at `http://www.rightactionscript.com/webservices/FlashSurvey.php`. If you request that URL in a web browser, you'll see a page that describes the Web service. You'll see that it has two methods, `getAverages()` and `takeSurvey()`. The `getAverages()` method requires no parameters, and it returns an associative array with two keys, `flash` and `actionscript`. Each of the two keys have number values. The `takeSurvey()` method requires two parameters: the number of years working with Flash and the number of years working with ActionScript.

You can complete the exercise with the following steps:

1. Open `flashSurveryWebService_starter.fla` from the web site, and save it as `flashSurveyWebService.fla`.

2. Open the `Classes` common library, and copy the `WebServiceClasses` SWC to the library for `flashSurveyWebService.fla`.

3. Note the instance names assigned to the text input and button component instances.

4. Place the following code on the first frame of the default layer:

```
import mx.services.WebService;
import mx.services.PendingCall;

// Specify the WSDL URL to a Web service published at
// www.rightactionscript.com.
var wsFlashSurvey:WebService = new WebService(
"http://www.rightactionscript.com/webservices/
FlashSurvey.php?wsdl");

// Declare a variable to use for the response.
var pcResponse:PendingCall;

// Register listeners for the buttons.
cbtReply.addEventListener("click", takeSurvey);
cbtGetResponses.addEventListener("click", getResponses);

// Request the response averages from the Web service. Tell Flash
// to handle the response with the onResponse() function.
function getResponses():Void {
  pcResponse = wsFlashSurvey.getAverages();
  pcResponse.onResult = onResponse;
}

// When the response is returned from the Web service method,
```

```
// display the response averages in the text inputs.
function onResponse(oResponse:Object):Void {
  ctiAverageYearsFlash.text = oResponse.flash;
  ctiAverageYearsActionScript.text = oResponse.actionscript;
}

function takeSurvey():Void {

  // If the user hasn't entered valid data into the form, exit
  // the function.
  if(ctiYearsFlash.text == "" ||
ctiYearsActionScript.text == "") {
    return;
  }

  // Call the takeSurvey() method on the Web service. Pass it the
  // values from the text inputs cast as numbers.
  wsFlashSurvey.takeSurvey(Number(ctiYearsFlash.text),
Number(ctiYearsActionScript.text));

  // Request the updated response averages.
  getResponses();
}
```

5. Test the movie.

When you test the movie, start by clicking the Get Responses button. Within a second or two the text input components will display the averages for every survey response. You can also enter years into the text inputs in the upper form. Click the Take Survey button, and the responses will get sent to the Web service and recorded. The code also sends a request for the response averages, which are then displayed in the lower form.

Dealing with Security Issues

Because the WebService class relies on the XML class to connect to Web services, it is subject to the same security restrictions. That is, if you are serving the Flash application from a web server, the Web service must either be in the same domain as the Flash application, or the server that provides the Web service must have a crossdomain.xml document that permits Flash applications from other domains to access the services. Because neither of those scenarios is likely to be the case most of the time, there is another possibility: You can create a proxy script on the same server as the Flash application. The WebService or WebServiceConnector can use the local proxy script as the URL, and the proxy script can relay all the messages between the Flash application and the Web service.

For more information regarding sandbox security and crossdomain.xml policy files, see Chapter 24. For more information on using a proxy script for cross-domain access, see Chapter 33.

We'd like to know what you thought about this chapter. Visit www.rightactionscript .com/asb/comments to fill out an online form with your comments.

Summary

✦ You can use the databinding feature to associate properties of various components so that you can quickly set up simple applications without much ActionScript.

✦ You can call Web service methods using the `WebServiceConnector` component or the `WebService` class. The `WebServiceConnector` component is available only in Flash Professional, whereas the `WebService` class is available in both Professional and Basic editions.

✦ Because Web service requests and responses use the `XML` class in the player, they are subject to the standard sandbox security issues as other data connections (`XML`, `LoadVars`, and so on).

✦   ✦   ✦

Introducing Flash Remoting

✦ ✦ ✦ ✦

In this Chapter

Learning what Flash
Remoting can do

Building Flash
Remoting Clients

✦ ✦ ✦ ✦

Flash Remoting is one of the most powerful and undermarketed technologies related to Flash. Flash Remoting is a way for Flash Player to communicate with server-side services more efficiently than using LoadVars, XML, or WebService. In this chapter, you'll learn what Flash Remoting is, what it does, and how you can use Flash Remoting.

Introducing Flash Remoting

Flash Remoting refers to a technology by which Flash Player can communicate with server-side services using a binary messaging format called AMF. Flash Remoting capabilities are native to Flash Player, so it runs very efficiently. And because the requests and responses are sent in a binary format, the bandwidth requirement is often drastically lower than equivalent applications utilizing uncompressed messaging formats like XML or SOAP. Flash Remoting gets even better than that, though. Flash Player uses the NetConnection class to send and receive Flash Remoting requests and responses, and the NetConnection class is capable of automatically serializing and deserializing standard, native ActionScript datatypes. That means that a String object or string primitive is serialized as a string, a Number object or number primitive is serialized as a number, and a Boolean object or Boolean primitive is serialized as a Boolean. Arrays are serialized, as are associative arrays and Date objects. Using one of the server-side gateways, that data is then deserialized into the corresponding native service datatype. In that way, AMF and Flash Remoting work a lot like SOAP and Web services. You have the convenience of automatic serialization and deserialization. But unlike Web services using SOAP, Flash Remoting sends messages in AMF, which is a significantly smaller packet size. Furthermore, nearly any standard service can be used as a Flash Remoting service with little to no Flash Remoting-specific modifications.

The basic elements of a Flash Remoting application are:

✦ Flash Player 6+ initiating Flash Remoting calls via the NetConnection **class**

✦ A Flash Remoting gateway

✦ A service

The Flash Remoting Client

Flash Player 6 and higher have a native class called `NetConnection` that can send and receive Flash Remoting requests and responses. Although nothing additional is strictly required to build a Flash Remoting client, there are a set of ActionScript 2.0 classes that are typically used because they provide a nicer API than working directly with `NetConnection`.

The Flash Remoting Gateway

One of the goals of Flash Remoting is to be as transparent as possible. That means that as much as possible, a Flash Remoting service ought to be able to work without having to know anything about the clients making the requests. A service should be able to get called by a JSP, ASP, or PHP client, as a Web service, or from a Flash client using Flash Remoting without any change to the code. Thus, the Flash Remoting gateway is a piece of software residing on the server that receives Flash Remoting requests from Flash Player, delegates the requests to the appropriate services, and relays the response back to the Flash client. Macromedia has three official commercial gateway products for Flash Remoting: one for ASP.NET, one for Java 2 Enterprise Edition (J2EE), and one for ColdFusion. The ColdFusion gateway is automatically distributed with ColdFusion. The ASP.NET and J2EE gateway products are available for sale from Macromedia. In addition to the official gateway products, there are several open-source, free, and third-party commercial gateway products. You can download the popular open-source PHP gateway product called AMFPHP from `www.amfphp.org`. A Perl implementation is available at `www.simonf.com/flap`. An open-source J2EE implementation is available at `www.openamf.org`. And there are third-party commercial J2EE and .NET implementations at `www.flashorb.com`.

The Flash Remoting gateway is located at a valid URL accessible to Flash Player. The specific URL depends on which gateway product and how you've installed it on the server. In each implementation, the gateway is accessible via HTTP such as a servlet, an ASPX page, a PHP page, or the like. All Flash Remoting requests are routed through that gateway resource.

Flash Remoting Services

As noted previously, one of the goals of Flash Remoting is transparency. Therefore, Flash Remoting services are typically not identifiable strictly as *Flash Remoting* services. Rather, they are simply "services." For example, Flash Remoting services can be ColdFusion Components, Java classes, EJBs, .NET assemblies, or PHP classes, to name a few. In most cases, little to no implementation specific to Flash Remoting is necessary within the service code. The Flash Remoting gateway is responsible for instantiating the correct service type, calling the requested method, and relaying any return data back to Flash Player.

Writing Flash Remoting ActionScript

Flash Remoting works over HTTP. Flash Player issues a request to the gateway. The gateway delegates to the appropriate service. The service responds. Then the gateway returns the response to Flash Player. In the following sections, you'll look at how you can write the ActionScript that drives that request-response chain of events.

Using NetConnection

Technically, all Flash Remoting requests and responses in Flash Player are routed through an instance of the `NetConnection` class. As you'll read in the next section, it's more common to use a set of ActionScript 2.0 classes so as to have a nicer API and debugging. However, it's entirely possible to work with Flash Remoting at a lower level by making the calls and handling responses directly using a `NetConnection` instance.

The first step is to make a new `NetConnection` instance. For that, use the `NetConnection` constructor in a new statement as follows:

```
var ncFlashRemoting:NetConnection = new NetConnection();
```

Next, use the `connect()` method to tell the `NetConnection` instance where the Flash Remoting gateway is on the server. The following line of code tells Flash that the gateway is located at `http://www.rightactionscript.com/flashremoting/gateway.php`. The gateway URL is the URL to the gateway as it has been installed on the server from which you want to call the service methods.

```
ncFlashRemoting.connect("http://www.rightactionscript.com/
flashremoting/gateway.php");
```

Assuming that you want Flash to handle a response from a service method call, you can make a new *response object*. A response object is any object for which an `onResult()` method has been defined. If you register the response object with a particular service method call, the `onResult()` method will get called when the gateway returns a response. Any return value is passed to the `onResult()` method as a parameter.

```
var oResponse:Object = new Object();
oResponse.onResult = function(oReturnData:Object):Void {
  trace("Response returned from Flash Remoting - " + oReturnData);
};
```

Next, call the service method. The name of the service is the name by which the gateway knows about the service. That differs slightly in each gateway implementation. However, in general the service name is the name of the class from which you want to call a method. The name must be fully qualified in most cases. For example, if you want to call a method in a class called `ExampleFlashRemotingService`, the name of the service would be ExampleFlashRemotingService. If the class is in a package called `com.rightactionscript`, the service would be com.rightactionscript.ExampleFlashRemotingService. In order to call a Flash Remoting service method, you must know the service name and the method name. You can then call the method using the `call()` method of the `NetConnection` object. The `call()` method requires one parameter specifying the service and method you want to call. The parameter is a string using a dot between the service and method. If you want to handle a response, you pass the response object as the second parameter. The following line of code calls the `exampleMethod()` method from the ExampleFlashRemotingService service. The response is handled by `oResponse`.

```
ncFlashRemoting.call("ExampleFlashRemotingService.exampleMethod", oResponse);
```

If the service method expects parameters, you can pass the parameters as part of the `call()` method parameter list following the response object. For example, if `exampleMethod` expects an array parameter, the following would pass an array to the method.

```
ncFlashRemoting.call(
"ExampleFlashRemotingService.exampleMethod", oResponse, aData);
```

Using the ActionScript 2.0 API

Macromedia has published a library of ActionScript 2.0 classes for use with Flash Remoting. While not strictly necessary, many feel they have a nicer API for working with Flash Remoting than using `NetConnection` directly. You can download the latest code from `www.macromedia.com/software/flashremoting/downloads/components`. Look for the download that says source code. Then follow the installation instructions after you've downloaded the files. The instructions will tell you where to place the files so that they are properly added to the global classpath in Flash.

Once you've installed the classes, you can start building Flash Remoting applications with them. The API of the Flash Remoting classes is similar to that of the Web service classes discussed in the preceding chapter. The primary classes with which you'll work are:

✦ `mx.remoting.Service`

✦ `mx.remoting.PendingCall`

✦ `mx.rpc.RelayResponder`

✦ `mx.rpc.ResultEvent`

✦ `mx.rpc.FaultEvent`

Since you'll use those classes, it's often a good idea to import them, as follows:

```
import mx.remoting.Service;
import mx.remoting.PendingCall;
import mx.rpc.RelayResponder;
import mx.rpc.ResultEvent;
import mx.rpc.FaultEvent;
```

You can construct a new `Service` object using the constructor. The constructor requires that you specify three parameters at a minimum: the gateway URL, a `Log` object, and the service name. It is not common to use a `Log` object with Flash Remoting because the NetConnection Debugger (which we'll discuss shortly) is a better option. However, to keep the API similar to the `WebService` class, Macromedia opted to require the `Log` parameter as the second parameter. Most frequently you'll use a `null` value. The following makes a `Service` object that maps to a service called ExampleFlashRemotingService using a gateway at `http://www.rightactionscript.com/flashremoting/gateway.php`.

```
var svcFlashRemoting:Service = new Service(
"http://www.rightactionscript.com/flashremoting/
gateway.php", null, "ExampleFlashRemotingService");
```

After you've constructed a Service object, you can call any methods associated with that service. Assuming the ExampleFlashRemotingService defines a method called `exampleMethod()`, the following code will call that method via Flash Remoting:

```
svcFlashRemoting.exampleMethod();
```

If the method expects parameters, you can pass those parameters to the method when calling it from the `Service` object. The following passes an array called `aData` to `exampleMethod()`:

```
svcFlashRemoting.exampleMethod(aData);
```

Flash Remoting method calls are asynchronous, as you've already seen. So, you need to tell Flash how to handle any response from the server if necessary for the application. Every call to a method of a `Service` object returns a new `PendingCall` object. The `mx.remoting` `.PendingCall` class is very similar to the `mx.services.PendingCall` class used with Web services. However, in order to deal with some scoping issues, the `mx.remoting.PendingCall` class defines a property called `responder` to which you can assign a new `RelayResponder` object rather than defining an `onResult()` method like for `mx.services.PendingCall` objects. The `RelayResponder` constructor requires three parameters: the scope object, the name of the result method as a string, and the name of the fault method as a string. The following code tells Flash Player to call `exampleMethod()`, to handle any return value response using a function called `onResponse()`, and to handle any fault using a function called `onError()`.

```
var pcResponse:PendingCall = svcFlashRemoting.exampleMethod();
pcResponse.responder = new RelayResponder(this, "onResponse", "onError");
```

The functions/methods that handle the server responses are passed parameters of `ResultEvent` and `FaultEvent` types, respectively. The `ResultEvent` class defines a result property that is a reference to the return value. For example, if `exampleMethod()` returns a value, you can display that value in the Output panel by defining `onResponse()` as follows.

```
function onResponse(reResponse:ResultEvent):Void {
   trace(reResponse.result);
}
```

The `FaultEvent` class defines a property called `fault`, which is itself an `mx.rpc.Fault` object. The `Fault` class defines `faultcode`, `faultstring`, `detail`, `description`, and `type` properties. Each of those properties tells you something about the error. The following defines a function to handle a fault response by displaying the code and description in the Output panel.

```
function onError(feError:FaultEvent):Void {
   trace(feError.faultcode + " " + feError.description);
}
```

Using the NetConnection Debugger

The NetConnection Debugger is a utility that you can use in conjunction with Flash Remoting applications to see what requests and responses are occurring. To install the NetConnection Debugger, you must install the Flash Remoting components. The Flash Remoting components are available for download from the same page from which you downloaded the Flash Remoting ActionScript 2.0 classes: `www.macromedia.com/software/flashremoting/downloads/components`. When you download the Flash Remoting components, make sure you download the ActionScript 2.0 version. Once you've downloaded the components, run the installation.

With the Flash Remoting components installed you can open the NetConnection Debugger as a panel within Flash. You can access the panel from Window ➪ Other Panels ➪ NetConnection Debugger. The NetConnection Debugger is simply an SWF file that runs as a panel because it's been placed in a specific directory. You may find that it's more convenient to run the SWF in the stand-alone player. If so, you can locate the SWF in the `en/First Run/WindowSWF` directory of the Flash installation.

The NetConnection Debugger uses `LocalConnection` so that the Flash Remoting client SWF can communicate with the NetConnection Debugger SWF. By default, the client SWF doesn't have any code that communicates with the NetConnection Debugger. However, conveniently you can use the static `initialize()` method of the `mx.remoting.debug.NetDebug` class to add that functionality to the SWF. Simply add the following lines of code:

```
import mx.remoting.debug.NetDebug;

NetDebug.initialize();
```

Then, as long as you are using the `Service` class to make Flash Remoting calls, any requests and responses will be sent to the NetConnection Debugger.

Taking a Flash Survey

In the Web services chapter, you built an application that used a FlashSurvey Web service. In this chapter, you update that application so that it uses Flash Remoting rather than Web services. The Flash Remoting version is more efficient than the Web services version. Fewer kilobytes are added to the SWF than when using the `WebService` class. The code runs faster because the serialization and deserialization runs natively in the player rather than using ActionScript code. And the AMF packets are smaller than the SOAP packets.

As with the Web services example, the FlashSurvey service used by the Flash Remoting implementation is published online. The gateway URL is `www.rightactionscript.com/flashremoting/gateway.php`. The service is called FlashSurvey. The methods are identical to those of the Web service example.

Complete the following steps:

1. Open the `flashSurveyWebServices.fla` file from the exercise in the previous chapter. Save the file as `flashSurveyFlashRemoting.fla`.

2. Edit the ActionScript code on the main timeline. Delete the `import` statements, and add the following new `import` statements to the top of the code:

   ```
   import mx.remoting.Service;
   import mx.remoting.PendingCall;
   import mx.rpc.RelayResponder;
   import mx.rpc.ResultEvent;
   import mx.rpc.FaultEvent;
   ```

3. Change the line of code that constructs the `WebService` object to the following:

   ```
   var svcFlashSurvey:Service = new Service(
   "http://www.rightactionscript.com/flashremoting/
   gateway.php", null, "FlashSurvey");
   ```

4. Add the following line of code that defines the `RelayResponder` object. Place the line of code just after the `pcResponse` variable declaration.

   ```
   var rrReturn:RelayResponder = new RelayResponder(
   this, "onResponse", "onError");
   ```

5. Update the `getResponses()` function as follows (the changes are bolded):

   ```
   function getResponses():Void {
     pcResponse = svcFlashSurvey.getAverages();
     pcResponse.responder = rrReturn;
   }
   ```

6. In the `takeSurvey()` function, update the reference from `wsFlashSurvey` to `svcFlashSurvey`.

When you test the movie, it ought to work just as the Web service example does.

We'd like to know what you thought about this chapter. Visit `www.rightactionscript` `.com/asb/comments` to fill out an online form with your comments.

Summary

✦ Flash Remoting is one of the most efficient and convenient ways to add client-server interaction with Flash.

✦ Flash Remoting uses AMF, a binary messaging format.

✦ Flash Remoting uses technologies that are built into Flash Player.

✦ There are three basic elements in a Flash Remoting application: the SWF client, the gateway, and the service.

✦ You can use the NetConnection Debugger to see what requests and responses are occurring.

✦   ✦   ✦

Managing File Uploads and Downloads

✦ ✦ ✦ ✦

In This Chapter

Uploading files

Downloading files

Security issues

✦ ✦ ✦ ✦

In previous versions of Flash Player, there was no built-in mechanism for uploading and downloading files to and from a server. Instead, you had to create workarounds for those tasks, using browser pop-up windows, DIVs, and such. However, with Flash Player 8, you can upload and download files directly from Flash Player using the new `FileReference` and `FileReferenceList` classes.

Introducing FileReference

The `flash.net.FileReference` class lets users browse for a file to upload or select a location to save a downloaded file using a system dialog box. In this chapter, you'll learn to work with the `FileReference` class and the `FileReferenceList` class.

Except when returned from a `FileReferenceList`, `FileReference` objects are constructed using the constructor method in a `new` statement. The constructor does not require any parameters:

```
import flash.net.FileReference;

var frToUpload:FileReference = new FileReference();
```

Optionally, if you want the user to be able to select many files at once, you can use a `FileReferenceList` object. Like `FileReference`, the `FileReferenceList` constructor requires no parameters:

```
import flash.net.FileReferenceList;

var frlToUpload:FileReferenceList = new FileReference
    List();
```

Uploading Files

The following sections explain how to upload files using `FileReference` and `FileReferenceList`.

Selecting a File to Upload

To upload a file, the user must first select the file. You can prompt the user to select a file by calling the `browse()` method. The `browse()` method is overloaded so that you can call it with no parameters or one parameter. When you call `browse()` with no parameters, it opens a new browse dialog box from which the user can select a file.

```
frToUpload.browse();
```

By default, the browse dialog box displays all file types. However, you can specify which file types from which the user can select by passing an optional parameter to the `browse()` method. The parameter must be an array of associative arrays in which each associative array has the following properties.

   ✦ **description** — A string describing the file type.

   ✦ **extension** — A list of file extensions with wildcards. The list items must be delimited by semicolons.

   ✦ **macType** — A list of Macintosh file types delimited by semicolons.

The `macType` property is optional. If it is not specified, the file extensions specified by the extension property are used for Macintoshes as well. The only caveat is that each associative array must be consistent. For example, the following is valid because every element specifies only `description` and `extension` properties.

```
frToUpload.browse({description: "Image Files",
extension: "*.jpg;*.gif;*.png"}, {description:
"Quicktime Movies", extension: "*.mov"});
```

Likewise, because every element specifies `description`, `extension`, and `macType` properties, the following code is valid:

```
frToUpload.browse({description: "Image Files",
extension: "*.jpg;*.gif;*.png", macType: "JPEG;jp2_;GIFF"},
{description: "Quicktime Movies", extension: "*.mov",
macType: "MooV"});
```

However, the following would not be valid because one element specifies `description`, `extension`, and `macType`, but one of them only specifies `description` and `extensions`.

```
frToUpload.browse({description: "Image Files",
extension: "*.jpg;*.gif;*.png"}, {description:
"Quicktime Movies", extension: "*.mov", macType: "MooV"});
```

The `FileReferenceList` class also defines a `browse()` method that uses identical syntax to the `FileReference` method of the same name. The only difference is that the browse dialog box opened from a `FileReferenceList` object allows the user to select more than one file.

Determining When a File Is Selected

Calling browse() causes the browse dialog box to open. However, it doesn't guarantee that the user will select a file. The browse dialog box has two buttons from which the user can select — Open and Cancel. If the user selects Open, the selected file data is sent to Flash Player before the browse dialog closes. If the user selects Cancel, the browse dialog closes without the file data being sent to Flash Player. To build a good application, you need to be able to determine which option the user has selected, and you can accomplish that goal using a listener object with the FileReference or FileReferenceList object from which you've called browse().

Listener objects for FileReference or FileReferenceList instances can define onSelect() and onCancel() methods that are called when the user clicks on the Open and Cancel buttons, respectively. In each case, the method is passed a reference to the FileReference or FileReferenceList object from which browse() was called. The following code defines a listener object with onSelect() and onCancel() methods that can be registered with a FileReference object:

```
var oFileListener:Object = new Object();
oFileListener.onSelect = function(frSelected:FileReference):Void {
  trace("A file has been selected.");
};
oFileListener.onCancel = function(frCanceled:FileReference):Void {
  trace("The file select has been cancelled.");
};
```

You can add a listener object to a FileReference or FileReferenceList instance using the addListener() method:

```
    frToUpload.addListener(oFileListener);
```

Retrieving File Properties

Once the user has selected a file via the browse dialog box, that file's properties are sent to Flash Player, and they are accessible via the FileReference object from which the browse() method was called or from an array of FileReference objects stored in the fileList property of the FileReferenceList object. The FileReference class defines the following properties that describe the file to which it is associated:

✦ **name** — The name of the file.

✦ **size** — The size of the file in bytes.

✦ **type** — The file extension (Windows) or Macintosh file type.

✦ **creationDate** — A Date object representing the date on which the file was created.

✦ **modificationDate** — A Date object representing the date on which the file was last modified.

✦ **creator** — On Macintosh, the property is a string value specifying the user type of the user that created the file. On Windows the property returns null.

The following code defines an `onSelect()` method for a listener object registered with a `FileReference` instance in which the file properties are written to the Output panel:

```
oFileListener.onSelect = function(frSelected:FileReference):Void {
  trace(frSelected.name);
  trace(frSelected.size);
  trace(frSelected.type);
  trace(frSelected.creationDate);
  trace(frSelected.modificationDate);
  trace(frSelected.creator);
};
```

The following defines an `onSelect()` method for a listener object that is registered with a `FileReferenceList` object. It uses the `fileList` property of the `FileReferenceList` parameter to write the file properties of each selected file.

```
oFileListener.onSelect = function(frlSelectedFiles:FileReferenceList):Void {
var frSelected:FileReference;
  for(var i:Number = 0; i < frlSelectedFiles.fileList.length; i++) {
    frSelected = frlSelectedFiles.fileList[i];
    trace(frSelected.name);
    trace(frSelected.size);
    trace(frSelected.type);
    trace(frSelected.creationDate);
    trace(frSelected.modificationDate);
    trace(frSelected.creator);
    trace("------------------------");
  }
};
```

Uploading a File

Once the user has selected a file or files, you can upload a file via the `upload()` method of the `FileReference` object you want to upload to the server. If you used a `FileReferenceList` object to let the user select more than one file, you have to call `upload()` for each element in the `fileList` array.

The `upload()` method requires one parameter — the URL to which you want to upload the file. The URL must point to a resource that can handle HTTP file upload requests such as a PHP script like the one used in the exercise in the following section. When the file data is uploaded, it is sent via HTTP POST with a content type of multipart/form-data and a name of `Filedata`. Therefore, to the server resource handling the upload it is as though the file is being uploaded via an HTML form with a file input named `Filedata`.

Listener objects get notified regarding several events as a file uploads. You can define the following methods for a listener object to get notifications about uploading events:

✦ `onHTTPError()` — There was an HTTP error. The method gets passed two parameters — a reference to the `FileReference` object and a number indicating the HTTP error type (for example, 404).

✦ `onIOError()` — A network error occurred, the URL is invalid, or the server requires authentication that the current player does not support. The method gets passed a reference to the `FileReference` object.

✦ onSecurityError() — An error occurred related to the Flash Player security model. For example, the requested URL may be inaccessible to Flash Player because of differing domains and no cross-domain policy file being found.

✦ onOpen() — The file has successfully started to upload. The method is passed a reference to the FileReference object.

✦ onProgress() — Some portion of the file has uploaded. The method is passed three parameters — a reference to the FileReference object, the number of bytes uploaded so far, and the total number of bytes to upload.

✦ onComplete() — The file has successfully uploaded. The method is passed a reference to the FileReference object.

Uploading files is subject to Flash Player security. That means that file upload requests conform to the same security model as any other HTTP request from Flash Player. Either the URL must be in the same exact domain as the SWF, or the server must have a policy file.

If the server resource to which the file is uploaded requires authentication, Flash Player will prompt the user for authentication only in the browser. Otherwise, in any non-browser environment the upload will fail.

Adding Uploading Capabilities to an Application

In this exercise, you'll build a simple application that lets users upload files to a server from Flash Player utilizing a PHP script on the server. To run the exercise, you'll need a Web server that runs PHP. PHP is fairly standard on most shared Web hosts. If your Web host does have PHP installed, then it's recommended that you use that Web server. However, in the event that your Web host does not have PHP installed, you can download and install PHP for free on your own computer. You can download PHP from www.php.net. PHP runs on Windows, Macintosh, and Linux, to name a few operating systems, so you shouldn't have difficulty installing PHP on your computer. If you opt to run PHP on your computer, you'll also have to run a Web server such as IIS or Apache. It's beyond the scope of this book to instruct you how to install a Web server or PHP, but you'll not have difficulty locating helpful resources for those topics on the Web.

1. Copy simpleFileUpload.php from the Web site to a PHP-enabled directory on your Web server that is accessible via HTTP.

2. Open a new Flash document, and save it as fileUploader.fla.

3. Add the following code to the first frame of the main timeline:

```
import flash.net.FileReference;

// Add a text field in order to display the data about the file
// and the uploading progress.
this.createTextField("tData", this.getNextHighestDepth(), 0,
0, 250, 250);
tData.border = true;
tData.multiline = true;

// Add a text field to use as a button to browse for a file.
```

```
this.createTextField("tBrowse", this.getNextHighestDepth(),     ⏎
0, 0, 0, 0);
tBrowse.border = true;
tBrowse.autoSize = "left";
tBrowse.selectable = false;
tBrowse.html = true;

// When the user clicks on the text call the browseFiles()
// function.
tBrowse.htmlText = "<a href='asfunction:browseFiles'>BROWSE</a>";
tBrowse._x = 275;

// Add a text field to use as a button to upload a selected file.
this.createTextField("tUpload", this.getNextHighestDepth(),     ⏎
0, 0, 0, 0);
tUpload.border = true;
tUpload.autoSize = "left";
tUpload.selectable = false;
tUpload.html = true;
tUpload.htmlText = "<a href='asfunction:uploadFile'>UPLOAD</a>";
tUpload._x = 275;
tUpload._y = 50;

var oListener:Object = new Object();

// When the user selects a file, display the properties of the
// selected file.
oListener.onSelect = function(frSelected:FileReference):Void {
  tData.text = "name: " + frSelected.name + newline;
  tData.text += "created on: " +                                ⏎
frSelected.creationDate + newline;
  tData.text += "modified on: " +                               ⏎
frSelected.modificationDate + newline;
  tData.text += "size: " + frSelected.size + newline;
  tData.text += "type: " + frSelected.type + newline;
};

// Display a message when the file starts to upload.
oListener.onOpen = function(frUploading:FileReference):Void {
  tData.text += "starting upload" + newline;
};

// Display a message as the file uploads.
oListener.onProgress = function(                                ⏎
frUploading:FileReference, nBytesUploaded:Number,               ⏎
nBytesTotal:Number):Void {
  tData.text += "uploading " + nBytesUploaded +                 ⏎
" bytes of " + nBytesTotal + newline;
};

// Display a message when the file has uploaded.
oListener.onComplete = function(frUploading:FileReference):Void {
  tData.text += "file uploaded" + newline;
```

```
  };

  var frToUpload:FileReference = new FileReference();
  frToUpload.addListener(oListener);

  function browseFiles():Void {
    frToUpload.browse();
  }

  function uploadFile():Void {
    // Specify the URL to the PHP script on your server.
    frToUpload.upload("http://server/simplefileupload.php");
  }
```

4. Test the movie.

When you test the movie, you ought to be able to browse to a file and upload it. When you check on the server in the same directory as the PHP script, a copy of the file ought to appear.

Downloading a File

Using the download() method, you can download a file from a URL to the user's computer. However, the user has to grant permission. When the download() method is called a new dialog box is opened, and the user is prompted to save the file. The user has the choice to click Save or Cancel.

The download() method requires two parameters. The first parameter is the URL to an HTTP resource to download. The second parameter is a string specifying the default save as the file name.

```
  frToDownload.download("http://server/file", "a_file.txt");
```

If the user clicks the Cancel button, the onCancel() method is called for any listener objects. If the user clicks the Save button, the onOpen() method is called. As the file downloads the onProgress() method is called. And when the file has downloaded, the onComplete() method gets called. If there are any errors, the appropriate error handler method [onHTTPError(), onIOError(), or onSecurityError()] is called.

We'd like to know what you thought about this chapter. Visit www.rightactionscript .com/asb/comments to fill out an online form with your comments.

Summary

✦ Flash 8 introduces file upload and download functionality.

✦ Using the FileReference or FileReferenceList classes, you can prompt users to browse to and select a file or files from their local drive in order to upload the file(s).

✦ The FileReference class defines methods for uploading and downloading files.

✦   ✦   ✦

Working with Flash in Context

Working with Flash in the Web Browser

✦ ✦ ✦ ✦

In This Chapter

Examining the HTML used to add Flash movies to pages

Communicating with JavaScript

Detecting Flash Player versions

✦ ✦ ✦ ✦

This chapter looks at Flash movies embedded in HTML pages. There are several things you'll look at in detail. First of all, it is important to familiarize yourself with the HTML required to add a Flash movie to an HTML page. Once you understand that, you'll next take a look at how you can communicate from Flash to JavaScript in the browser, and vice versa. And then you'll look at how to detect the Flash Player.

Understanding Flash and HTML

When you publish your Flash applications you have the option to publish the HTML pages as well. In order to do this, open the Publish Settings dialog box by choosing File ➪ Publish Settings. Then, make sure that you check the HTML option on the Formats tab. Figure 38-1 shows the Publish Settings dialog box with the HTML tag selected. (The HTML tag shows up after you have checked the HTML option in the Formats tab.) Notice the Detect Flash Version check box under the Template box, too. This option is discussed later in the chapter.

Using one of the templates to publish an HTML file can be a time-saver when you're getting started, or it might be all you need. In the majority of Flash targeted for the Web, publishing with the standard Flash Only template works well as is. Sometimes, you might need to communicate with the Flash Player, so you'll read about this process later in this chapter when you read about the FSCommand template. In other cases, you might need to customize or extend the template's output — for example, changing the generated HTML code to match the look and feel of your site. Or, perhaps the page in which the Flash movie is going to play needs to be dynamically generated by a ColdFusion page or a PHP page. No matter what your reasons for wanting to modify or copy and paste from the generated HTML, it is a good idea to familiarize yourself with the HTML necessary to add a Flash movie to a web page.

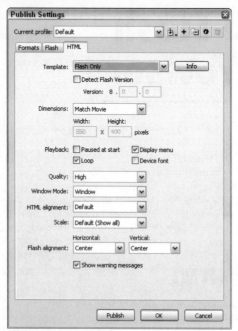

Figure 38-1: The HTML settings in the Publish Settings dialog box.

If you use the Flash Only template to publish an HTML page and open the HTML code in a text editor, you will see something that looks like the following. The bolded code is responsible for actually adding the Flash movie to the page.

```
<!DOCTYPE html PUBLIC "-//W3C//DTD XHTML 1.0 Transitional//EN"
"http://www.w3.org/TR/xhtml1/DTD/xhtml1-transitional.dtd">
<html xmlns="http://www.w3.org/1999/xhtml" xml:lang="en" lang="en">
<head>
<meta http-equiv="Content-Type" content="text/html; charset=iso-8859-1" />
<title>publishTest</title>
</head>
<body bgcolor="#ffffff">
<!--url's used in the movie-->
<!--text used in the movie-->
<object classid="clsid:d27cdb6e-ae6d-11cf-96b8-444553540000"
codebase="http://download.macromedia.com/pub/shockwave/cabs/flash/swflash.
cab#version=7,0,0,0" width="550" height="400" id="movieName" align="middle">
<param name="allowScriptAccess" value="sameDomain" />
<param name="movie" value="movieName.swf" />
<param name="quality" value="high" />
<param name="bgcolor" value="#ffffff" />
```

```
<embed src="movieName.swf" quality="high" bgcolor="#ffffff" width="550"
height="400" name="movieName" align="middle" allowScriptAccess="sameDomain"
type="application/x-shockwave-flash"
pluginspage="http://www.macromedia.com/go/getflashplayer" />
</object>
</body>
</html>
```

The `<object>` tag works with the ActiveX control that plays Flash movies in browsers such as Internet Explorer for Windows. The `<embed>` tag works for the plug-in that plays Flash movies in browsers such as Netscape. Therefore, for any changes that you make to the `<param>` tags or the attributes of the `<object>` tag, you'll need to also change the corresponding attributes of the `<embed>` tag.

Both the `<object>` and `<embed>` tags enable you to specify the width and height of the SWF file that is to be scaled to fit within those dimensions. The ID is important for specific JavaScript controls that you can employ, so you should generally make sure to assign an ID. And the `align` attribute specifies how the movie is aligned within the browser. The `movie` parameter/attribute is essential because it tells the browser where to find the SWF. The `quality` and `bgcolor` parameters/attributes allow you to override the settings within the SWF. If those parameters/attributes are left out, the values within the SWF are used.

The `allowScriptAccess` parameter/attribute determines the outgoing scripting access from a SWF (outgoing scripting typically meaning calls to JavaScript functions with `getURL()`). A value of `never` prevents all outgoing scripting calls. A value of `always` allows all outgoing scripting calls through. And a value of `sameDomain` allows all outgoing scripting calls to the same domain (that is, if the SWF is on the same domain as the HTML page to which the scripting calls are being made) but it disallows any cross-domain scripting calls.

If you want to add a Flash movie to a page other than the default, published HTML page, you can approach the situation in several ways:

✦ Memorize the HTML code, and type it each time you want to add a Flash movie to a page.

✦ Use an HTML editor such as Dreamweaver that has a built-in function for adding the necessary code to a page.

✦ Save the basic code in a text file, copy and paste it into each new page, and modify it as necessary.

✦ Publish the HTML from Flash and then copy and paste or modify the exported code.

Passing Initialization Values to Flash from HTML

You can pass values to a Flash movie from the HTML as Flash loads using the `FlashVars` parameter/attribute of the `<object>` and `<embed>` tags. The value or values you pass to the Flash movie using `FlashVars` are only passed when the Flash movie loads. That means that even if you update the values for `FlashVars` using JavaScript or VBScript, the new, updated values are not sent to the Flash movie. `FlashVars` is basically used for initializing a Flash movie with certain values. This is a very useful technique that is helpful in many scenarios, including the following:

✦ **Specifying the values for variables within the Flash movie that may update relatively frequently** — By using `FlashVars` instead of coding the values into the movie itself, you can change the values in the HTML rather than having to change the values in the Flash file and then re-export the movie.

✦ **Setting the values that may vary from environment to environment** — For example, the `FlashVars` technique is employed with Flash Remoting (see Chapter 36) to specify the Flash Remoting gateway URL — a value that will likely change from server to server. This way you don't have to maintain different versions of the Flash movie for each environment.

✦ **Initializing a movie with values retrieved from a database recordset or other server-side resource** — If you use, for example, a ColdFusion or PHP page in which you add the Flash movie, you can do a database query and pass some of the results to a Flash movie as it loads. This technique is not intended for passing entire recordsets or large amounts of complex data to a Flash movie. Flash Remoting is a more appropriate choice for that kind of functionality. But if you want to pass certain initialization values to a Flash movie, you can do so through `FlashVars`. For example, you might pass a Flash movie a session ID.

In order to use `FlashVars`, you should add a `FlashVars` `<param>` object nested within the `<object>` tag, and you should add a `FlashVars` attribute to the `<embed>` tag. The value for `FlashVars` should be in the URL encoded format. That is to say, it should contain name-value pairs in which each variable name is linked with the value by an equal sign, each name-value pair is separated by an ampersand, and all spaces or other non-alphanumeric (or underscore) characters should be escaped with their hexadecimal equivalents. For example:

```
<object classid="clsid:d27cdb6e-ae6d-11cf-96b8-444553540000"
codebase="http://download.macromedia.com/pub/shockwave/cabs/flash/swflash.
cab#version=7,0,0,0" width="550" height="400" id="usingFlashVars"
align="middle">
<param name="allowScriptAccess" value="sameDomain" />
<param name="movie" value="usingFlashVars.swf" />
<param name="quality" value="high" />
<param name="bgcolor" value="#ffffff" />
<param name="FlashVars" value="sLabel=circle&sDescription=a%20circle" />
<embed src="usingFlashVars.swf" quality="high" bgcolor="#ffffff"
width="550" height="400" name="usingFlashVars" align="middle"
allowScriptAccess="sameDomain" type="application/x-shockwave-flash"
pluginspage="http://www.macromedia.com/go/getflashplayer"
FlashVars="sLabel=circle&sDescription=a%20circle" />
</object>
```

The preceding code passes two values to the Flash movie: `sLabel` with a value of `circle` and `sDescription` with a value of `a circle`. This creates two variables on the main timeline of the Flash movie named `sLabel` and `sDescription`, and assigns them the associated values. If you want to pass Flash number or Boolean values you should, within Flash, use ActionScript to convert the values from strings to the appropriate types. For example, if you use `FlashVars` to pass a movie a variable named `nQuantity` with a number value then you should use the following code on the main timeline of your Flash movie:

```
nQuantity = parseInt(nQuantity);
```

If you want to pass your Flash movie a variable named `bIsVisible`, a Boolean value, you should use the following code in your Flash movie to convert the value to a Boolean:

```
bIsVisible = (bIsVisible == "true") ? true : false;
```

Communicating with JavaScript and Flash

When you deploy Flash applications in a web browser, you may want to be able to communicate with the container HTML page. You may want to call JavaScript functions from the SWF, and you may want JavaScript functions to be able to call functions within the SWF. That lets you make integrated applications, of which the SWF is just one component.

The following sections take a look at the ways in which you can communicate between Flash and JavaScript.

Calling JavaScript Functions from Flash — The Simple Ways

There are two simple ways you can call JavaScript functions from Flash — using `getURL()` or `fscommand()`. Typically, the `getURL()` method is the preferred technique for several reasons. The primary reason is that `getURL()` has greater compatibility with browsers. The secondary reason is that it is much simpler to use the `getURL()` technique than to use the `fscommand()` technique. The following should give you an idea of compatibility of each of these techniques:

✦ `getURL()` works for all 5+ browsers. It works for all 3.x browsers except in IE3 on Windows. And it works in all 4.x browsers except IE 4.5 on Macintosh.

✦ `fscommand()` does not work with the following:

- IE on the Macintosh

- Netscape 6 until version 6.2 (does work in all 6.2+ versions of Netscape)

- 68KB Macintosh (yikes!) or Windows 3.1 (double-yikes!) computers

In order to make a JavaScript call from Flash using the `getURL()` method, all you need to do is to use the `javascript:` directive followed by the JavaScript to execute in the browser. For example:

```
this.getURL("javascript: alert('hello');");
```

When you place the preceding code on the first frame of the main timeline of your Flash file and then do a publish preview (press F12), you see a JavaScript alert window with the message `hello`.

If you have custom JavaScript functions defined within the HTML page, you can call those functions in the same manner. For example, if you have a JavaScript function named `setStatusBar()` defined within the parent HTML page, you can call it from Flash as follows:

```
this.getURL("javascript: setStatusBar('message from Flash');");
```

Even though the `getURL()` technique using the `javascript:functionName(parameters)` syntax works for most browsers, it still is not supported by Internet Explorer version 4.x (including 4.5) on the Macintosh. However, if you must make sure that your Flash movie can communicate with the JavaScript, there is a workaround available.

Even though getURL() cannot be used to call a JavaScript function directly on version 4.*x* of IE on the Macintosh, it can still be used to open an HTML page. That includes opening an HTML page within a frame. Therefore, you can use this to create a simple workaround for the whole hitch posed by IE 4.*x* on the Macintosh.

The strategy is quite simple. You create a hidden HTML frame into which you can load various HTML pages containing the desired JavaScript that gets called when the page is loaded. This works for any platform that supports getURL() to open an HTML page into a frame.

Although the aforementioned workaround is a viable option, you may find it is simpler to work with ExternalInterface or the Flash/JavaScript Integration Kit as described in the following sections.

Note   The simple Flash to JavaScript calls discussed in the preceding section do not let you return values from JavaScript functions to Flash. If that is a requirement of your application, read the next few sections for ways in which you can accomplish that.

Using ExternalInterface with Flash 8

In Flash 8 content you can use the new flash.external.ExternalInterface class to both call JavaScript functions from Flash and call ActionScript functions from JavaScript. The ExternalInterface class works only with Flash 8 content, so if you need to author to previous player versions you'll need to use something like the Flash/JavaScript Integration Kit described later in this chapter.

The ExternalInterface class has been tested successfully in the following browsers:

✦ Windows Internet Explorer

✦ Windows Netscape 8

✦ Windows Firefox

✦ Macintosh Safari 2.0

✦ Macintosh Firefox

If you need the application to work in browsers other than those in the preceding list, consider using the Flash/JavaScript Integration Kit.

Calling JavaScript Functions from Flash

Using ExternalInterface, you can call JavaScript functions from within a Flash SWF. One advantage of using ExternalInterface over the getURL() technique discussed previously is that with ExternalInterface the JavaScript function can return a value to Flash.

To call a JavaScript function from Flash, you simply use the static ExternalInterface.call() method. The call() method requires at least one parameter — the name of the function to call. You can also pass additional parameters, each of which is passed to the JavaScript function as parameters. The following code calls the JavaScript alert() function with a parameter of hello.

```
import flash.external.ExternalInterface;

ExternalInterface.call("alert", "hello");
```

If the JavaScript function returns a value, you can simply use the `call()` method as part of an expression such as an assignment statement. The following example code assigns the return value from a JavaScript function `getStringValue()` to a variable:

```
var sValue:String = ExternalInterface.call("getStringValue");
```

Calling ActionScript Functions from JavaScript

You can also call ActionScript functions from JavaScript. To do so, you must do two things — register the function in ActionScript so that it is accessible from JavaScript, and then call the function from JavaScript via the Flash object.

You can register an ActionScript function within Flash using the static `ExternalInterface` `.addCallback()` method. The method requires three parameters: the name of the function as you want to call it from JavaScript, the scope to which you want the callback associated, and the reference to the function/method that you want to register. The second parameter may seem slightly strange. Much as when you use the `call()` or `apply()` methods of a function or the `Delegate.create()` method, you can specify the object that the this keyword will reference within the function/method when it is called from JavaScript. Assuming that the following code is on the main timeline, it registers a function called `runScript()` so that you can call it from JavaScript as `runFlashScript()`. It also specifies that the main timeline is the object within the function when it is called.

```
import flash.external.ExternalInterface;

ExternalInterface.addCallback("runFlashScript", this, runScript);
```

Once a function is registered, you can call it from within JavaScript. From JavaScript, you call the function as a method of the Flash object by referencing the ID of the plug-in or ActiveX object. As you'll recall from the earlier discussion, you can assign ID attributes to the `<object>` and `<embed>` tags. If you are using the ActiveX player (Internet Explorer), you reference the Flash object as follows:

```
window.flashObjectID
```

Otherwise, use the following:

```
window.document.flashObjectID
```

You can determine the correct reference by checking the value of the `navigator.appName` property within JavaScript. If the property value contains the string `Microsoft`, use the ActiveX reference. Otherwise, use the plug-in reference. The following code will help you accomplish that. Place this code in the head of the HTML document.

```
<script language="JavaScript">
function initialize() {
  if(navigator.appName.indexOf("Microsoft") != -1) {
    flash = window.flashObjectID;
  }
  else {
    flash = window.document.flashObjectID;
  }
}
</script>
```

Then, within the `<body>` tag, add an `onLoad` attribute, and assign to that a call to the `initialize()` function:

```
<body onLoad="initialize();">
```

That way, the `initialize()` function is called once the page loads in the browser. Then the `flash` variable will reference the Flash object. Next, you can call the function as you registered it using `ExternalInterface`. For example, assuming that you registered a function so that you could call it `runFlashScript()`, the following code will call that function from JavaScript (if the flash variable has been assigned the correct reference to the Flash object).

```
flash.runFlashScript();
```

You can pass parameters to the function. You can also use function call in an expression if the ActionScript function returns a value.

Making an Integrated HTML/Flash Application with ExternalInterface

You've had a chance to read about the theory of `ExternalInterface`. Now you'll use the theory to put together a simple demonstration application. The application uses a Flash movie with a rotating rectangle, a start/stop button, and a text field. The Flash movie is placed within an HTML page with a text input and a button. When the page loads, it uses some JavaScript to determine the browser that is being used. The Flash movie requests that data, and displays it in the text field. When the user clicks the start/stop button in the Flash movie, it pauses and resumes the rotation of the rectangle, and it also sends a message to the HTML text input to display the current status of the rectangle. The HTML button makes a new random color and sends it to the Flash movie. The Flash movie then applies that color to the rectangle.

To build the application, complete the following steps:

1. Open a new Flash document, and save it as `externalInterface.fla`.

2. Add the following code to the keyframe of the main timeline:

```
import flash.geom.ColorTransform;
import flash.external.ExternalInterface;
import actionscriptbible.drawing.DrawingUtilities;

// Draw a 200 X 100 rectangle so that when rotated it rotates
// around the center point.
var mRectangle:MovieClip =
this.createEmptyMovieClip("mRectangle",
this.getNextHighestDepth());
var duDrawer:DrawingUtilities = new DrawingUtilities(mRectangle);
duDrawer.beginFill(0xCC00CC, 100);
duDrawer.drawRectangle(200, 100);
duDrawer.endFill();

// Move the rectangle to the center of the stage.
mRectangle._x = 275;
mRectangle._y = 200;

// Make a new MovieClip to use as the start/stop button. Draw
// a 100 X 25 rectangle within it.
```

```
var mButton:MovieClip = this.createEmptyMovieClip(
"mButton", this.getNextHighestDepth());
duDrawer = new DrawingUtilities(mButton);
duDrawer.beginFill(0xFFFFFF, 100);
duDrawer.drawRectangle(100, 25, 50, 12.5);
duDrawer.endFill();

// Add a label to the button.
mButton.createTextField("tLabel",
mButton.getNextHighestDepth(), 0, 0, 100, 25);

mButton.tLabel.text = "start";
mButton.tLabel.selectable = false;

// When the user clicks the button, call the togglePlayback()
// function.
mButton.onPress = togglePlayback;

// Add the TextField object to display the browser data.
this.createTextField("tBrowser", this.getNextHighestDepth(),
150, 0, 200, 100);

// Call a JavaScript function, getBrowser(), that returns an
// object with browser, browserVersion, os, and osVersion
// properties. Display those properties in the TextField object.
var oBrowser:Object = ExternalInterface.call("getBrowser");
tBrowser.text = oBrowser.browser + " " +
oBrowser.browserVersion + "\n";
tBrowser.text += oBrowser.os + " " + oBrowser.osVersion;

// Define a TextFormat object to apply to the button label.
var tfFormatter:TextFormat = new TextFormat();
tfFormatter.align = "center";
tfFormatter.bold = true;

var nInterval:Number;

// Update the color of the rectangle to a random color.
updateColor(Math.random() * 0xFFFFFF);

// Call togglePlayback() to initialize the application with the
// rectangle rotating.
togglePlayback();

// Register updateColor() so we can call it from JavaScript.
ExternalInterface.addCallback("updateColor", null, updateColor);

function togglePlayback():Void {

    // If the button label is not current stop, then start
    // the rectangle rotating by setting an interval. Otherwise,
```

```
      // clear the interval to stop it rotating.
      if(mButton.tLabel.text != "stop") {
        nInterval = setInterval(rotate, 10);
      }
      else {
        clearInterval(nInterval);
      }

      // Call the JavaScript updateStatus() function with the message
      // of either started or stopped.
      ExternalInterface.call("updateStatus",
(mButton.tLabel.text != "stop") ? "started" : "stopped");

      // Update the label, and apply the formatting.
      mButton.tLabel.text =
(mButton.tLabel.text != "stop") ? "stop" : "start";
      mButton.tLabel.setTextFormat(tfFormatter);
    }

// Apply the specified color to the rectangle.
function updateColor(nColor:Number):Void {
  var ctRectangle:ColorTransform =
mRectangle.transform.colorTransform;
  ctRectangle.rgb = nColor;
  mRectangle.transform.colorTransform = ctRectangle;
}

function rotate():Void {
  mRectangle._rotation++;
}
```

3. Save the document, and export the SWF as `externalinterface.swf`.

4. To retrieve the browser data, you use a JS file. Copy `BrowserSniffer.js` from the web site to the same directory as the SWF.

5. In the same directory as the SWF and JS files, add a new HTML document called `externalinterface.html`.

6. Place the following code in the HTML document:

```
<html>
<head>
<title>ExternalInterface</title>

<!-- Import BrowserSniffer.js. -->
<script type="text/javascript" src="BrowserSniffer.js"></script>

<script language="JavaScript">

var flash;
function initialize() {

    // Note that eiMovie is the value of the id attribute of the
    // <object> and <embed> tags within the document.
```

```
    if(navigator.appName.indexOf("Microsoft") != -1) {
      flash = window.eiMovie;
    }
    else {
      flash = window.document.eiMovie;
    }
  }
  function getBrowser() {

    // The BrowserSniffer class is defined in BrowserSniffer.js.
    // Return a new instance. The class defines browser,
    // browserVersion, os, and osVersion properties.
    return new BrowserSniffer();
  }

  // Set the value of the text input control so it displays the
  // status of the rectangle rotation.
  function updateStatus(sMessage) {
    document.forms[0].playbackStatus.value = sMessage;
  }

  // Call updateColor() in the SWF with a random color value. The
  // updateColor() function gets called each time the button is
  // clicked in the HTML document.
  function newColor() {
    flash.updateColor(Math.round(Math.random() * 0xFFFFFF));
  }

</script>
</head>

<!-- Call initialize() when the document loads. -->
<body bgcolor="#ffffff" onLoad="initialize();">

<object classid="clsid:d27cdb6e-ae6d-11cf-96b8-444553540000"
codebase="http://fpdownload.macromedia.com/pub/shockwave/
cabs/flash/swflash.cab#version=8,0,0,0" width="550"
height="400" id="eiMovie" align="middle">
<param name="allowScriptAccess" value="sameDomain" />
<param name="movie" value=" externalinterface.swf" />
<param name="quality" value="high" />
<param name="bgcolor" value="#ffffff" />
<embed src=" externalinterface.swf" quality="high"
bgcolor="#ffffff" width="550" height="400" name="eiMovie"
align="middle" allowScriptAccess="sameDomain"
type="application/x-shockwave-flash"
pluginspage="http://www.macromedia.com/go/getflashplayer" />
</object>

<form>
  Status <input type="text" name="playbackStatus"
value="started" /><br />
```

```
Color <input type="button" value="new color"
name="newColorButton" onClick="newColor();" />
</form>

</body>
</html>
```

7. Save the HTML document. Test the page in a browser.

The Flash security settings will stop the `ExternalInterface` interaction with JavaScript if you are running the page as a local file (for example, the browser says something like `file:///path/to/file.html`). Either you can run the file from a web server (even if it's localhost) or you can add the location to the Settings Manager at `www.macromedia.com/support/documentation/en/flashplayer/help/settings_manager04.html`.

Using the Flash/JavaScript Integration Kit

There are cases in which the `ExternalInterface` technique won't work for your application. Specifically, it won't work if you are authoring to a version of the player earlier than Flash 8 or if you are authoring to a browser other than those listed in the previous section. In such cases, you can use the Flash/JavaScript Integration Kit, which is compatible with Flash Player 6,0,65,0+ and with the following browsers:

✦ Windows Internet Explorer 6.0

✦ Windows Firefox 1.0

✦ Windows Opera 8.0

✦ Macintosh Opera 8.0

✦ Macintosh Firefox 1.0

✦ Macintosh Safari 1.2.4 and 2.0

✦ Linux Firefox 1.0

Download the Flash/JavaScript Integration Kit for free from `www.osflash.org/doku.php?id=flashjs`. Once you've downloaded the kit, install it as follows:

1. Extract the files.

2. Add the `source/flash/actionscript` directory to Flash's global classpath.

3. Copy the `.js` and `.swf` files from the installation directory to a location from which you can use the files in HTML pages with which you want to use the kit. If necessary, you can simply copy the files to each project's directory as you're working on the project.

Calling JavaScript Functions from Flash

Calling JavaScript functions from Flash using the kit is fairly simple. There are three steps — one in the HTML page and two in Flash. Within the HTML page, import the `JavaScriptFlashGateway.js` file. Assuming that you copied the file to the same directory as the HTML document, add the following line of code to the document to add the necessary JavaScript classes to the HTML document:

```
<script type="text/javascript" src="JavaScriptFlashGateway.js"></script>
```

Then, within the ActionScript code you can construct a new `JavaScriptProxy` object. `JavaScriptProxy` is one of the classes defined within the `com.macromedia.javascript` package that you added to the global classpath when you installed the Flash/JavaScript Integration Kit according to the directions in the previous section.

```
import com.macromedia.javascript.JavaScriptProxy;

var jspProxy:JavaScriptProxy = new JavaScriptProxy();
```

Next, use the `call()` method of the `JavaScriptProxy` object. The `call()` method requires at least one parameter — the name of the JavaScript function you want to call. Optionally, you can pass it additional parameters that are passed to the JavaScript as parameters.

```
jspProxy.call("javaScriptFunction");
```

Unlike `ExternalInterface.call()`, the `call()` method of the `JavaScriptProxy` class does not return a value even if the JavaScript function returns a value. If you want to return a value from JavaScript, you have to use a callback technique in which the JavaScript function makes a call to an ActionScript function. You can learn how to make calls to ActionScript functions from JavaScript in the next section.

Calling ActionScript Functions from JavaScript

You can call ActionScript functions from JavaScript with the kit as well. Doing so requires some work to get the HTML page properly configured. To call ActionScript functions from JavaScript, do the following within the HTML page:

1. As when you want to call JavaScript functions from ActionScript, import the `JavaScriptFlashGateway.js` file:

```
<script type="text/javascript"
src="JavaScriptFlashGateway.js"></script>
```

2. Within a `<script language="JavaScript">` tag (so that the code will run when the page loads), define a new `FlashProxy` object. `FlashProxy` is one of the classes defined in the `.js` file. The `FlashProxy` constructor requires two parameters: an ID associated with the SWF and the path to the `JavaScriptFlashGateway.swf` file that you copied from the kit. You'll need to use the same ID as you use when you embed the SWF, so it's recommended that you have JavaScript make a unique number using a new `Date` object's Epoch milliseconds. The following code illustrates how to construct the new `FlashProxy` object, assuming that `JavaScriptFlashGateway.swf` is in the same directory as the HTML document.

```
<script language="JavaScript">
var nID = new Date().getTime();
var flash = new FlashProxy(nID, 'JavaScriptFlashGateway.swf');
function getBrowser() {
  flash.call("setBrowser", new BrowserSniffer());
}
function updateStatus(sMessage) {
  document.forms[0].playbackStatus.value = sMessage;
}
function newColor() {
  flash.call("updateColor", Math.round(
Math.random() * 0xFFFFFF));
}
</script>
```

3. Instead of writing the `<object>` and `<embed>` tags, use a `FlashTag` object. The `FlashTag` class is also defined in the `.js` file. The `FlashTag` constructor requires three parameters: the path to the SWF you want to place in the page, the width of the SWF, and the height of the SWF. Once you've constructed the `FlashTag` object, use the `setFlashvars()` method to add a new `FlashVars` parameter called `lcId` with a value equal to the ID you used when constructing the `FlashProxy` object. Then, call the `write()` method of the `FlashTag` object to write the HTML code to the document. You can add the FlashTag code within a `<script>` tag within the body of the HTML document at which point you want to place the SWF.

```
<script type="text/javascript">
  var ftMovie = new FlashTag('FlashJSIK.swf', 550, 400);
  ftMovie.setFlashvars('lcId=' + nID);
  ftMovie.write(document);
</script>
```

4. When you want to call the ActionScript function, use the `FlashProxy` object, and call the function. For example, if you want to call an ActionScript function called `runFlashScript()`, and if the `FlashProxy` object is called `flash`, you can use the following JavaScript code:

```
flash.runFlashScript();
```

You can pass parameters to the ActionScript function by passing parameters to the function when you call it from the `FlashProxy` object.

Within the Flash document, you need to construct a `JavaScriptProxy` object so that you can call ActionScript functions from JavaScript. When you constructed a `JavaScriptProxy` object previously you didn't have to pass it any parameters. However, to call ActionScript functions from JavaScript, you need to pass the constructor two parameters — the ID you passed to the SWF via `FlashVars` and the object to which the function calls are proxied. The ID is stored in a variable called `lcId`. The object to which you want to proxy the function calls is the object for which the functions or methods are defined. If you are constructing the `JavaScriptProxy` object on the main timeline, and you want to proxy the calls to functions on the main timeline, the code looks like the following:

```
import com.macromedia.javascript.JavaScriptProxy;

var jspProxy:JavaScriptProxy = new JavaScriptProxy(lcId, this);
```

Making an Integrated HTML/Flash Application with the Flash/JavaScript Integration Kit

In this exercise, you'll build the Flash/JavaScript Integration Kit version of the application from the previous exercise.

1. Open a new Flash document, and save it as `flashjavascript.fla`.

2. Add the following code to the keyframe of the main timeline. The code is very similar to the code from the previous exercise. The modifications are shown in bold.

```
import flash.geom.ColorTransform;
import actionscriptbible.drawing.DrawingUtilities;
import com.macromedia.javascript.JavaScriptProxy;

var jspContainer:JavaScriptProxy =
```

⤵

```
new JavaScriptProxy(lcId, this);

var mRectangle:MovieClip = this.createEmptyMovieClip("mRectangle", ⊃
this.getNextHighestDepth());
var duDrawer:DrawingUtilities = new DrawingUtilities(mRectangle);
duDrawer.beginFill(0xCC00CC, 100);
duDrawer.drawRectangle(200, 100);
duDrawer.endFill();

mRectangle._x = 275;
mRectangle._y = 200;

var mButton:MovieClip = this.createEmptyMovieClip(               ⊃
"mRectangle", this.getNextHighestDepth());
duDrawer = new DrawingUtilities(mButton);
duDrawer.beginFill(0xFFFFFF, 100);
duDrawer.drawRectangle(100, 25, 50, 12.5);
duDrawer.endFill();

mButton.createTextField("tLabel",                               ⊃
mButton.getNextHighestDepth(), 0, 0, 100, 25);
mButton.tLabel.text = "start";
mButton.tLabel.selectable = false;
mButton.onPress = togglePlayback;

this.createTextField("tBrowser", this.getNextHighestDepth(),    ⊃
150, 0, 200, 100);

// Note that the Flash/JavaScript Integration Kit version does
// not return a value. Instead, the getBrowser() function calls
// setBrowser().
jspContainer.call("getBrowser");

var tfFormatter:TextFormat = new TextFormat();
tfFormatter.align = "center";
tfFormatter.bold = true;

var nInterval:Number;
updateColor(Math.random() * 0xFFFFFF);
togglePlayback();

function togglePlayback():Void {
  if(mButton.tLabel.text != "stop") {
    nInterval = setInterval(rotate, 10);
  }
  else {
    clearInterval(nInterval);
  }
  jspContainer.call("updateStatus",                             ⊃
(mButton.tLabel.text != "stop") ? "started" : "stopped");
  mButton.tLabel.text =                                         ⊃
```

```
      (mButton.tLabel.text != "stop") ? "stop" : "start";
        mButton.tLabel.setTextFormat(tfFormatter);
      }

      function updateColor(nColor:Number):Void {
        var ctRectangle:ColorTransform =
      mRectangle.transform.colorTransform;
        ctRectangle.rgb = nColor;
        mRectangle.transform.colorTransform = ctRectangle;
      }

      function rotate():Void {
        mRectangle._rotation++;
      }

      function setBrowser(oBrowser:Object):Void {
        tBrowser.text = oBrowser.browser + " " +
      oBrowser.browserVersion + "\n";
        tBrowser.text += oBrowser.os + " " + oBrowser.osVersion;
      }
```

3. Export the SWF file as `flashjavascript.swf`.

4. Add a new HTML document to the same directory as the SWF. Save the HTML document as `flashjavascript.html`.

5. If you haven't already, copy the `JavaScriptFlashGateway.js` and `JavaScriptFlashGateway.swf` files to the same directory.

6. Add the following code to the HTML document. The code is very similar to `externalinterface.html`. The modifications are shown in bold.

```
<html>
<head>
<title>Flash/JavaScript Integration Kit</title>
<script type="text/javascript" src="BrowserSniffer.js"></script>
<script type="text/javascript"
src="JavaScriptFlashGateway.js"></script>
<script language="JavaScript">
var nID = new Date().getTime();
var flash = new FlashProxy(nID, 'JavaScriptFlashGateway.swf');
function getBrowser() {
  flash.call("setBrowser", new BrowserSniffer());
}
function updateStatus(sMessage) {
  document.forms[0].playbackStatus.value = sMessage;
}
function newColor() {
  flash.call("updateColor", Math.round(
Math.random() * 0xFFFFFF));
}
</script>
</head>
```

```
<body bgcolor="#ffffff">

<script type="text/javascript">
  var ftMovie = new FlashTag('FlashJSIK.swf', 550, 400);
  ftMovie.setFlashvars('lcId=' + nID);
  ftMovie.write(document);
</script>

<form>
  Status <input type="text" name="playbackStatus"
value="started" /><br />
  Color <input type="button" value="new color"
name="newColorButton" onClick="newColor();" />
</form>

</body>
</html>
```

7. Save the document, and test it in a browser.

Detecting the Flash Player in Web Browsers

Time and time again, one of the biggest problems that Flash developers face is making sure that viewers can actually see the content they are supposed to see. Many of the most frequently asked questions among new and veteran Flash developers is how to make sure that people will be able to see the Flash content across platforms, browsers, and versions. In the following two sections, you'll take a look at the two most sensible approaches to player detection.

Manual Player Detection

Often, it seems that companies and individuals want to make their web sites as fully automated as possible. However, one of the original methods for detecting the Flash Player is still one of the most foolproof. A splash screen can be used to alert users as to what player version is required and to allow them to enter the site/application once they have confirmed that they do have the requested player.

Automated Player Detection

Automated player detection used to be a somewhat complicated task. However, in Flash 8, Macromedia has built automated player detection into the publish settings so that you can have Flash publish all the necessary code and files. When you open the Publish Settings dialog box and choose the HTML tab, you can see a Detect Flash Version check box just underneath the Template combo box (refer back to Figure 38-1). By default, the check box is unselected. If you select this option, you also have the option to change the settings in the version detection settings dialog that is enabled.

Within the version detection settings dialog, shown in Figure 38-2, notice that the required Flash version is set to the version to which you are publishing the SWF. If you are publishing to Flash Player 8, for example, it will automatically set the required version to 8. If you want to require a major and minor revision, you have the option to enter the revision numbers up to the revision you have installed on your system.

Figure 38-2: The version detection settings dialog.

When you publish the HTML file, it automatically contains the JavaScript and HTML code used for Flash Player detection. If the minimum Flash Player version is not detected, the HTML code within the `<noscript>` tag is rendered in the browser. You can edit the code in the `<noscript>` tag to display custom content in that event.

Web Resource   We'd like to know what you thought about this chapter. Visit `www.rightactionscript` `.com/asb/comments` to fill out an online form with your comments.

Summary

✦ Flash movies are added to web pages with the HTML `<object>` and `<embed>` tags.

✦ You can call JavaScript functions in the parent web page by using the `getURL()` method in your Flash movie. When using `getURL()` to call a JavaScript function, you pass it a parameter containing the `javascript:` directive followed by the function call.

✦ An important but often overlooked step in working with Flash on the Web is detecting the Flash Player. Using the version detection system built into Flash, you can easily create player-detection systems.

✦   ✦   ✦

Making Movies Accessible and Universal

Flash Players 6 and later offer features to make your Flash movies more accessible. There is a need to create content that people with special requirements can utilize, as the population of those with Internet access steadily increases. The Internet can be especially important for those with additional needs because it can be much easier to access information online than by other means. Getting into a car, taking public transportation, getting into a building, and so on can be challenging for people with special needs. Macromedia has incorporated accessibility into Flash movies by enabling various parts of a movie to be recognizable to screen readers. Screen readers generate certain text, objects, and descriptions of graphic content into spoken word, thereby enabling visually challenged users to access the content. This chapter explains how to make Flash presentations that function successfully when played in conjunction with assistive technologies.

Standardizing Accessibility Concerns

Making computers and the Internet increasingly accessible to all users has been a long-time effort by many government and industry regulatory organizations, as well as software developers. These organizations have acknowledged the challenges that face individuals with physical and cognitive disabilities, looked at what challenges exist for Web users, and then developed guidelines and standards for the development of technologies to aid them. For example, programs integrating voice commands and text-to-speech have assisted visually challenged individuals in dealing with the navigation of their computers and the Internet.

Why is there such a need when it comes to electronic and online information? The Web, for instance, is full of content not suitably built for assistive technologies, such as images without `alt` tags, video without corresponding descriptions, improperly constructed image maps, and the like. Another problem, now of the past, was completely inaccessible Flash-driven content. Macromedia claimed Flash Player 6 to be the first "rich-media" player to be accessible to screen readers. Given that Macromedia says that about 25 percent of web sites include Flash content, many see this development as a giant step in the right direction.

Let's quickly look at why the development of accessible content is important and necessary in Web development.

Section 508

Section 508 is the 1998 amendment to the Workforce Rehabilitation Act of 1973 (a U.S. Federal Act). One of the requirements within it is that all electronic information produced for the U.S. federal government and agencies is to be made accessible to all individuals to the fullest extent possible. If web sites of a federal agency are not accessible, fines, penalties, or even legal action can be taken against the agency in question. However, this does *not* apply to the private sector or private agencies that receive federal funding. Section 508 follows the guidelines of the World Wide Web Consortium (W3C) in its Web Accessibility Initiative (see the following section). The initiative was implemented for several reasons, one of which was to encourage technologies to develop Web content with Section 508 standards and guidelines in mind.

Details on Section 508 requirements are available at `www.section508.gov`.

The United States is not the only nation to require federal web sites to be accessible these days. Canada and the European Union, as well as other nations, have implemented regulations similar to Section 508 in the United States. Therefore, companies and developers worldwide working with these sectors routinely face the issue of creating accessible web sites. Thankfully, Flash content can be seen as a viable accessibility-minded option for Web developers.

W3C Standards

The W3C is an organization devoted to creating universal protocols for Internet development. The W3C primarily focuses on the direction of the development of the Internet, present and future technologies involved in it, and the attempt to standardize the technologies and languages within this realm.

Not only does the W3C standardize the use of HTML, CSS, XML, and other languages, but it also sets standards and provides guidelines for accessibility on the Internet. The W3C is involved in making sure that Web technologies (HTML, XML, CSS, and so on) are supportive of accessibility. The W3C is also involved in outreach, education, and even the development of tools to facilitate accessibility. The program involved with accessibility is called the Web Accessibility Initiative, and it includes a set of guidelines aimed at helping Web developers achieve accessible design.

You can review the current W3C Web Accessibility Initiative and its guidelines at `www.w3.org/WAI`.

Web sites can achieve accessibility in a number of ways. As a result of the varied nature of assistive technology software and/or hardware found on the computers of a user, a Web developer can expect difficulty in creating a web site that is accessible by everyone. Depending on how you look at it, in one way we're "fortunate" that there are strict requirements for a Flash movie to utilize accessibility. The user must have a specific combination of web browser, screen reader software, and a compatible version of the Flash Player to view the accessible part(s) of a Flash movie. Despite this, it is still possible to note some differences among only slight variations in software. When more assistive technologies are developed to work with the Flash Player, we will have to cover many more variables and handle the unpredictable nature of this technology.

Microsoft Active Accessibility (MSAA)

Microsoft developed Microsoft Active Accessibility (MSAA) to improve the connection between assistive technology, such as software and Braille readers, and the Windows-based operating systems. MSAA standards help software developers create products for those with hearing, motion, or sight disabilities. MSAA also improves the communication between accessibility software and other Windows applications.

Macromedia built MSAA technologies into Flash Player 6 and higher to enable screen readers that also support this technology. As such, these screen readers can access the Flash content in web sites. MSAA is considered a basic requisite when working with screen readers in the Windows environment. Macromedia's adoption of MSAA signals a new era of Flash development where software developers can adhere to an already established standard in assistive software technology.

Note   At this time Flash Player cannot "talk" to equivalent system-level accessibility layers of Mac OS X.

Reviewing Current Assistive Technologies

Assistive technologies are special programs that help individuals with a disability to use their computers. These programs are varied and support individuals who face various challenges. One of the most prominent challenges for some computer users is an inability to see the monitor. Some examples of software to help these users in this category are JAWS for Windows, IBM Home Page Reader, HAL, and Window-Eyes. Currently, the only screen readers to work with Flash Player are Window-Eyes and JAWS.

Web Resource   For the most up-to-date information on Flash Player's compatibility with screen reader software, see `www.macromedia.com/macromedia/accessibility/features/flash/player.html`.

In the past, several methods were used to make a Flash movie more accessible. Some of these methods include allowing users to zoom into the movie, navigating by keypress controls, having a narrative in sync with the movie's content, navigating through pages by using Next and Back buttons as opposed to automated progression, and so on. However, this chapter focuses on the accessibility features available to ActionScript. The scope of the `Accessibility` class makes basic-to-advanced support in a movie possible for those with visual challenges. In order for a user to be able to hear your Flash movie content, at this time he or she must have screen reader software installed.

Screen readers are programs used primarily by the visually impaired. Individuals who can see, but still have difficulty reading text as a result of conditions such as dyslexia or aphasia, also use this technology. Screen readers generally work in conjunction with a speech synthesizer. They provide spoken vocal output of content on the monitor, and also when input devices are used (such as when a person is typing). Screen readers have been around for quite some time but were simply used to read text (for example, when DOS was used). Nowadays, with GUIs and multimedia web sites, more sophisticated solutions are required.

Screen readers are sometimes very complicated pieces of software. They are largely based on keyboard input, naturally to benefit the users. Understanding how they work, including the tabbing and keypress actions that are central to using them, can sometimes help your development in Flash. Therefore, it is a good idea to try out the software before or while you are developing your work. As mentioned earlier, there are only two products currently on the market that work with Flash Players. Because Macromedia is using MSAA technology, it is easier for third-party integration with the software. In time, you will probably see other MSAA-compliant screen readers support the Player. For now, take a look at what is already available.

Window-Eyes

GW Micro makes and distributes Window-Eyes, and the company recently released the newest version of its well-known and widely used software. The current release, which includes support for Flash Players 6 and higher, is called Window-Eyes Standard or Professional 4.5. It is compatible with Windows 95, 98, 2000, 2003, Me, and XP platforms.

You can purchase a copy of Window-Eyes at www.gwmicro.com. A demo of Window-Eyes, which runs for 30 minutes at a time, is also available at this site. After that time period, you must reboot your computer to continue using the product.

Window-Eyes is a fairly easy program to get up and running, and to configure based on your requirements or preferences. It should begin "talking" as soon as the program is up and running. If you are installing the program to test your Flash documents exclusively, you might want to make sure that you perform a custom installation and set it up so that the program does not load on startup.

JAWS

No, it's not the action-packed thriller movie with the infamous shark, but it is a popular screen reader for the Windows operating system. (Incidentally, the splash screen for the product does feature a rather menacing-looking shark.) JAWS 5 is the latest version of the application, developed by Freedom Scientific.

You can find more information about JAWS at www.freedomscientific.com. A free demo version is available for download.

For both JAWS and Window-Eyes, we recommend that you use the automatic or default installation option. There are many customized options that will likely be unfamiliar. If at all possible, you should install the screen reader on a separate computer — something other than your primary work computer. Screen readers tie up many system resources and increase your production time.

Setting Accessibility Options

One of the main differences between the accessibility options you see in Flash compared to other options such as QuickTime and RealPlayer is that Flash enables users to navigate around your movie. Previously, with QuickTime and RealPlayer, the only option was to add captions that could be read by screen readers. Flash Player 6 and higher offer many options beyond captioning, as you learn throughout the rest of this chapter.

Caution

It is important to understand that only the Flash Player 6 or higher, in conjunction with ActiveX technology, supports Microsoft Active Accessibility. Therefore, the only movies readable by Window-Eyes are in an Internet Explorer browser with Flash Player 6 or higher on the Windows platform. It's also important to remember that in order to support screen readers and MSAA, the Flash movie cannot be in the opaque or transparent windowless modes. You can control this setting in your Publish Settings and/or HTML attributes for the `<object>` tag.

Flash Player 6 and higher can "see inside" your Flash movie and send information to the screen reader about what is contained inside — such as buttons, movie clips, and text. The player also automatically sends a "load" message for the screen reader to announce when new accessible elements are loading into the movie. When scripting the accessibility of your movie, the first and foremost task is to ensure that every possible element of your movie has an instance name. Some of the most critical elements are your buttons and input text fields within your movie because they aid in the navigation of the movie. Static text fields create their own hidden names and therefore are not of the same critical nature. However, if you want to provide a description for static text or have the text read when the cursor is over it, you must convert it to dynamic text. Screen readers also automatically recognize dynamic text you can load into your movie. A screen reader will also read text when a mouse cursor is hovering over it. This works the same way when you have text loaded into a `TextArea` component. So, after you take care of naming your objects with instance names, let's look at the Accessibility panel in the Flash authoring environment.

Exploring the Accessibility Panel

The Accessibility panel enables you to control whether your movie and the objects within it are accessible to a screen reader. It also provides you the opportunity to assign names, descriptions, and shortcuts to these elements. Upon assigning your own names within this panel, you override the automatic labeling assigned to each object. You can also provide descriptions and shortcuts to these elements in this panel, or even turn accessibility off to objects or child objects within your movie or clips. You can find the Accessibility panel by using several methods:

✦ **The menu** — Window ➪ Other Panels ➪ Accessibility

✦ **Shortcut key** — Alt+F2 or Opt+F2

✦ **The Accessibility button on the Property inspector**

The Property inspector shown in Figure 39-1 includes a shortcut button for opening the Accessibility panel. The button is a small, circular graphic in the lower-right corner.

Figure 39-1: The Accessibility button is located on the Property inspector in the lower-right corner.

The following movie elements can be made accessible in Flash. The Accessibility panel options might differ, depending on which object you are currently working on. Note that these are the options that you set on elements that you manually add to the movie's stage during authoring time.

Tip

If you are using ActionScript to dynamically create `TextField` and `MovieClip` objects, the Accessibility panel's usefulness is limited to the global options of the movie, discussed first in the following list. All of other options must be assigned to the dynamic elements in ActionScript. You learn how to access these properties later in the chapter.

✦ **Entire movie** — Global attributes of the Flash movie can be made accessible in this panel. All of these attributes are applied to the entire movie. To view and change these settings, make sure that you have deselected any elements on the stage. You can press the Esc key to do this quickly. The Make Movie Accessible check box tells the screen reader to read the description and title of the movie. The Make Child Objects Accessible option tells the screen reader to read the object's attributes within your movie. Auto Label tells the screen reader to take any text fields next to an object and associate them with each other. Refer to Figure 39-2 for a depiction of the Accessibility panel with these options.

Figure 39-2: You can control global settings for the movie from the Accessibility panel.

✦ **Buttons and Input text fields** — Both of these objects are vital to properly name and describe your movie's functionality to a screen reader user. You can make buttons accessible, and it reads the name and description. However, embedded objects are ignored in buttons. The shortcut option only announces the keystrokes you want to associate with the button. You must write ActionScript to actually capture these keystrokes within your movie. The tab index option (available only in Flash Professional) enables you to specify the element's position in the tab order sequence for the given frame. With Input text fields, names and descriptions are critical. Figure 39-3 shows the options available in the Accessibility panel for text fields and buttons.

Figure 39-3: The Accessibility panel has the same options for both Button and Input text fields.

Note A `MovieClip` object that behaves as a button (that is, you have assigned button handlers such as `onRelease()` and `onPress()` to the instance) falls into the button category described previously.

✦ **Dynamic text fields** — These text fields can have a description added to them. This option can be useful when you want to describe text. As you can see in Figure 39-4, only a description field and tab index field are available in the Accessibility panel for Dynamic text fields.

Figure 39-4: Options for Dynamic text fields in the Accessibility panel.

✦ **Movie Clip instances (or MovieClip objects)** — Movie Clips have an extra option, and this is a check box to Make child objects accessible. This option tells the screen reader to recognize and read the objects contained within the Movie Clip as well. The other parts of this panel function the same way as the options for Button instances. Figure 39-5 shows an example of the Accessibility panel options for Movie Clip instances.

Figure 39-5: Movie Clip instances have an additional option to Make Child Objects Accessible.

All other media, including the following graphics, line art, and imported bitmaps, cannot be made directly accessible in the Flash authoring environment.

To work around this limitation, you can always convert your graphics into Movie Clip symbols, which support accessibility, and then assign names and descriptions of the container instance.

Tip   Some basic elements of Flash Player 5 content, such as static text and Button symbol instances, will be recognized when played in Flash Player 6 or higher.

Let's look at how to use some of the options in the Accessibility panel, and other considerations when developing your accessible movie:

✦ **Naming** — We recommend that you keep any names you assign to your objects exact, succinct, and simple. Also, for the benefit and support of screen reader technology, you should keep these names under 256 characters.

✦ **Auto Label** — In the main movie options of the Accessibility panel, you can choose to "Auto Label" parts of your movie. With Auto Label active, the movie associates any text close to buttons or input text fields as names for these objects. This is great if you are not providing custom names or descriptions to your objects. However, automatic labeling might not be the best option to enable because it leaves the task of assigning associations between text and buttons to Flash.

✦ **Shortcut** — The Shortcut input field can be a little confusing. Adding a shortcut to this field does not automatically create an actual shortcut assigned to the object. What you enter into this field will simply cause the screen reader to read the text out loud. You have to manually add a shortcut using ActionScript.

✦ **Hiding content** — There are several reasons why you might want to hide some of the content in your movie from a screen reader. It can range from a simple reason (such as that the object has no content or benefit in being heard), or you might have a very complex movie or series of objects that are best summed up in a single sentence. Hiding some of your content from screen readers might be useful to you if you find that it will potentially confuse the screen reader or conflict with other elements in your movie. For instance, you might have a group of objects within a Movie Clip, perhaps not containing any descriptive content. Or perhaps a group of items contained within the Movie Clip are best described as a whole. In this case, it is best to *uncheck* the Make Child Objects Accessible option, and the screen reader will not list off an illogical and repetitive series of names of the many objects. Instead, you can provide an overall description on the Movie Clip container, thereby avoiding the repetition of similar elements or causing confusion.

✦ **Changing attributes during playback** — You can change the properties of your accessible instance while your movie is in progress. You can let the screen reader know you are changing attributes at a certain point during your movie, such as at a keyframe. All you need to do is change the properties of that instance, and the screen reader *should* notice the changes you have made because the reader will treat this as a new instance. Actual results are unpredictable because sometimes only the new instance is read. In some cases, all instances within the entire movie might be read again by the screen reader.

Accessible Components

Some of the components provided with Flash support accessibility. For the component to work with screen readers, special ActionScript must be written into the component.

The components built with accessibility options include:

✦ `Button` (or `SimpleButton`)

✦ `CheckBox`

✦ `RadioButton`

✦ `Label`

✦ TextInput

✦ TextArea

✦ ComboBox

✦ ListBox

✦ Window

✦ Alert

✦ DataGrid

These components have specialized ActionScript that enables screen readers to recognize and read out the content of the components.

Tabbing

Allowing your users to use the Tab and Enter buttons for navigation is very important when constructing an accessible web site. They are common tools used for navigation by those who use screen readers. You might also find it a very efficient method of navigation, regardless of your abilities. As in the past, Flash Player 6 and higher automatically enable tabbing through text input boxes, buttons, and Movie Clips. The order is random, or "automatic," by default, although you can control the order of tabbing through the movie, thus increasing the logical progression through the objects or pages. Tabbing through a movie produces a yellow rectangle around each object as it progresses through, which is called the *focusrect*, short for "focus rectangle." It is possible to disable tabbing, the focusrect, and even certain objects from being "tab-able" if you do not want this functionality or if you want to alter it.

Setting the tab order benefits the accessibility of your movie and flow in data entry immensely. You cannot tab static text or graphics — unless, of course, you nest the items with Movie Clips. It is also possible for your users to use the arrow keys to move among the tab-able objects after they have pressed the Tab button once. The users must have the browser window and Flash movie in focus to be able to tab.

Using Keypress Actions

It is very important to understand the dependency that many screen reader users place on the use of navigation based on keyboard commands. A button's onRelease() handler executes when the Enter key is pressed while the tab focus is on the button. To make a movie easily accessible to screen reader users, you might want to design navigation using the Key class instead of mouse clicks or the Tab/Enter keys. Relying on tabbing and the Enter key might be enough functionality for you, although you might want some elements to execute on a certain combination of keys being pressed.

Cross-Reference   For a detailed description on how to use keypress actions in your movie, see Chapter 21.

The first thing you should do is make sure that each of the buttons or Movie Clips in your movie specifies the keypress you want to associate with it. You can put the shortcut in the Shortcut box of the associated Accessibility panel, making sure it is written with names spelled out (no symbols), using uppercase letters for letters, and joined by a + sign, such as Ctrl+N.

To apply keypress actions to your movies, you can place Key listeners that the movie will process when it loads. A sample of the code using the Key class is:

```
var oKeyListener:Object = new Object();
oKeyListener.onKeyDown = function():Void {
  if(Key.getCode() == Key.UP) {
     gotoAndStop("newpage");
  }
};
Key.addListener(oKeyListener);
stop();
```

As you can see, when the up arrow key is pressed, you are taken to the frame labeled newpage.

Detecting and Controlling Accessibility Options with ActionScript

The Accessibility class is available in Flash Player 6 or higher, and it's relatively simple to use — primarily because only two methods are associated with it: Accessibility.isActive() and Accessibility.updateProperties(). Like the Stage, Mouse, and Key classes, the Accessibility class is static. You don't use any new constructor to create new instances. Rather, you simply address the class's functionality directly through its class name.

Note   The Accessibility.updateProperties() method is available only in Flash Player 6 or later. Early releases of Flash Player 6 do not support this method.

Checking the State and Presence of a Screen Reader

The Accessibility.isActive() method makes the player check to see whether the user is actively using a screen reader on the computer and returns a Boolean value of true or false. This code enables you to enable or disable certain elements within the content of your Flash document based on the information returned. For instance, you might want to disable background music in your movie, thus leaving the focus on the speech generated by the screen reader. You might also want keypress actions available only to the users who are using a screen reader.

Caution   The Flash Player requires time to initiate a connection to the screen reader at the start of a Flash movie. Therefore, you have to build a slight delay into your movies if you use this method to check for a reader. If you can, set up any other movie attributes first, check for the screen reader at the last possible moment, and then perform any other actions you require to customize your movie. You can use the setInterval() function to delay the use of Accessibility.isActive() as well.

Let's have a practice run of using the Accessibility.isActive() method. Create a new Flash document. Select the first frame of the default layer, and open the Actions panel. Add the following code.

```
function checkScreenReader():Void {
  var bActive:Boolean = Accessibility.isActive();
  tDisplay.text = "Accessibility.isActive:" + bActive.toString();
```

```
        clearInterval(nCheckID);
}
this.createTextField("tDisplay", 1, 25, 25, 300, 30);
var nCheckInterval:Number = setInterval(checkScreenReader, 2000);
```

Publish your movie. When you test your movie in a web browser with the Flash Player 6 or later plug-in, your text box should report `true` if a screen reader is active or `false` if one is not currently active. If you do have a screen reader enabled, try setting the `setInterval()` time period to a lesser value. If you check the `isActive()` method too quickly, the Flash Player reports `false` even if you have a screen reader present.

You will use the returned Boolean value to control which version of the presentation in Flash the user sees. For instance, you might want to control the music in your movie. Essentially, your movie customizes itself, depending on whether a screen reader is present. If you want, you can also load a specialized movie for those using a screen reader program.

Checking the User's Browser for Accessibility Compliance

The `System.capabilities` class helps determine the attributes of a user's system, and part of this functionality includes determining whether the device meets accessibility standards. This class is available only in Flash Player 6 or higher. Specifically, the property related to accessibility is `System.capabilities.hasAccessibility`. This property is different from the `Accessibility.isActive()` method in that it returns information about the presence of MSAA compliance, not whether there is a screen reader actively running. For instance, if your user is running Netscape, which does not have the ActiveX control this technology requires, the property returns `false`. If your user is running Internet Explorer for Windows, the returned value is `true`.

Let's look at how you can use this object in a Flash movie. To see what is returned, you can run a test much like the previous example. Starting with the same sample document you created in the previous section, use the following code. The changes are bolded.

```
function checkScreenReader():Void {
    var bActive:Boolean = Accessibility.isActive();
    tDisplay.text = "Accessibility.isActive:" + bActive.toString();
    clearInterval(nCheckID);
}
this.createTextField("tDisplay", 1, 25, 25, 300, 30);
var bIsAccessible:Boolean = System.capabilities.hasAccessibility;
if(bIsAccessible){
    var nCheckInterval:Number = setInterval(checkScreenReader, 2000);
} else {
    tDisplay.text = "You do not have an MSAA compliant browser.";
}
```

Publish your movie. When you test your movie in a browser, you should see different results displayed in the `tDisplay` field, depending on which system and which browser or plug-in the system has.

Scripting Accessibility Properties Dynamically

You can also dynamically assign values to accessibility settings of ActionScript objects, such as `TextField`, `MovieClip`, and `Button` objects. Using the `_accProps` property, you can adjust the following accessible attributes of an instance:

✦ **silent**—This attribute accepts a Boolean value of `true` or `false` and controls whether the instance should be seen by the screen reader. If it's set to `true`, the instance is ignored by the screen reader. If it's set to `false`, the screen reader will see the instance.

✦ **forceSimple**—This attribute accepts a Boolean value and is the inverse of the Make Child Objects Accessible option in the Accessibility panel. If you set this attribute to `true`, any elements within the instance are ignored by the screen reader. If it's set to `false`, the screen reader can see internal elements of the instance.

✦ **name**—This attribute specifies a `String` value for the instance's name, as read by the screen reader. It is equivalent to the Name field in the Accessibility panel.

✦ **description**—This attribute specifies a `String` value for the instance's description, equivalent to the Description field in the Accessibility panel.

✦ **shortcut**—This attribute requires a String value to describe the keyboard shortcut that is read aloud by the screen reader for the instance. It is equivalent to the Shortcut field in the Accessibility panel.

Once you have changed an accessible attribute of an instance, you must let the screen reader know that the value(s) have changed by using the `Accessibility.updateProperties()` method. For example, the following code assigns a name and description to a `MovieClip` object named `mPhoto`.

```
mPhoto._accProps.silent = false;
mPhoto._accProps.name = "Conference Photo";
mPhoto._accProps.description = "Picture of attendees at the round table ⤳
    discussion";
Accessibility.updateProperties();
```

You can also use the `_accProps` property to assign the same global movie settings that you do in the Accessibility panel. Simply use the `_accProps` property without an object reference, and apply the update. The following code names the Flash movie and assigns a description:

```
_accProps.silent = false;
_accProps.name = ""Conference Slideshow";
_accProps.description = "This movie provides the lecture notes and diagrams ⤳
    from the session";
Accessibility.updateProperties();
```

Note that both of these code examples set the `silent` property to `false`. If you do not use the Accessibility panel to define initial options for your movie, all properties default to a value of undefined. Be sure to set the `silent` (and `forceSimple`, if applicable) property of dynamic instances in your movie.

Making the Most of Your Accessible Movie

Before moving on to building your own accessible Flash movie, take a look at some of the main things to remember about using screen readers to make a successful movie:

✦ **Avoid looping animation or movies** — The screen reader receives a command to return to the top of the page. It also says "Loading page, load done" after loading movies. This is something to keep in mind for your design because looping movies, animated buttons, and the like can cause unnecessary verbiage on the part of the screen reader.

Tip

It is possible to stop the "Loading page, load done . . ." verbiage by pasting the animation into a Movie Clip and then turning off Make Object Accessible in the Accessibility panel.

✦ **Hide objects** — Make sure you combine elements that might be considered redundant if read individually. Also, hide any objects that do not add any overall content to the movie, or hide graphics in accessibility-disabled Movie Clips if they interfere with screen reader technology.

✦ **Keep graphics/dynamic content to a minimum** — If you are developing your site with screen readers in mind, do not rely on graphics and dynamic content to display informational content. If you must use graphics and dynamic content, remember to add a detailed description to compensate for those who cannot digest this information.

✦ **Consider your audio** — If you have strong audio elements, you might want to disable them if your user has a screen reader. Limited audio does not usually interfere with the screen reader, and can still enhance the experience if used wisely and with due caution.

✦ **Consider navigation** — Your movie will be more accessible if you enable users to navigate by using only the keyboard (keypress actions and tabbing).

✦ **Consider scene (or state) progression** — A logical, user-controlled scene progression is best for screen reader users. Also, remember that screen readers might have a difficult time keeping up with rapid changes. Test your movie to ensure that all elements can be read in time if your movie cannot be made user-controlled.

✦ **Use simple language** — Remember that simple and concise language use is most effective when it comes to screen readers.

✦ **Consider text issues** — Be sure to include a description if you *rasterize* (break apart) any text. Remember that if you break text apart into separate objects, you should disable the screen reader action because otherwise it will read each letter individually. Remember that you can easily convert static text to dynamic text if you want to add a description.

✦ **Keep buttons simple** — Buttons are generally more effective with screen readers when they are kept very simple. Do not put any vital information you want the screen reader to see in the button's Down state. Try to avoid any invisible buttons in your movie; they will almost certainly not be noticed by a screen reader.

Web Resource

We'd like to know what you thought about this chapter. Visit www.righactionscript .com/asb/comments to fill out an online form with your comments.

Summary

✦ Assistive technology includes screen reader software, which reads aloud certain elements on a user's monitor. MSAA technology has been built into Flash Player 6 and higher and now enables users with a compatible screen reader to navigate through Flash movies using Internet Explorer.

✦ Flash movies can be made accessible with little effort by simply making sure the main movie Accessibility panel has Make Movie Accessible selected. It can be made highly effective by taking more time and care during production and by ensuring a logical order to events such as tabbing and movie progression.

✦ By using the `Accessibility.isActive()` method and additional ActionScript, you can tailor your movie to users with a screen reader active. There are many things to keep in mind when building a site for the visually impaired and screen reader technology, including concise language, logical tabbing progression, keyboard reliance, and brevity.

✦   ✦   ✦

Scripting for the Flash Stand-Alone Player

Although Flash is used primarily to develop multimedia for the Internet, you can publish executable versions of your Flash movies that can run without the use of a browser or a plug-in. This chapter explores how you can take control of your Flash movies in this unique environment.

Using the Stand-Alone Player

The stand-alone player refers to the Flash Player application that comes preinstalled in the Players folder of your Flash program folder. You can find the stand-alone player in the following default installation folders:

- ✦ **Windows** — `C:\Program Files\Macromedia\Flash 8\ Players`. In this folder, you will find an `.exe` file named `SAFlashPlayer.exe`.

- ✦ **Mac OS X** — `Startup disk\Applications\Macromedia Flash 8\Players`. In this folder, you will find an application file named `SAFlashPlayer`.

Note
Even though the Flash authoring application is no longer available for Mac OS 9, Flash projectors published from Flash can still be played on a Mac OS 9 machine.

There are two ways you can use SWF movie files outside of the browser and plug-in environment:

- ✦ Open your SWF file with the Flash Player application.

- ✦ Publish your Flash movie as a projector.

For the purpose of this chapter, these applications (Player or projector) are referred to as stand-alone. You'll see this term used in other Flash tutorials and books as well.

Most Flash developers rarely use the Projector options in the Publish Settings dialog box. Go ahead and open this dialog box now (File ➪ Publish Settings). Whether you author on Windows or Mac, you can create Flash movie projectors for either platform. When you publish a projector, Flash 8 bundles the movie's SWF file with the Flash Player engine. If you publish a Windows projector from either the Windows or Mac version of Flash 8, you get an .exe file. If you publish a Macintosh projector from a Windows version of Flash, you get an HQX file. HQX files can be decompressed on a Macintosh with a free utility such as Aladdin Systems' StuffIt Expander. If you publish a Macintosh projector from a Mac OS X version of Flash 8, the projector is an Application file type.

You can also create a projector from the Flash Player application. After you open a SWF file in the Flash Player, you can choose File ➪ Create Projector. However, this method allows you to create a projector only for your specific platform. In other words, if you open a SWF file with the Macintosh Flash Player, you can create projectors for the Macintosh only. One advantage of using this method is that it enables you to make a projector without recompiling the Flash document (FLA file). For example, if you were given a SWF file but not the FLA file from a business client, you could make a projector by opening the SWF in the stand-alone projector. This technique can also come in handy if you have an FLA file that uses embedded fonts that you do not have — if you have the SWF file already compiled with the embedded fonts, you can use the stand-alone to make a projector from the SWF file.

The file overhead of a projector varies between the platform versions. A Windows projector file is about 1.5MB alone, without the movie. However, an equivalent Macintosh projector file created with the Mac version of Flash is about 2.9MB.

In the following sections, you'll look at the pros and cons of using Flash projectors.

Tip   The file of an empty projector was calculated by publishing an empty Flash movie. An empty SWF file is 30 bytes. The Compress movie option in the Publish Settings dialog box has no effect on the size of an empty movie.

Benefits of the Stand-Alone Environment

Some of the potential benefits of the stand-alone are immediately apparent. Following is a short list of reasons why you might want to use a Flash movie in a stand-alone:

✦ No Web browser or plug-in is required for Flash movies in a projector. If you give a projector file to a client or friend, you can be sure that they can view the Flash movie on a Mac or PC.

✦ On Macintosh projectors that run in Classic mode, OS 9 or earlier, you can enable higher memory capacities for larger, complex movies. Windows operating systems dynamically allocate memory as needed. To allocate more memory to Macintosh projectors, select the projector application file, and choose File ➪ Get Info (OS 9 or earlier) or File ➪ Show Info (OS X) from the Finder to change memory settings.

✦ You can build hybrid CD-ROM presentations. Any larger media files and assets can be stored on the CD, whereas dynamic or routinely updated information can be downloaded from the Internet.

✦ You can run Flash presentations in places where Internet connections are unavailable.

✦ You can build presentations for kiosks in museums and other public places. Stand-alones enable you to play Flash movies full-screen and lock out the user's control of the keyboard.

Cross-Reference At the end of this chapter, you can find information about other third-party tools that enhance the capabilities of a Flash projector.

Although projectors can provide these features, there are some reasons why you would not want to use stand-alones. They are discussed next.

Limitations of the Stand-Alone Environment

Some of the benefits of a stand-alone can also be seen as drawbacks. Consider the following before you plan a project in the stand-alone format:

✦ Most Internet users are extremely wary of executables (.exe or application files). Why? Many viruses are spread from computer to computer via .exe files that are attached to emails and run by unknowing email recipients. It's best not to offer site visitors stand-alones as a download on your site, or as an attachment in your emails.

✦ Stand-alones are also unwieldy in file size compared to the SWF counterparts. Thus, it's not suitable for slower dial-up modem connections to the Internet.

✦ Stand-alones are available only for Windows and the Macintosh. Although the Flash Player is available as a plug-in for Linux, you cannot run projectors on this fast-growing desktop platform.

Tip You can use the POST and GET methods with server-side scripts with Flash movies in a stand-alone.

Now that you've been able to think about the implications of stand-alone use, you're ready to see the interactive commands that you can use specifically to control the stand-alone environment.

Applying fscommand() Actions with Stand-Alones

The primary function for stand-alone interactivity is the fscommand() function, also known as the FSCommand. The fscommand() function enables you to control the viewable area and size of the Flash movie stage, prevent users from using the keyboard to access the system (such as using Ctrl+Q to quit the projector), and more. The next section provides a brief overview of the commands and arguments for the fscommand() function. You also explore some examples of their use.

Overview of Commands and Parameters

The fscommand() function technically uses two parameters. The first parameter is referred to as the *command*, whereas the second parameter is the command's *parameter*. Both parameters of the fscommand() are string data types, as the following example illustrates:

```
fscommand("allowscale", "true");
```

In this example, allowscale is the command, and true is the argument for the allowscale command. From our experiments, we have found that you can also use Boolean data types for those commands that accept true or false as the command's argument. Table 40-1 lists the commands and arguments available to the fscommand() for stand-alone use. This table has four categories into which the commands fall: those that control the viewing area (View), playback, key capture, and external application use.

Table 40-1: Summary of fscommands for Stand-Alones

Category	Command	Parameter	Description
View	allowscale	true false	This command controls whether the size of a movie's stage can be changed from that specified in the Movie Properties (Modify ⇨ Document) dialog box in Flash 8. If this command is used with a "true" argument, the user can resize the dimensions of the movie by expanding the projector window. The "false" argument disallows any change to the movie's size.
	fullscreen	true false	This command tells the stand-alone whether the movie should play in a window ("false") or matted against a blank background that takes over the desktop ("true"). The color of the background matches the movie's background color, as set in the Movie Properties dialog box. Note that unless the allowscale command is used with a false argument prior to this command being executed, the movie's size will match that of the screen resolution.
Playback	showmenu	true false	This command, when set to "true", allows the user to right-click (or Control-click on the Mac) the movie's stage to access the contextual menu for player control. If this command is set to "false", the only options available in this menu are About Macromedia Flash Player 7 and Settings.
	quit	No arguments	As the name implies, this command tells the stand-alone to exit or quit its application from running. This is equivalent to using File ⇨ Quit from the stand-alone application bar.
Key Capture	trapallkeys	true false	This feature, when set to "true", enables you to prevent the user from using Ctrl-key combinations to exit or manipulate the stand-alone when the fscommand("fullscreen", "true") command is in use. Note that you must use ActionScript to capture all keypresses to enable keyboard features to the user. When set to "false", normal operation of the keyboard returns to the user.
External	exec	path to application	This command enables you to execute local applications on the user's system. You can execute only applications or files that are located in a folder named fscommand, in the same location as the projector file. You can also specify .bat files (Windows) or AppleScript applets (Macintosh) as files. Note that paths use forward slashes (/) on Windows, and colon characters (:) on the Mac.

Note The `fscommand()` is a global function. The `fscommand()` controls global properties of the entire movie.

Adding Controls to Projector Movies

Try some of these commands and arguments in actual Flash movies. In this section, you look at the `allowscale` and `fullscreen` commands to see how they affect the viewable area of a Flash movie.

Considering the Aspect Ratio for Full-Screen Movies

If you plan to create Flash stand-alones that will expand to the full size of the user's monitor, you should keep in mind the aspect ratio of standard computer screens, which is 4:3, or 1.33:1. Keep in mind that 4:3 is the aspect ratio of television screens and most computer monitors. Flash's default frame size, 550×400, is not a 4:3 aspect ratio — it's more like 1.37:1. This original size was determined by Macromedia by the "best fit" for Flash movies that play in a web browser window. It is recommended that you set your movie size to 640×480 or 800×600. Both of these computer resolutions are 4:3 aspect ratios. To calculate an aspect ratio, either divide the largest dimension by the smallest dimension, or divide each number by a common factor. For example, 640 and 480 have a common factor of 160, giving you the same fraction: 4×3. By using a 4:3 aspect ratio, you can be sure that scaled Flash movies will fit the size of the screen exactly.

Note Wide-screen computer monitors and HDTV sets use 16:9 aspect ratios. If you plan on presenting Flash projectors on an Apple Cinema display, for example, make sure you size your Flash movies appropriately. You can utilize the `Stage` class (discussed in Chapter 20) to reposition movie elements on a variety of screen sizes.

However, you do not want to make overly large frame sizes, such as 1600×1200, unless you are running the Flash projector on an incredibly fast computer. As you might have noticed, as Flash movies scale larger, playback suffers. Vector graphics, albeit small in file size, are mathematically intensive, especially when they are animated. If you want to design a smooth-running presentation that's likely to play back well on most computers, we recommend that you use a 640×480 frame size for your Flash movies, and set the system's screen resolution to 640×480. Even scaling a 640×480 movie to 800×600 can slow down the playback of a Flash movie.

Making a Resizable Projector Window

In this section, you see how to add the proper ActionScript in order to control the size of the projector window. You start with a template Flash document.

Now, take a look at the project file. Open the starter Flash document (FLA file), and look at the current objects on the stage. On the window control layer, you find a `MovieClip` instance named `mWinControl` in the upper-right corner of the stage. The `mWinControl` instance uses symbols from the `OS_UI_Elements.fla` library, which can be downloaded for free from the Macromedia Exchange web site at `www.macromedia.com/exchange`. The `mWinControl` instance contains three elements from this library, and will be the primary focus of this exercise. Here's an outline of the functionality that you want to achieve:

✦ When clicked, the minimize button (on the far left of the bar) should change the movie's size back to its original settings.

✦ When clicked, the maximize button (in the middle) should enlarge the movie's size to match that of the computer screen's.

✦ The close button should quit the Flash projector. However, it should first present the user with a warning box to make sure that he or she wants to leave the projector. We have already created this warning box as a Movie Clip symbol named winQuitClip, which is set to export from the movie's library.

Complete the following steps:

1. Open projector_starter.fla from the Web site, and save it as projector001.fla on your local disk. Note the instance names of the buttons and movie clips. Specifically, the three buttons in the upper-right corner are called btRestore, btMaximize, and btClose, the dialog box in the middle of the stage is called mDialogBox, and within the dialog box are two buttons called btYes and btNo.

2. Select the first keyframe of the Actions layer, and add the following code in the Actions panel:

```
// Make the dialog box invisible to start.
mDialogBox._visible = false;

// When the user clicks on the maximize button set the projector
// to full screen mode.
btMaximize.onRelease = function():Void {
  fscommand("fullscreen", true);
};

// When the user clicks on the restore button set the projector
// to regular mode.
btRestore.onRelease = function():Void {
  fscommand("fullscreen", false);
};

// When the user clicks on the close button make the dialog box
// visible.
btClose.onRelease = function():Void {
  mDialogBox._visible = true;
};

// When the user clicks on the yes button close the projector
// with the quit command.
mDialogBox.btYes.onRelease = function():Void {
  fscommand("quit");
};

// When the user clicks on the no button make the dialog box
// invisible again.
mDialogBox.btNo.onRelease = function():Void {
  mDialogBox._visible = false;
};
```

Once you've added the ActionScript code you can export the projector file, run it, and test the functionality. Figures 40-1 through 40-3 show the states of the application.

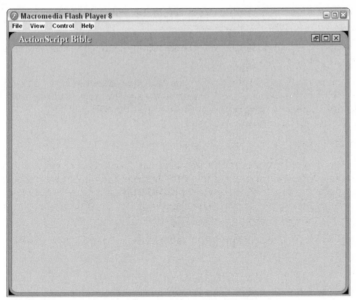

Figure 40-1: The projector in minimize (standard) view.

Figure 40-2: The projector in maximize (full-screen) view.

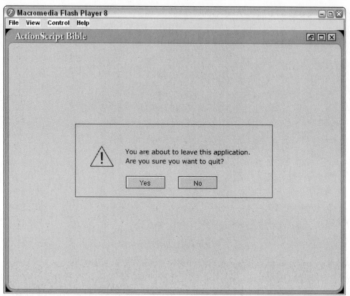

Figure 40-3: The warning dialog box.

 Note Some third-party projector utilities (mentioned later in this chapter) enable you to modify or remove the outer default window and title bar from projectors.

Using fullscreen and allowscale to Matte a Movie

In this section, you slightly modify the ActionScript created in the previous example. For this incarnation, you simply set `allowscale` to `"false"` directly in the `resize()` method. This prevents the movie from expanding in size, but it enables the projector to take over the desktop.

1. Open the `projector001.fla` file that you saved from the previous exercise, and save it at `projector002.fla`.

2. Select frame 1 of the Actions layer, and open the Actions panel. Modify the code such that when the user clicks on the maximize and restore buttons, it toggles the `allowscale` setting. Add a line of code that sets the `fullscreen` mode of the application to `true` as soon as the application starts. The updated code is as follows (changes bolded):

```
mDialogBox._visible = false;
fscommand("fullscreen", true);

btMaximize.onRelease = function():Void {
  fscommand("allowscale", true);
};

btRestore.onRelease = function():Void {
```

```
    fscommand("allowscale", false);
};

btClose.onRelease = function():Void {
  mDialogBox._visible = true;
};

mDialogBox.btYes.onRelease = function():Void {
  fscommand("quit");
};

mDialogBox.btNo.onRelease = function():Void {
  mDialogBox._visible = false;
};
```

You can export the new projector and test the functionality. This time, you'll notice that the project is maximized by default. The stage is matted as shown in Figure 40-4. Clicking the maximize button scales the content.

Figure 40-4: A matted, full-screen Flash projector.

Tip   You can press the Esc key to force the projector back to the original window and size.

Preventing Access to the Desktop

The `trapallkeys` command enables a projector to prevent the keyboard from being used to access any default system or application options, such as Ctrl+Q or ⌘+Q to quit, Esc to resize, and so on. If you want to create Flash projectors for kiosk displays in public spaces, you can make sure that the user of the kiosk can't access anything except that what you allow in the Flash movie.

In this exercise, you'll modify `projector002.fla` such that it prevents the user from accessing Ctrl+Q or ⌘+Q to exit the movie. The projector exits only when users press the Close button.

1. Open the `projector002.fla` file that you made in the last section, and save the file as `projector003.fla`.

2. Select frame 1 of the Actions layer, and open the Actions panel. Add the following line of code just following the `fscommand()` call that sets the `fullscreen` mode to `true`:

   ```
   fscommand("trapallkeys", true);
   ```

Although the `trapallkeys` command does capture most keypresses, it cannot prevent the user from pressing Ctrl+Alt+Del or Alt+F4 (Windows) or Option+⌘+Esc (Mac) to forcibly quit the application on a system level. Some third-party tools, such as Flash Jester's Jugglor, can trap other keys. Refer to the listing at the end of this chapter for a list of URLs to find such tools.

Executing Other Applications

Another feature of the Flash stand-alone is the capability to execute programs outside of the projector file. Using the `exec` command, you can specify another application file to be run concurrently with the Flash projector. In this way, you can use Flash projectors as front ends to software installers. For this scenario, you include the software installer `.exe` (or application on the Mac) file on the same CD-ROM or floppy containing the projector. For security reasons, any and all files that you want to run must be located within a folder named `fscommand`. This folder must be in the same parent folder as the Flash projector file. For example, if you had a software installer named `setup.exe` in the `fscommand` folder, you could add the following ActionScript to an install button's `onRelease()` event handler method in the Flash projector:

```
fscommand("exec", "setup.exe");
```

Note   The file name and path are relative to the `fscommand` folder. Therefore, you can use a forward-slash separator (/) to target files in subfolders of the `fscommand` folder.

You can also create applets or scripts with your favorite programming language. You can create Visual Basic `.exe` files that can perform operations with other installed applications.

Web Resource   It's beyond the scope of this book to delve into other scripting languages such as Visual Basic, but you can find an excellent tutorial on the Web at `www.flashgeek.com/tutorials/06_launchapp_01.htm`.

On the Mac, you can write AppleScript applets that can be executed from the Flash projector. However, the Flash Player (as a stand-alone) cannot be accessed via AppleScript. There are no AppleScript-defined objects within the Flash Player.

Caution You cannot specify document file names with the `exec` command. For example, `fscommand("exec", "readme.doc");` does not launch WordPad or Microsoft Word on Windows.

Expanding the Potential of the Stand-Alone Projector

Several third-party software applications allow you to enhance the functionality of a Flash projector. Unfortunately for Mac users, these products are usually available only for Windows. These add-ons allow you to embed files such as video and PDF documents into Flash projectors. Following is a list of web sites that offer Flash projector utilities:

 ✦ `www.flashjester.com`

 ✦ `www.multidmedia.com`

 ✦ `www.northcode.com`

 ✦ `www.screentime.com`

 ✦ `www.alienzone.com/screensaver_features.htm`

 ✦ `www.vanrijkom.org`

 ✦ `www.goldshell.com`

Most of these sites offer free downloadable trial versions of their software products.

Web Resource We'd like to know what you thought about this chapter. Visit `www.rightactionscript.com/asb/comments` to fill out an online form with your comments.

Summary

 ✦ You can publish self-running versions of Flash movies. These files are called *projectors* or *stand-alones*. You can also play SWF files in the Flash Player application that ships with the application.

 ✦ Projectors can be used to distribute your Flash content on floppy disks, CD-ROMs, or DVD-ROMs.

 ✦ Using the `fscommand()` function, you can control how a Flash projector behaves and communicates with resources outside the player. The function uses two arguments: a command and an argument for the command.

 ✦ The `"allowscale"` and `"fullscreen"` commands control the viewable area of the projector's stage.

 ✦ The `"trapallkeys"` command can prevent the user from quitting the projector or using system shortcuts to access other functions.

✦   ✦   ✦

Index

Continued